ENDLESS BEAT

VOICES OF THE NEW SARUM SOUND
1970-1999

Frogg Moody and Richard Nash

First published in the United Kingdom in 2010 by The Timezone Publishing Group (contact 07900 680 587)

Copyright © Jeremy B Moody and Richard Nash 2010

Cover Design by Pete Leyland

Design and layout by Pete Leyland, SWAPP Art & Design Ltd.

All rights reserved. No part of this publication may be reproduced, in any form or by any means, electronic, mechanical, photocopied, recorded or otherwise, without prior permission of the publisher and copyright holders.

The views expressed by individual contributors to this book are not necessarily those of the publishers or the authors. Neither the publishers or the authors can be held responsible for any errors or omissions in the views expressed by contributors, nor shall they be liable for any loss nor damage to any person as a result of these views.

Every endeavour has been made to ensure that the information published in this book is as accurate as possible. Neither the publishers nor the authors can be held responsible for any errors or omissions, nor shall they be liable for any loss or damage to any person acting on the information contained in this book.

ISBN: 978-0-9557410-2-9

Printed by Salisbury Printing, Greencroft Street, Salisbury, Wiltshire, SP1 1JF (01722 413 330)

CONTENTS

FOREWORD	by Tich Amey	v
CHAPTER 1:	FRESH EARS (The early 1970s)	1 - 26
CHAPTER 2:	DARK SIDE OF THE MOONRAKERS (The Progressive Rock Era)	27 - 60
CHAPTER 3:	SAVAGES IN THE CITY (Punk and New Wave)	61 - 94
CHAPTER 4:	THE PEOPLE'S FREE STATE OF STONEHENGE (The Stonehenge Free Festival)	95 - 116
CHAPTER 5:	EVERYTHING LOUDER THAN EVERYTHING ELSE (The New Heavy Metal Kids)	117 - 150
CHAPTER 6:	FLOWERS IN A DESERT (The 1980s)	151 - 212
CHAPTER 7:	INDEPENDENT'S DAYS (Into the 1990s)	213 - 256
CHAPTER 8:	THE BEAT GOES ON (The old and new scenes in the 21st century)	257 - 290
APPENDIX 1	Local Bands	291 - 301
APPENDIX 2	Discography	302 - 308
APPENDIX 3	Videography	309
APPENDIX 4	Concerts	310 - 322
CREDITS AND RECOURCES		323 - 324
INDEX		325 - 334
ABOUT THE AUTHORS		335

FOREWORD

I am delighted that Frogg and Richard have invited me to provide a foreword to this book. Reading their first publication, Hold Tight!, brought back many memories for me and 'The Boys' and this continues with Endless Beat, which covers a period that has given me – to some extent – even more personal satisfaction as a musician.

I have always tried to keep in touch with the Salisbury music scene but it is surprising to see how many local bands have made records and become well known outside this area. Endless Beat also teaches those of us who were around in the sixties that the local scene has remained just as vibrant and exciting across the following decades. Long may it continue!

Tich Amey
Salisbury, July 2010

DEDICATION

Endless Beat is dedicated
to the memory of

David 'Dave Dee' Harman,
Martin James,
Pete Maple,
Dave Stickley
and
Jason Stuart
who sadly passed away
whilst this book was being researched and written,
and to all those other musicians who are no longer with us.

1 Fresh Ears
The Early 1970s

The last chapter of our previous book, Hold Tight, examined the effect of the fallout of the psychedelic era on the UK music scene, which had split into two distinctive approaches: 'pop' and 'rock'. This continued into the early part of the seventies. The singles chart and the old ballrooms remained packed with guitar and harmony based classics, whilst the album charts, clubs and college circuit were dominated by the progressive, or 'prog-rock' scene, embracing rock, blues, folk, jazz, classical and eastern styles.

As was the case with the music scene, fashion at the start of the seventies basically continued the late sixties styles. While the high street boutiques sold afghans, denim, scarves, flowers and tie-dye, a cult simultaneously developing out of the mod movement was that of the suedeheads and skinheads. The latter in particular were presented by the media as mindless hooligans, but the brogues, crombies and button-downs worn by these youths represented a working class - and far more stylish - look than the hippy garb which is now thought to epitomise the era.

These early seventies fashions were fairly androgynous, compared to what had gone before, but one noticeable gender-specific change was the lowering of the hem-line - eventually to the lower calf - and the

ENDLESS BEAT

"Whatever happens we will call the next album Salisbury!"

raising of the neckline for a traditional, somewhat pastoral, female look popularised by Laura Ashley.

In Salisbury the once regular live shows at the City Hall had all but died out – replaced by the cheaper option (at least for promoters) of the mobile disco. Thankfully the Alex Disco[1] continued to thrive as a 'club' venue, putting on a range of acts from straight pop through to the most complicated prog. At the same time, the Students' Union at the newly opened College of Technology began to use the main hall of the campus as a live venue.

The Salisbury Journal reviewed the gigs put on during the college rag week in March 1970. The newly formed Uriah Heep appeared at the college and were described as having tight arrangements and keeping the crowd interested, which was thought 'no mean feat considering how critical Salisbury audiences can be'. Jelly Bread played the main Rag Ball at the City Hall and, although applauded, had not been fully appreciated.

Uriah Heep went on to play in the city on a number of occasions, and events following an Alex Disco gig in July 1970 inspired the title track of one of their best known albums, as guitarist Mick Box explains: "We had a situation with a gig down there where the bouncers would not let us have our equipment after the show. We remonstrated with a guy called Tiny - who was not tiny - as he was being aggressive with fans who just wanted a good time idiot dancing. We went back to our digs and in the night smashed the [Alex] window, got all the equipment out and drove away as fast as we can. On the way we said 'Whatever happens we will call the next album Salisbury!'"

The sleeve of the album carried an unsubtle image, although this was intended to reflect the mood of the times rather than South Wiltshire's strong military connections. It was, as Mick says: "A peace thing! It depicts something as dangerous and evil as a tank crushing a flower: very much flower power induced."

Despite the events at the City Hall and College, the Alex remained the only regular live venue, with a gig most Saturday nights - plus the occasional midweek date - throughout the first few years of the decade. Among the notable names appearing during this period were Chicken Shack, Manfred Mann (Chapter III), Yes, Caravan, Procol Harum, Black Sabbath, Thin Lizzy, Lindisfarne, Slade and Genesis. The bookings were primarily made by John Smith, an agent from Reigate.

Mike Robins took over as the Alex bar manager in 1970: "I was a City Councillor. John Stainer wanted to become a City Councillor but was busy - he was the prime leaseholder of the Alexandra Rooms and had no time to canvass. I said 'I'll canvass for you' and he became a Councillor. Some time after that I was at a loose end. I went to see John and said 'I don't suppose you've got a job for me?' He said 'I can give you a job at the Alexandra Rooms'. Within six weeks the bar manager retired and I took over."

"I became interested in what was going on there – there were so many interesting DJs and bands. I saw things that I had never been involved with before. It was anything from dinner jackets to leather jackets – you never knew what was going to come along next."

Keith Gale: "I can remember seeing bands like Black Sabbath, Genesis, Steamhammer, Geno Washington, Wishbone Ash. The thing about Black Sabbath was they were very scruffy – 'real metal' as I knew it – not the metal we have got nowadays which is commercialised."

Andy Sheppard: "You would get Slade, the next week Genesis, then a reggae band or something pretty middle of the road, and then suddenly I saw Back Door, a really heavy, improvising trio. That was

1: **Fresh Ears** (The early 1970s)

ALEX DISCO SALISBURY

★ **Spectacular Star Attractions for July** ★

Saturday, 1st July
HACKENSACK
MEMBERS 40p   D.J. Mad Mick   VISITORS 50p

Saturday, 8th July
EAST OF EDEN
MEMBERS 40p   VISITORS 50p

Saturday, 15th July
VINEGAR JOE
MEMBERS 40p   D.J. Mick C.   VISITORS 50p

Saturday 22nd July
GENESIS
MEMBERS 40p   D.J. Mad Mick   VISITORS 50p

Saturday, 29th July
STRAY
MEMBERS 40p   VISITORS 50p

PLUS: D.J. and Light Show.

Open Saturdays 8 p.m. till 11.45 p.m.
No Admission after 10 p.m. Rights of admission reserved

E. T. Price, 222 Highgate Road, Birmingham 12.   772 4829.

extraordinary - that somebody was booking all these different bands."

Andy Nicklen: "It was fantastic. You could be three feet away and shake hands, as the stage was only eighteen inches high. There was no restriction – it was a very close, intimate atmosphere, which was electric with the right bands."

Roger Raggett: "Slade started out a skinhead band known as Ambrose Slade but quickly dropped the Ambrose moniker when their hair started growing and the skinhead uniform of Dr Martens and check shirts gave way to more outrageous clothes. I recall seeing them at the Alex in their original incarnation and then later, as the hits started to pour in, as the Slade we all know and remember."

"At the time we slowly changed our clothes to reflect the new style and gradually went away from ska and Tamla Motown music. A shoe shop on Devizes Road[2] had opened and was making custom made platform boots, like the ones that Slade and other bands of the time were wearing. So, armed with my week's wages plus a lot of confidence, I went in one Saturday for a fitting, which consisted of placing each foot on some cardboard, choosing the height of the heel and how many platforms you required on the sole, and finally the colours of leather you wanted them made from."

"A week or so later they would be made and once money passed hands they were yours to totter around the streets of Salisbury in - I don't remember how much these unique creations cost but I sure would like them now! Combine this footwear with a pair of two tone tonic strides, a button-down collar shirt in bright colours and a jean jacket with sewn on leather and tartan patches, and by God your Mum and Dad - and probably everyone else - had a good laugh at your expense!"

"Of course we all thought we were the bees' knees that evening at the Alex, lined up playing our imaginary violins to Coz I Luv You. I can remember Noddy Holder commenting at the bar after they had performed on how he liked the boots and where did we get them!"

"Thin Lizzy at the Alex – now that was a big night out! As usual we started at the Bullring Café[3] and met up with our gang of hoodlums - the tension was high. As the reprobates gathered we got on our scooters parked outside and all trooped down to the Bull[4] to down a few beers - lagers for the young lads like me and Watney's Red Barrel or something similar for the elder, more respected, of the tribe. Looking back I was just sixteen, so really had no place in the pub legally, nor was it a wise idea to be drinking and riding a scooter!"

"At the given time again we all mounted up, rode around the town to the front entrance of the Alex and jockeyed for prime position parking in the street, in a long row. Once inside we waited whilst the girls danced around their handbags and the guys just yakked in anticipation, hanging out, trying to look hard and cool as teenagers do."

"Eventually Thin Lizzy appeared,

ENDLESS BEAT

"We had three or four encores - they wouldn't let us go..."

walking through the crowd from their changing rooms at the front of the building and let rip into their repertoire. Phil Lynott was a striking figure, very tall, skinny with a mop of dark curly hair and little moustache, a cross between a pirate and a gypsy from a different planet. It ended way too soon and we trooped out of the hall, mounted up again and rode off into the night, still with the sound of the opening guitar lick of Whiskey In The Jar ringing in our ears above the noisy exhaust – excellent!"

Some acts were of course simply too big for the Alex. In December 1971 Led Zeppelin were booked to play the City Hall. The date formed part of a tour to promote an untitled album, which has since become popularly known as Led Zeppelin IV or Four Symbols. Including such tracks as Rock And Roll, Black Dog and Stairway To Heaven, the album consolidated Zeppelin's position as the biggest act in the world at that time.

Using entrepreneurial initiative previously demonstrated when he played with The Purge in the late sixties, Suttons' employee Peter Coombs approached the band with a view to putting on a show in Salisbury[5].

Peter Coombs: "I was doing some promoting in Bournemouth and Salisbury with a very old friend of mine called David Strand. We realised the Led Zeppelin tour was going to be something special. Somebody mentioned to me that if you wanted to get to Peter Grant, who managed all of Led Zeppelin's affairs, you made contact with Mickie Most."

"I found out that he [Most] had a very modest office above Milletts in Oxford Street in London, and I managed to get the phone number. I rang and they said 'Yes, we can introduce you to Mr Grant, when would you like to come up?' David and I went up and Mickie Most was there, Peter Grant, and Richard Cole - who was their tour organiser."

"It was obvious they did business in a rather maverick sort of way, but they came across as being honest people and gave me a piece of paper saying 'We will come to the City Hall, we are happy for you to have 10% of the gross profit and we will not let you charge more than £1 admission'."

The popularity of the band ensured a quick sell out.

Peter Coombs: "I think it was one of the few promotions we did where we never needed to do any posters. Having said that, we did have a wonderful souvenir poster for sale, which has become an icon, but which we got nothing out of unfortunately."

The show was scheduled for 15 December but was cancelled after Jimmy Page contracted flu. This delighted the sceptics who had said the band would never play in Salisbury, but Peter Grant paid for the hall to be used that night so local fans could still enjoy a show.

Peter Coombs: "Very near the due date I had a phone call from Mr Grant saying 'I'm awfully sorry, we are going to have to pull out because Jimmy is poorly'. My heart sank, but Mr Grant said 'We'll pay for the hall and would like you to find a couple of decent local bands that play in the style of Zeppelin - it'll be a free concert on us. If you can find out from the City Hall when we can have a date, I'm sure by then Jimmy will be fit and well and we can do a replacement gig for you'. So, Jerusalem and Marble Orchard put on a very good free show. There would have been 1200 or so people there and I think everybody enjoyed it – and I wasn't lynched!"

Ethem Cetintas (Marble Orchard guitarist): "Nobody else would play.

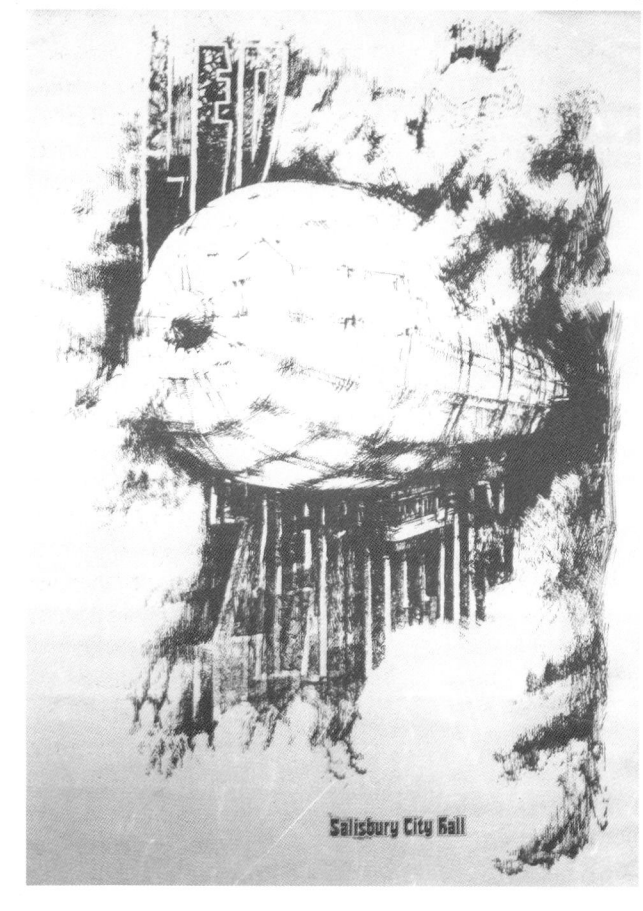

Salisbury City Hall

1: **Fresh Ears** (The early 1970s)

MARBLE ORCHARD - left to right: Martin James, Phil Milner, Ernie Parsons and Mark Howles

They were all scared shitless because there was no way they were going to face an angry crowd expecting to see Led Zeppelin. We had a brilliant night. We had three or four encores - they wouldn't let us go – a really keen crowd."

Tickets remained valid for the rescheduled date and six days later the Zeppelin landed in town.

Peter Coombs: "On the day a large Avis seven ton truck turned up outside Suttons and they said 'We're looking for Peter – can you tell us where we are playing tonight?' I jumped in the truck with them to the City Hall."

Roger Raggett: "My main recall was the wall of sound they produced and seeing Jimmy Page playing his twin neck guitar, with long curly-haired Robert Plant reaching an amazing blood curdling pitch at the end of Whole Lotta Love, whilst John Bonham thrashed the drum kit nearly to death. Cost me one pound to get the tickets out of my weekly apprenticeship wage of £5.40. What a sacrifice, what an experience!"

Sean Rice: "It was very loud, but they also did an acoustic set halfway through where they played Battle Of Evermore and Going To California, with the mandolin and John Bonham playing tambourine. That was a brilliant gig."

Keith Gale: "It was one of the most memorable gigs in Salisbury - sitting on the floor, absolutely jam packed – an atmosphere I haven't seen since in Salisbury. I think it was because they didn't turn up for the first gig and we were all given a ticket for the second one – there was such a hype then waiting for that gig."

Andy Nicklen: "It was probably one of the best gigs ever in Salisbury. The crowd just sat on the dance floor – no air, can't move - just had to sit for three hours and listen to the band. Zeppelin were extremely loud, That's probably why they put Martin James' band [Marble Orchard] on, because nobody could compete with it – Martin's band were quite loud."

Most people who were there believe that Zeppelin must have been the loudest band to have ever appeared in Salisbury, although some remain unconvinced.

Ethem Cetintas: "We were louder – ask anyone! I used to play through three Marshall stacks and they were all tweaked - we used to tweak them to get more out of the bins."

Zeppelin's reputation for excess and hell raising had mostly come about as a result of their offstage activities in the USA, rather than in their home country. Certainly the experience of the Salisbury support acts and promoter was that they were the very model of civility.

Ethem Cetintas: "We were backstage. They came and thanked us and I played Jimmy Page's guitar while they were doing the soundcheck. They were great guys – very polite."

Peter Coombs: "After the gig we took them to supper at the Provencal Restaurant[6]. Edward and Jerry Moss ran it and they did a super supper. When we arrived at the restaurant – this was late at night – at the door at street level, a journalist from the London Times tried to worm his way in. Mr Grant, who was not a small man, looked down on this journalist and said 'There is only one man in the world tonight who can invite you to this private party - and Mr Coombs doesn't want you at the party, so please go away', which made me feel ten foot tall. We had a very pleasant supper. I saw no sign of drugs, no unpleasantness, no drunkenness - it was a very, very civilised evening."

Led Zeppelin vocalist Robert

ENDLESS BEAT

"Rory Gallagher put on a wonderful show."

Plant has a reputation for eclectic tastes in music – particularly his leanings towards the pastoral. During the meal he made a tantalising suggestion, to which we would still love to see an outcome.

Peter Coombs: "During the evening Robert Plant said 'I am very interested in early history - if ever English Heritage said they would consider a folk inspired outdoor do at Old Sarum, please let me know'. I don't think I even thought it was worth talking to anybody from English Heritage, because how do you do crowd control for someone from Led Zeppelin at Old Sarum?"

One of the local crew from the Zeppelin show had a lift home to remember.

Peter Coombs: "A young man from Bishopdown called Tim Simons was helping me at Suttons at the time and he had been pretty well the senior steward at the City Hall that evening. He got chatting to John Bonham at the meal and said 'I know it's a bit cheeky, but any chance of a lift home?' I think Bonzo said something along the lines of 'Why do you want a lift home with me?' and Tim said 'Well, you are the only man I know with a white soft top Cornice. I live on a council estate and I would feel great if you took me home'. Bonzo actually took him home, in his white roller, and made Tim's evening."

Peter Coombs promoted other shows at the City Hall, notably Rory Gallagher in September 1971 and Free in February 1972, and has contrasting opinions of those artists.

Peter Coombs: "Rory Gallagher put on a wonderful show. I can't remember who was in his band, but I think his brother was the bass player and Joe Thorne, from Bishopstone, looked after him. I had supper with Rory. That was in another restaurant owned by Edward and Jerry Moss – where the Cross Keys now is[7]. Rory came across as a very appealing, gentle, Irishman - a real gentleman. It was just tragic that his battle with the grape was lost."

"I don't think Free played very well. The curtains opened to the first chords of Alright Now, which was fantastic, but they were just zombies on stage as far as I was concerned. They didn't give their money's worth - unlike Robert Plant and co, who really did give their all for the same ticket price."

"It was the winter of discontent. We only had three or four days power out of seven and I had arranged for a standby generator if our power was cut-off. Fortunately, because the Infirmary - which was then Salisbury's main hospital - was on the same electricity

Rory Gallagher at the City Hall

Rory Gallagher and Tom Thatcher

1: **Fresh Ears** (The early 1970s)

circuit as the City Hall, there was no drop in power. But Free had made it very clear they would not play unless they were connected to mains power – they would not play to a temporary generator supply and would not have given the money back. So it would have been very embarrassing, to say the least, if there had been a power cut."

The Enford based band Period provided support at the Rory Gallagher show.

John Hatchman (Period drummer): "In those days you all sat on the floor and it was absolutely heaving, so that was a nice experience. We didn't get much of a sound check - we didn't arrive until quite late because I was late coming home from work. Having said that you just got on and did things in those days and the technical side wasn't so big an issue as it is now - in those days it was just two columns and one little amp."

Marble Orchard, who stood in for - and then supported, Led Zeppelin had formed as a power trio in the late sixties. Led by drummer/vocalist Martin James they had built a reputation as a good live act, through support slots with the likes of The Who and success in a Melody Maker competition. Their new guitarist had drifted into Salisbury - and the band – almost by accident.

Ethem Cetintas: "I was born in Turkey. I went to Australia and in '67 came to the Isle of Wight and had my first proper rock band – it was the days of The Nice and all that lot. Then I floated around a few more bands. I never stayed in one place long enough to warrant a full time band – my first was Marble Orchard. I had come to Salisbury College, Mick Pinney suddenly left the band and Marble Orchard were stuck without a guitarist."

"I used to hang out in Suttons – the in place for all the musicians to go at the weekend. If you turned up there after three o'clock in the afternoon you would often catch a gig. Pete Coombs was very keen to get guys in, so they could teach each other - exchanging guitar licks - and if there was a bass player and drummer you would soon

PERIOD - left to right: Michael Bird (Birdie), Antony Philimore (Biddles) and John Hatchman

ENDLESS BEAT

"He played a double kit like Ginger Baker, who was his hero…"

MARBLE ORCHARD - left to right: Ernie Parsons, Martin James and Mick Pinney

have a band in the shop. Loads of people used to come to the windows and watch. It was a lovely time, and he was a really clever guy because he sold a lot of guitars that way! He was like the Peter Grant of Salisbury. He is quite an important guy from that period."

"I was already known as a guitarist, floating around and just jamming wherever I could. The word must have got to Martin somehow, because he sent word via a mutual friend, Eddie Barlick. It was almost like being summoned by the King: 'Martin James would like you to audition for Marble Orchard'. The audition was in Martin's ice cream warehouse at Churchfields[8]. It was an incredibly noisy, reverberant place - all concrete and steel. I did my bit, played louder than everybody else, and the next day I had a call from Martin saying 'Do you want to play with the band?'"

"Quite a lot of stuff we used to do was covers, but we used to modify them so they were almost unrecognisable. A lot of Mountain stuff – Nantucket Sleighride, Mississippi Queen and all that – we would modify those quite heavily, changing the chord sequences and everything. There were a few original songs – we used to all put our own bits in. We weren't just maniacs - we knew what we were doing. We were a very well practiced band - bloody tight. Some of the stuff we used to play was not 'ordinary rock' – the Mountain stuff was pretty complex."

"Martin was a great vocalist. I don't know how he used to do it - playing drums and doing the vocals at the same time. He played a double kit like Ginger Baker, who was his hero

– vocally he used to worship Jack Bruce."

"We were originally a three piece. Within a year we had a keyboard player. He was a real nutcase and came with the first synthesiser – a little suitcase you stuck pins in. He was this real geek, who knew how to use this machine when nobody else did. He could make these amazing stupid sounds out of it – we were all going 'How cool is that!'"

Marble Orchard provided a local example of a modern phenomenon: a band that audiences would stop and listen to rather than just dancing. This was even the case out in the villages around the city.

Benge Bennett: "I was a member of Langford Youth Club, getting to the age when senior members left and went on to other things. The lady who ran the club was moving away and they wanted somebody else to run the club - all the fingers pointed at me."

"You had the usual things like table tennis, a dart board and pool tables. It was fine but I thought maybe we could do something else. Salisbury was alright if you had a vehicle, but out in the sticks there wasn't much for youngsters to do. There weren't many areas the youngsters could go to and see a live group. It started as a casual remark by one of the girls in the club. She was friendly with a guy from Peacewave and said they were looking for somewhere to practice. I said 'Bring them along on a Friday night, they can practice, I can charge the kids a nominal amount to get in and we'll have a dance'. It went down fairly well so I thought 'We'll try that again'."

"I used to go in to Tony Moreton - in Ace Music in Salisbury - and book the odd group about once a month. Although I advertised locally and in the Western Gazette, word of mouth took it on and it snowballed. We were getting people from Shaftesbury, Gillingham, you name it. A dance was what it was most months, but occasionally we would get Marble Orchard and that wasn't a dance: the whole room just sat on the floor and watched them play - it was like a concert. They were very good – you could tell the quality."

Peacewave were one of the most popular local club bands of the early seventies. Active since the late sixties they were joined by a Malayan born guitarist, Yan Webber, who arrived in the area when posted to RAF Old Sarum in 1967. Having left the services Yan played briefly with Major Barbara before being introduced to Keith Daubney (vocals), Simon Reid (bass) and Dave Smith (drums) by a Wilton Royal Carpet Factory colleague.

Yan Webber: "I had a tuppenny hapenny guitar – a Jedson - it cost me twelve pounds and it was awful. I was approached at the factory by John Penny, who said 'I hear you're a guitar player'. My audition comprised having a pint at the Green Dragon at Alderbury

PEACEWAVE - left to right: Simon Reid, Keith Daubney and Yan Webber.

ENDLESS BEAT

"The hall was always jam-packed and it was a fabulous night."

and talking a bit about music. They decided they would like me and gave me a whole sheaf of music to learn."

"There was a keyboard player in Peacewave. He came up to me when I joined and said 'Welcome…but I'm the bloke who plays all the solos'. I said 'Yep, not a problem' but he didn't play the solos. I popped a solo in on one rehearsal and he said 'I told you I was the one who put in all the solos'. In the end he left the band – he said 'Yan's too pushy!'"

"They had carpet factory tannoy speakers nailed together as a PA. I thought even in those days that was disgusting and managed to persuade them to buy a pair of Vox PA columns from Andy Sheppard. We were then one of the first bands to buy the new H and H amplification with the bright green logo. Lights were home made - we had a little triangular box like a giant Toblerone bar on the floor. It had 'Peacewave' on a glass sheet, with blue gel behind it, lit by a fluorescent tube. Everybody thought that was frightfully modern."

"We thought we were fashion leaders with our loons, flares and tank tops and we invented the fashion of wearing sun specs with patterns cut out of day-glo on the front, like a pair of eyes or a rising sun. We all had pudding basin haircuts. We looked awful!"

"We had huge fun – the local scene then was absolutely thriving. It tickles me now that people I know from those days will still come up to me and say hello. We never played to a place that was less than packed – you just thought that was the norm."

"We all joined the Musicians' Union. Ken Dodson ran it and he was so influential to me in his egalitarian

BOB JAMES MUSIC with Roy Castle

ways and support for young musicians. These were big band people and we were guitar playing kids, but under the auspices of people like Ken we were well received and the atmosphere in Salisbury was really friendly and supportive."

"When you had functions like the Band Box Ball, which was a Musicians' Union run annual event it was a huge buzz. Each band in themselves didn't have the nous to fill the City Hall - but six of them did. The hall was always jam-packed and it was a fabulous night."

"The Musicians' Union also had what they called their 'Bang, suck and blow' nights - bearing in mind there was a lot of brass in those days. We did it above the Cadena[9] and also at the Green Dragon at Barford St Martin[10]. They were jam sessions and they were wonderful. You would get The Merry Macs playing strict tempo and we kids would love it. Then we would get up and the applause at the end of it….we thought 'Crikey! This lot actually enjoyed what we did'."

Dave Bennett, a drummer who had started playing at a very young age having been inspired by Lonnie Donegan in the fifties, agrees that the encouragement and advice offered by established dance band stalwarts such as Ken Dodson, Ken Palmer and Les Mant was a great help to younger musicians.

Dave Bennett: "You had to listen and learn from these guys. They understood music inside out and knew how the numbers had to be played. I've been very privileged to have shared a stage with them, especially being a mere kid at the time, and I've been grateful to have received such a wealth of their tuition – and some pretty heavy bollockings too!"

During the seventies Dave played with Bob James Music, The Dave Charles Sound, The Avonaires, Reform, Freeway and Recorded Delivery – he still plays today with

1: **Fresh Ears** (The early 1970s)

The Doghouse Boys and Fast Company.

With a line-up of Bob Rynn (vocals), Pete Lucas (guitar), Chris Lucas (bass) and Keith Small (drums), later joined by Dave Church on guitar, Bethany were another of the promising late sixties Salisbury hopefuls plugging away into the new decade.

Keith Small: "We didn't do a lot of gigs in Salisbury – most of our work was away. We were tied to Tony Moreton at the time and he got us a lot of work. Van Der Graaf Generator we supported up in the Midlands, at a big college gig. We did The Cavern – two support nights - one was a band called Tea and Symphony, they didn't have any hits but they had quite a following at the time. Bethany would have been about three or four years, then it changed to Jenny Lynn. We got John Ackroyd in on keyboards - we had only been guitar, bass and drums so that opened up a new world to us."

Keith also played live with a line-up of Plastic Penny, put together to capitalise on an earlier hit single and now based around Amesbury musicians: "The original band had Everything I Am, which was the one hit wonder - then they disformed. We did basically a rock'n'roll set with

PHOTO: TED SCHOFIELD. SALISBURY.

BETHANY.

Left to right: Chris Lucas, Bob Rynn, Pete Lucas and Keith Small

ENDLESS BEAT

"... it wasn't really rock'n'roll or heavy metal."

Everything I Am included."

The other Salisbury band that played on the cancelled Led Zeppelin date, Jerusalem, comprised Lynden Williams on vocals, Bob Cooke and Bill Hinde (guitars), Paul Dean (bass) and Ray Sparrow (drums).

Paul Dean and Ray Sparrow, together with their friend from St Probus School[11], Chris 'Kef' Skelcher, had decided to form a band the morning after seeing John Mayall play at the Alex in the late sixties. With Paul on vocals, the boys scrimped, saved and picked watercress to pay for their gear on which, quite unusually for the time, they had already decided never to play covers: Paul would take the main responsibility for providing original material.

After a few months of rehearsals the three-piece played their first major gig at Salisbury College, supporting Uriah Heep in front of some friends and a few German exchange students. Despite the unfamiliar material - and Paul making up or repeating lines when he had forgotten his own lyrics – the band went down well and were encouraged to continue.

On leaving St Probus, Paul went on to the College, and Kef to Bishop Wordsworth's School, while Ray joined the family post office and grocery business, which was useful as the band were able to practice in the basement of the premises[12].

Paul Dean was evidently a young man of many talents and had professional football trials with Southampton, AFC Bournemouth and Plymouth Argyle before he and Ray decided to concentrate on music as a career option. Meanwhile, Paul's sister Zoe was based in London working for record companies and had presented the pop/youth culture television programme, A Whole Scene Going.

Paul Dean: "Zoe briefly went to Leaden Hall School and then, as a boarder, Lyme Regis Grammar. On leaving school she went to London and worked for a music publishing company in Tin Pan Alley, then to Pye records where she got to know many of the artists of the day. She was quite a bubbly person and Liz Cowley - the BBC producer - pulled her in to do A Whole Scene Going, where she was one of a group of interviewers for celebrity artists from music, movie, dance, TV etcetera."

"She also worked for one of the pirate radio stations, so knew all the DJs who later became household names. She knew most of the artists of the time and eventually ended up with Ian Gillan, who she first met when he was in Episode Six - before joining Deep Purple."

Jerusalem had by now been joined by Paul's college friend Bill Hinde on guitar. Kef decided to go on to Cardiff University and was replaced by another college friend, Bob Cooke. The band then expanded to a five-piece as Phil Goddard joined on lead vocals.

Bob Cooke: "At Andover Secondary Modern I started out playing violin appallingly badly, but I had a guitar and went to lessons with Mr Dacre. By the time I was eleven we were doing gigs at the Country Bumpkin Club in Andover - myself and Tony Poole going out doing

JERUSALEM - left to right: Bill Hinde; Paul Dean, Lynden Williams, Ray Sparrow (obscured) and Bob Cooke (front).

Shadows and Jim Reeves stuff. We developed that into a proper little rock band called High Voltage."

"Everyone in Andover came over to Salisbury College by and large. That's where I met Bill Hinde, a really good mate. I was aware of Paul Dean but he was really quiet so I didn't really get to know him terribly well, but Bill said he was in band with him. Kef Skelcher was going to university and Bill invited me to join them. We were struggling to get a singer. Phil we did record some stuff with, but he had a very sweet voice - it wasn't really rock'n'roll or heavy metal."

Zoe Dean was pleasantly surprised when she first heard her brother's band and introduced them to Mickey Dallon, who recorded demos of Primitive Man and Beyond The Grave at Pye Studios. Zoe also invited her partner, Ian Gillan, to watch the band play.

Gillan was impressed and brought Deep Purple bassist Roger Glover to a farmhouse at Hurdcott, near Barford St Martin, where the band was rehearsing (and which they had named 'Pig Mansion') to record some demos on his new Revox four track.

Paul Dean: "[Initially] we didn't actually live there, but most days we rehearsed except when doing gigs. I knew a little three-piece band that practised there - they introduced me to the owner's son and we moved in. It was two semi-derelict farm cottages joined together. Great place, no neighbours to annoy - although once we did rehearse outside because it was a hot summer day and someone from the other side of the hills drove five miles to tell us to turn it down! Sound really travels in the countryside!"

"Deep Purple also used it for a couple of days before a UK tour. Ritchie [Blackmore] thought it was great and that weekend it was really foggy so he had his roadies build a huge bonfire, like something out of a horror movie - great night. We actually used the owner's mansion for the Jerusalem album cover photos. She was a lovely lady, related to the Walker whisky family."

Deep Purple manager John Coletta showed an interest in Jerusalem, but Zoe Dean and Ian Gillan decided they wanted to take the band on themselves. At this stage Phil Goddard decided to quit and was replaced by Lynden Williams.

Bob Cooke: "We advertised for a singer in Melody Maker, went up to London – Bill's brother had a big flat in Belsize Park where we auditioned everyone - and picked Lynden because he was pretty eccentric, full of beans and had written loads of lyrics. He was a trained actor - I think he was just about to go into Hair, which stupidly we talked him out of - I don't think he fancied getting his kit off...and nobody wanted to see it anyway!"

Despite being in a band with the acknowledged virtuosi Jon Lord and Ritchie Blackmore, Gillan told the music press he admired the fact that Jerusalem were 'entirely green' and had 'the completely abandoned qualities of Screaming Lord Sutch'. It was the band's rawness and refusal to follow rules that had attracted him to them.

The band's eponymous album was recorded by Gillan at his own Kingsway Studios in London before they had landed a record deal. Titles such as Hooded Eagle, Murderer's Lament and She Came Like A Bat From Hell reflected the band's Black Sabbath-Deep Purple style riffery and vocals, but the element of additional rawness was perhaps more in line with the so called 'new wave' of metal that would appear some ten years later.

Bob Cooke: "Amazingly, I think we made the album within six weeks of meeting Lynden. Ian helped us out, made loads of suggestions. He was allegedly our 'producer' but his idea was that we were rough as guts and 'Let them just do their funny thing and we'll put it out'."

The band eventually signed for Deram, the progressive arm of Decca Records. On the night the deal was clinched they played with Status Quo at the Red Lion in Leytonstone using

ENDLESS BEAT

"So, we didn't get paid – we got a whacking great bill!"

Deep Purple's old Marshall PA and speakers.

Following the 1972 release of the album, Jerusalem played all over the UK and Europe on the college and festival circuits, often alongside the big names of the day. At one event in Vienna they were the only 'unknown' band on the bill. Thousands of fans started walking off for a break when the band's name was announced, only to perform an about-turn when the introduction to their song Frustration was struck up.

Bob Cooke "Gillan had got us in with NEMS agency. We were in very small print at the bottom of their list of people who were available, but we got some quite good gigs. We didn't have a telephone in those days and my neighbour would say 'Hey, this guy's calling you up - he wants you to be in Vienna on Saturday!' We did a couple of festivals in Vienna and Heidelberg, in Germany. We were bottom of the bill – just above the local acts – but there were people like Fairport Convention, Juicy Lucy, Family, Black Sabbath, Deep Purple – it was quite amazing, but it never really went much beyond that unfortunately."

The band also played a number of venues in Salisbury including the College, City Hall and The Teacher Training College in The Close[13]. At the latter gig Jerusalem were using Deep Purple's PA and roadies but things didn't quite go to plan.

Bob Cooke: "They used to shut the [Cathedral Close] gates and we knew we had to be out before midnight, but they started shutting the gates of the college before half past eleven and we were stuck inside! This Liverpudlian [roadie] – he had been with the Bonzo Dog Doo Dah Band, so was completely bonkers – said 'I'm not having this' and just backed the lorry up and drove the gates down! So, we didn't get paid – we got a whacking great bill!"

Pamela Holman gave a supportive review of the album in the New Musical Express. She thought the quality of the songs was 'quite astounding' for such a young group and concluded by saying 'with so many new bands flooding the market there's always a danger of getting buried underneath the pile, but somehow I don't think this will happen to Jerusalem'.

The band had intended to release Hooded Eagle as a single – in an edited version of the album track, but Deram decided they wanted to release something new, so Paul Dean and Lynden Williams quickly came up with a song entitled Kamakazi Moth.

Bob Cooke: "I felt that was a huge improvement on what we had done previously. He [Gillan] got a bit of the hump because he was out of the country with Deep Purple and we produced this single without him, but it was still under the umbrella of Pussy Productions, which was his production company."

Despite the band's live reputation, neither album nor single would reap any success in chart terms and Jerusalem began to splinter. To Paul Dean and Ray Sparrow, the band was about rock in its purest and most basic state, while Lynden Williams and Bill Hinde were evolving and wanted to move in a more polished and progressive direction, taking advantage of rapidly developing studio technology.

Paul and Ray felt they had made their statement and didn't want Jerusalem to be forced into areas

---

BIOGRAPHY — DECCA GROUP RECORDS

| JERUSALEM | DECCA |

'Rough, raw and doomy' is but one way the music of JERUSALEM has been described. Although they are very young, the band consists of five solidly experienced musicians.

The line-up of the band is:

Paul Dean (20) .... bass
Bill Hinde (19) .... rhythm guitar
Bob Cooke (19) .... lead guitarist
Ray Sparrow (20) .... drums
Lynden Williams (22) .... vocalist

created by peer pressure and the accountants and lawyers who were beginning to take over and run the music business. After discussions with Ian Gillan and Decca A&R man Sam Hamilton it was agreed it would be a good time to avoid unwanted compromise and changes by folding the band. Bob Cooke joined Paul and Ray for the next project, a three-piece that would become known as Pussy.

The band was again managed by Ian Gillan. Although Paul Dean remained the principal songwriter, the direction was quite different from Jerusalem, but retained the raw, 'no rules' approach that had set them apart from many other bands of the period. At the time it was fashionable to record very long songs using the full repertoire of the latest studio equipment: Pussy did the opposite - all their tracks were around the length of a single and recorded virtually live in the studio.

The range of Pussy's lyrical topics was eclectic, including sex (in Feline Woman), politics (Riding Down The Red Flag), extraterrestrials (IFO), passion (The Knife), Ella Fitzgerald (Lady Ella) and alcohol (Moonshine).

Bob Cooke: "I can't believe we had a band called Pussy! Paul started singing – he seemed to be a big fan of Marc Bolan from the way he was singing. We became a sort of lighter-weight pop-rock band. We supported some strange people: Marsha Hunt, White Trash, Brian Auger and The Trinity. We were with Wizzard on Hastings Pier the night they became number 1 [sic] with their Christmas song. On Top Of The Pops the bass player used to be on roller skates, dressed up as an angel – they did all that on stage."

Ian Gillan

Pussy considered themselves to be a good-time band with no pretensions: if it seemed it might be fun they would try it and on stage anything could happen. The band gigged all over Britain and Germany, both headlining and as a support act. After the Wizzard gig, Roy Wood invited Pussy to play support on a world tour. Unfortunately the tour never materialised as Wood became involved in a wrangle with his old record company.

Ian Gillan was more proactive with the band than had been the case with Jerusalem, playing piano on a take of Feline Woman, co-writing Place in the Sky and contributing backing vocals on many tracks, and Pussy were regularly ensconced in his Kingsway Studios as well as Olympic, CBS and De Lane Lea.

There have been rumours for many years of a second, unreleased Jerusalem album, but this was actually recorded by Pussy. Deram decided to continue the Jerusalem contract with the new band, but the only release was a single, Feline Woman.

The record was generally well received but failed to make major commercial waves as the BBC refused to play it because of its sexual connotations. Alan Freeman took no notice and played the record anyway, saying he really liked it and it should have been a hit. At the time, the only pop and rock competition for the BBC was Radio Luxembourg, where the record was played by Kid Jensen.

Sam Hamilton then left Deram and as is common practice in the music business when the man who signed the act departs, the company lost interest. Ian Gillan decided to end the contract and look elsewhere but, although there was some interest, no one was willing to sign Pussy and the band eventually folded.

Paul Dean then worked on solo material and with Gillan on non-music related projects. A few years later, when the Ian Gillan Band were playing in France, Paul and Ian approached a few record companies about the possibility of completing the Pussy album in mainland Europe. To their surprise, there was interest from some major labels and eventually Ariola asked the band to reform.

Paul and Ray Sparrow invited Bob Cooke to join the band but he declined. Gillan knew a young American guitarist, Brian Goff - a good friend of Ritchie Blackmore and the son of the TV producer and screenwriter Ivan Goff – who immediately bonded with Paul and Ray. Brian rerecorded some of Bob's lead guitar on existing Pussy tracks, while Paul wrote new material and the Pussy album was completed - but not released, Ariola's plans having been hit by recession. The album was again put on the backburner.

Incidentally, between leaving

ENDLESS**BEAT**

"Being managed by Miles Copeland didn't help, ..."

Deep Purple in 1973 and forming his own band in 1975, Ian Gillan concentrated on business matters including investing in a motorcycle business in Salisbury with the assistance of Paul Dean.

Paul Dean: "A friend of mine and Ray's in Salisbury, Mick Eglington, ran a car garage, just along from Ray's parents' Post Office, but he was also a motorbike racer and a bit of a technical genius. He had already built a 500cc motorbike from scratch."

"Initially Ian, Zoe and I used to go to race meetings to watch Mick race his Norton production bikes. Once Ian got to know Mick better, he decided it would be a good idea to build a brand new British motorbike to combat the Japanese, who were beginning to monopolise the industry that had once been a flagship for Britain. Thus Mantis Motorcycles Ltd came into existence."

"The first idea was to build a rotary engine, but this was a long time target, so it was decided to come up with a highly efficient 4-stroke engine - the Japanese were concentrating on 2-stroke at this time. Gradually the Mantis design team grew bigger and included people like Jack Williams, designer of the famous Ariel motorbike. Ian and I spent most of our spare time on this project during that period, plus our own Norton race team."

"Unfortunately, the timing was not good, as Britain was entering a major recession. We actually finished the first running engine and a complete example of the production bike. Everyone agreed it was a great machine and already incorporated many features the Japanese would later use - monocoque frame, lightweight steel, alloy wheels, heated handgrips etcetera. To go into production would have taken major investment and, although there were many interested investors, the recession was making everyone nervous."

"There was one ray of light - to take over the now bankrupt Triumph factory at Meridan. The investors were okay, the Local Government and Member of Parliament were for it, but it was squashed by the then socialist Minister of Trade and Industry, Tony Benn, who wanted to turn Triumph into a co-operative. This he did, but with dire consequences - the end of the British motorcycle industry."

"Unfortunately Mantis eventually closed its operations, much to the satisfaction of the foreign motorcycle companies. A great British idea and product once again defeated by its own politicians! We also had shops selling other brands of motorbikes in Salisbury, Bristol, Dublin and Edinburgh, which were eventually meant to sell the Mantis once finished."

As well as the locally based bands, a handful of musicians with Salisbury connections were making a name for themselves on the national scene during the early seventies.

In the sixties, Mike Wedgwood had attended Bishop Wordsworth's School and been a Bishop's Chorister at Salisbury Cathedral (his father, the Reverend Keith Wedgwood, had been the Succentor at the Cathedral). Having played in a few local bands, notably Heap, Just Us and The Popees, Mike took his bass guitar to London.

Mike Wedgwood: "My parents moved to Canada and I was in the care of [Just Us bassist] Laurie Hamlin's parents while I finished at Bishop's and played sax in Just Us. Then I lived in a couple of sleazy flats and for a short period at Mick Smith's. I couldn't see anything to stop me going to London to seek my fortune and George Hart had a flat where I could stay, so I hitchhiked up there. On the way I got a ride with some people who were siphoning petrol from parked cars along the way. The police were called and I spent my first night in London in a cell!"

"After a few months I went to audition for the bass spot in The Overlanders - at that time the 'New' Overlanders. I had hair down to my something or other and the lads in the band were rather 'straight', but they let me join anyway. We went up and down the M1 and quite a few other roads playing in social clubs and cabaret clubs. One job was at the Edinburgh Ideal Home Exhibition where I stayed at Tom Thatcher's university pad and arrived rather thrashed the next morning! Quite an experience! The emphasis of the band was on three-part harmonies - which were rather good - and silk suits with frilly pink shirts."

"Then I was in Arthur's Mother with ex-Overlander and future member of John Entwhistle's Rigor Mortis, Graham Deakin. Later I arranged and conducted the orchestra on Rigor Mortis' Mad Dog album. Then came Curved Air - great musicians and ground-breaking material. I was extremely lucky to be playing with the band and it really was a challenge to keep up with the others, but I did okay I guess! I had my first taste of the USA on tour as opening act for Deep Purple and then for quite a few others."

"After a short period as a studio session player I joined Caravan and

1: Fresh Ears (The early 1970s)

CARAVAN with Mike Wedgwood (middle right)

although the music was very different, it was definitely just as great and original - and the touring was just as gruelling. The Blind Dog At St Dunstan's Tour was apparently the most intensive UK tour attempted to date - something like 28 concerts in 32 days. I left because I was too stressed to handle the conflicts and politics in the band. Being managed by Miles Copeland didn't help, since he was so intense and focused. No criticism meant - he was just a bundle of energy."

Mike's other big name gig was with Kiki Dee, with whom he played on a single and supported Elton John.

Mike Wedgwood: "I was friends with Joe Partridge. His sister was married to Davey Johnstone [Elton's guitarist] and when he got the job as Kiki Dee's guitarist he recommended me. The band started with Graham Deakin on drums - he left, leaving the spot for The Merseys' Pete Clark. BJ Cole was on steel guitar and Bias Boshell, composer of I've Got The Music In Me, was the keyboard player."

"I was in the band for about six months. We rehearsed and went on the Yellow Brick Road tour, and recorded one single, Hard Luck Story, which Elton produced. I left a few days later and just a short while later they recorded I've Got The Music In Me. Right place wrong time for me!"

"The tour was really a big experience. The final concert was at the Hammersmith Odeon and the reception afterwards included a rather large collection of well-known people. I met, among others, Ringo Starr, Mickey Dolenz, Rod Stewart, Bryan Ferry and two members of Monty Python. One of the two - I won't mention the name - was serving

17

ENDLESS BEAT

"... her nervousness turned into a weird aggression directed at us."

as the bartender! His boyfriend apparently left him during the evening. As a result he got steaming drunk and at the end the whole party filed down the stairs past the rather sad sight of him sitting crying his eyes out!"

"Elton was a very nice and generous man – here's one fascinating story about him: one evening the two bands and the stars stopped at a restaurant. We were given a back room and when the waitress realised who was there her nervousness turned into a weird aggression directed at us - she wasn't exactly a model citizen during dinner."

"Afterwards Elton gave her a tip. She didn't realise until we had left that he had given her £100 - of course a lot of money back then. He did it in an unusually effective way to point out her behaviour didn't go unnoticed. She ran out and apologised profusely, realising how awful she had been, and tried to give him the money back. He said 'Keep it and remember next time' - pretty impressive!"

Mike's former colleague in Heap, George Hart, joined Second Hand in time for their 1971 album Death May Be Your Santa Claus. Later the same year, the band became Chillum and released an eponymous album. Both records have become highly sought after and have been reissued on CD.

Mike Paxman, another ex-Bishop's School pupil, also moved to London where - in 1975 - he linked up with Judie Tzuke. As well as playing guitar in her band he co-wrote a number of songs, including the top twenty hit Stay With Me Till Dawn. Playing with the band until the mid-eighties, Mike continued studio work with Judie for a further decade. He also carried out other production duties, co-founding Big Ocean Studios and working with artists including Nick Kamen and Jimmy Nail. Since 1999 Mike has worked extensively with Status Quo and more recently has produced albums by Uriah Heep and Asia.

Kerry Minnear, born in Salisbury, became the vocalist and keyboard player with early seventies Portsmouth prog band Gentle Giant, after graduating from the Royal Academy of Music.

As for 'incomers': Before recording their debut album, Hark! The Village Wait, folk group Steeleye Span rehearsed at a bungalow in Winterbourne Stoke, north west of Salisbury. The line up at the time included Maddy Prior, Ashley Hutchings, Terry Woods (later of The Pogues), Gay Woods and Tim Hart.

Salisbury's sixties idols, Dave Dee, Dozy, Beaky, Mick and Tich, had split into two factions in 1969. Dave Dee went solo, aiming to develop a career in cabaret, films and television, while the rest of the boys stayed together as DBM&T, opting to pursue a more rock orientated path. The split initially came as something of a surprise to the musicians in the band.

Tich Amey: "It was at the Belfry in Birmingham. The dressing rooms were below ground but the windows came above ground and after the gig Dave opened the window, got his bag out and said 'See you lads' and that was it – off he went."

Although the band members were naturally disappointed, Dave never fell out with them. On the topic of 'friends' in his advice column for Fabulous 208 magazine, he talked about their ongoing good relationship, and many years later said 'it was not that I didn't like the boys anymore…it was just a career move really'.

Both factions remained signed to Fontana/Philips and the management team of Ken Howard and Alan Blaikley.

Alan Blaikley: "We didn't think the split between Dave and the group was exactly a good move, but it was probably unavoidable. All good things must come to an end and perhaps the kind of songs we were writing for the band had run their course."

"Maybe the Beatles' split had set a kind of unconscious trend. It became clear that Dave and The Boys had very different ambitions - Dave to become a more middle-of-the-road performer and The Boys to become much more experimental – avant-garde if you like - with songs no longer restricted to love stories, but more to do with the state of the world. Things had moved on from love-and-peace to a more political climate."

Alan's comment about The Beatles is interesting: The split between Dave

Mike Paxman

Dave Dee

Dee and The Boys was announced in late 1969 while, although they had effectively been falling apart for some time, The Beatles' last official recording sessions took place in January 1970, without John Lennon who was on holiday. At the start of a take of I Me Mine from that session, later issued on The Beatles Anthology 3 album, George Harrison makes a comment about Dave Dee no longer being there although Mick, Tich and he had decided to carry on the good work!

At the time of the DDDBMT split Ken Howard told Record Mirror that he and Alan saw Dave's solo career as 'a sort of cross between Rolf Harris and Englebert Humperdinck – comedy mixed with sex appeal'. Dave enlisted the help of a friend from Salisbury to launch his solo career.

Peter Mason: "It was the very end of '69 - I think it was December - that I joined Dave, playing guitar, singing harmony and being his personal assistant. We rehearsed for two weeks and then went and played Middlesbrough and Stockton-on-Tees. There was this really good nightclub there – Dave was going into nightclubs and all round entertainment."

As a new backing group for Dave Dee, Bob James suggested a trio he was managing, coincidentally named David and comprising Ian England (piano), David Martin (bass) and Phil Edwards (drums).

Peter Mason: "They were Welsh. They were quite heavy really – good in their own right. I played guitar. At the beginning of 1970, Dave said he was thinking about forming a publishing company, because I had written some songs and he was going to record them. That's when we started October Music."

"It was brilliant for me – the whole episode with Dave - I wasn't just on the road with the band, I was with Dave all the time doing the personal assistant bit. It was a godsend because I learned so much being in that position, seeing and meeting different people. Sometimes we would go to places like Holland to do TV, but it wasn't with the band, it was just Dave, and I would go with him. Another thing is I was in the studio for all the recordings, so you're just

ENDLESS BEAT

"Whoa, hang on a minute, where are you going?"

learning all the time."

The new right-hand man had to adapt quickly to the pace and pressures of the professional scene: "We wrote a song together called Hold On. I was in Salisbury and he was up in London. I got on the train to go to the session and the song wasn't finished. We had done the melody and I was thinking 'I've got to get this lyric done'. I got to Andover…Basingstoke…Woking…nothing. I was thinking 'My god, we've got all these musicians waiting', but as we pulled in to Waterloo I had finished it. It was all part of the learning process – learning to be a professional."

Peter was impressed at how generous established professional musicians were when dealing with the relative newcomer in their ranks: "There was one song called Sweden – I always remember this because it made me realise that there are some great professional musicians who are really lovely people. Big Jim Sullivan, who used to be in Marty Wilde's band, was a hot session player. We were doing the song with just a small rhythm section and Dave said to me 'Go in and show Big Jim the chord sequence'. So, I went in to the studio with my guitar and ran through it and Big Jim said 'That's real nice – lovely song'."

"As I walked away he said 'Whoa, hang on a minute, where are you going?' I said 'Well, Dave just said to come and show you how it goes'. He said 'Yeah, but what you play is lovely – I want you to play that and I will weave in and out of it'. I thought 'God, these are real hot London session musicians' – I was nervous as hell. We went through it and at the end he turned to me and said 'Beautiful, you did a great job'. I never forgot that – what a nice man he was – it gave you confidence."

Dave Dee had a good start to his cabaret career, including breaking a five-year box office record at the Talk of The Town in Manchester in January 1970. His first solo single, My Woman's Man, was released in March of that year, demonstrating the more middle of the road style he would now be pursuing. The single reached number 42 in the UK, spending four weeks on the chart. It might have been more successful, but the Philips label was having problems with a new pressing plant and although the track received extensive radio play, there were not enough singles available to actually buy.

This was followed by a run of commercially unsuccessful solo singles: I'm Going Back (credited to 'David'), Annabella, Everything About Her, Wedding Bells, Hold On and Swingy, the last of these apparently released as a tie-in with a new doll manufactured by Mattel.

Alan Blaikley: "I think My Woman's Man was right for Dave: quite a sophisticated song with good words and melody, and a twist in the tail which I'm not sure everyone got - the 'perfect' man in the girl's mind was in fact the self-deprecating singer of the song himself. We were also proud of Everything About Her, with its suggestion that you can love someone in spite, or even because, of their flaws - their 'blemishes and sweat'. Wedding Bells, though very catchy, was a - perhaps misguided - return to a less sophisticated, more innocent style."

Dave Dee also sang the theme to the 1972 film Rentadick, backed by the King's Singers. The film was directed by Ned Sherrin, apparently a big admirer of Dave's having also produced Every Home Should Have One, in which Dave appeared alongside Marty Feldman.

Despite his best efforts, Dave was struggling to find acceptance with the more mature crowds that his new musical style was aimed at. As well as recording and cabaret work he had also dabbled in television, including presenting the high profile German music show Beat Club, but could not develop a career meeting his own exacting standards in any of these fields. He eventually joined Atlantic Records as an A&R man in April 1973.

Peter Mason: "I think it wasn't working for him. Things weren't really going the way he wanted. I think it was down to the songs. Before - when Howard and Blaikley wrote for Dave Dee, Dozy, Beaky, Mick and Tich - they had all these songs which had storylines and different presentations, but it didn't really happen with Dave. Also the acting wasn't coming together and then he was offered a job at Atlantic."

DBM&T kicked off in a more blues and rock orientated direction, by recording an album of self-composed material, although their first single release, in 1969, had been a Howard and Blaikley composition, Tonight Today. The single had reached number 3 in Holland but did not make the charts in the UK.

Alan Blaikley: "We were pleased with Tonight Today, especially as its triple-layered melodic format enabled Dozy, Beaky and Tich to be showcased as singers and distinct individuals. The idea that all kinds of things, serious and trivial, go on in the world simultaneously had something almost psychedelic about it. Of course The Boys' own composition Mr President really should have been a world hit - a great performance and production."

Mr President was inspired by a discussion about the Vietnam conflict in a pub in Nottingham and showed off the band's superb three-part harmonies while providing clues to the influences that were informing their new direction. The track also made use of a new instrument.

Tich Amey: "An old roadie of ours, Pete Webber, quite liked some of the American bands and that's how we got listening to Buffalo Springfield and Crosby, Stills and Nash – we loved that kind of music. On Mr President we used the only Moog in this country. It was owned by Mike Hugg of Manfred Mann."

The band were invited to perform the song on Top Of The Pops, but didn't qualify for a second appearance, having – they felt – possibly been the victims of some 'promotional' shenanigans.

Tich Amey: "Johnnie Stewart was the producer. I think we were at 33. Johnny Johnson and The Bandwagon had this record out and we know we outsold them that week - but he jumped up to 25 or whatever and we dropped – a lot of that was going on. Johnnie Stewart did this, what he called, 'tip for the top' and said 'I've got you pencilled for next week - I just need you to plop into the 30'. It never did…that could have been a whole different ball game for us."

Mr President was somewhat ill-served by only reaching number 33 during a run of eight weeks in the UK Charts. However, apart from a surprise one-off week in the album charts for the 'Very Best Of' compilation in 2008, the single was the last hit involving any members of what remains Salisbury's most successful ever act. An interesting fact for local music trivia fans is that Dozy, Beaky, Mick and Tich enjoyed more weeks in the UK charts than their higher-profile former lead singer.

On completion of recording their proposed album, DBM&T decided to

ENDLESS BEAT

"The album we did mostly on our own, without management."

separate from Ken Howard and Alan Blaikley.

Alan Blaikley: "At first both parties were keen we should try our hand at writing material that reflected their new directions. In both cases Ken and I very much enjoyed the challenge - but when the records didn't do as well as we all anticipated the association gradually dwindled."

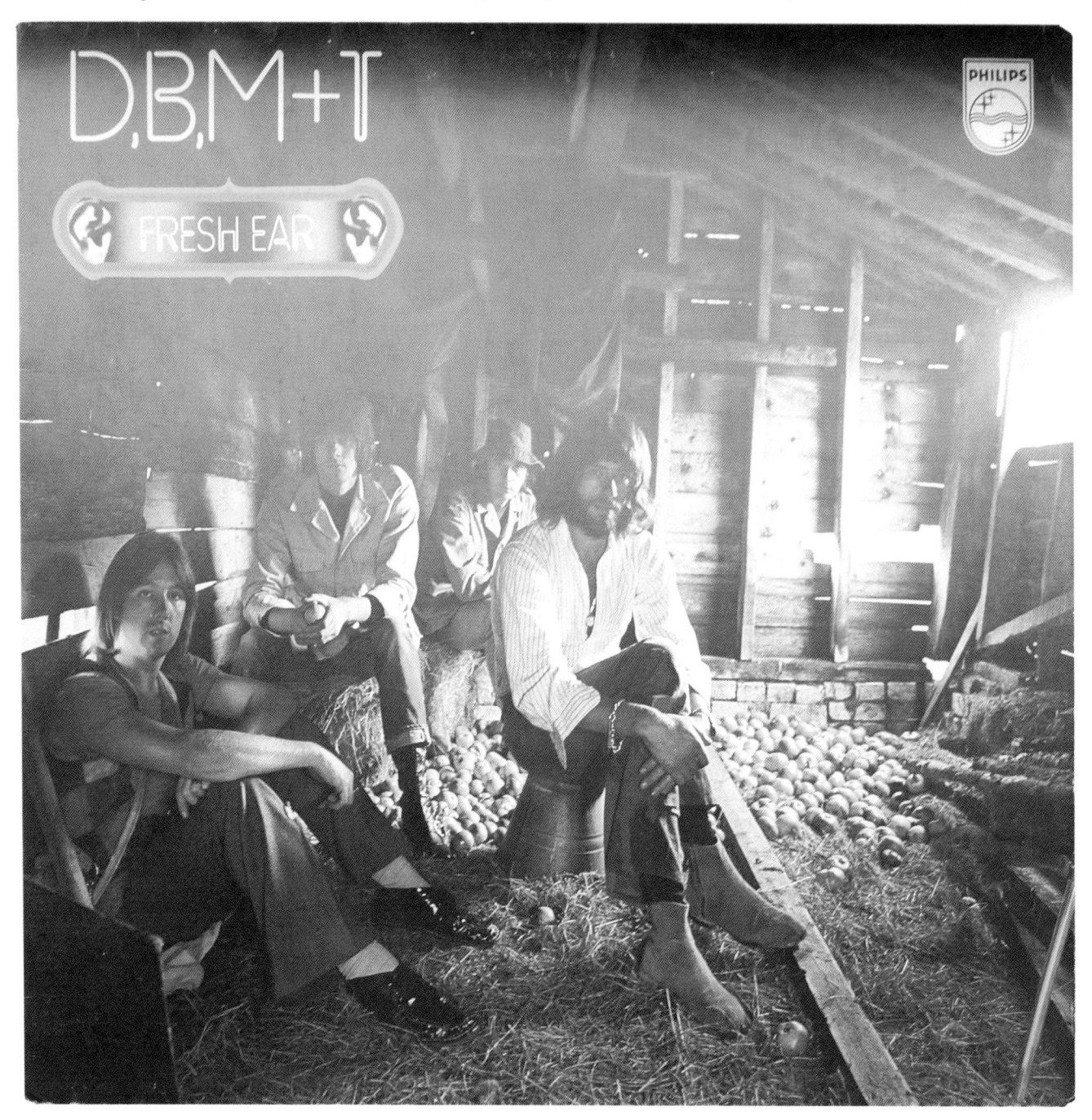

Tich Amey: "They tried writing songs for us but the nearest to a hit we had was a song we wrote ourselves – Mr President. The album we did mostly on our own, without management. We had a guy called Eddie Offord who used to do Yes and the Welsh diva - Shirley Bassey. Eddie was a really good engineer."

The final DBM&T release of 1970 was a single, Festival. The album, Fresh Ear, followed in January 1971. With the exception of Dozy's short piece of 'Propur-Wiltshur', Buttercup Joe, the album was characterised by Mr President-style harmonies, post-Led Zeppelin/pre-glam rock riffs and heavy drumming, with highlights including Too Much, Mystery Rider and World - the latter sounding like yet another blueprint for Oasis.

While the lyrics might seem a little simplistic, the music on Fresh Ear stands up alongside much of what is now considered the more acceptable face of early-seventies progressive music, although the perfectionism of the musicians meant they were not necessarily satisfied.

Tich Amey: "All the previous hits were quite simple little guitar things and I was never a big 'rocky' sort of player. Then we did the album and my guitar skills were not all I would have liked them to be - for me that came much later, with Tracker."

The straight pop scene underwent something of a minor revolution in the first years of the seventies as, reverting to basic rockabilly licks and Yardbirds riffs, a range of musicians – some of whom had already had a shot or two at the big time – donned mascara, glitter and stack heels.

The Sweet (brickies in make up), Slade (former boot boys), Wizzard (led by former Move member Roy Wood) and Roxy Music (musically untrained but innovative art rockers), were among those who released a string of distinctive – and brilliant – singles, leading to them being lumped together under the 'Glam Rock' umbrella with the likes of Alvin Stardust, Hello, Mud and the now disgraced Gary Glitter.

The Sweet appeared at Salisbury City Hall in April 1973. In an echo of the Led Zeppelin concert the original Sweet date had been cancelled due to illness. The band rescheduled for a month later and put on a show that, as far as the Salisbury Journal's Andy Golden was concerned, 'more than satisfied the fans' with an hour of entertainment, camp humour and their 'driving music', which Andy compared with the early Who.

The two most enduring stars of the period were friends of a similar age, and had followed a broadly similar career path – from teenaged mod through Peel-endorsed hippy philosophy and singer songwriting before camping it up and racking up the amps in the seventies.

Following their first major hit with Ride A White Swan, in 1970, T-Rex leader Marc Bolan become the first new teen sensation of the decade: the tabloid press delighting in a successor to Beatlemania – T-Rexstacy!

Although he had scored a major hit in 1969, with Space Oddity, David Bowie's first taste of superstardom came in 1972, with the release of The Rise And Fall Of Ziggy Stardust And The Spiders From Mars, an album tracing a vague concept of a damaged, space obsessed rock and roll star. Bowie had trained as an actor and would, of course, continually tinker with his musical style, appearance and persona. Consequently the line between the artist and Ziggy was never clear.

There is no record of Marc Bolan having played live in Salisbury, but

ENDLESS BEAT

"Is David Bowie really as weird as the papers say?"

Bowie/Ziggy came to the City Hall in June 1973, when a thousand people queued for hours to see him. In a rave review of the concert for the Salisbury Journal, Andy Golden's excitement leapt off the page under a headline of 'Brilliant Bowie Concert was Out of this World' - he called it 'the rock spectacular of the year – nay, the future'.

As the lights dimmed for the start of the show, lightning flashes and a strobe lit the stage and Walter (later Wendy) Carlos' version of Beethoven's Ode To Joy, from the soundtrack to A Clockwork Orange, was played. Drummer Woody Woodmansey took his place and sat motionless with both sticks held vertically over his skins. Mick Ronson (guitar) and Trevor Bolder (bass) arrived next and stood with their backs to the audience.

The intro came to an end and Bowie walked to the middle of the stage and also stood with his back to the hall. The band kicked into Hang On To Yourself, and Bowie, Ronson and Bolder all turned to face the crowd in a blaze of spotlights.

The show featured several costume changes for Bowie: a black costume with silver braiding; a multi-coloured outfit with a polo neck and separate legs and arms; a get-up with one arm and one opposing leg - accessorised with huge bangles; a striped suit with large padded shoulders; a white cloak with Japanese writing on it; a red 'woodland creature' leotard; a white dress with white boots and a see-through black shirt with black trousers.

Roger Raggett: "I was only a kid of about seventeen or eighteen and skint. I went with my girlfriend to the side entrance to try to listen. Between the opening and closing of the door I managed to pick up some of the songs but it was far from perfect."

"We walked around the rear and there was an old Daimler DS420 limo with the beautiful paintwork covered in gouged out remarks and signatures to Bowie. Whilst reading these a roadie - or perhaps he was the driver - opened the rear door and asked what we were doing. We started talking and remarked 'Is David Bowie really as weird as the papers say?' to which he gave us two backstage passes, opened the rear door to the City Hall and we were in watching the concert…brilliant!"

Roger Elliott: "Bowie launched himself off the top of the stack of speakers in the middle of Suffragette City - the bit where it gets to 'Wham bam thank you mam' – twisted his ankle on landing and had to do the rest of the gig sitting in a chair. So you've got David Bowie sitting in a chair singing a cover version of White Light/White Heat, which was quite interesting."

Roger Raggett: "To cap it off Bowie and Angie, his wife, sat in the foyer talking and signing autographs for anyone who approached them during the interval."

Material recorded at Bowie's City Hall show has since been released on a bootleg CD entitled Quaaludes and Red Wine. The concert was one of the last of eighteen months worth of dates played in support of the Ziggy Stardust album. Bowie announced from the stage of the Hammersmith Odeon, less than three weeks later, that it was 'the last show we'll ever do'. Given the blurring between the artist and the character there were reports that Bowie himself was going into retirement, but of course he had plenty more left to say.

Despite the memorable Bowie and Sweet shows, Salisbury was somehow never cut out to be a Glam Rock city. The art college scene, the serenity of the Cathedral Close and the mystical landscape of the surrounding area seemed more suited to long, lazy, stoned afternoons of pondering on the depth of topographic oceans, as opposed to the electronic garage stomp of a Jean Genie or the futuristic outlandishness of a Virginia Plain and, at least amongst local bands writing their own material, album-based progressive rock would remain the major influence.

1: **Fresh Ears** (The early 1970s)

Andy Golden

CHAPTER ONE FOOTNOTES

1. The Alex Disco was located in the Alexandra Rooms, at the junction of St John Street with New Street. The building was subsequently used as the city's Crown Court but is currently vacant.
2. Daniels shoemakers and repair shop was located in Devizes Road in premises now occupied by Hoi Fan.
3. The Bullring café was located in Fisherton Street in premises now occupied by Pino's Barber Shop.
4. The Bull was located in Fisherton Street in premises now occupied by Ladbrokes.
5. Suttons music and record shop was located in Endless Street, with an upper floor overlooking Blue Boar Row. The premises are now occupied by William Hills and The Collectors Room.
6. The Provencal restaurant was located in Ox Row in premises now occupied by Chang Thong and Julian Graves.
7. The East and West restaurant was located in Queen Street in premises now occupied by Salisbury Health Foods.
8. The Tonibell ice cream warehouse was located in Newton Road.
9. The Cadena café was located in Blue Boar Row in premises now occupied by Pizza Hut - the ballroom was on the first floor.
10. The Green Dragon has now been renamed The Barford Inn.
11. St Probus' School was located in Manor Road in a building now occupied by Hillcote CDC.
12. This section of London Road was renamed Estcourt Road after the construction of Churchill Way. The Post Office was located in premises now occupied by Salisbury Vineyard Church.
13. The Sarum St Michael Teacher Training College was located in the West Walk of The Close and has now been converted into residential use.

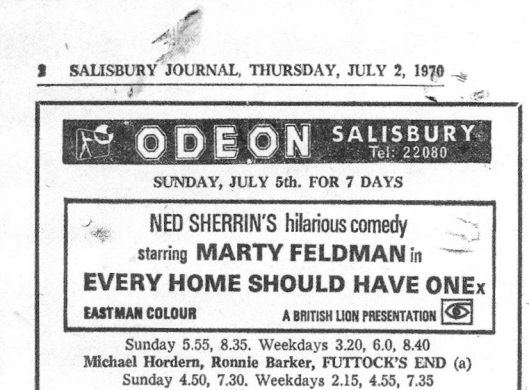

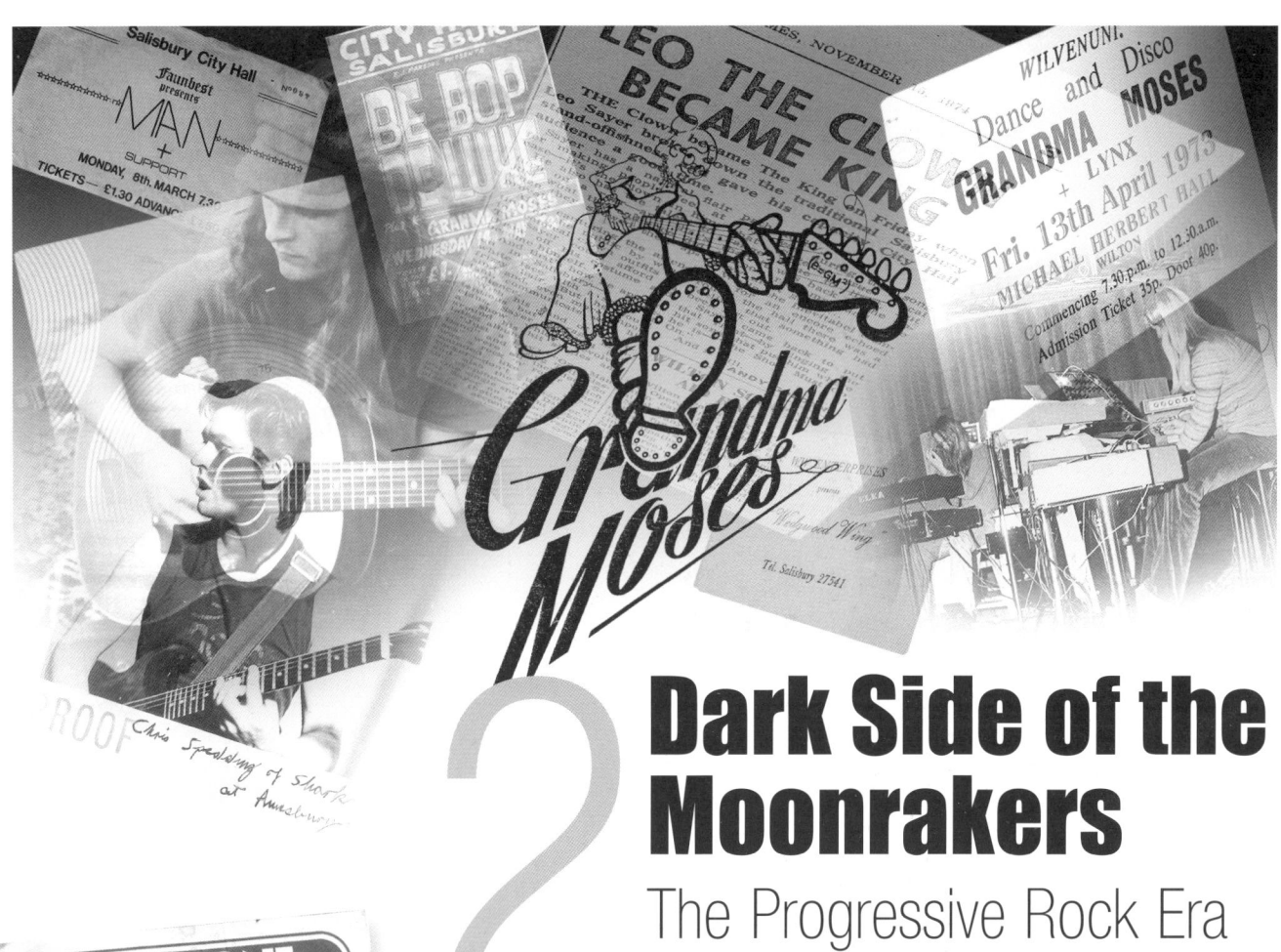

Dark Side of the Moonrakers
The Progressive Rock Era

Towards the middle of the seventies, renditions of current chart hits and standards could still be enjoyed in social clubs and at wedding receptions in the Salisbury area. However, those bands performing original material were largely drawing references from the sometimes bizarre range of subjects, styles and song structures utilised in the progressive field.

Whilst the prog rockers continued to dress down, smartly put together but exaggerated clothes - a sort of combination of the mod/skinhead and glam approach - became popular on the high street. Multi-soled platforms were topped off with ever-widening flares and jackets with giant lapels and patch pockets - all in a range of designs and colours. Bands such as The Faces and Mott The Hoople, who had evolved out of the sixties scenes, but not fully succumbed to glam, characterised this look.

During 1974, music fans in Salisbury were offered an unusual treat at the city's Playhouse Theatre[1] when a state of the art quadraphonic sound system was used to play two of the classic albums of the era - Mike Oldfield's Tubular Bells and Pink Floyd's Dark Side Of The Moon - to a live audience.

Although Floyd did not appear in the city during this period, a coach party from the College had been amongst those who witnessed what

ENDLESS BEAT

"We did something quite revolutionary for the time..."

was only the third ever live performance of the Dark Side album, at Bournemouth Winter Gardens in January 1972 – more than a year before its release.

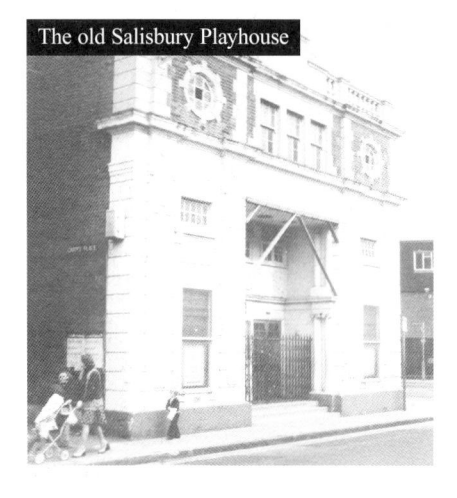

The old Salisbury Playhouse

The playing of unusual records as an integral part of the live experience during live shows was becoming more common, as demonstrated by Roger Elliott and Barry Webb's Dragon Disco when local folk singer Andy Sheppard supported Man at the City Hall.

Roger Elliott: "We got to play the music we liked - Captain Beefheart, Love and The Doors - in the first half. Then, in the interval, we did something quite revolutionary for the time – we played the whole of side one of Tubular Bells, which had just come out – incredibly hip at the time."

Tubular Bells had been amongst the wares available at the Salisbury branch of Sunshine Records[2]. Unfortunately the shop was only open for about a year as the company would only sell albums – exploiting the singles market being seen as 'selling out'. This ethos worked well at Sunshine's first shop in Oxford, where it was popular with that city's large student population, but failed in Salisbury.

Penny Elliott: "I managed Sunshine Records in 1972/73. We only sold albums and most of them, coming from an Oxford base, were totally unsuitable for Salisbury - so it soon closed. My best customers were the military from nearby barracks, who bought all my reggae albums!"

"It was a bit of meeting place for young music buffs at the time. Virgin Records had just started and the most professional thing the shop ever did was when a Virgin window dresser turned up and did a window display, which included a large photo of a naked pregnant woman. I was immediately confronted by loads of blustering older Salisbury citizens demanding the display be removed. At eighteen years old and in a completely rebellious phase of my life I of course refused! Richard Branson had just issued Tubular Bells, and every time I played it in the shop someone bought a copy. Amongst those Bishop's boys who hung out in the shop was Steve Sutherland, who went on to great heights in music journalism."

In June 1974, a relatively big name act played a storming gig under a marquee in the car park of the George Hotel in Amesbury. The original Sharks line up had included former Free bassist Andy Fraser. Although he had by now left, the band still featured top session guitarist Chris Spedding, who would have his own top twenty hit with Motor Bikin' a little over a year later.

A selection of early seventies German groups somehow became lumped in with the progressive scene and were to be shoved into a sub-genre: Krautrock. This catch-all term gathered up a disparate range from Can through Tangerine Dream to Kraftwerk – the only common factor being their nationality.

Tangerine Dream played at the City Hall in August 1974 when their show was described by the Salisbury Journal as 'more of a computerised love-in than a rock concert' and as having an 'ethereal space-sound'. In one of his earliest efforts to change the Journal's approach to music coverage, the paper's photographer incurred the wrath of the band.

Roger Elliott: "I started at the Journal in September 1973. Prior to that time, apart from Dave Dee and occasional visiting celebrities, the music scene really didn't get photographed at all. Andy Golden

Chris Spedding

TANGERINE DREAM at the City Hall

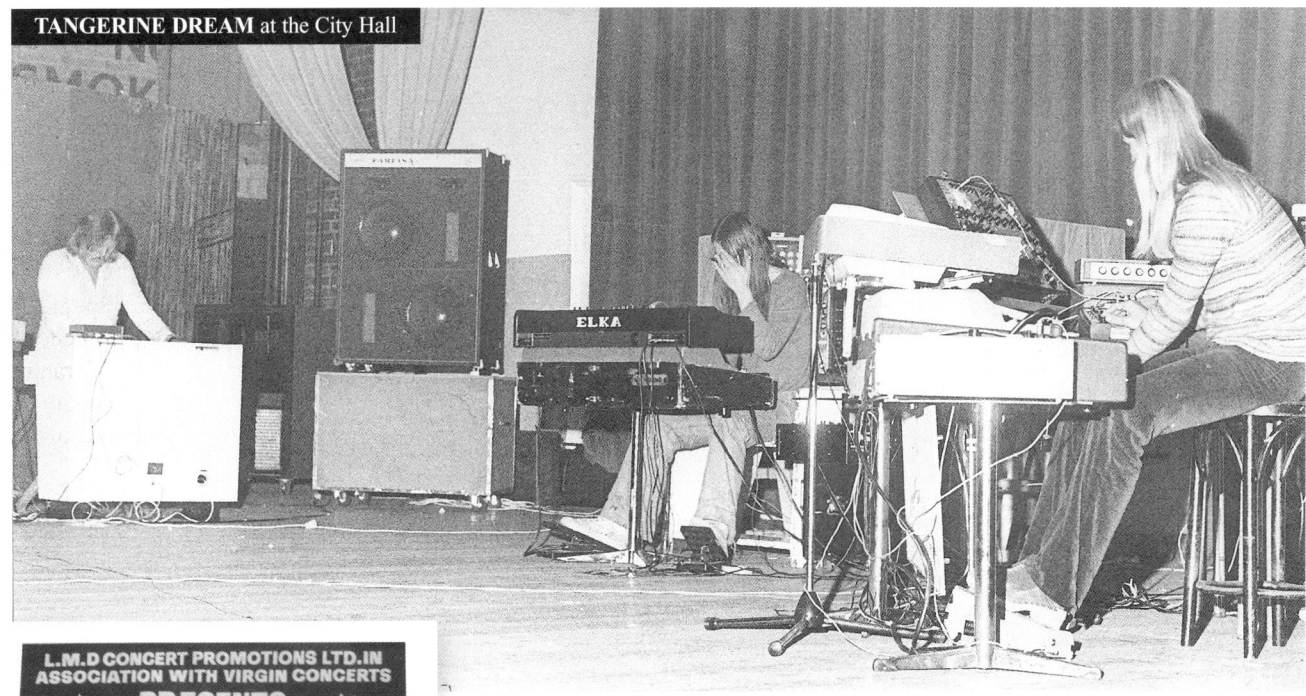

L.M.D CONCERT PROMOTIONS LTD. IN ASSOCIATION WITH VIRGIN CONCERTS PRESENTS
TANGERINE DREAM IN CONCERT
LAST DATE THIS SUMMER AT
SALISBURY CITY HALL
WEDS. 21ST AUGUST
DOORS OPEN 7-30 START 8PM. TKTS. £1-10P FROM WAX RECORDS SALISBURY 23306, BOURNEMOUTH 26501, SOUTHAMPTON 21866, VIRGIN RCDS. BRISTOL 297431 OR POSTAL APPLICATIONS - L.M.D 31, MARKET ST. TORQUAY & VIRGIN 130, NOTTINGHILL GATE W.11

used to review gigs and various reporters had taken an interest, but nobody had taken any pictures of all the bands visiting Salisbury in the sixties and seventies."

"I thought 'Well, I might as well start putting matters right'. The first one was Tangerine Dream - my first foray into the world of rock photography and realising the pitfalls. They performed under very low light and after a while I thought 'What the hell am I going to do here? I'll have to use flash'- so I took the photograph with direct flash. The music stopped and I was admonished in German from the stage, so realised at that point it was not a good idea to fire flashes off in semi-darkness at professional musicians!"

The concert prompted sixteen-year old Simon Kuczera of Amesbury to write to the Journal. Not only did he praise Tangerine Dream for their 'unique' performance, but also thanked both the promoters for arranging the City Hall's first top-line gig in eight months and the audience for their support and reaction to the band.

Discounting the occasional jazz act and sixties band, the number of 'name' gigs at the City Hall dropped to just two in 1974, with Leo Sayer appearing at the venue a couple of months after Tangerine Dream. The scarcity of good shows bemoaned in Simon Kuczera's letter had been compounded by the closure in March of the Alex Disco – the city's only club venue - after seven years of bringing an impressive number and range of acts to the city.

The last gig at the Alex featured local band All In The Mind – a neat coincidence as Pete Maple, father of All In The Mind bassist Colin, had opened the original Alexandra Rooms with his own band, The Merry Macs.

Little more than a week later, a new local authority, Salisbury District Council, was vested to administer the areas formerly covered by the City of New Sarum, Wilton Town Council and three Rural District Councils in the surrounding countryside.

A week before the Alex's last stand Liberal parliamentary candidate John Lakeman was involved in a demonstration against the Council over the lack of entertainment in the city, organised by local residents Cass Rawlings and Sandra Irwin.

John Lakeman: "Salisbury had been on the list of visits by major bands. For economic reasons that slowed down, but it had always been good to have the emerging bands playing and this was like having a door slammed in the face. Salisbury District Council had just been set up, so local politics was in a state of flux and they were much more concerned about matters that were of importance to them. I think they were oblivious to the needs of young people in Salisbury at that time."

ENDLESS BEAT

"We used to get shouted at in the street – 'disgraceful', 'get a hair cut'…"

"I was involved in local politics and felt it was something where I could share my own experience, to ensure there was something for young people of that day and later on – I felt strongly that it ought to be maintained."

The protest attracted a large crowd to the Old George Mall, where local theatre group Stage 65 provided a dramatisation of social life in the city, such as it was. This was followed by speeches from Cass Rawlings ('Why should we pay some of the highest rates in England and get nothing for our money?'), Sandra Irwin ('Your children will be sitting in pubs all evening if there is no disco to go to'), John Lakeman ('I am appalled to find that offices seem more important than houses and money more important than people') and the bar manager at the Alex, Mike Robins (who described its closure as 'another nail in the entertainment coffin of this city').

Mike Robins: "I had known the bar staff for a long time and we were all upset that the music scene in Salisbury was going to die because there was nowhere else really who put very much on."

John Lakeman: "Speakers climbed up on to the back of the seating areas and we listened intently. I went along initially just to observe - because I wasn't involved in the music scene - but I felt there were certain aspects which weren't being put across, so I got hauled up. It came quite naturally because there was a fairly sizeable Liberal representation on the Council and it was part of our manifesto to try to promote entertainment and culture - for the benefit of local people, but also to attract tourists."

During the week before the protest, a petition signed by 5,000 people (equivalent to around 15% of the city's entire population at the time) was handed in to the Council. Despite this, most official reaction was perhaps predictable.

The city's Conservative MP, Michael Hamilton, had already stated his opinion that the city had many 'lively organisations', quoting the examples of the Operatic Society, French Circle and Philatelists Club! Meanwhile Fergus Colquhoun, the outgoing Town Clerk, advised that (despite having granted planning permission to cease the use of the Alex for leisure purposes) the City Council had no powers to deal with the petition but hoped the new District Council would 'do what they can to help the youngsters in this city'.

The theme continued at a meeting of the new Council's Policy and Resources Committee, as Councillor Terry Heffernan dismissed the protest as 'just a big noise'. However, Councillor Austin Underwood - so often a champion of the people's causes – felt youngsters should be invited to join with the Council in a working party to find a new music venue.

The Alex wasn't the only venue to close down and there was a perception that the ultra-conservative (large and/or small 'c') city elders were determined to clamp down on anything considered to be out of the norm.

Ethem Cetintas: "We used to go and jam at the Saddle Rooms at Wilton and they shut that down as well. Salisbury was such a conservative place at that time. It was really prurience time – every other woman walking down the street was a Mary Whitehouse and they didn't like us. We used to get shouted at in the street – 'disgraceful', 'get a hair cut' and all this business. There was a lot of resentment and I think in the end the blue rinse lot managed to curb it through the Council to get rid of venues under the guise of causing too much trouble and noise."

Matters did not improve during the ensuing twelve months and a further protest was organised, this time by the Young Liberals in conjunction with Sandra Irwin and Bronwen Owen (described by the Salisbury Journal as 'Salisbury's charity and entertainment girls').

Publicity leaflets for the event pointed out that, as well as the Alex, three other dance venues had closed in the city since the end of World War Two: Victoria Hall, the Assembly Rooms and the Palais[3, 4, 5]. A further three venues were now more limited in their availability: the Cadena, Morrison Hall and Co-Op Hall[6]. Although the City Hall had opened in 1963, this was a different type of venue to those that had closed, for which there had been no replacements.

The desired outcome of the protest was that one of three scenarios would transpire: the Council would be spurred into finding a new entertainment site or hall; the city's Charter Trustees would find a hall to rent out to interested parties or; private concerns would move into the city and open a new venue.

This time the rally took place in the Guildhall Square, but the Council – perhaps in an attempt to halt the protest – asked for a £250,000 insurance indemnity. Councillor Ken Edwards felt this was 'utterly ridiculous' and told the Salisbury Journal he would support the protest even if it was

2: Dark Side of the Moonrakers

An Agreement made ..8th.. day September 1975 between Students Union hereinafter called the Management, of one part, and Neil Innes and Fatso hereinafter called the Artist, of the other part.

Witnesseth that the Management hereby engages the Artist and the Artist accepts an engagement to present .... to appear as known at the venue on the dates for the periods and at the salaries stated in the Schedule hereto.

Schedule: The Artist agrees to appear at ....Salisbury College Of Tech, Southampton Rd, Salisbury. on ..17th October 1975.. for a salary of £ ..200.. or ....% of the gross advance and door takings, whichever is the greater.

Clauses.
1. The price of admission is to be .... in advance .... at the door.
2. The capacity of the venue is .... seated .... standing .... total.
3. The venue has been set to gross £.......... and all receipts must be made available for examination by the Artist.
4. The salary is to be paid ..cash.. to Artist.. on/xxxxxx..night..
5. The Artist shall play for ..1 X 60 min.. minutes from .... to ....
6. The Artist should arrive by ..7.30.. and the equipment by ..5pm..
7. The other Artists appearing on the bill are (in order of appearance) ....
8. The Artist will receive ..100.. % Billing.
9. The stage size is .... ft. deep .... ft. wide .... ft. high, and .... ft. from the ceiling. It is/is not a permanent fixture.
10. There is to be a lockable dressing room for the sole use of the Artist.
11. The electric power available for the Artist's equipment is .... and for the Artist's own lighting is ....
12. The available lighting is ....
13. The mixing unit will be able to be situated in the centre of the hall at any position decided by the Artist's road manager on the day.
14. The Artist will not appear at any other venue within .... miles, ... weeks before and .... weeks after this appearance.
15. In the case of the Artist's wanting to cancel the appearance due to illness, the management has the right to demand a medical certificate.

P.T.O.

I/We the undersigned acknowledge that I/We have read the above clauses and agree that this will be adhered to in detail.

Date ..Neil Innes.. Signed ..22-9-75..
Address .... Telephone ....

---

technically illegal. His colleague Councillor Roger Hardy felt the City Council had acted inappropriately as, although the Town Map designated the Alexandra Rooms for cultural and leisure use, planning permission had been granted to use the building as offices.

The event was preceded by the carrying of a coffin from New Street, symbolising the death of live entertainment in the city following the closure of the Alex. However, although on this occasion there was more political buy-in, the protest was a failure with only a handful of people turning up in support.

Despite this setback the city's new Mayor, Anthony Stocken, pledged support to a new venture aimed at filling the void left by the Alex. Peter Coombs and his brother-in-law Ian Sutton had investigated using the former St Edmunds School as a nightclub, to be called Angie[7]. The entrepreneurial Coombs also had the necessary financial backing lined-up.

The building was eventually taken over by St Probus School, but as part of his investigations Coombs had also approached the owners of a nearby building that, however unlikely it might have seemed, would help resolve the issue of the a lack of 'club' venues in the city.

St Edmunds Church, in Bedwin Street, had been decommissioned and a scheme was launched to operate the building as an arts centre. The first public meeting of the St Edmunds Arts Trust was held in the redundant church in January 1975 and attended by eighty people. Trust Chairman Roger Townsend stressed the project's reliance on support from the District and Arts Councils, as the Trust was as 'poor as the proverbial church mouse and other than individuals putting their hands in their pockets, we have no capital whatsoever'.

The Diocesan Board of Finance had set a target of the end of July 1975 for the venture to be up and running and Trust President, Judith Buckland, urged attendees not to simply stand and criticise: 'If your ideas are exciting and you're prepared to work for them, you're just the person we're looking for'. Ideas suggested from the floor included dog shows, lectures, a craft workshop and use by the city's Studio Theatre.

The social secretary of the Students' Union at the College of Technology was also keen to address the lack of a decent live venue in the city.

Andy Pringle: "The natural course at that time was to go to Southampton or Bournemouth if you wanted to see a name band - or London even. The city and surrounding areas appeared to have very little, if any, live entertainment going on."

"Salisbury Tech leant itself to possibly being a replacement because it had its own hall and potentially a client base as well. I thought it would be a perfect opportunity to pull all those things together, maybe move the music scene on a little bit and make a place that was vibrant and had live music on a regular basis. I'd like to think we did make steps in that direction."

"The nice thing about the Students' Union is it does have a budget and people that would like you to book acts, which was a godsend. It wasn't just me, it was a committee of like minded people who wanted to promote acts - and maybe there was a growing awareness from the bands themselves that the college circuit could be exploited. Always they would go to universities but smaller colleges, like the Tech, were quite a good market for them."

"Booking agents were keen to become your friend because they needed to get their acts out and earning money, so there was never a shortage of supply and we could basically take our pick depending on what the budget was - in those days we could pay up to £300 for an act. They tended to be bands that were either on the verge of being good or had been good some time ago. We had Neil Innes – who wrote the music for Monty Python - he charged £100 for him and a band to come down. That was a bit different for Salisbury and it did appeal to students."

ENDLESS BEAT

"I was kind of taking a gap sort of thing – I'm still on it!"

Over the decades Salisbury music fans have missed out on the opportunity to see some very big names as shows were pulled because of the lack of a venue on the suggested date, controversy, illness or even death. In 1976 one potential superstar – or his agents – decided he had simply become too big a name to play in the city.

Andy Pringle: "I was approached by an agent who was given the job of launching the career in this country of a singer called Harpo, who was Swedish and an absolute monster star in his homeland - they thought maybe they could replicate that success in England."

"Salisbury Tech being an obvious place to launch the international superstar we agreed to put on Harpo and The Banana Band for the princely sum of £75. The contract was signed, it was all agreed, but in the interim Harpo released a single, Movie Star, and it made the charts. Obviously that boosted his appeal - and possibly the level of venue he could choose to appear in - and Salisbury Tech was quickly jettisoned, so he never did appear."

Movie Star having peaked at number 24 during its six-week chart run, Harpo never showed up in the UK listings again. Andy now wryly refers to this episode as having involved "The World famous Harpo and The Banana Band."

In 1975 Andy had promoted the first rock gig at the new St Edmunds Arts Centre, headlined by the Liverpool band Nutz. This however drew complaints from some local residents.

Andy Pringle: "It was unfortunate because it was a good concert, people enjoyed it - it was using the Arts Centre for what it was set up for. If it had been the City Hall or the College nobody would have batted an eyelid. The fact that it was an old church and people could hear it through the old windows was the only problem. I think you could have put on any rock act and if they made a noise the locals would have complained."

"We do live in a sleepy city and there is always going to be resistance. In the sixties, when there was a boom time in bringing in the Merseybeat acts, I bet the locals complained about that affecting the youth of the area and corrupting them. Now my daughter is eighteen and I am probably closer to being like the Bedwin Street people!"

Apart from the closure of venues, licensing issues and the rise of the disco were also impacting on the local live scene.

Andy Pringle: "We had problems because the Tech started to put restrictions on what we could do – the amount of door staff and the hours you could stay open. They would insist that music stopped by a certain time and didn't go over a certain decibel rating otherwise the power would cut out. We had several occasions where everything would just cut off halfway through a band's act."

"I think the Council would argue from another standpoint – I don't think they were right, but they were scared of everything that went with it. They associated live music with drugs, drinking too much, young people misbehaving and I think that clouded their judgement."

"The other side is it has to stack up economically. What happened over time is bands started charging more money and for smaller venues, like the ones in Salisbury, it just meant the figures didn't add up. The truth was that discos made money. You could bring in a local DJ for £25 and pack a hall, or bring an act down from London and pay £300 and they would play to a half full hall."

"I experienced it at the Tech – I brought Stuart Henry down, a former Radio One disc jockey - and put him on at the City Hall. We did get local bands to support him I have to say, but the reason for doing it was the figures stacked up. The figures have to add up, particularly out in the commercial world. It was less so in the Students Union - the aim was to break even."

Andy Sheppard

Yan Webber [of Peacewave]: "I have to say we hated the word 'disco' because we saw what it did to the clubs. They were paying us a fee, which you would have to split per person, and you went home with a fiver for about six hours hard work - they were paying a disco slightly less but the man was pocketing it all himself. The club scene died because of that."

A Salisbury solo artist who would find international fame was making a belated start in his preferred field.

Andy Sheppard: "I wanted to play saxophone when I was very young but was dissuaded by the system of education. In fact I never studied any music whatsoever at school because I was forced to decide between studying art or music. I think they still do that, which is completely crazy because I think you will find that most people who are interested in music are interested in the arts in general."

"I started messing around on the flute, but that was just because the music shop I was working in didn't have any saxophones. I was in that position where I could borrow stuff and check it out and the flute has very similar fingering to the saxophone."

"Then I was on my way to Art College, in Salisbury, but was kind of taking a gap sort of thing – I'm still on it! I bumped into Geoff Williams, who was a fantastic musician – great piano player. It was him who said 'You're a musician not a painter, have you listened to Coltrane, Davis, Monk?' I didn't really know about that music - he was the one who said 'You've got to check this out'."

"Hearing Coltrane I thought 'Oh shit! This is what I want to do with my life'. I took that decision, and it sort of becomes 'That's sorted then, I better get on and do it', even though it was starting ridiculously late. I practiced for eight hours a day and was completely addicted to the saxophone - and still am."

"Going to sign on for my student grant every week they would say 'Have you been working?' I would say 'Yeah, I've been playing eight hours a day'. They would ask things like 'Factory or clerical?' and I would say 'I'm a musician'. They would say 'No such thing' – literally! They used to send me for jobs like selling fishing tackle – they had me down as a

SPHERE - left to right: Geoff Williams, Pete Maxfield and Andy Sheppard

ENDLESS BEAT

"... in the jazz scene, you have to make an individual name for yourself."

salesman – so I used to go to these interviews and stutter so I would never get hired. But I was working my ass off - much harder than most students – learning to play the saxophone. At the end of two years they said 'we're not giving you any more money, you're on your own'! I got a phone call from a blues band and went on the road."

At the time Andy was living in a communal house in Milton Road with a series of housemates: "I took on the tenancy of this house, which became rapidly 'the hang' - it was party central, but amidst all that partying we were getting it together musically."

"We converted the garage into a rehearsal studio - soundproofed it as best we could with carpets and stuff. It was like having your own music college. It was great because you had the musicians on hand, could go 'I really want to get my head around this Monk tune' and play it all day long until you started to understand the harmonies and what was going on. It was a collective where any money went into the pot to pay for the rent and stuff. A whole bunch of musicians came through the house, loads of people came and went, kind of walked in from another planet, floated around for a bit and then disappeared."

Roger Elliott: "They used to have after dinner recitals where Geoff and Andy would play Bach and things. They always put on this album by Carla Bley called The Escalator Over The Hill. I photographed Andy playing with Carla Bley a few years ago – that's how things changed."

Andy Sheppard: "I took as my role model people like Miles Davis or Picasso. If you are an artist, then by definition you should be constantly evolving. Initially people get frustrated because they have heard a record and want you to be playing that music then find you playing a completely different style. It's not always to their taste but I think in a creative musician that's what it's all about – to be experimental."

"We formed this band Sphere - with Geoff Williams, Pete Maxfield, and a whole string of drummers. We realised that without any gigs the band didn't exist - it was just a concept. The whole thing about music is it only exists when you are playing with and for people. That's when the real dynamic happens – otherwise you are [just] practicing. Once you realise that it's 'We better get some gigs otherwise this band is just a figment of my imagination'."

"We bought a van and just went on the road. It was mad – we would go off

Geoff Williams

SPHERE

34

to Europe, with one gig, could be three days or could be two weeks, whatever. We would literally turn up in towns, find a bar and say 'You want a band in here – and here we are!' Sometimes it was great, we would pick up a gig and it would lead to other things – the story would unfold. Sometimes we were threatened with arrest. Sometimes we would find somewhere to stay. Sometimes it would just be ridiculous!"

"We recorded for a label called Cadillac - quite an important jazz label at the time. They had a lot of connections with South African musicians in London. We were getting reviews in the Guardian and playing at festivals and people were noticing us, because we were young and there was nobody else doing what we were – we were totally influenced by the Jarrett Quartet and just believed in the music."

"It's really rare to get a band like that. With my current band, two guys live in Norway, one comes from India and the guitar player lives in London but he's Italian – pulling everyone together is a major bit of logistical work, whereas we were all living in the same little house in Salisbury. It was a great learning experience, we had a little scene going and believed in it and tried to convince other people. Eventually we all went to London. We thought the streets were going to be paved with gold, but they were paved with shit! That's why I left the country because I found London so hard to earn a living in as a musician."

"Everyone from that band went on and did other things - you can't keep a band together forever and, certainly in the jazz scene, you have to make an individual name for yourself. It's not like the rock scene – where the [band] name stays but the personnel change around."

One of the premier progressive bands in Salisbury formed following the split of Wedgwood Wing who, although he wasn't a band member, had been named in honour of ex-Salisbury resident Mike Wedgwood.

Andy Golden: "I remember putting an advert in Melody Maker and New Musical Express for a guitarist/singer to join myself, Chris Glover and Nige Goode. We had people coming from all over the country – Manchester, Birmingham, Southampton, Bournemouth and other places. A lot of them were very good, but not quite the person we wanted."

"This went on for about a week – the auditions were in a cottage up in Hurdcott. We had sort of given up when at the end of the week I had a phone call from a guy, who said he would like to come along and have a go. He turned up - the voice was good, the guitar was good. We asked his name and he said 'Andy Bradbury'. We asked where he came from and he said 'Salisbury'. We had been all around the country and there was actually someone on the doorstep, literally living around the corner!"

"That kicked it off and we started writing our own material. There weren't many bands around Salisbury, as far as we knew, writing original material. We got as many bookings as we could at colleges and universities - because their mind was slightly more open to different music."

"Brad came up with the name Grandma Moses, based on an octogenarian artist, who had taken up primitive art in her seventies and became very successful. It was a very unusual name and people remembered it – and still do I hope!"

The cottage in Hurdcott, near Barford St Martin - where Grandma Moses rehearsed – was part of the same farm complex used by hard rock band Jerusalem.

Andy Golden: "Jerusalem were rehearsing in the cottage adjoining where we were. That's how we met Bob Cooke. When they split up we brought Bob in on guitar. Then in 1974 we got Tom Thatcher involved."

Tom joined Grandma Moses after his previous band appeared on the same bill at Southampton University.

Tom Thatcher: "It was a 'Battle of the Bands' type of thing, where I had my band Lizard, which had formerly been Gland Band – we had backed Cockney Rebel there a few days before. I got chatting to Andy and Brad and some time after Andy phoned and said 'Do you fancy joining Grandma Moses?' I said yes, but that I would rather go on keyboards and perhaps the other Lizard guitarist Paul McElhatton could come in on guitar. We both auditioned out at the cottage. Then we must have spent getting on

ENDLESS BEAT

"There was nobody around Salisbury doing anything like this…"

Tom Thatcher

Left to right: Mike Wedgwood, Graham Deakin and Tom Thatcher

for twelve months rehearsing."

Andy Golden: "It was a seminal moment for us because we hadn't had keyboards until then. The keyboard addition spread the music even further towards what we were trying to do, and two guitars were also important - the twin leads."

Grandma Moses developed a unique musical style through the members bringing their individual interests into play.

Andy Golden: "I was into Yes, Tom was very much into Genesis, the best pop and Rory Gallagher and Brad was into Clapton and the blues. That was the thing, the melding together of the ideas and interests we had."

Tom Thatcher: "One of my favourite musicians of all time was Tony Banks of Genesis. In as much as I was trying to play like anything that was the sort of stuff I was trying to put into Grandma Moses. Not that I can or could play like Tony, of course!"

Andy Golden: "There was nobody around Salisbury doing anything like this – with lots of different time signatures. It wouldn't be right to say we copied from anything, it was an amalgamation of all the different inspirations we had."

Tom Thatcher: "The main song writing was done by Brad and Andy. When I joined I brought about five songs, but the other eighteen or so were all Brad and Andy's. The idea was given to the band, and then things were added to it – layers, harmonies, solos."

Andy Golden: "To give you an idea, Brad might come along with three verses, but needing something else, so I would write a fourth – that's an example of our collaboration. Or I would turn up with a song and lyrics and Brad and/or Tom would suggest ideas or changes. Tom had some great original thinking. One of my favourites is Porridge Man, which had a great opening line: 'Christ! He's seen me, as he strides in through the pub door…'"

Tom Thatcher: "We weren't a rock band, we weren't a pop band. I suppose 'prog' was the nearest thing, but it was just what we thought were good songs. We weren't an easy listen but we did it to the best of our ability and I think some of the songs still stand up pretty well."

The new line up of the band made its debut at the Teacher Training College.

Tom Thatcher: "We started with the song Astral Spiral – it started with twittering birds on an old, primitive S1000 Roland synthesiser then sort of segued into a gentle guitar introduction. Then off it went – like all our songs – thirteen different timings, an instrumental section in the middle and, to come back in, the gentle twittering birds."

"What I actually managed to programme it to was what was described as 'an ack-ack attack'. So, instead of this gentle noise there was this extraordinary bombing and crashing. Chris Glover told me he literally nearly shit himself because he thought we were under attack! He completely forgot his parts after that. Also, the audience had thought it was a good old rock band and were trying to dance – hopping around on one leg and turning in circles."

During this period, Brad and Andy were also playing in a duo as a side project, whose name occasionally resulted in some unfortunate billings.

Tom Thatcher: "When we played

ENDLESS BEAT

"Brad had a major sense of humour bypass about it."

at the Teacher Training College, Andy and Brad also had a duo called Ferry - but there was a poster up saying 'Next Week – The Fairies'. Brad had a major sense of humour bypass about it."

Andy Golden: "We got called 'Fairy' quite a lot actually - on posters at various pubs."

The shortage of suitable venues in the Salisbury area impacted on local bands. A Salisbury Journal review of a Grandma Moses' gig at the Playhouse noted it was only their fourth live appearance in nine months and suggested their stagecraft had suffered accordingly. Furthermore, some of the music was felt to be overly complex.

Even so, the reviewer ignored 'the lack of polish which, in an old half-full theatre it was so easy to pick out' and welcomed 'a dazzling array of talents by any standards'. Songs picked out as highlights included Brand New Day, Goodbye Suzanne, Rainbow Chaser and the satirical Porridge Man.

The generally negative tone of the

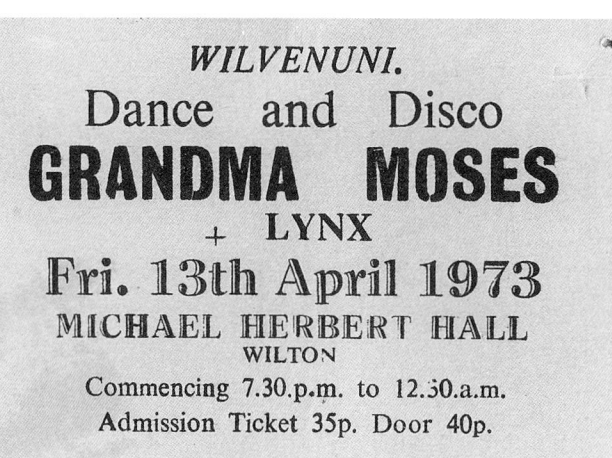

WILVENUNI.
Dance and Disco
GRANDMA MOSES
+ LYNX
Fri. 13th April 1973
MICHAEL HERBERT HALL
WILTON
Commencing 7.30.p.m. to 12.30.a.m.
Admission Ticket 35p. Door 40p.

review drew a response from Christina Cox of Hamilton Road, who felt that 'once again a wealth of talent goes overboard and drowns for want of recognition'. Although there had been no 'frontals, horizontals or abusive language' the show had inspired her to 'rock, rig and reel in the upper part of the theatre'. Christina wouldn't have blamed the band if they rewrote Porridge Man and dedicated it to 'the stodgy porridge people of Salisbury'.

Grandma Moses attracted the interest of Ian Gillan, who had produced the Jerusalem and Pussy releases on Deram. Drummer Andy Golden had in fact previously had the briefest of brushes with him while playing with one of his previous bands.

Andy Golden: "I first met – if I can put it like that - Gillan in around 1969/70, with Wedgwood Wing. We went to a 'Battle of the Bands' in Weymouth. About halfway through our set four or five guys dressed in long black coats came in and just stood there. Afterwards we found out they were Deep Purple, who had been playing locally."

Gillan took note of Grandma Moses having overheard them rehearsing when he and Zoe Dean were visiting Jerusalem at Hurdcott.

Andy Golden: "We went to his place near Reading – a fantastic place with a guitar-shaped swimming pool. He liked the music and put us in touch with his manager, whom we called 'Fearless Dennis'."

Tom Thatcher: "What we played to Ian Gillan on that occasion was a demo we had just done in Gooseberry Studios in Soho. We had somehow managed to do five of these toe twisting, tongue curling epics in twelve hours. Thank God Mike Wedgwood and Pye Hastings of Caravan came to help mix it – we would never have done it in a million years."

"We played the Dagenham Roundhouse in London with Dr Feelgood. Ian and Zoe and a gang came along and he said he really enjoyed it. He was a great guy. Fortunately Wilko Johnson was horribly out of tune, so we came up smelling of roses on that one. We played an impromptu heavy rock set at the end, with Brad on superb slide guitar, and did about three encores. Lee Brilleaux was good, but Wilko was just awful."

Andy Golden: "Gillan was the name we could open doors with. Cube Records liked us - Olaf Wyper was the MD and said he would sign us, which

Bob Cooke

GRANDMA MOSES - left to right: Nige Goode, Andrew 'Brad' Bradbury, Chris Glover and Andy Golden

was fantastic. We went along to the meeting, went away and waited to sign the contract – then we went back and there was a new guy sitting behind the MD's desk. This guy said he was going to listen to all the acts again and never picked us up."

Grandma Moses also played support slots to Decameron at Farnham Playhouse and Be Bop Deluxe at the City Hall back in Salisbury and came away with contrasting views of the headliners.

Tom Thatcher: "Decameron were fantastic and we had a good chat with them at the end. Mike Wedgwood mixed for us that night. They were very nice and I have actually kept in touch with Johnny Coppin the guitarist/singer from time to time - they were very kind about us."

"Be Bop Deluxe weren't the easiest. I think their roadies had a bit of an attitude problem - we were not there to be watched at all, they had come to see Be Bop Deluxe. I suppose if I was arrogant I could say we had five hundred people jumping up and down, and they had three."

Ethem Cetintas of Marble Orchard

ENDLESS BEAT

By the time the companies said 'Let's talk…' the band had disbanded."

also recalls Be Bop Deluxe as being somewhat aloof: "They didn't really see themselves as a 'rock band' like the rest of us. I think that's one of the reasons they were keeping their distance – because they weren't part of our crowd. If you looked at the way they dressed, they had beautifully manicured hands, beautifully done hairstyles and wore really clever suits, and there was a whole bunch of us oafs coming out with ripped jeans, smelly t-shirts and stuff. They weren't the kind of guys we would have mixed with – not like Led Zeppelin for instance."

Ethem had left Marble Orchard towards the end of 1973, to pursue a career in TV, film and recording: "I left the band and Dave Eppel was the next guitarist and a guy called Mick Smith was the next keyboard player. I moved away to the London Film School so it was not possible to stay with the band. Then the band became more soft – they were trying to become more mainstream."

"Me and Martin were very close friends and always kept in touch. I used to do all their recordings because I worked as an engineer at the BBC. Martin had a studio down in his basement, at Barrington House on Churchfields Road."

In 1975 Marble Orchard keyboard player Mike Smith landed a contract as a songwriter with Marty Wilde's company Rockhard. In their final days Ethem recorded Marble Orchard professionally, although possibly off-the-record, at the BBC. He had hoped that Ahmet Ertegun of Atlantic Records, who knew Ethem's father from his days in Turkey, would pick up on the demos.

Ethem Cetintas: "Ertegun knew me as a child. I said 'I've got this band called Marble Orchard and I've recorded them – these guys are a pretty good rock band, can I send you a tape?' He told us to also send one to Decca. The two were listening to the tapes, but in the meantime the band were having a huge amount of arguments – they just weren't getting on. By the time the companies said 'Let's talk and do another demo' the band had disbanded.

Marble Orchard leader Martin James had attempted to organise a pop festival in Salisbury over the 1974 August Bank Holiday weekend - at The Butts off Ashley Road - with 25% of the proceeds to be donated to the Mayor's charity appeal. The Council agreed to the event, but then effectively quashed it by demanding a £5000 deposit (in lieu of potential damage: 'broken cars and trampled flowers') and a £250,000 third party indemnity.

Martin was disgusted, telling the Salisbury Journal 'the Council are supposed to be helping the youngsters of Salisbury to get some entertainment together and this would have been good for five or six thousand people… they don't want a festival, it's as simple as that'. He also drew a comparison with the conditions imposed by the Council on the city's Hospital Carnival: £100,000 indemnity and no 'damages' deposit.

Although the festival never materialised Martin, along with fellow ex-Marble Orchard member Ernie Parsons, put on his first show at the City Hall in early 1975, when The Groundhogs appeared, supported by Halcyon.

Around 500 people attended, which meant a loss for the promoters. A Salisbury Journal review felt rock fans had become 'fussy' and 'a band blasting its way on the pretence of past successes' was no longer enough to

Andrew 'Brad' Bradbury

40

satisfy them. This was followed by an even lower turnout of 300 for a Global Village Trucking Co gig – despite their having topped a poll of bands the locals would most like to see. Although Martin was disappointed he would not give up on his quest to provide entertainment in the city.

The farm cottages at Hurdcott, where the seeds for both Jerusalem and Grandma Moses were sown, also saw the formation of the first 'serious' band of a member of an Amesbury musical dynasty.

Steve Collinson's parents Jo and Ted had formed one of the first skiffle bands in south Wiltshire – The Red River Group - and by the dawn of the seventies Ted had moved into the country and western field with The Midnite Ramblers. Having been approached by producer Alan Green after an appearance on the BBC's Country Club, The Midnite Ramblers recorded an album, Midnite Breakdown, in a converted barn on a remote Welsh hillside. Steve sometimes stood in on bass with his father and had previously played rhythm guitar in a teenage late sixties band.

Steve Collinson: "Dad taught me how to play guitar but being in bands you soon learn the hard way. I remember being in a band called The Pippins. I was only about fourteen, my brother Jerry was on guitar, we had a bass player called Paddy Cox and a drummer called Ronnie Starbecker."

"Paddy was in the band because his dad brought all the gear. He wanted to be a drummer but we went down to listen to him and said 'No, we've got a better drummer than you - you play bass'. It worked very well - going around youth clubs playing anything that was in the charts – this was about '67. We did one gig in a Bournemouth hotel and Paddy got electrocuted. He got taken to hospital but, being the showmen we were: 'The show must go on'. So, I said I would play bass. That's why I first started playing bass – because he got electrocuted."

"I joined the Bob James Band playing loads of dance band gigs and would be depping for anybody who needed a bass player – for money. I was doing at least three or four gigs a week. The dance bands financed the rock bands. That's how you got your gear together – went out and played with dance bands to get the money, to put your own band together and go out and play for nothing."

Steve's first 'rock' band, Bullfrog - with Anton Hayman on guitar and vocals and Andy Golden on drums - spent the summer of 1971 on the farm at Hurdcott.

Steve Collinson: "Bullfrog was very heavy blues influenced - along the lines of Leslie West of Mountain. We rehearsed all

The Midnite Ramblers (left to right): Tony Griffiths, Phil Bryant, Ray Gulliver and Ted Collinson at rehearsal.

Ramblers record first album

SALISBURY'S country and western cowboys, The Midnite Ramblers, have recorded their first

41

ENDLESS BEAT

"... whose gonna put a band on the radio called The Homosexuals?"

through the summer, relentlessly. It was that 'get it together in a country cottage' ideal, which was lovely for the summer, but two gigs later the band broke up."

"We did a gig – I think with Keef Hartley, it was something to do with Pete Coombs - down in Bournemouth at a place called the Jump Ballrooms. There were about eight people there, so I was a bit despondent. I remember driving home in the van thinking 'Where did Anton go? What happened to Andy? As we came off the dual carriageway I saw Andy walking with his drums - we had left him behind! We did stop and pick him up but that was the end of that band."

Following the disintegration of Bullfrog, Steve and Anton returned to Amesbury and formed Never Bend Over, with Steve's brother Jerry on second guitar and Reggie Maggs on drums. They were later joined by Ernie Cartmell on synthesiser.

Steve Collinson: "We did a club down the Kings Arms. There was nowhere to play, so we thought we would go and ask the landlord if we could use his back room as the Rock Club of Amesbury, which we did, until he came down one day when we were rehearsing and said 'Look, the people in the bar' - which was like three rooms away - 'their drinks are shuddering across the table'. That put an end to that. We did have volume problems, but most bands did because you had to play as loud as the drummer. Drummers just don't play quietly – and it was Reg Maggs, who was an absolute monster – so as loud as he played we just turned up to match him."

Anton Hayman had a reputation as a driven and innovative individual.

Steve Collinson: "We were rehearsing and Anton had just got this Les Paul Junior guitar. We sat working out all our stuff for the evening and he put his guitar on the settee. His son Sam leapt on one end of the settee - the guitar leapt off the other end and broke the head off. End of the gig you might have thought? Not to Anton – he immediately said 'I've got some horse glue in the car. He got it on the cooker, boiled up this glue, stuck the head back on the guitar and played the gig - worked a treat."

Never Bend Over claim to have been the first band to ever play at Stonehenge, as Steve explains in Chapter Four. After about a year the band folded and Steve and Reg Maggs set out on a new venture.

Steve Collinson: "Anton eventually went to London and formed a band called The Homosexuals. That was his 'death wish' - he was a fantastic player, playing with really good people, but calling the band 'The Homosexuals' immediately ruled you out of getting played. He made a couple of records but in those days – '75/76 - whose gonna put a band on the radio called The Homosexuals?"

"At the time we were doing that Kings Arms club we used to get John Priestley along to play in the intervals. We were good friends anyway and when Never Bend Over finished I started working with John a lot more. We went out and did duos and then formed a band called Eskimo."

Eskimo featured a young guitarist who would become a familiar face on the local punk scene.

Nick Kemp: "Steve came round to the house and asked the old man if it would be okay - always polite under all that hair. I started playing when I was sixteen - give or take. I restrung a Spanish guitar left-hand and taught myself the basics inside three weeks. Why? Hendrix. I liked everything about his sound – I especially liked that a lot of people considered it noise. I thought 'Wow - if all that feedback and shit is making these assholes so miserable then it's got to be something."

In common with many of Steve Collinson's band projects, Eskimo folded after about a year.

Steve Collinson: "At a gig at Boscombe Down John was drunk and we had just done this horrible rendition of Positively Fourth Street. I turned around and said 'What do you want to do next?' and he just sort of slurred at me 'Positively Fourth Street'. After that we decided to knock it on the head."

As had been the case with Dave Dee, DBM&T's career foundered largely because of a perceived lack of credibility with their new (albeit different) target audience, resulting in a lack of general recognition for a series of very good records.

Alan Blaikley: "The trouble we found was, with the closing of the pirate radio stations, the BBC had become the only avenue - other than live performances - by which the songs could be heard. On Radio One there was by this time a new breed of producer who wanted at all costs to be thought 'hip' and were not prepared to give DBM&T, in their new incarnation, the benefit of the doubt. There was no way John Peel was ever going to play their records - though he should have. Radio Two should have been the natural outlet for Dave's records, but he certainly wasn't given a fair crack of the whip there."

"Although both Dave and The Boys were always very much liked personally throughout the music industry, their 'crime' was the fact that they hadn't written their own songs from the word go. This, absurdly, ultimately robbed them of the stamp of 'authenticity', despite their undeniably superb and original musicianship."

"Ken [Howard] and I were always immensely fond of all the band members, and this didn't change, though inevitably we felt sad we weren't able to help them achieve the much greater success they deserved in their later careers."

DBM&T had released two further singles, I Want To Be There (in 1971) and They Won't Sing My Song (1972) with negligible sales. In early 1973 Philips turned down the track Sarah for a single release, and the band folded.

Tich Amey: "We did the cabaret thing for a while and went back into doing the hits but it just wasn't us really. The band just filtered out - Mick went and got himself a pub. I think he just decided he had had enough and the best of luck to him."

Trevor Davies also took on a pub, leaving John Dymond and Tich to consider their options before getting in touch with an old friend.

Peter Mason: "I had written a bunch of songs and wanted to do an album. Just about the same time Beaky and Tich contacted me. They said 'We want to form a band – would you be interested?' They were very experienced and innovative."

Beaky and Tich were anxious to start afresh and had no desire to be the 'stars' of the new project.

Peter Mason: "Beaky and Tich had got so involved and contributed to it, I said 'Why don't we make this the first [group] album and go on from there – it doesn't mean a lot to me that it has to be a 'Peter Mason' album. Why don't we just call it 'Amey-Dymond-Mason', but they didn't want any association with Dave Dee, Dozy, Beaky, Mick and Tich. I really wanted

ENDLESS BEAT

"You name it he would give it a go!"

'Amey-Dymond-Mason' because I thought it was such a great name, but I gave in to their wishes."

The three musicians began working on arrangements of Peter's songs at Beaky's shed before moving into a rehearsal room in Salisbury. At this stage they were joined by Martin 'Cuddles' Smith (formerly of The Meddy Evils, The Mojos and Gentle Giant) on drums and David Rose and Bob Taylor (both formerly of David) on keyboards and bass respectively.

Having refined the songs, the band went into Advision Studios during late 1972 and early 1973, where they were augmented by another ex-David member, Ian England, on piano and joined for guest appearances by Mox Gowland on harmonica – who had played with Alexis Korner among others, former Family and New Animals member John Weider on fiddle and sixteen-year old Weybridge schoolgirl Judie Tzuke.

The Mason sound featured strong harmonies and was heavily influenced by American bands such as Poco. The recordings were produced and engineered by Martin Rushent, who would later work with quite different bands, such as The Buzzcocks and Joy Division.

Beaky and Bob Taylor thought of the album title - Starting As We Mean To Go On – and a cover art concept and Dave Dee secured a deal for the band with Dawn, a company set up in 1969 as the 'progressive' arm of Pye Records, but which by now had the likes of Brotherhood of Man on its roster.

Dawn advised the band that they wanted to issue a single initially but the album, in their opinion, didn't contain anything commercial enough to interest the radio stations. Mason therefore returned to the studio to cut additional material. When Freedom Comes was issued in April 1973 on the Pye label itself, with Dawn putting out Fading (with guest lead vocalist and drummer Chas O'Brien) five months later. Neither single became a hit although band members believe this was at least partly due to a lack of promotion.

Despite the lack of commercial success, Mason embarked on a tour of the Netherlands in early 1974, before supporting Man on a UK tour.

Peter Mason: "We were doing universities and were known as a sort of country rock band. We were playing somewhere and doing a sound check with Man's sound engineer. Man came in and said 'What are they like?' and the engineer said 'They're great – they remind me of Poco'. We were rather

MASON - left to right: Bob Taylor, David Rose, Peter Mason, Tich Amey, Beaky Dymond and Chas O'Brien

flattered of course. We got on great with them – they watched us and we watched them. After the tour they went into the studio to record a new album and invited us in. We went along and they had got in to harmony vocals and all that. So, we obviously impressed them!"

Mason attracted a great response from their audiences, but Dawn seemed to have lost interest in the project and decided there was no point in releasing the album.

Peter Mason: "In the end we found out that the record company didn't know what to do with us. They thought we were great but didn't know how to promote us, but I enjoyed it and learned a lot from the guys because they had more experience. In a way I learned about the business with Dave and with Tich and Beaky I learned more about being in a band."

Having been released from Dawn, Mason signed with Atlantic for a further single, Follow Me, in July 1974, but this too failed to reap any success and the band subsequently folded.

The Mason album was finally released in 2010, as a CD on the Cherry Tree label. It seems that to date only two 1973 'originals' have surfaced, a white label with mocked up sleeve given to the promoter of the Dutch tour and an Apple publishing acetate that eventually showed up in Japan. If anyone else has a copy, please contact the authors!

1974 saw a short reunion for Dave Dee, Dozy, Beaky, Mick and Tich, with John Dymond moving to drums and Peter Mason replacing him on guitar. This line-up released a one-off single, She's My Lady, on Atlantic subsidiary Antic.

Tich Amey: "Beaky has always been versatile. He wouldn't make a lead guitarist but he was a good right hand rhythm player. He could play drums, a bit of bass, squeeze box - you name it he would have a go."

Peter Mason: "Dave had this job at Atlantic Records and he called me one day and said 'What are you doing?' Mason had split up, he needed somebody to help him and I went and worked for him. That was a great experience. Manhattan Transfer, Yes, even The Rolling Stones were with Atlantic at the time. Also coming out of WEA – which was the umbrella company – was things like Emmylou Harris and Fleetwood Mac."

MASON - left to right: Beaky Dymond, Peter Mason and Tich Amey

ENDLESS BEAT

"Everybody used to say 'Who's Charlie Harwood?"

"I had written She's My Lady and we did a demo - Beaky, Tich and I. Bob James got it to The Hollies and they loved it. There was talk about them doing it, but previous to that I had played it to Dave and said maybe the boys could get together and do it. Dave initially turned it down but then heard that they [The Hollies] liked it, so thought maybe it was worth getting together. It was my one 'official' time of being a member of Dave Dee, Dozy, Beaky, Mick and Tich."

Somehow She's My Lady was not a hit - despite Dave Dee's potential influence on promotion at Atlantic, despite its similarity in style to The Hollies' huge hit of the same year, The Air That I Breathe,

DDDBM&T - 1974 with Peter Mason (right)

and despite its being a simply superb record – one of the very best in the entire DDDBMT and related canon.

Dave Dee had also recorded some tracks with Martin Rushent at Advision, at around the same time Mason had been active. By further coincidence Rushent was also working with former Salisbury resident Mike Wedgwood - with Curved Air - at Advision during this period. The Dave Dee tracks were apparently canned because they didn't suit his image.

It could well have been the case that the gap-toothed, grinning sixties pop idol might have been one of the last names of his generation of musicians to be expected to become involved in the progressive movement. Nevertheless, in 1975 he collaborated with French avant-garde composer Jean Musy on a single, I Have No Hold On You, and album, Few And Far Between. Dave provided un-credited vocals (singing lyrics written by Ken Howard and Alan Blaikley) on one of his most interesting recordings – and also one of his rarest: in 2008 Dave told Record Collector that he was still looking for a copy!

Following the reformed DDDBMT interlude, Dave went back to the day-job at Atlantic – working with the likes of The Heavy Metal Kids and AC/DC. The other four band members performed occasionally in an ad-hoc band, Charlie Harwood and The Pub Beats, at the Duck at Laverstock.

Tich Amey: "Everybody used to say 'Who's Charlie Harwood?' It wasn't anybody in particular - it was just Beaky thought it was a good name."

Occasional Pub Beats' member Pete Lucas - formerly with Bethany - then joined Tich, Beaky and Dozy in a new project, playing covers of Steely Dan and Cat Stevens and a show stopping Beatles medley, as well as original material.

Peter Mason: "They went into Tracker. The guitars were very prominent and I didn't really want to do that. I didn't feel I knitted into it. They took on board some of the songs that DBM&T did. They were brilliant at what they did but I left. I was a bit sad in a way but it had moved on to a heavier band – but the harmonies were still there."

Tich Amey: "Tracker formed through doing the record with Dave. They wanted to do a live radio show for the BBC and I said 'Well, I can't play guitar and pedal steel'. So Beaky said 'We'll get Arkle in' – Mr Lucas. Pete came along and played a bit of guitar and we got through this live radio show."

"A friend of Dozy's happened to be with him and said 'You've got the makings of a good band there' – Pete, Beaky, myself and Dozy – and offered to give us a few quid to go and rehearse. Of all the bands ever it was probably my favourite because I probably played better then than I do now. It was an interesting band to be in, with some funny arrangements. If I could have any band back it would be that band."

"The Dave Dee band was a growing up experience and we got pushed into lots of things, but challenging playing and singing and doing something different – it was definitely Tracker."

The first incarnation of Tracker showed tremendous potential but with no prospect of any recording deal on the horizon, Dozy and Beaky left the band in 1975. However, Tich and Pete carried on with two new members.

Steve Collinson: "After Eskimo, I met up with Tich and Pete Lucas. Dozy and Beaky had left, so they were looking for a drummer and bass player, and me and Reg [Maggs] were hauled in. That was intensive rehearsals – four nights a week."

"Instrumentally it was spot on. We did a recording of Eleanor Rigby once and the engineer Tony Arnold stopped it and said 'I can only hear one guitar' - but it was Tich and Pete playing so tightly together that it sounded like one big fat guitar. What it missed - from 'Tracker One' with Dozy and Beaky - was those extra vocals. Reg didn't have vocals and my voice didn't really suit what they were doing."

Tich Amey: "Steve used to sing but he wasn't really what I would call a 'harmony' singer as such - and Reggie didn't sing. So it wasn't quite there – but it was enjoyable."

Steve Collinson: "Tich had got me and Reggie in with promises of Scandinavian tours,

ENDLESS BEAT

"... we couldn't get the Hammond through the studio door..."

but I think he got disillusioned with it. As you can imagine, if he had rehearsed Tracker for a year with Dozy and Beaky and got it just how he wanted it and then had to go through all that material again – it makes you despondent."

Tracker recorded demos at Arny's Shack[8] and Pathway Studios, but the initial promise dissipated and as the band folded John Dymond came back on the scene and picked up two of the ex-members for his new project, Band Of Gold.

Steve Collinson: "Beaky was into nightclubs and discos, so he put a disco band together. He was a good mate with Pete Lucas who could play all that funky stuff. It was me on bass - playing my funk role – Steve Clasby on keyboards and we needed a singer. I knew John Hatchman, so I persuaded him to come along and audition."

John Hatchman, a native of Enford, started playing drums at the age of six or seven during breaks in a trio's set at Netheravon Working Men's Club…he later bought the drum kit. While he was still at school he played with Period, an Enford Youth Club based band who also gigged in the North and Midlands, playing Cream and Edgar Broughton songs. Period had also supported Rory Gallagher at Salisbury City Hall before eventually folding.

John Hatchman: "The other lads didn't carry on, but I knew it was what I wanted to do - and to do anything you've got to push yourself. I joined Scallywag from Marlborough and other local bands."

"Beaky put an advert in the paper – 'vocalist and percussionist required'. I answered and had the audition at The Grange. They had a little Dansette and an album by a guy called Jess Roden. They put the album on - a song called Blowing. Beaky said 'Listen to it, get the lyrics off and then we want to hear you sing it'."

"I got a pen and paper and wrote it down and he said 'I'll give you five minutes to get the tune in your head'. They struck up and I just went [sings] 'Blowing, feels just like the wind across my face…' Pete Lucas looked at me and said 'That's the man…that's it!' We started rehearsing that day and that's the first time I met Tich - being nosey as he is [laughs], anything new going on in Salisbury he had to suss out and obviously Beaky had told him about it."

Steve Collinson: "I hated the disco from day one. The only thing that was interesting to me was the actual bass lines and Beaky was a great drummer to work with - his timing was fantastic. He wasn't a fantastic player as such but his timing was so good, and he was a good singer."

Steve Clasby's keyboard set up - a Hammond organ with the requisite Leslie speaker – occasionally led to logistical difficulties.

John Hatchman: "We did a song – I think Pete Lucas wrote it – called I Love You and we went down to Arny's Shack to record it. It was a cold evening – a frost – but we couldn't get the Hammond through the studio door – it was a side door going in to the garage. Tony Arnold said 'What about if you get your keyboard player to play outside?' So Steve sat outside and we recorded it inside!"

A preference for a good night out

S.J. 22/5/75

New Salisbury group "Tracker" (standing) "Beaky" Dymond, "Dozy" Davis, with Paul Lucas and "Titch" Amey.

'TRACKER' ON DUTCH TOUR

A NEW Salisbury band has just left for a three-week tour of Holland — hot on the trail of record success.

They're called "Tracker" and were formed from the dying embers of "Mason" (formerly known as Dozy, Beaky, Mick and Tich).

Drummer Mick Wilson gave up the pro music scene several years ago in again . . . this time hoping for a recording contract with Atlantic.

Of course, one of the boss men at Atlantic i their old singing star Dav Dee. Dave's heard the nev band play — doing up dated versions of ol Beatle's songs like "E'le nor Rigby" — and he' convinced they've got future.

perhaps resulted in one band member missing out on a great opportunity.

Steve Collinson: "At the time of Band Of Gold I was still doing duos with John Priestley. Talk about 'The Nearly Man' and that's me – I had a choice of doing a duo gig with John down The George, or going up to Porton and playing with Band Of Gold. I thought 'Well, Band Of Gold is much more fun, so I'll go up there and do that'. John did the gig down The George on his own and ended up being spotted by John Denver's lawyer. So, John ended up going to America and I'm still playing up at Porton!"

Steve's career to date had been typified by talented, interesting bands and ideas that didn't last for very long – his twelve month stints with Tracker and Band Of Gold matching those of his previous bands Never Bend Over and Eskimo. His comments on shows at the City Hall might throw some

48

light on the reasons for this: "I left Barclay James Harvest - I thought it was abysmal. They had that big sign on the back 'BJH' and didn't one of the letters fall off? I was thinking to myself 'Even the letters are falling to sleep', but I have got a low threshold. I remember going to see Status Quo as well, and I left after about half an hour. That's why my bands never last – I even get bored with my own bands!"

Tracker and Band Of Gold were among the locally based acts regularly appearing at a new Salisbury venue. Former Alex Disco bar manager Mike Robins went to work in Somerset for six months. On his return, with his partner Jofie Allenby, he took on the Grange Hotel, a mock-Tudor building originally built as an out of town mansion for the Woodrow family, but now owned by the Gibbs Mew brewery[9].

Mike Robins: "One of my old waitresses from the Alex said 'The Grange is empty – I'm sure you could do something with it'. Jofie and I knew Roger and Peter Gibbs well. We acquired the lease and thought 'We're going to put the Salisbury scene back on again'. Jofie drew the plans for an Alexandra Rooms-like function room at the back, and we built what became the Dragon Suite – we called it that because of all the dragons around the roof of The Grange."

"We realised the only way we could handle it properly was to get a late night licence. We went to see David Kirkconel, a local solicitor, who said 'I'm the King where licensing is concerned in Salisbury'. When we

BAND OF GOLD - THE GOODTIME DISCO BAND
Representation:- ACE MUSIC ENTS. (Salisbury). Tel: (0722) 28755/6.

Left to right: (back) Steve Clasby and John Hatchman, (front) Steve Collinson, Pete Lucas and Beaky Dymond

ENDLESS BEAT

"... he caught hold of the stand and just collapsed."

said we wanted a late night licence he said 'Nobody in Salisbury goes out after midnight'."

"We thought a bit differently. I bought a little book on licensing laws. It said as long as you have premises - a room specially built for entertainment – where there are sufficient fire exits, a permanent bar, a permanent stage, you're able to provide food ancillary to alcohol – the judges are obliged to grant. Mr Kirkconel said 'It will never go through - I don't think it's advisable'."

"Jofie and I took it to court on our own. I had a big plan with all the hours that I handed to the magistrates and they granted it, but I misread it and for nearly a year we ran The Grange illegally. We had so many people coming from Bournemouth and Southampton. We couldn't understand why we were so popular until David Howell, who I think was a Chief Inspector, phoned me up and said 'I don't think you can open this Sunday – you're breaking the law – you had better stop'."

"We contacted loads of our old friends – Dinger Dell, Mike Parr, Chris Sandford – Dave O'Reilly from The Premiers often played. They used to play in the lounge on a Thursday and a Sunday. One time Chris Sandford had rather too many parking tickets. The law came along, took him away to have a talk down the police station, brought him back and as he walked back in he got a round of applause from everybody, sat down and continued playing where he had left."

Among the former Alex staff employed by Mike at The Grange was the legendary bouncer Bill 'Tiny' Mackerel, now assisted by his brother.

Mike Robins: "He wore a red jacket, bow tie, leather gloves and a chain mail vest. He was six foot nine and twenty two stone and his brother was a mere slip – only being six foot seven – and an ex-Regimental Sergeant Major in the Military Police. Between them they could run my whole place. The army could be…challenging… but my bouncers were awesome – it was like walking through a field of wheat when they walked through the hall - chest, shoulders and head above everybody else – incredible guys."

David O'Reilly (aka Dave York) - a regular performer at The Grange - was to die tragically young following an accident at the Kings Arms in Amesbury, where he was rehearsing with Reform – a reconstituted version of popular local covers band The Premiers.

Brian Saunders: "About halfway through the evening Dave suggested he would like to do a Jim Reeves number. I hadn't heard of it, so he said 'Give me your guitar and I'll show you the chords – it's pretty simple'. As he went to adjust the microphone he caught hold of the stand and just collapsed. I was leant on my speaker cabinet, so I leant down and whipped the mains plug straight out, which broke the circuit, but alas it was too late, he had received a massive shock. The ambulance crew were marvellous – they came from Amesbury and were there within five minutes and spent fifteen to twenty minutes trying to revive him."

Following the tragedy, Brian Billen helped Reform out on a few outstanding bookings. Brian was lead vocalist with Recorded Delivery, another popular local covers act.

Hannah Billen: "Don [Reynolds - keyboards] and Brian would do all the arrangements. The whole band would be wearing matching white suits with big bell bottoms and silk shirts - normally different colours per member. Sometimes they would wear matching white suits with pin stripes. All the suits would be professionally tailored to fit."

"They played in many places around the south including The Lions

THE PREMIERS

50

Club, Southampton Guildhall, Salisbury City Hall, Corfe Castle, Hammersmith Power Station in Poole, The Fisherton Club and Longleat. They did many gigs that would raise money for charity – for example raising money for incubators at Odstock Hospital. One time they went to Sparkford in Somerset to perform and found the Scottish Band Slik rehearsing and didn't know what was going on. Turned out Slik were meant to be playing in Sparkford in Bristol - so Recorded Delivery did get their gig in the end."

"Recorded Delivery recorded at Arny's Shack - a disco version of Bless You For Being An Angel. Freddie and The Dreamers stopped in on their way to do a tour in Australia and expressed a great deal of interest in that version of the song."

"In 1978 Recorded Delivery made a song for the Eurovision Song Contest. Brian wrote the lyrics and Don the music. It was unfortunately not picked that year but they were contacted later and asked about the song, but the band were very busy and - absorbed in their live success at the time - passed it up."

After Tracker split, Tich Amey had joined up with Peter Mason again, to form a trio alongside another old friend, who had been the vocalist with Theodore Watkins.

Peter Mason: "Beaky formed Band of Gold. Tich and I weren't into that and we got in Robin Gair – we were looking for another vocalist to do harmony stuff. That was the start of Amey-Gair-Mason."

Robin Gair: "Theodore Watkins

Brian Saunders and Dave O'Reilly

RECORDED DELIVERY

ENDLESS BEAT

"It was probably the happiest live performances I ever did."

was a dance band – pretty much all covers of the day and standards - things like Whiter Shade Of Pale. We were really busy, in fact at one stage we were earning so much money we thought it would be good to invest in a house or something – as a band. We did a lot of work in the Swindon area – we were very popular up there. It seemed that bands in those days were almost better off out of their own town – although having said that we did do quite a lot of prestigious gigs at the City Hall – things like the Conservative Association. There was six or seven of us in the band. Theodore Watkins basically took over from Ricky Vernon and The Pathfinders. We called ourselves initially the Theodore Watkins Organisation."

"I was gigging with Theodore Watkins at a club somewhere and Tich came in and had a chat. He said 'We're thinking of starting this band up, would you like to come in?' We started rehearsing and I remember clearly he was very much into The Eagles and lots of other American acts. When we started our rehearsals it fell together quite well and he said he was amazed at how quickly I picked up all the harmonies, but what he probably didn't realise was that I had been harmonising since I was six, so it was quite natural to me!"

"I tell people now that if they want to do well with their singing they have got to put a lot of hours in. They say 'What's a lot of hours?' and I say 'Well, when I was attempting to get a recording contract back in the seventies I used to rehearse for four or five hours a day, five days a week'. I'm absolutely serious – that's what we used to do, because that's how passionate we were."

"Initially we decided we would have just two acoustic guitars and three voices and wouldn't go into the drummer and bass thing – it was just going to be us three. But before long we decided that if we were going to do the live thing then the least we needed was a bass player – Nigel Dixon. Then Reg Maggs drummed with us for quite a while."

Peter Mason: "You could say that we introduced Salisbury to The Eagles. Judie Tzuke was a good friend - she used to come down and play songs and did back-up vocals for me. She came back from America, where her father lived, and said 'Peter, I've got two great albums for you – you'll love them' and she showed me The Eagles' first album and the Pure Prairie League. I was very into that country rock kind of stuff – great harmonies, good songs, good lyrics."

"They weren't just 'pop' lyrics either, they were meaningful. That suited me because when I first started writing, although I wrote some things like Gotta Make You Part Of Me for Dave, it was because they wanted that kind of stuff. Amey-Gair-Mason carried on doing what we wanted."

Robin Gair: "Peter was quite active with his song writing, although I didn't write much. We were passionate about Peter's songs – they were really quite good – so we introduced some original songs."

The band played the same venues as Band Of Gold and with the Tich-Beaky connection comparisons were inevitable.

John Hatchman: "Amey-Gair-Mason and Band Of Gold went hand in hand really, although it was different types of music. We were disco funk. We used to do a lot of stuff like Wild Cherry, Osibisa and all that sort of stuff. We weren't trying to compete with Amey-Gair-Mason or vice versa. There weren't many bands of that sort of calibre in Salisbury at that time - they started to call us the two worst bands in Salisbury [laughs]."

Amey-Gair-Mason's growing reputation led to some memorable nights at their regular gig: The Duck at Laverstock.

Roger Raggett: "I have to thank Amey-Gair-Mason for introducing me to the American West Coast sound at The Duck. They were doing great covers of Eagles, Doobies, Orleans and Marshall Tucker Band mixed in with their own material, of which one I distinctly remember should have been a hit single - called Starmaker, written by Pete Mason."

Robin Gair: "It was probably the happiest live performances I ever did. To sustain something week in-week out, month in-month out, year-on-year is quite incredible and the audience just seemed to grow – it didn't diminish at all. Sometimes it was just unreal, you literally couldn't get in the door - it was shoulder to shoulder stuff. Initially they put seats down the front but in the end it got so busy that it was just wall to wall stood up. It was a great atmosphere."

"It seemed whatever we did was accepted and enjoyed. I used to sing an old scouts' song - Green Grow The Rushes'o – there was about twelve verses to that and they all used to join in and sing along! Then we had a Christmas song that Peter wrote – that went down well."

At one stage there was a suggestion the band might release the Christmas song, put forward by a famous face with a track record of supporting Salisbury artists.

2: **Dark Side of the Moonrakers**

Amey Gair Mason Band + Disco, at South Wilts School Hall
April 1st 7:30
admission 60p Refreshments included

AMEY-GAIR-MASON - Left to right: Peter Mason, Nigel Dixon, Robin Gair, Reg Maggs and Tich Amey

53

ENDLESS BEAT

"I beat Paul McCartney and Pink Floyd to number one!"

Robin Gair: "I was a bit naïve about the rock scene. Tich came across while we were onstage and said 'Do you know who that is at the front? That's Ian Gillan'. I said 'Ian Gillan?' He said 'Yeah - lead singer with Deep Purple' and I said 'Oh…I've heard of them!' He was stood in front of me all night and I felt a bit unnerved in the end, but it was a good night – well received. He took me to one side and said 'Are you going back to [Duck landlord] Stan Scott's afterwards? I'll have a chat with you…you're a great vocalist'. I didn't know what to say, but I was obviously thrilled. He wanted to talk to us about doing the Christmas song as a single but in the end that didn't materialise and I ended up doing the single on my own."

Despite Tich's reputation in the business, Amey-Gair-Mason were unable to land a record deal.

Peter Mason: "We did demos and got some record companies interested. We nearly signed with DJM, which Elton John was with, and I think RCA were interested, but in the end – maybe it was more 'cool' to like Yes and Zeppelin, but we weren't really into that."

Robin Gair: "Peter had written some good songs and we had a couple we thought were pretty close to singles. Tich only had to ring up and say who he was and he would get A&R people to at least see the band."

"We went to EMI and played them the latest songs. The guy was pretty interested, we had our meeting and they said – normal story – 'We'll call you when I've had a chance to play it to the team'. We walked out – Peter led the way, I was close behind and Tich was right behind me. EMI was quite a big office - there were a number of girls on typewriters, really busy - Peter opened the door and walked straight into the broom cupboard! It was like a cartoon! Brooms went everywhere, I fell into the back of Peter and Tich fell into the back of me!"

"What was even funnier - or more ironic - was when we went down to Arny's Shack. We bumped into this guy who had seen us at EMI. When we said to Tony Arnold 'What's that guy doing with you?' he said 'He's the coffee boy here'. I said 'That's no good Tich, you're being seen by coffee boys now, not A&R men!' So, they

WHY DO WE HAVE TO WAIT 'TIL CHRISTMAS

Featuring **DOWNTON SCHOOL CHILDREN**

A new Release by ROBIN GAIR and Friends on P.V.K. Records No. PV 32.

GRAPHICS BY SARISBERIE DESIGNS, 20 OATMEAL ROW, SALISBURY. PRINTED BY TEMPSFORD PRESS, GREENCROFT STREET, SALISBURY.

had palmed us off a bit, but it kind of told you a bit about how the industry worked."

Tantalisingly, a recording of one of the band's gigs seems to have become lost forever.

Roger Raggett: "A bunch of us followed the band around the local area and one night at Shaftesbury Rugby Club we set up a very basic Philips cassette recorder and taped the evening. That recording stayed with me for years, being transferred from car to car until one night many years later I mentioned to Yan Webber that I still had it. Yan told Tich and I took it around to his home in Ashley Road."

"Somewhere down the line after that it went missing - probably thrown out when I changed from cassettes to CDs or left in a car when I sold it. It would have been great to have still had it twenty years later when, after a lot of manipulating, Tich, Robin and Pete got together after a few practice sessions at my factory on Old Sarum to reform for a couple of gigs."

Given Tich and Peter's connections, it would seem the band had missed a trick in not exploiting Dave Dee's position with WEA.

Robin Gair: "We did try to get a deal with Dave, but with Tich in the band it might have been a bit awkward – not 'correct'. Tich was a great artist – a very tasteful player – I learned a lot about harmony and singing in general from Tich. He would talk about the old times, but not in an egotistic way, it was very much the fun things he would relate to, but one thing I would say about him is that he is not a great businessman!"

"You'll probably laugh at this: I tried to persuade them to do New Faces. It was a big thing and what was happening was a lot of the old sixties bands were turning up on New Faces in different guises. I said to Tich 'Look, if you do this with Amey-Gair-Mason we would clean up'. There was an audition, which I put us in for, but Tich and Pete said they weren't doing it. I did it on my own - but I didn't get in. They would have jumped at Amey-Gair-Mason, but they didn't jump at Joe-Bloggs-Gair!"

In 1979 Robin released the Amey-Gair-Mason composition Why Do We Have To Wait 'Til Christmas on PVK Records, backed by pupils from Downton Secondary School.

Robin Gair: "In Salisbury it was a huge hit - I beat Paul McCartney and Pink Floyd to number one – for about ten days [laughs]. It sold about 2,000 in ten days. It was quite incredible - I got on Wogan - on the radio. I was an engineer at the time. I was working away and all of a sudden all the blokes gave the normal 'Wa-hey, you're on the radio!' We all stood around while Terry Wogan said 'You know it's this time of year when these singles come out of the woodwork – it gives me a real headache!'"

"Apparently when it came on again – a few days later – he had had loads of complaints from people in this area and he said 'I know he's a lovely chap, I know he's a good singer…but I just said it gives me a headache!' So he continued with the joke, but its fine – I'll live with that!"

More notable chart success had been enjoyed by former Studio Theatre actor (and St Michael's Church choirboy, Coaster and Folk Blues Inc (aka FBI) member) Brian Jones, by now known as Brian Protheroe.

He returned to music in the seventies, recording four decent albums as a singer-songwriter on Chrysalis and achieving a number 22

ENDLESS BEAT

"... one night he put an axe through the main cable."

UK hit single with the atmospheric Pinball in 1974. Pinball summed up Protheroe's particularly British style, with its tales of running out of pale ale and flies in the bathroom evoking the 'Rising Damp' grubbiness of the seventies bed-sit land the artist was then living in, amplified by the break up of a relationship.

Other highlights of his catalogue included Fly Now, Enjoy It and Running Through The City. Although Pinball was his only hit, it did get Brian on Top Of The Pops, where he refused to wear the velvet suit suggested by his record company.

The efforts of Salisbury's biggest sixties names - and their various cohorts - to sustain their earlier success had by and large failed, commercially if not artistically. Their time would come again to some extent, but by the mid-point of the seventies popular music had fallen into something of a rut. There was still interesting, challenging and exciting stuff around - but it was getting harder and harder to find amongst reams of uninspiring country rock, prog rock and insipid pop – technically brilliant though much of it might have been.

Zebeck, Cooler and The Exit Band seem to have been the first gigging bands formed from a new generation of South Wiltshire musicians emerging in the mid-seventies.

Simon Kuczera: "I went through Swan School in Salisbury and ended up at Dauntsey's, and became very miserable - the last few years of my time there I was dreaming of becoming a musician. I became aware of bands like Black Sabbath, Alice Cooper, Led Zeppelin, Genesis and Yes, and had aspirations to become the next Chris Squire."

"I persuaded my father to buy me a cheap Jensen Gibson Signature bass copy, learnt to play that as best I could and was introduced to a local drummer called Lloyd Collinson. We used to rehearse – just the two of us – in an old workshop next door to my parents cottage in Amesbury, at the corner of Flower Lane. Lloyd got Nick Kemp to come along, who was a great guitarist. Within a month or two I found myself sacked and supplanted by Nick's brother Jez as the bassist – and for the first time in my life emotionally traumatised [laughs]."

Neil Dalziel: "I first started writing songs when I was about fifteen when I bought an acoustic guitar. The first people I started playing with, in Amesbury, were Simon Kuczera and some of his friends from Dauntsey's - then at some point Lloyd Collinson got involved."

"I started at the Tech College in 1974, where I first met Colin Holton. We got friendly with Nick Kemp and started playing with Lloyd on drums and Simon on bass. I don't think we ever got as far as

Neil Dalziel

playing any gigs. I remember going out to Amesbury Rec to rehearse - it was bloody freezing. That started to fall apart when Nick was whisked off by the Collinsons to Eskimo."

Simon Kuczera teamed up with a crew of other youngsters to form Zebeck.

Simon Kuczera: "Through Lloyd I met Jeremy [Frogg Moody]. We used to jam together and eventually met up with Chris Walsh, a guitarist, and Mike 'Jackboot' Jones - who was a drummer. We used to rehearse at Jackboot's house out at Ebbesbourne Wake in a caravan, until one night he put an axe through the main cable because his parents were fed up listening - probably to me playing my bass!"

Frogg: "I come from what you might call a musical family. My father Jack played sax with a local dance band in the fifties called The Conroy Sect and could also play guitar. My mother played piano, as did her twin brother Brian Whitehorn who, like my dad, also played in jazz bands around Salisbury."

"On leaving school, I continued my good friendship with Lloyd Collinson, who also came from a very musical family. Lloyd had been playing drums since our school days and I remember hearing him practicing in the garden shed at the bottom of his garden – the noise was probably too much for his family!"

"Lloyd and I started drinking in the local pubs and playing table football – we became quite a formidable doubles team. Our local was the Star and I distinctly remember the favourite song on the jukebox was Pinball, by local boy Brian Protheroe[10]."

"Eventually Lloyd started jamming with local bands and I wanted a piece of the action! I bought a drum kit from Honest Alec[11] and rehearsed for what seemed like ages – but I was completely hopeless. So, back to Alec, where I managed to swap the drums for a bass guitar – this was even more frustrating than the drums and I was becoming increasingly disillusioned with the whole idea."

"Then, one day whilst in Suttons, I heard a noise that made the hairs on the back of my neck stand on end. On investigation, I found the instrument to be a Moog Satellite synthesiser – a one-note-at-a-time keyboard with sounds that were so unique that I had to have it. Locked away in my bedroom I practiced to classical records, picking out and playing along with the major melodies and loving every second of it – at last, an instrument I can play!"

"Lloyd and I by this time had drifted apart somewhat but I remember being invited to hear a rehearsal of a new band he had joined called Cooler. The band had Colin Holton on bass guitar – probably the first time I had seen him play and little did I know how much our paths would cross just a few years later. I left that rehearsal completely hooked – this is what I wanted, I had to find a band."

"I have no recollection of how I met Simon Kuczera but he was a bass player and for a young lad seemed very confident and self-assured. We started jamming and after a few months, Simon introduced me to Chris Walsh, a guitarist with real natural talent – we all started jamming in my bedroom. It was Simon who then persuaded me to purchase a polyphonic string synthesiser from Suttons to help 'fill-out' our sound and it cost me an absolute fortune! It was also the best thing I ever did because it improved my playing 100%. My musical influences at this time were Focus, The Doors, PFM, Yes and Genesis."

Mike Jones: "I came from a musical family - all played instruments and sang. In the sixties I got to see Cliff Richard, The Walker Brothers and The Beatles! I had training on the piano and trumpet, but was rubbish. I got into rock at about thirteen years old and saw Uriah Heep in Salisbury City Hall - they were so loud the best place to hear the vocals was in the Guildhall Square! I took up drums at age fifteen - and found something that suited my mentality - just like Animal from The Muppets."

"I played with a band in school, doing rock covers - they were quite good, surprisingly. I then joined a band in London via a Melody Maker advert - doing prog rock. When that broke up I moved back to the Salisbury area."

"Rehearsing in the hut in Amesbury was bloody cold at times! I ended up doing the singing. Then Simon left and one of my mates, Andy, joined us - often rehearsing in an old caravan at my parent's house."

Frogg: "The band became Zebeck and billed as a 'Melodic Rock Band' we played a few gigs around Salisbury and Amesbury. We also developed a concept idea based on a gangster theme and this had some people turning up to our gigs dressed in thirties pin-striped suits and carrying violin cases!"

Simon Kuczera: "I came up with this riff which was a sort of very intimidating gangster-ish bass line. Jeremy came up with the idea of

ENDLESS BEAT

"I remember being really drunk… no change there then…"

The Story

The dawning of the Twentieth Century and a New Era. A young Boy wanders down a dusty outskirt street of the suburbs of New York. His only friend his brother Paul. The boy fights to live, and begs to live by being a Shoe Shiner. Its not long before he falls in love with a girl called Eleanor Maybury. For a brief time his world consists of a beautiful Fantasy, reality though is cold and Paul elopes with Eleanor. Our friend is left totally alone in the world. As time passes by hatred replaces the love he had for Paul and Eleanor. Now he sets out to have revenge and gets it. Coldly on behalf of a Local Gang he murders Paul and Eleanor for blood money. Soon guilt sets in having spent the dirt Cash, his conscience hurts-but not for long, he becomes a dope peddler and lives off his racket. One day he travels deep into the heart of Town and discovers the system, overwhelmed by its speed and efficiency he strives to become the pinical of it and succeeds. Now the Gangster he tries the big job-he fails and nothing but death avails.

ZEBECK, 1976.

The Songs

Opening Overture	The Scene is set
Shoe Shine Boy	Hardship for Him
Eleanor Maybury	His first Love
Brothers	Some Help!
Dark Journey	A Murder
Rain	A Guilty Conscience
Street Punk	A New Living
Rush Hour	The Speedy System
The Gangster	The End of the Line

The Band (Formed February, 1976.)

Simon Kuczera	Bass-Vocals
Frogg	Keyboards
Chris Walsh	Guitar
Mike Jones	Drums lead Vocals

All Songs written and Copyrighted by ZEBECK. Dedicated to Sandra Bailey : The most beautiful girl in the world. Special thanks to the Jones'es and all our friends. (and following if we got one.)

ERIC & CHANDERIKA

ZEBECK PRESENTS The Gangsters Story

(The life of a Gangster, from Childhood to his Death.)

This programme is aimed at further Enjoyment, Understanding, and promotion of the Concert for the general Audience.

WELCOME

10p Official Programme 10p

---

inserting a sequence of sirens, as if there was a police chase in the middle. So, that song was based around a gangster and somewhere along the line the idea came of putting a story together – in that era of course concepts were quite a big thing: Topographic Oceans, The Lamb Lies Down On Broadway and whatever - and we compiled a set of songs around a story about a shoeshine boy that ultimately became a gangster. For our first gig, at Salisbury College above the refectory, we dressed up in 'era' clothes."

Zebeck's bassist opted to abandon his dreams of stardom, although the other members of the band persevered.

Frogg: "Simon decided that girls were high on his wish-list and left the band, resulting in various bass players joining and departing. Mike had taken on lead vocal duties and the band decided to record a demo tape somewhere in deepest Hampshire. The songs were all original and not at all conventional – lots of different timings and styles all rolled into one."

"There was one song that stood out from the rest called March of the Zombies, and we decided this was more the style we should adopt for future song writing. It was also decided we should advertise in the local press for a lead singer and bass player."

Simon Kuczera: "I realised there was a thing in the world called women, which distracted me somewhat. I don't know if it was all a fantasy about becoming a rock'n'roll musician, or the novelty wore off, or perhaps I actually didn't enjoy playing live as much as I thought I would – I certainly remember it being a quite daunting experience - but I sort of drifted away. Sadly that was the end of my formal bass playing days."

Simon's former rehearsal friends, the Kemp brothers, played in the Exit Band alongside Tremayne Roden (vocals), Colin Holton (bass) and Steve Hutchinson (drums).

Colin Holton: "My elder brother got me into music. He was into Deep Purple, Led Zeppelin and the original Fleetwood Mac. It trailed off a bit because music got a bit up its own arse with the prog stuff and country rock – great bands but I found it all a bit starched and twee and self indulgent. We used to go over the Porton Hotel on a Thursday night to watch the Old Grey Whistle Test with a pint of Ben Truman. I started seeing bands on there like the New York Dolls and Bowie – something a bit different."

"We rehearsed on Sundays, 11.00 'til 6.00 going over the same two chords…nothing has changed… wailing and screaming. Anything out of all those hours that sounded remotely melodic we would be pleased with. The amplification was a Marshall amp and a speaker in a Fyffes banana box – cardboard, not wood…if it rained we'd had it!"

"The first gig I ever did was at

Porton Memorial Hall. They were original songs but we put Jumpin' Jack Flash in there. I remember being really drunk…no change there then… we did four songs and it was the best thing in the world at the time – we had done it!"

Tremayne Roden: "Colin approached me about joining. He'd been with them for a short while and they were looking for a singer. I went with Colin on the bus to Nick Kemp's house and joined from that meeting. It was a real culture shock for me as Nick was well educated, read books with no pictures, suffered with teenage angst/tortured soul syndrome and had a girlfriend. I liked Nick but could never connect with him as a person."

"Jeremy on the other hand was a different soul, down to earth, approachable and great fun to be with and Colin…well, he lived at my house, I lived at his house and at weekends we played 'Argentinean Football' - ball on centre spot, kick ball into touch….kick each other! - and talk and play music. Steve Hutchinson was an incredibly talented drummer but was more interested in beer, fags and darts and would never commit to anything."

"For our age we were quite sophisticated .We played three gigs in total, our first being at Porton Village Hall. Afterwards we went to a party in Winterbourne Gunner, at Spike's house - he helped us out carrying kit. It was great – fourteen-fifteen, alcohol, basking in the glory of our first gig and I got my first snog with a girl. We then played Salisbury College supporting Snafu, and our final appearance was at the City Hall - I think it was supporting some famous DJ of the time. For the life of me I can't remember how it all came to an end but I enjoyed every minute of being in Exit."

After their first forays into the world of bands had petered out, Neil Dalziel and Colin Holton joined forces with Steve Le Hardy and Lloyd Collinson in Cooler.

Neil Dalziel: "A lot of the stuff we did was self written and that was quite exciting, because it was the first time I had managed to get my own songs performed by other people – that's quite a buzz. Steve had quite a few as well. Cooler sacked me because my guitar wasn't good enough. Lloyd phoned me on my eighteenth birthday to sack me – I think he drew the short straw. They didn't carry on for long after that."

Colin Holton: "Cooler did quite a lot - because it was different people from different bands we had more outlets to go and gig. We did mostly parties and one at Sarum 76 and then we cracked it - we went down and played in Bridport! It was a rough, rough place but a good experience - the first gig I played out of town."

After Cooler, Colin had a spell with some older musicians in Fairlane, led by James Ferguson and Tommy Pugh, both on vocals, guitar and bass (James would play guitar and Tommy the bass on a set of original material – then they would swap over during Steve Hutchinson's drum solo for a set of covers). Chic Duggan was also in the band.

James Ferguson was born in Denver, Colorado - where he remembers a Doors concert at Denver University as having been "pretty exceptional" - had married an English girl and moved over to Salisbury, where he started playing with others in a "sort of hippie hang out" in Pennyfarthing Street.

James Ferguson: "I had been to England before and always liked the whole feel - it always felt like home to me. A parallel between Denver and Wiltshire is that one of the biggest bands in Denver was The Moonrakers. I never knew what 'Moonrakers' meant until I came to Wiltshire and heard the stories."

Colin Holton: "They were the coolest dudes around. Tommy had a great technique, Steve Hutch was great, Chic was Chic - a hard drinkin' Scotsman - and James was the laid back American. I learned a lot off James – it was great."

One of James' compositions was to win a prestigious songwriters' award.

James Ferguson: "Just as Fairlane was breaking up I had gone to Chic's

ENDLESS BEAT

"I sent it off to the NME and won first prize..."

house one Sunday and recorded Suicide Blonde (Dyed By Your Own Hand). I sent it off to the NME and won first prize - a reel to reel tape recorder and some microphones. Charles Shaar Murray was one of the judges so it was quite good to be the one they liked the most, even though it didn't get anywhere."

After Fairlane split Colin and Chic move into a heavier project – Chicken Pox.

Colin Holton: "That was some real hard gigging. It was all local bikers' pubs – doing ZZ Top and Rory Gallagher. That was when new venues were opening up like the Royal George, Pheasant and King and Bishop[12]."

Despite a solid grounding in the traditional rock scene, the young members of Zebeck, The Exit Band, Cooler and Fairlane would play significant roles in the local response to the change in popular music that was bubbling up in London.

James Ferguson

CHAPTER TWO FOOTNOTES

1. The old Salisbury Playhouse was located in Fisherton Street. Following its demolition the building now occupied by Multi York was built on its site.
2. Sunshine Records was located in Ox Row in premises now occupied by Hawkins Bazaar.
3. The Victoria Hall was located in Rollestone Street in part of the premises now occupied by Plant Life.
4. The Assembly Rooms was located at the junction of High Street with New Canal in premises now occupied by Waterstones.
5. The Palais was located above Fisherton Working Men's Club in Wilton Road.
6. The Co-Op hall was located on the first floor of the Co-Operative Stores in Winchester Street in premises now occupied by McDonalds.
7. The original St Edmund's School was located in School Lane in premises now occupied by The Farringdon Centre, part of the Five Rivers Project.
8. Tony Arnold's Arny's Shack studios, established in Parkstone in 1973, have been used by hundreds of musicians in subsequent years, including many from the Salisbury area.
9. The Grange was located in St Mark's Avenue. Following its demolition the Ventry Close housing development was built on the site.
10. References to the Star within this book all relate to the public house that was located in Brown Street in premises now occupied by Rai D'Or, rather than the public house in Fisherton Street that has now been renamed Deacons.
11. Honest Alec's second hand shop was located in Pennyfarthing Street in premises now occupied by Urban Hardware.
12. The King and Bishop was located in Crane Street. It was subsequently renamed The Steam Rock Café and is now The Old Ale House.

3 Savages in the City
Punk and New Wave

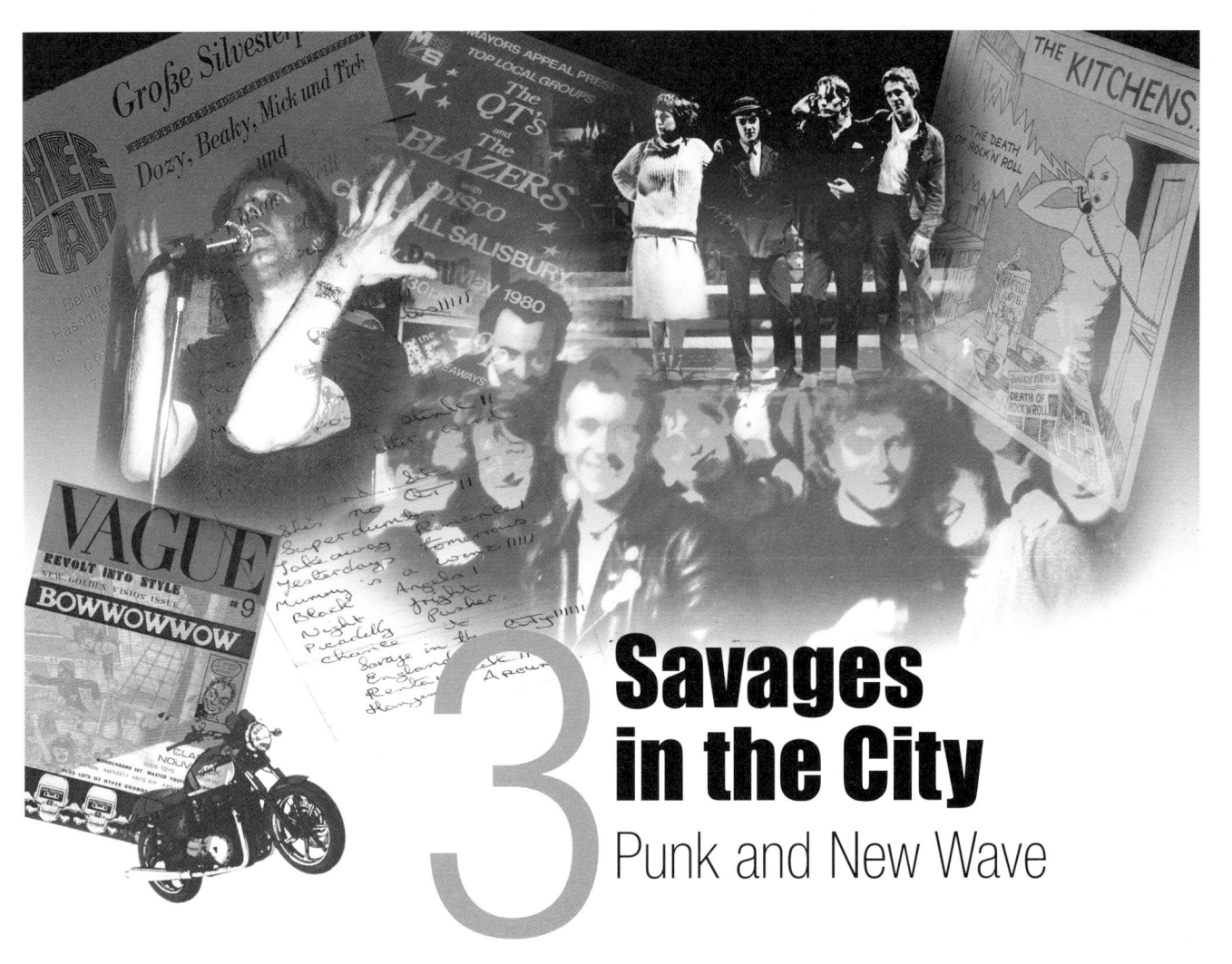

During the mid-seventies there was a strong revival of interest in fifties and sixties music. Reissued singles by acts such as The Beatles, Beach Boys and Small Faces were in the charts, and several great compilation albums were around: The Rolling Stones' Rolled Gold, The Very Best Of Eddie Cochran, The Beatles' 'Red' and 'Blue' albums, The Story Of The Who, Buddy Holly's Legend, The Beach Boys' Twenty Golden Greats and more.

Perry Harris: "There was quite a few good second hand record shops and junk shops around, where I would go and rifle through old 45s. Honest Alec had great big six foot piles of records that you would look through, and there would quite often be some interesting sixties stuff. I think a lot of punk was influenced by the sixties – it seemed a lot more interesting than the early seventies music that was in the shops."

Two young bands in particular had adopted something of a retrospective playing style whilst wearing different clothes than the mainstream rock stars of the day: Dr Feelgood and Eddie and The Hotrods, both of whom hailed from the Southend area.

Richard Nash was a Rolling Stones fan and was struck by the change in the air. In 1976 a version of (I Can't Get No) Satisfaction was played on the radio that seemed faster,

ENDLESS BEAT

"But at this stage they were known as 'freaks' rather than 'punks'."

louder and even more exciting than The Stones' version. According to the DJ it was by somebody called 'Eddie and The Hotrods'. The Hotrods appeared on Top Of The Pops a few weeks later, playing Get Out Of Denver. They didn't look like a pop group. They looked like some of the older lads in Downton - wearing jeans, bomber jackets and Robin Askwith haircuts – as if they had dropped into the studio on their way to The Kings Arms. They looked normal, which was an incredibly appealing feature.

That same year Dr Feelgood had a number one album - somewhat out of the blue - with their live set Stupidity, which captured the amazing high energy of their gigs. Although they had largely played on the pub-rock circuit these two bands had more of a snotty-faced edge and their importance in paving the way for punk is often overlooked.

The raw fifties and sixties styles certainly influenced the Sex Pistols – who included Small Faces, Who and even Dave Berry covers in their early set - and their manager Malcolm McLaren, who idolised Eddie Cochran and whose Sex clothes shop in the Kings Road (ran with Vivienne Westwood) had previously been named Let It Rock.

The Pistols and the other early London punk bands also drew from then still largely unknown American bands – The Stooges being a particular influence on Brian James of The Damned: ditto the MC5 on Mick Jones of The Clash.

As with every youth cult before or since, punk fashion soon became a high street cliché. However, although Sid Vicious represents the 'classic' but 'cartoon' punk image, in its earliest days the look could encompass anything that was out of the norm but – McLaren and Westwood notwithstanding – was cheaply available in flea markets and bric-a-brac shops. So, army trousers and restyled old drapes were as common as custom-made bondage gear and leather jackets.

Neil Dalziel: "Whilst I liked the whole punk thing, I never wanted to look like 'a punk'. I thought the whole fashion thing was a bit silly. Any uniform like that is daft in my book. If you look at the Sex Pistols – the way they looked then – they looked less punkish than any other punk band. They were just a band of ragamuffins thrown together."

Following the 'Bill Grundy Incident', the details of which do not require repeating here, punk exploded out of London (and the few other larger cities where it had gained a foothold) and into the provinces.

Tom Vague: "When I started at Salisbury Tech in September 1976, on an O-level retake course, there was already an Art College punk scene featuring Richard and Nancy - green hair, Oxfam clothes, plastic sandals - and Gareth, who looked like Alex Harvey. But at this stage they were known as 'freaks' rather than 'punks'."

"Richard knew the Buzzcocks and they saw the Sex Pistols at the 100 Club Punk Festival. Richard and Gareth were photographed at the front of the queue and duly brought the word back to Salisbury. There was a poster up the stairs to the common room between the Tech and Art Colleges advertising a trip to see the Pistols, possibly at the 100 Club or the banned Bournemouth Village Bowl gig on the Anarchy tour."

"In '76 the jukeboxes in the college common room and the Star featured Lynyrd Skynyrd's Freebird and Sweet Home Alabama, Genesis' Ripples, Supertramp, Led Zeppelin and Black Sabbath. But the common room jukebox also had the Ramones' Blitzkrieg Bop, Eddie and the Hot Rods and The Count Bishops EP. To be honest, at this stage I was more of

Dave Berry on stage in Salisbury

a football hooligan than a punk rocker, with glam, prog and soul records, mostly Bowie. I got into punk going to college on the train from Gillingham to Salisbury with Pat Sheridan and Chris and Deb the punk hairdressers."

Perry Harris: "The punk thing happening in London had kind of filtered down to the West Country, but there was quite a mixture of people that were still into hippy type things and a few people into punk. I think it was quite shocking for some people to see short hair and straight trousers."

Nick Heron: "I think that people who weren't around when punk happened can never really understand what a fundamental change it was to music and a lot of other things. I had got really bored of the music that my mates were into – rock music had become incredibly conceited and decadent, but more to the point plain boring."

"Suddenly, punk seemed to come out of nowhere. Listen to it now and it seems fairly ordinary but at the time it was a bolt out of the blue - full of energy, loud and dangerous. Punks looked scary - they challenged authority wherever they saw it and it genuinely did change society in some ways."

"It's ironic really when you realise it was only a Malcolm McLaren fashion stunt to earn a few quid that blew up into something much, much bigger. It caught the zeitgeist of the time. For me, it made me think that if they could play three chords and sound great then so could I. Off I went and bought my first electric guitar and started my journey into becoming a musician of sorts. I still listen to a lot of punk today so for me it has stood the test of time."

Mike Jones: "Musically it varied from crap to very good, but it was great because it opened up the music industry to lots of new talent and companies. We desperately need something like it now! During that period UK artists accounted for 30-35% of the US charts. Now, thanks to music colleges and the likes of Cowell, we are lucky if it is 2%! We

ENDLESS BEAT

"... it was so simple it was brilliant."

need some originality - watch YouTube newbies, not X Factor!"

On the nationally emerging scene, Colin Newman of Wire was born in Salisbury in 1954. Wire appeared on the seminal Live At The Roxy album and were central to the subsequent development of post punk.

The first punk band in Salisbury itself appears to have been an ad hoc outfit put together at Christmas 1976 and featuring Jon Maple, a rebellious former Bishop Wordsworth's School choirboy whose previous experience had included a tour of the cathedrals of northern France. The Maple pop pedigree was solid – Jon's cousin Colin played with All In The The Mind and his uncle Pete with The Merry Macs – but Jon had somewhat different tastes.

Jon Maple: "Duncan Howell was a big influence - he introduced me to the Velvet Underground. They used to have Saturday morning art classes at the old art school[1], which my mother sent me to. I was eleven years old, listening to Slade and T Rex, and suddenly this avant-garde stuff came in. Then it was The Stooges and The New York Dolls. That was deeply influential – the basic approach. I never got into prog or anything of the sort – I've always thought rock'n'roll was a primal thing."

"In 1976 I went to art school - at the age of sixteen - and of course that was when punk hit. Being a youth of the type I was, I was pretty sold on punk rock and it was ideal in an art school full of young people, who were a bit mad of disposition and alienated from what was going on, to fully engage with punk."

"My first live experience was at the Students' Union common room playing the Christmas gig with a band called Elliott Ness and The G-Men. This was a scratch band – never to be repeated - and the only person in it who later figured would have been Tim Darlow, who played guitar. I did the singing. I remember doing Suffragette City and

---

CHARITY FOOTBALL MATCH

The following charities are supported:-
 British Heart Foundation
 British Red Cross Society
 British Council for the Rehabilitation of the Disabled
 British Empire Campaign for Cancer Research.

TOP TEN XI SQUAD
(subject to availability)

Kevin O'Shea - Manager and former player for the side which was formed in 1968.
Bryan Marshall - Starred in the TV programme 'Warship' and appeared in 'Lisa of Lambeth'.
David 'Diddy' Hamilton - Popular Radio One Disc Jockey. Has his own radio show between 2.00 & 4.30 pm daily.
Junior Campbell - Member of Marmalade, writes & produces many hits.
Troy Dante - Troy is the other half of the group 'Men' and can be heard on Radio One.
John Lyons - Appeared in United, On the Buses, Z Cars, and Never Mind the Quality, Feel the Width.
Dave Dee - Former member of Dave Dee, Dozy, Beaky, Mick & Tich.
John Taylor - Captain of London Welsh Rugby Football Club & played for Wales on many occasions.
Jess Conrad - His shows Oh Boy & Six-Five Special were great television successes. More recently he starred as Jesus Christ in Godspell.
Jimmy Clugston - Ex Portsmouth Defender.
Miki Anthony - Miki records for RCA. Produces Goodies' records.
Del Grant - One of the best known DJs, ex BBC Radio Manchester.
Doug Fielding - Best known as PC Quilley in Z Cars.
Bill Oddie - One of the fabulous BBC TV Goodies.
Patrick Mower - Star of Callan & Special Branch.
Michael Whale - Michael is a member of the ITV Today team.
Andy Walton - Up & coming drummer with the young pop group, Kenny.
Wally Hinshelwood - Ex Chelsea footballer. His sons Martin and Paul play for Crystal Palace.
Nobby Bracket - Trainer for the Top Ten XI. The man with the magic sponge.

John Cohen - Commentator.
Rick Wakeman - Highly talented musician. Recent record White Rock.
NOTE: *The team will be picked from the above list subject to the commitments of each personality.*

SALISBURY COLLEGE OF TECHNOLOGY INVITATION XI SQUAD

Richard Sharp - (Manager) Plays in Midfield. Founder of the College team which is pushing for league status.
Simon Davis - (Captain). Leading goalscorer for the team.
Peter Rattue - Goalkeeper. Reliable member of the defence.
Andrew Pringle - (Defence). Manager of Debenhams Shoe Dept.
Chris Ellis - (Defence). A good prospect.
Steve Thomas - (Defence). Comes from Dorset.
Peter Slater - (Defence). Comes from Warminster.
Kelvin Hudson - (Utility). Art student.
Emad Bahsoon - (Midfield). Comes from Sierra Leone. Mr. Handsome.
Ahmed Sasso - (Utility). Also comes from Sierra Leone.
Gilbert Durosaro - (midfield). A remarkable resemblance to Stevie Wonder. Comes from Nigeria.
Andy Mercer - (Forward). Rarely has a bad game. Scored many vital goals since his debut last year.
Scott Deacon - (Forward/Midfield). Lightweight member of side.
Wally Afuwape - (Winger). Student Nurse. Comes from Nigeria.
Derek Turner - (Attack). Mancunian. Fast winger often scores.

COLOURS: SHOWBIZ - Red & White stripes.
 TECH DYNAMOS - Either green shirts with white sleeves or Orange shirts.

Final Acknowledgements

Sarah Bristow and Virginia Barstow for providing teams with refreshments.
Janet MacLennan for typing and help in producing this programme.
Programme edited by Richard Sharp.

* * *

The promoters of this match between the Top Ten XI and Salisbury Tech XI can accept no liability for any loss or damage to property or any accidents to those attending this match, either in the ground or in its precincts.

64

Anarchy In The UK - despite the fact it had only just been released. None of us owned copies, we had just heard it once or twice on the radio. I've no idea what it sounded like but I imagine it didn't matter because everyone was so pissed anyway - they all said it was marvellous!"

"In order to see live punk I had to go to Bournemouth Village Bowl, which was a kind of underground concrete bunker. I remember standing next to Paul Weller at the urinal and I noticed he didn't wash his hands after he had a piss – I thought 'Well…that's punk rock!'"

"It was almost Stalinist, the rules of punk. Anything with more than two or three chords in it from before 1976 was like Stalin's Politbureau - where they would wipe out people by changing their pictures. It was like a rebirth I suppose. There was a whole group of people waiting for punk to happen and I'm glad I had the experience because it influenced me right up until…I was in my thirties before I could bring myself to listen to Neil Young for example – just on principle…on prejudice."

In March 1977 a Salisbury College team played football against a Celebrity XI featuring Dave Dee, Bill Oddie and Rick Wakeman. This was at the time that Rick Wakeman was signed with A&M Records, who were about to tear up their contract with the Sex Pistols.

Tom Vague perhaps took the punk ethos of kicking out the old school a little too literally: "I hacked down Andy Walton, the drummer from Kenny - of The Bump fame. By then The Ramones' Sheena Is A Punk Rocker was on the college jukebox, but not much continued to happen in Salisbury throughout the early punk period. The '77 scene consisted of hanging out in the common room playing cards and Katz punk/vintage clothes shop[2] run by Nick - the West Country Malcolm McLaren - or going to the Star and on pub crawls from the college to the station. There was also a Salisbury Art College fanzine called either 'Unite' or 'Ignite'."

A young, but already established, face on the Salisbury scene was inspired by the new sounds – in particular a support act at a City Hall concert.

Colin Holton: "It really gave it a meaning – really opened your eyes. It was 'below' what we were doing ourselves but it had something about it. I remember hearing the Buzzcocks and The Damned on John Peel and thinking it was so simple it was brilliant."

"Then I went to see Babe Ruth at the City Hall - you had all these sort of old blues and rock bands regurgitating their same old stuff. The opening band was The Stranglers, who were playing to me, Lloyd [Collinson] and about four other people. They started off with Grip and we thought 'Wow! There's something here!' A couple of weeks later they were on telly and we were like 'Bloody hell – we've seen this lot'. Then we all bought their album [Rattus Norvegicus] - one of the best albums ever."

In September 1978 Adam and The Ants, supported by Glaxo Babies and The Screens played in the main hall of Salisbury College. This was well before Adam's attempts at becoming a mainstream pop star and at the time the Ants performed dark songs in freakish clothes. Examples of their subject matter included sado-masochism, the need for plastic surgery after a car accident, Mussolini, the assassination of Kennedy, death camps, Ruth Ellis and Cleopatra's proclivity for oral sex.

Along with the likes of Siouxsie and The Banshees, the Ants were at the forefront of the contemporary underground scene and were certainly the hippest London punks to appear in Salisbury to date. Unfortunately things turned nasty as a result of an incident in the Star before the gig.

The headliners were edgy, dangerous and stunning, but during their set bikers and various other non-punks gate-crashed the hall and began to drag people outside to give them a hiding - there were claims that some people were stabbed.

Tom Vague recalled the event in a post-pop star overview of Adam's early career: 'Salisbury had never seen anything like it. I was used to having exams in the hall, but there we were waiting to see Adam and The Ants: students dressed up punky for the night, everybody from Southampton and Bournemouth, a large contingent from London…Most of the London lot looked really young and they had their own style, consisting of cardigans, Ants or Seditionaries T-shirts, studded belts, bondage trousers and kung fu slippers – and there was rather a lot of bikers'.

'At the time nobody knew what was going on, even when it was actually going on, but I later pieced together roughly what happened. A couple of bikers went into the Star, which was full of punks including the London contingent, generally taking the piss, and one of them came off worse in an 'incident'. However, there was a United Bikers rally on, and after a few phone calls bikers started infiltrating the Ants gig. When there were sufficient numbers amassed, they began picking punks at random and dragging them out to the foyer for a kicking.'

ENDLESS BEAT

"... the Ants were really stunning - tight and intense..."

'In the hall things were relatively calm, although there was a generally uneasy atmosphere and the word soon got round. The 'Weekend Swingers' (Salisbury was the only place the Ants ever played this song) realised it wasn't such fun after all and started frantically flattening their hair and wiping off their make-up – they really did!'

'I missed out on most of this because, for once, I was more interested in what was going on onstage. The converted were apprehensively paying homage. Most everybody else had either gone home or was outside getting beaten up…the Ants were really stunning - tight and intense - and everyone who stayed was bonded together as they did a defiantly long set. You just couldn't leave till the end - and it was just as well we didn't, as the early departees were being picked off one by one outside. I only just got out in one piece, as a bouncer stopped me walking right into the middle of a gang of chain-wielding hairies.'

The story has always been that the trouble was sparked by tribal rivalries. However, Adam had allegedly proclaimed from the stage that the Ants had a disturbing effect wherever they played and at least one local fan thought the headliners might have been partly to blame.

Simon Kuczera: "I think I was a bit inebriated at the time but there was a lot of anger from the audience towards the band. They didn't like the sound and the image and the way Adam Ant presented himself - I think that was one of the causes of the friction."

The Ants gig was put on to mark the start of the academic year in which Tom Vague returned to Salisbury College. It was during this second stint of skipping class that Tom started Salisbury's – in our opinion - greatest ever popular music, cultural and lifestyle magazine.

Tom Vague: "I had left college to work in Gillingham for a year. In September '78 I went back to do a Building Studies course and started Vague fanzine in 1979 with the cartoonist and local reporter Perry 'M' Harris, the Dutch poser Iggy Zevenbergen, Sharon Clarkson and Chris Johnson from the art college, and Chris Nugent and Jane Austin from Mere."

66

30p
VAGUE
THE POPGROUP #6
SEPT/OCT. 1980.
CRASS
D-E-V-O
COSMETICS
MPs will debate
bringing in a register
of people eligible for

VAGUE
REVOLT INTO STYLE
#9
NEW GOLDEN VISION ISSUE
BOWWOWWOW
IT WORKED, LET'S GET INSIDE!
CLASSIX
NOUVEAUX
GODS TOYS
PROGRAM
MONOCHROME SET
WASTED YOUTH
DAMNED
NTNON
AMNESTY
ANTS RIP
FASHION
V.NEWS
PLUS LOTS OF OTHER GOODIES,
ALL FOR
30p.

VAGUE
12
THEATRE OF HATE
UK DECAY
DANSE SOCIETY
POPSTARS !!
30p
Tales From The Blank Generation

VAGUE
[THE 20th CENTURY AND HOW TO LEAVE IT]
#16/17 : PSYCHIC TERRORISM ANNUAL : £3.50

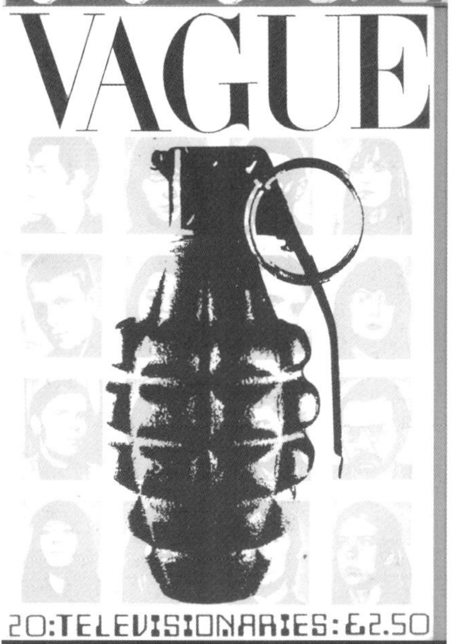
VAGUE
20:TELEVISIONARIES: £2.50

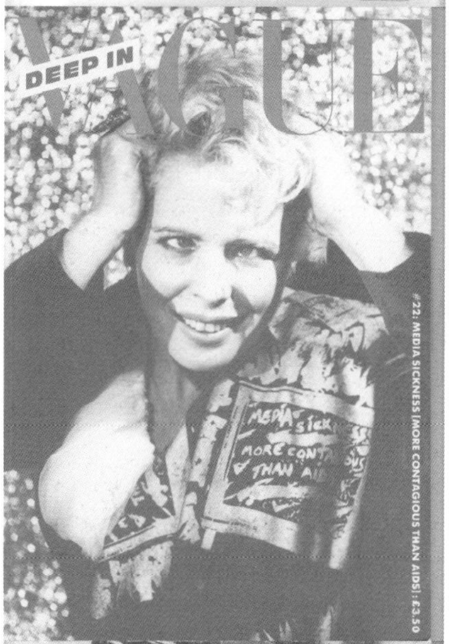
DEEP IN
VAGUE
MEDIA SICKNESS
MORE CONTAGIOUS THAN AIDS
#22: MEDIA SICKNESS [MORE CONTAGIOUS THAN AIDS]: £3.50

VAGUE
#24
THE WEST ELEVEN DAYS OF MY LIFE
NOTES FROM THE PORTOBELLO STYLE UNDERCLASS.
Longhair, Beatniks, Druggies, Free Love... £2.50 Mate. I call that equitable.

VAGUE
14
ARE YOU POSITIVE, PUNK?
THINGS ARE HAPPENING BUT YOU DONT KNOW WHAT
THEY ARE DO YOU? ALL THAT
SORTA STUFF, THAT WE INVENTED YEARS
AGO, ENDING IN A SUDDEN INDEPTH CULT
FEATURE THAT GOES TOTALLY OUT OF CONTROL...
40p

THE GREAT BRITISH MISTAKE
VAGUE 1977-92
A FOURTEEN AND A HALF YEARS' STRUGGLE
AGAINST LIES, STUPIDITY AND COWARDICE:
A RECKONING WITH THE DESTROYERS OF THE
PUNK ROCK MOVEMENT

ENDLESS BEAT

"A truce was arranged with the Salisbury rockabillies in the Star."

Perry Harris: "We knew each other at college and became friends because we were both into punk - not many people were really at the time - and we decided to start a magazine. I was at Art College doing graphics – I was interested in cartooning. I did a few interviews but I'm not an interviewer really - I was just interested in the drawing."

"Initially we just liked the idea of doing a magazine and then it evolved into what it became. We didn't sit down and say 'Well, it's going to be like this'. For the first issue we got a few pounds together just to get a printer. I think Tom took the burden of the finance over the years. He did everything really – it pretty quickly became his thing, and I just contributed to it. It started off as just basically a big pamphlet, to [become] quite a lavish magazine."

Tom Vague: "Iggy and Sharon lived on Nelson Road and their house was the hub of the Salisbury punk scene. There was also Spanish Alf, Bournemouth Christine, the catering punks Martin Butler and Tim Aylett, the black post-punk artist Dave Somerville, Mike Muscampf - who was later in the Goth group Dormannu, Simon Loveridge and our hippy correspondent Frank Stocker. Our local was the Star and later the Cathedral Hotel. The good record shops were Derek's[3] and Wilmer's[4]."

The ever independent minded Suttons also supported the punk scene and had no qualms about selling the Sex Pistols' single God Save The Queen and album, Never Mind The Bollocks, neither of which were available at the high street record outlets in the city.

THE KITCHENS - left to right: Ruth Jones, Andy 'Sprog' Ford, Andy Lovelock and Duncan Fulton

Tom Vague: "The scene largely consisted of going to gigs - mostly at the Bournemouth Village Bowl, but also in Bath, Bristol, Southampton and London. Inspired by Tim Aylett's Channel 4 fanzine - reggae and post-punk, Adam and The Ants, Siouxsie and The Banshees, Joy Division, The Pop Group, Public Image, The Slits and Rough Trade groups - we launched Vague on the world."

"On the back cover of Vague 1, Iggy, Alf and Dave Somerville are pictured outside the college common room. The first issue was designed and printed by Mark Cross from the Art College, who went on to design album sleeves. The second issue, featuring 'Salisbury Calling' by Mike Dyer, was photocopied down Fisherton Street. Perry's 'Lovable Spikey Tops' cartoons best documented the evolution of Vague and the Salisbury scene - attempting to put on gigs, avoiding bikers, teds, rockabillies, squaddies, smoothies, young farmers, etcetera. A truce was arranged with the Salisbury rockabillies in the Star after their American car – possibly a Cadillac - pulled up behind my Mini on Churchill Way and we invited them for a drink."

In his 'Salisbury Calling' article, Mickey Dyer reflected that 'Entertainment in Salisbury must be at an all time low. Throughout the early seventies it saw gigs by the likes of David Bowie, Led Zeppelin, Groundhogs, Alex Harvey, Tangerine Dream, Genesis, Budgie, to name but a few. Over the last two years only Adam and the Ants, XTC and The Pirates have graced us with their presence'.

As well as the lack of visiting bands, Mickey also bemoaned the shortage of venues for local bands to play: 'At the moment all we have is discos and lots of pubs, which is all very well, but what we want is an alternative scene, a place where bands can play regularly, a club perhaps, regular College or City Hall gigs, anything'.

Spearheading the first wave of local bands lumped in with the punk movement, The Kitchens, The QTs and Identity Crisis all included musicians who had played in previous local bands.

The Kitchens probably had the best claim for being Salisbury's first serious punk band, with an original line up of Duncan Fulton (bass and vocals), Fred Phillips (guitar) and Andrew Lovelock (drums). Their first gig was at Amesbury Church Hall, followed by the Stonehenge Free Festival in June 1977. Duncan Fulton had played locally for a number of years, first as a solo artist and then with The Shining Hearts Band.

Duncan Fulton: "My mother brought me a guitar home from school, where she was working as a secretary. When I was a bit younger a cousin of mine had turned up with this guy that played guitar – he was really cool, had a couple of good songs and inspired me to think in the future I would like to play. My mother brought me the guitar a few years later. I was twelve and started playing protest songs – Donovan and stuff like that – I wrote my first song after a couple of weeks. I was listening to early Rolling Stones, Beatles, all the beat groups - and the folk scene had just started – Donovan, Bob Dylan and that sort of stuff."

"John Pook was also at Bishop's School – a year older than me – was a good singer and got me to accompany him on guitar. He was singing Paul Simon songs, but a bit operatic inclined – he had a good voice. There was a folk scene: Barnard's Cross was where all the trainee teachers were living, off St Ann Street. That was a neat place – a good venue – all women like! This must have been about '68."

"Steve Ryall, a good friend of mine at college, said 'We're gonna put a band together and you're playing bass'. So that's why I became a bass

THE KITCHENS

ENDLESS BEAT

"… Ruth came by with a guitar on her shoulder…"

guitar player. That was the Shining Hearts Band. That was a dodgy band really - hippy band. I was a contributor in songs – Steve wrote half of it and I wrote the other half."

"Me and Fred Phillips left the band when the punk scene started with The Ramones and all that. Fred said to me 'This is crap what we're playing with this band Dunc, we've got to get out. Come round to my place and I'll show you these songs I've composed'. I went round and he was just playing flat out, jumping off chairs as he was showing me the stuff saying 'It's all action, man – its ACTION!'"

"I knew it was on the scene because I used to read the NME right? I had seen the pictures of Johnny Rotten wading into the front row of the audience. Fred was out on the roads tarmaccing so he was high energy and fit as hell. I got the message – I saw him playing this Ramones' style guitar and thought 'Yeah, this is good – let's go this way'."

"So, we formed The Kitchens. We phoned up Andy Lovelock because he had told me 'Anytime you want to make a new band give me a ring' and that was it – a three piece band. Fred wrote most of the material - like Hell's Angels - really good stuff. I composed a couple. Then Fred left and we had Paul Kelly playing guitar for a while. Colin Holton came up and played with us a couple of times, but couldn't handle the pace! [laughs]"

Perhaps unlike the popular conception of most drummers, Andrew Lovelock was a noted academic and apparently worked out his drumming patterns using mathematical formulae.

Duncan Fulton: "He was a genius. His father was well known as a professor - he brought the world the Gaia theory, which is all about the ozone layer. He warned of all the bad things that were gonna happen – and Andrew used to do work like measuring the ozone layer and was one of the first

THE KITCHENS

Duncan Fulton and Ruth Jones at the Cathedral Hotel

people on computers. I met him at Bishop's School – he was the same age as me but they put him a year ahead because he was so brilliant. It was hard to know what his method was, but if you actually examine it he was drumming in a strange way – he seemed to be going backwards as he was playing rather than forwards. It sounds quite rhythmic – it never slows down or speeds up – the timing is excellently good."

After Colin Holton left the band The Kitchens continued as a three piece, with Duncan back on bass. Paul Kelly then departed and Duncan took over on lead guitar, with Gavin Lear and Ian Stramm joining on guitar and bass respectively. The new members then also both left and Andy 'Sprog' Ford joined the band – who were once again playing as a three piece.

This line up supported Wild Horses at the City Hall, where the headliners' guitarist Brian Robertson, formerly of Thin Lizzy, suggested The Kitchens might benefit from a female bassist. Duncan approached Ruth Jones – who at the time was still attending South Wilts Grammar School. Ruth turned up to a practice session on her moped and struck up an instant rapport with the band.

Duncan Fulton: "Me and a bloke called Steve – a bit of a local character – were doing a bus survey and were sent all around the area giving out questionnaires to people on the buses. We were on the Woodford bus and on the way off the bus Ruth came by with a guitar on her shoulder, plus the questionnaire, and said 'You make sure you read my comments' – so she made an impression. Next time I met her was over in the Cross Keys Mall. I said 'You play guitar don't you? We're looking for a bass player' and she said 'I could do that' and that's where it came from."

71

ENDLESS BEAT

"... they didn't see a sandwich... didn't even see a pickled onion!"

"Talking Heads was an inspiration – I liked the female bass player and thought it fitted well. I saw them live when they first came over. They looked normal when they came on the stage right? Really normal - American, preppy, cord jeans and everything - but after a few numbers David Byrne started to look a bit edgy and twitchy."

"That was the classic Kitchens – that was what we were looking for. When we found Sprog that was the big one because he plugged in and just instantly was great – he's a star right? He's got the sound and he's great technically. Andy and I just looked at each other and said 'Wow! This is the guy we've been waiting for!' When he was playing with The Kitchens he was using a Selmer treble and bass amp – a 2 x 12 I think. He had a distorted sound – he had an Ibanez in those days with a pedal on it, which you could switch to to get that."

"He looked good and had his own fans as well – people would come to see him - so we doubled our audience. Then we brought Ruth in and we had a lot of her friends - she was quite a well known starlet around town. She had played clarinet – she was a musician…she studied music."

By now the scene in Salisbury was becoming more vibrant with new local bands and venues appearing.

Duncan Fulton: "It was great. There was The QTs – we were the first two bands that were playing that sort of music. Then there was Nick Kemp's band – The Crimmos – they were good, so there was lot of high standards of competition. Everyone was conscious they had to get their act together."

The Cathedral Hotel was a popular venue for the new crowd.

Duncan Fulton: "That was a great gig but it didn't pay very well. The manager was a really cool dude - looked just like Manuel out of Fawlty Towers – but used to pay about three quid a gig. That was our favourite gig because we were right with our audience. Communication with the audience was strong in those days. We weren't playing like 'stars' – we were playing to people we knew and people were talking to us from the front row."

"I liked the social element of it – that's what I was writing lyrics on. The early Kitchens' stuff had things about Anthony Stocken, the architect from Salisbury who built all this stuff everywhere. I wasn't really thinking politically but I was thinking about what was interesting."

The Kitchens were involved in a mild controversy in the city.

Duncan Fulton: "We played at Gordon's nightclub[5] – we had a couple of dates there. There was a tragic consequence – they lost their licence! They had undercover police in the nightclub. In those days you could have a late licence if you provided food. These policemen testified in court that there was a punk band playing who were 'Pretty rough like' – and they didn't see a sandwich…didn't even see a pickled onion!"

This 'classic' version of The Kitchens recorded a single, The Death of Rock'n'Roll, backed with Lies and A Bomb. Issued on Red Square Records, the single sleeve depicted the band near Salisbury's then infamous 'Pier' or 'Road To Nowhere' - the full story of which would probably be better told in a book about the triumphs

3: **Savages in the City**

QTs'

and disasters of the area's Local Authorities[6].

Duncan Fulton: "I had come off the fast punk and was going into the new wave really – introducing minor chords – but we still had the muscle. It had a bit of rhythm but was slow - like Vanilla Fudge [laughs]. A-Bomb was a very popular live number. I had written it at the end of the very punky version of The Kitchens. It had a great chorus but it was punk by numbers."

Reviewing The Kitchens' single in Vague, Perry M though the A-side was 'slow and vaguely bluesy'. He felt A-Bomb was the best of the three tracks but that overall the record hadn't shown the band's full talents.

Early in 1980 guitarist Sprog Ford left the band and they reverted once again to a three piece. This line up didn't last long, although before the band finally folded they supported The Martian Schoolgirls at the Rising Sun[7] and in London.

Duncan Fulton: "Sprog left the band and really that was it, because that was the 'model' of The Kitchens. It was a pity because it was an excellent combination. We went on – it was good but different – it wasn't the same without Sprog because you need a great guitarist in a great band I think."

The legend lived on: In the late nineties, a list of 'best ever gigs' compiled by the staff of Q magazine included The Kitchens at Magnums in Basingstoke.

Colin Holton

THE QTs

The Kitchens first serious rivals on the Salisbury punk scene, The QTs, formed out of the remnants of Zebeck. After Simon Kuczera left the band the remaining members – Chris Walsh (guitar), Frogg Moody (keyboards) and Mike 'Jackboot' Jones (drums) decided to change musical direction and advertised for new members.

Frogg Moody: "I saw The Stranglers for the first time on The Old Grey Whistle Test. They were playing a song called Hanging Around,

73

ENDLESS BEAT

"... this is what our band should sound like!"

recorded live at the Hope and Anchor, London. I already loved The Doors and The Stranglers were in the same vein with a modern edge. After probably being the first person in Salisbury to purchase Rattus Norvegicus, I played the album to Chris and Mike and announced 'this is what our band should sound like!'"

The band brought in a lead singer who was not well known on the local scene.

Mike Vickers: "At junior school in Wylye we used to pretend to be The Beatles out in the playground – I was John. I used to love singing. I was always jumping up on stage and singing with bands when I could. A lot of them didn't like it - well the singers didn't anyway! I had interviews – I think I would have got a job with Wedgwood Wing but they said I was too young - I was about sixteen-seventeen."

"There was an advert in the Journal for a band – they wanted a singer. So I got on the coach and went out to Ebbesbourne Wake and that's when I met Frogg, Jackboot and Chris. There was two other people on the coach. I overheard them and thought 'I don't stand a chance with this' – they were well to do with music. I nearly got off but thought 'I'll stick it out'. I got there and they took me on."

While working under the name of Zebeck, the now un-named band had made an acetate recording of a ballad entitled Living.

Mike Vickers: "I remember hearing that and thinking 'These guys are too good for me'. I didn't have the confidence at all then. The confidence just grew with that band. I thought it was fantastic. The guys were coming

Mike Vickers, of the QTs, at the Rising Sun

3: **Savages in the City**

up with music that needed lyrics and melodies and I found that I could do it. That's when I discovered I could really sing and I could write songs. The guys would come up with ideas – like Savage In The City - I completely changed it around from there being a savage in the city to it being savage in the city."

After Steve Collinson had turned them down, Mike helped complete the line up by finding a bass player – Colin Holton, then playing with Chicken Pox: "I went to the Rising Sun and seen this guy. I didn't know him at all but I thought 'Bloody hell – he's fantastic!' I went up to him and said 'Do you wanna join our band?'

The QTs wrote new songs, rearranged older material and rehearsed for about two months before their debut gig, supporting The Kitchens at the Coach and Horses. With a set comprising all original compositions apart from The Stranglers' Hanging Around and Princess Of The Streets. The band then gigged throughout the end of 1978 before playing at the City Hall at Christmas - where they impressed their old friend Simon Kuczera enough for him to suggest he become their manager.

Simon Kuczera: "I heard them practicing and thought 'there is great potential here'. I probably quite liked

75

ENDLESS BEAT

"We listen to it now and think 'God that's crap'..."

the idea of - power, control, you name it – managing a band and putting on concerts."

Simon arranged gigs for The QTs in and around Salisbury, Basingstoke and Devizes and the band began to attract a solid local following. He also stumbled upon a coincidental link with the leading lights of the London scene.

Simon Kuczera: "One thing to try and get things moving formally was to see if we could [legally] get the name 'The QTs'. I ended up meeting with a lawyer in Oxford Street - I think his name was Simon Butler - about copyrighting the name. It turned out he was interested in what we were up to because he was the ex-lawyer for the Sex Pistols and at some stage the band had been called 'The QTs' – so he was interested to know how we had arrived at the same name. It didn't really come to much apart from a nod and a wink and 'carry on as you are'."

With Simon's encouragement The QTs recorded an EP entitled Savage In The City at Arny's Shack, although ultimately the band were disappointed with the results – apart from the sleeve designed by Mark Cross.

Simon Kuczera: "We ended up at Arny's Shack because we knew Robert Fripp had used the studio, a few other musicians had recommended it and it was fairly local. I remember us turning up there very early one morning to record in one day what was going to be the band's first single."

"We ended up doing an EP consisting of two tracks a side. Unfortunately, nobody knew - least of all me - that putting four tracks onto a seven inch vinyl you actually degrade the quality of the sound, because the grooves are thinner, so the reproduction quality was very poor. The overall effect was the tracks sounded as if they were a bit rushed."

"We also thought, to add a bit of novelty, that at the end of one of the tracks we would have a crowd cheering as if it was a live concert. Unfortunately five or six people down in the studio did not make for a crowd – it sounded quite pathetic [laughs]. That said the songs were very good for their time and the cover was quite novel."

Despite the band's feelings about it now, the EP proved very successful locally.

Mike Vickers: "We listen to it now and think 'God that's crap' but there was kids all the way down the path, right out to the road, queued up to buy the single. I couldn't believe it – here I am with a couple of little kids – all of a sudden I'm famous [laughs]. I didn't even have a car at the time – I would walk over to the bus stop and all around our record would be playing, it was fantastic."

The EP also gained some radio plays. During a road show at Wilton House, The QTs gave Tony Blackburn a copy of the record. He passed it on to John Peel, who duly played it on his show. However, Mike Vickers and Colin Holton's interview with Oliver Gray in Winchester, for BBC Radio Solent, did not run quite to plan.

Mike Vickers: "We had a bit of funds from the band to get the bus down there and back but we hitchhiked and were there nice and early - so we went to the pub. When we finally got to the interview we

QT'S'

ENDLESS BEAT

"I interviewed The QTs, it was unbroadcastable..."

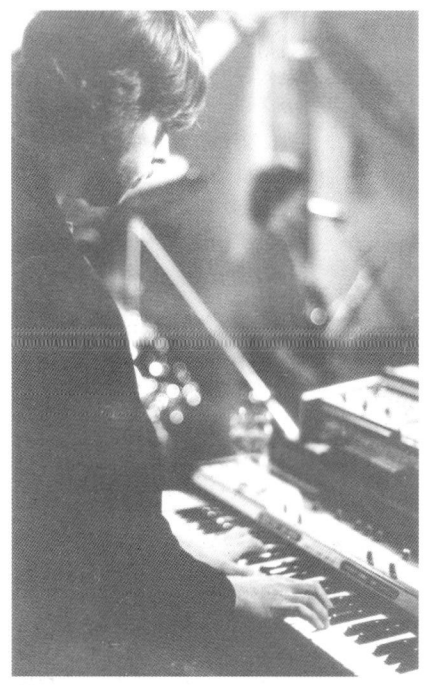

were quite pissed. I kept calling him 'Ollie' and trying to sing into his microphone. He didn't like being called 'Ollie'. He didn't play the interview at all – he just mentioned 'I interviewed The QTs, which was unbroadcastable' – but he did play the single."

There are rumours that, having hitchhiked back as far as Stockbridge after the interview, the pair unofficially 'hired' a series of bizarre vehicles to get them home.

The popularity of Savage In The City perhaps demonstrated The QTs' strong relationship with their audience, in comparison with other local bands.

Mike Vickers: "They were the 'in' thing with the college and we weren't really a college band. We never had the same connections they did. They were all quite tight-knit together and all of a sudden we appeared and developed a big fan club, I think they lacked that. We weren't 'cool' – they were 'cool'."

Colin Holton: "It started a buzz and you knew wherever you played it would be ram-packed. That band did the business. It had everything. We were a bit naïve by not taking certain chances or doing certain things but we had great songs. Chris and Frogg's stuff had a real edge to it. Before I was just learning my trade - this was the first band I was in where I thought 'Yeah, this has got something'."

Mike Vickers: "We got the name as the bad boy band. We did a song called Rent-a-Wreck, which went 'We're on a rent-a-wreck, what a nice house you had…' Up by the railway station there was a party and there was things flying out of the windows. We wrecked the place and hence the song came about – which all the fans loved singing."

"The audience loved us. They used to mimic everything I did. My arm went up – their arms went up. If there was a gap in the song they used to fill it out – '2,3,4' – and they learned the songs so quick. The other bands used to try and be too clever I think. We were learning all along as we went, that was the edge we had. If all the guys had been trained musicians we wouldn't have had that edge to create what we were."

Frogg: "We became a really tight outfit and attracted a fantastic following, often taking coach loads of

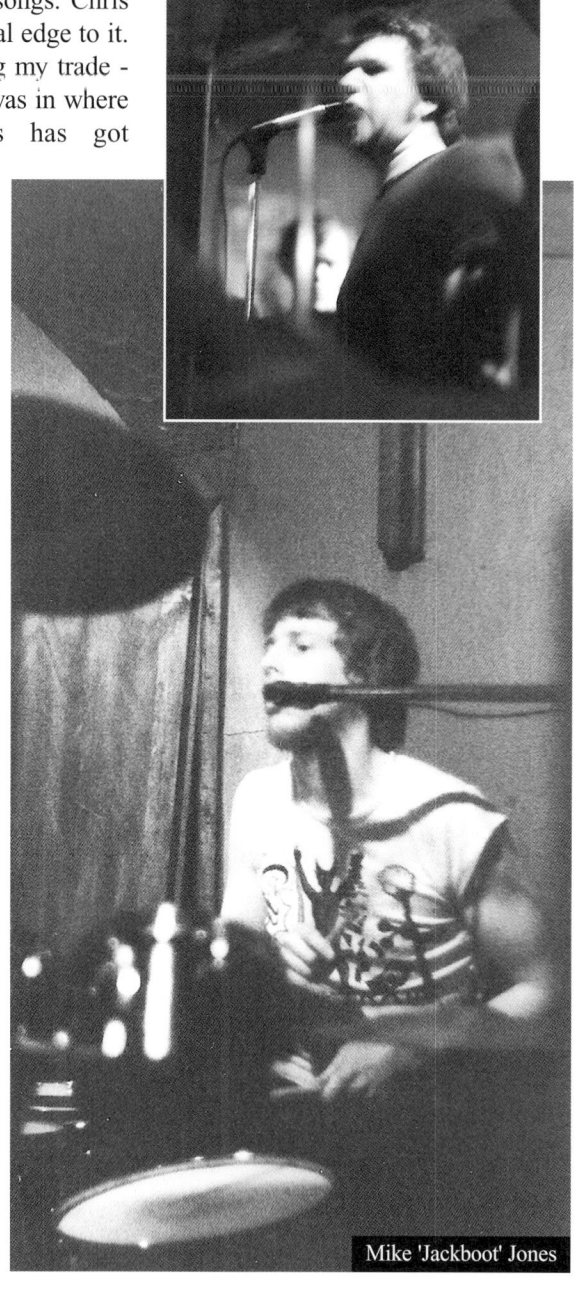

Mike 'Jackboot' Jones

78

3: **Savages in the City**

loyal fans to various venues around the south. There was a really great bunch of lads from Bemerton Heath called 'The Bemerton Boys', who followed us to many gigs."

"The atmosphere ushered in by the punk explosion had created a great new music scene in Salisbury and the pubs were always packed – especially the Cathedral Hotel and the Rising Sun. The QTs would be nose to nose with the audience and the walls would be running wet with sweat. It was so packed sometimes that it was impossible to reach the bar - resulting in punters buying pints at the Red Lion and taking them back to the Cathedral to drink!"

Although untrained, The QTs attempted to present something beyond basic punk thrash, which attracted the attention of some of the older music fans in the city.

Tich Amey: "I quite liked that band because it was a completely different sort of music to what I had ever played."

Andy Nicklen: "I'd seen The QTs at the Blackbird[8] and said to Pete [Lucas] 'You want to have a word with some of the boys' because I personally thought The QTs

79

ENDLESS BEAT

"... how the hell is it going to get into the car park!"

were in with a very good chance. The reason I liked The QTs was it was basically a straight up sixties type of sound with a different slant on it. Also, I thought the energy coming from the band projected very well. I thought perhaps one of the boys might be able to push them or give them a chance."

The QTs impressed local folk singer Chris Sandford enough for him to contact Hal Carter, manager of a number of established artists. Carter came down from London to see the band play at The Conquered Moon[9].

Frogg: "We didn't believe for a second that he would travel down to see a band he'd never really heard of, but come the day there was Hal Carter wearing black trousers and a black bomber jacket with 'Warner Brothers' emblazoned across the back, tapping his foot and seeming to enjoy the gig. This led to an offer of a publishing contract which, if he had thrown his overcoat over it, I think I would have signed it through the button hole! 'We're on the way' I thought to myself…'this is our big chance…'"

Simon Kuczera: "The general dissatisfaction with the quality of the single and a bit of an argument over the fact my name ended up along with the band as producer caused a bit of friction. I felt entitled to have my name on there along with the band because I had spent the whole day down there as the tracks were laid down, discussing the pros and cons of individual tracks and how it could be improved or changed."

"As things came to pass the band was having discussions with another management company and signed a contract with them. The first I found out about this was when I went around Chris's house having not heard from people for a week or two!"

Frogg admits that "We were probably guilty of not doing the decent thing by telling him that our association was over. The Hal Carter Organisation was now in charge of The QTs' future and we were soon booked into a London recording studio. This resulted in two tracks, Over You and Piccadilly Pusher, which didn't sound too bad."

"However, The QTs were at their best live and Hal decided to record our whole set. This in turn would give him some idea of which track might make a decent single. There were also, Hal informed us, contacts waiting to hear our material in Germany, which might result in a tour – we were excited by what was happening."

"When it came to recording The QTs live, Hal suggested we book a hall in Salisbury that would capture the atmosphere and in turn, The QTs' sound. We booked the Rising Sun which had a decent sized function

The QTs by Perry Harris

room at the back of the pub. What we didn't know was Hal had called in a favour. Mobile 1 Remote Studio had been on tour with Supertramp in Paris, recording what would become their best selling live album. The next location after Paris was a back room in a Salisbury pub!"

"On the afternoon of the gig, Mike Vickers and I were sitting in Rose's Café[10] when a monstrous articulated lorry with 'Mobile 1' splashed in large red font came thundering down the road and stopped outside the Rising Sun. 'Bloody Hell!'said Mike as we sipped our tea, 'how the hell is it going to get into the car park'."

"The answer was quite simple. The lads in Mobile 1 contacted the Wilts and Dorset bus depot just down the road, and they promptly poured oil onto the road and then, with the help of a crane, proceeded to push the back end of the lorry around until it was able to drive straight into the car park!"

"That night was electric and the Rising Sun was packed to the rafters – some of the audience took the opportunity of going into the control room on board the lorry and said it was 'like the Starship Enterprise!' One thing I remember after the gig was my dad who said 'This is your big chance, don't blow it'. There then followed a sound that must have been reminiscent of the Titanic hitting the iceberg as Mobile 1, powering forward, proceeded to demolish a tree on it's way out of the car park!"

Mike Vickers: "We had never seen the likes of it. We had to take the gate post out of the back of the Rising Sun where we used to rehearse in the beer cellar, which was a garage basically. Hal took that [recording] away and tried to get it around. I think the mistake he made was he should have invited record companies to see us with our audience – showcased us. We should have tried other people. We went straight with Hal Carter and that was it but being so naïve we didn't know."

The QTs were extensively covered in Vague. In a somewhat tongue in cheek interview their aims were stated as being to first 'get a drink' and then 'be famous and earn lots of money'. Referring to recent gigs, Colin Holton claimed Basingstoke had been good as 'I only got bottled twice'.

Mickey Dyer reviewed a QTs gig at Magnums in Basingstoke for Vague, where a coach load of fans had travelled from Salisbury. 'The Infamous Bemerton Boys' cheered the band on and by the third number everyone was on their feet, including 'the local greaser contingent…jumping like nuns on nails'. Towards the end of the set some skinheads turned up looking for trouble, but were soon dancing along with everyone else.

At another memorable out-of-town gig – this time in Guildford - The QTs brushed shoulders with a band who were soon to enjoy a degree of commercial success.

Mike Vickers: "We were playing at the Royale, which was Mick McManus' pub – the wrestler. We went up this other pub and started talking to these guys, and they were called The Vapors. We said 'We've got this song Takeaway Romance'. Next thing we know The Vapors have got Turning Japanese out - I always say they pinched that idea from us!"

The QTs at the City Hall

ENDLESS BEAT

"...the writing was on the wall for The QTs - we decided to split up."

"We got back and a lot of locals started dancing. The wrestlers they had behind the bar tried to stop them, so we just invited them up on stage. I don't think they paid us for that gig – we tried to threaten them with the union…but none of us was in the union. We were all singing on the way back down the M3 when all of a sudden it was 'bum-bum'…there was a dead body in the middle of the motorway."

In 1980 ex-Kitchen Sprog Ford replaced Chris Walsh in The QTs. In a Vague interview the band claimed Chris' departure was down to the traditional 'musical differences' problem. Colin Holton felt Sprog's playing style was more suited to the band whereas 'Chris has a very unique style'.

Mike Vickers: "Colin thought of the name – The QTs – and was a big influence on the band, but I think there was always a little bit of differences between Chris and Colin's styles. We were all quite good buddies but I think Colin slowly was taking over the band, and it was pushing Chris out a little bit. Colin was churning out song after song and Chris was having to learn these songs, which wasn't giving him the chance to put his influence through the way he should be."

Colin admits he was more inclined to write material of an 'epic' nature: "I just didn't know when to stop! It was based around Boomtown Rats and Clash – the way they integrated stuff. Living In The Country was like 'well, that's three minutes but let's put in a bit of reggae, make it interesting and tell a story'. Nothing was too precious – it was like 'let's put that in and see how that works'."

Although they might have been an influence, in the Vague interview Colin had taken the opportunity to offer some opinions on Joe Strummer and The Clash: 'He contradicts himself so much. He said when Sid Vicious died he broke down and cried for two weeks [but] when Johnny Rotten left the Pistols, Joe Strummer said the rest was crap. I think he's a twot. Mind you when I saw The Clash I thought they were great, they put a lot into it. It was a really good gig, but they're very pretentious, they're trying to out-pose each other'.

Sprog Ford added a new dimension to The QTs but they had lost momentum and their change in style to a more bluesy sound signalled the end of a promising band.

Mike Vickers: "Chris's brilliant way of playing was just unique – different from anything else around at the time. I thought The QTs were never going to be the same. We got Sproggy in – more of a bluesy player but it lacked Chris's influence. Sprog is a very capable guitarist but nobody is quite like Walshy."

Frogg: "We had waited for the results of the live recording. Eventually, a tape arrived in the shape of an unmixed demo, badly edited and a disappointment. We waited for Hal to come up with some decent gigs and the proposed tour of Germany…. nothing happened. Then Chris left and although we gigged for a while, the writing was on the wall for The QTs - we decided to split up. 'You bloody idiot!' said my dad on hearing the news. Soon after, I found myself in my bedroom looking at the publishing contract I had signed with Hal Carter's 'Moggie Music'…the small print informed me I was still contracted for a further five years in the event of The QTs splitting up!"

3: Savages in the City

Identity Crisis was formed by the Collinson brothers - Steve and Lloyd - on bass and drums respectively, with guitarist Nick Marchant. Vocalist Neil Dalziel was added to the line up and the band, still as yet unnamed, made its live debut at a private party in August 1977.

Steve Collinson: "Reg Maggs went off doing Caribbean cruises as a painter and decorator – a sort of handyman. So I had lost my drummer and also lost John Priestley, who had gone to America. But Lloyd by this time had become a very good drummer and I thought 'Well, I could boss him around'."

Neil Dalziel: "It started as a sort of partnership between Steve and Nick Marchant - they got some ideas together at Nick's place out at Steeple Langford. Then they decided they wanted a singer and that's when they got me in."

For their second gig, at the Hamster near Andover, the landlord demanded a name for advertising purposes and after various ideas were kicked round, a band member complained they had an identity crisis. The band thought this was apt and kept the name beyond that date.

Neil Dalziel: "It seemed The QTs and ID Crisis were always playing at the same places and following each other around. People told me there was a rivalry but I didn't think there was particularly. Identity Crisis was much more conventional rock and QTs was a bit more new wave tinged."

Steve Collinson: "I didn't get on with punk at first. The only band that did it for me – after their first album – was XTC. There was something about XTC I loved, and I'm still keeping up with them. I did get the first Talking Heads album and carried on buying their stuff for some time, but I couldn't get into the Sex Pistols and didn't like early Jam. Looking

> GRANGE HOTEL, SALISBURY
> FRIDAY, 8th FEBRUARY, 1980
>
> **Q.T'S**
> PLUS
> **IDENTITY CRISIS**
>
> Admission Ticket £1

IDENTITY CRISIS - left to right: Nick Marchant, Neil Dalziel, Lloyd Collinson, Steve Collinson and Colin Gray

83

ENDLESS BEAT

"Logo Records... replied and that was just to say 'Sod off'!"

Steve (above) and Tim (right) Collinson

back now, it was full of great energy and did start a whole new way of playing, but I wasn't really into it."

"The whole thing about punk seemed to be speed playing. Identity Crisis would play fast and loud but it wasn't just three chords. There was lot of weird timings and riffs and things. We were still being what we thought was clever musically."

Neil Dalziel: "I loved the attitude and some of the music. I found a lot of the more contrived stuff a bit painful. I thought the Pistols and Clash were great and I liked the American stuff – Television, Talking Heads."

Nick Marchant: "Before punk took off I had been trying to get a rootsy R&B band going. All the other musos thought I was mad so it never happened - prog and guitar hero stuff being the order of the day – so punk to me was a breath of fresh air. Duncan Fulton was an old mate and lived in the same village, so I got all the latest punk stuff from him. Musically I found it a bit limited hence ID Crisis tried to take something from punk and the music that had gone before - the name of the band actually represented our musical mindset."

Steve Collinson: "Nick would write most of the licks and I don't think he listened to anything but the blues – there weren't any modern bands that Nick liked. Then we got Colin Gray in and he was sort of jazz rock influenced. So putting that with a high energy drummer and pounding bass we came up with some weird things. Andy Sheppard used to come out and jam with us. Andy had just started learning sax then so he wanted to play with anybody. We used to let him come and play with us – that was wicked."

Steve's former colleague in Eskimo, Nick Kemp, had – with his brother Jez - also formed a new wave band - The Crimmos. Nick's new material reflected the change in his taste from his original influences "Hendrix Man, Hawkwind and a bunch of guitar-based outfits to whom time has not been particularly generous."

"All that sort of ended with punk. For whatever reasons, The Doors got a hold of me and there was a brief nasty affair. At the same time there was Iggy Pop's Lust for Life and The Idiot, which really blew me away, and - I hate to admit - the shadow of Mr Bowie loomed large, but I was listening to a lot of stuff - anything I could get my hands on: dub, rockabilly, Kurt Weill, trashy pop, Television, T-Rex, Eddie Cochran, The Residents. PIL's Metal Box album made a big impression. And of course the two guys that have made the biggest impression of all: James Brown and Captain Beefheart."

"Punk made a big dent in my pompadour - the whole scene, not just the music. As far as the music goes it really pulled the scales from my eyes and showed me what's possible - revealing the virtuoso as more often than not an embarrassment, a dexterous clod, the tool of corporate semi-demi-quavers and contrapuntal ass-wipes."

Nick wasn't particularly impressed by his local rivals and feels that punk has generally not aged very well.

Nick Kemp: "Stand out bands? Hell, I was young and competitive and

Nick Kemp

Nick and Jez Kemp

would admit to no such thing. My viewpoint was if a band wasn't doing what I was doing it just couldn't be any damn good [but] I always enjoyed Colin [Holton]'s Mummy Is A Wino routine."

"Very few bands made it out of the era in good odour - and not always the ones you would have supposed. The Clash still sound good - in fact better and better - ditto The Fall, and The Stranglers' first effort has acquired a certain mystique, but most of it – Jesus, talk about undercooked. The technology sure didn't do anyone any favours. I mean, those crappy snyths – Diablo!"

Between The Eyes were formed from musicians who had largely not previously had a profile on the local scene.

Johnny Fellows: "I always fancied myself as a singer. I never really thought I would do it until I met Colin Crook – a hundred years ago – who was living the guitar. What he couldn't do was pace himself very well, because he didn't have a metronome or anything like that."

"I said I would go around his place one Saturday afternoon and sing. He had some sheet music – Beatles Songbook and that sort of thing. I just started singing at what I thought was good time and he was playing along. He joined the Musicians' Union and got a club band. They didn't have a singer, so I went along, and that's how it started."

"It was after the initial punk explosion but still in that new wave period. Strange sort of band because two of us really liked that sort of stuff – me and Micky Lavender - but the others were more into rock stuff – AC/DC, Thin Lizzy – so we were a bit of a mishmash really."

"Micky was a good songwriter, he wrote some of our stuff, as did Colin. I helped with a few lyrics and things. It's like a lot of those bands - you learn somebody else's songs so you can go out and actually play, then you try and get as much of your own stuff in there. We made a couple of tapes, up in Andy Partridge's studio in Swindon. We took a tape up to London. Logo Records were the only ones that ever replied and that was just to say 'Sod off'. We didn't have grand designs - but it was good fun."

During the early stages of their partnership, two members of Between The Eyes experienced the community spirit prevalent among Salisbury musicians.

Johnny Fellows: "Chris Lucas used to live in the flat below me and Colin Crook. Tich Amey came round to talk to Chris, who told him Crooker had a Les Paul. He came up to have a play and broke a string. He promised to replace it and we both thought we would never see him again - we were both a bit star struck that a sixties star would even talk to us - but the next day six new strings were posted through the letter box. I've always had a lot of time for him ever since."

The new local bands naturally inspired other aspiring musicians. The lead singer with Kinetic NRG (formed at Westwood St Thomas School[11]) would go on to build a reputation on the local scene – as a drummer.

Alex Mundy: "I was about fourteen or fifteen, still at school and trying to get into pubs to listen to music. Local bands that were inspiring us were The QTs and The Kitchens. Our very first gig was in the break of a QTs gig - Frogg Moody and Colin Holton were certainly an influence on us at the time. I had gone from one day playing football and messing around being a kid, to suddenly wanting to be in the pubs listening to, and playing music."

"I was at school with Gary Clements. He said to me one day 'We're starting a band' and he couldn't think of a name. It was only because some bands - like XTC - were using initials to abbreviate names, that I said 'Why don't you call it 'Kinetic N-R-G, as in ENERGY!' He said 'That's great - do you wanna join?' So I went and did an audition - as the singer."

ENDLESS BEAT

"... people like Jon Nicholas and Jon Stone were the ones to look to."

"We used to practice at the scout hut up at Hudson's Field. We would get a bit bored and I would ask Andy Clements 'Can I have a go on your drums?' He taught me my first couple of drum beats. Then I got a little kit and started from there. When I first started drumming people like John Nicholas and Jon Stone were the ones to look to - and The QTs' Jackboot was always a good drummer – it was just soak it all up really."

Skid [Kinetic NRG guitarist]: "The first band I was ever in was at school, with Andy Clements and a couple of other kiddies. It was about 1978 so we were doing songs by The Members, The Undertones and stuff like that - we were called The Singing Nuns of Alcatraz."

"Kinetic NRG did our first gig in September 1979, supporting the fabulous QTs at the Cathedral Hotel, in the interval. That was the first time I had ever played and it was absolutely brilliant - Alex being sick beforehand, me having to go to the toilet loads and loads of times, but it was fantastic. It was all due to Colin Holton walking up to us at a gig at the City Hall."

"I went to school with a kid called Carl Moody. Through him we got to know Mike Buxton, who was with The Shining Hearts Band. They had just got a load of new gear so were selling an old Rema drum kit, which Andy bought, a Selmer bass amp and 4 x 12 cabinet, which Gazza bought, and I borrowed £100 off my mum and bought a 100 watt Marshall and 4 x 12 cabinet. We had to carry the stuff home right across Bishopdown downs - it took us nearly all day!"

"We used to rehearse on Wednesday nights at the scout hut at Hudson's Field, which meant that with Gazza's dad's Volkswagen Beetle roof rack on, the first trip would be the Selmer bass amp and half the drum kit…drive back…my amp and some of the drum kit…drive back…pick us up and take us over…and then it all had to be done in reverse - but we loved it – that's what its all about!"

KINETIC NRG - left to right: Andy Clements, Alex Mundy, Gary Clements and Ian 'Skid' Browne

"Also we never had any phones in any of our houses. If you wanted to phone somebody to book a gig you had to go and queue to use this phone box up on Bishopdown. If you wanted to go and see a band down Southampton Gaumont you had to go and queue up on a Saturday when the tickets were released. You couldn't get them sent to you."

Having been influenced by The QTs and The Kitchens, the youthful Kinetic NRG were themselves inspiring other young musicians.

Clive Roper: "I had no interest in music whatsoever. The only connection I had was my aunt ran the record department of Style and Gerrish and bought me a copy of Sparks' Propaganda[12]. The other thing was my dad was in the Army with Dennis Bullis whose brother was Ronnie Bullis [i.e. Troggs drummer 'Ronnie Bond'] – that's how I met Ronnie's son Dave – I didn't know that Dave and I would play in a band years later."

"Punk came along and everyone said 'You must listen to John Peel'. Every night I had one of those little white ear pieces stuck in my lughole and a little transistor radio, trying to stay awake until midnight listening to the sessions. Just before I left school somebody there formed a band - Kinetic NRG - I overheard them practicing and thought 'I want to be in a band too'. I persuaded my dad to buy me a Kay Telecaster copy, which you would normally get from Woolworths - but he bought it from a friend for a fiver."

After his relationship with The QTs ended, Simon Kuczera promoted local gigs before hitching up with a Dorset based band who had shared bills with Salisbury acts on a number of occasions.

Simon Kuczera: "I got involved with a few local bands, putting on gigs at the George Hotel in Amesbury. Then I put on some concerts at the City Hall, starting with a Christmas concert with all local bands – I think it was called 'A Christmas Rave Up'. The great thing was we had crowds of four, five, up to six hundred and the evening would last from 7.30 to 1.00 or 2.00 in the morning. People used to come up and say 'that was really fantastic – when's the next one' and that meant more to me actually than making a bit of money out of it."

"Through that somebody asked me to go and look at this band called The Martian Schoolgirls, from the Wimborne/Blandford area. They were looking for a manager and had great potential. I remember driving down to see them play and struggled all the way back to Salisbury after the gig because it absolutely snowed down - the area was snowbound for two or three days. I was pretty lucky not to have got trapped on the old Coombe Bissett road, but heartily impressed by this band – their professionalism, their sound and the great songs they had written."

"One of the guys from the band, Dan Kelleher – the lead guitarist and songwriter - had played with Joe Strummer in a band prior to The Clash [The 101ers], so he gave quite a good pedigree as it were. The drummer had

Cathedral Hotel gang with Mr Nardell (manager) far left.

ENDLESS BEAT

"I had all the bass lines written down on paper,..."

done some work with, I think, Boney M of all people."

"I became their manager and invested quite a considerable amount of money in terms of buying a full blown monitor PA stage system and a double wheel base Transit and set about trying to get some decent gigs and finding A&R people that would be interested in signing them. I spent quite a few days up in London going around record companies and arranged some quite good gigs at the Music Machine and the Acklam Hall."

"We had some interest from Europe and New York. Unfortunately it just wasn't viable to get the band over there [the USA] so that never happened, but we did get a residency in the Gibus Club in Paris and I set up a mini tour in Holland."

"The band had a single [Life In The 1980s], which got to number 16 in the independent charts. It was the first single of 1980, released at just gone midnight, and was reviewed on Round Table[13] with very favourable comments. We had fan letters appearing in Melody Maker and NME, including one spoofed-up photo spread of the band walking down a quiet country path down Blandford way, with a flying saucer in the background coming through the mist."

The Martian Schoolgirls landed a prestige tour support slot with Robert Fripp's latest project The League of Gentlemen. Fripp was a native of Wimborne and his new band were rehearsing in an old hunting lodge near Sturminster Marshall, on the Kingston Lacey estate, where Martian Schoolgirls guitarist Steve Burden lived. Their bassist having left on the eve of the tour, the band called on the services of an ex-Kitchen to help them out.

Ruth Jones: "I came across The Martian Schoolgirls when I was playing with The Kitchens. They came to see us and got us loads of gigs in Dorset and we did quite a few gigs supporting each other. Steve thought The Kitchens was a great band – actually they covered Lies and another couple of Kitchens' songs, and later one of my Courgettes' songs – Riding In My Car."

"At the time they had troubles trying to keep a bass player. Robert Fripp had been rehearsing a new band at their cottage and I had met him a few times out there, and Barry Andrews the keyboard player - who used to be with XTC. We also met the Roche Sisters and Brian Eno - I jammed on Great Balls Of Fire with Robert Fripp and Brian Eno in a pub in Tarrant Hinton."

"They were due to go on the UK leg of their tour and asked The Martian Schoolgirls to be their support band. Their bass player let them down literally two days before the tour so they came to me and said 'Will you do it?' I had to leave my job at Derek's Records, learn all the songs in one night and then go on tour – I had all the bass lines written down on paper, pinned up on the back of the PA speakers at the gigs."

"Our instruments went in luxury – on the tour bus - and we piled into a Ford Cortina. It was 'Does anybody know anybody in Birmingham? Can we sleep on any floors?' It was hard, hard work - we would get to the venue, do the sound check [then] we all had to be back there at a certain time, run on, the lights would go on and we would play. It was a really professional tour - apart from the fact that we had nowhere to sleep and nothing to eat!"

"Robert Fripp's band were in

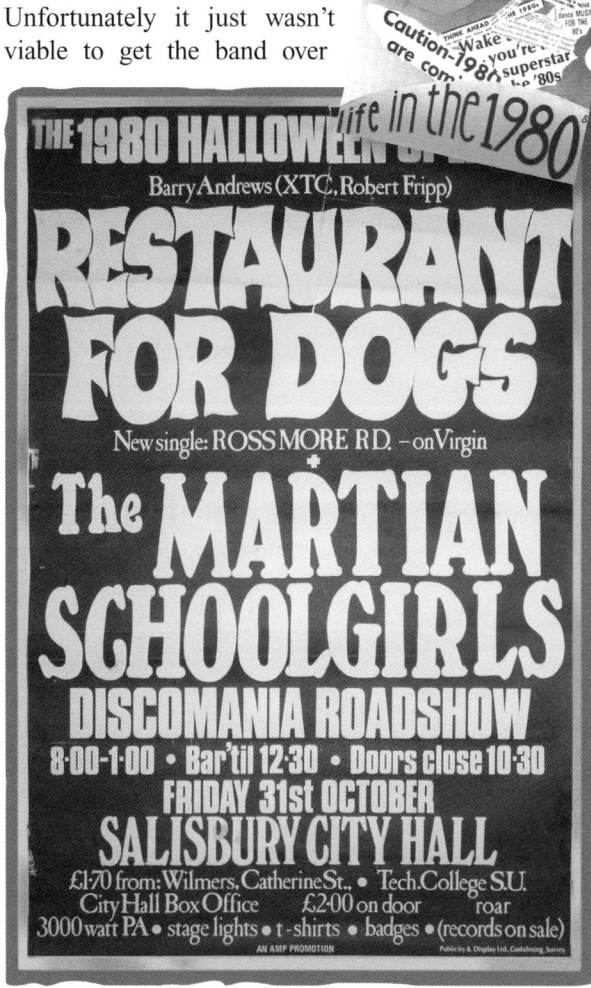

hotels - and we were sleeping in the venues! I remember getting up after sleeping on the floor, getting in the Cortina and eating one meal a day, which was usually a takeaway curry at about six o'clock."

Unfortunately, The Martian Schoolgirls never capitalised on their rising profile and, as the band folded, their manager dropped out of the music business and in to the civil service.

Simon Kuczera: "Everything was looking really good and I am absolutely convinced that within another six months that band would have been a pre-Prefab Sprout or Beautiful South but, as is often the case with bands, it started to disintegrate, which was very sad because they really had, I believe, huge potential."

"As a consequence of the Martian Schoolgirls I got my hands severely burned financially because I had put a lot of money into the band. I sadly ended up having to get a court order and bailiffs involved to recover some of the equipment I had paid for, so it got very stressful. I made a conscious decision at that point that it wasn't worth fooling myself I could attain what the likes of Simon Cowell have now established!"

Grandma Moses, a band that had already demonstrated a range of influences, moved on from the progressive era and were able to change to a more up-to-date sound.

Tom Thatcher: "The band started changing again. Chris Glover left, Paul McElhatton left, and George Hart joined on bass - I had played with George in my first band [Heap], back in the late sixties. That was a much more funky version of Moses. We were getting much more into blues-rock. George Hart was as mad as a coot, but a great, great, bass player. We played in a field once – that was one of George Hart's things – 'Come and play at a festival man, you'll love it'."

Andy Golden: "It was a most bizarre gig. We went down to Milborne Port and drove up this track – there were signs saying 'festival this way'. It was a weekend thing, big stage, generators, lights and everything, but there was nobody there – nobody at all! We put the gear up and thought 'What shall we do?' So, we had a smoke…..and then had another one."

"We thought after a while 'Well, we'll play then'. We just went on and started jamming – on and on for twenty minutes - and still there was nobody there. Then someone appeared out of the bushes and came into the clearing. We kept on playing because we were out of it by then – it didn't matter. Other people came and suddenly this whole place was filled up with all these hippies – all doing the forest dancing with the twigs in their hair – and it was a great gig!"

Tom Thatcher stood as a candidate in the 1979 General Election and achieved the second highest independent vote in the country. As a result he became friendly with Alexander Thynne, Viscount Weymouth - now Lord Bath of Longleat – leading to another unusual gig.

Tom Thatcher: "He rang up one Friday. He was putting on a gig in Gough's Cave in Cheddar Caves, of all places, which I don't think anybody had ever done before. He had a young band playing called The Violent Daffodils or something, but they had actually broken up during that week. He said 'I've got hundreds of people coming – can you organise a band?' I rang Brad, who was up in London and said 'I'm not coming down for any gig at short notice'. I said 'We're going to get £200 each' and he said 'I'll be there at nine'."

Derek's Records with Rob Morrow behind the counter.

ENDLESS BEAT

"I'm gonna stick this bottle of champagne right up your arse, matey."

"We went along into this deep, dark, dripping cave – right down inside Gough's Cave – and it turned out to be a great gig. It was a straight set of pretty heavy rock and blues and it went down an absolute storm."

"Brad had terrible trouble getting out of the traffic in London. He stopped at a phone box and said 'I can't possibly get down there before nine - I will be there - but just be patient'. At quarter past nine he came staggering up through the cave with his AC30 and his guitar under his arm, and Lord Christopher – Alexander's brother – said 'My brother has paid good money for this party, what do you mean by turning up late like this?' Brad leant over and said 'If I hear one more word from you, I'm gonna stick this bottle of champagne right up your arse, matey'. Christopher said 'Ah, suddenly I see your point of view – carry on, whenever you're ready, no rush, in your own time'."

There were some famous guests at the party, but Andy Golden failed to recognise a well-known fellow drummer.

Andy Golden: "I think Joan Collins was dancing with Oliver Tobias in the front row. In the break I went to the bar to get a drink. This bloke came up and said 'Excuse me mate, any chance of me playing your kit?' I said 'No, I don't let anyone play my kit' and off he went. Tom came up and said 'What did Simon Kirke say to you then?' I said 'Who?' Then it dawned on me who it was - the drummer out of Free – oops! I've recently met some friends of his in Cyprus and I've been invited to their place to meet him…so I'll have to confess everything!"

1977 is remembered as the year punk exploded. However, the following year saw another musical phenomenon, which had a huge, worldwide impact – the nightlife of Salisbury was no exception.

Roger Raggett: "Growing up during the sixties and seventies was a heady experience as the musical styles and fashions were so diverse, plus they seemed to change on a regular basis, which ultimately culminated in the mid-seventies in the Disco sound."

"I at that time was working at Gordon's - initially in the downstairs part, but later in the nightclub as one of the house DJs. Gordon's was owned by Chris Ling and Alf Bowley, and managed by Alf's son Mark. Working there at that time was fun with a capital F and the hip place to be! We always opened at 9.00pm but it was never busy 'til the pubs shut. After about 11.00pm the line stretched to the entrance of the Old George Mall and beyond. The bouncers had their hands full trying to keep order up the narrow stairwell, inside it got hot, humid and noisy, which in turn created a great atmosphere. It was also a great place to be to meet your mates - and of course girls - plus I was getting paid and my beer and food was free!"

"The club had an account at Suttons, where I used to go on Saturday mornings to buy the latest singles or - what were becoming really popular - extended mix singles. Just released was the Saturday Night Fever album with all the hits from the film. I bought a copy plus a couple of extended mixes and took them back to the club, only to be told by Mark that we had to cut the budget on buying records and I had to take it back for a credit - which I did after a heated discussion."

"That evening, when Chris and Alf asked if I was okay, I brought up the subject of the album and they backed up Mark. As the evening wore on Chris came into the DJ box, only to be requested over and over again for Staying Alive, Night Fever, More Than A Woman and all the other tracks from the film contained on the album."

"Needless to say, next week Gordon's had it's very own copy of Saturday Night Fever, which actually got replaced about three months later, as the original was so full of scratches, beer spills and finger prints it would not play. Never again was there a discussion about music expenditure!"

Away from these new scenes, many of Salisbury's previous generations of musicians were still working. Peter Mason invited the guitarist from Peacewave to join him in a new project with Robin Gair.

Yan Webber: "Peter said 'I'm getting a rehearsal band together and I don't know if you would be interested in playing?' Of course I would! The drummer didn't turn up but the rest of the band was there and comprised Peter and Robin Gair – they had just finished Amey-Gair-Mason so were local luminaries and I was absolutely gobsmacked to be in their company – two young Amesbury sisters, Linda and Christine Taylor, and Nigel Dixon was the bass player."

The band were later joined by Andy Golden on drums and John Hatchman on percussion, but lost a founding member.

Yan Webber: "It was supposed to be a rehearsal band for Peter but in the end it drifted away from what he wanted and the band became the Taylor-Gair Band. The band had a funky edge with elements of country

3: Savages in the City

– the Little River Band were very influential but we did Earth, Wind and Fire and things like that."

"I thought Band of Gold were absolutely brilliant. They had – I thought – a young South American looking singer…who turned out to be from Enford…John Hatchman. We got to know him and eventually he joined us on congas – of course he was the looker and all the girls fluttered their eyelids at him. He was more of a focal point than the two girls sometimes!"

Trevor Davies had formed a country rock duo named Woodsmoke, with Phil Boardman – a former member of Liverpool band The Thoughts. Polydor considered putting out Woodsmoke's versions of Slow Dancin' (Swaying To The Music) and Lonely Boy as a single in 1977. The duo also played live on Wally Whyton's Country Meets Folk show on Radio 2. By all accounts the recordings were excellent and Boardman told Zabadak magazine that Dozy was 'devastated' and 'wanted to throw his bass guitar into the river' when Polydor decided not to proceed with the release.

At the end of 1975 Andover band The Troggs, whose line up now included former Bethany, Tracker and Band Of Gold guitarist Pete Lucas, had found themselves in a quandary. Bassist Tony Murray had left the band with three shows in England and a tour of Holland and Germany booked to play in the New Year.

Tich Amey had recommended Pete Lucas to the Troggs and he now returned the favour by approaching Tich who, although he didn't normally play bass, agreed to have a go. An interesting curio in the Troggs discography is the 1979 album Wild Thing, the sleeve of which featured a picture of this line up of the group, despite neither Pete nor Tich having played on the record.

The Troggs' German dates were

TAYLOR GAIR BAND - left to right: (back) Nigel Dixon, Andy Golden, Yan Webber and John Hatchman (front) Robin Gair and the Taylor sisters

ENDLESS BEAT

"...they were probably the best sixties band on the circuit."

promoted by Rainer Haas. While the band was in Hamburg he put a suggestion to Tich.

Tich Amey: "He said 'It's lovely to have The Troggs – what are the chances of reforming Dave Dee, Dozy, Beaky, Mick and Tich?' I said 'Well, Dave Dee you can forget. I could probably get Beaky, maybe Dozy, but Mick you can forget because he's got his pub'. He said 'But you've got "Mick" – and pointed to Pete Lucas [laughs]."

Pete agreed to the promoter's suggestion and DBM&T reformed in 1978, with John Dymond playing drums and taking on lead vocals.

Tich Amey: "It was the Tracker band, but became the DBM&T band. We played all the Dave Dee hits but we also had all the Tracker stuff and you could go out and give the German audiences two or three different sets."

The first recorded output by the reformed band was a Peter Mason song, You've Got Me On The Run, released in Germany and Holland in 1979. The single was produced by Dave Dee but, although a decent effort at a mainstream modern sound, suffered from minimal promotion and airplay and failed to make an impact.

The signs were not looking good for a successful comeback. In a thoroughly disparaging NME review of a gig at Dingwalls in London, Charles Shaar Murray summed up DBM&T as follows: 'where these guys are is the definitive end of line. They're stranded and the last bus home left years ago'.

At the time, the NME was of course expected to present such matters from the angle of 1976 having been 'year zero'. However, longstanding fans of the band felt they still had something to offer.

Andy Nicklen: "I was using the same pub as Tich, Beaky and Pete. They had a sound engineer but were one short for the humping. I was self employed at the time so I got asked to go. They were going down an absolute storm – it was almost like the middle sixties. It wasn't only people of their own age – it was young people turning up as well. At that time they were playing mainly in Germany and Holland."

"I was totally surprised at how good they were without Dave. They developed a completely new persona – I couldn't believe how professional and confident they were. Beaky was doing more talking and throwing a few jokes in, they also had a stage act with capes and a few UV lights and fireworks. I thought they were probably the best sixties band on the circuit – and probably still are."

The band could also hold their own in younger company.

Andy Nicklen: "They were on a gig with Dr Feelgood in Holland. Dr Feelgood were in the charts in England and I thought 'Bloody hell... they [DBM&T] might struggle tonight'. I was wrong. Dr Feelgood went on first and were absolutely, stunningly good, and I thought 'Well, you've gotta do something to follow that'. They did - they went on and did a superb show and the audience went absolutely bananas."

DBM&T were among many acts – at many levels of popularity - proving that punk, rather than killing off everything that had gone before, had provided a much need shot in the arm all around. It was perhaps ironic that in the eighties the long-hair dominated free festival and heavy metal scenes would reap the benefits.

CHAPTER THREE FOOTNOTES

1. The old Art College was located in New Street, in premises subsequently occupied by Trethowans but now vacant.
2. Katz clothes shop was located in Catherine Street.
3. Derek's Records was located in the original Old George Mall in part of the area now occupied by BHS.
4. Wilmer's clothes shop had a small but very tasteful record section and was located in Catherine Street in premises most recently occupied by Confetti and Lace but currently vacant.
5. Gordon's nightclub was located in Catherine Street and was later renamed Raffles and then Bentley's. The premises are now occupied by Goldfinger's.
6. The 'Road To Nowhere' – also known as 'Salisbury Pier' - was intended as a high level link from the then newly opened Churchill Way East, across one of the oldest parts of the city to a proposed multi-storey car park in Brown Street. The car park never got built, but the link road did and remained there for many years as a 'flying car park' and as a testament to civic disaster…but hey…'Road To Nowhere'…what a gift for a punk band looking for a slogan!
7. The Rising Sun was located in Castle Street, opposite the entrance to Wyndham Road. Later renamed Sunny's, the building has now been demolished and (along with the the adjacent Edward's Brothers garage) replaced with retirement apartments.
8. The Blackbird was located in Churchfields Road and has now been converted to residential use.
9. The Conquered Moon was located in Woodside Road. Following its demolition the Collingwood Mews housing development was built on the site.
10. Rose's Café was located at the junction of Hamilton Road with Castle Street in premises now occupied by Mandarin House.
11. Westwood St Thomas school was subsequently renamed Salisbury High School and is now The Sarum Academy.
12. Style and Gerrish was located in Blue Boar Row in premises now occupied by Debenhams.
13. The Radio One Round Table was a weekly record review show featuring the stars of the day as pundits.

ENDLESS BEAT

Tim Collinson

4 The People's Free State of Stonehenge
The Stonehenge Free Festival

The story of the Stonehenge Free Festival is not just about music. The Festival's founding, development and eventual demise are symptomatic of wider social and political movements – arising from, and reacting to, sixties ideals of 'freedom' - and their relationships with one another as the less tolerant eighties dawned.

The aim of this book is to tell the story of the music scene in South Wiltshire, in which the Festival has a very high profile. We cannot help but touch on the wider social importance and impact of the events, but this has already been well documented by people who are far better placed than us to explain its significance. We have therefore attempted to concentrate on the local perspective.

The spirituality and mysticism of the stones have long held a fascination for musicians and this developed with the hippy movement of the late sixties and early seventies - Ten Years After, Richie Havens and Graham Bond were among those who utilised the monument for album titles and sleeves. However, festivals aside, its best known appearance in rock history was probably that - in miniature form - in the Spinal Tap movie.

Whatever the original reason for their construction, crowds of up to 3,000 had been gathering at the stones to celebrate the Summer Solstice since the 1890s, entertained by portable

ENDLESS BEAT

"Do you want to come and play at Stonehenge?"

gramophones and jazz and skiffle bands. These ad-hoc events were mostly trouble free but by 1962 the authorities had become so concerned about the rowdy behaviour of a minority, that temporary barbed-wire fences were erected round the site. By 1964 access during the Solstice had been restricted to everyone but the Druids.

However, exponents of the counter-culture were no respecters of such restrictions and in 1969 around 2,000 of them gate-crashed the Druidical ceremony and held their own alternative festivities. The following year, by which time the wider free festival movement was beginning to take off, 3,000 people held a huge party around the perimeter of the site.

September 1970 saw the first event held at Worthy Farm in Pilton or - in common parlance - Glastonbury. The site owners, Michael and Jean Eavis, hatched a plan to hold a similar festival at Stonehenge to coincide with the summer Solstice of 1971, but soon abandoned the idea as they felt the authorities would never allow such an event to take place.

Over the August Bank Holiday weekend of 1972, the first Windsor Free Festival took place. Although the organisers had hoped for a crowd of a million, only around 700 people actually attended, almost being outnumbered by the police presence. However, the festival was a landmark and the following year's Windsor event saw around 8,000 attending over a ten day period. Unlike Glastonbury, Windsor was a genuinely free festival – not only was there no entrance fee, there was also no licence.

A 'pop' gig of some description is reputed to have occurred at Stonehenge during the summer Solstice of 1972 but no evidence has come to light as to what actually happened. However, a low-key event certainly seems to have taken place during the following year.

Steve Collinson: "Never Bend Over was the first band that ever played at Stonehenge. Some hippies were camping, came down and said

NEVER BEND OVER play Stonehenge - Reg Maggs and Steve Collinson

'Do you want to come and play at Stonehenge?' We said 'Well, you get a generator and put a stage up and we'll come up there', which they did. That would have been '73."

The first 'organised' Stonehenge Free Festival was held in 1974 after a meeting at Windsor, where Philip Russell (aka Wally Hope) drummed up enthusiasm with other hippie figureheads such as Sid Rawle.

Of all the British media institutions, the Daily Mail is probably that which one would least expect to have been first on the scene at Stonehenge, but the morning after the Windsor site had been cleared by police, the small group who had moved on to the stones were approached by a man in a suit. He introduced himself as a journalist from the Mail and said he had heard the Windsor Festival was relocating to Stonehenge.

Although this idea hadn't particularly occurred to anyone else, it sounded good and the hippies pointed to a lorry, telling the reporter it contained a stage from Windsor. The

4: **The People's Free State of Stonehenge**

Steve talks to his son Luke as Anton Hayman looks on

ENDLESS BEAT

"...a few hippies, six or seven bands and tents – that was the first Stonehenge Festival."

following morning a front page article commented on Stonehenge becoming a new Camelot.

Duncan Fulton: "I reckon I was there the first year the Festival was on. I just happened to be walking along the leylines. I came up from Woodford and when I got to Stonehenge there was a little field with a few hippies, six or seven bands and tents – that was the first Stonehenge Festival."

After the event a small group of hippies remained camped along a track near the stones before moving into a squat in Amesbury for the winter. Wally Hope was among them and the group called themselves 'Wallies' in his honour.

Hope was a legendary but ultimately tragic figure in the freak-hippie-

'KEEP AWAY' WARNINGS IGNORED
Campers in robes at Stonehenge festival

FARMERS said "keep away". So did the Department of the Environment. But over the weekend thousands of young people ignored the warnings and transformed a field alongside Stonehenge into a vast medieval-style encampment.

They brought their goats and their dogs and even their own bakery and, with many of the campers wearing long flowing robes, they could easily have been the army of Henry V at Agincourt.

Playing in turn on the makeshift-stage — built in line with the central arch of Stonehenge and the Heelstone — were 20 groups. They included members of the cult recording band Hawkwind, Lightning, Sphere, Jupiters Child and Solar Ben, with Elizabeth Taylor's son, Michael Wilding, on flute and saxophone.

LOCAL BANDS

Local bands also used the opportunity to play to a vast audience of people from all over the country. Shining Hearts, based in Salisbury, long being their own gener- impromptu where wholemeal bread was being baked and the tiny stalls selling tea, fruit and home-made candies — all at rock-bottom prices.

Food supplies were being bought locally and a farmer in the area, for example, agreed to supply daily churns of milk. Perhaps the biggest problem was sanitation — although the toilets at the entrance to the monument were left unlocked.

Amesbury people had mixed feelings about the festival which was declared illegal by the Department of the Environment last week.

But one middle-aged man said: "I only came to laugh but now I'm here I think it's great." And many of the traders in the town agreed that the festival had "not been detrimental."

NO PROBLEMS

The manager of the Co-op, Mr Ken Allen, said: "They've got their rules and I've got mine but we've had no problems of shoplifting or anything."

On the other hand, the manager of one cafe said he was only serving his "recognised customers" otherwise he would have had to take the salt, pepper and mustard from the tables.

Wiltshire police kept a the public address system. And they even directed traffic through the wide open gate at the entrance — past a Department sign warning people of possible jail sentences for remaining on the site illegally, for organising or taking part in an "unauthorised assembly," or for "erecting or using apparatus for sound transmission."

By yesterday (Wednesday) 52 arrests had been made, mostly on drug charges. The arrests were mostly outside the festival but in the vicinity of Stonehenge.

SORDIDNESS

Chief Supt Frank Lockyer said: "While perhaps the numbers of arrests and crimes may be low considering the numbers attending, the figures really reflect the amount of effort the police were able to put into it, rather than the extent of the problem. One should not ignore the fact that the festival is illegal; neither should one ignore the sordidness of the circumstances on the site."

Earlier this week the DoE were accepting the festival as a fait accompli which they were powerless to do anything about. A spokesman said he was just keeping his fingers crossed and hoped everyone would be gone from the field by the weekend.

As for the local branch of the NFU, which first tried to nip in the bud any possible festival in the area, a spokesman said he was simply relieved that the festival-goers had kept off valuable farm land. Told about local farmers selling milk to people on the site was a "very sen-

98

4: **The People's Free State of Stonehenge**

ENDLESS BEAT

"When are these heavy metal kids gonna get off?"

festival going circuit. In 1975, just before the second Stonehenge Festival, he was committed to a psychiatric institution where he was 'medicated' after being busted for possession of three tabs of LSD.

He was released a few weeks after Stonehenge '75 but was never the same. He had been given huge doses of Modecate to counter the effects of Largactyl, which he had been surreptitiously avoiding actually taking due to its lobotomising effects. This had induced a condition of chronic and incurable dyskinesia - characterised by repetitive, involuntary, purposeless movements.

Not wishing to continue in this state, Wally Hope committed suicide in September 1975, despite the efforts of Penny Rimbaud (later of Crass), who knew him well and had earlier tried to extricate him from the psychiatric hospital. The sprinkling of Wally's ashes at Stonehenge the following summer was said to have been a particularly moving occasion.

Meanwhile, there had apparently been an increase in numbers of head lice in Amesbury. Parish Councillor Grace Lumley felt the infestation centred on the houses where 'people who call themselves Wallies' had moved in. The Parish Council requested an investigation into this and the Wallies' other misdemeanours, which allegedly included overcrowding of the squats and the cutting down of trees in the Lords Walk area.

Barry Pritchard: "They squatted at the stones and then, when evicted, took up and squatted properties in London Road. I was involved at that stage as the detective in Salisbury dealing with drug matters and got to know a few of them – I went in to all the squats at that stage."

The contrast in lifestyles no doubt resulted in some local tensions, but many residents were no more than amused by their new neighbours and the annual influx of festival-goers. An article in Wobbly Jelly fanzine would recall an Amesbury childhood where apples and barrels of water were left out for the visiting hippies, and many local music fans were of course delighted.

Johnny Fellows "I lived in Amesbury so it was absolutely brilliant. I loved it because it would give us something to do. On a Friday night we would have a few beers and just wander up the stones and watch the bands until the morning – I thought it was absolutely fantastic."

Stonehenge 1975 was far more organised than previous events, as a result of co-ordination between various groups following police intervention at Windsor. There was a feeling of a need to give the free festival movement a new site to focus on. The Stonehenge event was held in an open field with the campsite in adjoining woodland, and at its height was attended by 3,000 people.

Helping to boost the attendance was the new phenomenon of large numbers of curious locals and servicemen from the camps around Salisbury Plain. Some festival-goers found this something of a disturbing intrusion, particularly when 'visitors', influenced by alcohol, chemicals or both, turned violent around the stage area.

However, as dawn approached people moved onto the site of the stones to watch the sunrise and the festival spirit returned. It has been said that what happened to a number of people by the Heel Stone, at that time still outside the wire perimeter fence, as the sun rose on that morning, was such an intense spiritual experience that it fired them up to sort out the problems back at the festival site, which then settled into a more relaxed mood.

The loosely organised bills of the festivals were bolstered by local musicians.

Steve Collinson: "In '75 me, Anton [Hayman] and Reggie [Maggs] went up and did an off the cuff set. This guy came up and said 'When are these heavy metal kids gonna get off?' It was Joe Strummer - it was just coming up to that era, and he was trying to get on with a band called the 101ers."

Although crowd numbers grew year-on-year, the early festivals did not cause much concern to the authorities.

Barry Pritchard: "Trespass on land on its own was not necessarily a criminal offence – not a policing matter. When it comes to mass trespass it becomes a bit different, with all the other issues that brings along – illegal issues. When you were talking about a few people having a bit of a jive or whatever it may be – call it a 'festival' but it wasn't really that, they were just enjoying themselves with music and staying together in a field, maybe using dope or whatever."

At this stage the police and festival goers had a good relationship and Paddy Morrison, the Chief Inspector at Amesbury, was able to walk among the crowd unthreatened.

ENDLESS BEAT

"… it was a band finally finding its audience!"

Barry Pritchard: "There wasn't a difficulty. It was light hearted, fun and enjoyable in the early days. Let's not get away from the fact that stages were put up very well – a lot of the groups that came were national and international – the music was bloody great! I quite enjoyed it I must admit."

The 1976 Festival attracted a crowd of 5,000 at its height and although the first day was wet, cold and very windy the following two weeks were blisteringly hot. The Salisbury Journal described the scene as Department of the Environment warnings to keep away were ignored and 'thousands of young people… brought their goats and their dogs and even their own bakery and, with many of the campers wearing long flowing robes, they could easily have been the army of Henry V at Agincourt'.

Amesbury residents were reported as having mixed feelings about the event. One middle age man said 'I only came to laugh but now I'm here I think it's great' and many traders agreed the event had 'not been detrimental'. Co-Operative store manager Ken Allen confirmed he had experienced no problems with shoplifting, although one café manager said he would only serve 'recognised customers' for fear of otherwise having to remove the condiments from all his tables!

Chief Superintendent Frank Lockyer acknowledged the festival crime to attendance ration was low but felt this was largely due to the efforts of the police and stressed 'one should not ignore the fact that the Festival is illegal. Neither should one ignore the sordidness of the circumstances on the site'.

At one point there were six stages spread around the site, with one main built stage, resulting in an unpleasant listening experience at the centre of the site as each band's sound polluted the others. Local bands were again invited to make up the numbers.

James Ferguson [of Fairlane]: "We were sitting in the Star and someone

4: **The People's Free State of Stonehenge**

came in and said 'Do you want to go out and play at the Festival?'. We got all our equipment together in Tommy [Pugh]'s Mini van and drove up there. I think we were supposed to play at nine or ten o'clock and ended up not going on until after midnight – we were all freezing by then. It was the only stage there. It was a bit ramshackle – it got a bit more polished later on.

We were in a field opposite the Stones and on the first number the bass amplifier fell over, but I think we seemed to go down quite well."

Duncan Fulton: "I played with the Shining Hearts Band up there – it was a band finally finding its audience! Most of our numbers drifted off into obscurity after about ten minutes, when the band forgot what they were originally playing. Everyone used to play Waiting For My Man in those days I seem to remember. It was a great number but you would get really deadbeat rock bands doing it."

In 1977 the Festival was held well to the west of the Stones and the attendance approached 6,000. The event was well organised with regular on site meetings. There was no trouble and the police were content to remain off-site, although they had taken a pro-active approach at the gate by advising queuing drivers not to enter the site, as the event was illegal. This advice seems to have been largely ignored!

Richie Havens unexpectedly arrived at the site and approached a stage where Here and Now and the Bombay Bus Company were jamming. Havens set up an amp and over two hours played most of

Nudes, drugs and theft at rock festival

STONEHENGE'S Midsummer Solstice ceremonies may be over for another year for the Druids, but for 2,000 or so hippies, the field around the ancient monument is still a site suitable for them to pitch their tents, tepees and mobile homes and carry on with the rock festival they started last week-end.

Although there have been no incidents on the site, the number of arrests for theft and drug offences, both on and off the site, has steadily increased.

Offences have ranged from a 'streaker,' caught inside the monument site during a Druids' ceremony, to theft of food and equipment from other campers. Complaints were made to the police on Tuesday after a number of hippies were seen bathing nude in the river Avon at Amesbury.

One American visitor — Lisa Anne Thacher, from Wisconsin —had £112 worth of property taken from her tent, including her passport, return air ticket and cash. Miss Thacher had stopped at Stonehenge to see the stones and camped at the site not realising it was a hippie commune.

Store fire

On Tuesday, a food store on the site was destroyed by fire along with most of its contents. Fans put out the blaze themselves.

So far there have been close on 60 arrests for offences of one sort or another and a handful of the hippies have already appeared before Magistrates at Salisbury and been remanded.

The number of fans built up towards the end of last week and by the week-end, close on 5,000 were camped on the site adjoining Stonehenge. Pop music blared out day and night, but by Wednesday the numbers had dwindled to 1,500 and fans were still leaving the site in small groups or singly.

Cloudy

Despite a large number of visitors from the festival being held in the next field, the annual Druids' ceremonies at Stonehenge at dawn on Monday proved the most orderly and least attended for some years.

Several hundred sightseers and visitors to the ceremonies were joined by about only 1,000 or so of the 3,000 rock festival fans.

But the Druids and their visitors were unlucky with the weather and because of cloud did not see the sun rise over the Hele stone as is hoped on the Summer Solstice.

Among the Druids was 'Coronation Street' star Ken Barlow (Bill Roach) who sounded the trumpet during the dawn ceremony, which included some 60 white-robed members of the Order.

The stone circle was heavily barricaded with barbed wire fencing and illuminated and the police were out in strength with dogs.

Visitors, including many from overseas, who had come to visit Stonehenge found a bonus attraction in the festival and many paid a visit to the site to see what was going on.

Answering questions about the likely cost falling on the County Council of the festival at Stonehenge, the County Council Chairman, (Group-Capt. Andrew Willan) said any cost would fall on the police.

'The people there are breaking the law if they trespass and the police will be expected to carry out their duty,' he said.

NO WHEELS

Warminster W.R.V.S. Meals-on-Wheels service will be maintained by private cars after it was found on Sunday that three wheels and tyres had been stolen from the service's Ford van, in an unlocked council garage on Portway Lane Estate, Warminster.

ENDLESS BEAT

"... the monument is effectively hijacked!"

his best-known songs, before heading off to his next scheduled gig.

However, the highlight was an appearance by Hawkwind with their 'Atomhenge' stage set and Liquid Lem's light show. The Hawks' show flattened the on-site generator but the band continued playing acoustically, illuminated by torches and car headlights, while new diesel was drained from vehicles.

In general there were fewer rock acts in 1977 than in the previous year. This helped lessen noise pollution between stages but there were still complaints that acoustic sets could not be heard above the louder electric acts.

The New Musical Express carried a two page feature on the 1978 Festival, trumpeted by a full page front cover picture showing the stones behind barbed wire. By this stage the Festival was still a relatively small scale event, but the NME coverage perhaps indicated how it was becoming an established part of the musical calendar, although the feature tended to lean towards hippie-baiting rather than reporting on what was actually happening.

Lord Pembroke, who owned land adjoining the site and provided wood

---

Officials in the dark over Stonehenge pop festival

WHILST large rolls of barbed wire were being put up around the world-famous prehistoric monument Stonehenge early this week, up to about 100 hippies drifted into a neighbouring field with vehicles and tents for what one of them described as 'a pop festival likely to attract 15,000 fans.'

The festival they were talking about and which has never been officially notified to the police or local authority, seems to be 'a happening' which could last for about seven days from tonight (Friday). But local landowners, the Department of the Environment, who are responsible for Stonehenge, and the District Council are in the dark over the event.

On Wednesday under 100 hippies were in the field and were just recovering from a not-too-pleasant night of rain. They were finding themselves in a seige position for the field entrance through which they had gained access the day before was now padlocked and they were, according to one of their spokesmen, unable to get water from the nearby toilets at Stonehenge car park.

A Welsh rock group leader, 'Solar Ben,' said the water and access to the public toilets had been denied them, but the police had been friendly and helpful towards them.

He said they were at the site for the Summer Solstice which meant a lot wo them and was a highlight of the year as it was for the Druids.

Bedraggled

'We are nothing to do with the "Wallies,"' he explained, 'they're dead, man,' he added. He pointed out a stage which was in the course of being erected in such a position that the sun, if it shone at the Summer Solstice dawn, would light up the stage and the performers upon it.

But the Festival spirit was not abroad mid-week for the scene was decidedly damp and bedraggled and not a note of music could be heard drifting from the vans, cars, or tents in which men, girls, and one or two tiny tots had spent a dreary night.

In the meantime the Ministry workers were putting up the protective barbed wire wall around the monument preparatory to the week-end Druid ceremonies, an annual precaution made necessary a few years ago through rowdyism and vandalism.

'Happening'

One of the hippies said he and his friends had been let into the field through a gate by someone who seemed to have something to do with the land, and he thought eventually about 15,000 fans would be turning up for 'the happening,' many of them from the North Devon Pop festival which finished recently.

Police will be keeping an eye on the area and on Wednesday head of Salisbury Division Chief Supt. Frank Lockyer, said the hippies were occupying the field illegally and in contravention of the Stone...

But yesterday (Thursday) a question-mark was put over the rock festival. As more hippies slowly drifted in, the Department of the Environment in London announced that the festival was off.

In a special statement a spokesman said: 'There is no free pop festival at Stonehenge this week.'

He said regulations governing the monument forbade any assemblies at the site without previous permission from the Secretary of State.

YET MORE ALTERNATIVE SOCIETY PROPAGANDA NA

A STONED LOVE-IN OF FREE THINKING People, CELEBRateing the Midsummer Solstice, is going to take place AT STONEHENGE THIS SUMMER

ACCompanied by Lotsa Rock'N'RoLL and all the other paraphanalia of the usual FREE FREAK FESTIVAL, DA DATe is 17th JUNE 1977 for at LEAST 10 DAZE, an its all happening in WILTSHIRE on the A-303.

BRING WOT YOU EXPECT TO FIND ♥ if you want to contribute in anyway dont wait to be asked, :: DO IT ::

By the very definition of a FREE FESTIVAL their can never be enough bands n things. :: DO IT :: Organisers dont exist --- co-ordinators are secret - so dont ask

POWER TO THE PEOPLE   FREEDOM OF THE SOUL
PASS ALONG   PASS ALONG   THIS IS A TURN ON

WALLY LIVES

for festival goers, wrote to The Times deploring the use of barbed wire around the stones, adding that it was hard to believe anyone who had come to revere the stones would cause damage to them.

This prompted a response from local MP Michael Hamilton who agreed about the barbed wire but was vehemently against the festival, and hinted at a threat of damage to the stones if the police attempted to act against the event: 'The Wiltshire Police are highly efficient but, if they move in to clear it, the one per cent of trouble makers are ready with their paint pots, and the monument is effectively hijacked'.

This encouraged a letter of complaint from the Director General of the National Trust concerning damage to archaeology and the risk to the stones, which in turn elicited a lengthy response from Sid Rawle, in which he suggested, amongst other things, that the National Trust treated both the public and its tenant farmers 'worse than any feudal baron'. He also, not unreasonably, felt that a single military exercise might do more damage to the ancient landscape of Salisbury Plain than twenty years of festivals.

The growing popularity and profile of the festival led Salisbury Police Chief Frank Lockyer to make the radical suggestion that legalisation of the event would relieve policing pressures to some extent.

ENDLESS BEAT

"...wrapped in a blanket, as bikers chased punks about..."

In 1979 the festival grew considerably in terms of attendance. As in other years the event was an example of pure democracy. The 'organisers' would call general site meetings and several hundred people would debate what to do about the stage, the toilets, liaison with other parties and general financial and administrative matters.

There was improved liaison between organisers, landowners, welfare groups and the authorities. The site was kept relatively clean with the District Council's Environmental Health department having provided rubbish bags and arranged for a refuse cart to visit the site, and the stage was directed away from Amesbury in response to a police request. The police provided information on arrests to Release so that proper representation could be arranged and festival goers co-operated in investigations into an accident involving a child and a cot death that occurred on the site.

LSD was scarce on the site in 1979 but there were copious amounts of hash and a big supply of Diconal – a powerful painkiller, which later received notoriety in the hands of Harold Shipman. The word went around the site that Diconal had to be taken intravenously. However, it should be taken orally and injection intensifies its impact. As a consequence, people were crashing out everywhere and organisers resorted to making regular announcements over the PA to request that users stayed inside their tents, possibly because of the amount of children now attending the Festival.

During the early eighties, the Festival grew from a gathering of a few thousand hard core freaks into a major attraction. Along with the increase in popularity and associated media attention, there came a proportional increase in pressure on facilities such as toilets. Extra fields had to be used, which did not please landowners, and there was an increase in police presence.

Barry Pritchard: "People felt a draw towards Stonehenge and the mystical side, there were people who wanted to stay on longer than a couple of days and suddenly it started to take off. There was this opportunity to join together for an illegal event that could last some time, where anything went."

Despite the increases in attendance, there was a decrease in the acts of worship and celebration at the stones themselves. In 1977 there were less than 2,000 people at the Festival and 1400 were believed to have visited the stones. By 1984 nearly 40,000 attended, but less than 1,000 went into the circle.

The weather was atrocious in 1980 as it rained over a period of two weeks. Notwithstanding this, numbers attending the Festival gradually built from 200 on 13 June to more than 15,000 for the Solstice. Observers suggested the event had a 'very pleasant' atmosphere, but unfortunately this year saw the worst example of on-site violence during the Festival's existence.

Crass attempted to play alongside, among others, Poison Girls, The Mob, The Epileptics - who later became Flux of Pink Indians – and various local bands. The punk flavouring of these acts upset the bikers at the Festival and led to scenes reminiscent of Adam and The Ants' gig in Salisbury in 1978.

Tom Vague: "I remember wandering round, drunk rather than stoned or speeding, with flattened hair, wrapped in a blanket, as bikers chased punks about, in protest at the anarcho-punk bill."

Derek Johnson reported on the Festival for the NME under the headline of 'Bikers Riot at Stonehenge'. Trouble erupted late on the Saturday night when some bikers went on the rampage, attacked every punk they could lay hands on and effectively prevented Crass and Poison Girls from playing their sets.

Nik Turner's Inner City Unit, The Mob and The Snipers had been reasonably well received, but when The Epileptics took the stage they were greeted with a hail of flour-bombs, cans and bottles. Their lead singer was knocked to the ground by a

4: The People's Free State of Stonehenge

STONEHENGE FREE FESTIVAL

By Perry Harris

ENDLESS BEAT

"... a festival of peace and love... but we're not having the bike nicked"

bottle and their stage banner set alight. The site generator was damaged and the crowd took over the stage.

Skid: "The singer turned around to look at the guitarist, a bottle hit him on the side of the face and he went down. The bass player ran up to the microphone and said 'Right - whoever fucking did that fucking get up here now' and this hippy ran up and said 'Don't say that!' By that time there were all these Hell's Angels clambering up on to the stage! They told all the punks to get off the site by morning or there would be serious trouble."

"Me and Andy Clements had gone up on my moped – an FS1E Yamaha. We got up there and I thought 'I know this is a festival of peace and love… but we're not having the bike nicked. I know…we'll put it with all these other bikes'. So we put my FS1E in the middle of the Windsor Chapter's bikes and then had to smuggle it out when they were gonna beat everybody up afterwards!"

To avoid further trouble Crass and Poison Girls decided not to play and spent the rest of the night trying to break up fights and ferrying their fans to the safety of Salisbury railway station. Crass drummer Penny Rimbaud described the events as 'a four hour nightmare' including 'the most savage attacks I've ever seen'. People complained to the police but John Loder, a soundman at the Festival, claimed they were 'totally uninterested' and refused to take any action.

Superintendent Maddock of Salisbury Police Station told the NME he had no knowledge of the violence or any complaints. He did however say that 67 arrests had been made, mostly for drug offences or stealing wood, and added that in the view of the police 'the entire festival was illegal' as it was held on squatted land.

Penny Rimbaud acknowledged the presence of Crass at Stonehenge had attracted several hundred punks, to whom the festival scene was a novelty. This in turn attracted interest from some factions to whom punk was equally new. He had been involved in the free festival movement for many years and was appalled at the bikers' attitude: 'They said they didn't want punks taking over 'their' festival, they only wanted to hear 'real' music. This is supposedly an open festival, of peace and freedom. After this, I don't think Crass will play there again - we won't expose our fans to these experiences and risks'.

In retrospect, the events of 1980 were probably the beginning of the end for the Stonehenge Free Festivals. As well as the friction between various groups of attendees, contributory factors may have included the presence on site of several 'businessmen' – not traditional festival goers – who were supplying strong home made scrumpy and miscellaneous substances.

Barry Pritchard: "Things started to get a bit nastier. Underground issues started to come to the fore - drugs, alcohol, women, whatever – there was money to be made and the illegal side of it became quite ugly."

"There was a series of festivals at that time – illegal festivals – and people that travelled would go from one to another, linking and being in that frame of mind throughout. If you were dealing drugs, that was part of your game – you would go from one festival to the next and carry on your business."

Jon Maple: "I went there every year from '74 – at least to have a look if not to stay – just for its sheer oddity as a social scene. It was a huge educational experience to a fourteen year old grammar school boy, who should have been at double PE instead of hitching to Stonehenge and witnessing what was in effect a shanty town, which appeared to be a police no go area tolerated for reasons I could never fathom to this day."

"It was an open air drugs market - there were signs up on tents and marquees with price lists. Not just like you would find in Amsterdam or places where they have cannabis cafes, but they had something called the 'Loco Coco' tent - where you could buy a line of coke for a quid or a wrap for more. It was very structured with two queues - one for a line and one for a wrap - and the queues were right out of the tent for 24 hours a day!"

Skid: "There was drugs everywhere. I remember queuing up for an ice cream and he had blues and a jam jar of spliffs for sale on the ice cream van."

The following Stonehenge stories are told by a former Salisbury biker who would prefer to remain anonymous.

"We had a few years there. We used to go up in a little gang with about six motorbikes and hang out. There were little tents and caravans where you could go in for the 'Hot Knife'. You get two knives over a gas cooker until they are red, get a bit of dope on them and put them into a plastic bottle, and just go [sucks in breath] and inhale every last bit of smoke you can. You can't hold it in your lungs for more than ten or fifteen seconds. Within a minute your mind is invaded in every aspect: your walking ability, your thinking, your attitude, your reaction and how you talk to people."

"It's almost impossible to describe…like you're watching a programme and suddenly the programme changes into something completely out of the norm. You could be introduced to enormous paranoia or you might get a feeling you are on another level. It's unpredictable but very powerful!"

"I was stoned out of my head at one stage and went to see this band and I've got to say that in my memory they were the best rock band I have ever seen. I hadn't lost the plot - it was just I was really heavily stoned, which makes your ears much more sensitive."

"Then I got lost. It was so dark and I was really out of my head, and I walked into the Hell's Angels' camp. I stayed cool, quickly scanned, thought 'That looks like a good exit' and walked through the middle of them all. There were about sixty of them and they didn't say anything…. fortunately."

"After a couple of hours it used to wear off a bit and you would want to go up or down. We decided we wanted to buy a bit of pot, so we came up with ten pounds each and drew straws – the short straw had to go to the Hell's Angels tent. It was M who had to take the sixty quid to this frightening place and he came back about a quarter of an hour later with a big piece of tin foil."

"We opened it up and were chatting away rolling this joint and passing it round. It got to me and I was sort of [inhales – looks puzzled] - it was horse shit! We said 'M you've got to go back and get our money' and burst out laughing…that was the end of our finance. We were given sixty quid of horse shit but what are you gonna do about it? [laughs]. I just

ENDLESSBEAT

"Just walk in… saying 'we're arresting you!' What do you think is going to happen?"

couldn't stop laughing!"

So why didn't the police attempt to stop drug dealing on the Festival site?

Barry Pritchard: "When it comes to the illegal selling of drugs and you've got ten or twenty thousand people in there, who want that sort of thing to be going on, what do you do? Just walk in with a half a dozen officers in uniform saying 'we're arresting you?' What do you think is going to happen?"

"Uniform and Drug Squad Officers carried out intelligence-led stop checks and searches of persons attending and leaving the Festival site. Drugs and weapons were seized and arrests made."

"It was [also] done by undercover officers. Afterwards there were some very serious sentences dished out by the Magistrates for dealers that had dealt at Stonehenge or other festivals. It didn't hit the press at the time the festivals were going on because it didn't happen then – you had to gather your evidence, make sure you had it correct, arrest these dealers after they had gone away from the Festival and bring them before the courts. They received substantive sentences for dealing at those festivals."

"It didn't become too big to police, it just meant the policing had to go on in a different way. Whether it was armed robberies – a lot of those happened – offences of a sexual nature, other offences that were not drug related - and there were many of those – they all had to be policed, but in a different way. There was no opportunity to go bowling into the site and carry out the normal enquiries you would on a day-to-day basis in the centre of Salisbury or wherever."

In 1981 the Stonehenge stage generator was hired from a builders' suppliers in Devizes, along with some scaffolding poles. The pyramidical Polytantric stage also appeared at many other eighties free festivals. It was originally used by the band Sphynx in the late seventies, having been designed by Harry Williamson who played with Mother Gong. The Sphynx stage set was based on the Egyptian Book of the Dead – hence the pyramid.

The scale of the event was beginning to impact on the wider area as people invaded nearby woods for fire fuel. This became such a problem that the police formed special plain clothes squads to arrest those found wood hunting. Those who ventured off site were also liable to be stopped and searched for drugs, as well as having their vehicles checked for MOT and Road Tax infringements.

Peter Beasley: "I did go to the, possibly 1981, Stonehenge Festival briefly during the day, with a mate who had a clapped out old Land Rover but wasn't into music at all. Consequently I didn't get to stay very long but I do remember it being chaotic and filthy! I believe I did see part of Here & Now's set. My abiding memory is post-festival when many of the people from college who went for the entire festival ended up with a nasty rash – the rumour was that somebody had had inappropriate relations with a sheep; the rash spread like wildfire! Highly unlikely but boy did the unfortunates get a ribbing!"

By 1982 numbers had swollen to 35,000 and there were growing concerns that the existence of the Festival might be threatened by hard drug dealers using the event as an opportunity to sell their wares without police intervention. However, some regulars disputed the level of such impact, claiming that festival etiquette would not allow the open sale of opiates on site.

This year saw more violence – a

large scale disturbance between several biker gangs and some travellers. This naturally clashed with the ethos of the Festival but compared to large scale can throwing at official festivals and the football violence and general rioting happening around the country during the period, Stonehenge remained relatively peaceful and safe. Notwithstanding this, for some the potential for violence was an underlying part of the Festival's ambience.

Perry Harris: "I did go a few times but it was quite an aggressive atmosphere I always found."

Increased media attention resulted in Stonehenge now being trailed in the music press as much as any other festival. In 1982 it was suggested that more than forty bands would play the main stage, including a number of big name acts coming over from Glastonbury. However, the most significant occurrence was the formation of the Peace Convoy - a massive collection of travellers in vans, buses, trucks and caravans - which made its way from Stonehenge to the Women's Peace Camp at the Greenham Common airbase.

The local press, which had always taken an interest in the strange events taking place on its doorstep, was by now becoming aware of the wider importance of the Festival.

Roger Elliott: "It got covered like a regular gig. We would just go up and see Misty In Roots and Roy Harper or whatever, write about them and take pictures. It did exist for a long time under the radar. I would go and photograph the Druids, particularly William Roache from Coronation Street - Ken Barlow - he used to blow the trumpet there every year. Across the road there would be a pop festival - and we would just ignore it."

"Then of course there was an occasion when lot of cars got burnt out and it became Europe's biggest drug market and suddenly it became big news. The Journal has never had a political stance as such – it is supposed to be impartial in these things - but we did pick it up as being a major story."

Local bands were still appearing on the loosely arranged bills at the Festival.

Johnny Fellows [of Bangkok]: "We played there twice. Back then – about '82 – it was easy to go up there and play. We went up, talked to a couple of the guys and they just said 'Come on up, we'll try and fit you in'. That was on the main stage. Nick Kemp's band was playing there the same year - they came on after us and did quite well."

"We just pitched up. The back line was all there - we just had to bring up Colin [Crook]'s Marshall stuff. We went down alright I think. It was difficult to tell – people were all over the stage and sitting on the front of the stage. We played well but anything that wasn't nailed down was nicked – guitar stands, spare strings. Colin had this thing that he used to use Johnson's baby powder on his hands - they even nicked that!"

In 1983 a crowd of around 30,000 attended Stonehenge during the week, peaking at 70,000 during the Solstice weekend. For comparison, the combined population of Amesbury and Salisbury was at that time a little under 40,000. There were far more casual visitors and the hardcore old school hippies and travellers were now in the minority, as a result of which some aspects of festival etiquette declined.

The Kemp brothers at Stonehenge

ENDLESS BEAT

"...they were losing control and had done for the last couple of years."

Increasing numbers of dealers – as opposed to festival goers selling drugs – were on site. Heavy drugs were contrary to the original ethos of the Festival, which for many had been a spiritual event in which the ingestion of hallucinogens was an essential part of the pilgrimage to the stones. Opiates dulled the senses, whereas hallucinogens heightened awareness and were far less dangerous in terms of overdose and the spreading of diseases and infections.

In order to prevent the continuing decimation of trees near the site, the National Trust provided free wood. Convoy News sought to address the problem by pointing out the requirements of the Country Code as well advice on how to enjoy the Festival itself: 'Label your children with their names and where they belong - Try to stop rip-offs - Get to know your neighbours – Be nice to each other'.

By now the barriers as to what sort of music would be accepted at the Festival had relaxed somewhat and a wide range of bands played to a far more mixed and tolerant audience than at the start of the decade. Hawkwind played Silver Machine at exactly the point of the Solstice sunrise as, right on cue, an F16 jet flew across the horizon leaving a trail through the middle of the emerging red sun.

The 1984 Festival was the biggest ever. The change in ethos was reflected in the fact that the late John Pendragon – one of the original attendees - helped set up a small scale 'Alternative Free Festival' within the main site, with a more intimate stage in a dealer-free zone, as an attempt to recreate the spirit of the early events.

Two separate crews filmed Stonehenge '84 and footage of sets by Roy Harper, The Enid, Here and Now and Hawkwind has been released on VHS and DVD. The footage captured Hawkwind's entrance to the stage replete with 'Vestal Virgins', fire eaters and the Tibetan Ukranian Mountain Troupe, and provided a useful record for those that were not there…and even for some that were…

Phil Manning: "My memories are quite sketchy – for obvious reasons [laughs]. I retired to my tent for a bit of a lie down, due to excesses of certain things including rough cider from Essex. I was woken up fairly early in the morning by people coming back saying 'You should have come. You missed Roy Harper, Gong and Hawkwind. I was quite cheesed off really."

The Liberators played during the early hours of the last day of the 1984 Festival, having only arrived on the site at about midnight. Their set finished at about 3.00am and no other rock band has played at the stones since.

The increased crowd numbers left behind a huge amount of debris, including a dozen burnt out or abandoned vehicles (some said to have belonged to unwelcome heroin dealers who had been 'dealt with'). The authorities would now lobby formally for the prevention of the Festival.

Barry Pritchard: "There was a lot of political talk about whether these things should be allowed to go on or not and if they were allowed to happen whether they should be legalised, in what shape or form – all that work was going on."

"This is what you are down to: the landowners didn't wish the Festival to take place on their land. That's not their game – their game is managing and running a World Heritage Site that has millions of visitors a year, and a new visitors' centre that they have been chasing for years - did that [the Festival] put a stop to the visitors' centre coming on a lot earlier?"

"At the same time there were issues being discussed as to how you put a stop to what is now growing? The Festival at Stonehenge in '84 was something along the lines of 50 to 60,000 people and lasted for five to six weeks – a long time. When it was over the site itself, I know, contained in excess of fifty stolen vehicles, many of them burnt out and left behind. The rubbish left behind cost thousands of pounds to clear up – and trying to put back together what was pasture land."

"With those that were managing the Festival at the time when it was growing it was a very good relationship. But those organisers were overcome by pressures from elsewhere that led to them losing control. In '84 I had a lot of dealings with Sid Rawle and others around him. Knowing how they felt, they were losing control and had done for the last couple of years, of how the Festival should be run. Things were going away from them. They did not want the use of heroin on site at Stonehenge and yet it was forced upon them so much that it was very difficult for them."

"The control they had was not control that you and I may know as being within the law. It was an illegal gathering anyway so it was outside the law – but they had an element of control about who set up stages, who got the bands in, who was allowed to sell ice cream and alcohol. These things happened in their way, but they lost it – so much so that there were injuries and difficulties."

Jon Maple: "It was a madhouse and a lot of damage was done to individuals - it was an anarchy environment. At a time like that, when the police were really becoming more and more like a Government militia than a police force – especially under Thatcher - clearly it couldn't go on. It was so much about irregularity that it wouldn't be tolerated and you knew it would end."

Skid: "As you went in to the site [in 1984] there was a Volkswagen camper van turned on its roof and burnt out, with 'Heroin Dealer' sprayed along the side. A lot of heroin had started getting up there. They had to do something - you couldn't allow that sort of civil unrest to go ahead."

The Thatcher Government had handled other national unrest – particularly with regard to Trade Unions - in an uncompromising manner, encouraging police tactics

ENDLESS BEAT

"We've got to put a stop to this somehow!"

that the British public had previously only associated with less democratic states, and had no compunction in supporting measures that would restrict the activities of the travelling culture.

In 1985 English Heritage, who administered the stones, and the National Trust, who owned 1400 acres of land around them, spent £10,000 on a campaign expressing their 'regret' in having decided the Festival would not be allowed on the land cared for by them at Stonehenge 'this year or in future'.

The two organisations made plans to seal off the stones over the Solstice period and took out an injunction against the Festival 'organisers'. Wiltshire County Council supported the moves by using the Road Traffic Act 1984 to give the police discretionary powers to close the A344 and six other rights of way around the site between 13 May and 15 July.

The 'organisers' showed no inclination to abandon plans for the Festival and on requesting help in enforcing their injunction, English Heritage and the National Trust were advised the police would require complete control of any situation that might develop. It was made clear that anyone who attempted to stay on the site after its 'closing time' of 6.00pm on 20 June would be forcibly removed and a ring of police would prevent any further access overnight.

With the memory of the miners' strike still fresh there was a suspicion that certain factions on both sides were looking forward to what might transpire in Wiltshire and the local information officer for the National Trust expressed 'a very strong worry' about the potential for confrontation, admitting that 'Stonehenge and the land around it is meant to be public'.

Somewhat confusingly, the Trust claimed to have no problem with the majority of festival-goers who, as 'ordinary music lovers' would now – they believed - stay away from the site. Referring to drug use and £6,000 worth of damage cause over a six-week period in 1984, it was explained that the injunction was solely aimed at the 'disruptive element': in other words the very people that would relish the challenge of resisting the ban.

John Pendragon suggested the Trust could have helped reduce the damage of the previous year. This was countered, not unreasonably it must be said, with the argument that it was not the Trust's business to run rock festivals: in any case the organisation had previously co-operated with Festival Welfare Services to some extent.

In using the law to eliminate the unruly elements of the Festival, English Heritage and the National Trust – whose position can perhaps be empathised with – had a simple choice: all or nothing. They chose all – even the Druids would not be allowed to gather at the stones – and because of police requirements the situation would be beyond their control. The irony of course was that if a riot was to break out close to the monument, the resultant damage to the landscape and archaeology might be worse than that which would have been caused by the Festival itself.

Due South magazine set the scene: 'the stage is set for a clash between two intransigent parties. Barbed wire is up around the stones, the A344 is blocked off with mounds of sand and the police are preparing for a possible repeat performance of the battles at the Nottinghamshire coalfields'.

On 1 June 1985, what became known as 'The Battle of The Beanfield' took place near the junction of the A303 with the A338 at Cholderton, approximately 7½ miles to the east of Stonehenge. A convoy of travellers had left Savernake Forest en route for the stones and were stopped by a large police contingent with, in very simplified terms, violent consequences.

Barry Pritchard: "Things got to the stage where you say 'We've got to put a stop to this somehow'. From the police perspective, that's what forced the 1985 situation, when there was a drive by the Chief Constable of Wiltshire, Don Smith, with backing from the Home Office, to say 'No, the convoy is not going to take the fields and start the Festival'."

There has long been a widespread belief among the festival community that allowing one more event to take place would have legitimised the Stonehenge Festival – as a result of a 'twelve years squatter's rights rule'. However, this was apparently not on the minds of the police.

Barry Pritchard: "There was never any grounding in law for that. It was the political backing to say 'We need to put a stop to this, can we do it? Can we stop a convoy of heavy vehicles? – and the plans were laid that we could."

Many of the police on duty at the Beanfield did not wear identification numbers, leading to suggestions that they were members of outside forces and still 'hungry' from involvement in quashing the miners' strike. Again, the official line was that this was not the case.

Barry Pritchard: "Public order training within the police service took place nationally, but it was all local officers involved in the actual stopping of the convoy and the Battle of the Beanfield - from the surrounding forces: Wiltshire, Hampshire, Dorset, Somerset – it was the local officers."

"I was in the Beanfield, but not in

Buster Bloodvessel (right) at the festival

ENDLESS BEAT

"I think it was a wider thing than 'protecting the stones' per se."

uniform. I actually got thrown out of the Beanfield, so I saw both sides of what was going on. At one stage I had a travellers' coach being driven straight at me and, as far as they were concerned, I was in there 'with' them. There was chaos in that field – they were just driving around and around, the last thing they wanted was to be stopped – and it was bloody dangerous. There was only one way to put a stop to that which was to stop those vehicles and the police did it."

The incident was later immortalised in song by The Levellers whose sympathies, along with many locals, were not in doubt.

Sean Rice: "I wasn't at The Battle Of The Beanfield, but the next morning I stopped off to view the aftermath, which was swarming with reporters from all the newspapers. When I found out what happened it was very sad. To me it broke the back of some kind of alternative movement that was gathering momentum. Maybe In hindsight it was a defining moment - in a national sense."

"I'm sure the authorities would have been well aware of all these old rules and laws that allow you to establish a precedent whereby no one can then stop you. I think it was a wider thing than 'protecting the stones' per se. I think it was just 'undesirables' - at the time I was very angry about it."

Readers with an interest in the politics of the time might like to consider whether it was just the Festival that was the issue. The Government seemed determined to stamp out, by any means possible, attitudes and ways of life that did not conform to their own. Major steps had rightly been taken towards dealing with football hooliganism, but disenfranchised inner city youth, unions and new age travellers were wrongly seen as all being part of the same 'problem'. Perhaps some issues of contention might have been solved by better investment, rather than in such a crude and cruel manner.

Measures to prevent festivities at the stones continued for a number of years, but have been relaxed to allow increased access in recent times. A crowd of around 20,000 attended the 2010 summer Solstice, although this was not as high as the estimated 36,500 that witnessed the sunrise in 2009.

Barry Pritchard: "Policing was put in place for a number of years to ensure it didn't occur. After that there were a lot of meetings with those wishing to manage a festival again – after South Africa, they called themselves 'Truth and Reconciliation'. I was there with the director of Stonehenge, Clews Everard, and others. That led to a gradual - after ten years, opening of the stones to those that wished to go at the Summer Solstice to celebrate peacefully, openly and lawfully. That now, thankfully, still continues."

"There's no doubt in my mind those years of discussions led to the large legal festivals that we now have, within the law, run for the safety of the public. I know it's really expensive to put that sort of scene together but if you are going to be kept safe and look at all that's on offer it's a fantastic experience – I've been several times."

A 'fantastic experience' no doubt but how might all the fun of the modern Glastonbury Fayre compare with the old festivals?

Jon Maple: "Glastonbury commercialised all that and became an internationally renowned event. That could have happened to Stonehenge I suppose - had it not been on a site of international scientific and archaeological interest. It was part of the monetarist economics of the time - driven by the bottom line profit motive. Everything had to become commercialised or alienated to the point of being wiped out."

The travellers will tell you one set of stories about what happened at the Beanfield in 1985, and the 'Establishment' will tell you another. One thing that is certain is the police were left in no doubt as to what was expected of them.

Barry Pritchard: "You read which press and what side of it you want. The Festival didn't go ahead. There was only one objective - and that was it."

As authors we are principally concerned with the music scene in the Salisbury and South Wiltshire area, in which the history of the Stonehenge Free Festival plays a major part. We weren't at the Beanfield, we have no axe to grind either way and we have no particular views on the travelling lifestyle - other than to support individual freedom of choice.

5 Everything Louder than Everything Else
The New Heavy Metal Kids

The early seventies had seen the rise of a genre of rock music that fell somewhere between the most basic garage rock'n'roll and the worst excesses of progressive rock. The American band Steppenwolf have been widely credited with the first high profile use of the phrase 'heavy metal' – in their signature anthem Born To Be Wild – but the term wasn't actually in widespread use at that time – 'hard rock' being the preferred label.

Although Led Zeppelin were the hardest rock band of them all, their music covered a wider range of genres than the forerunners of the new style – Black Sabbath and Deep Purple. As we have already seen, Salisbury had its own leaders in the field as Jerusalem - managed by Purple vocalist Ian Gillan, but perhaps closer in style to Sabbath - briefly flirted with fame.

Whilst the punk movement took aim at all the old school bands and genres, heavy metal – a term by then in general use - was in reality at least equally popular in terms of being 'the music of the streets'. Indeed, in pockets of East London, the Midlands and the North it was more popular, and – although punk had a good foothold in the city itself – the Salisbury area has always had a large biker contingent, for which metal was of course the preferred musical style.

A raft of younger bands – inspired

ENDLESS BEAT

"... and there was Chris with his old Galaxy guitar."

not only by the original hard rockers, but also by the spirit and DIY ethics of punk – began to appear in small venues and on small record labels, all but unrecognised by the popular music press. This groundswell built into a movement that would become known as 'The New Wave Of British Heavy Metal' (or 'NWOBHM').

In February 1981 a band who, although destined not to reap great commercial success, would be feted as a huge influence on later metal giants such as Metallica, performed in Salisbury.

Peter Beasley: "The gig I recall best is Diamond Head at the City Hall. I had bought their self-financed and self-released debut album through a mail order advert in Sounds and played it to death. They didn't disappoint and played the entire album, a couple of songs that were only released as singles and a couple that appeared on the two albums subsequently released on MCA. A brilliant gig – probably one of the best I have been to."

Salisbury's metal buying public was well served by both WH Smiths[1] and Rod's Records, opened by Rod Fry on the upper floor of the Fisherton Arms, the pub he ran with his wife Liz, alongside his day job as a fireman[2].

Peter Beasley: "The only outlets for information, record and gig reviews were Sounds and the Friday Rock Show - and then Kerrang! I got a few albums through mail order but I did buy a number in Salisbury. Smiths were probably the best stockist until Rod's came along, though it was mainly albums on the major labels, which suited me as I was trying to catch up with the classic seventies albums I was too young to appreciate

GENGHIS KHAN - left to right: Alan Marsh, Tommy Mafflyn, Alwyn Lovell, Ian Frost and Rob Boston

when they were first released. Most of my Led Zeppelin, Deep Purple and Hawkwind albums came from Smiths."

"I found out, from one of the ladies that worked in Smiths, they had harsh trading terms that most independent record labels couldn't finance, particularly in regard to credit - much like big companies such as Tesco requiring ninety day credit terms."

"The ladies that worked in Smiths were very knowledgeable, which I always found amusing, because they seemed so old. In reality they were probably in their fifties, but I guess when you are seventeen-eighteen anybody over thirty seems old! I recall one of them advising me to wait an extra day before I bought the album Glory Road, by Gillan, because they had limited editions due in that had an extra album included called For Gillan Fans Only."

"Rod's Records, for me, was the ideal shop – any album that got a decent review in Kerrang! was guaranteed to be in stock at Rod's the following week. I assume Rod had music industry connections as there were gold discs over the bar of the Fisherton Arms."

"I bought many albums from Rod's that at the time were extremely difficult to find elsewhere – by artists such as John Verity, Russ Ballard, Frank Zappa, Manowar, Anvil etcetera. There were also American imports - I remember seeing a copy of an import of Ozzy Osbourne's Ultimate Sin, which would have been 1986. I wasn't prepared to pay £8.99 for it, which is ironic considering five years later HMV had domestic CDs for twice the price!"

"Rod's was also a ticket outlet for smaller venues – I remember getting tickets there for Bernie Torme at Bournemouth Town Hall in 1984. I continued to visit Salisbury after I had stopped going to college, and continued to visit Rod's, until one visit when it was no longer there. A shame really as there were, and are, so few specialist record shops – the only comparable shop I can think of was the late great Shades in Wardour Street, London. It was a classic owner/proprietor shop - the type that went to the trouble of checking both sides of the album for scratches."

Two former members of Salisbury's youthful and short-lived Exit Band went on to join mid-seventies metal act Sonofabitch.

Tremayne Roden: "I got introduced to them at a wedding. I was sixteen-seventeen - the others, besides Jeremy, were in their mid to late twenties - maybe older. What a bunch! I was taught the art of sarcasm, the dynamics of sarcasm and sarcasm the history of. Band members were Roy Shergold (guitar), Jeremy Kemp (guitar), Maxwell Strange (bass), Trevor Frampton (drums) and Peter Dennis (big hair). We were most probably not the greatest musicians on Earth, but together we gelled and made, I think, a great sound - very simple loud heavy rock. Roy was the main songwriter but it was down to me to come up with the words."

"We played mainly in and around the Avon valley and our audience were bikers. We played at the Teacher Training College and were thrown off stage for being too loud, singing songs about the Devil and not knowing Blockbuster by The Sweet. Jeremy left the band - I can't remember why or who took his place but for me it was never the same and eventually the band split. I ended up going to Israel in 1979 and on my return in 1980 moved to Leicester, where the music scene was the beginning of the new wave of heavy rock."

Genghis Khan formed in Salisbury in 1975 and became early leading lights on the NWOBHM scene. The first line up comprised Alan Marsh (vocals), Alwyn 'Coke' Lovell (lead guitar), Eddie Johnson (guitar), Rob Boston (bass) and Trevor Harris (drums).

Rob Boston: "I met Eddie Johnson at school. We both picked up the guitar in about '71/72 when I first moved to Salisbury - we were twelve or thirteen. There was a lad from Canada called Dave Lowry who came in to school one day with an Epiphone semi-acoustic and taught us to play twelve-bar and we were immediately hooked."

"We bought guitars and Eddie introduced me to Chris Walsh. I was knocked out with Chris's technique – he was a great guitarist playing this kind of Jimi Hendrix style. The three of us used to jam above St Edmund's Church in a vestment room. It was still a church then and you would go through a back door up some winding stairs to a top room - and there was Chris with his old Galaxy guitar."

"I had always seen myself as the new Chuck Berry – you know, 'the great rock'n'roll guitarist' - and Eddie and I were vying for who was going to be lead guitarist. As soon as I met Chris I realised I should rethink and that's the moment I bought myself a bass guitar. We formed a band with no name and rehearsed on and off for a year or so but we could never get a drummer with a kit – a few drummers but no kits - and that drifted."

"Eddie had told me about a lad he had heard of called 'Coke' – Alwyn

ENDLESS BEAT

"Alan was the only one with a driving licence..."

Lovell – although he hadn't met him. I was actually introduced to Alwyn by Baz Stapley – we arranged a meeting at the Star. Alwyn had been playing with Alan Marsh and Trevor Harris and we arranged a jam session with Alwyn and I and Trevor – who I hadn't met at that stage. The three of us got together, it worked really well and we decided to form a band."

Alwyn, Alan and Trevor had been playing, with Chris Percy and Ray Dismore, in an informal band of Westwood St Thomas' school mates.

Alan Marsh: "We all liked your Slades and Marc Bolans then all the older kids used to say about Deep Purple and Black Sabbath. We were always interested in bands and I ended up doing vocals because I had been in choirs and I couldn't play anything properly. That was just kicking stuff around and trying to start somewhere."

Alwyn Lovell: "My parents were very heavily into music. My first recollection is being taken to see A Hard Day's Night, when I was about seven and my mother would always be buying singles – especially The Beatles – so they were a major influence on me. I started playing guitar when I was about twelve. I got a bashed up old acoustic off someone - a pretty bad Woolworths type thing - bought myself a chord book and started learning and trying to play along."

"Me and Trev used to walk down to Alan's parents' place, carrying our gear from the Heath and making a noise in his garage. That was just me, Trev and Ray and Alan used to give us a critical appraisal afterwards, which as you can imagine was pretty dire."

"I remember meeting Rob and the thing we had in common was John Lennon – he had an Elephant's Memory album that Lennon produced and I was still totally into The Beatles."

Rob Boston: "I said we would definitely get Eddie in on rhythm guitar and Alwyn said the vocalist from his previous band would be available – Alan Marsh. We arranged another session with all five of us and we all got on like a house on fire. The first rehearsal we had was at St Gregory's Church Hall. One of the great things was they had a shared minibus that they all chipped in for - eight of them were co-owners. Alan was the only one with a driving licence – so we used to get about in that."

"It was heavy rock stuff – Led Zeppelin, Deep Purple, Black Sabbath – we were all into that. I was more Sabbath-Zeppelin and they were more Sabbath-Purple and that was the formula. We were writing straight in – we were doing a few covers but not many, it was mostly our own stuff. By '75 the major acts were touring America and we weren't seeing much of them so the middle range – Judas Priest, Budgie, Groundhogs – were big news. They were the bands we were going to see on a regular basis and were trying to emulate."

Alwyn Lovell: "We started off, like everyone, doing covers but we were writing our own stuff at the time as well. We would have two or three of our own songs and some rock standards – things like Highway Star. I would write musical stuff and Alan would stick lyrics over the top, Rob would come in with whole ideas and Ed was putting in stuff. So it was a mixture of all of us – quite a healthy thing."

Genghis made a few recordings and played a number of local gigs, including a fundraising show at the old Salisbury Playhouse in 1976. £120 was raised for the new Playhouse appeal and eventually a seat in the new theatre was named in honour of the band. Even in these early days the band were noted for their stage act and the effects used.

Rob Boston: "A lot of the PA companies were trying to promote lighting effects. I remember someone turned up with some flashes at the Playhouse gig, which almost set Alan alight. We didn't know what to expect – they just went off like bombs. Some of the PA companies would turn up with a dry ice machine often not knowing what to do with them and would put kids in charge – kids plucked from the audience – and say 'At a given moment drop this'. More often than not there would be far too much dry ice – you couldn't see anything!"

At the Playhouse fundraiser Genghis Khan were also using some home-made equipment, with unfortunate results.

Alwyn Lovell: "The PA wasn't earthed and a few people did get some slight shocks off it. Rob had made this thing we called 'The Genghis Box', which was just a plywood box with jack sockets in it. He had taken the trouble to put carpet around it to make it look really nice but it wasn't electrically very safe. I think it was Lloyd [Collinson] who noticed it needed to be earthed."

The band underwent the first of many personnel changes during 1977.

Rob Boston: "Eddie was going to university and that's when Ray Dismore stepped in. He was a friend of Alwyn's and was drafted in for a brief period. Ian Frost came in after Ray left. He was from Romford and had some connections with UFO. What Ian brought to the band was a whole new range of connections in Essex and East London. We switched our attentions from Salisbury-Bristol to Salisbury-London-Bristol and that was when it got quite interesting, because at that time there was a core of what became the heavy metal scene in East London."

Alan Marsh: "That's when it started to get a bit serious. Rob's dad was managing the band at the time and he was very good - he was supportive and eventually converted his basement into a studio for rehearsing."

Drummer Trevor Harris also left the band during 1977 and was replaced by Tommy Mafflyn. Using Ian Frost's connections the new line up of Genghis Khan became a part of the movement emerging in the Capital.

Rob Boston: "There were three main bands as I remember - Angelwitch, Iron Maiden and Genghis Khan. The three bands played the same clubs and pubs – places like Crackers in Wardour Street and the Bridgehouse. There was a core of young bands with the same audience, so it was building up a ball of froth and interest. It was really down to a couple of people – a DJ – I can't remember his name, a youngster like us – who had a big following of rock fans, and a lad called Jim Norcott who was a very good friend of Ian. They kind of created that whole thing."

Of the three bands, Iron Maiden would of course become the best known and go on to enjoy huge world success. However, perhaps not everyone on the scene would have predicted this.

Rob Boston: "We thought Angelwitch were going to be the monster band – we backed the wrong horse! [laughs]"

More personnel changes came in late 1978 and early 1979 as one of

Alwyn Lovell

ENDLESS BEAT

"It was just people caught in the cross fire."

Genghis Khan's regular intra-band arguments got out of hand.

Rob Boston: "The biggest bust up of all happened after a gig in Bristol. We had a soundcheck [scheduled] at seven. Tommy walked in at nine. We went on at five past nine with no soundcheck. It was a very good gig but there was bad blood. There was a huge argument basically a fight in the dressing room and it spilled outside. It was me on one side, Alwyn on the other and Ian and Tommy on another side. There was also aggro with the landlord over volume - we often had volume problems. We blamed the soundman and the soundman blamed the back line, so he was involved as well."

Rob hasn't seen Ian Frost or Tommy Mafflyn since they drove way from Bristol that night. He humbly recognises his own part in the inevitable friction in a band full of strong opinions and volatile personalities.

Rob Boston: "There were a lot of personnel in a few years and I think it was down to Alwyn and me. We were really good mates - and still are - but artistically we were at loggerheads all the time. There was lots of bust ups and each new member of the band had to align himself politically, so we always started on rocky ground. The longevity of the partnership was productive but it was just a shame that so many musicians parted ways along the route."

Alwyn Lovell: "The characters were very different but we made it work, but as I look back on how things evolved I think how we split and who we split off with speaks for itself… with me and Rob there were probably no bigger egos around Salisbury at the time!"

Rob Boston: "It was just people caught in the cross fire. Alwyn and I would have a row and it would spread like wildfire among the five. Not all were responsible I must admit - Alan Marsh is always a calming influence, one of the nicest blokes I've ever played with. I can't lay any blame at Alan's door, but certainly Alwyn and I and lots of the other members that came in were fiery."

"I always loved the way Alwyn played. He was a very choppy, riff orientated guitarist. He would come out with these riffs and we would jam around them and see what happened. I would write my own songs and he would write with the singer - so a lot of the clashes were my songs versus songs written by Alan and Alwyn."

"The truth of the matter is their songs were superior to mine, but it was ego and I think because I was into Zeppelin and they were into Deep Purple we were always crashing into each other. I would tell Alwyn how good and how much like Jimmy Page he was…and he would take it as an insult – he wanted to be Ritchie Blackmore! [laughs]"

An influx of Scottish blood would lead to the line up of Genghis Khan that made the biggest impact on the NWOBHM and is most fondly remembered by fans.

Rob Boston: "Alwyn and I decided we had to go on. By fluke I picked up a copy of the Evening Echo and there was an advert – 'guitarist and bassist

Early **GENGHIS KHAN** line up - left to right: Alan Marsh, Trevor Harris, Alwyn Lovell, Rob Boston and Ray Dismore

Trevor Harris

required…to form a jazz band'. I don't know why but I phoned and spoke to this lad, Billy [Morrison]. He was into Hendrix and jazz-funk and living in a squat in St John's Wood, but his sister was living in Bournemouth where he had spent a few weeks with his pal Jimmy [McTurk] – a guitarist. I said 'Maybe we can get together and jam?'"

"At the time we were rehearsing in the basement under my old man's place in Wilton Road. It was a fantastic, magical jam session lasting all afternoon, but one thing that was apparent was they were into a completely different type of music to us. We were sort of AC/DC-Deep Purple and they were kind of Jimi Hendrix-Kool and The Gang! After the weekend I was speaking to Alwyn and said 'Well, maybe we should just go for it - get them into Genghis Khan and let whatever is going to happen, happen'."

Although he hadn't been involved in the bust-up in Bristol, Alan Marsh's tenure with Genghis came to an end at this time.

Rob Boston: "Alan was part of the Genghis Khan thing and was a great singer but, if anything, he lacked a bit of self-belief I think. He did meet the Glasgow boys briefly but the chemistry wasn't there and it was almost as if Alan took a back step – he didn't fancy it. Maybe he thought we were going in the wrong direction. He didn't quite leave and he certainly wasn't thrown out, but it just didn't happen. On a personal level it was quite upsetting but the whole thing had a momentum of its own."

"Jimmy and Alwyn were going to take care of the vocals. We were rehearsing along those lines and then, about a week before we started gigging, they said 'We've met this guy from Birmingham staying in Bournemouth – John Butcher. We've seen him singing in a club and he's fantastic'. They brought him up and he was like Roger Chapman from Family - he had a kind of bleating quality - and was absolutely superb."

"We were still a driving rock band but these other influences came in and I think that was the Genghis Khan that people remember. John was a fantastic

GENGHIS KHAN - live 1978

ENDLESS BEAT

"… if it had been a bit fiery before, this new mixture was really incendiary."

performer and singer, Billy played a fourteen piece Tama kit – plus octave arms - he was virtually stood up at the kit. Jimmy had an old fifties Telecaster that someone had spilt their breakfast on a few years previously. It had been left in his kitchen to dry out and when he came back in he just varnished it! It had this wonderful texture…kind of eggs and bacon."

"It was a mad band…if it had been a bit fiery before, this new mixture was really incendiary. These guys used to fight their way in just so they could fight their way out…we had some hairy moments. Alwyn went to Glasgow with them that Christmas and said it was the most phenomenal experience of his entire life! But they were fantastic musicians and blokes."

The NWOBHM was held up as a good, solid, working class alternative to punk, but in reality there were many similarities.

Rob Boston: "We didn't really play what you would now call 'metal'. We were playing stuff that sounded like UFO, Budgie and Deep Purple – it was just rock. All the time clubs were closing their doors to rock bands so there were fewer and fewer venues. It helped create the heavy metal scene. It was like the heavy metal kids in East London felt like they were in a ghetto. It concentrated their minds and they were on a crusade to 'save' rock from new wave."

"It was affecting the way we thought, Alwyn and I, because we were basic rock'n'rollers anyway. A lot of things happening in the better punk stuff we liked because it was good rock – like Never Mind The Bollocks. Malcolm McLaren described it as 'a swindle' – somehow we had been hoodwinked by crap – but we listened to it and thought 'What a brilliant rock'n'roll album'. Bands like The Stranglers, Sex Pistols, Ruts and Clash we secretly admired. What developed after that period…there wasn't really a lot of difference in the music, it was just the packaging was different."

Alwyn Lovell: "We were very much taking in what was going on. To me rock music was becoming preposterous and I had had enough of it - and I think Rob had. I was never 'punk' with the hair business, but what I liked was it made me realise I could do what I wanted. It felt like up until then, in Genghis Khan, it was almost like an apprenticeship where you were trying to be someone else. I found that whole new music was nothing to do with safety pins – it was to do with finding what you particularly wanted to do."

Genghis Khan had by now linked up with a manager who had strong presentational ideas linked to the band's name.

Rob Boston: "We were introduced to Tony Waldron – a kind of PR man in the music business. He wanted to get to grips with a rock band. I remember him asking us the big question – 'Do you want to be famous?' We said 'Yeah…we do'. He said 'Will you do anything to be famous?' We said 'Of course'. He said 'Will you wear Oriental clothes and goat skins as 'The Mongol Nation of Genghis Khan?' We said 'Yes! We will!' He said 'Will you shave your heads like Genghis Khan?' We said 'Fuck off! We're not doing that to be famous'."

"He proved a point – there was a limit to what we would do - but it was cutting edge, no one had ever done that. To turn up at a hot, steamy basement club in the West End wearing a goat skin was quite an experience - low ceilings and lighting two or three feet from the band – I often opted for the kimono rather than the goat skin!"

The Genghis Khan live experience developed in line with the image.

Rob Boston: "It was the classic joke – everything turned up to eleven. We didn't have a clue about back line levels. It was literally all tone controls up, all volume controls up. No pre-amps in those days – just whack it up and the guy with the PA had to do what he could. We were happy because the audience seemed to like it. They had been to see The Groundhogs and Black Sabbath and had their heads blown off – they expected raw volume – and it was exciting…if not hi fi."

"I was very much the man at the back playing the bass – Bill Wyman if you like – but from my perspective, the band with Billy, Jimmy and Butcher was better than Iron Maiden for songs and performances…but it takes more than that."

"We were building an audience and packing places. We were always exciting – Alwyn was a very good performer - we were flashy and a little bit arrogant I suppose. Bristol and London seemed to be the places we would think of as our home territory. It was great when we played in Salisbury – we tried to do it once a year and I think there was local interest to see what we were up to."

Although the band enjoyed returning to Rob and Alwyn's home city, there is a question mark over how Salisbury felt about them.

Rob Boston: "Over the years it has come to light that certain people did have a bit of an attitude - not that I was aware of it. The musicians I knew – Colin Holton, Chris Walsh, Nick

Cowan - were like brothers really. My attitude was I wanted them to be successful."

"Colin Holton for example I always looked up to because I thought he was a far superior musician to me - in some ways I aspired to be Colin. I remember going to see him rehearse with The Exit Band. I thought they were fantastic. In fact we did a cover of one of their songs. Tremayne [Roden] wrote a song called Evil Deceiver, which now seems so…twee…but at the time it was a great riff."

In time there was another split in the Genghis Khan ranks with the departure of Jimmy McTurk and Billy Morrison.

Rob Boston: "I can't remember the circumstances of the Scots boys leaving…but it was another bust up. John knew a drummer – we were just getting ready to go into the studio and he got Dave Pounds, who had been a bit of a session musician - not flash but he could do everything on four drums that Billy had knocked out on fourteen. He was a dream to work with - what a nice bloke. We went straight into the studio and recorded the great Genghis Khan song the audience always loved – Mongol Nation."

The tracks recorded by this line up were later issued as a double seven inch single on Wabbit Records. Dave Irwin then came in on second guitar and became the last new musician to join Genghis Khan, by now in its seventh different line up.

GENGHIS KHAN 1979 - left to right: Jimmy McTurk, Billy Morrison, Rob Boston, John Butcher and Alwyn Lovell

ENDLESS BEAT

"We decided to leg it all around the country."

Rob Boston: "We needed a new guitarist, so we put an advert in Melody Maker and met Dave, who had just left Fist. They were a very good band – one of the Saxon type bands - out of Newcastle. He was probably the only guitarist I've played with who was on a par with Alwyn. That was another fantastic version of the band – probably not the showmen but technically the best version."

Despite the talents of the latest incarnation, three members became sidetracked with The Ghosts - a project that would contribute to the ultimate demise of Genghis Khan.

Rob Boston: "We were introduced to a man called Adrian Miller. He managed The Babys – not so well known in the UK but massive in America. John Waite, the singer, went out with Britt Ekland and their biggest hit, Isn't It Time, was on Top Of The Pops. There had been a bust up and the two founding members – Mike Corby and John Waite - had fallen out. Mike was back in the UK looking to form a new band."

"Mike was very sore about leaving The Babys. He had two main gripes – first of all any time he stepped off an aircraft in America there would be a limousine waiting for him, but when he flew into Heathrow he would have to hail a taxi – that was the difference in his career between the UK and USA. The other thing was that he had a big grudge against Steve Marriott. I think The Babys had toured with Steve and he had picked on Mike, who couldn't retaliate because Steve's friend Joe Brown was always there to protect to him."

"Adrian wasn't interested in Genghis Khan, but he was interested in John Butcher, Alwyn and I, to form a band around Mike. Next thing we know Mike is down in Salisbury. It was a very dodgy situation because Adrian was very specific – he wanted to work with three of us not five of us. So, there was this very ugly overlap of two or three months where Genghis Khan were still playing, rehearsing and gigging and we had this secret project – The Ghosts – going to London and recording - at Morgan Studios - two songs we didn't like, written by Mike and Adrian."

"John, Alwyn and I found ourselves in a hotel, feeling really shitty at the fact that the rest of our band were back in Bournemouth and Salisbury - rude, blind ambition forcing us along against our moral judgement. The two other guys had no idea."

"Mike was a great bloke, he had great charisma – he was a big star. To be honest the first session we did with him I was totally awestruck, it was difficult enough talking to him. He was the real McCoy. I'm sure we could have worked happily with him but we just didn't like the project – The Ghosts were ill-fated because we hated the music. One morning we just walked out – we said 'We're not going to do it'."

"That was also the end of Genghis Khan: Dave Pounds realised something had been happening and John told him, and Dave Irwin went back to Newcastle - thinking we were a bunch of bastards - reformed Fist and went on to do even better with them."

Alwyn Lovell: "Adrian Miller wanted to put a more rocky version of 'The Babys' together using me and Rob. It dwindled our attention away from the thing we were doing with Genghis Khan – I think it was all just a natural dying process in the end."

Although Genghis Khan were an important NWOBHM band both locally and nationally, the most widely known Salisbury metal act were Tokyo Blade – whose roots lay in an informal school band, the members of which would go on to play varying roles in the city's music scene.

Andy Boulton: "My earliest influence was hearing Brian May on the first Queen single Keep Yourself Alive. Nobody else locally had heard of them at the time and for me it was something really new. I got into playing guitar because my family are very musical and it was kind of destined I was going to play something. I started off on violin and when I was about thirteen got a guitar. The only person in my year at school that had a guitar as well was Andy Robbins."

"Andy and I started a band up. We had Elwyn Toomer on bass and vocals, and John Nicholas on drums. When we left school we kept the band going for a while but John lived in Bemerton Heath and the rest of us were more over towards the Laverstock side of Salisbury, so it was getting difficult. We were young and in those days, if you were very lucky, you might have a moped - but that was all you would have, so after a while John drifted off out of it."

Elwyn Toomer - who would later manage Toucantango as well as being resident DJ at the Saddle Rooms and Concorde's nightclub - also left the band, which then took on a more formal approach under the name of White Diamond.

Andy Boulton: "Andy and I kept the band going. We got Steve Pierce in on drums, Steve Rushton on vocals and Andy's brother Martin played bass. We were doing quite well locally and making a little bit of money – enough to buy some decent gear."

Following a change in personnel and format the band was renamed.

Andy Boulton: "It then became Killer. We had an argument with Martin one day because he just wouldn't come to a gig – he wanted to stay home and watch the football. So Andy said 'Well, I'll play bass'. Then we wanted to get a better singer and I said to the lads 'I remember going down to Salisbury College and seeing Genghis Khan. They had quite a good singer – this guy called Alan Marsh'. We did a bit of tracking down and he came in."

Alan Marsh: "They were doing the working men's clubs, doing a shed load of covers. They approached me and I said I was interested, and it went from there. We sat down at my house and both Andys said 'We want to write our own stuff and see how far we can take it'. I thought 'Well, that'll do for me'. We started to try and write our own stuff, but I think on reflection the amount of covers we did gave them all a damned good sound - they were one of the best bands of that type at that time."

Killer recorded a five track demo cassette and, although low on budget, aimed for high production values.

Alan Marsh: "We used to spend hours – me and Andy Robbins in particular – making stuff. What we tried to do was what you expected to see with a big band in a big venue - we would try and do that in the corner of a pub. We built a dry ice machine in the days when you were allowed to handle a dry ice machine without about 6,000 risk assessments and health and safety protocols, and lights and pyrotechnics – Cliff Stafford used to run all that for us."

"We decided to leg it all around the country. We got this truck, took a gamble and went off. We dropped all the covers except in emergencies - some of the gigs we did in South Wales, if we didn't have a couple of Black Sabbath covers we would have been in trouble. Halfway round we decided all these gigs were no better than those we were doing locally - we needed a decent demo."

Andy Boulton: "Then we decided to change the name of the band to Genghis Khan, which we did for a while, but the former Genghis Khan got a little bit sniffy about it."

The new 'Genghis Khan' had in fact got as far as issuing their demos as Double Dealin' - a four-track double seven inch single.

Alan Marsh: "The demos turned out quite good, and that was the time Rod Fry got involved with us. We took the single to his shop and he thought 'Oh, it's just a load of local lads' but he heard the first song and thought 'Bloody hell!' He was quite happy to sell it. If it wasn't for Rod we probably wouldn't have done anything - God rest his soul."

The single was however withdrawn as members of the original Genghis Khan asked the 'new' band to desist from using the name.

Alwyn Lovell: "There was some European band using the name and then Alan started using it as well. In

127

ENDLESS BEAT

"Let's throw away all the claptrap..."

some venues that Genghis Khan used to play they weirdly wanted to book us as 'Genghis Khan' when we were The Prams – places like The Granary in Bristol – the name had a pulling power."

Rob Boston: "There were two things surrounding the name that were a bit of a problem. First of all a Eurovision song contest band from Sweden used the name Genghis Khan when we were gigging with the name. We wrote to their management and basically got ignored."

"The other thing was the Alan Marsh connection, which lots of people have asked me about. I've noticed on the Internet there are lots of misquotes – one thing listed Genghis Khan members who were actually Tokyo Blade members, then listed Tokyo Blade releases on my label, Wabbit Records, so there's lots of confusion."

"There was no bad intent by anybody but, I think, when Alwyn and I were gigging as The Prams, Alan assumed the name Genghis Khan was vacant and their manager printed their single release labels as 'Genghis Khan', which caused problems for us as most of the promoters were selling us as 'Genghis Khan'."

"We called a meeting at my dad's place between Alwyn and I, Alan and Alan's manager and said 'We know you've invested money in this, but you

THE PRAMS - Rob Boston and Alwyn Lovell, live in London, 1982.

5: **Everything Louder than Everything Else**

haven't spoken to us and we're still gigging with this name and earning from it'. They withdrew their single. It left a nasty taste in the mouth between Alan and us for a number of years but we only did what we felt we had to. We were cornered – we had no other option."

Andy Boulton: "Al didn't want to fight them on it – he said 'Let them keep the name and we'll change it."

Alan Marsh: "Obviously 'Genghis Khan' was no more because they had dropped it and called themselves 'The Prams', but the minute we used it they came out and said 'Oi! You can't use that!' I think for a point of law that wouldn't have held up, but what's the point of causing any grief? So, we didn't pursue that."

After the final split of their own Genghis Khan, Rob Boston and Alwyn Lovell had formed The Prams, with Rob's brother Nick on drums and their original Genghis colleague Eddie Johnson on guitar.

Rob Boston: "Alwyn and I decided 'Let's throw away all the claptrap. Let's play the rock'n'roll music we like. Let's get away from the image'. I said 'I've got an idea for a band, let's market it as a product - we'll be The Prams. We'll wear suits and get away from the goat skins. We'll still play Budgie type driving rock'n'roll but we'll look like a new wave band and we can play on that theme - the difference between the music and the image'."

"I don't think he thought much of my new songs but he was up for the project. We got Eddie Johnson back in and my brother Nick was a very good drummer – he was very young – fifteen or sixteen with a tiny little Hayman kit with an 18" bass drum… but a power house."

The Prams embarked on providing a whole package for their new approach to playing traditional rock, including

129

ENDLESS BEAT

"To be honest we regret doing that album…"

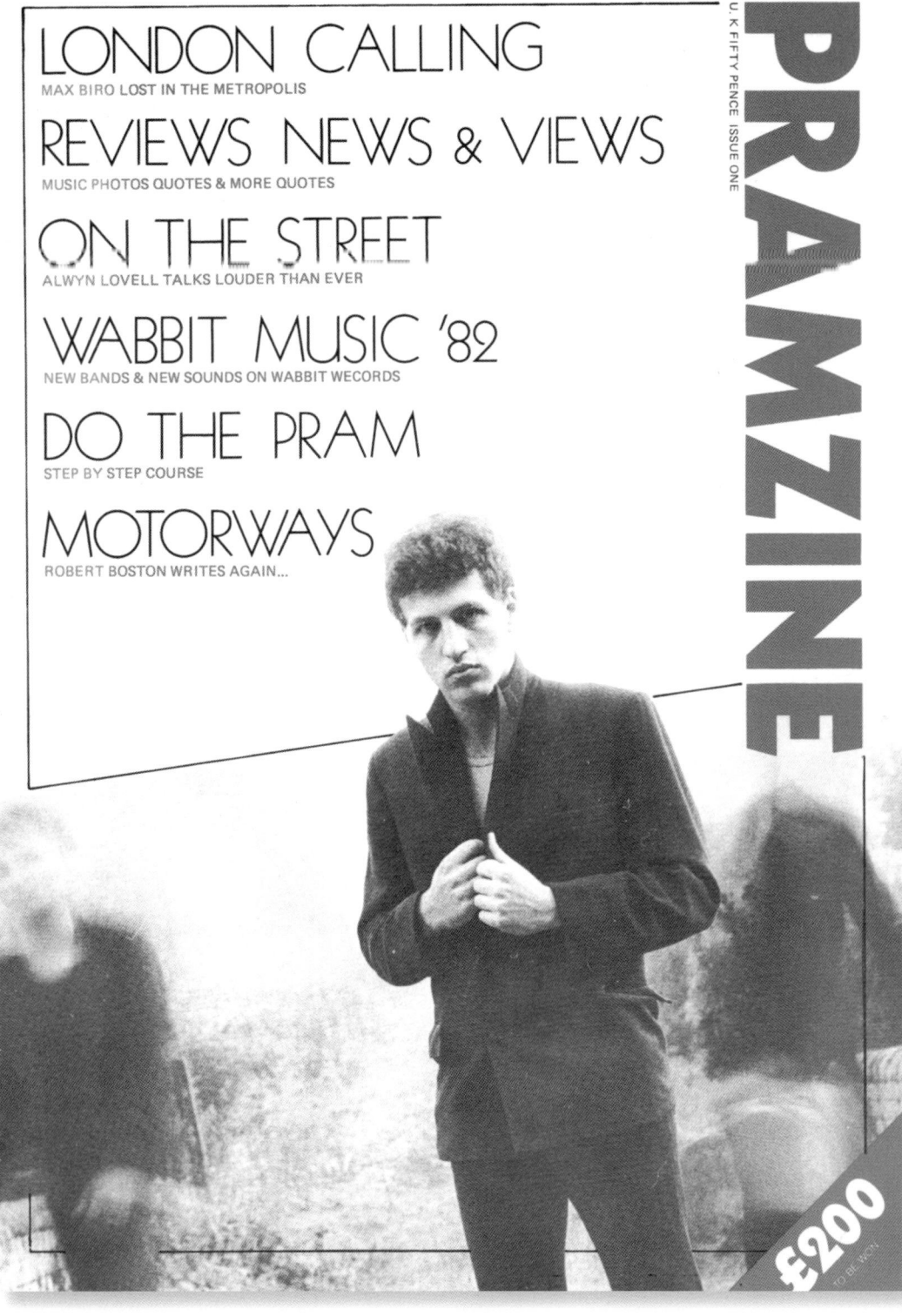

PRAMZINE — U.K FIFTY PENCE ISSUE ONE

LONDON CALLING
MAX BIRO LOST IN THE METROPOLIS

REVIEWS NEWS & VIEWS
MUSIC PHOTOS QUOTES & MORE QUOTES

ON THE STREET
ALWYN LOVELL TALKS LOUDER THAN EVER

WABBIT MUSIC '82
NEW BANDS & NEW SOUNDS ON WABBIT WECORDS

DO THE PRAM
STEP BY STEP COURSE

MOTORWAYS
ROBERT BOSTON WRITES AGAIN…

£200 TO BE WON

the production of their own fanzine, Pramzine.

Alwyn Lovell: "Trying to get stuff played – even with people like John Peel – was difficult. We felt if you had some product it would be something you could give to people rather than just knocking on the door and saying 'Please sign us'."

Rob Boston: "It was a nice fun project, and the Pramzine was fun - that was supposed to be tongue in cheek. We were trying to get away from all the pretension of Genghis Khan and be in your face boy next door, looking like we were rubbish."

"It was a fantastic new set. The problem was all the venues wanted to book us as Genghis Khan, so we were playing to heavy metal audiences. We were walking out on stage in double breasted suits and drainpipe trousers and getting things thrown at us and booed - but as soon as we started playing it went down really well."

5: Everything Louder than Everything Else

In 1981 The Prams released a single, A's Okay, on the Wabbit label. An album, What's The Time Mr Wolf?, was issued during the following year. The band were, however, disappointed with the recordings.

Rob Boston: "The album was a disaster - we couldn't afford to record. We knew what we wanted but had no money, so we borrowed some stuff and started recording the album in the basement in Salisbury."

"Halfway through Eddie left – we had half an album. We decided to restart from scratch and by the time the thing was mastered it was tired, it was flat, all the energy had gone out of it. We were recording it ourselves so all the technical side was rubbish. To be honest we regret doing that album because it wasn't what the band was about. Lots of people have said, over the years, they came to see the band – we were regulars at Dingwalls and the Greyhound in Fulham Palace Road, with big audiences - bought the album and were disappointed – it just didn't have the sparkle."

The band were happier with their final release, How About Emee?, issued in 1983.

Rob Boston: "Things got better for us. We had a new manager called Patrick Williams who introduced us to Steve James, who had worked with Neil Innes and the Sex Pistols as a technician. He was a budding producer and was working with a band called The News, who were owned by the

131

ENDLESS BEAT

"It was basically the tea boy that was the engineer..."

wrestler Kendo Nagasaki. Steve was also interesting because he was the son of Sid James, the Carry On actor."

"Kendo and his manager Gorgeous George lived at the Elephant and Castle and they had a basement studio. Kendo said we could use the studio and Steve was a fantastic producer. We did one single there, How About Emee? We got a lot of radio plays and it really caught the band as it was. Steve worked in the studio with us on the arrangements for a few weeks, changed some of the rhythms and things and he produced it really well. So, that's how I like to remember The Prams, from that single...not from the album."

Alwyn Lovell: "We sent How About Emee? out to radio stations and were starting to get good airplay. The most thrilling thing for me was when Stuart Henry on Radio Luxembourg played the single - and hearing him introduce it."

Wabbit Records - the band's own custom label – also released recordings by some of the musicians whose paths they had crossed, including Richard Patrician from Coventry and The Fluffy Vikings - described by Rob as "the first rap band ever, circa 1981" - whose lead singer Dave Forecastle sadly committed suicide.

Rob Boston: "We put them out on cassette – we couldn't afford to have them pressed, but we got limited edition cassette albums and singles. That's what Wabbit Records was about - it was low budget just for people we liked the sound of. It was a terrible failure – we lost what money we had, but I'm proud of it."

Following the earlier resolution of the band-naming issue, Wabbit also issued a double seven inch single - by the Boston-Lovell Genghis Khan, featuring the tracks recorded with Dave Pounds and John Butcher. Both this and the Double Dealin' 'Genghis Khan' double pack are now highly prized by collectors. The sleeve of the first Tokyo Blade album would carry the comment 'Pooh's not happy with wabbit!' possibly a reference back to this incident in the band's history.

The Marsh-Boulton Genghis Khan changed their name again and repackaged unsold copies of Double Dealin' as two separate singles with new labels and sleeves.

Alan Marsh: "Andy Robbins was driving and me and Andy Boulton were passengers, going down to Kestrel Music in Ringwood. We were saying 'What the hell are we going to call ourselves – every time we pick a name somebody else has got it'. We started bouncing names around. We came up with 'Tokyo' but we wanted a double barrelled name – everybody had a double barrelled name – Thin Lizzy, Deep Purple, Black Sabbath, Iron Maiden. Somebody said 'Blade' and we put it together, and thought "That's got potential - nobody else is going to have that'."

With the name and line up more settled, Blade embarked on what would become a successful career – in terms of their art if not financially. They played their biggest gig yet at Salisbury's Arts Centre, becoming the first rock band to play at the venue since the 1975 show by Nutz drew complaints from nearby residents.

Alan Marsh: "At that time there wasn't any rock gigs going on at the Arts Centre. I remember going down to see John Curry and saying it would be alright but he said 'I'm not having that - it attracts the wrong kind of people', but we managed to get a gig there and sold out - much to their surprise - and there wasn't a great deal of aggro. We weren't ridiculously loud - but loud enough - and they didn't get any complaints."

The band also began to build a wider audience.

Andy Boulton: "We did a four track EP [i.e. Double Dealin']. I took a copy to Tommy Vance, who was opening up Oscars nightclub at Longleat. He said he would play it if he liked it – he did luckily. That got the attention of a couple of record companies."

A deal was obtained with the assistance of Rod Fry's brother Colin.

Alan Marsh: "He took us to see a guy at Stage One, which was a distribution company, and when he heard it he got us to one side quietly and said 'I'm starting a record company – don't go with this lot I can offer you something better'. That's how we got involved with Powerstation – that was Kevin Nixon."

With a striking cover designed by Brian Shepherd, Tokyo Blade's eponymous debut album was released in 1983 and showcased the band's self-composed material, although the circumstances of its recording were not exactly the epitome of rock star grandeur.

Alan Marsh: "They put us in a studio in Mitcham and we had three days, and I had about four and a half hours to do the vocals. It's at times like that you think 'This isn't quite what I thought it was going to be' [laughs]."

Andy Boulton: "It was basically the tea boy that was the engineer because our record company wouldn't pay for anything. It was done in three days and we literally started work at eight in the morning, carried on until about two the following morning then straight into sleeping bags on the studio floor. We had three days to record it and one day to mix it – that's what we were given and it had to be done in that time."

"It was all original stuff. It was always Alan and I because nobody else wanted to get involved. Alan is a very good writer – he's got lots of ideas. He changes things a lot, which can be frustrating because you get the song in your head and he'll come back and say 'You know, I don't like that bridge I'll just need to change that' but I have to say he pretty much always changes a song for the better. He's good at what he does."

The album proved popular and increased Blade's fan base further – particularly in mainland Europe.

Andy Boulton: "It was very well received, especially considering the

TOKYO BLADE - left to right: Alan Marsh, Andy Robbins, Steve Pierce, John Wiggins and Andy Boulton

ENDLESS BEAT

"We wanted him to stay, but in the end he went…"

poor production. A big following started to come together out of that and the offer of a couple of big festivals in Holland came through. It was all good stuff."

Alan Marsh: "It took us by surprise really. We were put on at the Aardshock Festival in Holland. We tipped all the stuff as usual in our little van and went abroad. The week before we were playing down the King and Bishop to our normal faithful following - next thing we knew we were in front of 15-20,000 people and on the front cover of all these magazines. You sort of think 'Hang on…is this happening?' It was a bit surreal to be honest."

"Over here we were like 'Who are you lot?' but over in Europe we were doing really well. One of the singles got to number 13 in Germany – Midnight Rendezvous. Needless to say we didn't see any money, but we were doing alright."

Andy Robbins – who went on to play with Jagged Edge and Skin - was replaced by Andy Wrighton before the recording of the second Tokyo Blade album, Night Of The Blade - released in 1984, for which Powerstation pushed the boat out just a little more.

Andy Boulton: "It was much, much better than the first album in terms of production quality. Again it wasn't exactly what we wanted, but it was okay. They were prepared to spend more on us – not a lot, but some - it was two weeks this time. It wasn't so bad although it was to be done in York where they said they could keep an eye on things - but it actually turned out they could get a cheaper studio rate up there."

"Initially they put us in this really, really, really bad accommodation. It was a doss house, it really was – an awful place - and we had to do some negotiating to get into a slightly better hotel. The first two nights we stayed with one of the guys from the record company…who later billed us for it!"

Alan Marsh: "This time we actually had a couple of weeks, which was much better. Then we went back to Europe and headlined the Earthquake Festival[3]. They used to do them in what I can only describe as cattle markets - but massive - a bit like some of your indoor arenas here."

The band were pleased with the new album and, aiming to build on their growing reputation abroad, a slot was secured for them prior to its release on a European tour supporting the Irish band Mama's Boys. However, preparations for the dates were thrown into disarray as a fundamental component of Tokyo Blade left the band.

Andy Boulton: "Just before the tour started we lost Alan as vocalist. That was down to the fact that the record company, for whatever reason, weren't happy with him – they wanted him out. We wanted him to stay, but in the end he went…that's just the way it is."

Alan Marsh: "The record company were quite high up on the instigation of all this from what I've heard. It was twenty five years ago and I can't remember all the details, but it's what you piece together from what you have heard and what you are told."

"I was told by Andy and Ian Rossiter, our manager, that they weren't confident I was the right man for the job. As far as I'm aware they were looking for somebody like David Lee Roth who would bounce across the stage. I'm six foot two and that's not the sort of thing that's easy to do. I just went for the standard heavy rock thing – I didn't dance around the stage."

"You look back now and think it's quite sad, because we were all from the same school – except Steve who came from Highbury[4]. We did all that hard work to get it where it was and the minute a record company gets involved…that's when the pain starts."

"Unfortunately, with bands, if you want to get on somebody becomes the weak link and they have got to go.

Then somebody else becomes the weak link and they have got to go. You end up with a different band - very often musically better, but on reflection you sometimes wonder if that was the start of where you lost the plot. It turns into a business and nobody is safe."

"I don't blame the others for not standing in my corner, because they were protecting their own interests. It had stopped being a thing that four friends do and become a business, and if the record company is standing there saying 'The singer's not up to it' then…"

"I think it was a mistake because we had started to get a style and a big fanbase for that sort of music. When the third album came out, which was written by Andy and Vic [Wright] mainly – it's quite a good album, there's nothing wrong with it - but it was such a change in direction that everybody just went [blows raspberry]…'What was that?' It was not quite what they wanted from Tokyo Blade. Even now people say the first two albums are what they remember, which is nice in a way for me but a shame in a sense because God knows what we could have done if we had stuck together."

Andy Boulton: "We advertised for a singer in Sounds. Tape after tape after tape came through. The time was ticking on – it was getting

TOKYO BLADE - left to right: John Wiggins, Steve Pierce, Alan Marsh, Andy Boulton and Andy Robbins

ENDLESS BEAT

"I looked over and our manager was crying – he couldn't take it in."

nearer and nearer to the start of the tour. The record company had paid a so called 'buy-on' to get us on the tour so they wanted us to do it - we had to find somebody quick."

"It worked out that the day before we left for the tour I spoke to Vic Wright, who was the only person who sent a tape worth listening to. He had sent photographs we thought he looked pretty good. I said 'Can you do it?' He said 'Yes' and I said 'Right, be at my place tomorrow night' He came into the house at about six o'clock. All the band were gathered there because we were leaving in the morning for Dover - for the tour. Vic said 'Hi', sat straight down in the corner and I gave him a cup of tea, the lyrics to all the songs and a Walkman."

"He sat there learning it…and on the way to the ferry…and on the ferry…and carried on doing it. His first rehearsal was the soundcheck for the first gig. On the second or third night in the van got broken into and all our duty free cigarettes and booze were taken…and my Walkman. Luckily by then he had memorised most of the set."

"He had told us he was seventeen but we now believe he was fifteen or sixteen, but he was just Mr Confident. There was nothing he didn't think he could do. I have to say I don't think he was a great singer – but he was a great front man, and that's how he pulled it off – because he was just extreme."

The change in vocalist gave the band a dilemma in terms of the album they were supposed to be touring in support of.

Andy Boulton: "We approached the record company and said 'What do we do now?' We wanted to rerecord the album because we thought that would be the proper thing to do. The record company said 'No – we're going to remove Alan's vocals and get Vic to sing over the top', which at the time we thought was really unfair, but they were the ones with the money, so we had no choice. I don't think Al was particularly happy about it - I can't blame him to be honest."

Tokyo Blade were extremely well received on their continental jaunt.

Andy Boulton: "We couldn't believe our own success. When we did the Breaking Sound festival in Paris, we pulled in through these huge gates in this big limo and started going through the crowd, and they were swarming all over the car. We were on the same bill as Metallica, Dio and Ozzy and I said to Ian [Rossiter] 'Look at these idiots - they think its fuckin' Ozzy in the car'. He said 'No they don't – look'. I looked and they were all holding our first two albums! They had brought them there to get them signed."

"It was a beautiful, sunny day. One of the sponsors was a beer company and backstage each band had its own caravan for a dressing room, and great big tubs filled with ice and this beer and cigarettes. It was just a mountain of beer and fags – we were in seventh heaven. I remember, very distinctly, walking on to the stage – it was probably one of our biggest moments – and seeing about 15,000 French fans going completely ballistic."

"They absolutely went crazy. I stood there and grinned ear to ear. I looked over and our manager was crying – he couldn't take it in. It was like there had been no other bands on worth mentioning until we hit the stage. Vic ran on and they just erupted again. We could have played complete crap and they wouldn't have cared less. We weren't supposed to have an encore but they had to give us one. We did the encore and I remember our manager

5: **Everything Louder than Everything Else**

Ian coming through crying, saying 'Did you see that?'"

Tokyo Blade's success at the Paris event even resulted in the UK's leading metal magazine writing about them in a complimentary way - for a change.

Andy Boulton: "Kerrang! hated us. When they came to review a gig when we were touring the first album they basically ignored us - they were hanging about in another band's dressing room. We were so sick of being ignored by them that I made the – some people would say – mistake of storming into this little…twat…for want of a better word – and giving him a piece of my mind: 'You're a bunch of wankers, you're only interested in American bands and only then if they've got enough eyeliner on, you're not interested in us blah blah blah'."

"It kicked off again at this festival because they were there and I thought 'This is going to be interesting, because if we go down half as well as I've got a feeling we're going to, they're not going to be able to ignore it'. Kerrang! actually wrote – much though they hated us – 'Tokyo Blade were the band of the weekend'."

Adulation of the Blade continued across the border.

Andy Boulton: "Steve and I went to McDonalds to get something to eat – we were in Spain, for another festival. It was chock-a-block with people and

Alan Marsh and Andy Boulton

ENDLESS BEAT

"We had that success because we turned our back on England."

Steve and I joined the queue, and this guy that was serving burgers was just staring at us. We were like 'What's with this guy?' and with that this guy leaps over the counter, comes running up and...'It's Tokyo Blade! Andy! Steve!' All these people in the queue are obviously miffed because this guy is talking to us, and they now don't know who we are but think they should. The next thing is we've got everybody in McDonalds - even old people - asking for autographs. They have no idea who we are but this kid is running around saying 'It's Tokyo Blade! Its Tokyo Blade!'"

Despite the admiration of the European audiences, the band members were somehow unconvinced of their popularity.

Andy Boulton: "I still think, even to this day, that in the back of everybody's minds we were still thinking 'They've got us wrong - they've mixed us up with some other band'. I don't know if it was because we went from playing pubs to stadiums without anything in between but there was always that element that we could never quite believe it."

"A lot of bands weren't having the success we had abroad. We had that success because we turned our back on England. The press here were against us so we said 'Sod you – we'll go over there'. Eventually over here it started to pick up and we did Friday Rock Show sessions and some other work for Radio One. We also did the Camden Palace video for London Weekend Television. We were actually paid £800 to play the Marquee, whereas when we first played the guy came up to us at the end of the night and said 'That'll be sixty quid please!'"

A Tokyo Blade compilation, Warrior Of The Rising Sun, was issued by Raw Power in 1985, a year which also saw the release of the third album proper, Blackhearts and Jaded Spades.

Andy Boulton: "This was going to be a big departure, because for the first time Alan and I weren't writing the album, and I have to say the album as a result did not sell in the quantities it was expected to. Vic had made it clear he wanted a different sound for the band. We were not experienced enough to say 'We've got this fan base and they're expecting this'."

"We started getting very highbrow – 'Let's not do the heavy metal thing, let's make it more American'. That's what we did and it didn't go down well. There are some people who absolutely love it - there are a few people who think it is the best thing we've ever done - but most of the European fans voted with their wallets. There was a

5: **Everything Louder than Everything Else**

Alan Marsh

ENDLESS BEAT

"Another ridiculous situation – we wrote that album when we met."

couple of ballads on there - and the metal-heads of Germany and France don't want any ballads - plus a couple of unusual tracks, and it was just too much for some people."

With another European tour approaching, the band's problems increased with another singer's unexpected departure.

Andy Boulton: "We had been to America and did a tour. Vic loved America – the sunshine, the big lorries, big cars, the highway, the openness, the freedom that you feel. His brother already lived there so he did some wangling and moved to America… without telling us. The reason he didn't tell us was the album was just about to be released and he didn't want his vocals to be taken off, like had happened to Alan."

Having not been able to contact Vic directly for some time, the band finally learned about his move during a phone call to his parents.

Andy Boulton: "We were about two weeks away from a tour with Blue Oyster Cult, and we've got no singer. We found a guy called Carl Sentance who used to sing for a band called Persian Risk. Carl did a very good job – he's a very good, classical heavy metal singer and he did it – but it was difficult for him. He was coming into a band that had quite an image and was being asked to replace Vic, who was blond and eyeliner and all this, and Carl wasn't like that at all. He gave himself a bit of a hard time over that."

"This tour wasn't quite so good because it was a mismatch. Blue Oyster Cult weren't big enough in Europe to do justice to a proper tour. So, their management approached ours and said 'If we do it as a double bill Tokyo Blade fans will, we're hoping, like Blue Oyster Cult as well. We'll make some new fans and you guys are bound to make some new fans along the way'. They always played last but it was billed as a double headliner."

"It didn't go down as well as expected because we were playing largely to the wrong sort of people, but

Ian needed us back out on the road making a noise. We didn't have any money to do our own tour and this was the only thing he could get us."

At least one Salisbury ex-patriot got to see Blade, in just one case of the blatant blagging he had been carrying on while living on the continent.

Skid: "I saw them in Berlin supporting Blue Oyster Cult. Being English you could get into any gig free – you could just walk up and say 'I'm with the band' and they would let you in."

"I did make a mistake once – The Damned were playing in Amsterdam, I walked up to the door and said 'I'm one of the lighting crew – I've lost my pass'. They said 'Thank God you're here', grabbed me and took me up to do the lighting. I had to say 'Actually… I'm not' and got thrown out again. I also got beaten up by The Ramones' road crew. The guitarist I was playing with was a writer with ZigZag, so I walked up backstage and said 'I'm John Travis from ZigZag'. I got in with Joey and Dee Dee in the dressing room, they ended up throwing me out and then there was some tear gas and the road crew, and it all got very embarrassing."

"We also got in fights with Nick Cave – he used to drink in our local bar - and The Cult - never pick a fight with Billy Duffy…he's a right hard bastard. I was always very jarred up over there."

Following the disappointment of the Blue Oyster Cult tour Tokyo Blade fell apart, although there were subsequent reincarnations.

Andy Boulton: "There was a fourth album a lot later. After it all fell to pieces I was determined to keep it going and managed to piece together a very average band, and we did a very average record - which sort of got forgotten about - under the name of 'Andy Boulton's Tokyo Blade'."

"Then I did another 'Tokyo Blade' album with some German guys, which was actually a good record but very different. Another ridiculous situation – we wrote that album when we met. The record company said 'Come over on such and such a date'. I had four songs and four guys I had never met in my life, some of whom had very sketchy knowledge of English – 'Hello lads, let's make an album' - two days to write it in. That album turned out amazingly well considering."

Following the unexpected end of his tenure with Tokyo Blade, Alan Marsh needed some encouragement to begin again.

Alan Marsh: "I went and sulked for quite some time - I moved down to Poole to get the hell out of it. Rod Fry

SHOGUN - left to right: Danny Gwilym, Alan Marsh, Bob Richards and Toby Martin

ENDLESS BEAT

"We're going to send you out to Los Angeles..."

saved my ass. He said 'Look you're too good to sit around feeling sorry for yourself, let's see what we can do' and put some adverts out trying to pick up some guitarists."

"We ended up getting Danny Gwilym from Portsmouth. He had been in London for a long time working with a band called Chinatown. He came down and I clicked with him a bit like I had with Andy with the song writing."

The initial line up of the band that was to become Shogun comprised Alan and Danny with David Gochaux on bass and Bob Richards on drums. As had been the case with Tokyo Blade, Colin Fry's contacts proved useful – this time putting them in touch with a man who had formerly been involved with The Move and Black Sabbath.

Alan Marsh: "We were rehearsing at the scout hut in Downton – how the mighty had fallen [laughs]. He brought this guy to see us, who was setting up his own record company, and that was Wilf Pine."

"We did an album with Steve Tatler. Me and Danny were trying to write heavy metal stuff, but we wrote a few what we called commercial rock as well. Wilf picked the songs and went for the commercial rock and we lost five what I would call really good heavy metal songs. It wasn't quite what me and Danny wanted and I think the biggest mistake that was made with Shogun was not really explaining what it was they wanted. If they had said they wanted Bon Jovi right from the start we could have tried to adapt."

Shogun's eponymous debut album and their single cover of Amen Corner's High In The Sky, both released on Attack in 1986, received airplay and bought the band to the attention of Jet Records, home of Ozzy Osbourne and the Electric Light Orchestra. Having signed a deal with Jet, a new - yet familiar - rhythm section was recruited prior to the recording of the second album, 31 Days.

Alan Marsh: "Tokyo Blade were falling to bits. We were in the Fisherton Arms talking with Wilf and he said 'Look we've got to get a drummer'. Danny was on about how good Steve Hopgood was, but Steve Pierce was at home that weekend and he came into the pub. We said to Wilf 'This is Steve – he's a drummer' and he offered him the job there and then! It wasn't the 'Steve the drummer' we were on about but it didn't matter. We still needed a bass player so we got Andy Wrighton in…also from Tokyo Blade!"

The opportunities offered by a major label contract were not always obvious to the band members.

Alan Marsh: "Me and Danny were sent to America to remix a couple of songs. We went into Jet's office, Don Arden was there and said 'We're going to send you out to Los Angeles - we've got Bob Ezrin'. He waited for the response and me and Danny looked at each other…'Who's Bob Ezrin?' Now we know who he is…he did Pink Floyd and Alice Cooper! [laughs]"

As opposed to the traditional hard rock approach of Genghis Khan and Tokyo Blade, Shogun were more aligned with the hair-glam-metal genre of the late eighties. They were described by the New Musical Express as 'fakes - bank accountants in wigs'…but then they weren't really an NME sort of band.

The Second Coming described Shogun as being 'no worse than 99% of the other 'Kerrang!' type stuff around' and somewhat cheekily suggested that '…these boys are all extremely cute and with a little luck, Peter Powell and the right breaks on kids TV could easily be this year's Jonbons' (i.e. Bon Jovi).

Meanwhile, although she acknowledged the successes of Shogun in her Salisbury Journal Soundtracks column, Sally Anne Lowe confessed to not being a fan of their style, finding it 'extremely cliched and macho'. Sally peppered her writings on the band with phrases such as 'local boys make good – well I suppose it depends on what you mean by good' and 'Shogun may take off…I hope they don't become one hit wonders…'

Sally's article provoked a reaction from Shogun fan Stuart Taylor of Harnham, who rightly pointed out that heavy rock remained extremely popular in Salisbury, and felt it therefore followed that the Journal should take a more positive approach to the genre.

The Journal editor defended Sally's right to express her opinion. With the paper having a single writer focusing on the local music scene(s) it was inevitable that such issues would arise – we very much doubt that a hardened metal fan would have written sympathetically about the indie pop bands that Sally herself was so fond of.

By coincidence, the Soundtracks column had been introduced by the Journal following previous complaints from local metal fans.

Roger Elliott: "Soundtracks came about because somebody came in who had been to see Genghis Khan and complained to the paper that this was a sold out gig and wasn't covered."

The initial Shogun line-up was later augmented by a keyboard player who had been classically trained during his time at Marlborough College and came to the city to work at the Arts Centre.

Atilla: "I stopped being classically trained at the age of about sixteen when I'd had enough of it, decided to play guitar instead and formed my first band. They were called Hellspawn - an early black metal band. I didn't know it was black metal at the time, but I realise it was now…mainly because it was shit. I was shit at guitar and eventually turned back to playing keyboards again."

"I was playing in a band called Spirit of St Louis, who were out of Newbury. We had done an EP and quite a few gigs, but nobody was really biting at it, so I got bored with that. I joined an American band called The Acrylics who came over here and got a deal with Mute Records but that fell apart as well. I needed a new scene and there was a job going at Salisbury Arts Centre in the publicity department.

ENDLESS BEAT

"It was disappointing in that we were so close and yet so far…"

That's how I came to Salisbury and met the Holton…its dogged me ever since…he still owes me £42.75!"

"It was quite vibrant at the time. There was half a dozen pubs putting music on, the Arts Centre was doing something nearly every Thursday and there was a lot of bands happening in Salisbury in different styles. Playing-wise I did a couple of guest appearances with Holton, but I don't know what the band was called – he changed it every couple of weeks. Then Al Marsh asked me to join Shogun."

Alan Marsh: "Danny didn't want to work with another guitarist if possible and we wanted a keyboard player to put a bit more padding in it. Rod knew Atilla because he used to pop in the pub now and again so we had him up and chatted to him. He set up in the corner of the Fisherton Arms and Wilf just said 'Right…play something'. Obviously he is a very competent keyboard player so luckily, even under those circumstances, he managed to shine."

Atilla: "I can't particularly say I had heard them, but I knew of them, they were going well in Europe. When I heard the album I thought it had great potential to be a British Bon Jovi, but it soon became fairly obvious they didn't actually want to be that - they wanted to be a much heavier band."

"It was my first introduction to hairspray – we had big, big hair – it used to take forty minutes to do before you went onstage. Hairspray and trousers – those were my abiding memories of Shogun."

"I was never particularly attracted to that AOR, stateside music, which was what was happening in the mid-eighties. It was a bit poncey for me, but hey, it was as good a job as you were gonna get as a keyboard player - unless you played for some awful indie band."

"Mainly, the music was written by Alan and Danny, great songwriters and Danny – given the chance – a great riff writer, but that music wasn't necessarily about riffs - it was about big choruses. Some of the music was very, very good, there were some great hook lines but the trouble is, with all English bands who attempted to emulate the success of American bands of that genre…Bon Jovi, Foreigner – the Americans have this massive production and millions of dollars are spent on the albums."

"The budget for the British bands tended to be about a tenth of that, so you would get a tenth of the sound. In the eighties it was all big production, like Phil Spector to the nth degree. The only British band who could remotely be called AOR who made a massive splash was Def Leppard – and they weren't that to start with. They came, like Tokyo Blade, from the New Wave of British Heavy Metal."

Shogun eventually drifted apart, partly as a result of the inertia caused by their contract being tangled up in a conflict between Jet and CBS.

Alan Marsh: "That was way above our level but in the end we were just so tied up from doing anything, because there was no money and we were in litigation. I'm not privy to all the stuff that went on and I wasn't overly interested. As a musician – and a dopey one at that - I just want to play music. We just drifted apart. I think it had played its hand out anyway and to be honest it wasn't quite the sort of music we wanted to do so we let it go. It was disappointing in that we were so close and yet so far - we had touched it again."

Of course, the band might have been cursed by a high profile support slot…

Atilla: "There was a tour with Meatloaf, which everybody knows is the kiss of death. Any band who has ever supported Meatloaf almost immediately disappears! Blind Heart, Terraplane…have you ever heard of them again? Mind you…I wasn't there…I got sacked just before it!"

After the demise of Shogun, the original Tokyo Blade songwriting partnership was reunited in a new project, Mr Ice.

Alan Marsh: "Me and Andy got chatting about trying to do something again. We remembered this geezer that had wanted to put money into the band in the early days – Jeremy Hayes - so we went and saw him, and he said he would be interested in helping. Danny wanted to get involved and Andy said 'Yeah, why not?' Colin Riggs did bass and we advertised for a drummer and got old Jocker up from Southampton – Marc Angel - and Atilla came in on keyboards."

Danny Gwilym did not stay with Mr Ice for long.

Alan Marsh: "There was a bit of a fracas. The rot set in when Danny had a bit of a punch up with Till and a couple of the roadies. I don't know the ins and outs because I wasn't there but it got heavy. There was lots of alcohol… and then there was much fighting... Danny went and we were down to just Andy on guitar. The music sort of settled down because there was no longer a conflict. When you get two really good guitarists together…we had to have twenty minutes of solos in each song because of politics."

Andy Boulton: "That was quite a happening little band. It was looking like it was going to go somewhere. We did a City Hall gig and no expense was spared - we got in a big light rig and a decent PA and spent a lot of money on new equipment."

Despite the band's promise, Andy was replaced by Steve Kerr. Mr Ice then crossed paths with a band that had once 'enjoyed' Salisbury so much they had named an album after the city.

Atilla: "What had been Mr Ice got called 'Tokyo Blade' to go and do this tour, because Uriah Heep wanted that name to draw extra people. We did a six week European jaunt with them and they are some of the nicest people I have ever met in rock'n'roll."

Andy Boulton: "They went off and did the Uriah Heep thing – started off as 'Mr Ice' and then changed their name at the start of the tour to 'Tokyo Blade', because their manager said it would have more clout in Europe. They were a band that people went to see and said 'Tokyo Blade? Where is Tokyo Blade?'"

Mr Ice fizzled out – partly because their music was no longer in sync with modern rock tastes.

Alan: "We did some demos in the Chapel in Winchester, which was a beautiful studio. I played the songs to Cliff [Stafford] and he said 'They're too classy' [laughs]. That was right smack bang at the time when Nirvana had emerged and it went back to basics again."

Atilla: "It wasn't happening. Same story as before…trying to be American but having no budget. We had a ridiculous management company, who tried to rule us like a prep school class. I remember Jocker nearly getting sacked for putting a fried egg in his pocket at a motorway services."

"At the time when the main protagonists of Mr Ice thought you should still be playing Foreigner or Bon Jovi a la 1987, what was beginning to happen was the threads of punk like Faith No More were coming in. It was getting harder, nastier. Bands like Nirvana were coming up and things were getting very much more point blank and riff orientated. So, clashes of egos and fried eggs notwithstanding, it never stood a chance."

ENDLESS BEAT

"Spinal Tap is funny… but we were the sad reality"

Alan Marsh next put together a project named Pumphouse, with Jez Lee and Steve Kerr on guitars, Colin Riggs on bass and Marc Angel on drums - augmented by Atilla on keyboards and samples.

Alan Marsh: "I liked Pumphouse. It went back to the raw energy that we started out with. It wasn't heavy but it was raw and powerful. The stuff we produced was really good. Jez was fabulous - absolutely brilliant. He was one of those guitarists – a different generation I suppose - that wasn't bothered if he did a solo or didn't. The old metal guitarists have got to do a solo otherwise they sulk for a month. He wasn't so precious - he would do exactly what was needed for the song. If it wanted a solo he would do a solo if it didn't he would leave it out."

"We did an album at Aldbourne with Nick Beer producing. At that time we got involved with the management company that was running Venom and some other bands but politics got in the way and we got thwarted again."

In an echo of the Mr Ice project, the Pumphouse album was eventually released in 1998 as a 'new Tokyo Blade' product.

Andy Boulton's side project Saigon issued a CD, Soul Shaker, in the early nineties before, perhaps surprisingly, he and Alan Marsh got back together again as Tokyo Blade in 1994. This latest incarnation of Blade - with John Wiggins on guitar, Colin Riggs on bass and Marc Angel on drums - recorded the Burning Down Paradise album.

Alan Marsh: "We were approached by a label about re-releasing all our old stuff. That never panned out particularly well but they did put it all on CD for us. Ollie Hahn heard about it, got in touch and said 'Why don't you stick the band back together? I'm sure I can get you a deal in Germany'."

"We did a festival in Europe and the album did quite well…and that was it. Paul Di'Anno asked Colin, Marc and John to join his band Battlezone. They had a tour booked and we were stagnating at the time – didn't know where to take it – and they went, which left me and Andy. I think by then we had just about had enough."

This was the story of Salisbury's favourite NWOBHM bands, but we obviously couldn't let this chapter pass without reporting on some of their on and off stage excesses – as Rob Boston says "Spinal Tap is funny…but we were the sad reality".

For starters there is Alwyn 'Coke' Lovell's seemingly classic rock star nickname.

Alwyn Lovell: "That started when I had quite long hair and decided to cut it all off myself. It was really, really short - almost like a skinhead - but parts of it were still long because I didn't do a very good job on it, and my father said I looked like a 'bloody coconut'. My brother was the first to cotton on and it got condensed down from there…it was nothing to do with cocaine!"

Rob Boston: "When we formed the band, a friend of mine of at art school called Dave Compton said 'The sound you make is like Genghis Khan and the Mongol hordes coming over the horizon'.... light bulb! 'Genghis Khan!' Our sound engineer at the time, Bob Burnell, worked at Salisbury Playhouse and said 'I'll get one of the actors to make up an intro tape'."

"He got Gilbert Wynne – a brilliant old TV actor who had done Z-Cars. It started up with these horses, drums and horns, and you could hear the army coming. It lasted two or three minutes then the sound would stop and Gilbert would say in a huge pantomime voice 'Ladies and gentlemen… Genghis Khan' and this gong would go and the band would come onstage. Real Spinal Tap, but no irony - we believed it!"

"I remember one night playing in a club in Wardour Street – it was the Vortex some nights of the week, a punk place – and other nights it was Crackers. Some kids at the side of the stage had been swinging on pipes. One was a water pipe - it came down and the dance floor flooded. We played the gig with dry ice and everything and the soundman and lighting bloke were getting zaps through the equipment. When we got off stage we were halfway to our knees in water!"

Andy Boulton: "One night we had a massive dressing room and we were riding chairs - like horses - in a sort of race-type situation and it got really serious - people were betting on it! I sat there and thought 'This is so ridiculous'. You find yourself in situations that are so surreal it's almost like you get home and tell people and they say 'Did that really happen?'"

"One hotel we stayed in, I had gone to bed early and heard a terrible commotion that night - I had no idea what was going on. When I woke up the next morning, came out of my room and got to the lift the first thing I saw was a group of people gathered around. There was a huge wardrobe wedged into the lift, so it wouldn't go up or down."

"I got downstairs into the restaurant where the lads were having breakfast, all sat there very bleary eyed, and they gave me a little tour of the night

SHOGUN - left to right: Andy Robbins, Danny Gwilym, Alan Marsh, Ian 'Atilla' Marshall and Steve Pierce

before…'Well yeah, the wardrobe, that was us, and if you look out there…' There was a set of telephone wires from the hotel to the town square and there was a mattress hung over them, and a load of bed clothes blowing around the square. In the restaurant there was one of these fish tanks where you go up and say to the guy 'I'll have that one' and pull out your lobster… there was a turd floating around in that."

"At a Holiday Inn in America I went to Andy and Steve's room to borrow their hairdryer. I walked in and they've got everything off the walls, out of every corner of the room. They had broken it up and made a pile of it - basically like a bonfire - and there's Steve sat on top having his photo taken by Andy. I just wandered in and said 'Can somebody lend me a hairdryer?' I got it, walked out and took no notice until I got back to the room and suddenly thought 'I've just been into a room where two people that I know very well, who wouldn't dream of doing that under normal circumstances, have taken a room to pieces and built a little mountain in the middle of it!' Totally bizarre – why would you do that?"

The behaviour of one of Salisbury's larger than life metal figures was even too much for one of the genre's most notorious hell raisers.

Alan Marsh: "We used to rehearse in Paul Webber's studios, in Putney, and Girlschool also used to rehearse there and one day Lemmy came down. There was a pub at the back and we all used to pop down there for a beer, and Lemmy asked us to remove Atilla from his vicinity. I think Till was a little bit three parts to the wind…he was getting a bit boisterous…I don't know what he had said to him…"

Lemmy had in fact crossed paths with alcohol and another Salisbury keyboard wizard a few years before.

Frogg: "A mate of mine, Mitch,

ENDLESS BEAT

"... no wonder he got rid of all the records!"

invited me to see Motorhead at Southampton Gaumont. His brother was their tour manager and arranged for us to meet the band backstage. Lemmy was on form that night and after the gig was in the mood for a good drink. 'This is Frogg' announced the road manager to Lemmy. 'Fuck me – what sort of name is that?' said the great man. 'Well, what's Lemmy short for? Lemming?' I replied. 'Right you little bastard, let's see how much of this you can drink – and I'll tell you when to stop' said Lemmy, handing me a bottle of Jack Daniels. A volley of expletives followed as I downed a fair quantity of the drink, resulting in Lemmy snatching his bottle back and pulling me onto the floor in a mock fight – great fun!"

Despite the typical hard rock antics of our local bands, the Salisbury Journal Soundtracks columnist found Tokyo Blade to be quite affable.

Penny Elliott: "I interviewed them in his [Andy Boulton's] mother's house, in his bedroom. They were quite shy and quite scared of being interviewed. They played me some music and were really co-operative and nice…sweet as can be. As soon as they got on stage they rampaged…"

Of course, the taste for excess had been going on for many years before the NWOBHM era – even in Salisbury.

Ethem Cetintas [Marble Orchard]: "There wasn't a big drug scene but you could always get hold of it. There were people who spoke to people and they knew people. Young people were divided: like Martin [James] was a pub-goer, he would go to the pub every lunchtime and evening and down twelve pints or whatever, but there were a lot who were more drug-orientated, just going down each other's places with a bunch of records and a bit of grass instead."

Then there were the roadies - Cliff Stafford and Noddy Dudman have both worked with many bands, but are legendary characters in their own right on the Salisbury scene.

Dave Taylor [Afro Dizzy Acts]: "We had some cracking times. Cliff Stafford was our roadie. We were driving back from Oxford in two transits, after doing a gig. Ten miles outside Oxford he said 'Will you stop here?' Everyone thought he just wanted a pee. He got off and said 'See ya – bye' and disappeared. He had met a woman, obviously, and had somehow worked out that she lived in a village we were going to drive past. He just got off at two o'clock in the morning in the middle of nowhere!"

Tom Thatcher: "I rate Noddy as one of my dearest, dearest friends of all time. We had a band called Inside Job very briefly. One of the first jobs we got was at Salisbury Police Station - for their annual bash. Noddy said 'I'll have a go on the fruit machine'. He was there cranking away and in came these particularly heavy looking coppers – they were very nice, a great audience to play for – and one of them said 'Hello Nod, how are you?' with genuine affection."

"This went on for most of the evening. I said 'Nod, I know you have never been a cadet policeman or anything, but you seem to know every copper in here'. He said 'Yeah, I've been up here five times actually: twice for gigs and three times in an official capacity.'"

"The ESB Band played the Waldorf Hotel in London when Noddy tried to duff up the MD – who was saying [in a French Accent] 'You cannot play so loud. We 'ave Mr 'arry Enfield next door and it is 'is wedding party, you are disturbing the guests'. Noddy stood up and went 'Ferrrcoff!' and the bloke disappeared! He did not reappear that evening!"

Andy Golden: "I played for a while with the Taylor-Gair band. We played at the Red Lion and the grammar school girls were there, and the Bishop Wordsworth boys, for some sort of celebration. We were doing a quiet song with acoustic guitars and stuff to help the feeling and atmosphere, and so on. There was a lot of chatting going on in the audience and after maybe half a dozen bars of this Noddy - who was doing the lights - marched onto the stage, barged the two singers out of the way, took the microphone and said 'Shut up, will yer, they're trying to sing this song', and walked off stage again. They did shut up – there was total silence."

Tom Thatcher: "Just after the [Grandma Moses] EP had come out we played a gig at the Cathedral Hotel. It was absolutely packed. There were actually people out on the street dancing and so on. It was one of the first times we had the EP for sale so in

Lemmy and Frogg

148

5: **Everything Louder than Everything Else**

the interval I said 'Nod, pop round with the EPs, we only need to sell a few hundred before we start to get some money back'."

"He went off with the box, came back and said 'I've sold the lot', so I said 'Great' and got some more from the car. We did the second set and went down even more of a storm, people were jumping up on tables, the beer ran out and everything. At the end Nod came up and said 'Cor, fuckin' good gig - I'm gonna sell some more EPs'."

"I saw him standing over a table, until a chap had bought an EP…..and then another one. The chap came over to me at the end and said 'That was a fantastic gig, we really enjoyed it, but your roadie came up at the end and was incredibly insistent that I should buy one of your EPs'. He got quite upset by it and I said 'Oh, don't take any notice, it's just that he's very fond of the band'. The chap said 'I wouldn't have minded but I had already bought four in the interval!' Noddy was so full of enthusiasm that he didn't recognise them, so he kept going around and selling EPs to all these poor buggers who had already bought one – no wonder he got rid of all the records!"

Is there an explanation for the onset of such examples of aggression, excess and road fever? The man that - entirely against his natural disposition - became known as 'The Dark Lord of Laverstock' as a result of his role in band sackings, has some theories.

Andy Boulton: "We did the whole nine yards - don't let anybody tell you otherwise – we wrecked just as many hotels as anybody else. It's surreal - you come home, you're on the dole and you're the only one around in the daytime because all your mates have got jobs, and you've just been away with a rock band trashing hotels. It's a very weird life. You do understand why people turn to drink and drugs – most of it comes from hours and hours of doing nothing. You fill your days with total crap, just to give yourself something to do."

"It's a bit like a child. You have the idea to start this band. You give birth to it. You raise it. You nurture it. You keep it going - building and building and building and everything's a challenge. First of all you've got to get some management, then a record deal and each thing feels like a big step. Then you've finally got everything in place and you're out there doing it. You've got the fans absolutely loving you, you're playing the venues."

"You do get sucked in to a certain extent. I've always tried to stay as down to earth and focussed as I can possibly be, but you do get this funny, disjointed idea of life - because it's a very surreal life that you live. You're with a band earning money out of playing rock'n'roll, which your parents have told you is never going to earn you a penny. You're doing crazy things, riding in these limos and tour buses. You've got everybody carrying your stuff for you. You have to keep one foot really planted on the ground…because it's very easy to start feeling like something that you're actually not."

149

CHAPTER FIVE FOOTNOTES

1. WH Smiths was at this time located at the junction of High Street with New Canal, in premises now occupied by Waterstones. Smiths also had a rear entrance – directly into the record department – on the original Old George Mall, approximately in the area now occupied by The Body Shop.
2. The Fisherton Arms in Fisherton Street has now been renamed Bar 44.
3. The Earthquake Festival was held at Kaakshuvel in Holland.
4. Highbury school has now been renamed Wyvern College.

6 Flowers in a Desert
The 1980s

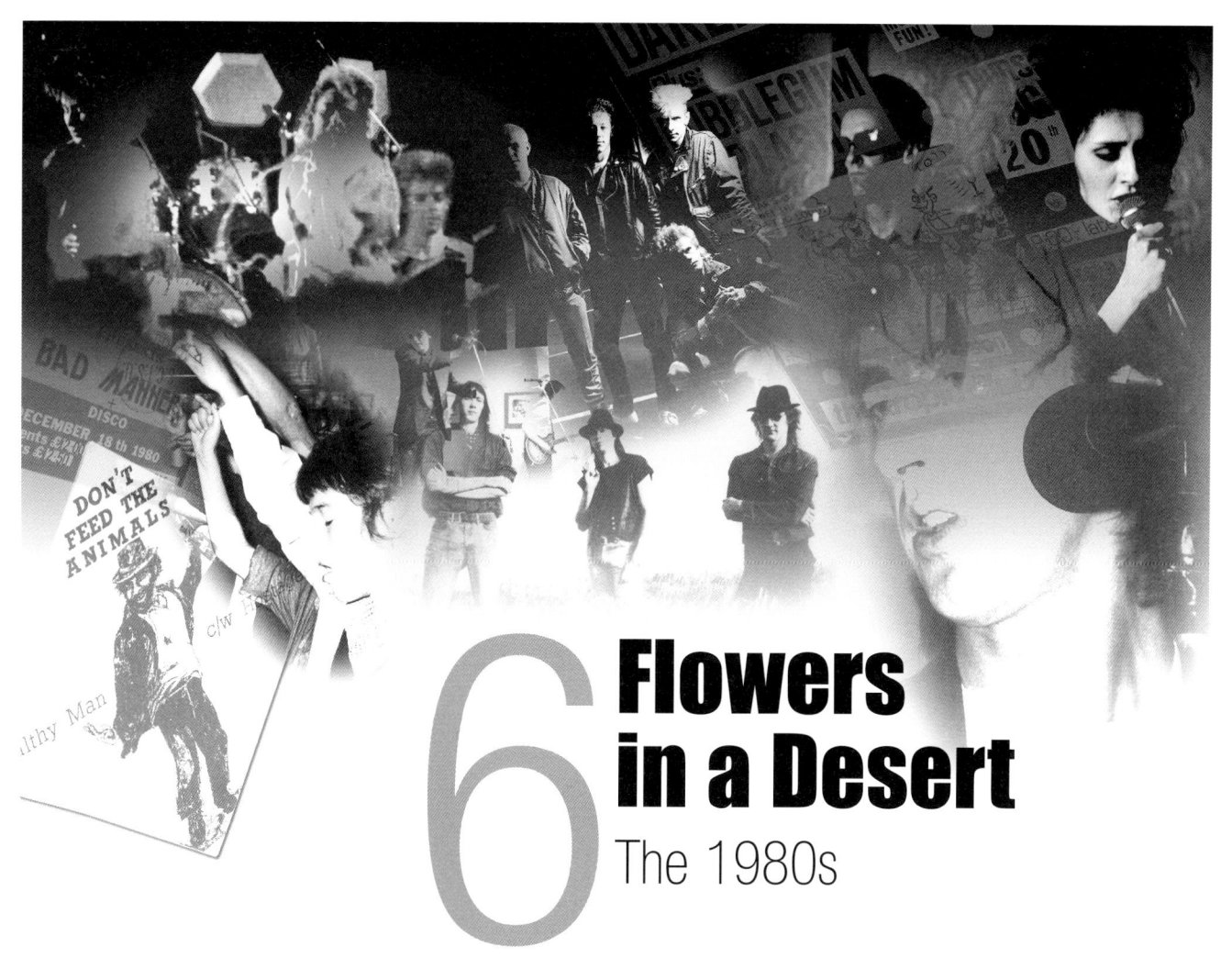

The greatest legacy of the punk movement arose from its 'anyone can-Do It Yourself' ethic, resulting in what might be called 'The Billy Casper Effect'. The downtrodden guttersnipe-poet of Barry Hines' Kestrel For A Knave (whose image is cast in stone by Ken Loach's cinematic interpretation, Kes) had little prospect of escaping the coalfields of South Yorkshire. However, if he had been born ten years later, Billy could have been in a band.

By 1978 all manner of spotty, speccy, lank haired, nylon parka-wearing kids from what were still being called 'the provinces' were making a name for themselves: Feargal Sharkey (of Derry's Undertones), Jake Burns (Belfast – Stiff Little Fingers) and Mark E Smith (Salford – The Fall) were among those appearing in the NME, on the John Peel show and making singles – genuinely great, classic singles - on independent, and sometimes locally based, labels.

At this stage, 'indie' didn't signify a particular style. All manner of genres were presented by the smaller labels: punk, heavy metal, reggae, ska, rockabilly, electronic, ex-pub rockers, hippies, avant-garde – anything drifting away from the mainstream.

These genres came with their own uniforms. If you followed the bands seriously then you had to wear the

ENDLESS BEAT

"Where have you been over the weekend?"

gear. The sixties copy suits of the mod revivalists were also worn, alongside Fred Perrys and Doc Martens, by the rude boys who had latched on to the 2-Tone movement, and then there the new generations of punks, bikers, teddy boys, hippies and random freaks.

Chris Hartford: "In terms of youth there were some demarcation points. I used to go to the Star, never the William IV – I think I went there once and walked out very quickly[1]. I was at home in the Star with the goths and hippies. They had one of the best jukeboxes in Salisbury."

Skid: "I used to go to work and they would say 'Where have you been over the weekend?' I would say 'The Star' and they would say 'Ooh…you go in The Star do you?' It was the most peaceful lovely pub you could go in but I suppose it had such a horrible reputation nobody went in there… apart from the people in the know."

Chris Hartford: "I was on the punk side of things and remember being chased out of the Liberal Club once by ten mods[2]. Olivers[3] were the only shoe shop in Salisbury that did winkle pickers and I had a pair that were too big for me. I was running across the road outside the library, one of my shoes fell off and I just had to leave it!"

Peter Beasley: "I recall a clothes shop on Catherine Street that had the early Space Invader machines on the first floor[4]. The owner was not particularly welcoming – he used to sit on the stairs so he could keep an eye on both floors, and a friend I was with accidentally kicked his coffee over while coming down the stairs. My friend apologised but we were still banned from the shop!"

"We also got banned from the County Hotel. We discovered that by rubbing your feet on the carpet, the static electricity that was created channelled through a coin touching the coin slot and gave you a free go on the fruit machines and Space Invader/Pac Man machines - until the management rumbled us!"

Chris Hartford

Vague had by now outgrown Salisbury - and was to eventually outgrow the music scene - but the mantle was taken up locally by a new fanzine during 1980.

Tom Vague: "I left college for good and briefly moved the Vague office to Bournemouth as I sold issue 7 - the programme for Adam and The Ants' Kings Of The Wild Frontier Tour - and started writing for ZigZag. Point Of View, the post-Vague and more traditional punk Salisbury fanzine was started in late 1980 by Kev, Luke Brignel, Simon Poffley and Chris."

In November 1980, The Passions played at the College, followed a month later by Bad Manners - led by Buster 'Fatty' Bloodvessel for the College Christmas dance.

Perry M reviewed The Passions' gig for Vague and noted 'the usual mixed crowd of bikers, skins, punks, mods, trendies…which usually means the gig ends in some sort of fight'. The Passions went down well with the mixed crowd, although their show was spoilt by the main hall lights being switched on towards the end of the set, causing Barbara Gogan, the band's vocalist, to believe that trouble had in fact started. It hadn't - so the band continued and was called back for an encore.

Bad Manners' gig was reviewed in Point Of View, although this nearly didn't happen as ITV was screening a documentary about Toyah on the same evening and the reviewer was torn between the two. This might seem odd in these days of multi-channels, recording media and I-Players, but very little music was being broadcast on television at the time.

The gig was sold out and the crowd included a large skinhead gathering. As the band took the stage the skins let up a chant of 'Fatty! Fatty!' The band played one number without Buster and then he appeared, dressed in a boiler suit and flicking his ample tongue in and out in time with the beat.

The crowd stomped and jumped around through tracks such as Ivor the Engine, Here Comes the Major and their various hits before, halfway through the set, the power was turned off after Buster Bloodvessel mooned the audience. After much shouting the power was switched back on and the band eventually left the stage after three encores.

Unlike the Ant-riot of just over two years earlier, the gig was trouble-free, proving that 'the majority of skinheads are just like the rest of us – out for a good time'. The reviewer was also happy because 'most people said the programme on Toyah was crap'.

In October 1981, Vague promoted a gig at The Grange, headlined by anarcho-punk band Crass.

In an article published in Vague, and later ZigZag, Tom Vague described how the gig came about. He returned home to 'Vague Mansions' (his family home in Mere) to be told by his mother that 'Andy from Crass' had called. His immediate reaction was 'Who's taking the piss?' but a few days later Andy Palmer called again enquiring whether Vague would promote a gig for the band. Tom declined at first having had difficulties with previous promotions, but reconsidered as 'Crass can't rip me

ENDLESS BEAT

"I was there ten years and everyday was an eye opener."

off, it would ruin their image'.

The venue was swamped by locals and Crass' bunch of travelling fans. Eventually the manageress informed Tom and his Vague colleagues that she wouldn't allow any more people in because of fire regulations. However, by means of the fire exit and backstage door they got most of the remaining fans in, leaving about half a dozen shivering outside until Tom simply let them in the front door.

Although the break-even attendance figure was exceeded, the takings on the door didn't work out - Vague were still £50 short of the £250 Crass had charged as a number of forged tickets had been sold. Tom approached the band expecting a repeat of a response to a similar difficulty with his previous promotion of a Martian Dance gig, but was stunned by the reaction: 'That's fine, but do you need any more to cover your expenses?'

The management team at The Grange had been surprised at the turnout for the Crass gig.

Mike Robins: "We were unsure about punk. When they advertised I thought 'Nobody's going to come'. On the afternoon before these people started arriving. We had a lot of woods and trees and banks around us and they came in and pitched tents up. All amongst the trees there were two to three hundred people pitched up overnight ready to come to the punk do the next day – absolutely amazing!"

Mike left the Grange in the mid-eighties and now runs a hotel in Somerset. Martin James took over the venue soon afterwards and it later became Concordes nightclub. Former Alex and Grange bouncer Bill 'Tiny' Mackerel moved to Brighton but has now sadly died. Both manager and patrons have fond memories of The Grange.

Mike Robins: "I was there ten years and everyday was an eye opener."

Peter Beasley: "The Grange was a

Martin James at Concordes

6: Flowers in a Desert

GETTYSBURG ADDRESS - left to right: Mark 'Kenny' Kenchington, Steve Rushton, Chris Walsh, Jon Nicholas and Frogg Moody

popular haunt of many people at college and many end-of-term parties were held there – I still have the invite for the party organised by the class I was in. The place reminded me of Fawlty Towers!"

Local band Gettysburg Address supported Jools Holland and The Millionaires at the Grange, giving Frogg Moody the opportunity to meet a fellow keyboard player.

Frogg: "The bass player with Jools was a fantastic player called Pino Palladino, and we spent the afternoon playing Space Invaders, chatting and drinking. He invited me to meet Jools, who was in his hotel room and obviously not in the mood for being disturbed - a shout of 'piss off' greeted our knock at the door. Revenge was sweet later on because, in front of a packed Grange, we blew Jools Holland off the stage!"

In July 1983, another rare show by a national name took place in the city as the newly rising Big Country, led by ex-Skids guitarist Stuart Adamson, appeared at the City Hall. On the afternoon of the gig Frogg Moody encountered a relaxed Adamson outside the venue.

Frogg: "Prior to the gig I found Stuart Adamson sunbathing on top of the band's camper van. Climbing up to the roof, I said 'Hi, I'm Frogg Moody from a local Salisbury band, would you mind listening to our demo tape?' Fully expecting a Jools Holland type of reply I was surprised as he not only invited me up, but listened to the full demo. 'Great songs' he said, 'here's the phone number of our management and tell them I recommend you!' I couldn't have expected anything else – I had loved his guitar style from the days of The Skids - a great bloke as well."

The show itself expressed everything that Big Country's music was about at this stage of their career: freshly filled with faith and hope, spiritual and life-affirming. Afterwards the band spent a long time talking, shaking hands and signing autographs outside the venue before going to a party at a house in Kingsland Road, hosted by local face Vincent Clayden.

Big Country were very much a people's band – approachable and unassuming - perhaps even more so

155

ENDLESS BEAT

"I broke him down over a period of weeks..."

Phil Lynott

Legend has it that just before Lynott passed a nurse heard him whispering. She bent towards him to hear more clearly and realised he was singing My Way. An alternative rumour has him asking the nurse for 'a wank'.

Although for the purposes of this book we have tended to focus on local acts that predominantly performed their own material, the Colin David Set – one of the most popular club and function bands of the era – warrant a mention for their 1981 album, Limited Edition. Recorded at the ever popular Arny's Shack, the album did in fact include some original material. The band members at the time were Colin than the punk bands had been. In our overly melodramatic modern world, Stuart Adamson's suicide in 2001 represented the very real tragedy of a soul we could have done without losing.

Another tragic death, which it must be said was probably less surprising than that of Adamson's, occurred in Salisbury in January 1986.

While attempting to overcome his addictions at Clouds House near East Knoyle, Phil Lynott of Thin Lizzy was taken into the city infirmary and sadly died there at the age of 36. He was suffering from pneumonia, heart failure, kidney malfunction and severe liver deterioration. For all his personal problems Lynott was a great talent and a proper rock'n'roll star: there really ought to be a blue plaque up there now.

Mitchener (keyboards, saxophone and vocals), Colin Maple (bass and vocals), Alan Young (guitar and vocals) and Dave Goddard (drums and percussion).

The aforementioned Gettysburg Address had formed following the teaming up of former members of punk bands The QTs and Kinetic NRG with a new vocalist.

Frogg: "Chris Walsh had teamed up with singer Steve Rushton and I invited myself to one of their rehearsals armed with a keyboard. I was invited to join and we recruited Andy Clements on drums and his brother Gary on bass. Rehearsals were at Britford Hall. During the winter the hall was like the inside of a fridge - so cold was it one day that we ripped all the parish meeting notes off the wall, smashed up some wooden chairs and proceeded to light a fire in the strategically placed grate. Little did we know that someone had long since blocked off the chimney resulting in the whole hall becoming like a pea-souper and the band almost choking to

Limited Edition — The Colin David Set

Initially I bought a guitar lead – one of those curly ones - wrapped it around the strap on my acoustic guitar and stood in front of the mirror, pretending I was in a band."

"I remember trying to make contact with some of the local musicians, like Ruth Jones, trying to pester them. Then I met Frogg and started pestering him to get into Gettysburg Address. He wasn't that keen initially because he didn't know me very well and I was a couple of years younger - but I persevered."

"I broke him down over a period of weeks and eventually Frogg and Chris Walsh relented. Steve Rushton was the singer and I was always impressed by how quickly he could come up with lyrics to the music that Frogg and Chris had written. Within a

GETTYSBURG ADDRESS - at the Coach & Horses

death! Somehow we managed to get away with it and continued rehearsing there for ages."

"Gettysburg Address gigged continuously around the south and although the band took on different personnel, Chris Walsh, Steve Rushton and myself remained at the helm. The band probably reached its peak with the line-up that included Jon Nicholas on drums and Mark 'Kenny' Kenchington on bass."

Mark Kenchington: "I got a guitar for Christmas when I was about ten. I was really keen on trying to learn all the theoretical side of playing so I took lessons – at the bottom of Wilton Road. I moved into being in bands but initially it was classical guitar."

"I used to go to the Arts Centre. It looked really cool – being on stage – and I thought 'I would like to do that'.

/ ENDLESS**BEAT**

"He had been at Abbey Road for a long time..."

GETTYSBURG ADDRESS - at Foxhole Studio, Bristol

couple of run throughs Steve would come up with a lyric, which I thought was amazing – real talent."

Gettysburg Address had one track, Dance Feat, released on a compilation album entitled Young Blood, but the band split soon after its release. Chris Walsh (now on bass) and Frogg Moody then became involved in The Processors, alongside former Fairlane guitarist James Ferguson and the teenaged Baker sisters Karen and Sarah on vocals.

The Processors were the first band to be featured in the Salisbury Journal Soundtracks column, with a photograph taken in the suitably state of the art Castle Street offices of UK Provident (now Friends Provident). The concept for the project revolved around electronic music and space travel and was conceived by Peter Bown, who wrote the lyrics – set to music by James Ferguson - but did not perform with the band.

James Ferguson: "Peter liked all of that. The computer thing was still new and the whole idea was space travel, and that kind of stuff appealed to him. I've got a very wide taste in music so I like something that gives me something new to think about. They were all three minute songs trying to be commercial, with musical hooks, and the lyrics had a real strong sense of form about them."

Peter Bown was a well respected name in the music industry and had a connection with The Beatles.

James Ferguson: "He had worked with The Beatles on a lot of stuff – it started around the Ticket To Ride time - he used to do most of the engineering. He had been at Abbey Road for a long time, working with Cliff Richard and a lot of classical music. In George Martin's book he says Peter was the top in his field."

Frogg: "The band gigged around the Salisbury area and recorded a selection of songs at Peter's home studio in London. This recording took place over a weekend and the father of Karen and Sarah, Roger Baker - who

THE PROCESSORS - left to right: Karen Baker, Frogg Moody, James Ferguson, Chris Walsh and Sarah Baker

ENDLESS BEAT

"John Peel played it a few times – he really liked it..."

had the Anchor and Hope in Winchester Street - must have trusted us, because Sarah was only fourteen and Karen sixteen!"

"Peter's studio consisted of recording equipment that had been discarded over the years from Abbey Road and looked like something from a Buck Rogers movie! There were wires everywhere and large dials which didn't really do anything – Chris and I had the girls in hysterics as we pulled wires out all over the place whilst the recording continued completely unhampered! The recording wasn't too bad and Peter thought we had a chance of hitting the charts, although his contacts probably had other ideas….."

James Ferguson: "It had the most going for it than anybody I have ever worked with. We had a good sound – up to date with what was going on at the time – and Peter had connections with the industry. When the girls came in that added another dimension to it.

It seemed to snowball along for a while but we never did any London gigs or things like that. I think Peter did ask some people to come down and see us, but I don't think anyone ever did, so it just didn't take off."

The Processors eventually stalled having to some extent become sidelined by another project.

Frogg: "The Processors provided all the backing music for a community rock musical at Salisbury Arts Centre - Maria Martin and The Red Barn. This involved a large cast and took months of rehearsals. The show was a great success but, for The Processors, it was the straw that broke the camel's back – one rehearsal too many."

Despite being decidedly non-new wave, Grandma Moses were featured in Vague and continued performing into the eighties, as well as entering into the spirit of the times with a self-released EP.

Tom Thatcher: "A good gig we played was up at the High Post Hotel. It was crowded with disco lovers and we thought we were going to die a complete death. Andy Golden is famous as the loudest drummer on the planet. I was crawling around on the floor because the PA wouldn't work and just as I went past the snare he went 'cushhhh' – I bit my tongue so hard that I've still got a chunk out of it!"

Andy Golden: "The DJ at the end said 'Thank you very much, but you would like one more wouldn't you?' and the whole place erupted."

Tom Thatcher: "We ended up with a version of Tom Rush's I've Lost My Driving Wheel, which Brad had arranged and onto which I tagged the last bit of Hey Jude - na na na na na na na etc."

"The EP was recorded in Phoenix Studios in

THE PROCESSORS - at The Boot, Shipton Bellinger

MICRO CHOP

ELECTRONIC space popsters Micro-Chip and The Processors have cancelled their proposed gig at Salisbury Arts Centre on August 26 and are concentrating on studio work for the time being.

There's consolation for fans, however, in the form of a tape of their songs, obtainable from the arts centre, price £3.

James Ferguson, the guitarist, is playing live with the Peter Mason Band as well as working at EMI's Abbey Road Studio with chief recording engineer Hazelmere, who co-wrote many of the Processors songs.

Frogg (keyboards) and Chris Walsh (bass) of course have their other band, Gettysburg Address, who often play gigs in the Salisbury area.

Still, it's a shame we won't be seeing the Processors for a while.

160

Euston and Pickwick Studios in Corsham. With that same line-up we got two tracks on a sampler called Influx One on Zygo Records, which actually sold quite well – I got my first royalty cheques."

"I thought the songs were good enough to risk a bit of a punt, so I got the tapes properly mastered. We had the single pressed ourselves, got the cover designed by a very good artist called Ray Smith – we also had t-shirts and posters and such like. We sold just under a thousand copies, so it made a heck of a lot more than we spent on it. It gave us quite good publicity actually, John Peel played it a few times – he really liked it - and he also played the tracks from the Zygo album."

Despite the promise of their recordings, Grandma Moses eventually split in around 1984.

Tom Thatcher and Andrew 'Brad' Bradbury

Andy Golden: "I left because I got a full-time job in London. It carried on for a bit with Chris Williams. The music changed then – it was a bit more punky - but I didn't leave because of the band, I left because of the job."

"I suppose the decision was made for me to not do music anymore - I was working on a newspaper [the Sunday Mirror] and the news editor took me out for lunch, to get to know each other. He said 'What are your hobbies?' and I said 'I like playing drums'. He said 'I used to be a drummer as well – my drums are up in the attic. Are you still playing?' I said 'Yeah, and I hope to keep on doing it'. He said 'You won't anymore, because on this paper we work 24 hours a day, 7 days a week, 52 weeks a year'."

"The nice thing was I met him some twenty years later and reminded him of the conversation. He said 'Oh yeah, when you join a paper like that you have to give it up' and I said 'Well, I have made a couple of albums and done some tours since then'."

During the early eighties Andy also played with Britz, alongside Lynden Williams (vocals), Bob Cooke (guitar), Yan Webber (guitar) and Henk Leerink (bass).

Yan Webber: "We were frightfully avant-garde. We did the Greyhound at Wilton once and Lynden came down covered in a sheet, said 'I don't want to see anybody tonight' and sang the whole evening covered in the sheet. I also made my own FM radio transmitter - when we were in the dressing room at the Greyhound I started playing chords, which came through on my amp. This absolutely shocked the crowd - they had never seen anything like this before and we came downstairs on to the stage while I was playing."

"I remember doing a song Lynden wrote called Polaroids - with this one I was probably at my most avant-garde. I would put my guitar on top of my amp and jam plectrums in all my strings except the top E and bottom E. They would burst into feedback and give this horrible droning E while everybody else played – wearing

161

ENDLESS BEAT

"Kerry was a sort of 'Hell's Angel with a hairdryer' type..."

polaroids of course. I would sit cross-legged on the floor surrounded by my effects pedals and beat them with my fist to change the sound in time with the music."

Until joining Britz, Yan had been a reluctant song writer.

Yan Webber: "I realised the joy of going your own path and writing your own stuff. To me the finest times were when we were playing in the Cathedral Hotel and everybody used to dance on the tables singing the songs that

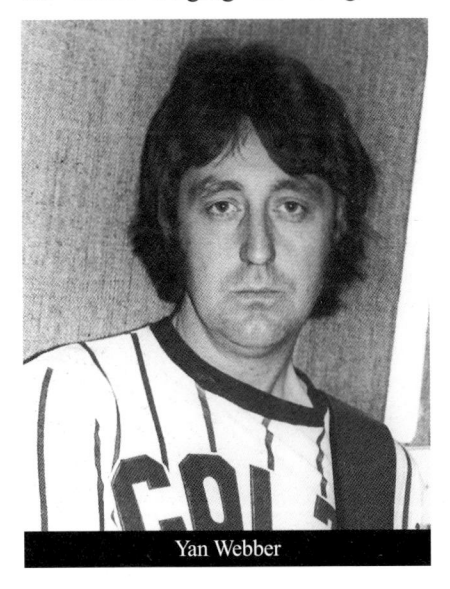

Yan Webber

Lynden had written. That's when I started to realise we were painting the sound, and started to enjoy the process of making music rather than skimming across the surface and just playing it."

Ex-Kitchens vocalist Duncan Fulton tried his hand at some different musical styles, before returning to a more standard set-up.

Duncan Fulton: "Andrew [Lovelock] and I continued playing together. We got Nick Marchant in – he played bass and I went on to guitar. We were called The Menthol Jaggers and were making more experimental music – a bit pretentious you know? We were trying to make music sound like groups of secretaries on typewriters – some songs like that."

"That was short lived. Then Andrew retired from the music business so he was off the scene. We got Big House together with Colin Holton on bass, Jon Nicholas on drums and Tim Collinson and Ruth Jones on sax."

"That was a good band. I wrote solo and with Nick. You could dance to a lot of the stuff - that was the idea – we were going a bit cooler with a nice brass section. Nick was a fantastic guitar player. Colin was brilliant - doing slap bass. Often they used to get into grooves – Jon Nicholas is easily the best drummer of all time in Salisbury I would say. That went for a few years but never really took off."

"After Big House I got back together with Sprog. I wrote all the lyrics, Sprog came up with the music and the melodies. He's a great composer Sprogger - that's where he discovered his style. I used to encourage him in certain directions."

Duncan and Sprog's new band was named Red Book. The initial line up was completed by Kerry Waite on rhythm guitar and Robert Gridge on drums. Kerry was younger than the band's leaders and had never previously played in a formal band, but he was certainly not lacking in confidence.

Kerry Waite: "One day a friend of mine, John Cliff, said 'This new band are looking for another guitarist. Sprog Ford and Duncan Fulton are going to be in the Star this afternoon - why don't you go and speak to them?' So I rushed in on my bike, walked into the Star and said 'Hi, I'm Kerry. I hear you're looking for a guitar player – I'm the one'. I think Duncan said 'Oh…are you? Well, you had better have a couple of auditions'. I turned up and played and they accepted me then and there."

"I was a very eager young man and very confident about what I could do. I had spent the time since I was about thirteen really getting into rock music and by the time I was fourteen or fifteen I was playing AC/DC stuff. By that point I was thinking 'Well, whose gonna get higher than AC/DC? If I can play their riffs then I'm good enough' [laughs] – so I was cocky."

"We did about three months rehearsing and the material was all Andy and Duncan's – I was the new boy. February '84 at the Saddle Rooms was my first ever gig and that went really well. Then Robert Gridge left – he had a job as a tennis coach. My friend from school, Jim Blackwell, came for a jam audition and the others accepted him warmly."

Duncan Fulton: "Kerry was a sort of 'Hell's Angel with a hairdryer' type – he was big, but a peaceful guy. Him and Jimmy were tight – they went to school together. Jimmy was aggressive the way he played, but right on time, great to play with."

In response, Kerry recalls how he and Jimmy described Duncan: "Yeah, we had quite a partnership - he was known as 'the coat hanger with a ginger wig…' It was great working with Duncan and Sprog. They were much more experienced and it was all stuff they had written, so right from the beginning I had the idea of creating – it was nothing to do with cover versions. Duncan said 'If you've got any material just come around with it. If we think it's good enough we'll use it'."

Duncan Fulton and Caroline Holt-Keen

"My first two pieces he said 'Yeah that's good - just keep working on what you're doing'. The third one he said 'That's great' and it ended up being titled Thin White Life - Duncan was the lyricist and I wrote the music. That went down well. It's a mind game if you like - if you actually perform publicly something you have done you wait for the reaction, and if the public like it that's quite pleasing - so that psychologically encouraged me that what I was doing was acceptable."

"Red Book developed really well. We had an interview on Bournemouth radio and there was always fresh material and lots of gigs - everything seemed fine. Then Duncan said 'Maybe we could move up by getting a front woman'. Duncan was in touch with Caroline Holt-Keen and brought her along for a jam - I don't think she needed an audition because we knew what she could do. It fixed really quickly - she enjoyed what we were doing and we enjoyed what she was doing, so we were very quick of accepting one another. Then Duncan came up with a new name - Dark Star."

Duncan Fulton: "We got Caroline as lead singer. She was nineteen or something at the time, beautiful looking. She had a public school accent – quite posh and a great singer, really powerful – much better than most female singers…better than any singer. It's a shame and a waste that she didn't become more well-known really."

Kerry Waite: "Caroline was very fast to learn – eager and enthusiastic.

ENDLESS BEAT

"I went back and told the band she wasn't coming back."

You get a new vibe when a lady comes into a rock band so things were different. Caroline was a great pleasure to work with - fantastic voice and a very pretty girl. She had an edge to be professional, a very healthy attitude, full commitment to the band, very dedicated and a gem to work with. She could immediately communicate with the audience - there was no separation at all - she had great movement on stage and her voice was just as good as if she had spent a week in a studio – she didn't lose anything. A perfect live performer and a great artist – it's a great shame that she didn't get somewhere."

"There was always new material, nearly every week, and lots of songs we would only play for a month. I was doing more stuff working with Duncan, trying to get my elements in of what I wanted to do with riffs, and that was working very well with Caroline. It was a very active band that was going really well – lots of gigs, lots of support. The Journal was always giving us good write-ups and had a good photographer – everybody was really helping us."

"After a period I thought 'Well, playing in the south is alright but London is the way I see would be a good place to go'. The others didn't seem over eager so I went up on my own and got us a couple of gigs. We had coach support, which was fantastic – I'm grateful for that – I didn't think about that at the time because it just happens…you don't reflect until years later."

"We did some recording at Arny's Shack. We did five songs in one afternoon - very quickly – one soundcheck then through the songs

DARK STAR - left to right: Duncan Fulton, Jimmy Blackwell, Caroline Holt-Keen, Kerry Waite and Sprog Ford

bang, bang, bang. Duncan sent the tape to different people and got some feedback – promises that people would be turning up at such and such a place but to our disappointment they didn't, but it was just all starting – having the confidence to send stuff and believing there may be an interest that people could believe we were worth something."

Duncan Fulton: "We had a bit of record company interest from RCA. I was up in Scotland with my father, on a holiday. I phoned Jim's mother and she said these guys from RCA had been on the blower. They had heard our demo tape and were really interested, so we arranged a gig in London. We brought a coach up and it was a good night, but the guy didn't turn up."

Kerry Waite: "Unfortunately there was a band dispute and Caroline decided she was going to leave. We were all very disappointed and I personally went to speak to her to try and resolve what had happened, but she seemed adamant that she didn't want to come back with the existing line up. I had to accept that so I went back and told the band she wasn't coming back. We did a few gigs as a four piece without her but then I lost interest – it felt like going backwards really. Jim was quite happy to leave and Duncan and Sprog went their way with their original partnership and that sadly was the end of Dark Star."

Another band rising from the ashes of a Salisbury punk band was the short-lived Marseilles Frame, formed by ex-QT Mike Vickers.

Mike Vickers: "Things had moved on from punk to new romance – the Spandau Ballets and Duran Durans and I just changed with it. I had pleated trousers and the shirts, long hair down one side and short up the other and all that. In Marseilles there was this guy stealing all these paintings and I just thought…paintings… frame… We started adding a bit of French into our songs. Mark Sheldon - a brilliant guy, great guitar player, keyboard player and songwriter wrote Valentine and Guillotine."

"Mark's dad paid for us to go to Arny's Shack, I think it cost about £400. Tony Arnold really took a liking to us and wanted to introduce our stuff to Sting, but I think they [The Police] were too busy doing their own thing. Mark had done an interview to join the RAF and train to be a pilot. Time was running out and though we had interviews with Virgin and lots of other labels he said 'If nothing definite comes up I've got to choose' and obviously the sound bet was to go in the RAF."

Mike's next band would be Nosferatu, with Graeme Pinder (guitar), Ray Goodge (guitar), Graham Rose (bass) and Nigel Emm (drums). Ray Goodge was later replaced by Ray Dismore - formerly of Genghis Khan. The band played only original

MARSEILLES FRAME

ENDLESS BEAT

"'Yeah, that's a good idea – I'll do that', because I liked writing."

material including Prince of Darkness and Realms of Reality. Their gigs included the King and Bishop, Coach and Horses, Fisherton Arms, the Saddle Rooms, Oscars at Longleat and venues in Southampton and Bournemouth.

In a 1983 review from the Salisbury Journal entitled 'Masters Of Darkness', Nosferatu were described as emerging to be 'one of Salisbury's prime pub crowd pullers, seemingly made to measure to go down well with a pint or two and add a little atmosphere to our local hostelries'. Nosferatu were among the many local bands benefiting from the Journal photographer's innovative sense of fun.

Roger Elliott: "I photographed Nosferatu in the churchyard of St Martin's - standing around the graves holding candles. We would go to great lengths and spend ages doing shoots. I remember shooting The Kitchens sitting in a bath once – that was one of the strangest ones. Bands used to love it. Everybody used to throw in ideas and it would take on a life of its own. They would start enjoying themselves so you would get some great shots. My usual mode of operation was to just let people do what they do naturally."

The Journal's music coverage had taken a turn for the better since the introduction of the new Soundtracks column, written by Roger's wife Penny. The paper previously had a column reviewing major album releases, but hadn't really covered the local scene until the early eighties when the editor, Gareth Weekes, was bombarded with letters from Genghis Khan fans, as explained in Chapter Five.

Roger Elliott: "We had a friend, Sandra Jones, who worked at the Journal and lived in our village. She became good friends with Penny and encouraged her to write – she gave her a few reviews to do, which Gareth liked."

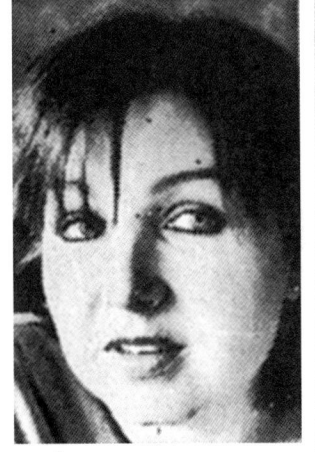

Penny Elliott: "We knew a lot of people in Salisbury bands and had the idea to start a column. Roger was the one who pushed and I was the one who said 'Yeah, that's a good idea – I'll do that', because I liked writing. Gareth was very forward thinking and progressive and said 'We'll give it a go'."

"We contacted a few local bands we knew, put an advert in for anyone that wanted to contact us and took it from there. I would do one big piece, Roger would do record reviews, I went to a local independent record shop to

6: Flowers in a Desert

ENDLESS BEAT

"... looking back, maybe I thought that was the end of that."

get their top ten for the week and also to a chain, like WH Smiths - who would also give me a chart - and anyone who wanted to advertise their gigs or anything else could ring or drop stuff off at the Journal. I was allocated roughly half a page. I can't remember being seriously cut down or subbed, although sometimes they would maybe leave out one of the charts."

"Local bands would contact me and I would meet them in various drinking establishments around Salisbury. I would scribble on pieces of paper and we would probably have a few drinks, and out of that would come some semblance of an interview, a history of the band, what they were planning to do, roughly what sort of music they played, whether they had any recording ambitions and where they were playing."

"I covered the so called 'straight' music scene as well, so bands that had been around for years and years suddenly discovered they could get a nice bit of publicity. These were the bands that played at working men's clubs – Peter Pod and The Peas and bands like that."

"Once the column got known about I had several people who supported me a lot. Richard Hayward was in publicity at the Arts Centre – he was the brother of Justin Hayward from The Moody Blues. Richard was fantastic and when he was trying to launch young bands, Soundtracks got involved. I remember one night when I was dragged up on stage - which is not my scene at all - and him saying I had done my bit to help the Salisbury music scene and needed a round of applause…which was horrible [laughs]."

Roger Elliott: "Me and Pen suddenly found ourselves at the heart of a very healthy music scene. I think there was only one week when we actually invented a band – most of the time there was something to actually write about. We got very ambitious – we would go further afield. Then there was a girl who put a lot of things on at Bournemouth Town Hall and we used to go down and see people like Lee Perry, Cabaret Voltaire and The Fall."

Among those bands exploring the opportunities offered through mixing a classic pop sound with a new wave edge were Ambulance Beat, with Chris Binns (guitar), Pete Leyland (bass) and Steve Barker (drums) - fronted by Neil Dalziel.

Chris Binns moved to Salisbury in 1984 to work for Naim Audio. He had previously worked as a tea boy in Island studios and for

Virgin at The Manor where he did "anything and everything - except drug running - the Manor had a special department for that", and then with Martin Hannett and for music agent Nick Hamilton. After leaving Naim he formed Primary Acoustics, specialising in the design of studio monitors and associated electronics.

Neil Dalziel: "After Identity Crisis finished, in about 1980, I didn't do much band-wise for three or four years. I did a few solo gigs and, looking back, maybe I thought that was the end of that."

"I first met Chris around '84 or '85. In the early days we were rehearsing with Nigel Finn and Jim Blackwell above the hairdressers in Fisherton Street – Jim's Mum's. Musically it was okay, but there were obviously some differences between those two on one hand and Chris and I on the other – I think they found us a bit childish actually. Ambulance Beat I thought was a really good band with good songs, but was kind of kicking against what was prevalent – horrible synthetic drums and eighties production. Thank God for The Smiths!"

Colin Crook and Johnny Fellows of new wave band Between The Eyes joined forces with some older musicians in another power pop styled project, Bangkok.

Johnny Fellows: "I knew Reg Maggs socially and knew he was a very good drummer. He knew Chris Lucas and suggested we got together. Chris couldn't put in the amount of hours we were and we got Simon Viney in. We did a lot of power pop with rocky stuff which the majority we ended up writing ourselves."

"We played in places like

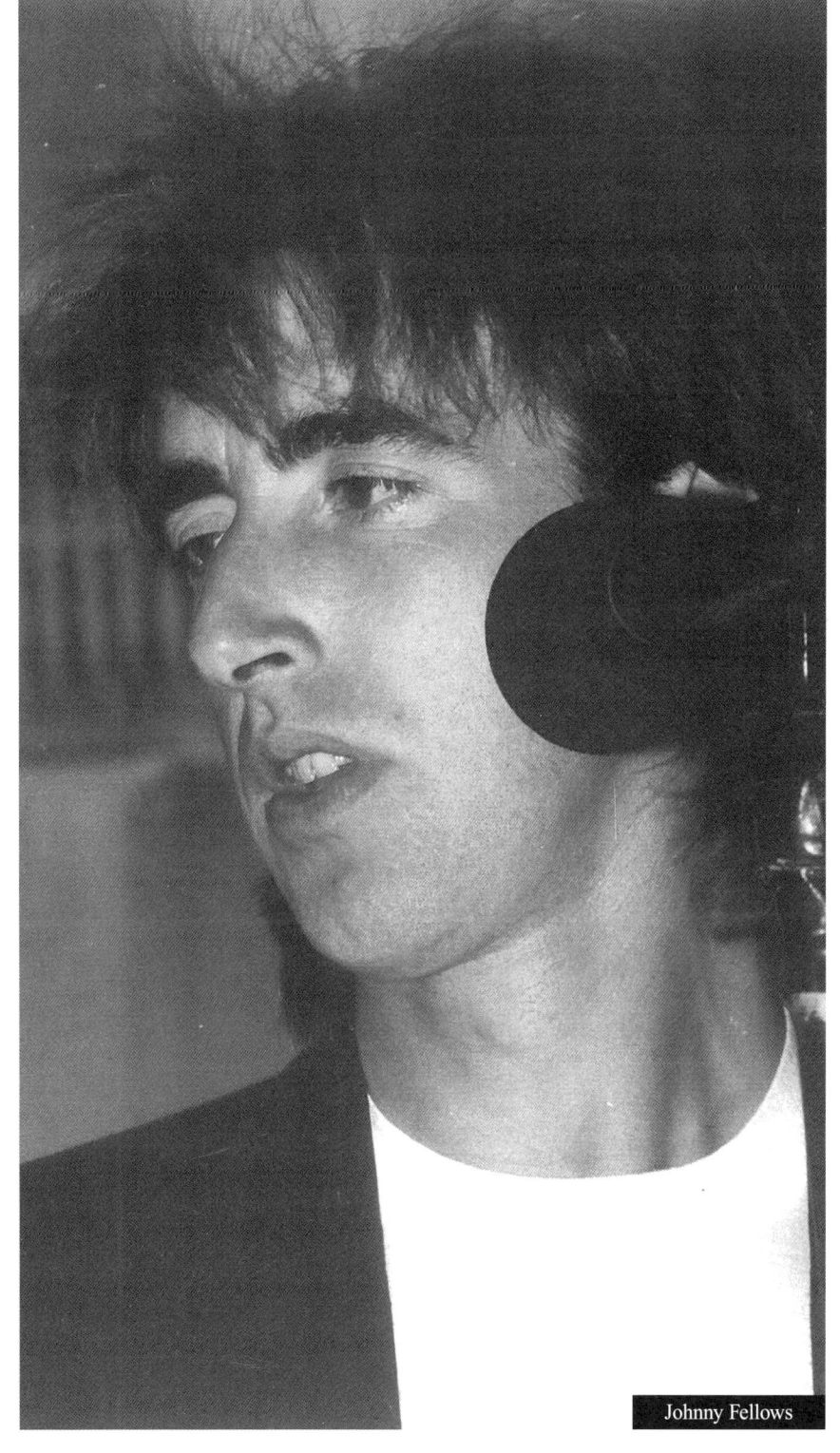

Johnny Fellows

ENDLESS BEAT

"This is where it gets a bit incestuous."

Bournemouth, Southampton, Basingstoke Magnums. We bought a van, which was an old Gibbs Mew transit - falling apart but we could just about get everything in there - that lasted for a few miles."

Illness then forced Johnny to separate from his long-term musical partner: "Colin - in his mid-twenties - had a stroke, which was unbelievable. A bloke who didn't smoke and rarely drank, was fit and ate pretty well – it was bizarre. Because of that he had a problem with coordination. It was quite gut wrenching for him. He gave up for quite a while after that."

"We formed Money For Guns. Colin Gray used to be the guitarist with ID Crisis. Colin knew Jon Stone – a really good drummer. Simon Viney was the bass player from Bangkok and Mickey Norris was a friend of Simon's."

"We were once compared to Talk Talk, which I thought was a pretty good reference point. It was pretty much all our own stuff - any covers we did would be our favourites that people didn't know, so we could pass them off as our own. It was the first band I had been in with keyboards – it had gone from the power-poppy sort of stuff to a more mature sound. I thought we had some good original stuff."

"With Bangkok we were quite a rocky sort of band and I'm not sure my voice really lent itself well to that type of music - I didn't have a rock n roll scream. It was more sort of melodious, so when we started Money For Guns there was a conscious effort on my part not to sing like a 'rock' singer."

After Money For Guns folded in the mid-eighties, various members found their way into Don't Ask, along side Matt West on guitar, Mike 'Spike' Pizing on keyboards, Simon 'Min' Viney on bass and drummer Graham Hughes.

Johnny Fellows: "This is where it gets a bit incestuous. Mickey used to be in Don't Ask as well as Money For Guns. Simon was playing for us and then joined as well - there were two bands on the go at the same time with two mutual personnel. I was without a band for quite a while then one day Min came round and said 'We're sort of mix and matching on vocals. How

DON'T ASK - left to right: Simon 'Min' Viney, Mike 'Spike' Pizing, Johnny Fellows, Tim Collinson, Matt West and Graham Hughes.

do you fancy doing it?' So I started singing with them."

"The majority was self-written by Hughesy – and Matt was writing a lot. What I really loved was for once it wasn't 'my' band. I'm not saying I was carrying the other bands, but if it's down to you to produce the material then every rehearsal you get a little bit 'Oh God, we've still got the same songs we had six months ago', but joining a band where I've got to learn all their material was brilliant. I could contribute to new stuff but going over their old stuff for them was a bit of a refresher - it gave it a bit of a kick. What gave us a real big lift was Tim Collinson joined. He was playing sax but he was a really strong songwriter as well and brought a lot of new songs to the band."

"We played a lot all over the place. At the Whitgift Centre in Croydon we probably played to about 10,000 people over the course of three hours – people that were walking through the shopping centre…most of them running to get out of the way of the hideous noise! Matt's dad knew somebody there and we drove our van into this underground car park, came up in a lift, hooked all our gear across to the stage, set up and played."

"We played a lot in Southampton. At the time Hughesy was a sales rep, which was one brilliant thing we never had in the other bands. He would take tapes around and drop them off in pubs while he was working. It generated so much more work in places we had never even heard of. To get gigs outside Salisbury you had to send a tape and you knew that would be one of a thousand. So we decided the best thing was to make a tape and take them round – because when they are face to face it's more difficult to say no."

"A school friend of Hughesy's was at Keele University doing a music degree. They had a studio up there, so one time when all the students were away we went up for a weekend and recorded a tape. It was the first time we had ever seen a Fairlight computer, so our tape was totally overblown with these huge amounts of horns and strings. A total mess really I suppose but at the time we thought 'Wow - this is mega production'."

One of Salisbury's most popular live acts of the early eighties was Un Deux Twang! The band's seven piece line up - Candy Hill (vocals and keyboards), Nikki Kozak (vocals), Phil Hill (vocals and guitar), Malcolm Wilkinson (guitar), Colin Holton (bass), Neil Nicholson (trumpet and saxophone) and Alex Mundy (drums) – certainly offered something different

UN DEUX TWANG - relaxing!

ENDLESS BEAT

"They became a sort of burlesque thing, with a touch of the Alex Harvey's thrown in."

UN DEUX TWANG - left to right: Malcolm Wilkinson, Nikki Kozak, Phil Hill, Alex Mundy, Colin Holton and Candy Hill

6: **Flowers in a Desert**

to local fans.

Roger Elliott: "They became a sort of burlesque thing, with a touch of the Alex Harvey's thrown in - Phil Hill had that sort of striped t-shirt severe look about him. They were wonderful."

Un Deux Twang! Also had a great reputation in the music community for their musicianship, professionalism, polished sound and live act.

Alex Mundy: "Playing with this band upped my game. I looked up to Phil Hill, whose band it was along with his wife Candy. Phil wrote most of the songs - he was like a big brother to me - and obviously playing with Colin Holton was great because going back to the QTs days Frogg [Moody] and Colin were musical heroes. I first met Malcolm Wilkinson playing in Twang. He was a very accomplished player and probably raised the standard a bit. He'd not been in a band before, but nothing floored him."

Some professionals were not however convinced of the band's potential.

Alex Mundy: "We did make a couple of recordings down at Arny's Shack, which was a good experience, and I'll never forget one comment that Tony Arnold made when we were recording there. Nikki Kozak was saying 'We're gonna be the next big thing' and stuff like that. He obviously wasn't very diplomatic, and said to her 'Look love, it's no good thinking you look like a Porsche when in fact you look more like a Ford Cortina!'"

The band's sense of personal fun sometimes impacted on their performances.

Alex Mundy: "There was a really good camaraderie, and I remember one gig at the Fleece and Firkin in Bristol. Colin and I had a bit too much

ENDLESS BEAT

"...fifteen teenage girls are rushing towards us, screaming..."

to drink, and his guitar strap came off and his bass fell onto the floor, and I did a drum roll, missed the floor tom-tom and also fell onto the floor. So the rhythm section was completely out of it – we ended up in the audience dancing and the band carried on without us. We had to get back home to Salisbury that night, as we were playing in Dingwalls in London the next day."

Although very popular, Un Deux Twang! provoked comment in some quarters for their unabashed stage show where, among other things, Candy Hill would perform a number called The Sadist, and strip down to a leather corset for another entitled Anna Rexsick.

Writing in the Salisbury Journal, Penny Elliott was particularly disappointed that 'as they progress musically, their cruder element is also increasing, I had hoped to see the reverse'.

Nikki Kozak

Penny thought anyone 'sympathetic to the advancement of women in society' would find the band 'an embarrassment', although punters who enjoyed 'a full-blooded male thrill at whoever's expense' would have 'a good laugh'.

The band folded after Phil Hill tragically took his own life in September 1984.

Dave Taylor: "The previous weekend we had been to a party at Broad Chalke. It wasn't an organised gig but various people turned up and played, and I found myself at one o'clock in the morning, with Phil, playing guitar. He had this beautiful white guitar – made for him by Nick Marchant. He said he was thinking of selling it and I arranged to meet him for a drink in the Pheasant on the following Friday."

"We both turned up, started talking about this guitar and I saw nothing at all – bearing in mind this is nine o'clock of the evening – he was perfectly calm, totally in control. He said he was going to the Arts Centre to see Jonathan Hyams. Apparently Jonathan wasn't there, but he borrowed some gaffa tape off John Curry and then drove off and did what he did – up under the railway arch near Petersfinger. When I found out I just couldn't believe it."

Alex Mundy: "We were in the middle of doing a recording and Nikki had to go down and finish the vocals after Phil had died, so that was pretty traumatic for her. He wrote most of the songs and that band was based around him and Candy. Nikki was keen to try and do something else in a folky vein, but I wasn't interested."

In an affectionate tribute, published in Due South, Penny Elliott remembered Phil Hill as 'an artist, devoted dad, musician and prolific wordsmith' but above all as 'a one-off, irreplaceable, light years away from any human production line'.

Another Salisbury band trying to introduce a fresh approach were Afro Dizzy Acts, formed by Arts Centre Director Jonathan Hyams.

Nick Heron: "Jonathan had a deep love of African music. This was going back to the days before anyone really had heard of world music. I'm not sure even if that term had been coined back then."

"He decided it might be fun for a few of us to get together and try and play some of this music. I'm not sure if at the time he ever thought we would go out and gig it. After a few faltering starts the band got together and consisted of two very good guitarists - Jonathan and Charlie Davis, and Julie - Jonathan's then wife - on sax, Mike on trumpet, Andi Glashier on keyboards, Dave Marsh on drums and me on bass."

Dave Taylor: "Jonathan was a fairly decent guitar player – he had a really nice looking Les Paul. He had recently heard and gone bananas about African music – particularly the guitar style. I liked listening to it but had no desire to play it. My friend, Charlie Davis, was an exceptionally talented guitar player. The two of them got together and Jonathan introduced Charlie to African music – and they decided to put a band together."

"I worked with Charlie every day so I knew about the progress of the band. I was beginning to like the music a bit. Pretty soon they got rid of the trumpet player, who was fairly limited, and the keyboard player, because they wanted a more guitar orientated sound. They wanted another guitar - so the two of them could interweave the lead parts. That's why I was brought in, but even that wasn't enough because then they brought Malcolm Wilkinson in – so there were four guitars."

Nick Heron: "A bunch of mostly middle class white people went off and played a style of black music that most people had never heard of back then. We did quite a few gigs and had a lot of fun. Because we were nowhere near as good as the music we were copying we had to do it with a sense of irony. Lots of people got the joke and enjoyed it for that reason."

"Then, for me, the worst thing happened - some of the band started to take it really seriously. I really wasn't good enough to play at that level, but more to the point I didn't want to play that sort of music unless it was a bit tongue in cheek. It was much better coming from the guys who actually were black and steeped in the culture of that type of music in the way that we never could or should. The band underwent a lot of changes and I was one of the ones to leave."

Before Dave Taylor joined, Afro Dizzy Acts had released a single. It was while playing with the band that he experienced his closest brush with stardom.

Dave Taylor: "I always considered myself peripheral – I was sort of eighteenth guitarist really - but we went up to Capital Radio to do a session. The curious thing was, Charlie is about four foot two and looks like a bank clerk - and I certainly don't look much at all! We went out for a fag, turned and looked up the road and fifteen teenage girls are rushing towards us, screaming, we looked the other way to see who they were following…and there was nobody else…it was us! So we set off running – we stopped and these girls stopped and we said 'What are you chasing us for?' and they said 'We thought you were Spandau Ballet!' [laughs – loudly] Apparently they were doing a session somewhere else in the building!"

"When it was broadcast the guy said 'Of all the English bands that have tried to do African music, this is the best yet'. I think guitar-wisc he was right because Jonathan and Charlie were spot on, and Tim Collinson's sax worked, but it's the singing – it just wasn't right. I made myself very unpopular once because we were talking about this and I said 'To me it's a rhythmic music - like a chant – and you sing it melodically'."

The early eighties also saw the rise of a second wave of punk bands.

Thick Dick and The Green'eds had formed at Salisbury College in the winter of 1979 and initially comprised Jeff Watkins (vocals), Richard Grocott (guitar), Andy Murphy (drums and keyboards), Dave Notley (bass) and Carl Hutson (drums). Later members included Jim Clay and Andy Moores.

They cited their influences as cider, lardy cake, The Stupid Babies, John Peel and Suttons 30p bargain record bin, and had ambitions to be The Undertones crossed with the

ENDLESS BEAT

"Within three or four weeks we were supporting Chelsea at the college."

Damned. The Green'eds' first gig took place close to Christmas and complimentary mince pies were handed out, which the audience naturally used as ammunition to bombard the band with.

Despite their 'punk joke' name and somewhat tongue in cheek approach the band stayed together for a lengthy period. Their live highlights included gigs at The Grange, Arts Centre and City Hall - all of which featured excessive use of crazy foam.

The band were runners up in Salisbury's 'Young Rock Bands' competition of 1985, where the Salisbury Journal described how 'four, or sometimes five, bouncing green haired monsters exhumed the ghost of Devo and spun it on a spit'. Their best loved song was I'm In Love With A Waste Disposal Unit and their proudest moment was a mention on the John Peel show. The Green'eds disbanded in 1988 but reformed in 1999 as 'Thick Dick and the Greenheads' – a subtle 'grown up' change - and released a ten track CD entitled Dum De Dum De Dumb.

Another band from the Point Of View generation, Last Orders, were formed from a mixture of street and art punks.

Colin Mundy: "I was into Slade and stuff at junior school. Then when punk came along that was it, I was hooked on music forever really. I think it was on my twelfth or thirteenth birthday, my girlfriend of the time bought me three records – The Skids' Into The Valley, Clash's English Civil War and one by The Cars - and from then on I collected seven inch singles all through my life."

"The first live band I went to see was the Buzzcocks, which was in '79. Myself and a couple of mates skived off school and got the bus down to Bournemouth, hung around all day and went to the gig. The band supporting them was Joy Division. I fainted because I was crushed down the front. There was quite a few parties where bands were playing, Alderbury Village Hall used to have a lot of bands and we went to the Arts Centre a lot, and up to The Grange."

"I was a bit in awe of some punks who were a couple of years above us. There were Westwood punks and Bishop's punks and there seemed to be a line through the middle: the arty ones and the street ones. There was a guy from Bishop's, Mark Palmer, and his cousin Dave Boyes, and they knew me from years ago – we used to play football together as kids. They said did I want to join a band and that was it really. I still can't play but it was the punk ethic wasn't it? - 'Just give it a go'. If you know a chord, then you're in the game basically."

In local terms Mark Palmer had a distinguished musical pedigree. In the sixties his father Dave had played bass with The Coasters and The Avengers. More recently his cousins Rob and Nick Boston had been with Genghis Khan and The Prams.

Mark Palmer: "My dad is the quietest man in the world and it wasn't until I read Hold Tight that I really understood about the bands he was in. When I was about fourteen or fifteen, for some reason I decided I wanted to be a bass guitarist, I didn't know why but now it turns out Dad was a bass guitarist. I picked up a bass for about fifteen quid, took it home and my dad picked it up and could play it! He taught be some basic twelve bar and riffs and it took off from there, but to this day Dad still doesn't talk about the bands he was in."

"Me and Dave Boyes, my other cousin, used to roadie for The Prams – these guys were playing at the Rock Garden, Dingwalls, Dublin Castle, Marquee…for me and Dave to actually be in these places… I also interviewed Rob for ZigZag – that was my first proper piece of journalism. I owe a hell of a lot to Rob."

"There was always an underground movement at Bishop's. There was a gang of us who were into the fringe of punk and new wave. Somehow we congregated together and a lot of us ended up doing music - essentially an excuse for us to play things like Stranglehold by The UK Subs and dissect that. We had a music teacher who enabled us to act with freedom as it were."

Colin Mundy: "There was myself, Mark, Dave and a drummer. Then the drummer left and they asked if I knew a drummer. I said 'No, but my, mate taps along to songs when we are

LAST ORDERS - left to right: Dave Boyes, Mark Palmer, Ian Hamilton and Colin Mundy

listening to them – The Angelic Upstarts and Stiff Little Fingers'. I brought him down to rehearsal and they said 'Yeah, he'll do'."

"Within three or four weeks we were supporting Chelsea at the college. That was fantastic and Ian [Hamilton], who had only just started playing the drums didn't even have a drum stool, so he just nicked one of the stools from the classrooms."

"We did some gigs down Bournemouth and Weymouth. The big thing in those days was to get a demo tape done – these days anyone can record a CD or download – in those days to get cassette done was a real achievement. We went down to a place in Somerset and recorded a tape."

Mark Palmer: "I think we were very arrogant, and in being arrogant I found we didn't really have contact with any other bands. So it was very much a do your own sort of thing. It depended on what me, Dave and Colin had been listening to. If we had been listening to UK Subs that week we would suddenly come up with a couple of tracks which we thought sounded like The UK Subs. In my dreams we sounded like The Clash - in reality we were a third rate UK Subs."

"Initially I was into Stiff Little Fingers, who to this day I still adore and go and see, but The Clash to me are the greatest rock and roll band ever - full stop. I have to thank Colin for that - Colin had the best record collection of all of us. The problem is you are never going to get a band like The Clash coming from a place like Salisbury. I remember walking around the back of the Gibbs Mew brewery[5] at the time of the Toxteth riots. There was this rumour going round there were going to be riots in Salisbury – any city that has a road going to nowhere deserves a riot - and we were gullible, or maybe arrogant, enough to think that was going to happen. I remember us waiting for this so we could write a song like White Riot, but it never happened."

Following a further change of drummer, Last Orders became Obvious Action.

Mark Palmer: "We felt we had gone as far as we could go with that sort of UK Subs/Clash/Stiff Little Fingers sound. We were listening to bands a bit more like Big Country and 999. I think they experimented a bit more musically - and we tried to. We had this big backdrop with a big soviet red star with 'Obvious Action' painted over the front."

Colin Mundy: "We got rid of Ian, because he had his limitations, and got Steve Christey. He lived at Nomansland and his mum and dad had a massive garage, which was always handy. He was a really good drummer but too technical – putting in fills all over the place – it was difficult keeping him to 4/4."

Steve Christey: "I got my first drum kit from an uncle – cleaning out the shed, usual thing. I took lessons from various people - still really naïve, thinking I knew everything - and from the age of sixteen I started getting involved with the Salisbury music scene. My parents were very supportive because it's horrific listening to a drummer first starting – it really is!"

"I was quite flamboyant. I think the thing is that when you're young you think bigger is better [laughs]. I was really into just trying out different things, bringing all sorts of percussion into the kit. I would say looking back I was a fair drummer but improved a lot through working with musicians."

Mark Palmer: "Steve Christey was a big Duran Duran fan. There was a song we did called Problems, which was almost the same chords as Girls

ENDLESS BEAT

"Everything we did was always after... in the wake."

On Film. We broke into that at one gig and Steve thought it was fantastic… but normal service was soon resumed."

Colin Mundy: "I remember practicing at Sarum 76 – we always practiced in the kitchen rather than the main hall because the acoustics were dire. It makes me think that bands these days have it so easy for rehearsals – if you're a kid in a band you just ring up Grosvenor House: 'Yeah, yeah, come along, we've got a room for you, all the amps are there'. Back in the old days you would have to go to Britford Hall and collect the key and take it back, and it was freezing cold…at Sarum 76, practicing in the kitchen, you could turn the cookers on to keep your fingers warmer."

Mark Palmer: "My mum was involved in running Sarum 76 and me and Dave Boyes were the cleaners. It was set up by some sort of charity for use by the community. It was cheap – even cheaper for us because we used to rehearse there for nothing – not in the big hall because the sound was awful, but in the kitchen."

"It was also important for us because there was the infamous gig when The Mental played there and wrecked the place. Me and Dave got the gig to redecorate it and the twenty five quid I got enabled me to get this WEM 50 watt bass amp from Kingfisher Music[6]. There were these two guys - they've probably been forgotten in punk history in Salisbury - Vince and Tony Clayden from Downton. They got The Mental to play…in punk rock circles in Salisbury that is as infamous a gig as was Adam and The Ants."

Colin Mundy: "One of our big gigs was supporting New Model Army at the College. They had a bit of a reputation so we were a bit cautious, but we went down okay. We did some tapes and loads of gigs. We did a couple of cover versions but I have always been in bands that predominantly used our own material. In Last Orders it was Mark and Dave writing, but as we progressed into Obvious Action I started putting a few ideas in – I would hear a riff and think 'Yeah, I could rip that off' and put it in to my own song."

"Nick Shirfield came in on bass, Mark went on to guitar and Dave concentrated on vocals. Then Dave left – I think he was going on to a job somewhere - and Mark took over on vocals. Then Nick went on to Don't Feed The Animals, Kev Barnes came in on bass and Russ Whatley came in on drums. We became a bit more hardcore - like Discharge and GBH and all that kind of stuff - veering away from the poppier stuff. It was the

OBVIOUS ACTION - left to right: Russ Whatley, Colin Mundy, Kev Barnes and Steve Marlowe

times, loads of new labels were springing up - No Future, Secret Records - so we were getting into that more."

Focussing on following the latest punk trends perhaps resulted in a lack of originality in Obvious Action's material.

Mark Palmer: "Everything we did was always after…in the wake. Essentially we were flogging a dead horse. The problem me and Colin had - we ended up writing most of the music – was whatever band we had just been listening to we tried to replicate. As such there was no originality, but we were arrogant enough to think we could get away with it."

"Penny [Elliott] wrote an unfavourable review of us saying we were trying to sound like The Clash and Stiff Little Fingers. It wasn't helpful and we were a bit upset because we wanted a hand up – but what she wrote was the truth. A few of our friends wrote in to complain and the next week she issued an apology – in some ways she shouldn't have done."

"The Journal interviewed me and I was moaning that we were new and different and all the other bands consisted of people who had been in various other bands previously. Karen Baker had a go at me about this and I was trying to defend my line…and I had no line to defend…I was totally wrong. On reflection I wish we had melded and welded more into the local scene."

This line-up of Obvious Action split shortly after a potentially high-profile charity gig turned sour.

Colin Mundy: "When we had the infamous 'Rock For Africa' gig at the Arts Centre we were disappointed we were going on first, so three of us made our own political stand and got trashed out of our heads. Mark was pissed off because he was stone cold sober and he just picked up his amp and guitar and walked off stage. Pictures were in the Journal the following week and I had my t-shirt on back to front, where I had been bathed to get me sober and had dressed myself wrong."

Mark Palmer: "I went off to study and, even though I was only in Bournemouth and tried to get back once a week for rehearsals, it wasn't working. Colin said 'Look we can't go on like this…we've got another singer'…fair enough."

Colin Mundy: "Then we got a guy called Steve Marlowe, who Kev had known for years [but] Obvious Action split up – there was a bit of a problem between me and Russ – and I took a break from being in bands, because I was a bit disillusioned that we never really made that breakthrough out of Salisbury."

Although Colin would play in bands again at a later date, he now took the opportunity to set up a business venture, which would provide an essential outlet for music and fashion in Salisbury.

Colin Mundy: "I started up the shop around about the same time – Stand Out[7]. I had left school without any qualifications and just wanted to do something for myself."

"If I ever had any money me and my mates would go up to London and spend it, so I just thought 'Let's bring a bit of London down to Salisbury'. It started off as clothes but then went into music as well, we started stocking bootleg cassettes and vinyl and it went from there really."

"In some ways I hated it because it kept me in Salisbury – I couldn't just get up and go - but in other ways it gave me a great lifestyle for fifteen years. We opened another shop in Bournemouth, in Old Christchurch Road, when it was down in the dumps. We had started just about breaking even when it was time for a new lease and they wanted to double the rent, so we had to get out."

In league with another entrepreneurial figure, Colin also ventured into promoting bands in the city.

Colin Mundy: "Rod Fry was a seminal guy in Salisbury. I was sick and tired of bands I wanted to see not coming down to Salisbury. I wanted to see 999. I talked to Rod and did the legwork - got the contact details through the record company they were with - got the bass player's number and gave him a call."

"Later on myself and Colin Holton put on loads of gigs at the Arts Centre, and stuff outside Salisbury as well, but the trouble with 'Smallisbury' is everyone wants to be on the guest list – no one wants you to make any money!"

Colin Holton's brother Gary formed Against

ROD RECORDS

Presents

999

+ OBVIOUS ACTION

AT

SALISBURY ART CENTRE

5th JULY   7.30 - 11.30

£2.00 in advance (£2.50 on night) *BAR

ENDLESS BEAT

"...cars parked all the way down the hill... we couldn't believe it!"

The Wall in 1982, with Nick Wells and Grahame 'Chalky' White.

Chalky White: "I had three older sisters so there was always music in the house, our tastes however were quite different! The first band I went to see was Status Quo at the Gaumont, Southampton in 1977. I wanted an electric guitar after that but it would be three long years until I got one - a very poor quality Vox from the junk shop [Honest Alec's]."

"I really liked more 'new wave' stuff - The Vapors, The Jags, The Only Ones, Hazel O'Connor. I was still into Deep Purple, Led Zeppelin and Bad Company when the punk thing started!

Gary was into Barclay James Harvest and the Eagles...until he fell in love with Paul Weller and The Jam!"

"I first played in a band in 1982, rehearsing with the embryonic Against The Wall. Why? To pull birds, drink copious amounts of alcohol and have good fun with my mates...everything happened but the first bit!"

"I replied to an advert in the Salisbury Journal and arranged to meet Nick at The Chough for two weeks on the trot at the same time but we didn't manage to meet – it was well before mobile phones and we didn't know what each other looked like! I eventually met up with them at a Thick Dick and the Green'eds gig at The Grange."

"Our first gig was at the Saddle Rooms supporting one of Duncan Fulton's bands. We played all over the place - Bristol, Bath, London, Ferndown, Winchester, Andover and Salisbury. We became a permanent

Colin Holton and Frogg Moody

fixture at the Porton Hotel. We came second in the Salisbury Battle of the Bands in 1985 – I think a band from Swindon called Midnight Express won. When we announced our final gig at the Porton Hotel it was absolutely rammed - cars parked all the way down the hill...we couldn't believe it."

"After that Nick went off around the world sight seeing. Gary and I did other bands then Nick came back, we reformed and had a blast again, but Nick got fed up, we got fed up and we recruited a young bass player called Dicky Watts and Against The Wall's style changed dramatically. More mature songs followed with the writing partnership of Holton/White but the world wasn't ready for us...Against The Wall had run its course and ideas were drying up. It was time for a change - for both of us."

"The Against The Wall times were good as it was all new to us. We were youthful and optimistic that we could achieve whatever we wanted....then reality hit us after doing gigs out of town. However, we had great support for gigs in Southampton and Winchester where we regularly took coaches of supporters for a night out in another town."

"Against The Wall used to rehearse at the Holton brothers' family garage in Gomeldon – our gear used to be left in the garage. Colin used to weld people's cars there and a regular at the Anchor and Hope asked him to do some welding. Whilst welding the car it caught fire taking the car, the garage and our equipment with it. Luckily Colin was unhurt. A fireman was sent in with breathing apparatus...and promptly disappeared down the pit inside the garage! He was okay and I subsequently got introduced to him whilst attending the Salisbury Beerex...he wanted to meet Colin!"

"We lost everything except the bass and electric guitars. The only good thing to come out of the incident - besides the anecdote - was that Gary got a new Pearl Export drum kit and could now pretend to be Mark

WINNER

Winner of our recent competition to win a free day's recording at the new Recluse Studio, Landford, is Clive Roper, bassist with Salisbury's Don't Feed the Animals. Clive will be going into the studio shortly to claim his prize by laying down two songs for a solo demo tape he has long cherished recording. Congratulations Clive.

DON'T FEED THE ANIMALS - left to right: Colin Holton, John Ulicsny, Clive Roper, Karen Baker, Frogg Moody and Alex Mundy

181

ENDLESS BEAT

"Colin was always a fantastic front man with the gift of the gab..."

Brzezicki from Big Country."

"Rumour has it that the Anchor and Hope regular phoned Colin on return from his holiday and informed him it was very hot where he had been and he had got burnt, and Colin retorted 'Not half as burnt as your fucking car is!'."

Described by Due South as 'a refreshing tonic from some of the songs in the charts at the moment', Don't Feed The Animals originally comprised Karen Baker (vocals), Colin Holton (guitar and vocals), John Ulicsny (guitar), Nick Heron (bass), Frogg Moody (keyboards) and Dave Marsh (drums).

Colin Holton: "I really got into acoustic rock based stuff like The Alarm – it had taken punk and refined it. It was something we put together just to see how it went down at the Arts Centre. It changed around quite a lot and then it got into recording. We gigged everywhere and it just sort of took off."

Frogg: "Colin was responsible for writing the songs and lyrics and with Karen would work out the vocal harmonies. My main musical input was working out musical intros, lead solos and middle eight sections, although I did co-write a selection of songs with Colin – most notably Wealthy Man, Call Of The Wild and Wagons West."

"DFTA attracted a large, loyal following in Salisbury and could pack out most venues – I remember taking two 53 seat coaches to the Kings Head in Fulham and also two coaches of fans to Golddiggers in Chippenham. There were great times including supporting Happy Mondays in their home town of Manchester. They were the most miserable bunch I had ever met in my life - their fans gave us a great reception which probably added to their misery!"

"We also supported Eddie and The Hotrods in Bournemouth and they were unable to play their hit single Do Anything You Want To Do - they had the hump because we played it in our set before they played! We did a few gigs supporting Dumpy's Rusty Nuts - these were always drink injected sessions and great fun! Another highlight was supporting Shogun at London's Marquee Club – a venue full of history and one that most bands would love to play."

Nick Heron: "Don't Feed the Animals was the band I enjoyed playing with most. I was very flattered when Colin asked me to join – he was probably the best bass player I had ever met. The band gelled very quickly and we seemed to build up quite a following. I learnt a lot playing in that band and actually got to be a reasonable player by the end of it all."

"It kind of realised that teenage dream of being a rock star in a small way. We released a single, got it reviewed in Melody Maker (even if they reviewed the B side rather than the A side), got a bit of local radio play and people I didn't know would come up and ask me if I played with 'The Animals'…and there were some girls too..."

Frogg: "Colin was always a fantastic front man with the gift of the gab – a great man to have on your side if the audience was proving difficult. We had loads of excellent reviews in the local press but perhaps the best review, for me personally anyway, was the one that appeared in Sounds in August 1985."

"After mentioning the 'heavenly keyboards' the reviewer continued 'the appallingly named Frogg is the man responsible for these synth noises. It is the keen vocal edge and the

6: Flowers in a Desert

unrelenting melody of the keyboards which set Don't Feed the Animals apart from the herd. Frogg's fingers swirl crisply, underpinning the excellent Plumb Stones and their self-financed single Wealthy Man' - fame at last!"

The Don't Feed The Animals single was issued on Rod Fry's own label in 1985. The record peaked at number 1 in the Salisbury Journal local charts, although it should be noted that the listings were being supplied by Rod's shop at the time.

Nick Heron and Dave Marsh were later replaced by Clive Roper and Alex Mundy.

Clive Roper: "Overnight they lost their rhythm section and I joined. My first gig was at the Angel in Southampton, which got reviewed by Sounds. Don't Feed The Animals was alright – all I did was play bass and yell into a microphone. The drummer was Alex Mundy, who I had heard practicing in the band when I was at school. I enjoyed it except for one little thing that really got on my nerves…trying to get Holton to shut up! [laughs]"

Clive was also involved in The Strugglers - a Don't Feed The Animals spin off playing 'punk's greatest hits'.

Clive Roper: "We would learn songs in an afternoon and play the gig in the evening – that was good fun. Colin was saying he wanted to learn something really different. I said 'Let's do Ernie'. I went over Harnham, where he was sharing a house with Nick Shirfield and Ruth Pooley, and me and Colin worked the song out - but we could never finish it…we just kept bursting out laughing. I ended up playing the bass line from Donna Summer's I Feel Love under it."

Clive eventually left Don't Feed The Animals – to be replaced by Nick Shirfield – and formed his own band.

Clive Roper: "I had songs in my back pocket and formed View From A Bridge with Richard Atkinson – or 'Buzzard' as he is known - and Steve Christey. Steve was a bit of a find. He was a really, really good drummer – technically great. The best thing was his mum and dad lived in the New Forest, so we could go out and make as much noise as we liked, then end up in the Lamb or the High Corner absolutely hammered."

"It was strange because I found I couldn't sing unless I had a guitar in my hand, so Buzzard played bass and I played guitar. The only problem was my guitar playing wasn't that good… but it slowly brought me up to speed. Widdly-widdly guitar bits I couldn't play, but I always liked Ennio Morricone and things like that, and it was far easier to do the twanging spaghetti western-like licks. That came through in quite a few songs. We

DON'T FEED THE ANIMALS - left to right: Jimmy Blackwell, Colin Holton, Karen Baker, Nick Shirfield and Frogg Moody

ENDLESS BEAT

"... obviously we never stood any chance of replicating what they were doing..."

did quite a few gigs but the problem was I ran out of songs and the initial enthusiasm ground to a halt."

Although short lived, View From A Bridge holds the distinction of being the only band Frogg Moody has been sacked from – he normally walks. Clive describes this as "my proudest moment".

After his spell with View From A Bridge, Steve Christey replaced Alex Mundy in Don't Feed The Animals.

Steve Christey: "The band was established anyway and full of characters - big characters - and that was really enjoyable. The thing with anything musical, as well as being serious, is to have humour because it makes it more enjoyable and a lot more relaxing. They were a very good live band – taught me a lot about tempos, timing…laughing. I remember having a great time."

"Colin enjoyed himself because he was actually quite a good player and a good songwriter. I think when you have established yourself as a good all rounder you can relax a bit and start enjoying playing. I enjoy playing a lot more now than I did, just because I feel able to tackle any situation."

Don't Feed The Animals eventually folded when band founder Colin Holton began to return to a hard-edged sound.

Frogg: "After quite a few years in DFTA, I felt the time had come for a change. Colin had started to veer away from the pop-rock style that was more

VIEW FROM A BRIDGE -
left to right: Steve Christey, Clive Roper and Richard 'Buzz' Atkinson

suited to my keyboards in favour of a harder rock feel – one that I think he has kept to this day."

Colin Holton: "My personal influences to start with were heavy metal - I love anything like that and it just went around full circle. By the time I got back there it was really thrashy, but not to the extreme – it was just before the likes of Napalm Death and those sorts of bands."

There were many contenders for the title, but the Horizontal Bulgarians claimed to be 'the drunkest band in Salisbury'.

Phil Manning: "I was living in Green Lane, the hippy caravan site, in the very early eighties and Mickey Dyer used to pay occasional visits[8]. He suggested getting a band together and I thought I'd give it a try. I had been in a band in Basingstoke called Horizontal Bulgarians, which is where I stole the name from – I used to do a bit of vocals and play drums rather badly."

"My memories of it are unfortunately rather sketchy because of a head full of college and coping with life up at Green Lane, but slowly we got people like Tim Darlow, Matthew Finn…drummers were always difficult, we used to try and do a lot of things with drum machines but we eventually found a collection of drummers."

The band's unusual name reflected their rather idiosyncratic style, as did Tim Darlow's guitar method.

Phil Manning: "He's a left handed guitar player but he used to play a right handed guitar, with a string missing. He used to say 'Well, I never use that one so that can come off'. But he used it strung as a right handed guitar, so he kind of played it upside down. I think he was quite fond of the Keith Richards style of guitar playing - tuned to E, and he would bar across a lot and just thrash things out."

"Tim liked a lot of old school rock'n'roll, being that bit older. Mickey and my influences were very much things like Fall, Joy Division…obviously we never stood any chance of replicating what they were doing, but we stumbled across a few things that we could make work. We found it a lot easier to write our own stuff than learn other peoples. We did occasionally attempt covers but probably quite obscure – things by Wire…Mickey got us doing a couple of Can numbers…and Pere Ubu…"

The Bulgarians played the Arts Centre many times and at venues in London including North East London Poly. They were also responsible for organising two 'Rock for Africa' charity gigs at the Arts Centre, one of which took place well before the Live Aid event, but ultimately didn't have the drive to take things further.

Phil Manning "We were fairly indolent. We used to rehearse fairly irregularly under the clock tower at the Arts Centre – in the small room there. We played maybe once every couple or three months. Because we were quite a lazy band, we got to a stage

Local Salisbury musicians gather for the 1985 Ethiopia Benefit Gig

ENDLESS BEAT

"Phil was absolutely brilliant – like Marty Feldman on speed really."

where we had a certain amount of material together and would only rehearse if we actually had a gig coming up."

"I think people had to try a lot harder in those days to get things together. It was very much a case of going out and playing in village halls - hauling your equipment out there. I think kids these days are a bit luckier because they have got facilities like Grosvenor House. I think it's a very good thing."

The Horizontal Bulgarians' best known numbers were Chicken Head, Pictures In The Rain, Dracula's Daughter and Emma/Mild Thing (later covered by Dennis for the God's Great Tape Head Cleaner compilation). Demos were recorded at Steve Collinson's Orchard Studios in Amesbury. Phil isn't sure if anything was ever released, although there are rumours of Pictures In The Rain being available on a compilation tape from Yorkshire.

A number of local bands in fact recorded demos at Steve Collinson's studios, set up after his own band, Identity Crisis, had folded in 1980.

Steve Collinson: "After that I started working in a studio down in Corsham - Pickwick Studios. I had everybody in from up this way because that was one of the only studios around this way - the main ones being Nick and Jez [Kemp] in The Crimmos. We spent hours in there doing stuff with Nick – he was so pedantic."

"I then set up Orchard Studios, working with Phil Stanford, who I had met at Pickwick. There was a couple of people came in who I thought would have done really well. It was always odd people within bands, like a singer who you thought 'He's got a fantastic voice – I might pinch him for something later' or the occasional great guitarist, but I never heard a band I thought were really going to make it."

The Horizontal Bulgarians split in the mid-eighties, but soon reformed under the new guise of Newcombe and Roach, with Alex Mundy on drums.

Phil Manning: "Newcombe and Roach started up because Tim and myself were sharing a flat. Tim was thrashing away on guitar and I was coming out with lyrics, so we would attempt to do things. We tried playing a gig in the corner of the Star – just

HORIZONTAL BULGARIANS - left to right: Micky Dyer, Tim Darlow, Gary Holton and Phil Manning, with Jim Crouch reclining

NEWCOMBE AND ROACH

guitar, vocals and drum machine – and Mickey [Dyer] joined us. Mindful of the publican's thing about only having two musicians playing, Mickey smuggled himself in and played his bass from underneath the bar football table, so as to remain unseen."

As had been the case with the previous incarnation, the band's new name seemed somewhat obscure.

Phil Manning: "We used it as a double meaning – obviously 'Newcombe and Roach' the doubles tennis team, and 'Nuke' em' because it was the eighties and we were all under the shadow of the bomb and 'Roach' because people liked to smoke a bit of spliff."

"It was fairly thrashy, punk style stuff I suppose. Mickey's very keen on what he calls 'light and shade' in music – different sections - so it's not always verse, chorus, verse chorus, bash it out. We were very lucky to get Alex, because he was one of the better drummers in town. Mickey is an exceptional bass player and it's hard to find somebody who is up to his standard."

Alex Mundy: "I don't know how I got into that - all these people are your drinking buddies – especially around the Star on a Saturday, because it was one of the only pubs in town open until three o'clock in the afternoon. Then you would wander over to the Cathedral Close and sit on the riverbank with a few bottles."

"Phil was absolutely brilliant – like Marty Feldman on speed really. It was always a bit…'Let's just have fun'…and we did! It was amazing how we ever got through a whole set really, because we were very drunk a lot of the time."

ENDLESS BEAT

"It would have been nice... even if it was a little piece of seven inch vinyl with a picture."

Phil Manning: "We used to go on very drunk, probably nerves as much as anything - and the fact that rough cider was starting to get into Salisbury in quite a big way. We would usually be outside of two or three pints of that by the time we went on stage."

"We played a lot of support slots. We played one supporting Tokyo Blade at the Arts Centre. Tokyo Blade had all their sort of gutted Marshall stacks and their goat's head with the lighty-up eyes - and us, performing in front of some four or five hundred bikers, with me togged up in a pair of leather jeans and leggings…bare chested. I can't remember them booing, I can't remember them cheering. I remember a few people turning round saying 'I like 'em', but that was probably Bootsy McCauley!"

"We had no management, ever. The guy who managed Mad Cow Disease [Mike Smith] spoke to me once and said 'I wish I had been around Salisbury when you guys were playing', but I'm quite glad he never got his hands on us. I regret the fact that we didn't actually get anything released. It would have been nice just to have – even if it was a little piece of seven inch vinyl with a picture."

Former Kinetic NRG guitarist Ian 'Skid' Browne was honoured to be asked to join Newcombe and Roach when Tim Darlow moved to Spain.

Skid: "They were the first Salisbury band, apart from The QTs, that I used to follow around - if they were doing gigs out of town I would go and see them. They were fantastic, original and a bit more imaginative. They were quirky, rocked out at the right times and had a really good attitude."

"They turned around and said we need a guitarist instead of Tim and we would like you to do it, which was the biggest honour I have ever been paid in all my guitar playing years. One of the first things I had to do was go and lock myself away for months to try and work out what he had been playing."

Despite, or perhaps because of, their somewhat offbeat approach, Newcombe and Roach are fondly remembered.

Wiggy: "There was one band in Salisbury where you knew you were watching something two or three steps up from the usual local stuff, and that was Newcombe and Roach - excellent band."

Jon Maple: "Newcombe and Roach were a brilliant outfit. They did some great stuff - very influenced by bands like Pere Ubu – American arty punky obscure stuff but at the same time Darlow had a very loose bottleneck guitar style, with a special tuning. They weren't technically brilliant, although saying that Matthew Finn was a very good musician and Mickey Dyer has always been an astoundingly good bass player."

Clive Roper: "I would put Mickey Dyer in front of any other bass player in town - he was the most original. I used to like watching him because he

NEWCOMBE AND ROACH

6: **Flowers in a Desert**

NEWCOMBE AND ROACH - Tim Darlow, Micky Dyer, Matthew Finn and Phil Manning (kneeling)

ENDLESS BEAT

"With our long black hair, silver earrings and gothic clothing it was ideal."

used to walk backwards on his heels and play upstrokes – he was a perfectly nice chap as well, which was a bonus."

Newcombe and Roach – and Phil's musical career – fizzled out after he had to move away from the city for work purposes.

Phil Manning: "I was working at the Arts Centre as a front of house manager and my contract was coming to a close, so I had to look for more work. There was nothing local so I moved off to the Midland Group Arts Centre in Nottingham, which unfortunately folded after about three months."

"I got as far [back] as Bristol and didn't move back to Salisbury for another seven or eight months. By the time I got back things had moved on. Tim had decamped to Barcelona, Mickey was doing other things - I don't think Matthew has played with anybody since. I fell into working at Salisbury City Hall in about 1990 and because of the nature of the work I just never managed to make the time again to get it together with anybody."

Members of Newcombe and Roach had also been involved in odd one-off projects with a former art school punk who had returned to the city.

Jon Maple: "I was living all around the west country for the early eighties. I came back and managed the Oddbins shop when it was in the High Street. I wasn't sure if I wanted to come back, but I sank into the womb like environment of Salisbury."

"I got back with old mates and made new mates who were doing music, and did some singing with various line ups of local bands. Pope Shenouda and the Coptic Orthodox was one silly name, where we did a kind of psychobilly-blues orientated Gun Club-Cramps type noise. I've listened to demos we did in recent years and thought they were not too bad – I thought it was shite at the time. I had no onstage confidence at all - it was just sheer effrontery in my performance – an attitude of 'I don't care whether you like it or not I'm going to do it anyway you bastards'."

After Dark Star folded, Kerry Waite had taken some time out before deciding to get back into the scene and found himself as a front man for the first time.

Kerry Waite: "I spent a year drinking but it was time to get my act together and try and form a new band. I originally wanted to get a four or five piece, but couldn't find another vocalist or guitarist I wanted to work with - I did a few rehearsals with people I didn't know very well but nothing seemed to gel."

"Then I approached Jim Blackwell again and said 'If you've got some spare time would you like to give me some support?' He got approval from [Don't Feed] The Animals – so thanks to them - and suggested Nigel Finn. Nigel came out for a rehearsal jam and it went really well but we also clicked as friends – that was quite important, we were focussed on the work but there was no friction…

which was quite a rarity."

The three-piece came up with an unusual name to suit their sound and image – Oglala Sioux.

Kerry Waite: "It came from a book that Mike Smith gave me about American Indians. We thought that 'Sioux' wasn't enough – we wanted a complicated name - so we called it 'Oglala' and someone had to explain to us how to pronounce it [laughs]. With our long black hair, silver earrings and gothic clothing it was ideal."

"I wasn't a front man and I wasn't a lead guitarist - I had just been a rhythm guitarist - so I struggled away about what to do. Working with Nige, because of his lovely melodic bass lines, gave me ideas to weave around and Jim was a real pleasure with his drumming ideas and patterns. It was tribal beating – a bit like The Heartbreakers with Johnny Thunders in '77/78 - that kind of style really appealed. I wanted to carry those sort of drum beats into the eighties but with melodic bass and hard edged guitar."

This direction suited Jimmy Blackwell's approach to playing the drums perfectly.

Kerry Waite: "I think the word 'tribal' really got to him – he was thundering the arse off the old tom-tom and became obsessed with power. He came up with double skin snares – very expensive and he would be there cherishing them - and then smash them to bits. You can hurt people in the room, almost physically, and he got quite a buzz doing that. It was

OGLALA SIOUX - left to right: Nigel Finn, Kerry Waite and Jimmy Blackwell

ENDLESS BEAT

"... why don't you play at the Rock Garden?"

"We were quite calm and said 'Let's tighten up - spend a week rehearsing not scratching our heads when we get there'. We went out for a meal to celebrate and then - one week before we were due to go up there - I collapsed and that was, almost, the grinding end of Oglala Sioux."

obviously a childhood problem that led to that [laughs]."

Oglala Sioux secured some high profile support slots through Kerry working with an interview picture disc company based in Fisherton Street.

Kerry Waite: "I was working with a guy called Chris Jones – his job was to go and interview professional bands. I thought 'Yeah, I might get in touch with some professional people - what a great idea'. We met Girlschool in Southampton and I said 'I'm in a band - any chance we could support you' and they said 'Yeah of course you could'. We also became acquaintances of Lords Of The New Church and an opportunity came when they were doing a little tour of France. We had to get our own van and that but were really excited to get the experience - it really tightened us up a lot."

"After about a year we did our first demo at Kurt [Cooper]'s studio. Mike Smith came to see the band and said 'I would like to be your manager'. Mike did his very best for us, took our demo to A&M in London and had a good reaction. They were going to record us for a week and, if they were happy, it would go out on BBC Radio."

OGLALA SIOUX

6: Flowers in a Desert

THE LORDS OF THE NEW CHURCH

APPEARING at :- the Passenger Club
DATE :- 23rd JULY (saturday)
TICKET PRICE :- £4/£3.50

PLUS !!!
D.F.T.A.
AND
THE STAND

Bedwin Street – Salisbury – Wilts – SP1 3UT
Telephone : Salisbury (0722) 21744

SAC
SALISBURY ARTS CENTRE

Kerry had suffered a brain haemorrhage – a main artery burst and he lost four pints of blood. With such haemorrhages categorised on a scale of 1 to 10 he was judged a '10' - the worst possible. At the time 70% of people suffering haemorrhages in this category were expected to die and the remaining 30% were highly likely to need care for the rest of their lives. Kerry survived and, against all the odds, returned for the last stand of Oglala Sioux.

Kerry Waite: "Thanks to Jim and Nige - they waited nine months after my illness struck. I started to go back rehearsing…as ill as I felt. Then I decided to move to London. Chris Jones said 'I think you can still play well – why don't you play at the Rock Garden?' You had to take your tapes down there first but we pulled off an acceptance."

"It was a fantastic evening - it really was. I think we played great and we had a great night, but I had to decide what I was going to do. I decided to stay in London and it sort of fizzled away…but I had to get my life back together. It was nothing to do with the music - I had a great time with Jim and Nige and I miss it, but it had to come to a halt…I was so ill."

Having "run out new of songs" in View From A Bridge, Clive Roper took a break before forming a new band, Cameras In Paris.

Clive Roper: "This has been one of my curses in bands so, what do you do? - Split that band up, have a sabbatical, go home and write more songs, record some demos…and form another band."

"I had a phone call from Dave Bullis. By then I had written a load more new songs. To be honest Cameras In Paris was 'View From A Bridge Mark II' with different people – the only difference was by then I could just about pull out a guitar solo."

"The very last gig we played was in December 1989 at the Arts Centre. It was the only time we played with a big PA and we were absolutely gob-smacked at how good it sounded. As is always the way that's when the band split – at the high point. They lived in Andover, I lived in Salisbury, I didn't drive… what can you do?"

Simon 'Sox' Oxborrow's father had played guitar in dance bands and Simon had jammed with friends at school, but his first formal band was What The Butler Saw.

Simon Oxborrow: "They had been going for a few months before I got involved. It came about because Steve Burton and Johnny Bell worked together down Mitchell Music[9]. Johnny knew Andy Penny and Steve Christey, who used to work on the tugs down Southampton. Johnny approached me in the Pheasant one night and asked if I would be interested in coming in as a guitarist."

ENDLESS BEAT

"... and it was one of those real tumbleweed moments..."

Left to right: Johnny Bell, Jav and Simon 'Sox' Oxborrow

"Even though people would say we had a definite sound, I think the influences individually were quite different. Johnny was into The Skids and bands like that, Steve was jazzy and soully and personally I love funk and rock – a bit of a cross between the two."

Johnny Bell developed an unusual stereophonic live sound whereby the twin guitars would bounce around between two speakers.

Simon Oxborrow: "That was courtesy of the good old Boss DD3 digital delay unit, which had two outputs on it. I don't know where he got the idea from but you could take one output to one combo on the left hand side of the stage and another to the right hand combo, so you had almost like a ping-pong effect going on through your speaker cabs. It was a very atmospheric sound."

"The reason we were so disciplined was we rehearsed an awful lot. We were fortunate that Andy's dad was a vicar and had this place up in Bouverie Avenue - a huge detached house with a huge spare bedroom. We put three layers of carpet on all the walls and sound deadened it as much as we could, and we pretty much used to live in there."

"We did untold amounts of demos - if we weren't gigging we were in a studio somewhere. We did some up at Kurt Cooper's studio and also down at Recluse. Johnny came up with most of the scratch ideas, they would be presented to us and we would all put our little bits and pieces on."

"We used to go quite far afield. The very first time we played at The Angel in Southampton I knew nothing about it – I had heard no stories. Getting the gear out the back of the van and taking it in to sound check I was the first one through the door and it was one of those real tumbleweed moments – just forty hardcore looking men staring…'There's nothing for you around these parts' you know? I have never been so frightened setting up and sound checking in my life but they absolutely loved us - we went down a storm and ended up playing down there every month."

"I look back at What The Butler Saw and still think they are some of the best musicians I have ever played with. We were all late teens/early twenties and we sort of stumbled into each other, and it worked…and there was so much laughter. One time we had done a demo and decided to take it up to London around the record companies and Johnny managed to blag this brand new Austin Montego."

"It was in the days when you had to run a car in but Johnny went steaming up the M3 - with us in the back - at ninety miles an hour. We got just past Fleet and I saw the biggest plume of smoke coming out of this car looking over my shoulder. It only had about 63 miles on the clock and I remember it going off on the back of a recovery wagon. We hitchhiked up to Woking and got a train, and still managed to get around the A&R departments."

Of course the eighties music scene was not all about the 'serious' side. Indeed those times are now viewed as somewhat frivolous, although in reality they had no more of a share of pure pop bands than any other decade.

Salisbury shop girl Shelley Preston hit the headlines when she was selected as the replacement for Jay Aston in the Eurovision winning Bucks Fizz. Back in her home town Toucantango, one of the most popular local live acts of the period, made no bones about being a 'good time' band.

Neil Leacy: "It began in 1979 when Trevor Webb bought his first drum kit (second hand and paid for with his first ever wage packet) and I bought my first keyboard (a mono synth - Korg MS10 – purchased on a dodgy hire-purchase loan)."

"We got together with two Daves, Walker and Woods, and became Blue Haze - so called from the cigarette smoke we would end up looking through as every Sunday afternoon was spent in the old hall at the back of the Stonehenge Inn, Durrington, banging out rock cover versions and our own brand of Hawkwind and Rush style prog-rock numbers about mage-lords and such - no, I don't know what a 'mage-lord' is either."

"We didn't actually play live. Dave Wood left and we were joined by Andy Shepherd - I think that was his name - on guitar. Dave Walker and Andy shared rhythm and lead guitar duties and I doubled up on bass and keyboards. For a brief time Adrian Weeks joined as vocalist before deciding it wasn't for him - he went on to manage Millets in the Old George Mall - and was replaced by Ian Gillan sound-a-like Nick Walker."

"Renamed Snowblind - from the Black Sabbath album track - for Trevor, myself, Dave and Andy our first ever live gig was at Durrington Comprehensive School[10]. Highlights included storming versions of Deep Purple's Child In time, Queen's Tie Your Mother Down, AC/DC's Whole Lotta Rosie, and an out of tune synth solo on Rush's The Trees - and almost losing my wedding tackle standing too close to a stage pyro! Our second and final gig was at the [King and] Bishop Inn. A highlight for that gig was watching a frisbee skimming across the audience, just missing Trevor as he bashed away on the drums and continued without flinching."

"Trevor and Nick went off to play with previous members of Nosferatu in the newly formed Nighthawk. Dave and Andy stopped playing altogether for a while and I joined a local club/cabaret band called Astral Plain, formed by Steve [Thompson] and Charlie [Marsden]. We worked clubs and military messes around the South of England."

"It was a great learning time on how to judge audiences and gee them up when needed. However, there was always the very dodgy mid-show comedy stint that included a raucous 'punk' tribute that would end with an exploding speaker cabinet. One night Charlie decided to make the bang louder by wrapping tape around the stage pyro inside the cabinet. Yet again I almost lost my vitals as splinters shot off everywhere when the cabinet literally disintegrated."

Neil Leacy

ENDLESS BEAT

"... Nick walked on wearing a pink leotard!"

"Meanwhile Nighthawk played many local gigs and one memorable one at the Marquee, London. They played the last live gig at the Cathedral Hotel - rumour has it that the owners lost their live licence because the gig was so loud police were called in to pull the plug."

"Roundabout Christmas 1982, Mark and I had grown tired of playing club standards. So when Nighthawk split we joined Trevor, Dave and Nick to form Mercedez. From February till November 1983 we wrote and played our own brand of 'futuristic funk' - often inspired by Mark's solid slap and pop bass riffs mixed with a little rock, soul and whatever we felt at the time."

"As with most new bands in the early eighties, visual style was an added part of the show. Bright clothes and make-up were the order of the day - especially one memorable night when Nick walked on wearing a pink leotard! We played all over the south in pubs and clubs; gaining a small but loyal following. Eventually we had enough money to work in a Bournemouth based studio, to record a three-track demo used to gain more gigs and hopefully a contract."

"As it was, soon after a gig at the City Hall the band split as Nick starting insisting that if we wanted to continue working with him it would be as his backing band, going out under his name. This didn't sit well with the musicians as we had always wrote the music and Nick would add lyrics afterwards. It was a group effort and no one deserved to be given overall credit for any of our songs."

"Nick left without the rest of the band realising he had plans to re-mix our demo tape and release it under the name 'Niki True' as his own double A-side seven inch single, Too Much, which reached the heady heights of number

MERCEDEZ - clockwise: Mark Hogarth, Nick Walker, Neil Leacy, Trevor Webb and Dave Walker (centre)

two in the local chart supplied by Brian's Records - a favourite haunt for any music fan of the time[11]. To say I was pretty pissed off was to put it mildly, so I wrote to the Salisbury Journal."

The Journal ran an item on the row under the immortal headline 'Top Ten Turmoil For Big Hit Niki'. Niki told the Journal 'I paid for the whole thing – it was my money and it's my song because I wrote it. I wanted to change the guitarist but the rest of the band said I would have to leave first – so I did. I always copyright everything I record – to protect the band as much as anything'.

Neil Leacy: "Nick's version of why the band split is very different from the musicians, but the last paragraph of the article was right: 'Mercedez have decided to find another singer and change their name'. While Nick went on to form Dance Factor with keyboard player and programmer Steve Burton, the remainder of Mercedez teamed up with Kurt Cooper."

Kurt had previously played guitar and sang backing vocals with Xtrax, a promising band who had formed at Bishop Wordsworth's School.

Kurt Cooper: "It was Beatles, Rolling Stones - the general bog standard covers that every club band did. We signed up with Tony Moreton at Ace, so we were doing a lot of Army camp work. The band was about earning cash to be able to do our own thing eventually. We signed a recording contract with Chris Denning – one of the original Radio 1 DJ's – it was a six month retainer but nothing came of it."

"I was getting restless with the band because I wanted to sing. I was only doing guitar and backing vocals, so there was a little bit of unrest in the camp and I moved to Oxford to join a band. We did about fifteen gigs but by the time we split we still didn't have a name - we were still 'the band'. Then I moved back to Salisbury."

Neil Leacy: "We hit it off from the start and decided we would be a fun new-wave band - think Wham, Spandau Ballet, Blancmange - where it would be good-times at every gig. As before the musicians would write the music and Kurt, as the vocalist, would write the lyrics."

"In essence our songwriting sessions, either at the Moose Hall in Devizes Road or Britford Village Hall, would consist of jam sessions where anyone with a riff or chord sequence would put it forward and we would see if it could be worked in to something more solid. Kurt would join in adding a vocal melody, usually with nonsense rhymes and words we affectionately called 'banana lyrics'."

Kurt Cooper: "We gave people what they wanted - time to switch off. It was just music to enjoy. That was the whole ethos of the band - get people up and get them moving. They were not interested in what I was singing so I would probably write lyrics for a song in half an hour – pap, banana lyrics. I've always been a rhythmical singer and long words don't fit in with rhythms normally, so it was easier just to go with short, sharp choppy lyrics that meant nothing."

Neil Leacy: "When anything gelled in to a song we'd rehearse it until we knew it through and through, becoming an ever-tighter band. One thing that set us apart from any previous bands we had been in was the arrival of Sarah Tolly as

XTRAX - clockwise: Pete Gallagher, Mark Sheldon, Jon Nicholas, Pete Leyland and Kurt Cooper (centre)

ENDLESS BEAT

"... work on clothes and hairstyles became almost as intense as that on our songs!"

backing vocalist. With voices that complimented and harmonised with each other so well, Sarah and Kurt were a classic front for a good-time band."

"We invested in a Luton Bedford van as well as designing and building - mainly Dave - our own PA and light show. Trevor was also one of the first local drummers to use an electronic drum-kit, which helped as we wanted to be able to control the sound and lights as much as possible - to give the punters a memorable show."

"The only thing left was the image and with the help of Kurt's wife Jackie - who as well as being the then manageress of local hair-salon Blinkers also came up with our name - work on clothes and hairstyles became almost as intense as that on our songs!"

"In March 1984 - four months after forming - Toucantango played our first ever gig, in the junior ranks mess at UKLF in Wilton. After a nervous start, caused in part by our PA amp playing up, it turned in to the first of many storming gigs. We really were a very tight band and wowed audiences wherever we played, building a loyal following in a very short space of time. At the end of May we played a then record-breaking gig at the Saddle Rooms, taking almost £200 on the door. In fact we returned the following weekend - 'by popular demand' - and almost did another £150 on the door."

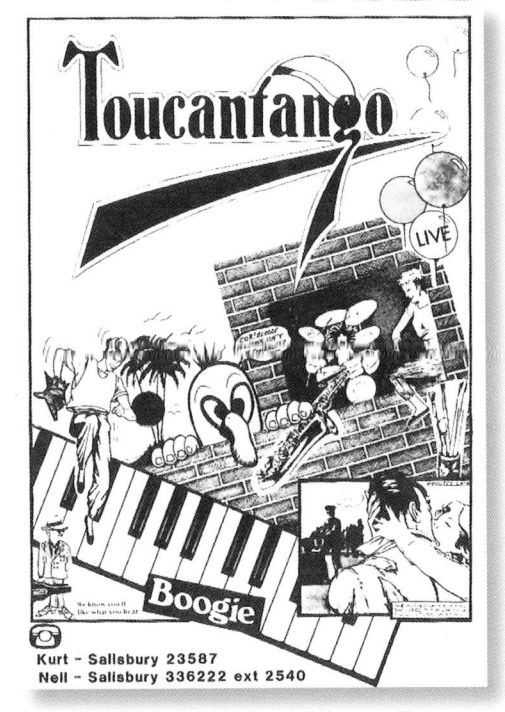

"At that time Elwyn Toomer, the resident [Saddle Rooms] DJ, started taking on the duties of manager. All we needed was a decent demo, and with Kurt's investment in a Tascam 244 cassette-based studio we started to record. The demos got us into clubs like The Grange, Raffles[12], The High Post, Oscars in Longleat, Goldiggers in Chippenham and places further afield in Bournemouth, Southampton and Basingstoke."

"We decided to take it a step further and record our own cassette album. Listening to it again it is quite incredible the quality we got out of that little Tascam recorder. Mind you, we spent hours recording the various tracks - in the Moose Hall, Britford Hall and various band members' houses. Recording, and then tweaking and re-recording - I still remember one night in Mark's house in Durrington trying to all clap in sync - just to sound

TOUCANTANGO - left to right: Trevor Webb, Neil Leacy, Kurt Cooper, Sarah Tolly, Dave Walker and Mark Hogarth

6: **Flowers in a Desert**

like a clap-machine! Heaven only knows what the neighbours thought. After all that Kurt then spent even more hours on getting the mix right."

"Released in August 1984, Toucantango - essentially all the tracks we played live, eventually sold over 450 copies at gigs and through Brian's. People still tell me how they have kept their copy. Even cookery Goddess Delia Smith received a copy, which I sent to her tongue-in-cheek, after she mentioned on a Saturday morning kids TV show that she didn't know a lot about new bands."

Left to right: (back) Trevor, Mark and Dave, (front) Kurt, 'Style Guru' Jackie Cooper and Sean (lighting).

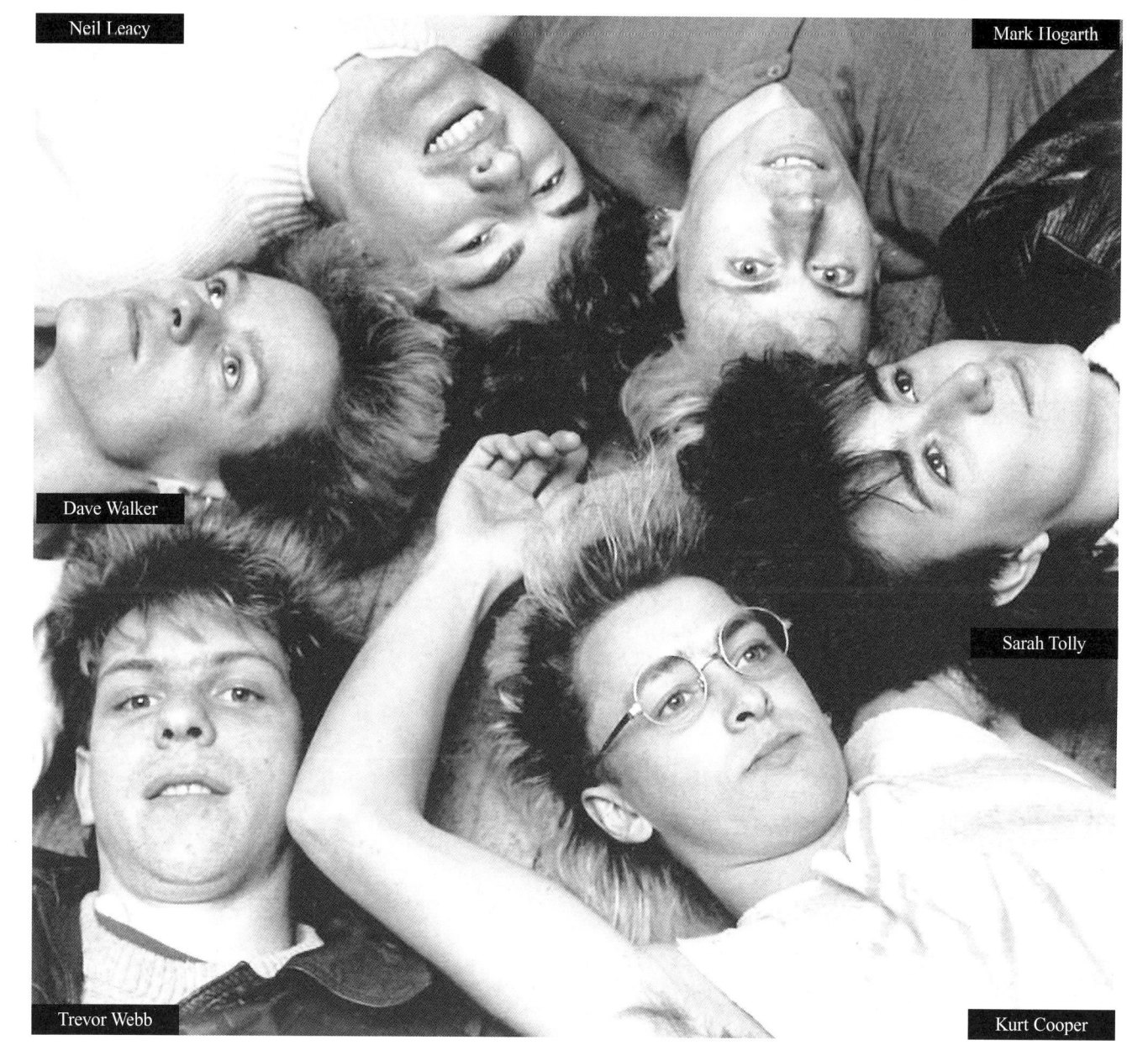

Neil Leacy

Mark Hogarth

Dave Walker

Sarah Tolly

Trevor Webb

Kurt Cooper

199

ENDLESS BEAT

"It gave a whole new meaning to scratching and jumping!"

The cassette reached number 1 in the local chart and Penny Elliot tipped the band for success, calling them 'local representatives of the teen dream, spinning into a carefree world where you need no longer fret about the nuclear bomb or famine in Africa, but escape for a while into the brightly coloured world of disco music'.

Neil Leacy: "We also started printing and selling our own t-shirts. For a while we were a hive of activity - albums, t-shirts, coaches to gigs - and all within nine months of getting together. This was a time when we were gigging at least once, twice - sometimes three times a week. We supported Roman Holliday at the College. The crowd were fantastic, even though we only had a postage stamp area of the stage to set-up on: a classic good-time gig followed by autograph signings galore."

"We travelled to Chippenham to support Jim Davidson at Golddiggers. I still don't know how we got the gig - we had been told we were in-line for supporting

S.C.T.S.U. (Salisbury: 338655) Proudly present

ROMAN HOLLIDAY

Toucanfango + [support]

Friday October 5th - 8:00 pm.
Technical College Main Hall
Tickets £2:50, £2:00 (with N.U.S. card)
Available from S.U. Common Room, college, Refectory, union adviser, Rod's Records, Brian's & Carousel (Amesbury). Postal applications accepted with S.A.E (cheques & postal orders, made payable to S.C.T.S.U.).
Any UNSOLD tickets, sold on night

TOUCANTANGO - live at Salisbury Arts Centre

Tears for Fears at the time - but we arrived to find a note on the door that the gig had been cancelled."

"Sadly, in December, Sarah decided to leave the band and we were left without her harmonies or one of my own favourite Toucantango songs, Change of Heart, which she wrote and only ever sounded good when she sang it. So we were left to fulfil a Christmas/New Year residency at Raffles with just Kurt fronting the band. Carting the gear up those steep stairs was no great fun. Neither was bringing it down again - or trying to dance to the DJ's set when the groove on the dance floor made the decks bounce more than the crowd. It gave a whole new meaning to scratching and jumping!"

"After a few auditions we invited Carol Chu to join us on backing vocals, and Jon Nicholas on percussion. The second gig of the new line up was back at Golddiggers for the re-scheduled gig supporting Jim Davidson. We went down well with a mixed but appreciative audience - even if it was a bit bizarre to be a good-time, get up on your feet and dance band and have the audience sit all the way through our set."

"However, things were still changing. In February [1985] Dave decided to leave the band because he wasn't prepared to give up his job like everyone else - we had got it into our heads that without spending all our time rehearsing, writing, gigging and recording we wouldn't get anywhere, and so took the decision to go and live off of the dole until our ship or contract came in."

"Kurt invited Pete Smith to join us as Dave's replacement and within a very short space of time we were back recording, gigging. With new blood came new ideas for writing songs and a newly recorded demo."

"March 27th 1985 was a special gig for us. Katy Grant, one of my wife's closest friends and a big fan of the band, had been diagnosed with leukaemia earlier in the year. An appeal fund for donations to leukaemia research was set up on her behalf and we organised a fund-raising gig at Salisbury College, which featured

Mark Hogarth and Carol Chu

ENDLESS BEAT

"...too much time in each other's company... was not good for anyone."

ourselves, Obvious Action, Kid Charlemagne, and I Am 7, raising a total of £480. Katy, now over twenty-five years in remission, is still a friend."

"May '85 saw Kurt and I being interviewed by Radio Solent DJ Gethyn Jones. Turning up in our full

Dave Walker

regalia of stage clothes, hair and make-up - for radio! It wasn't until listening to the show the next day that I realised I basically repeated whatever Kurt said in a slightly different order and with a lower voice, but Gethyn liked the tracks and us. In the meantime we also heard the demo had got to A&R people at Virgin, Chrysalis and Elektra. We were on our uppers!"

"Then we got our first public slagging after I sent a copy of the demo to Electronic Sounds and Computer Music magazine - one of my favourites at the time. A very wry review concentrated more on our photo than the music, while slagging off a number of the bands we admired. I was so pissed off I wrote a letter to the editor who replied, in a hand-written letter, to my criticisms and agreed to differ on what makes a good review - but they did put a couple of our tracks on a later cover cassette."

"We also entered the 'England Entertains' amateur talent contest, which saw us playing in front of large audiences at the Bournemouth International Centre before losing out to a solo singer, Pauline Burr, in our semi-final heat. We were still arranging coaches to bus out our fans to gigs around the South but, as the year went on we started to do fewer gigs. A couple at Godolphin School were crazy, a real taste of that Duran Duran screaming mania."

"It seemed important to get demo recordings out there - beyond our circle of regular venues. Kurt decided it would be a good idea to build a recording studio in the garage at the bottom of his garden. A little on the cramped side and soundproofed by carpet and cardboard, the fondly named 'Not So Tacky Studios' was to be the band home for the next six months. It was also a time when our sound started to change, becoming a little darker, rockier and edgier."

"We wrote some good songs but the time spent recording, criticising, re-recording and over-dubbing songs that rarely saw the light of day was, in hindsight, when things started to turned sour; too much time in each other's company in a box of a room was not good for anyone."

"We'd also lost Elwyn as manager and had been approached by a guy called Colin – I can't remember his last name - based in London. Colin was planning a showcase gig at Busby's in Charing Cross: also he'd arranged professional studio time for us."

"1986 started with Mark Hogarth, our foundation bass player, leaving. This was hard as Mark had been a lynchpin for so many of song writing sessions as well as a great character both on and off stage. Pete Smith moved from guitar to bass while Kurt's friend Pete Woo came in on guitar. The music definitely became darker and our look was the same. As we prepared for the gig at Busby's the Journal ran a story on us, and didn't we look a miserable bunch - EMO before EMO was cool."

"Prior to the gig we spent two days at Etude Studios, somewhere on the outskirts of London, trying to record more professional versions of a couple of our tracks. Not a very productive time and a great disappointment. Still it made us realise how well we'd done with a reel-to-reel and four-track cassette recorder."

"Come the showcase gig and a coach load of our die-hard fans were with us. It was a very strange night. We were nervous but played well, however we weren't the only ones there and it was confusing as to who was the main band and who wasn't. We went home wondering what would come out of playing what was then a major venue in London."

"What did happen was Kurt decided he was better off on his own and decided to leave the band, possibly having Colin as a manager. Rumour had it that an A&R rep had been there and was interested in the band but nothing would come of it as we started looking for yet another singer and guitarist - Pete Woo had decided to leave too."

Kurt has a different memory of the circumstances surrounding his departure from the band.

Kurt Cooper: "I walked off stage at Golddiggers. We had an A&R bloke down…they wouldn't let us take our three coach loads of screaming fans with us. It was a Thursday night, there

Left to right (back) Pete Smith, Neil Leacy and Kurt Cooper, (front) Carol Chu, Mark Hogarth and Trevor Webb

ENDLESS BEAT

"Musically I felt more fulfilled, singing old jazz covers and all the greats."

was about twenty people in there and I basically threw my hands up in the air and said 'What's the point' and walked off."

Neil Leacy: "At this point I wonder why we still continued to call ourselves Toucantango. Trevor and myself were the only original members left and the music was very different from that original, fresh sound of 1984. However we found a guitarist in Andy Webley and a vocalist, Mike Vickers."

Mike Vickers: "They gave me a tape of all their stuff that Kurt used to do and it was disco – it was like 'up and dancing' – stuff that I really didn't like at all. I said 'There's no way I'm doing that - if you want me to be in the band I'll rewrite all the lyrics and melodies but we'll still keep your music."

Neil Leacy: "As Kurt had written the lyrics for all the songs we asked Mike to write new lyrics - we were worried about copyright arguments. Give him his due Mick had a good bash at it but it was hard to hear different words to old music, so we made an effort to write more new songs. Again we were moving far away from the original Toucantango sound and even our fans were getting confused."

Mike Vickers: "I think a lot of the girls that used to come and see Toucantango were disappointed because they were all in love with Kurt!"

Neil Leacy: "Even though we recorded a decent demo at Orchard Studios, I realised my heart really wasn't in it so much and early 1987 saw the last Toucantango gig, at the Old Manor Social Club[13]. What goes around comes around - just as at my first live gig at Durrington School [with Snowblind] I almost lost part of my body to an itinerant stage pyro!"

"Actually that wasn't the last ever Toucantango gig, as in September 1987, as a favour to one of the teachers - a friend of Kurt's - we held a re-union in the drama studio at Godolphin School. With local musician and hi-fi guru Chris Binns standing in on guitar it was an absolutely cracking gig, as tight as that first gig in Wilton, and featured all the classic good-time Toucantango sounds - a fitting end to a band that, for four years of more highs than lows, had been such a major part of my life."

Following his departure from Toucantango, Kurt Cooper had teamed up with a new keyboard player.

Kurt Cooper: "I had known Steve Burton for quite a while and seen the bands he was playing in. I got together with Burty as The Fondell Brothers. We used to go out in tuxedos, he would play his electric piano and I would sing - do all the old jazz classics, get drunk and have a bloody good time."

"It opened my eyes to how narrow-minded I had been for so many years and how seriously I had taken it. Musically I felt more fulfilled singing old jazz covers and all the greats. I just felt at home with that sort of music

At Orchard Studios

TOUCANTANGO (final line up) - left to right (back) Mike Vickers, Neil Leacy, Trevor Webb, Andy Webley and Pete Smith

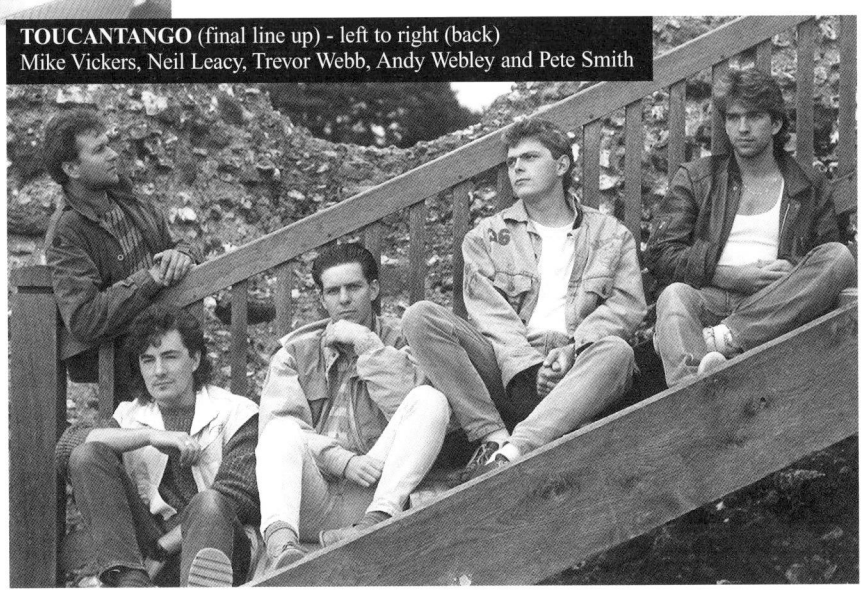

SHOOT THE TOUX - left to right: Simon 'Sox' Oxborrow, Kurt Cooper, Jo Charrington and Steve Burton

and that sort of skill behind me."

Kurt and Steve then brought in ex-members of their former bands Toucantango (Peter Smith and Trevor Webb) and What The Butler Saw (Simon Oxborrow).

Kurt Cooper: "We wanted to do other things so we formed Shoot The Toux. Steve came up with the name. We [Toucantango] were always called 'The Toux' by all the girls that followed us around, so it came from that. It wasn't a two fingered thing - it was basically 'That's gone, let's move on' from my point of view."

Neil Leacy: "Kurt was trying to lay the Toucantango name to rest I think. They entered the Battle of the Bands (South of England) in 1990 and were played on the Pete Wardman Show [on Power FM], and won two studio sessions at Landford."

Simon Oxborrow: "That was very funky. There was a lot of that sort of music around at the time – Terence Trent D'Arby, George Benson and Luther Vandross. We were incredibly tight because we were well rehearsed - we rehearsed two or three times a week for nine months, writing a set before we even did a gig – it was pretty full on. Sometimes we would literally write from the drums up – it was all about getting a groove."

From the younger generation of musicians appearing on the scene, Mrs Taylor's Mad were together between 1984 and 1986 with a line up of Dave Ware (vocals and harmonica), his brother Andy (guitar and vocals), Paul Read (bass), Trevor George (drums) and Tom Power (saxophone).

Andy Ware: "We had loads of energy, enthusiasm, and misplaced belief - influences were Stranglers, XTC, Undertones, Bunnymen. I don't know how you would categorise our sound - a racket I guess. I couldn't and can't play guitar and that's probably why we eventually disbanded - I was hopeless."

"The name of the band derived from when we began practicing at Trevor's house in Netheravon. The

ENDLESS BEAT

"We only had about fifteen minutes of material but we managed to blag our way on."

neighbour was a certain Mrs Taylor, who was of an elderly dissuasion. When we would kick-off practicing in the living room, she would thump the walls, which of course we would ignore. Unfortunately, one evening, she took it upon herself to come round to the house and put her fist through the front window, screaming and hollering. We called the ambulance as we saw a trail of blood going back to her house and they took her away. We never saw her again and, in a fitting tribute, we named the band after her."

"We got a spread in the Journal and thought we were there. We also had a big picture in the Journal with me singing, playing guitar, and a sign saying 'Ladies' from the toilet behind the stage, that looks like it's stuck to my head! We played local venues including the Amesbury Fleapit[14], Saddle Rooms, Fisherton Arms and the Arts Centre. We made a cassette, Brain Drain, with a booklet, in 1985 - given away at the gigs we played around Salisbury."

In 1986, after attending a Jesus and Mary Chain and Shop Assistants gig, Jim Harrison and Dave Todd were inspired to form Bubblegum Splash! Prior to forming the band Jim, Dave and Marty Cummins had produced a short-lived - there were two issues - fanzine named Family Entertainment.

The initial line up of musicians got together between March and June with Jim (guitar), Dave (bass) and Marty (tambourine and backing vocals) being joined by Alan Harrison (stand up drums - no relation to Jim). Nikki Barr was then recruited on vocals, after being spotted wearing a Jesus and Mary Chain t-shirt in the Star. The band's name came from a cut and paste exercise, in the best traditions of Burroughs and Bowie.

Dave Todd: "We didn't want to be 'The' something or other and we put all these sort of indie pop names down on paper - 'bubblegum', 'candy' and

MRS TAYLOR'S MAD - left to right: Andy Ware, Trevor George, Paul Read and Dave Ware

that sort of thing - and the two that stuck together were 'Bubblegum' and 'Splash' - always with an exclamation mark!"

Bubblegum Splash! turned out to be a perfect expression of how the independent 'just do it' attitude could lead to a modicum of success, no matter what the level of technical aptitude.

Jim Harrison: "I knew Dave from school, the rest we all met in the Star. It really was almost overnight: 'Let's form a band - we can do that'. Musically we were one of the least competent bands to come out of Salisbury I would have thought… ever…we really couldn't play."

"Dave's fret had letters written in because he didn't know where the notes were. At our first gig I asked him to play an E and he looked at me and goes 'Which one of these is E?' It was about two weeks after we first formed – taking the mickey really, we shouldn't have been playing live at all."

Dave Todd: "Jim knew three chords and told me what to play. To start with I had A4 pieces of paper and it was like 'third string-second fret' - when we did our first gig I barely knew what the notes were called. Our first gig was at the Arts Centre with Newcombe and Roach – on the altar stage. We only had about fifteen minutes of material but we managed to blag our way on."

Jim Harrison: "Influences were all the really basic garage punk bands from the time – Jesus and Mary Chain, The Primitives – which you heard and thought 'I could play like that'. It was only when you tried it you thought 'Well, actually it's quite difficult this innit?' We played in Bristol a couple of times, which was good, and the Fisherton Arms, and with The Darling Buds, who had a couple of hits - they were a similar band but quite a bit better!"

The Bubblegum Splash! discography comprised a flexidisc featuring If Only - coupled with a Darling Buds track (given away with the Norwich-based So Naïve fanzine), an EP, Splashdown (which cost £200 and was recorded on the day Andy Warhol died) and two tracks on a compilation album entitled Surfin' In The Subway. The EP and compilation were issued by one of the trendiest labels of the day.

Jim Harrison: "We recorded the seven inch for a Bristol label called Subway - they printed up 2,000 copies. It made the independent charts, which at the time we thought was quite a big thing. We also got to number one on Radio Lille - independent music radio - in France. Musically it was very simple but it was the right time to release that sort of record."

The EP reached the Network, Catalogue and Melody Maker indie charts and – probably most credibly – spent a week at number 28 in the NME listings – alongside such giants of the indie-world as The Wedding Present, New Order and The Smiths, but the band was of its time, and its time was brief.

Dave Todd: "Whether that [success] was because people collected

BUBBLEGUM SPLASH! - left to right: Alan Harrison, Jim Harrison and Dave Todd

whatever was on Subway I wouldn't like to say - but it was quite an achievement. Of all the bands from Salisbury it probably shouldn't have been us, but I think we sort of kick started The Mayfields in to doing a bit more - and The Badgeman as well. There wasn't a rivalry but you would see a band getting a good review and it spurred you on. It was about a year and a half, fifteen gigs and seven recorded songs. That was the way it was meant to be really. I think it had run its course."

ENDLESS BEAT

"I still have the pics, but think they're better off being kept private!"

Jim Harrison: "We never did a tour – we probably only played a total of twenty-odd gigs all together. We were on a couple of compilation albums and then we split up. I think we realised probably we needed to go away and learn how to play a bit. I think that was as far as it could have gone – you couldn't have listened to an album of it, four songs was enough!"

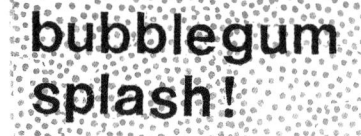

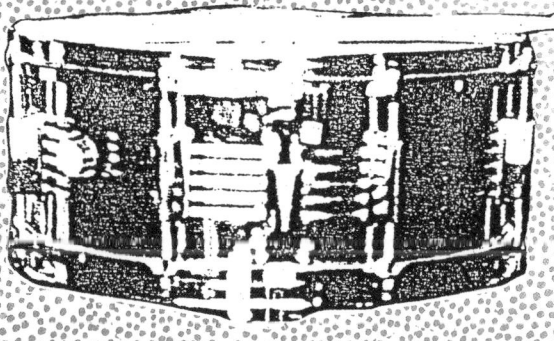

Away from the local scene, an ex-Salisbury resident had a short spell managing one of the rising bands of the early eighties.

Andy Nicklen: "Alan Crompton-Batt, who in 1971/72 was in the sixth form at Bishop Wordsworth's School, was going on to big things. In the end he went to London and started one or two enterprises – mail order in the Sunday magazines - then he was working for Heron Books, and the next thing he was managing the Psychedelic Furs – but he called it a day, probably after about a year. He went on to great things in PR - he started off the whole aspect of promoting chefs as 'pop stars'. He was quite famous in the end, considering he started off in the Chough…drinking cider!"

Meanwhile, singer and songwriter Robin Gair, by now a well known face on the Salisbury scene for over a decade, was trying a new approach to promoting his material.

Sally Anne Lowe: "My induction into the Salisbury music scene came

BUBBLEGUM SPLASH! - live debut at Salisbury Arts Centre

BUBBLEGUM SPLASH! - left to right: Alan Harrison, Dave Todd, Nikki Barr (front), Marty Cummins and Jim Harrison

with Your Special Day, Robin Gair's Eurovision entry, when I was sixteen. My school music teacher asked if I was interested in singing on a record for a local musician and I said 'Yes!'"

"With two girls from my school, and three others, we recorded backing vocals for the song. When the song was entered into the contest - via Dave Dee, I think - we had our picture taken by Roger Elliott for the Journal, on the swings in Churchill Gardens. I went off on a school exchange to Germany, where I received a phone call from my mum telling me to stand by because there was a chance we might have to go on the Song for Europe programme.

All very exciting, but sadly it came to nothing."

"A long time later I was walking past the Pheasant when I heard the strains of the song coming from the Liberal Club opposite - bringing back loads of memories. I still have the pics, but think they're better off being kept private!"

In 1980 Dave Dee made a cameo appearance as a record executive in the Sex Pistols' Great Rock'n'Roll Swindle movie. During 1980 and 1981 he ran his own record label, Double D Records. Nine singles and four albums were released, but unfortunately the label folded because of financial problems.

The best known Double D artist was probably the former Sun page-three model Jilly Johnson (fronting The Features). The London Cowboys – including former Sex Pistol Glen Matlock – were signed, but the label folded before they could release anything. Dave also just missed out on signing Australian band The Church - he had wanted to release their single, The Unguarded Moment, one of the truly all-time greatest non-hits.

In 1982, in unofficial support of England's World Cup effort, Dave Dee released his first solo record since 1971, The Ballad Of Bulldog Bobby,

209

ENDLESS BEAT

"... when it came to vocals we could pitch with any band on our day."

DBM&T - left to right: John 'Mick' Hatchman, John 'Beaky' Dymond, Trevor 'Dozy' Davies and Ian 'Tich' Amey

issued on Panache and credited to 'Dave And The Bulldogs'. Unfortunately it proved to be about as successful as Kevin Keegan's appearance as a substitute during the tournament.

In a far more worthwhile venture Dave Dee headlined (with DBM&T), and was involved in the organisation of, the Heroes and Villains Concert staged at Hammersmith Odeon in September 1982 to celebrate Radio One's fifteenth anniversary, with all proceeds going to the Nordoff-Robins Music Therapy Centre.

The reformed DBM&T had issued a second single in 1981 - Peter Mason's In The Coven backed with I Can't Stop Wanting You, a Mason-Amey composition, released on Earlobe Records in the UK. The single received airplay on Radio One, but failed to make any significant impression. Peter Mason's own single, Rock 'n' Roll (Look What You've Done To My Life), on which he was backed by DBM&T, had been issued in Germany in 1980.

Following his stint with Beaky Dymond in Band Of Gold, John Hatchman had become involved with a successful continental show band.

John Hatchman: "I first went pro when I was approached by a great friend of mine called Billy Bowers who used to be the roadie with The Troggs. He was over in Switzerland with The Troggs and when he came back he came to see me and said 'I've got a proposition. We were working with this band called Magic Power – they are absolutely brilliant. I was talking with the guitarist and he said 'Do you know of any English singers?'"

John landed the job as lead singer with Magic Power after an audition in Switzerland. The band gigged constantly touring Switzerland and John was offered the chance to record a track for a French film soundtrack, although the band refused to let him out of contracted gigs.

In 1982 Peter Lucas left DBM&T to rejoin The Troggs. As lead vocalist Beaky Dymond was keen to use this as an opportunity to vacate the drum stool and get back out front on guitar. By fortunate coincidence John Hatchman was in the UK during a break in Magic Power's hectic schedule.

210

John Hatchman: "I went out to see Beaky, who lived at West Wellow. When I arrived Beaky was painting his house and Tich was there as well. We were chatting away and Beaky said 'We're looking for a new 'Mick'' I said 'Well, I hope you've thought about me'. He said 'To be honest I hadn't - if you like we'll give it a go, but you've got to audition."

"I hadn't played drums for a few years as I had been concentrating on vocals and I thought 'Can I hack it?' Beaky knew I could sing because I was in Band Of Gold with him, but it was convincing Tich and Dozy. Tich didn't think I would cut the mustard but Beaky said 'You've got to give the guy a fair crack of the whip' and in the end I came through."

Following a proposal from DBM&T promoter Rainer Haas, Dave Dee also appeared at occasional gigs, the band having rehearsed with him upstairs at the rear of the Coach and Horses back in Salisbury.

Tich Amey: "The German promoter said it would be great to have Dave come and do a gig in Hamburg where we did the Top Ten Club in the early sixties. I rang Dave and he was coming out of the record business and wasn't doing a great deal. We did a place called the Machtel and Rainer said it would be nice to have him on a couple of other gigs. We had quite a good long set because we used to do an hour on our own – Eleanor Rigby, the b-sides and the Dozy, Beaky, Mick and Tich stuff – then on Dave would come and we could do an hour and a half of hits and rock'n'roll."

John Hatchman: "They couldn't just forget about the Zabadaks, Bend Its, Hideaways and Hold Tights, because that's what people wanted to hear, but at the same time we were trying to create something new and fresh and our ability was always vocals. I'm not saying we were the best musicians in the world – we weren't…Beaky always used to have a saying: 'The four conmen from Salisbury have done it again' [laughs] - but when it came to vocals we could pitch with any band on our day. We would blow them all away."

John was impressed by his new colleagues' versatility: "Beaky could put his hand to anything musically. We used to do Bend It with a squeeze box – he used to get black gaffa tape and tape the notes, so he knew where to hit it, and think nothing of going on stage. If he cocked it up he was the type of guy that had the personality to get out if it."

Dave Dee also joined up with The Boys for two single releases in 1983: the German only issue of Do Wah Diddy, and Staying With It (a cover of a minor American hit for Firefall) issued in the UK on Atlantic. The latter was performed on the Rod Hull and Emu Show and made a chart of sorts – reaching number 28 in the top 50 compiled by the writers of Music magazine. However, despite its contemporary sound it was another commercial failure.

In late 1984, the band recorded a version of the then popular football terrace chant, Here We Go. There were moves to release this as a single but this was eventually scuppered when Everton Football Club released a version of the song to commemorate their appearance in the 1985 FA Cup Final. A few copies of the DDDBMT effort were sold at live shows, on white labels and credited to 'The Boys'. Also available at gigs around this time was an album of recently re-recorded versions of their old hits, on the Heartbreak Hotel label.

Following a trip to Spain, DBM&T embarked on a new venture, opening their own bar in Marbella.

Tich Amey: "We had a small bar for the first year and then moved into a bigger place next door. Beaky originally put the money up for the first bar and then got a couple of English guys to help with the bigger place. It was just called 'The Sixties Bar' and it didn't take long for people to know whose bar it was."

"The first place held probably about a hundred people and they were like sardines. We had everybody there - Hurricane Higgins we had to remove a couple of times – George Best was another one - and the racing driver James Hunt".

In the ten years or so following the punk explosion, independent record labels had predominantly acted as a springboard for artists to move in to the mainstream, or as an outlet for those who would never be likely to attract much interest outside of a hardcore fan base.

However, acts such as The Smiths had demonstrated how commercial success could be attained whilst remaining true to the independent ethos and this, combined with an increasingly strengthening network of labels, distributors and fanzines would lead to the 'Indie' style becoming predominant in the traditional pop and rock fields during the nineties.

CHAPTER SIX FOOTNOTES

1. The William IV - one of Salisbury's bikers' pubs - was located in Milford Street and was subsequently been renamed The Hobgoblin and now The Vestry.
2. The Liberal Club was located in Salt Lane in premises now occupied by Conrans.
3. Olivers shoe shop was located in Silver Street in premises now occupied by Starbucks.
4. We believe this refers to Wilmer's in Catherine Street.
5. The Gibbs Mew Brewery was located in Gigant Street - on certain days the whole of the old city would smell of hops. Following the demolition of the brewery buildings the new housing to the north of Brewery Lane was built on the site.
6. Kingfisher Music was a music shop in Fleet.
7. Stand Out was located in Fisherton Street. The premises are currently vacant.
8. Green Lane was located near Odstock (now Salisbury District) Hospital and was occupied by a selection of locals and over-wintering travellers in an assortment of vehicles.
9. Mitchell Music was located in Queen Street in premises now occupied by London Camera Exchange.
10. Durrington Comprehensive School has now been renamed Upper Avon School.
11. Brian's Records was located in the former Derek's premises in the original Old George Mall in part of the area now occupied by BHS.
12. Raffles nightclub was located in the former Gordon's premises in Catherine Street and was subsequently renamed Bentleys. The premises are now occupied by Goldfinger's.
13. The Old Manor Social Club was located in Wilton Road on part of the site now occupied by Salisbury Law Courts.
14. The 'Amesbury Fleapit' was the Plaza Cinema in Salisbury Street. Following its demolition St Melor House Surgery was built on the site.

7 Independent's Days
Into the 1990s

The indie scene grew and with it the number of bands looking for places to play. The Passenger Club, launched at Salisbury Arts Centre in January 1988, was to provide the best regular series of gigs in the city since the closure of the Alex Disco in 1974. The Passenger's main drivers were the tireless Colin Holton and a new face on the city scene, who vividly remembers one of their talent spotting trips.

Ant Roberts: "'The back of the van' has an immediate resonance for those of us connected with music making. On this occasion, the dodgy van - they're always dodgy - rather than bearing the lumpy paraphernalia of amps, speakers, pedals and noise making stuff in general, was carrying the still reverberating young promoters and inventors of the freshly formed Passenger Club - we were the passengers."

"We and our chums were returning from one of our frequent forays that took us out to London, Bristol, Portsmouth and yes, Ringwood, in our quest for breaking music, new voices, new sounds and rock'n'roll. Fuelled only by sheer enthusiasm - and pockets stuffed with amyl nitrate - our passion would lead us to back rooms in pubs, swanky venues, plucky promoters' clubs and downright dives."

"Arriving at Salisbury Arts Centre in 1987, I had been appointed the humble marketing officer. Although I

ENDLESSBEAT

"... it would have been a real 'I was there' moment!"

hadn't known it at the time, small arts venues are often very fluid in their job descriptions, which is another way of saying that day to day there exists within the seeming organised structure, a freefall of panic that demands everyone do everything they can on whatever occasion to make the venue operate. I rapidly acquired the role of looking after the rock and pop."

"In the mid to late eighties there had emerged out of the apocalyptic but now diffused punk scene an indie scene. This scene, contrary to the current associations of jangly guitar bands, drew its 'indieness' from its independence from major labels and not as a music genre. The venues would spring up and disappear and clubs would occupy one space, vanish and appear the next week somewhere else. It was a London thing - bands like Bogshed, Stump, That Petrol Emotion, would pinball across the city on bills that listed usually five or more bands on the night. It was vibrant, truly independent, artistically risky and loads and loads of fun. This was where I'd come from, and what I brought to Salisbury under the respectable façade of marketing officer."

"I was new, the director – Jon C Struthers - was new, and I had a new friend. The friendship was instantly enormous - and so was he, in talent, knowledge, creativity, musicality, charisma, charm and girth - Colin Holton no less, and believe me, nothing is less than Colin Holton. The slot that had been previously set aside for the local rock bands had carried the less than inspiring title of 'Another Thursday Night'. We ditched it - we gave our slot the title of 'The Passenger Club', lifted straight from Iggy for no other reason than we liked it."

"Had the exercise been subjected to the type of market research or risk analysis necessary for any new venture these days it would have never have happened. The idea wasn't even properly formulated. Now, thirty years later, I would say we were trying to 'place quality cutting edge contemporary music into a strongly branded context that allowed local youth culture access to ownership whilst bringing together national benchmarks of innovation with a strong sense of community and shared ritual'. Back then we were just putting on gigs - of stuff we liked."

Leeds Indie band Cud made an attempt at reviving the spirit of the Stonehenge Free Festival in October 1988, after playing at the Arts Centre.

Dave Todd: "They were playing the Arts Centre on the Thursday and had stopped off at Stonehenge on the way down and had their photo taken, which is on their single Lola. They had a day off on the Friday and said 'Oh yeah, Stonehenge Festival – great. We'll go up and do a gig at Stonehenge'. We said 'You won't get within yards. How about doing something at Old Sarum?' They played for a bit until some traveller managed to almost reverse his lorry into the moat and the police were called."

Since the band's formation, the members of Bubblegum Splash! had utilised their contacts in the independent network to put on a series of gigs in Salisbury.

Alan Harrison: "We did everything under the banner Toothpick Productions. These events included fanzines and gigs and I think we managed twelve in total. We got contacts from the gigs we did, and the gigs we were going to in Bristol and London at the time."

"I was mainly responsible for putting together the bills for the gigs. They all took place at the City Hall, either upstairs or in the foyer. The idea was to put on three or four bands combining local bands and indie chart names including Mega City Four, Rosehips, Groove Farm, Blow Up, Jazz Butcher. The intention was for the gigs to be cheap and a little shambolic and in the main that was what we achieved."

Despite the best efforts of local promoters, and as had often been the case since Jerry Lee Lewis returned home in disgrace in 1958, the city missed out on some potentially big events.

Alan Harrison: "One Sunday in the summer of '89 I got a call from an agent - someone from the Arts Centre had given him my number. He was looking for a small gig for his band just before their single, which was

*Rudi Protrudi of **THE FUZZTONES** at Salisbury Arts Centre*

forecast to be their break through. Unfortunately he was looking for a specific date at pretty short notice and I couldn't put anything together to meet his requirements. The single was Made Of Stone, the band was The Stone Roses. If it had happened it would have been a real 'I was there' moment…and they were only £50!"

American garage legends The Fuzztones appeared at the Arts Centre in August 1989, supported by local punks The Stand. Richard Nash maintains this is the best gig he has ever seen in Salisbury, although the psychedelic fallout of having spent a couple of hours in the Wyndham Arms beforehand might have had some influence on this.

Practically every space in the city had been plastered with posters for In Heat - the headliners' then current album. The Rambler magazine reported that 'The Fuzztones took the stage looking like the coolest rock'n'roll band on the planet, dressed completely in black from their winkle pickers to their raven barnets, launched into Jack The Ripper and never looked back'.

Jon Maple reviewed The Fuzztones' gig for the Salisbury Journal. He referred to the amount of covers played as being justified as 'the original artists were so obscure that the records were not much heard outside the area of the local radio station'. Although he felt the band's range was limited in style, their performance of it was nevertheless excellent.

Carter The Unstoppable Sex Machine came along in January 1990, supported by local band Dennis. The gig was on a night of severe gales with weather warnings for people to stay at home, and consequently only around forty people witnessed a storming set by the then little known headliners.

In June 1990, Napalm Death and The Cardiacs were filmed at the Arts Centre for a video release. Napalm Death had been booked for the venue after the organisers of the Passenger Club had seen them playing in Southampton.

Colin Holton: "Me and Ant would listen to John Peel and look at the NME – we saw this band Napalm Death and thought 'What a name!' We tracked them down to this gig at St Mary's and saw this bunch of completely nutty Birmingham guys. All the Jamaican old boys were sitting in the corner playing dominoes and drinking their rum and this thrash concert was straight in front of them, and they didn't bat an eyelid. It was a great night out."

Ant Roberts: "The gig, if memory serves, had been organised by the anti fox hunting campaign in the days before fox hunting was, supposedly, banned. The venue had been a tiny back room, the stage lighting came from one bedside light at the back of the stage - I kid you not. God knows what PA had been hustled together to

215

ENDLESS BEAT

"I don't want to play bass I want to play guitar!"

make the gig happen, but happen it most emphatically did."

"The band not only rattled the eardrums, but also the sensibilities of the audience and the rules of all that preceded them. There had been about twelve of us in the room. In four weeks time there would be four hundred people plus watching as mayhem descended on the Arts Centre. The lunatics, on this occasion, really had taken over the asylum."

Manic Street Preachers, a Welsh band whose strong social and political views, mixed with crunching riffs, glammed-up appearance and a touch of pale ordinariness, resulted in their becoming a huge act in the nineties, played twice in Salisbury during the early part of the decade.

In November 1990, having only issued a couple of singles on small labels, they supported The Levellers at the Arts Centre. They returned in March 1992, as headliners at the College of Technology, having recently released their debut album Generation Terrorists.

In June 1992 The House Of Love played what was almost the last ever gig at the Arts Centre. Earlier in the day a few hundred individuals had marched through the streets of Salisbury in support of an ultimately successful campaign to save the venue, following a threatened closure.

To the south west of the city a new event that would attract name acts to the area had first been held in July 1990. Drawing inspiration from the Bracknell Jazz Festival, James Shepard organised the 'Larmer Tree Jazz, Blues and Folk Roots Festival' at the Larmer Tree Gardens near Tollard Royal. Headlined by Dick Heckstall-Smith, the event was such a success that, apart from a break in 1992, the festival has been held annually ever since, and in recent years has been complemented by the End Of The Road Festival, catering for a different audience in the same setting.

South African singer-songwriter Alexa Mackenzie arrived in Salisbury in the late eighties.

Alexa Mackenzie: "I had made this recording with two friends and it got to number three in the university charts. We were supporting all the biggest bands in South Africa –

MANIC STREET PREACHERS at Salisbury College

7: **Independent's Days**

Alexa MacKenzie and Ruth Jones

whatever that means – and I was approached by EMI in Johannesburg. They wanted me to fly up to demo. I said 'No thank you – we're emigrating to the UK'. My attitude was 'Who wants to be a big fish in a small pond?' Off we jetted to Salisbury - I arrived pretty confident in my song writing abilities."

After her arrival Alexa began to develop material and recruit personnel for a band that would become known as The Gurus.

Alexa Mackenzie: "I demoed some stuff at Recluse Studios and that got played on Spire FM. I was looking for a bass player and somebody said about Mark Kenchington. Ken came along and said 'I don't want to play bass I want to play guitar', so Ken taught me to play bass and we had a drum machine."

"Our first gig was in Hale Hall – we had Peter Wilks on keyboards. We did six or seven songs and that was where Nigel Finn saw us. Then we had a gig at the Pheasant and I remember Nigel telling us he so loved us he had invited all his musician friends. So everybody was there and I was quite nervous. The guy from the Journal, Jon Maple, was there. The first two or three songs were absolutely dire and Nigel said he was just standing there falling through the floor with disappointment. Then all of a sudden it kicked in and everybody loved it, and we got a great review from Jon."

"I was prolific in the way I wrote

217

ENDLESS BEAT

"I wish I could go back in time and slap myself round the face."

songs – we had a different set every time we went out - and we had a gig every six weeks. Only a certain amount of music made it to the tip of Africa and it was only the extremely successful music. You had to really scratch around to get the indie underground stuff. Consequently I had a real pop edge. I also loved Siouxsie and The Banshees, The Cure and The Smiths, but as a writer pop was running through me. What Ken brought was that edge that I lacked. Ken was coming from a darker side - melancholic – something that I didn't have."

"We only played two gigs with Pete. He was a brilliant keyboard player but we wanted to try something new so we threw all those songs out, I wrote a whole new set and then we got Frogg in and did the second set of demos at Recluse."

Frogg: "My time with the band was quite short lived but I loved the experience and the songs remain some of the best I ever played on. There was no doubt in my mind this band should have become rich and famous, because Alexa's songs were pop classics - I still play them to this day."

"I only played a handful of gigs - highlights being London's Mean Fiddler and Salisbury Arts Centre. I also completed a couple of recording sessions with the band. They were essentially a duo and after a while went their own way, eventually to live in London and pastures new – leaving me to concentrate on a classic Victorian murderer, a studio and a rock musical!"

Alexa Mackenzie: "We were doing well in the Salisbury scene - Jon Maple used to regularly trash the guesting band and always favour us, no matter how weird our set was. I was coming from this complete Bananarama edge but the irony is when you try and write the perfect pop song it always goes wrong in an interesting way - the mistakes make it indie - which is probably why he liked us."

"At the Mean Fiddler Russ Conway from Polydor saw us. He phoned the next day, sang New Heaven down the phone to me and said 'Come in and talk to me'. I went up to see him and he said 'I would like to buy this song for Kirsty McColl'. I was absolutely devastated - because I wanted to be the pop star - and said 'No – it's my song'. I wish I could go back in time and slap myself round the face."

"We decided we wanted to try a jingly-jangly guitar sound so we got rid of the keyboards and hooked up with a couple of chaps from another band. We rehearsed again a whole new set – a new sound. I think we were trying to become edgier. The Sundays were in the charts, The Darling Buds, The Primitives. It was all going that way. Then we decided we were going to London."

After some time away from the scene, former Kitchen and temporary Martian Schoolgirl Ruth Jones became involved in a new project.

COURGETTES - Ruth Jones and Graham 'Chalky' White

Ruth Jones: "We started off as Mission Impossible - with Lloyd Collinson - then it really quickly went into The Courgettes. It was the first time I was allowed to do some writing – or felt comfortable writing. It was Graham Hughes [drums], Chalky [White - guitar] and me on bass and lead vocals. I used to write the stuff, bring it to the band and they would work on it and shape it up – and sometimes Chalky would come with an idea for guitar and I would put some lyrics to it."

"Steve Burden [of The Martian Schoolgirls] at one point was looking to be my manager and got me a kind of deal with EMI – but it was really complicated. It meant ditching Chalky and Hughesy and going out as 'Ruth' – not The Courgettes – and I just thought everything I was doing was to do with The Courgettes: I needed their support to do the writing."

"That was the point at which I realised the reason I was involved in music was to play with a band live and enjoy it – it wasn't to get in to the business. They were talking about having clothing consultants, a photographer and an image, and I was saying 'Well, what's going to happen to my daughter Anna? How can I go on tour – she's got school'. That was the point at which I thought 'I know why I play live music – to do gigs and have people clap if they like it. I don't play to get involved in…legal arrangements'. It was a revelation to me – it really was."

"I had done this showcase gig in Dorset for EMI, and they had smoke machines and a light that was burning my face and I was given this pep talk - you know, like a football manager? Then it was proposed they could have this biblical marketing thing about 'Ruth' and all this crap – and I thought 'Actually, I just want to play in a band with my mates'."

"Not long after that I was involved in a Radio One Road Show debate. Muff Winwood was there and my song Fashion Queen was played on Radio One! I was asked because I was a female bass player and they were talking about image and the whole thing about women dressing up and using sex to sell music. My approach was it depended on how I felt on the night – if I wanted to wear a cardigan and jeans I would and if I wanted to dress up I would."

Having been inspired by Ruth, Soundtracks columnist Sally Anne Lowe was part of a short lived band, Six Miles From Huesca, with Mark Palmer (bass), Duncan Howell (guitar) and the late Alex Sharpe (drums).

Mark Palmer: "I had never been in a band with a girl singer and I wanted to see what it was like. We were named after a group of anarchists who dug a trench six miles from Huesca at the start of the Spanish Civil War - at the end of the war they were still in that trench. I just loved the fact they did fuck all for three years."

Sally Anne Lowe: "Rehearsals at Sarum 76 and one gig in Bournemouth. I said I wouldn't play in Salisbury because I would get lambasted, but someone from Salisbury came to Bournemouth! He was very kind to us thank God!"

"I was terrified to perform in public - but the boys were brilliant. I had Marty [Cummins] of Bubblegum Splash! tambourine, but my hands shook so much I had to put it down! Alex was the best drummer I have ever come across but he never really got the chance to shine. I think he's remembered by lots of people. He was a great friend and I was heartbroken when he died, as were many people. I last saw Duncan at Alex's funeral - fortunately we didn't perform. Mark left us for the glamour of the BBC, and Ruth Jones tried to convince me that I could sing and play bass at the same time - sadly I'm not as talented as Ruth, but thank her for her misplaced confidence in me."

Jane From Occupied Europe emerged from those members of Bubblegum Splash! who had decided to take a more studied approach to their music.

Jim Harrison: "Three of us decided we would carry on but try and improve our ability in a slightly different style. Within a year we formed Jane From Occupied Europe, which was me, Dave Todd, Alan Harrison and another guitarist, Colin O'Keefe. After the first two gigs Dave Ware joined and he did guitar and keyboards."

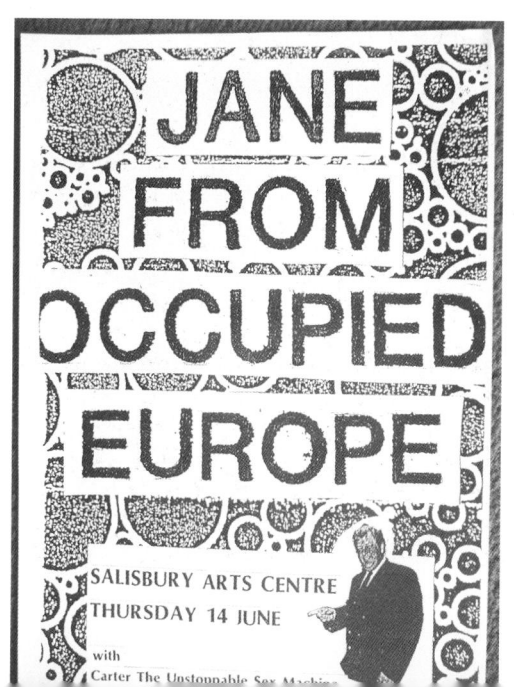

ENDLESS BEAT

"... they played at the Arts Centre in front of about thirty people."

"It was definitely a lot more competent than Bubblegum Splash! We could play a lot better. We did our first single after about a year, with a drum machine which Dave Ansell programmed for us - Alan had left and moved to Brighton. Then we got a guy called Phil Eason to drum for us, he is now a cameraman - he has worked for Aardman Animations."

Dave Todd: "Me and Jim were always going to carry on as long as we were in the same town. Colin was an old school friend of Jim's and was a virtuoso musician compared to the rest of us. He helped out on guitar because Jim was taking over the singing."

"The early Jane From Occupied Europe stuff was very much a continuation of Bubblegum Splash! - it wasn't until later on that it developed. Naturally you play more and learn your instrument but it wasn't like 'Right - we're gonna get our heads down'. Over time you stop just copying and start doing your own stuff more."

The band's unusual name was borrowed from one of their influences.

Jim Harrison: "We nicked it from a Swell Maps album. They were quite an offbeat band - punk but quite... almost unlistenable... experimental. They did an album called Jane From Occupied Europe, which I think was based on a cartoon strip in the war."

"We played a lot more than Bubblegum Splash! - from Exeter up to York. We played with Carter The Unstoppable Sex Machine, who stayed around our house at East Street when they played at the Arts Centre in front of about thirty people. We played a lot of little clubs – they were called 'clubs' but they were normally the back of a pub."

'The Janies' evidently had a lot more confidence in their ability than had been the case in the Bubblegum Splash! days, and preferred to let the music provide 'the show' during live appearances. Reviewing one of the band's gigs in June 1988 for the Salisbury Journal, Sally Anne Lowe reported: 'This band make almost no attempt to perform. So the whole gig relies heavily on the songs, and it's just as well that on the whole they are dead catchy'.

The band played original material and, with the help of Andy Ware, formed a label - 7% - apparently named after Sherlock Holmes' preferred cocaine solution.

Jim Harrison: "We would each come up with little riffs and then all play together. The first single I pretty much knocked up on my own – Ocean Run Dry. Once we got Dave Ware in, who was a good musician, we all used to write together."

"We did two singles – they didn't make the indie charts but we got NME coverage – reviews and little interviews. Dave Ware's brother set up the label. We probably sold about 500 to 1,000 copies of each – we had a distribution deal with Revolver – so we got in all the 'Chain With No Name' type indie shops."

Andy Ware: "When I returned from working in Saudi in 1990, I moved to London and had a bit of spare change in my pocket. JFOE were

220

7: **Independent's Days**

Jim Harrison

ENDLESS BEAT

"We sort of created a little scene in Salisbury..."

releasing their first single, which did pretty well, and were looking for funding for a follow up and perhaps an album. I attended a music management course at North London Poly - run by Horace Trubridge from Darts no less - and took on the dubious mantles of music mogul, cash benefactor, and owner/manager of 7% Records."

Jim Harrison: "The first single got played on Peel - it was about six minutes long, but he played it once or twice. It was noticeable that, in the week he played it, it sold like 400 copies on the strength of that and maybe an NME review that said 'These lot are alright' – we were in their 'Bands To Watch' column."

"There was one album - Coloursound. We always used the same place – Pete Lamb in Devizes. He had a little studio in his garage. He had Jesus Jones in there and some other quite big bands in their early days – but a lot of country and western, but he was cheap. We knew him through Dave Ansell, who recommended him. He's a lovely chap - brilliant little studio, and whatever you want to do he'll do it."

"Kevin Russell of The Mayfields used to work with Fred Fieber and they did the cover. A cartoonist did the insert, a mate of ours - it was like most of these bands, you get your mates in. A couple of other people played on the album - a violinist who was Jon Maple's sister, Sarah [McCauley]."

Andy Ware: "I helped to fund and manage the records. I also helped with the funding of a tour bus - a shit Renault Trafic van, the fastest thing about it was the rust - as well as sorting out gigs and publicity. I interestingly worked with a chap named Angus who was the publicist for Carter the Unstoppable Sex Machine. I also paid for a ridiculous fly posting campaign around London for the album. It cost a lot of wonga, a visitation from the Metropolitan

THE MAYFIELDS - left to right: Tim Waterman, Kevin Russell and Adrian 'Swannie' Martin

7: Independent's Days

Police, and probably got about three extra sales of the album."

Dave Ware: "Andy was really supportive - I think he had some fun being a record company el presidente."

Another element to the hive of activity involving the Janies and their cohorts - living at various 'houses of cool' dotted around the city - was the production of a fanzine, Wobbly Jelly, the name of which was apparently partly inspired by the city's then MP Robert Key. In a neat parallel with their earlier effort, Family Entertainment, the fanzine only lasted for two issues.

A few other low-key fanzines appeared during the eighties including the Fovant and metal based Defenders Of Rock and The Rambler, something akin to a 'lifestyle' magazine for the young pub-going men of Downton, but with a generous musical content.

Despite a fair smattering of coverage in the national music press, the Janies folded soon after the release of the Coloursound album.

Jim Harrison: "We split up shortly after we released it pretty much! Dave Todd, who was an original founder member, decided he was going to move up north with Wendy, who is his wife now. We did a few gigs without him but it never felt quite right. It was about mid-91 we called it a day."

"I have very fond memories. The Badgeman were doing very well and everyone was playing gigs – not just locally, we were all playing out of town. The Mayfields were playing all over the place, The Nuthins – everyone knew everyone else."

The Mayfields were formed by Kevin Russell and Adrian 'Swannie' Martin.

Swannie: "In 1986 I found myself lost - after getting out of the mod scene in about '84. I met Kevin who was a mod with me and I grew up with. He was just getting into indie music and I started knocking about with him. He used to play guitar and I played tambourine – in his bedroom – and that was the original Mayfields. We didn't do any covers – it was all original music. Kevin was the main songwriter."

"The Mayfields was in the era of C86, which was a very good indie time, when bands like Primal Scream, Soupdragons and My Bloody Valentine all started. It was a scene that was very DIY, so you would set up your own gigs and be friends with all these bands and it really took off from there."

"We sort of created a little scene in Salisbury with The Badgeman and Jane From Occupied Europe. We hung out with them most of the time because we were into similar things. Half of us used to live together. We used to play with each other at gigs outside Salisbury a lot. We were making our own vibe. It was a nice little circle and we were meeting bands that were actually doing quite well."

In June 1988 The Mayfields and Jane From Occupied Europe played at a self-promoted gig at the College Common Room.

Swannic: "We were fed up with playing horrible little pub gigs so we decided to do up the hall ourselves - which took about five to six weeks of hard work – cleaning the floors, redecorating, making sure the toilets worked. We made all our own posters, flyed out all the pubs, organised the bands, organised the bar. There was one local band and one bigger band that we happened to be friends with – The Razorcuts. We were hanging out with the college crowd at the time and all the people that used to go in the Pheasant, so it was well attended."

As was the case with The Janies,

223

ENDLESS BEAT

"We got fed up of playing gigs in Salisbury and nothing happening."

The Mayfields left a small but fondly remembered recorded legacy.

Swannie: "We decided to make a flexi to promote the band, with The Badgeman. Just as we paid for it we signed two deals – Ambition Records in Southampton and Bus Stop in Iowa."

"The American guy just rang up and said 'You go and record two tracks and I'll pay for the recording time', and the guy in Southampton came in the studio with us, recorded two tracks and organised some gigs. Distribution was mostly through gigs, fanzines – not through shops, because of the underground ethos of it all."

The lead tracks on the singles were World Of Your Own (on Ambition) and Deeper Than The Ocean (Bus Stop), both issued in 1989. A future member of The Nuthins made his debut on World Of Your Own.

Bob Taylor: "Through knowing Swannie I started playing a bit of glockenspiel and keyboards on a couple of songs. They released a single and – that sort of cute scene – Kevin wanted a glockenspiel on it. I never played any instruments then so I learned it, put it on in the studio and played it live for them a few times. That's how I started."

The Mayfields also appeared on a number of compilations but didn't see any financial reward, despite reasonably healthy singles sales, and struggled to adapt to the changing indie scene.

Swannie: "They were rubbish [deals] as in we didn't see any money, although we did sell about 10,000 copies of our single in Iowa - we were actually number 2 on the college chart in Iowa. The label was very small so they couldn't really afford to pay us to go over and we didn't really have the money because we were poor students as it were."

"After the indie self-promoting thing times changed. Bands like Primal Scream grew up and we had to sort of go along with that, and we got involved in the Madchester scene. We had a demo done and got a producer in - this producer was mixing in things like Led Zeppelin and Jungle Brothers – he was very ahead of his time. We sent it to some companies and A&M loved it. They came and saw us play a couple of times at London gigs. The first time they loved us but they came again and unfortunately Kevin got very drunk and they didn't bother after that."

"To be honest, looking back at it, the excitement was getting to that point. I don't think it would have been exciting when we were under pressure to make records and tour. The fact that you were doing it yourself and going up to London in a beaten up old van – that was the exciting part."

"Being together for about five years, people change, you get different members come and go - it was only me and Kevin who were original and we had literally about fifteen or twenty people coming in. We got fed up of playing gigs in Salisbury and nothing happening. The trouble is when you get to a certain high and then that scene disappears, you end up getting relegated to doing local gigs - and that's not for us."

Despite the unsatisfactory end to the band, Swannie recalls the highlights of his Mayfields days with fondness.

Swannie: "We supported the Las in Portsmouth Guildhall – our height of fame. We had supported quite a few other bands like Pooh Sticks and The Wedding Present but the Las was the big gig – big audience, big venue. We loved doing it. We had a lot of fun. We would go to gigs and get girls coming up and saying 'We know you', because they had read about us in a fanzine. So we were like mini pop stars – and it was great."

Old friends Kevin Russell and Swannie continued playing together.

Swannie: "We started The Spoils with two younger guys. We were in that band for about a year and then the age difference got the better of us. Then we got together with two members of The Badgeman - who we were mates with - to form Parma. We were like a 'super group' from Salisbury and I loved that, but unfortunately it was at the end of 'our' time. We carried on with Parma until 1998 and then knocked it on the head – people were getting married and having kids."

The Mayfields were among the acts featured on a Salisbury compilation tape, God's Great Tape Head Cleaner, put together by Dave Ware and issued on 7% in 1991.

Dave Ware: "It was a really interesting time musically in Salisbury and my motivation was to represent that. My friend Andy Brown designed the cover and it was quite interesting pulling all the tracks together. I wanted to do a kind of C86 compilation tape. I had a couple of DATS from those that didn't record at Pete Lamb's great studio in what is the English version of Memphis - Potterne."

"The nice thing was being able to choose the tracks with some help from friends – it's all about the mixture of friends, music, beer, pasties, crap jobs broken up by stints on the dole and trying to get a girlfriend - for me that is!"

"I think all of us were on the dole at the time so I got in touch with the Prince's Trust and to my surprise got a £500 loan. I got all the bands I wanted. The only toss up was between Shady Lady – a popular Wiltshire covers band - and The Badgeman. The Badgeman got it because they needed the publicity."

"We sold a lot, but to be honest I was not the most driven person. What is important is it reflects a really good patch of music. I don't even have a copy of the tape. I worked out that from the age of seventeen to thirty-one I lived in about twenty-five different houses - I kid you not. I have not held on to anything."

Andy Ware: "If you're wondering what happened to the £500 Dave got from the Prince's Trust - he failed to mention that a very large crowd of people just happened to co-incidentally dine out on a very nice Indian at the Asia when the money was deposited!"

A highlight of the tape was a cover of Newcombe and Roach's Emma (Mild Thing) by Dennis.

Skid: "I got Dennis up together with Mickey Dyer. We had Sarah McCauley on violin and Andy Clements on drums. We used to play at the Arts Centre a lot – we all worked behind the bar so we could always get gigs down there. We supported Carter, Ride and a few other decent bands of the time."

"All we were trying to do with Dennis was write very nice little pop songs that once you heard them you couldn't get them out of your head, but played at a deafening volume with very distorted guitars and a screechy violin over the top."

The Stand, whose gigs included The Fuzztones' support slot, were formed by Stand Out proprietor Colin Mundy – once of Obvious Action: "I wanted to get another band together, so we did The Stand – I stole that [name] from the Alarm."

Comprising Colin on guitar and vocals with Kev Barnes (bass) and Terry Whatley (drums – later replaced by Rich Walker), the band had an uncompromising pure-punk approach, as noted by Sally Anne Lowe in a live review for the Salisbury Journal: 'Try saying The Stand without saying 1976'.

The band also had an alternating second guitarist position.

Clive Roper: "Nick [Shirfield] couldn't always play so I used to wear the number 12 shirt and play the odd gig. It was quite good fun because I had no responsibility whatsoever – all I had to do was turn up, play and possibly drink the occasional drink if I was required to."

With his former View From A Bridge cohort Richard 'Buzzard'

ENDLESS BEAT

"...we could do better than this – do you fancy doing it?"

Atkinson, Clive put together his own band, the unusually named Going Out With God.

Clive Roper: "There was a single by a band called Kinky Machine called Going Out With God, and I thought that was a really fun title [but] Dave Marsh told everybody that Hannah Burton, who I was going out with at the time, had said it was 'like going out with God'."

"Buzzard came up with this idea that we could make a pretty penny by forming an acoustic rock trio. We ended up playing at the Salisbury Comedy Club with Jonathan the Jester[1]. It was quite enjoyable. Frogg joined us on keyboards - and beer - and we had Dave Marsh on bongos until one day he bought his drum kit."

"We ended up with a residency at the Wig and Quill. The landlord Adam Heaton was an XTC and Jam fan and we used to get him up to sing - and members of staff. It was the slippery slide doing covers but there was more people coming in – all of a sudden you couldn't put a foot wrong."

Clive's occasional colleagues The Stand would evolve into The Magnificent.

Colin Mundy: "Kev [Barnes] and I had become a bit of partnership – if I was in a band Kev would be the bass player. Nick [Shirfield] suggested this guy Gary James, who had been in loads of Gothic bands. We did a rehearsal above the shop and just gelled straight away – it was a good mixture and we did some good stuff. Gary had confidence in his voice and a good stage presence. He could write lyrics as well – much better than I could - so we let him get on with it. We would give him a title and he would write a song about it."

Gary James had been the lead vocalist with Rose Coloured Nightmares, a Bishop Wordsworth's School based band, and had spent some time writing songs with Don't Feed The Animals bassist Nick Shirfield after both bands had split.

Gary James: "I met and started chatting with Colin at The Nuthins' first gig, about how cool I thought The Nuthins were but wished for something inspired by stuff that came a little later on. We discussed the idea of forming a band based on Electric-era Cult, Hanoi Rocks, New York Dolls, Damned - and both suggested we knew a bass player for the job."

"When it came to setting up a first meeting I didn't know they all knew each other from Obvious Action. I brought along drummer Ian Rudorf to complete the line up and we got it together pretty quickly."

In his role as a local promoter, Colin was able to ensure the band got some decent support slots.

Colin Mundy: "The best gig we ever put on was The Macc Lads - I made sure we were in the support slot. It was a fantastic night. The Macc Lads were renowned for people throwing beer at them and we benefited from that as well. Kev and I were at the front and loving it because we were punk rockers, but Gary wasn't used to that kind of treatment. When The Macc Lads came on it was like a tidal wave of fluids from the crowd all across the stage – it was a fantastic sight."

Gary James: "I remember it very well for two reasons: one, I watched a skinhead piss in a pint pot and then launch it at me - I still remember saying 'that was warm' mid-lyric - and two; as soon as we left the stage Colin sacked Ian. To this day I have no idea why but no-one seemed to question his decision and we set about auditioning for a new drummer. Ray [Hunt] was I think the third out of eight drummers due to audition one evening above Stand Out and we just told the last five we had our drummer without even hearing them."

Whether playing headline or support, The Magnificent were able to crank the excitement up while playing live.

Colin Mundy: "Even if there are only ten people out there, if the lights are on the stage and not on the crowd, there could be thousands. One of the best ones was when Mr Chesils was a venue[2]. We did the first ever gig there when they got a licence to put bands on and it was absolutely rammed."

Mr Chesils was also the venue for a storming, indeed magnificent, double header with The Mayfields - a favourite local band in Colin's memory: "I was always impressed with Kev Russell. He was so single-minded, he would even tell you how to hold the plectrum – he was very pernickety. He ruled the band with an iron fist but they had some good 'Wonderstuffy' type songs going on."

Internal frictions within The Magnificent eventually led to Colin dropping out of the band scene, but other band members would persevere in a new project.

Colin Mundy: "We did quite a few demo tapes and had some quite strong interest from Warner Brothers, but we would just argue all the time. I loved it – it kept things healthy - but Nick and Gary took it all personally. Gary, Nick and Ray wanted to go in another direction. I decided to concentrate on the shop and they carried on as a three-piece. I then made a conscious decision that I wasn't going to waste any more time playing in local bands."

Gary James: "We started recording and did more gigs until it started to become fairly obvious there was a musical pull in two different directions. Nick and I demoed some songs and asked Colin if he was into them to which he replied 'No' - and that was the end of The Magnificent."

"Nick, Ray and I started rehearsing - often for twelve hours a day - at Britford Village Hall. As there were no available guitarists we wanted to work with it was essential that I learned pretty quickly. We needed a name quick as we wanted to get out and play as soon as we had a set together, and called ourselves Swing Syndicate. The sound at first was influenced by the lead bass sound of New Model Army, mainly to cover up the fact that my guitar skills were extremely limited."

"Our first gig was supporting The Troggs at Salisbury Arts Centre, which I was really proud of - they were fantastic, really nice guys. I knew Pete Lucas from drinking in Mr Chesils but hadn't met any of the others. I remember The Troggs sound checking without Reg, we sound checked then all of us went to The Five Bells where some die hard Troggs fans from France were waiting with gifts for the band. When it came to show time The Troggs went onstage and started playing, and Reg Presley appeared on stage in a puff of smoke, right on cue, to start singing – fantastic - what a brilliant loud English rock'n'roll band!"

Mad Cow Disease, initially featuring Jon Maple on lead vocals, Colin Holton and Dan Bunce on guitars, 'Mad Mark' on bass, and Rob Arney on drums (shortly to be replaced by Jimmy Blackwell), provided Salisbury with an experience of a new sound - a blend (although that is probably too gentle a word) of metal, punk, sampling and general noise buffed up with as much grunginess as possible.

Colin Holton: "That was started as a complete joke. It's one of those things - everything we have done with any of the bands we never really pushed it, it just came to us. It was the same with Mad Cow."

"Jon Maple was bar manager at the Arts Centre and he goes 'Some of these bands - we could do better than this – do you fancy doing it?' We sat at this table with my old acoustic guitar and wrote Give Me Tea Or Give Me Death and Jesus Wants Me For A Vegetable. He's a fantastic lyric writer."

"We thought we needed a sampler so I went to a junk shop and bought this thing, and after about five gigs it melted – it went really soft. We were playing the altar stage at the Arts Centre and people were just going mad."

Jon Maple: "The first thing I did that met with any great success was Mad Cow Disease, and I was getting on a bit by then. It was about '89/90 when we got together, which would have made me thirty - which was old, although not as old as Colin it has to be said."

ENDLESS BEAT

"... we were very much at that point taking the piss to be honest."

"Colin and Ant Roberts used to put on a lot of gigs by hardcore thrash bands, which were then cutting edge. We were quite influenced by this but at the same time had an ironical take on it. Me and Colin wrote a few sort of…parodies I suppose you would call them, of death metal. I remember one called Death Metal Fatigue, which was a typical Maple-Holton pun, but based on a very efficient Slayer-style riff that Holton came up with."

"Our first gig I remember because I was electrocuted. It was at Amesbury Sports Centre supporting BTF, who were an Amesbury crusty punk thrash outfit – BTF stood for Blasted To Fuck I seem to recall. One of these crusty hippies had constructed what you might call a junk sculpture out of scrap metal, on which he had put lights. Metal obviously conducts electricity and somehow as soon as I touched the mic stand I got 240 volts, which sent me six foot backwards onto my arse and completely knocked out all the electricity in the building for ten minutes. That was quite a good start…I think it was somehow symbolic - we had started as we meant to carry on – in chaos and disaster and almost death!"

"We were very much at that point taking the piss to be honest, but we developed through line-up changes and the influence of different musical forms – American industrial stuff like Revolting Cocks and Ministry – who took us away from the death metal parody into a more grinding noise-based approach."

The band's name summed up their general approach of having a laugh, but seeing how much they could get away with – it would soon attract some notable attention.

Colin Holton: "You had to be a bit controversial, so we called it Mad Cow Disease. Then John Peel said 'It's a wonder no-one has called themselves Mad Cow Disease', so I sent him a fax saying 'There is a band called Mad Cow Disease' and he read it out on his show."

"We then went to Atilla – who wasn't anything to do with the band at the time - and recorded four tracks on a cassette. I sent it up to Peel and didn't think anything else of it, until I put the radio on one night and he was

MAD COW DISEASE - left to right: Colin Holton, Ally Gamble and Jon Maple

MAD COW DISEASE - left to right: Jimmy Blackwell, 'Mad' Mark Andrews, Jon Maple and Colin Holton

saying 'on the show tonight…blah blah, Mad Cow Disease, blah blah' and I was like 'Did I hear that right?' He said 'Here's a band from Salisbury' and played Jesus Wants Me For A Vegetable. I phoned Jon and he's saying 'What are you on about you fucking idiot?' – I said 'he's playing it!' Peel gave us a call and said 'We're playing another track tomorrow night!'"

"Then we got these faxes coming in with people asking for our names, so I thought I'm gonna be 'Thrax The Herdsmen', then we had 'Crazy Daisy', a real gloomy name for Jon… and 'Pat' – as in cow pat. We thought 'Let's see how far we can get with it', so we sent Kerrang! this list of names and gigs – one real gig and the rest we made up – 'West Country band, John Peel's favourites blah blah' and then I started getting letters saying 'Dear Mr Herdsman'! That's how it went – it made a complete mockery of trying to make it with blood, sweat and tears."

The band line-up changed as bassist Mad Mark left and was replaced by Ally Gamble, an impressed member of a band Mad Cow had supported.

Jon Maple: "We were taken on as support for Wench – a bunch of New York women who played thrash metal. A right cack-handed do it was - we were down for gigs right across the country and I reckon two out of three of them were pulled, which was soul destroying - I think it broke up Wench."

Colin Holton: "This promoter said 'I've got this band called Wench. Do you lot want to tour with them?' I did a deal for a van for two weeks and we went all around the country. Then Mad Mark left and Ally [from Wench] said 'I wanna join your band' - we didn't have a record deal or anything."

Jon Maple: "She stayed in this country, got a work permit and joined us. Our bass player – a gentleman from Bournemouth, a big ginger bugger and a mental case on stage - was replaced by this tiny woman, with lots of tattoos - from Queens - with this underground New York attitude, which I was very impressed with."

"On her bass she used to have a big sticker saying 'pre-menstrual and in tune'. She introduced a feminine aspect to what had been a very testosterone fuelled experience. I think when women join bands it alters the whole dynamic for the better. That's my sociology for heavy metal - bring a woman in and it'll bring a different atmosphere."

Catalina Records signed the band, whose dirty sound was now augmented by samples and keyboards.

Colin Holton: "The whole thing was detuned down to D – just enough so the strings didn't flap around – so it was a really heavy guttural sound. Atilla had joined after that first tour so we had keyboards and samples."

ENDLESS BEAT

"... like young male stags rutting in the moshpit."

Jon Maple: "Sample copyright was a very grey area then so you could sample anything and get away with it. We were sampling things like Eraserhead and Blue Velvet dialogue. It was very imaginative I thought - we spent hours going through our record and video collections with a sampler."

"The song writing became more influenced by Atilla, who has classical musical education so he could do orchestration. It's like a trade to him - he knows music theory like a carpenter knows wood and saws, and that would have been a huge influence on our harmonic development and coherence. Me and Holton left together were just doing this sort of noisy riffy punk rock. Holton can certainly write a catchy riff but Tilla's thing was to structure it – Tilla came from a heavy metal background and of course metal is very influenced by classical music structures."

Atilla: "It was fabulous, they were my favourite band I have ever been in because everything was so exciting - it was fresh. I not only played keyboards but also provided noises. It was exactly what I didn't know I had been looking for. There were certain songs where I would play riffs that would back up the bass guitar and just add to the grungy bottom end of it, but a lot of it was firing samples."

"In the late eighties you had the hardcore scene – Napalm Death, Extreme Noise Terror et al - who had a real influence because they had this real rage, this real blast beat sound, which was a new thing. I think we were wanting to emulate some of that, but also adapt it in to our own thing. People called us 'industrial' but real British industrial is bands like Throbbing Gristle and 23 Skidoo. We were punky metal noise, but this whole movement came to be called 'industrial'."

Colin Holton: "We went up to the Monty Python studios in Camden. Michael Palin was there and we used the original sheep noises off the sheep sketch on one of our demos. We mastered at Abbey Road and that's how that took off – we were thinking 'This is silly'."

For Mad Cow's first release, the Costermongerin' EP, Catalina employed a plugging company, who promised the band a spread in the UK's leading rock magazine.

Colin Holton: "I go up the shop and buy Kerrang! and I'm walking back looking in the singles…nothing in there…typical! It was only on the front page - I had missed that! It was a massive great picture - and it was single of the week!"

"Then we started getting the interest. Alan Freeman on Radio One - we turned up at the Joiners[3] and as we pulled up he said 'This is Mad Cow's version of Masters Of The Universe…and this is another song called Bullshit Acres! It was great!"

The band's stage act was developing in line with their big personalities.

Jon Maple: "Holton has always been a presence. A gig by a band with Colin Holton in is generally a gig by 'The Colin Holton Band', in that he is the main source of attention and plays up to the audience. He'll do anything to get the audience's attention. One night at the Jericho Tavern[4] for example, there was a moshpit going. He pulled a baseball cap off a kid at the front, pissed in it and put it back on the kid's head! That was the sort of extremities to which he was capable of going to draw attention to an act."

"It was a spectacular scene I think – Mad Cow Disease on stage. There were a lot of physically big people with big egos and big characters in that band and I think that came across live. It was a constant battle for attention between me, Colin and Atilla

MAD COW DISEASE

and you have to fight your corner. So each gig – it wasn't macho posturing at all but there was an aggressive atmosphere."

"It seemed to work on certain audiences - biker club houses and stuff - but we were quite often out of control, especially on drink. When touring in the Transit there is nothing to do and your whole day is comprised of hanging about or driving somewhere - you turn up at a venue, you're loading in your stuff at two in the afternoon and then waiting 'til ten at night to play - what do you do? You drink…or at least we did – as a band. We were big drinkers. We normally kept it together, although when we didn't I think it probably added to the chaos of the moment."

"I used to enjoy the performances but I always found it very nerve-wracking and really had to work on developing my performance ego. I was unapproachable for about an hour before going on. I was rather enamoured of Iggy Pop as a performer but of course didn't have the physique or musculature to do that kind of stuff - but I liked his arrogance and venom and attack. It's about testosterone that kind of music - like young male stags rutting in the moshpit."

The band spent little time in Salisbury as they were mostly off gigging in support of their records, although their memories of being on the road are somewhat hazy.

Atilla: "We were doing loads but don't ask me too much about them because that was a particularly… 'confusing' time…we drunk a lot of alcohol and kept going on tour with bands whose bass players were drug dealers…"

Mad Cow Disease recorded two albums for Catalina. Goat Lung (The Mexican Approach) was produced by the band with Martin Johnson and released in 1993. The follow up, Tantric Sex Disco, was issued two years later but failed to live up to expectations, despite the use of a name producer – Gang Of Four guitarist Andy Gill.

Atilla: "The first album was under our control and came out better as a result. The second album had a different sound to it – I wasn't happy with Andy Gill's mix. We had some massive riffs on the album and there were some songs every bit as good, if not better, than the first album. In fact I think the demos we did were better – they had more energy, the songs were captured better. Andy Gill is a very talented producer and musician but it didn't really gel with what we were wanting, we were all about massive riffs, with hook lines, but with a nasty punk rock attitude."

Jon Maple: "I think the first one was more representative of our live approach and loose way with playing. I thought Gang of Four were great and was impressed when the management company suggested we use Andy Gill but he made us far more clean and precise and the second album hasn't the…disorder…of the first."

"It became too computerised – to the point where some of the tracks couldn't really be played live. There was going to be a battle of wills because we were opinionated big noisy bastards who all had their own ideas and he was a very strong character. He had produced the Red Hot Chilli Peppers. I remember saying to him 'How did you get on with Flea and all them?' He said 'I had a great deal of trouble about drum programming' and I thought 'Yeah, I bet you bloody did - sitting at your computer sorting their loose funk arrangements into something precise for digital reproduction' and that's the kind of thing that happened to our songs."

"He had his way by and large on that album. Although we wrote the tunes, he sculpted the sound into something that was not quite representative of what we were. However that's by no means unique – that happens all the time."

As well as the regular band releases, the Mad Cows were also involved in a typically tongue in cheek one-off single…that some took more seriously.

ENDLESS BEAT

"It didn't really split it just kind of petered out."

Jon Maple: "We did a piss-take of The Levellers and the whole crusty punk movement called The Dishevellers. We released a song me and Colin wrote one afternoon, with an acoustic guitar and a bottle of scotch, called Crusty Girl - about getting married at Stonehenge as a pagan ritual and the whole crusty phenomenon - in the style of The Levellers. The Levellers got in touch and said 'Can you do a support'! We said 'That's all we've got' – we had to turn it down."

Sadly, Mad Cow Disease became the latest Salisbury band to show great promise but end up fizzling out as the band became disillusioned with decisions made by their management.

Jon Maple: "We were just about to embark on this tour, so we were in rehearsal for that - using the Joiners Arms' stage while it was closed in the afternoons. We did that for about a week and on the last day of rehearsals I collapsed with some terrible infection of my kidneys. I was hospitalised that night and wasn't in a healthy enough position to continue, and it folded."

"I think it was on its last legs anyway to be honest. It wasn't the band itself - we were getting on alright, we were a unit - but we were so pissed off. We had such trouble with the record company and management, who seemed to be working in opposite directions to us and more interested in pouring money into recording processes."

Atilla: "We had the bones of the third album coming together, which was really gonna sound exciting – it was using a lot of the then up and coming drum and bass and jungle rhythms – I think it would have forged a whole new thing. There was a comedy of errors on the part of the record company-cum-so called management we had. I'm sure it's not all their fault but quite a lot of it has got to be laid at their door. It didn't really split it just kind of petered out."

"After Mad Cow Disease Jon and I formed E-Coli – basically taking the concept that we were exploring what would have been the third Mad Cow album and went in this hard dance-cum-jungle-cum-hard techno route. We produced an album's worth of stuff, which garnered a lot of interest from people like Sony but didn't quite get bitten on. We had this totally insane guy who offered to manage us and went to see Sony and threatened to dangle the guy out of the window – so that kind of fell through."

Jon Maple: "Till and I spent a summer in his house recording an experimental electro digital techno sample thing involving all sorts of things like trying to sample Leadbelly, Gene Krupa and Hungarian throat singers and banging down beats on the programmer. We sent it off to Skint but they weren't interested, so me and Tilla sort of lost interest."

Although in Colin Holton's words "You get sick of the hassle. You lose faith in it. It could have been managed better", he still has fond memories of what Mad Cow achieved.

Colin Holton: "In the Champs Elysees HMV they had a massive collage of our

BLITZED HIPPIES FINALLY MAKE THEIR CRUSTY GIRL

14 DAILY SPORT Tuesday, October 6, 1992

IT'S only taken "Oo-Aar, Oo-Aar" urchins the Dishevellers 11 years to come up with Crusty Girl, their debut single for Catalina Records.

Frig, guitarist with the Swindon, Wiltshire, outfit, said: "We met in Boggy's all-night cider and mushroom tent during the 1981 Stonehenge Festival.

"Our playing was so rusty we couldn't even tune our instruments, which isn't surprising because we were blitzed out of our brains on magic mushrooms most of the time."

Goats

Now Frig and the lads are getting maximum airplay in England and also making it big in American universities.

Frig, who rears goats in his spare time, added: "We've just completed a college tour over there. And all the students were fascinated to learn a little bit about Wiltshire history.

"We told them it's not only the ancient site of Camelot and Avalon, but also the lost city of Atlantis."

He reckons: "They swallowed our drivel hook, line and sinker."

Talking of Wiltshire, rock radio DJ Tim Oakes, whose job with BBC's Wiltshire Sound was terminated after his hippy lifestyle was discovered, tells me that Britain's travelling folk are ditching their motors for horse-drawn gipsy caravans.

They're cheaper to run and the horse-shit can be sold to eager rose growers.

Warnings

So does this mean Oakes will be selling his Transit home, complete with souped-up V8 engine?

MAGIC: Frig, left, and Dig, are making it big with their first hit

---

stuff – it was really big news in Europe. We recorded two really good albums – really clever stuff. Andy Gill was a great bloke to work with – a genius. When he did his top ten in NME our song Death Squad was one of his favourites."

"We were just having a laugh all the time but we got a lot of respect from other musicians. That was a good band. It was an exercise in seeing how far you could push things and then coming out the other end was some pretty good stuff. Jon Maple being a rock star was completely not on - but he just did it and we had a great laugh."

Swing Syndicate had by now changed their name and were ready to enter the studio themselves.

Gary James: "We demoed with Clive Roper and played a lot of gigs before deciding to record properly. By this time we had renamed ourselves Suicide King, taken from a song by an American band I was into called Mary My Hope. We went into the studio in Aldbourne near Marlborough that Mad Cow Disease did their best ever recording in - they demoed Tantric Sex Disco there and the recording to my mind was tons better than the finished album, there was audible bass on there for a start!"

"We did gigs at the Hobgoblin[5] and The Tavern and spent a week rehearsing in Shrewton Village Hall. With Dan Bunce appointed producer we recorded Go Go Juice in two days. The bass and drums went down in two and a half hours and the whole recording, including ownership of the reels, cost £500."

"Caroline [Holt-Keen] did her vocal for Setting Sun in one take but Dan and Nick Beere, the engineer, insisted on her doing it two or three more times as she was easier on the eye than us. Ally Gamble did the artwork for us and we played gigs around Salisbury, Southampton, Bristol, London, Bournemouth, Gillingham and Wales among others, selling the cassettes at the gigs."

"It was a fun time. We played with Crazy Gods Of Endless Noise, Ban Jyang, Atom Heart Mother, Gravity Hill from Bristol, Mad Cow Disease, Sidi Bou Said and others. Sidi Bou Said were on their 'Bring The Cabaret' tour so we decided to get Ray's girlfriend - now wife - Jayne [Holloway] and her two sisters to dance for us. They turned up in hot pants and little bra tops and gyrated away while we played. Sidi Bou Said were not happy. It kind of went against their feminist attitudes but really it was just our little bit of cabaret, no harm was intended."

"By the time we did this gig I had moved to North London and travelled down to play, it was getting awkward keeping the band going between Salisbury and London and the following year Nick and Ray moved up and we shared a flat in Hornsey where not a fat lot was achieved. We rehearsed and recorded there but it was like The Monkees meets The Banana Splits on the wrong stimulants, and after playing all the toilets of London we eventually stopped doing it."

Alongside the younger acts The Hopback Blues Band, led by a Salford born and bred self-confessed 'child of the sixties', were part of an unexpected blues boom in Salisbury.

Trevor Kay: "My interest in music

ENDLESS BEAT

"Fortunately Malcolm and I agree on everything to do with blues music."

started when I first heard a lot of folk and blues. Josh White was on TV in those days. He was an acoustic blues folk man from the States and I was really taken by that. Then I started to hear a lot of stuff on the Light Programme. In '73 I went to work in Germany and lost contact, and of course it had gone into prog rock then anyway."

"In the mid-eighties I really got interested in playing again. I set up a folk club in Shipton Bellinger with Colin [Masson] and Cathy [Alexander] from The Morrigan and thought I would start a band again. I met up with some people at Porton Down and one of those was Duncan Brown, who was eventually the saxophonist in the first incarnation of the Hopback Blues Band."

"I met Charlie Marsden, who was a drummer with Astral Plain – a very good covers band. His wife was managing the Wyndham Arms. I was in there every day and said to him one time 'I don't suppose you like blues music do you?' He said 'Come with me'. We went upstairs and he's got shelves and shelves of videos, albums and CDs of blues music."

"I had just started working for the Council and was being shown around, and a sister of Pete Catlin worked there – now Wendy Lawrence. I was chatting about forming this band. She said 'My brother plays blues guitar – why don't you have a word with him? Actually one of our Environmental Health Officers, Rick Wells, plays bass guitar' - and at that moment he walked in the office. So I said 'I'm Trevor, this is what I'm doing, are you interested?' and he said 'Yep. I'll have go at that'."

"We had our first rehearsals at Quidhampton Village Hall – a stone's throw from the White Horse, where of course they used to do all this blues stuff. After a while Pete said 'It's not really what I want'. He was being very polite – basically he was saying 'You're crap and I don't want to do this - but I know a man who does – Pete Sherburne'. He was wheeled in and off we went at more than a canter."

"We came in on a big blues revival. In '91/92, when we were at our zenith, we were gigging two or three times a week. We played in a sort of 'diamond shape' in the south west from Bristol to Bournemouth and Weymouth to Wokingham. We would travel long distances and not just, as we tend to do these days, play in Salisbury."

Already at the forefront of this local blues revival were The Rhythm Blasters. Lead vocalist Dave Taylor was coincidentally also from the Manchester area. His first guitar had been owned by one of Billy J Kramer's Dakotas and he had played in a covers band with a 10cc session guitarist before moving to Salisbury in 1979.

Dave Taylor: "I had heard my sister's music – Beach Boys, Beatles and Stones – and I definitely knew it was the Stones sort of stuff I liked, but I heard a Muddy Waters track on the radio and thought that's it - I was aware that whatever he had been singing he had actually been through it."

"He wasn't singing 'la la la' lovely stuff - he was talking about his car being repossessed, having a really bad time and getting drunk and I knew he had actually experienced exactly what he was talking about. That to me was a rebellion because you weren't accepting what was coming your way."

"I came down here to sell second hand books. I worked for a rather upmarket new book seller in Manchester, saw an advert in the trade press to work in a shop and that's what brought me here."

"The first place I went to – virtually the first week I arrived - was The Chough on a Sunday. It was a sort of a musical get together - Pete Catlin was playing, an older gentleman with a Hammond organ, Ken Lailey and there were two sax players – Andy Sheppard and Tim Collinson. I remember thinking 'There's a lot of talent here but they're still sticking to twelve-bar blues' – that seems to be the universal language."

"Within a very short space of time I got to hear about Malcolm Wilkinson who taught classical guitar and classical lute – but I was told he also did blues. I found his address and wrote to him - could he teach me a few things on the guitar? I maintain he wrote back and said 'Fuck off'. He says he didn't…but he basically did."

However, the former Un Deux Twang! guitarist got in touch with Dave shortly after that band had folded following Phil Hill's tragic death.

Dave Taylor: "Malcolm - who I had never actually met - came in the bookshop and in his usual style said 'You Dave Taylor?' I said 'Yes'. He said 'You wanna start a blues band?' I said 'Yeah, I'll have a go'. 'Right – Arts Centre – Monday'. 'Okay'."

"I turned up and there was Alex Mundy - looking about four years old – on the drum kit, Colin Holton and me. I was waiting for a singer to turn up, because obviously I was going to be rhythm guitar – and no singer did turn up. They said 'You do a bit until somebody turns up' – and that's how we started."

Alex Mundy: "There was a bit of a hiatus at this time when Twang had finished, and Malcolm was organising a guitar festival at Salisbury Arts Centre, and Colin was going to do a bass guitar workshop. Malcolm and I backed him on a couple of songs and I said 'Can't we carry on and do something?'"

"Malc's roots were in the blues and he said he was going to do this blues band. I said 'Yeah, I'm up for that'. He said 'I've got someone in to do the vocals for now', which was this off beat bass drum thing, which threw me if you're trying to sing or phrase blues. I think Colin can probably play anything – he got into it very quickly indeed."

Alex Mundy: "I didn't know anything about blues - I couldn't even play a shuffle. Everything I had done up until then had been on straight beats - eighth beats or quarter beats, but blues and jazz is very triplet based – three beats to the bar. So I had to learn - but it seemed to work."

"Really you've got a free range mini tour. I watched the drummer and he just hit his bass drum four to the floor, doing a shuffle on his hi-hat, and back beat on two and four on the snare. I thought 'Well, if that's good enough for Chicago'."

Dave Taylor: "Fortunately Malcolm and I agree on everything to do with blues music. We hate the English stuffy way of playing – we find it incredibly tedious. Most white English blues bands – you could see they had been formed by the guitarist, who did not care about the song or anything else – his fifteen minute guitar break was all he was interested in. They hadn't understood the song was the thing – the guitar solo was just the froth on the top. If you heard a Muddy Waters song you would think 'That's brilliant'. I couldn't understand how these people then went away and reproduced it so badly – they ironed out all the rough edges."

Although Dave, Alex and Malcolm Wilkinson played together in The Rhythm Blasters for more than twenty-five years, the bass role has rotated and at one time included a musician with no previous grounding in the blues at all.

Ruth Jones: "The Courgettes was going great guns then Chalky had a very nasty road accident – he was

THE RHYTHM BLASTERS - left to right: Malcolm Wilkinson, Alex Mundy and Dave Taylor

Dave Taylor – twenty-five years later he's still doing it!"

Dave Taylor: "We had a problem with Alex at the start, because he had been playing with punk bands. He had because there were no drums on some of those old tracks. I remember a Eureka moment for me was when we were going to Southampton to watch a Chicago blues band, over here on a

ENDLESSBEAT

"Dave Marsh was a great personality from the punk days in Salisbury."

hospitalised for quite a while. That kind of slowed it up a bit and then I had Florence [Ruth's second daughter] in '93 – and then I was playing with The Rhythm Blasters. That was my introduction to the blues, quite an interesting education – it's good for you to learn how to play the blues."

"After being classically trained and doing a bit of punk, trying to get into the feeling of the blues was really good, because you have to sit in the pocket. Blues bass lines on the face of it are very simple, but it's the feel and the way that you play with the drummer."

A local scene had also developed around an interest in 'roots' music blended with a punk spirit. For a small city Salisbury has a sizeable community of Irish immigrants and their descendants, some of whom took up this new style in the band Slainte (named after an Irish drinking toast).

Sean Rice: "I had a guitar from my teenage years. I wasn't involved in any bands because I was a bit of a Bohemian, wandering around the world – I didn't settle anywhere. My father came from Ireland – he was a farm labourer – and when I was about twenty my mum and dad moved to Ireland. I used to spend quite a lot of time over there – not just in one place but in different areas."

"At that time Ireland seemed more influenced by American culture than English, and in some ways they seemed more advanced as regards to implementation of ideas. Also Ireland had a brilliant literary tradition as well as musical. It's not surprising that Bob Geldof, U2, Sinead O'Connor – a lot of really good innovative artists - have come out of Ireland."

"When I came back to Salisbury, in the early eighties, I really started to get into music. I didn't have an avenue as such - I just used to go along to wherever I was going - seeing all the bands around the pubs. I started going to the folk club in Burke's Bar[6]. It was pretty funny – all these cranky people playing songs – but very hospitable. I wouldn't say folk music was my primary influence but I've always liked it."

"The old Irish community in Salisbury had come over to work in places like the Old Manor and on the roads, building and agriculture. There was always an Irish club down at St Osmund's and things at the Old Manor Social Club. Remnants of the second generation of a lot of those people then wanted to get involved in Irish culture. The Winchester Gate had an Irish landlord so that kicked off and a really good mix of people used to get in there. Banks of musicians, the Guinness was flowing and it was a really good atmosphere."

"In Slainte we had Tim Madden, Doug Sheriff, who is no longer with us, on accordion and Matt Carter on bass. The local Irish music promoter, Finbar Sheehan, got us bookings. We were playing down Bournemouth one night and I had got my slot of playing this really sensitive Scottish song. We got halfway through it and a bloke in the audience dropped dead on the dance floor – that sort of killed it a bit, it was surreal really."

THE STATUES - left to right: Simon Dickinson, Mark Torokwa, Sean Rice and Dave Marsh

After the demise of Slainte, Sean joined The Statues, an outfit with a wide range of influences.

Sean Rice: "Dave Marsh was a great personality from the punk days in Salisbury. He was a great character and a very helpful guy who put a lot into what he was doing. He would sit in on any type of gig – even ceilidh type bands – but essentially he was a punky guy. In The Statues he did everything he could to promote the band – driving people around in his little mini with his drum kit – he was the main part of the band really."

"We had Simon Dickenson playing guitar - he was a bit bluesy/heavy in his approach. We had a guy called Mark Torokwa, originally from Uganda, and he had a good take on African music – he played fretless bass. A girl called Debbie Fulton played bass with us when Mark wasn't around, and also rhythm guitar - and we were augmented by a keyboard player, Dave Wilds."

"Other influences were probably The Cure and an undercurrent of Siouxsie and The Banshees, but with this pop feel as well, so it was quite a good little mix in our sound. I think our band was described initially as power pop, which I think was probably a fair description of our songs – building to choruses and kicking out."

"I would like to think that, once I got over the early stages of rubbish song writing, the skill of it remains constant, but the styles can be all different music - dance stuff for my stepdaughter, folky, rock stuff, blues and country and pop. Hopefully a certain standard is there for whatever style it is. It comes out of what your 'space' is like around your brain."

"We entered a couple of talent contests at the City Hall. They were really funny because it was like Butlins - the compere wore a wig and had a bright red jacket. We went out to perform but the microphone didn't work. I started singing and there was no sound – halfway through the song it came on and the whole audience burst into applause!"

"On the same bill was Jonathan The Jester – before he was Jonathan The Jester – a bloke who was completely crazy. He used to run a comedy club which was itself a joke - he was a rubbish comedian…terrible! He's got better now - good luck to him, he's done really well - but as far as his own jokes went…nobody laughed at them."

"He was trying to get an alternative comedy scene going in Salisbury and Wilton. He got up on stage and I thought he was incredibly funny. His jokes were so bad that I started laughing at him. He got told he was not allowed under any circumstances to use water in his act – he wanted to throw a bucket of water off stage. He got halfway through and he went and done it and got chased offstage by the bouncers."

Originally from Basingstoke, folk band The Morrigan were named after a character in an Alan Garner novel, although the name might also refer to the Celtic Goddess of death, destruction, war and pestilence. The first Morrigan album, Spirit of the Soup, was released on cassette in 1985 and during the same year band members Cathy Alexander, Colin Masson and Cliff Eastabrook moved to the Salisbury area.

ENDLESS BEAT

"Penny Elliott had written me up as 'an anarchist poet!"

The Morrigan built a reputation of playing an unusual blend of folk and rock, with Cliff Eastabrook in particular gaining notoriety for his theatricality and reciting of poetry. However, the band were generally considered too rocky for the average folk club and too folky for the average rock venue, and decided a drummer might help to refine their sound.

Archie Stone was invited to join The Morrigan at the beginning of 1988, having been spotted playing in Downton based covers band Vulture Squadron. Taking a more focussed approach, by the end of the year the band were playing an average of two gigs a week in places ranging from Cornwall to Felixstowe. Melanie Byfield had by now also joined and plans were laid for the recording of a full blown vinyl album.

Recording began in a farmhouse near Tintagel on Hallowe'en 1988 followed by sessions at Jon Hayward's home 'studio' and in Weston-Super-Mare. A friend of the band named 'Spam' put up the money for 1,000 albums to be pressed and The Morrigan Rides Out – replete with a rear sleeve photo taken at the Wig and Quill - was issued in 1990.

By 1992 Melanie Byfield had left the band while Jon Hayward, having been heavily involved in the recording of the album, had drifted into becoming a full-time member. In June The Morrigan played the Field of Avalon at Glastonbury Festival. Although not playing on one of the main stages, the band attracted a large crowd, with whom they went down a storm. The following morning, the band were at the site's Wise Crone café when they heard the festival radio station playing their Fingal's Cave, recorded from the sound desk the night before.

Along with his studio gear, Jon moved in with Colin and Cathy – who were living on a farm near Coombe Bissett - and plans were hatched for the band's next recording project: a live album to be recorded in a barn at the farm, in front of an invited audience of neighbours and friends. The gig proved to be a great event but, unfortunately, after the first number the equipment failed somewhat as the drums did not record properly.

The salvaged track, Fingal's Cave-Spirit of the Soup, was issued on a CD EP, War In Paradise. The EP title, and its content, sadly reflected the band's mood at the time as individual factions were looking to explore different styles of music. Around this time Jon Hayward left the band, although he did contribute to some of their future recordings.

In 1993, shortly after a successful return to Glastonbury, bassist Cliff Eastabrook left The Morrigan to join Press Gang. Having been part of the line-up for ten years, Cliff's departure almost led to the band's complete implosion. However, their ever cheerful drummer Arch rallied their spirits and it was thought that a new album might rejuvenate them.

With Jon Hayward now at university, and his intermittently reliable gear having been put in storage, Colin and Cathy purchased an eight track Portastudio and work began on what was to become the Wreckers album. Recording began as a trio but the band soon realised they would need to reconvene a full line-up to achieve the sound they were looking for. Arch had been sidelining in a covers band known as the Bolt-on Parsnips and their guitarist Dave Lodder and vocalist Mervyn Baggs were invited to join The Morrigan in time to complete the recordings.

Wreckers was initially issued on cassette in 1996, but around the same time – to the band's surprise – their first album, Spirit of the Soup, showed up in Spain on vinyl. These releases attracted interest from independent labels, and The Morrigan signed with English Garden Records. Wreckers was put out on CD and gained a number of favourable reviews and radio coverage, and English Garden subsequently issued the band's first two albums on CD.

With the support of a record company behind them The Morrigan were able to obtain better gear, although with new members having to learn the old material live appearances remained sporadic. However, notable dates from the era included the Talking Heads club in Southampton and a gig on a specially hired ferry sailing around Poole Harbour.

Although the band missed Cliff Eastabrook's presence and theatricality, the new line up had more flexibility in terms of multi-instrumentalists and two excellent vocalists. Prospects were looking bright and in 1997 The Morrigan were booked to play at the Cornish Morwenstow Festival, followed two days later by a third Glastonbury appearance. However, because of dreadful weather the Morwenstow event had to be relocated into a large barn, and at the end of the gig the pregnant Cathy began to feel pains in her leg. The following day she was admitted into hospital with a deep vein thrombosis.

Band activity was put on hold for a year, but thankfully 1997 ended with the birth of Cathy and Colin's son Ryan. This forced some further adjustment as their spare room, home of their Amek recording desk, was converted to a nursery. The gear was moved into the garage and, as Cathy's health improved, occasional gigs were played again – although personal commitments meant the previous level of live appearances had to be reduced. Notwithstanding this, a new album, Masque, was recorded and issued in 1998 to critical acclaim.

A further example of the diversity of talent emerging in the city came in the form of a true one-off.

Chris Hartford: "My mother made me learn the piano when I was about six – so I'm a classically trained pianist. Then I went to Bishop's School and wanted to learn the guitar – the guitar teacher at Bishop's was Malcolm Wilkinson. It was all Greensleeves and that sort of thing - I didn't really take to it and threw in the towel."

"When I was sixteen I got my first electric guitar – for my birthday – and an old WEM Copycat echo machine, and just started messing around. At the time I was into The Cure. One of the tracks on the Cure's 17 Seconds album was In Your House, which had a very hand-picked structure to the guitar playing. I learned to play that, which meant I avoided using a plectrum, and I stuck with that kind of style."

"By '84 I had become a bit of rebel, a punk, an individualist. I had always been writing bits and pieces – I wrote my life story when I was at school every two years [laughs] and turned all my disasters into humour. I don't how, but I wrote a couple of songs and then wrote the music for them in this whole adopted style from this Cure track."

"My songs were based around things like not being able to go to toilet in the urinal if there was someone else there at the same time – social angst. Quite a few of the songs I would never be able to perform in today's world, but there are a few that I think would stand the test of time."

"I had a friend whose social circle included The Siren – they were a sort of very pretentious, back-combed goth band. I supported them at the Saddle Rooms – my first ever gig – and, according to my notes, went down very well. I stuck with supporting The Siren, which took me to The Grange and, eventually the Arts Centre."

"The first time at the Arts Centre, my mother never knew I was playing. I remember Roger Elliott taking this picture and I said 'Don't put that in the Journal because if you do I'm going to get killed' – my mother slaughtered me: Penny Elliot had written me up as 'an anarchist poet'!"

"It was a case of promoters saying 'Do you want to do a bit on the small stage whilst we change bands at the other end?' A couple of times I did a gig with no notice whatsoever. I would be in the audience as a punter and Holton would come along – or Ant Roberts – and say 'Do you want to do a bit?' I would borrow a guitar and get on up there."

"It would be an interesting experience because the guitar would be a pretty good one – whereas I always used a pretty bad one! It was a Hondo that I picked up in Stangers for £25. I think he was selling it off cheap because one of the strings would never tune in with the rest, so it always

ENDLESS BEAT

"Okay, let's try and do something else."

sounded really trashy. I jollied the guitar up with some pages from an old atlas - I always wanted to be an individual."

"Malcolm Wilkinson would be in the audience quite often. We would catch each other's eye and I would be so embarrassed because I really struggled to play guitar – Malcolm used to bury his head in his hands. It became part of my act that in fact I couldn't really play at all – at one of my gigs I actually sang a guitar solo! I was so bad at the delivery – forgetting words and having to make lines up on the spot - but that used to get the laughs and it got to the point where I would actually build that into the set."

Chris perhaps suffered more than most from the variable sound quality at the Arts Centre: "Cliff Stafford used to do the PA there and I would say 'Look, people have got to hear my words or I'm just going to die out there'. I would go on and I knew people were struggling to hear – it was such a shame sometimes."

"I did rehearse with a band called Snakespear in the late eighties. I had started wearing really outrageous clothes. They wanted me to play bongos, but I didn't have any - I just used to turn up and pretend to be playing. They just wanted a bit of colour at the back of the stage."

"Ant Roberts put me on at the Old Bull Arts Centre in Barnet in October '90. That was the first time I got paid - £50 for ten minutes – and either Newman or Baddiel was on the same bill. That was my brush with the big time but sadly was at the tail end of the list of gigs. I had made it – got my fifty quid - and thought 'Okay, let's try and do something else'."

Two local bands from this period went on to achieve significant national and international recognition, releasing a number of records and touring in Europe.

The Nuthins were inspired to form – initially as The Good For Nothings – following the Fuzztones' Arts Centre gig and their first full rehearsal took place at St Birinus' Hall, Woodfalls (now Woodfalls and Morgan's Vale Village Hall) at Hallowe'en 1989.

Bob Taylor: "There was a bloke called Mike Brunt, down from Scotland. Lee Tea was down from Oxford. We all got talking because we looked the same – bowl cuts, button down shirts and all that stripeyness. Then we met Mojo – I used to know him as a mod – he was a bit younger and a bit of a hippy but because we were more or less interested in the same things we got talking and formed a group."

Mojo: "For me it all started at an early age – Top Of The Pops on the sofa with my mum - aged three I was already a fan of Sweet. By the age of five or six I heard oldies on the radio, which were really only ten years old max! As a result I delved into Mum's Beatles, Stones and Animals 45s and they had a huge impact. I was about six or seven when punk hit, and even then I drew a correlation between Get Off Of My Cloud and the new brigade - to me it was the same. The first single I bought was on my ninth birthday - Turning Japanese by The Vapors. After a dalliance with Adam and The Ants - my first fave band - it was Madness into The Jam and the whole sixties mod thing, which I fell in love with aged ten."

"I started playing classical guitar at Downton Secondary School, then progressed onto electric and played in a fifth form covers band. It was far from cool, but I learnt my trade before moving onto the mod thing with my pals in Landford, The Ghosts, who performed one gig at the local youth club. For fourteen-fifteen year olds we were cool. We looked the part and covered sixties garage and freakbeat,

THE NUTHINS - with Lee Thornton (far right)

THE NUTHINS - left to right: Bob Taylor, Andy Cornick, Richie Walker and Jon 'Mojo' Mills

including The Eyes and The Del-Vettes…I may have forgotten to say we were crap."

"When doing my A-Levels I chummed up with Salisbury eccentric and Johnny Rotten look-a-like Jonny Blamey, to make merry hell and start a revolution...of sorts. A collective of eighties rebels - Rob Arney (biker), Scud and Cath (goths), Jonny and I formed The Sackville Baggins. We rehearsed at Jonny's parents' house and made rather odd music, which may or may not have sounded quite good. A few gigs were played: Salisbury City Hall (alongside future Nuthin Richie Walker, who was drumming for The Rose Coloured Nightmares) and a party with BTF and other goth and anarcho punk bands."

"Like a fairytale in reverse the

ENDLESS BEAT

"... two other people that very same evening had the exact same idea!"

Ugly Sisters met at the ball! The Fuzztones were supported by The Stand - my fifteen year old buddy Richie Walker was playing drums with them that night. As I was a mate he told me he was supporting a band I would like. At the end of the mod thing I had discovered US garage bands after reading about the Pebbles and Nuggets compilations, but I wasn't aware of the new bands from the eighties that played this style - The Fuzztones were new to me."

"Although a tad punkier and gothier looking, The Fuzztones embodied the spirit of all those great garage records I had adored since age fifteen. I was won over and decided I had to be in a garage band. Fortunately for me two other people that very same evening had the exact same idea - Bob Taylor and Lee Thornton."

"I had seen Bob resplendent with moptop in The Bishop's Mill, when my pal Ingsy and I would go in dressed up like the [13th Floor] Elevators. Lee I did not know, but I remember eyeing him and his girlfriend Tash in their sixties clobber at the gig and calling out 'Nice one mate. You look like Iggy Pop circa 1969'."

The original Nuthins were Mike Brunt and Lee 'Lee Tea' Thornton (vocals), Jon 'Mojo' Mills (black and white Vox Phantom guitar and vocals), Bob Taylor (Vox Continental organ and vocals), Carol Galpin (Eko bass) and Richie Walker (drums and percussion).

The band were unapologetic about their retro style and are described on the Bluemoonraker website as having played 'authentic McGuinn-fringed garage rock for the loved-up generation'. A Salisbury Journal review of their second ever gig also took particular notice of their haircuts: 'like Byrds-nests, shaggy and heavy of fringe, very sixties'.

Bob Taylor: "Lots of people wanted to take photographs from Salisbury College and we had a video made by two students there - because we were so visual. It [the equipment] was all authentic stuff. Then you could pick it up a lot easier - I used to kick over my organs and not necessarily respect them - now you can't find them anywhere and they are worth a lot more money. It was the same with the clothes and records…and scooters - then you could find them in gardens all over the place, for a pittance, now they are thousands and thousands…if you can find them."

"In the American garage scene they used Voxs and Farfisas, and in the British mod scene Hammond organs. I had a Vox Continental, a Farfisa and a Hammond – I had all three. The problem is moving them around because they have got speakers as well – Leslies. Nine times out of ten we would get to a venue and they would all disappear because they didn't want to help me!"

Although there was a desire to look and sound 'right' the bulk of the Nuthins' material was original.

Bob Taylor: "We always did covers but the main idea was to write our own stuff. When we started we were quite psychedelic and hippyness, as well as the garage. Everybody tended to write so it was a bit of an eclectic mix at first – it was all over the place - indieness, alternative, garage, mod, hippy stuff - all rolled into one. As we got more into our 'career', as such, we became more beat and garage, whereas when we started we were quite

242

7: **Independent's Days**

Inspiration

THE NUTHINS - with Carol Galpin

ENDLESS**BEAT**

"We hung out together like a gang..."

psychedelic. We honed our writing towards how we thought the band should sound – not necessarily better, but different."

"There was no actual [local garage] scene - we just latched on to the indie scene and alternative stuff in Salisbury to get gigs and it built from there. I used to like Bubblegum Splash!, The Mayfields, Farley 708 – all those groups just before us. Salisbury at the time was pretty good. Pubs were easy to play and there was obviously the Arts Centre. I think it was better then and people like Jim from Jane From Occupied Europe were putting on groups – there were plenty of places to play and people were willing to do things as well."

Mojo: "The Nuthins were totally at odds with the early nineties and in Salisbury the only band mining sixties beat-punk and garage bands as our influence. We wore the clothes, played old equipment and were for real. We hung out together like a gang, listened to music and behaved no differently than a sixties US garage band would have done in a small town."

"What influenced us? The classic sounds of Nuggets and Pebbles. The bigger mid-sixties garage gods: Electric Prunes, Seeds, Music Machine, Blues Magoos – and, far closer to home, The Troggs! Of course, we also liked The Byrds, The Beatles, The Who, The Animals…you get the picture."

"Although to many locals we were that unforgettable looking sixties influenced band, we subtly changed as we went along with various dalliances with psychedelia, raw Kinks-like beat, folk-rock, punkier trashier garage, to end with a more purist form of musical late sixties psych-punk/garage."

The Nuthins' 1992 debut single, Allergic Kiss, was described in The

FARLEY 708

7: **Independent's Days**

Lee Thornton

ENDLESS BEAT

"... that would never have happened in the UK."

THE NUTHINS

Rambler as 'proper rock and roll music with proper guitar and keyboards, not a bunch of old tossers strutting around the stage with a poodle perm and a cucumber down their boxers'. The review also raved about the record being on seven inch black vinyl with a paper label, packaged in a card sleeve with a purple tinged picture of the band on the front and a black and white rear: 'They really DON'T make records like this anymore'.

Allergic Kiss was the first of a range of singles and compilation appearances on a number of worldwide record labels, all of course with that authentic sound in mind.

Bob Taylor: "Eve Records liked us but we were very retro and they were unsure whether to sign us. That created interest and other labels came to see us. We didn't want to change but there were labels that were custom for us – Twist Records from Guernsey, Detour Records in Midhurst - which is a mod label but they do garage as well - and we did a one off single with an Italian label."

"Our earlier stuff we recorded in local places – Pete Lamb's and a place in Coombe Bissett – they were proper studios but not built for sixties stuff so what we got there I don't think we were happy with. Toe Rag in London was where we did our LP and a couple of singles and that catered for a retro sound. They had original four-track and two-track machines from

246

Abbey Road, so there was a brilliant retro sound."

Before recording the album, One Step Forward (released on Twist in 1996), Lee Tea had been replaced by Marcus, who in turn also quit. The band had then reverted to a four-piece with Mojo on lead vocals. Bassist Carol Galpin had also left the band to be replaced by Andy Cornick.

The Nuthins had by now received airplay on Radio One and had become a big name on the modern garage scene, playing gigs all over the UK and Europe.

Bob Taylor "We did a small tour of Italy and played in France, Belgium and Germany. It was hard work but it was paid for. In Europe they are really good because they will pay for you to go over – obviously not flying – in cars or vans across the Alps. It was mod clubs, sixties clubs, big garage events. We were playing in front of anything from 50 to 5,000, which was in Perpignan. In Europe they used to love the sixties stuff – right down to the way they lived in their houses – furniture, the whole thing, they were fanatical."

Mojo: "It was wonderful - France, Belgium, Germany and Italy. We played to over 500 people in Berlin and were the main band - that would never have happened in the UK. We headlined The Festival Beat - an annual garage festival in Italy, near Verona. It was beautiful and we headlined it…The Nuthins were a draw. As an aside, I also met my missus whilst playing in Perpignan. She was in Spanish garage band The Flashback V…so there you have it…Garage - it's a way of life."

The band preferred to stay true to their initial love of the music rather than take a step away to try and reap wider commercial success.

Bob Taylor: "Doing our LP was really interesting because that makes you feel like you have half made it – somebody is paying for you to record and put it out. We were played a lot on radio in Europe and Mark Radcliffe played two of our singles quite a lot. It was enough to make it great for us. We would have had to change considerably to get any bigger – but we were happy as we were. We weren't the best musicians or writers but we were totally into it. We believed in it - it wasn't false."

The Badgeman emerged from Amesbury based band The Hunny Monsturs and comprised Neale Hancock (vocals and guitar), John Packwood (guitar), Simon 'Wiggy' Wigglesworth (bass) and Tim Kerley (drums). Many years previously Neale Hancock's father Terry had been a member of The Moonrakers, one of the area's most notable skiffle bands.

Neale Hancock: "My influences were Echo and The Bunnymen, Psychedelic Furs, very early REM. My first singing experience was being asked to join the band…. I still can't sing!"

THE NUTHINS

Left to right: Carol Galpin, Marcus Turner, Bob Taylor, Richie Walker and Jon 'Mojo' Mills

ENDLESS BEAT

"... all of a sudden we realised the possibilities."

Wiggy: "I had quite catholic tastes really – quite broad – Beatles and Stones, psychedelia, punk, reggae – the usual stuff that kids growing up in the seventies liked. My granddad, who taught me to play trumpet, told me I wasn't very good - so I took up the bass instead. I went through a succession of little bands with the few people in Durrington and Amesbury who played something and were my age."

"When you're in those sort of bands it's funny because it reflects all the things the different people like, so you would be doing AC/DC, Cramps, Black Sabbath and Clash covers – trying to please everyone in the band."

Neale Hancock: "The Hunny Monsturs formed with Wiggy, me, John and Tim. Personnel wise it was early Badgeman but it was a very different band."

Wiggy: "It was John's band really – John asked me because they wanted a bass player – to come and play some AC/DC songs! It was the first time we thought 'Okay, we'll go out there and try and gig properly'."

From playing covers the band struggled to develop their own sound at first…until inspiration suddenly struck.

Wiggy: "I got Neale in because he's my mate and liked the same things as me – Bunnymen, Teardrop Explodes. I wanted to go like that and it was a real struggle to get there until one day we were rehearsing and we suddenly wrote, out of nowhere, Go Insane! We were jamming and it was like the spirits came through the amplifiers."

"It literally came out of nowhere - like suddenly we had hit the motherlode. We just knew then we were a good band."

Neale Hancock: "I played very limited rhythm guitar, but knew enough to thrash out chords. I kind of explored it, repeated it over and over again and it just threw out this riff. It kept going and going – then John went off on one and made it great."

Wiggy: "Tim is a great drummer - really made me a much better bassist. He also liked a lot of very good music,

THE BADGEMAN - left to right: Neale Hancock, Simon 'Wiggy' Wigglesworth, Tim Kerley and John Packwood

and brought a lot of good ideas, energy and commitment to the party. We always credited the songs to the band. Even if 90% of it had come from me, Neale or John, the fact is it wouldn't have been the same without all four – it would have been a different animal. We were never going to make any money anyway!"

Neale Hancock: "No one was coming to the band saying 'I've written that song or this song'. A lot were ideas generated by the band - which made it a lot easier to say 'Okay - it's a band song'."

The band decided a name change was required to herald the arrival of the new style.

Neale Hancock: "We weren't 'The Hunny Monsturs' anymore - sugary sweet – it's a cereal for Christ's sake!"

Wiggy: "We were a proper rock'n'roll band. We had done it and we didn't know how but we had got to treat this with some respect. We changed the name and decided we would only write good stuff from now on – which was what we tried to do."

Inspiration struck while Neale and Wiggy were watching a documentary on the Kennedy Assassination at Wiggy's 'mobile home' in Amesbury. The band took their new name from the mysterious figure said to have been standing behind the bushes on the so-called 'grassy knoll' overlooking the spot in Dallas where the killing took place. Some conspiracy theorists, believing they had seen the glint of a police badge in the foliage, believe the murder was not the work of Lee Harvey Oswald, but of 'The Badgeman'.

Wiggy: "I think we were both quite interested in paranoia and conspiracy!"

The band received support from the promoters at the Arts Centre, and were soon encouraged to make their first recordings.

Wiggy: "Ant Roberts was a real dude. Him letting us gig with good visiting indie bands really gave us an idea of where we needed to be in terms of quality and commitment. Gigging with bands seems to have more of an effect than just turning up to watch the show for some reason."

"There was stuff going on in Salisbury at the time but I think before there was that kind of 'We're crap and nobody from here does anything anyway'. Bubblegum Splash! managed to have an indie hit and all of a sudden we realised the possibilities - it opened up a whole new vista."

"I was into the fanzine and indie scene and used to go off all over the place to watch bands I liked. There was a real DIY thing coming through, which Bubblegum Splash! had harnessed beautifully. I thought 'We'll have some of that - why don't we do a flexidisc?' So, we shared a flexi with The Mayfields – we tossed a coin to see who would be first on it."

"I knew plenty of writers to get it into fanzines and we sent some to labels as well. We had two offers to sign - from 53rd and 3rd – a great label up in Scotland who released records by people like The Vaselines - and from Glass, who at the time had Spacemen 3 on their books."

"We recorded an album for Glass in 1988 but we kept getting stories about why it wasn't being released and the studio wasn't getting paid. This went on for about a year and a half… of course the label was going bust. So, there is a lost Badgeman album out there."

"The guy who ran Glass was a shit businessman – which is fine, I've got plenty of time for shit businessmen – but a great fan. He really knew about music. He had just signed Teenage Fanclub as he went bust – they were pretty hot. He decided he would take us, them and The Walking Seeds - a band from Liverpool who invented grunge in my opinion, the most underrated rock band this country has ever produced – to a new label Fire Records had set up, called Paperhouse."

The first Badgeman album, Kings Of The Desert, was released on Paperhouse in January 1990. The album and its companion single, Crystals, received extensive airplay from John Peel.

Wiggy: "We thought we had arrived with that album. We really thought we were the dog's bollocks. We were doing gigs on the same circuit as Blur and people like that - names that were going to be big. We were there or thereabouts – getting reviewed regularly in Melody Maker and we thought we were an excellent indie band, we really did…but we got a lot better than that."

In support of the album the band toured in Europe with Paperhouse colleagues Teenage Fanclub.

Wiggy: "They did some gigs with us in the UK – for their first show in London they supported us. They weren't billed – they had come down to do some business with the label and just asked if they could come along and play with us at the Bull and Gate."

"Their big influences are Badfinger, Big Star and that kind of power pop – good quality song writing. I thought they were better song writers than us but weren't as good live. We went to see them quite a lot - we were

ENDLESS BEAT

"... it sounded less like a pick'n'mix and more like 'The Badgeman'."

always on the guest list and then we did this tour of Germany and Switzerland with them in 1990, which was great fun. I could tell you a few things about Teenage Fanclub…but I'm not going to!"

Neale Hancock: "I could tell you a few things about our roadie…but I'm not going to [laughs]!"

THE BADGEMAN
KINGS OF THE DESERT

Wiggy: "I'll just say that Brendan O'Hare, the drummer, could have been one of the most bizarre rock'n'roll deaths ever recorded and we were there…but he didn't die, luckily…."

As The Nuthins also found, visiting musicians were treated well on the continent.

Neale Hancock: "You would go up to the bar and say 'I'll have a Bacardi and Coke and he'll have a vodka and orange' and you would get a bottle of Bacardi, bottle of vodka – 'There you go' – and you would get fed properly, in a restaurant, before you went on stage."

The Kings Of The Desert album sold well, particularly in Europe, despite a lack of proper promotion.

Wiggy: "I remember having to take calls from Greek and Italian journalists. It didn't do fantastically, but it did do reasonably well. The critical acclaim it got was bigger than the sales but it did sell all around the world. We were a lot of people's best kept secret."

"Our label were a bit of a shambles really – but that's what I liked about them. Their attitude was 'We don't do bullshit we just do good music' – that was where they were coming from. Of course sometimes you've got to do the bullshit and we sort of paid for that in a lot of ways, but despite their shambolic uselessness they were principled people who cared about the music."

"The lad who made tea, did paperwork and basically held everything together at our label was called Laurence - I remember him telling me he was forming his own label. That label, Domino Records, is doing very well thank you - Arctic Monkeys anyone?"

Despite the warm reception the album received, The Badgeman had already started to explore new styles.

Wiggy: "I think the first album sounds like an indie band from the early nineties doing a sixties rehash. It was good but by the time the album came out our set was entirely different really. We had written so much new stuff - and it was so much better. It was more coherent for a start – it sounded less like a pick'n'mix and more like 'The Badgeman'. It was in our style not someone else's. I think it anticipated a lot of what Muse and Radiohead and people like that did early in their careers – that sort of folk-prog-darkness."

The band's next release was the Curse Of The Badgeman 12" EP. Sadly this proved to be aptly named and, what's more, was released on the 13th of the month.

Wiggy: "The EP was going to be the thing that took us, in terms of popularity, to new heights. It was scheduled for release but the Cartel – the big indie distributors - went bankrupt the week it was coming out. So it was stuck in warehouses going nowhere. We had a little tour to promote it but no records to sell. Sounds magazine went bust at about the same time and they were going to do a page on us. That was really where the chances of us ever 'making it' went down the pan – if those things are important."

Neale Hancock: "Sounds was big and – as far as I was concerned – the one decent, true music paper around. They had phoned and talked to us personally – 'We want to do a thing on this – we really like this'…and they went bust…thank you very much…it all went tits up at the same time."

The EP demonstrated the new sound that would crystalise on the album Ritual Landscape, the pinnacle of The Badgeman's achievements – and perhaps those of the entire Salisbury scene.

Neale Hancock: "The one thing I'm very proud of is our second album, which unfortunately was at the arse end of our career as The Badgeman. I knew when we were making it that it was quite interesting. This was quite off the wall from everything else that was going on – even for the indie scene."

Wiggy: "We had written all this stuff we knew was good and…it wasn't a concept album but…we felt musically it was conceptual. You hear a lot of repeating motifs through the album – we put a lot of work into that kind of thing. We put a lot of effort into making sure it was coherent, but without being poncey musos – it was still punk rock."

Despite the band being pleased with the finished album, it received minimal recognition at the time of its release.

Wiggy: "Nobody was doing anything like that when we made it - I defy you to find anybody in 1992 who made a record like that. We knew it was a good album but it came out to nothing. I think the label had sort of moved on with us and thought 'Have we backed a lame horse here?'"

Neale Hancock: "To be fair to Paperhouse, they signed us up on the strength of Crystals and Go Insane! and we had given them Ritual Landscape two or three years later - they were like 'What the….!'"

Wiggy: "I think they still thought we were that little garage band doing sixties pastiches, so all the promo copies went to people who liked stuff like that. The reviewers were completely nonplussed by it – you could tell that the people didn't know what to write about it, what hole to put us in."

The first sign of frictions in the band had appeared during the recording of Ritual Landscape as John Packwood was not entirely comfortable with their new direction.

Neale: "We still got on with each other but it was very much Wiggy's album lyrically and mine and his musically, and I think we kind of dragged John along kicking and screaming. Tim drums and as long as it's not banal he's happy – the better the band the better his drumming – but John…what he did was brilliant but…I think he was thinking 'I'm not sure if I really want to be going down this road'."

Wiggy: "John would have liked to have written more songs that sounded like The Who or The Kinks, which we

ENDLESS BEAT

"... slung my guitar, said 'I'm off' and walked away – and we never gigged again."

all liked, but that was not where we were anymore. John never got how good he was on that album – what he was doing was fantastic."

Following the failure of the album the band became disillusioned and eventually imploded.

Wiggy: "We were sick of it I think. We had had enough – the previous year had done us in."

Neale Hancock: "We could see Teenage Fanclub getting a lot of press and going up - not that we were jealous, they were a different type of band entirely - but they were on our label, signed at the same time as us and were going on to have a career. They went on to Creation and we were stumbling around trying to get our EP out... so we were just hacked off."

Wiggy: "The thing is though I think it made us really brilliant. It made the album and our gigs great because our attitude was 'It's us against you' wherever we went. We never did that thing where you take a coach load of mates up to the Rock Garden or whatever, for us it was 'Us against you and you're gonna fucking like us'."

"We played at the Cavern in Exeter with Eugenius, or someone like that. It was rammed and we blew the fucking place to bits. It was that 'Us against Exeter' and we blew holes in the walls - but when we finished there was still so much of that left – that was the trouble. We had to get it all out and we had a dust up – me and Neale had a fight…'hold me back' sort of stuff [laughs]."

"It sort of ended in Exeter but we limped on. We were scheduled to headline at Bath Festival the week after. We went up to do the gig and just said 'We'll honour this but let's go on first'. We said to the support band 'Do you fancy headlining', played our ten songs and never played again."

Despite an initial feeling of relief three of the four Badgemen soon found themselves back together again as Neale, Wiggy and Tim Kerley linked up with three guitarists - Ian 'Skid' Browne, Darren 'Dazman' Blake and Mickey Dyer – in a new project named Big Bird.

Wiggy: "For a few weeks I felt really free but then I was saying to Neale 'Shall we form a band? Let's do it all again! Our final Badgeman cheque came in - £500 from the publishers – which we went and spunked away on a demo for our new band."

Neale Hancock: "We were very different – it was a happy band."

Wiggy: "We just made happy, chaotic music - rock'n'roll but very sort of literate – with lots of referencing for people with record collections. You would hear a bit of a Jonathan Richman song and if you were in on it you liked it. It could have turned out to be something quite good."

"It was great doing that with Skid, Daz and Mickey - I admired them both as musicians and people. We needed three guitarists to take John's place, as well as Neale, and therein lay the seeds of our next problem – the ill fated gig at the Arts Centre."

"Colin Holton was promoting this gig and Dave Marsh was doing the sound. I genuinely love Colin – he is Mr Salisbury Music and he's done a lot of good things for us - but at this particular point in time I was quite angry with him. He put us on at the altar end - I think he thought it was just a new local band…'It won't be busy, I'm not going to spend lot of money on a PA'. I said 'Colin…we used to fill this venue and people used to write about us all over the world. I know it's a new band but trust me this is gonna be busy'."

"We got there and Dave couldn't get the PA working properly. There were four guitars, bass and drums – you needed a proper PA. Not only that but Dave was going off to do another gig – he wasn't even going to be there while we were playing – and Colin had okayed this."

"I was saying to the guys 'I don't think we should do this gig – I think we should go home now' but everyone was up for it. We did it and we couldn't hear a thing. I got really angry, slung my guitar and said 'I'm off' and walked away – and we never gigged again. It was the only show Big Bird did."

Neale Hancock: "It was rammed - that's what really pissed me off. There were 200 people there and no one could hear us. We had worked our arses off since the end of The Badgeman with all the rehearsals we had at Enford Village Hall, and got this band together that was actually fucking good. We had got our sound together. A lot of guitars - okay a sound man's nightmare but all backline - all we needed was the vocals and they couldn't deliver. I was devastated."

Despite the ignominy suffered, the band's first and last hurrah at least gave the Salisbury Journal a great headline: 'Big Bird Get In A Big, Big Flap'!

A vital facility for young bands in Salisbury developed in the mid-nineties, when the late Rose Gale and her husband, Keith, set up Bass Connection at Grosvenor House in Churchfields Road.

Keith Gale: "Grosvenor used to belong to the college and was taken over by the youth service in the sixties. At that time myself and my younger brother Richard put in beams which are still there – they originally came from the cathedral. Miss Whatley, who was then in charge, wanted something a little bit different - we called it the 'Thieves Kitchen', put these oak beams up and had a few pews from a church. It was almost a beatnik type of coffee bar - that was the idea. I went off doing village youth work in Quidhampton and lost touch with Grosvenor until I went back for a brief spell in the eighties to do some training - then I went back to start Bass Connection in '96."

"Bass Connection actually started in Durrington Youth Club - a group of young people wanted to start DJ-ing. In late '95 we got them decks and vinyl, but they wanted to have a name – we came up with 'Bass Connection'. From early '96 Rose was running both Durrington Youth Club and Grosvenor, but we gradually had to move out of Durrington."

"We started transporting the young people from Durrington into Grosvenor, where we had a basement that was fairly soundproof. I had about forty DJs coming in, but with one pair of decks there was a lot of unrest – a ten minute slot wasn't long enough, but it was good fun."

"One day me and Rose were walking through town, when a young lad came up called Dan Foot, who said 'I hear you've got DJs in Grosvenor but I'm in a band. Can I bring my band down?' Dan comes down with John Birch and another lad called Lee, who went on to be a DJ in Ibiza. They were called The Haemorrhoids, which I didn't really think was a particularly good name, but they changed to Sweet Children and then to Uncle Brian."

"We had one room soundproofed. Then the caretaker left and I said to Rose 'I think we can have two rooms now' - because there wasn't the worry about the caretaker and his young children. We committed to two rooms which we opened up twice a week, so we had four bands coming in."

"I wasn't a musician – I didn't know anything about bands, apart from watching them in the past and what I liked and disliked. I had to learn about PAs, drum kits, guitars and amplifiers and myself and Rose had to convince the youth service – we both worked for Wiltshire County Council – that it was good youth work."

"They said 'You're just providing a rehearsal space'. I said 'Have you ever been in a rehearsal? Don't you think that young people communicate when they are in a band? They've got to learn about health and safety, to negotiate…' – all the things that were in the youth and community curriculum. I think we had to fight for about five years to convince the service it was good youth work."

Rose and Keith also had to look for somewhere for the bands to play in front of an audience.

Keith Gale: "I found the Fisherton Arms, which was a bikers' pub. Chic [Duggan] was the landlord and I said 'Can we have these bands coming in here?' He said 'Yeah, bring 'em in mate. I can't pay 'em much'. I said 'I don't think they're expecting to be paid - they just want somewhere to play'."

ENDLESS BEAT

"... but we were treated like royalty!"

"Taking Sweet Children - who were about fourteen-fifteen - into a bikers' pub was quite an experience, but we were treated like royalty. They got paid and there was something quite magical about that time – Sweet Children, Cast Iron Shores, Tracer, Junk DNA and Stormfly were the original bands at Grosvenor - they all played down there."

"Then, through Beth Doyle and Colin Holton we started putting on gigs in the Gallery Club. We needed a new drum kit because we were going from two rooms to three, so we put a gig on and raised all the money for the kit. I also met Chas Pinder who did the lights for us – all those people were a very big part of Bass Connection."

"It really took off in the late nineties. Everything we had to fundraise for ourselves. At one stage we had over £100,000 worth of equipment - all young people fundraised. We had gone into a building in '96 with virtually nothing – not even tables and chairs."

The Salisbury area had seen a small influx of established rock stars in recent years: Robert Fripp and his wife Toyah moved into Reddish House - Cecil Beaton's former home in Broad Chalke, and Sting into a mansion in the Woodford Valley. Toyah would take advantage of the available local talent.

Chris Binns: "Paul Nicholson persuaded me to get involved in recording an album for her - summer 1993 I think. It involved taking over the whole of my house with different mics in lots of rooms. It should have been a week but ended up about three with Paul Beavis sessioning on drums and her young band - only two of which I remember, Paul Luther and Jolyon [Dixon]."

Jolyon Dixon, son of former Amey-Gair-Mason bassist Nigel, has become an in demand session guitarist, playing with Scarlet, Mark Owen and Amy MacDonald among others.

Having survived through punk into the indie era, many of the city's 'old boys' continued to play.

In 1987 Reggie Maggs replaced the ill-fated Ronnie Bond as The Troggs' drummer. Of course there could only ever be room for one Reg in that particular band and to avoid confusion Maggs took up his middle name of Dave for professional purposes.

Pete Lucas and Dave Maggs both played on the band's 1992 album Athens/Andover – recorded with the assistance of REM. This line up also played at the wedding reception of local celebrities Trudie Styler and Sting, where the original band members were held in awe by the attending rock stars of the day.

The Troggs were augmented by another local musician for live shows during this period.

Steve Collinson: "In about 1993 I started working with Pete Lucas again - in The Troggs. They had made that album with REM, which of course had loads of jangly guitar, but they only had Chris Britton and they needed an extra guitar to try and replicate this jangly sound live."

"We learnt three songs off this new album, but it was pretty grim. We were going off all over Europe playing big arenas – it was great fun doing it, but The Troggs were there playing this fantastic set, then I would come up to do these three songs off the new album and they went down like a lead balloon! It trickled down from three songs, to two songs, to one and in the end it was like 'Can you do the PA?' I ended up doing the PA for them for three years."

"All this time I'm still working. I would be going to Heathrow at four o'clock to catch a plane, phoning work and they could hear the tannoy: 'Where are you?'… 'Sainsburys!' In the end they knew because we had a tour of America coming up. As it

TRACER

turned out – typical Troggs – we did the first gig and the money didn't turn up, then did the second gig and the money didn't turn up, so Reg said 'That's it - I'm going home' – we were back within four days!"

During 1989 Peter Mason had released Bergen Blue Eyes as a single in Norway - his first new record in almost ten years. His next single, Walking On A Tightrope, would not be issued until 1998.

Following DBM&Ts relocation to Marbella, Dave Dee had been approached by fellow sixties-survivors Marmalade to join them for dates in the UK and Germany. This led to the German release of a single, Scirocco, a commercial failure but one of the better recent offerings from the DDDBMT camp, with a similar feel to their 1967 hit Zabadak. It was certainly a better effort than DBM&T's last new single - a pedestrian cover version of Cat Stevens' Matthew and Son, a record rendered even worse by its eighties production values.

1989 saw the return of most of DBM&T to England, although John Dymond chose to stay in Spain and was replaced by Rochester-based guitarist Paul Bennett.

Tich Amey: "By then my wife had opened up a residential home for the elderly, and I thought 'I need to be back in England'. I came back and so did Dozy and John. The only one that stayed was Beaky and he's still there now. He still goes out and gigs and he likes his golf and fishing."

When Paul Bennett was first approached about joining the band he apparently exclaimed 'Good Lord! Are they still going?' He had a thorough grounding in the business, having first played with his schoolmate David Jones (i.e. Bowie) in 1962, progressing through various beat and harmony groups before performing with Barry Ryan, Fats Domino, Cliff Richard and many others.

In 1993 Tony Carpenter replaced Paul Bennett as the third 'Beaky'. Tony had previously worked with Phil Collins and David Essex, as well as on a number of musicals.

The band continued to perform regularly at sixties revival shows in the UK and Europe, regularly crossing paths with Dave Dee and Marmalade along the way. Despite their general lack of success in terms of record sales, both Dave Dee and The Boys remained hugely popular live draws: Dave estimated that during 1992 he had played live to 350,000 people – the equivalent of five sell out gigs at Wembley Stadium.

In 1994 Dave contributed a couple of tracks to a German Christmas compilation CD. At around the same time, he claimed to have never heard of an up and coming band named Oasis, although he did recall a nightclub in Manchester of that name: somewhat ironic as he also later covered the band's Don't Look Back In Anger for another compilation.

Dave's long promised solo album finally saw the light of day in 1995. Unfinished Business, released on CD on Dave Dee Records, was produced, performed and almost entirely composed by Dave with Sandy Newman and Steve Morris. Ironically, the biggest Salisbury name of them all had released a truly independent record while 'indie' had become a style as opposed to an ethic.

At its onset, in the mid-seventies, the indie scene was never about creating new stars – quite the opposite

Peter Mason

ENDLESS BEAT

"We're too small – promoters want to see a big capacity."

in fact. Inevitably though, some of the acts who started out on the small labels, whether through luck, charisma and/or sheer talent, became big names.

In November 1999 the biggest British indie star of them all - former Smiths' vocalist Morrissey - appeared in Salisbury in an early example of the new management's plans to reintroduce the City Hall to the contemporary circuit. The artist appeared at the same venue ten years later to the month but, whilst the number of notable shows taking place here has increased in the meantime, there is still room for improvement.

Phil Manning: "It was really running on a shoestring for a couple of years, the management was pretty poor. I don't think there was much interest from the Council or even the local populous – obviously they weren't programming the right things."

"When the management changed in '96 and Phill Smith took over he pulled the place up by its bootstraps and turned it round within about eighteen months. Over the last ten or twelve years it's been run pretty well. We have difficulty getting bands because we're just not on the national circuit anymore. We're too small – promoters want to see a big capacity."

By the middle of the nineties the term 'indie' was almost exclusively being applied to four-or-five piece, predominantly white, guitar-based bands – regardless of who was issuing their music, and had effectively become the mainstream, encompassed in Britpop.

As with any other era, this undoubtedly resulted in some great records: this time by the likes of Blur, Pulp and Oasis, the latter providing a phenomenon as inevitable as any musical revolution of the previous forty years – the only surprise being that it hadn't already been achieved by The Stone Roses.

Incidentally, Oasis were yet another big name act that Salisbury fans missed out on. During their early rise the band were booked to play at the Arts Centre but cancelled for unstated reasons (although Colin Holton thinks "They were probably beating each other up").

The lower ranks of the Britpop movement, including Menswear, whose vocalist Johnny Dean was born in Salisbury, generally failed to demonstrate much originality, thereby surely missing a vital component of independence. Where was the next Alternative TV or Cabaret Voltaire – or Mike Oldfield for that matter?

They are probably out there somewhere, but it will take a lot of trawling through the Internet to find them. Thankfully, the 21st century music scene in Salisbury is already providing some great bands, events and stories. We look forward to - physically or virtually - reading a younger chronicler's account of them.

CHAPTER SEVEN FOOTNOTES

1. The Salisbury Comedy Club was held in the Circolo Bar, which was located in the part of the City Hall fronting on to Fisherton Street.
2. Mr Chesil's, at the junction of Fisherton Street with Water Lane, has now been renamed Cactus Jacks.
3. The Joiners Arms is a venue in Southampton.
4. The Jericho Tavern is a venue in Oxford.
5. The Hobgoblin, in Milford Street, has now been renamed The Vestry.
6. Burke's Bar and Buttery, in New Street, has now been renamed The Wig and Quill.

8 The Beat Goes On
The Old and New Scenes in the 21st Century

Sound Tracks by Penny Elliott

Some of our players have touched on their later lives within the previous chapters of this book - as for some of the others…

After the demise of Pussy, Ray Sparrow played with a number of bands in the Salisbury area and Brian Goff joined the Los Angeles band The Sights. Bob Cooke also continued playing in the Salisbury area with bands including Grandma Moses, Britz and the Faith Healers.

Paul Dean moved mainly into the business-side of things, working with Ian Gillan on non-musical projects as well as finding new bands for his companies and managing and producing some of them. In 1984 he recorded an album with Ian's sister Pauline entitled Rocks On, released on the Thunderbolt label.

He has subsequently moved around the world and now lives in Asia. Whilst living in Africa he took up golf and eventually turned professional, he is also a fully qualified golf coach. He remains active in the music industry as a record producer, promoter, advisor, PR man and journalist. He has also written articles for a number of publications and had small parts in feature films such as Reign Of Fire, The Count of Monte Cristo, Veronica Guerin and The Actors.

Paul has fond memories of his relationship with Ian Gillan: "Great guy, very down to earth and good fun. We were good mates for many years and used to do many things together outside of music - scrambling, horse

ENDLESS BEAT
"It all fitted in beautifully"

riding, golf, darts, snooker, cards, boating, playing and watching football and cricket, horse racing…drinking, whatever came to mind!"

There are now plans to issue the previously unreleased Pussy album. The Jerusalem album has been issued more than once on CD and has gained a cult reputation.

Bob Cooke: "I've never seen a brass bean out of the whole thing – ever. It's been reissued all over the place – I can't believe I've not ever made anything out of it because it's sold quite well over thirty odd years."

A footnote to the Jerusalem story is the issue of a CD under the band name in 2009, entitled Escalator. Although this release included re-recordings of some original Jerusalem songs and is not without its own merits, claims that it is a long awaited 'second Jerusalem album' are perhaps somewhat fanciful as neither of the original band founders, Paul Dean and Ray Sparrow were involved in the project: it was recorded by Lynden Williams and a band including Bob Cooke and Geoff Downes.

Bob Cooke: "Lynden writes all this mad stuff and we go and record it - it's a good laugh but Jerusalem had a bit of credibility, so for the last three or four years he's been trying to rebuild Jerusalem. I've got mixed feelings about it. Lynden has got this obsession with re-recording some of the old stuff and trying to restore what he thinks the legacy of Jerusalem should have been. We were all sort of eighteen-nineteen years old, he was a bit older – twenty two-twenty three – he's always had it in his mind that Jerusalem wasn't right and he can do it better now - but there you go."

Paul Dean: "This is not the original Jerusalem band. Jerusalem has never reformed, nor will it ever reform and certainly could not without the founding members, plus of course the late Bill Hinde." [Bill was sadly killed in a car crash in 1975].

Mike Wedgwood emigrated from the UK very shortly after leaving Caravan: "I got married to an American girl and moved to Hollywood! I left England a few days after my last concert with Caravan, and when we

Mike Wedgwood

got to Los Angeles I played with local bands and made a living – barely."

"Then there were some studio jobs and a little production work. I had a bad reaction to the smog and we moved to Denver - much the same work there. I joined a band I thought could do better than the ski lodges and bars of Colorado, so we moved back to LA and lived in a less smog-infested area. The band didn't become rich and famous, I'm afraid."

"I met someone who said musicians were needed and well paid in Alaska, so I moved up there and stayed for fourteen years - amongst other things helping to start the state's first 24-track studio. Now I'm in Denmark with my own studio and The Wedgwood Band, and very happily married. I play a fair amount of solo gigs, and bass with four or five other bands and sometimes sessions in other studios - and I love it!"

After Grandma Moses split, Tom Thatcher formed Government Property. This morphed into the ESB Band, in which Tom was rejoined by Andy Golden.

Tom Thatcher: "With Bob Wallace on vocals and my son Dominic on saxophone and various other people, we have played some great gigs. We played a gig for Feargal Keane, the BBC correspondent – one of the first guys to report on Rwanda. He works with a charity called MSADA and we played a gig for them."

After leaving Grandma Moses, Andy Golden and Bob Cooke had formed Rocky Cockerel and rehearsed original rock and blues songs, but only gigged once before being joined on vocals by Lynden Williams. The band re-named and changed direction into high energy music, very fast and with a punk edge. They released a single, Good Night Roxy, under the unlikely name of The Men of the Doomsbury Lifeboat. The name was changed again, to OXOXOX at which point former Radio One DJ Peter Powell got behind them and the band almost picked up on a record deal.

Andy later became involved with some well known names.

Andy Golden: "When I joined the Mirror, one of the people I met and became very good friends with was Mick Green, who used to be with The Pirates – a consummate guitarist and a lovely bloke. We talked about music and he said 'Do you still play?' I said 'I play in The ESB Band occasionally'."

"We were booked to do the Sunday Mirror Christmas party. Mick came along and the next week I had a call from him. He said 'What are you doing next Tuesday?' He asked me to come along to this address in East London and I asked what for. He said 'Never mind that, just bring your sticks'. I went along – there was a drum kit there and we did a whole hour or two of Pirates' stuff. I didn't know all the material but it was good r'n'b. At the end of it he said 'Right, you're in'. I said 'In what?' and he said 'In The Pirates – I've reformed it', which was fantastic! There were some tours in Scandinavia, some work in England and a couple of albums."

"The bass guitarist dropped out for a couple of gigs and a guy called Denny Newman came in. He had a gig in Romford where his normal drummer couldn't turn out. I went over to do the gig and their manager was there, and he made a call the next weekend to a guy called Tony Williams, who was the bass guitarist with Eric Bell. They had been looking for a drummer for some time and I got a call while I was in Harrods – waiting to see Mohammed Fayed! Eric said 'Come over for an audition and bring your sticks'."

"Instead of going to a hall with drums, guitars and amps, he just invited me to his house. We went into one of the rooms and he had an electric guitar, but no amp. He gave me a cushion and said 'These are the songs we do' and we just went through his set with me playing on the cushion. At the end of it he said 'Yeah, that'll do, you're in'."

The offer of work with Eric Bell landed Andy with a dilemma that was perhaps normally faced by far less-experienced musicians - whether to give up the day job.

Andy Golden: "We had a three week tour and I thought 'Well, this is a bit tricky' because I was working for a national newspaper - but the weekend [Princess] Diana died I wasn't called into the office, so I realised there was a bit of a problem. They had decided they were going to revamp the office and I wasn't part of it. I was given my marching orders, which was perfect…. it all fitted in beautifully. That's what made me decide I should do music from now on."

Although he has gone on to higher profile work, one of Andy's old Salisbury bands is remembered fondly: "I've found that, when you are out for a drink or something, people go 'Weren't you in…' Then the name 'Grandma Moses' comes in and they say 'I saw you at…' when you're involved in it you don't recognise it like that, you just do what you do. You go along, play somewhere and go home again, but I'm always very pleased that people remember the name and want to talk about it."

ENDLESSBEAT

"... finding your voice in a way where no-one is laying down the rules."

Tom Thatcher: "Debbie Thrower [a local TV presenter] came up to the farm some years later to do an interview – we had some rather extreme giant cattle. After the interview she said 'You weren't in a band called Grandma Moses were you?' I said 'Yes' and she said 'I remember going with a boyfriend to see you playing in Salisbury!' People were really kind about the band on the whole, we always seemed to be appreciated – never made an enemy."

Andy Pringle, one-time social secretary of the Salisbury Students' Union later achieved a modicum of fame in certain circles with a book on British football grounds.

A former legend of the Salisbury punk scene relocated to the continent after the mid-eighties demise of Dark Star.

Duncan Fulton: "In '87 I upped and moved over to Germany. I was working for the railway and I cultivated a bad back - I decided it was time to get back at my employers, who had been annoying me with inconvenient night shifts, low pay and hassling, so I took a holiday."

"I was over in Amsterdam for a while, playing on a houseboat. Then I moved to Germany but I was flying back every month or so to get a renewed doctor's certificate. It was a great little life – I was earning out on the street and making a transition. Andrew Lovelock was living in Oldenburg at the time – that's how I came to go over. He was working at the university and I stayed with him, and when he finished I took over his flat. After a year or so I had to resign from the railway and became a professional busker, playing mainly covers but 30% my own stuff."

One of Duncan's former colleagues from the Kitchens has kept in touch with the local scene.

Ruth Jones: "I have ended up being a professional in the arts world but campaigning for arts provision for young people, and not just at school. It's not the classical music side of things, for me it's the 'I've got a guitar - I can express myself' and finding your voice in a way where no-one is laying down the rules."

"There is a really good band scene

THE JAMESONS - left to right: Graham 'Chalky' White, Steve Collinson, Gary Holton and Ruth Jones

but it's not just that, it's DJ-ing, skateboarding, whatever. Everything comes and goes and it's relatively easy for a bunch of kids to get together, record some stuff and release it on YouTube or myspace or whatever, but now there is a new respect for any band who can play live for more than half an hour. You can use technology and make stuff up but a band that can play in front of an audience, without technology, there is a new respect for."

After Toucantango folded Mike Vickers landed a part in the Salisbury Amateur Operatic Society's production of Jesus Christ Superstar - performed in St Mary's Cathedral. He still performs live using backing tracks and with the occasional band.

Mike also appeared in fellow-former QT Frogg Moody's Yours Truly, Jack The Ripper production and co-wrote his own show-stopping number, The Innocent Man, which he believes is the best work he has ever done. Although Frogg has played keyboards with many bands over the years, 'The Ripper Show' has probably been his finest musical achievement.

Frogg: "I became interested in the subject from watching the Jack The Ripper TV series of 1973 and following this I was given a present: Stephen Knight's book, The Final Solution. In 1996 I started a project with scriptwriter Dave Taylor and decided to do a concept album. I contacted Clive Roper and asked him to help demo up some of the songs. This took us to Steve Collinson's studio where we laid down the first ideas of the album."

"Sue Paramore helped with lead vocals and we decided to record the project at her new studio at Burcombe. Sue had engaged a superb engineer and producer, Paul Gulliver, who became vitally important in shaping the recording. I also called upon various musicians and vocalists to take part including Sue, Alan Marsh, Sean Rice, Dave Ansell, Chris Walsh, Simon Oxborrow, Colin Holton, Paul Abbott and Ian Marshall. I played most of the keyboard parts and additional bass parts, with Paul Gulliver adding extra keys and programming all the drum parts. The narrative was written by Dave and

ENDLESS BEAT

"It won't be too long before old Jack is back"

recorded in a fine cockney accent by Colin Burden."

"Dave and I decided to call the album Yours Truly, Jack the Ripper and the whole recording took around a year to complete. Once released, it started to attract good reviews and was accepted by leading Ripperologists as a masterpiece!"

"Dave then said 'Do you realise we've got a show here?' The first show at Salisbury Arts Centre in 1997 was fantastic and the audience response electrifying, but the material on the CD only gave us forty-five minutes - we decided to add more material and make it a full length show. Rosemary Howles was at this time organising the first Jack the Ripper National Conference in Norwich, in 1998, and invited our Midnight Theatre Company to perform Yours Truly as the Saturday night highlight. The show went down a storm and received a favourable review in the Ripperologist magazine. The cast at this time consisted of only eight people - we knew that bigger and better things were to come."

"1999 was a busy year, with good reviews for the CD coming in thick and fast. The show continued to tour extensively including a four day stint as part of the Salisbury Fringe Festival, and was enhanced by the superb vocals of Alan Marsh and a new narrator, Graham Paramor. Dave Taylor and I also finished extending the show into a ninety minute format."

"The strangest performance we've ever given was at the request of the Gatehouse Masonic Lodge in Redhill, Surrey. We could hardly have turned down such a request given the conspiracy theories involving Jack the Ripper and the Freemasons. The Grand Master was relieved that the old conspiracy theories were not relived - the show was based on the true facts of the case."

"By 2000, the show was going from strength to strength and we were invited by Christopher George to take part in the American conference, Jack the Ripper...A Century of Myth, in New Jersey. By now we had a full backstage crew - Backstage Antics - and they performed a minor miracle in transporting scenery, props etcetera across the Atlantic. Before leaving we staged a press conference and photo-call in the London Dungeon to launch our transatlantic adventure, which led to my appearing on the radio - London Today, with Julia Somerville."

"We realised a show about Jack the Ripper, being synonymous with London, should be performed there. After a prolonged search of suitable venues we hit upon the Wimbledon Theatre and ended 2000 with our London premiere - a five day run - which attracted good audiences and much press coverage. We continued touring throughout 2001- by now the cast had swelled to fourteen with a backstage crew of seven. After many successful performances, including at the Theatre Royal, Portsmouth, we found ourselves back at Wimbledon Theatre by popular demand. During the autumn of 2002 we made a short film documentary on the show."

"By 2003, the show had taken on a new style, thanks to the talents of new narrator and director Richard Clarke. Soon, after negotiations with film maker Philip Peel, an agreement was reached to produce a full length film, involving our stage production running parallel with a modern storyline. Locations included landmarks in the East End of London and the auditorium of the Athenaeum Theatre, built in the late nineteenth century and used by Oscar Wilde during his lecture tours."

"The film, Jack - The Last Victim, was shown in full at the Jack the Ripper Conference in Brighton. It was well received but, due to contractual problems, was never released or marketed. This was a great shame as a lot of work went into the production but it looks as though it will never see the light of day."

"Perhaps the disappointment of the film has resulted in Yours Truly, Jack the Ripper not reaching its true potential, because the show has not been performed as much in recent years, although it was performed in Washington, USA by an independent theatre company complete with a live rock band. The American version received some fantastic reviews in the major USA press which, in turn, gave the show some excellent publicity."

"Yours Truly, Jack the Ripper has been a wonderful experience and brought together some outstanding performers and musicians from Salisbury. I am still continuously asked when the show will be performed again and my answer remains pretty much the same…'It won't be too long before old Jack is back!'"

After The QTs folded drummer Mike 'Jackboot' Jones played in Elite and then sang and programmed in Aku Aku. He still has his own recording set up and writes music - currently a new type of dance music in 3/4 time that he calls 'Bounce'. Prior to The QTs he had played in a London based band with a guitarist who has gone on to build a career in the music business.

Mike Jones: "Jules Hardwick is still a good friend. He is currently doing a lot of work for the BBC, as well as gigs with various guitarists and production for many new bands such as The Ting Tings. After our band broke up he helped form a band called Writz, who were moderately successful. He then was involved with writing, production, session work - indeed he has helped write a lot of fairly well known songs, such as Enola Gay by OMD. However, a few years ago he was persuaded to re-record a Spanish track for a producer friend that I am not sure I have yet forgiven him for - it was called The Birdie Song!"

Neil Dalziel, of Identity Crisis and Ambulance Beat, now plays in Forbidden Fruit with Chris Binns and Steve Collinson: "From the mid-nineties onwards, for some reason, I started to have a real rebirth in terms of writing songs and recording them in my own little Portastudio. I was getting more into it than I had ever done before in terms of quality and quantity. When I look at the stuff from then until now I think it's far better than anything I did before. I had all this stuff I had recorded on my own and phoned Steve, who I hadn't spoken to for a few years, went out to his studio and spent months and months recording one song, which was called Forbidden Fruit. It kind of grew out of that song."

Chris Binns has been working for Spike Stent, a successful mix engineer

THE CATALOGUE MEN - left to right: Neil Dalziel, Nick Heron and Dave Marsh

ENDLESS BEAT

"Guess who I've met' and I said 'George Harrison?' He said 'The Pope!"

and producer, for ten years. He also worked for Robert Fripp doing mixes in around 2005. He has mixed feelings about the old Salisbury scene.

Chris Binns: "I honestly can't pretend to have been much of a part of it. I seem to recollect I was a horribly arrogant individual when I first came to Salisbury, and as such I was always surprised at how quiet it was compared to say, Bath – there should have been something akin to Moles Club. I took more of an interest when I taught sound recording at the college from 1996 to 2001."

Nick and Jez Kemp of The Crimmos are still remembered in Salisbury as artists that had the potential to have gone a long way in the music industry.

Nick Kemp: "I made an album with Duncan Fulton in Dusseldorf in '91. Since then it's been home recording all the way - I ain't finished with this sucker yet. I quit playing for a couple of years disgusted - listened to nothing but orchestral music in the interim. Then I realised I couldn't live like that, got a guitar, recording gear and started over. I wouldn't say it's all I do, but it comes pretty close. Jez is still playing – band's called Spicy Chutney - a Celtic traditional thing – made a CD a couple of years back."

Nick Marchant of Identity Crisis still plays with The Kings Of Lounge. In the late seventies he started building electric guitars in his spare time, teaching himself inlay work and various finishing techniques, before moving on to acoustic, steel strings and jazz arched-top designs. In 1983 he set up his own guitar making and repair business, which is still going strong today. Clients have included Charlotte Hatherley of Ash and Jimi Volcano – 'the hottest hard rock ukulele player in the world'. Nick's website is at www.guitarrepairsuk.com.

Founder member of Genghis Khan and The Prams, Eddie Johnson, now lives in America. He is fondly remembered by his former colleagues.

Rob Boston: "He was really into music and introduced me to lots of people around town. He was always

HORSE LATTITUDES - left to right: Nick Kemp, Barry Stevens, Caroline Holt-Keen and Jez Kemp

ahead of the game - he knew about new bands coming in and was just a motor-mouth, energetic, funny kid. Very entertaining to be with and a kind of catalyst – he made things happen."

Alwyn Lovell: "Ed wasn't technically the best guitar player in the world but a funnier bloke you could not wish to play with. He was always in and out because he had a career planned for himself but he was very influential, especially on me and Rob. He was a very funny guy who would often interject good ideas into the band and take it off at a different tangent."

Alwyn, who alongside Rob Boston was the only musician to have been with all incarnations of Genghis Khan, The Ghosts and The Prams, had no desire to find a new project after the last of those bands folded.

Alwyn Lovell: "For me the band wasn't musically led – it was characters that made the band – especially when Ed was in it. It was four really solid characters. With me it doesn't always boil down to musical ability, it boils down to character. Because of the high of The Prams and what I thought of it I found it quite…[long pause]…it takes a lot of work to get the chemistry right in a band. It's difficult to do and I felt that going for an audition to just be the guitar player in a band was not what I wanted to do."

In 1984 Alwyn moved to Iceland, as he had met an Icelandic girl. He took his guitar and finally found a degree of fame as a sideman to a local pop star.

Rob Boston: "Alwyn became a celebrity out there – he met the Pope. He phoned me up one day and said 'Guess who I've met' and I said 'George Harrison?' He said 'The Pope! I was walking through Reykjavik and there was a bit of a scrum of photographers. I was trying to get by to get home and as the crowd parted I suddenly found I was in front of John Paul II, and we shook hands – it was really surreal'."

Alwyn has not performed with bands since returning to the UK but still plays for his own amusement and has recording facilities at home. He does not have a high opinion of the current music scene.

Alwyn Lovell: "If you want my take on the scene at the moment I think it's worse than it has been in living memory. It is so bad. When you've got people like Jo Wiley judging people, and whether they are any good or not, it speaks for itself - because she knows nothing about music. She wouldn't know a good band if it came up and bit her on the ass."

After the demise of The Prams, Rob Boston never quite returned to the music scene: "I became a parent in '83 - my eldest son Luke was born. I was a completely broke musician and needed to earn money and, although I never meant to walk away from the band, it kind of took second place. Then his brothers came along and I never quite got back into it. The biggest regret of my life was not carrying on."

Despite the advice of their father, who told them "not to go into the music industry as it would break their hearts", the Boston boys (Luke, Beau and Vic) are making their own way in one of Salisbury's best current bands, Big Num.

Rob Boston: "You always do the exact opposite of what your old man says. They were very keen, I've got recordings of them playing Howlin' Wolf songs when they were ten, all strumming along and doing the voice. They formed a band and started gigging and asked my opinion – 'Do you think we're good enough to do it?' I said 'Technically and artistically, yes, you are good enough…but you would be better off playing football – if you're going to do it I've warned you – it's a tough old road'."

By strange coincidence, the paths of Rob Boston – who lived in East London as a child - and ex-Iron Maiden vocalist and fellow modern day Salisbury resident Paul Di'Anno, crossed for a third time at a Big Num gig. Despite both having been part of the nascent NWOBHM scene many years before, it wasn't until now that they realised their first meeting had in fact occurred many years before that – at the Thomas Gamuel primary school in Walthamstow in the late sixties.

Rob Boston: "I met him at a gig in Pewsey. We started talking and when we compared notes we came from the same place. We had been at Thomas Gamuel in Walthamstow. I couldn't remember his name because there were family changes and he was actually at school as Paul Taylor - I

THE PRAMS - Eddie Johnson and Nick Boston 1980

ENDLESS BEAT

"I'm shit at everything. All I can do is play guitar!"

knew him when we were seven or eight years old. It's such a weird story – from Thomas Gamuel through the heavy metal thing - I didn't click then – to twenty years later in a pub in Pewsey!"

Rob's cousin Mark Palmer, of Last Orders and Obvious Action, now works in political journalism for the BBC. He owns a bass played by Ali McMordie on the first two Stiff Little Fingers albums. While studying in Bournemouth he formed a band called the Cadillac Babies, who still reunite to gig once a year.

Mark Palmer: "I think we are nothing without music. It's a release, an escape, it makes you think. Everything I am today I owe to The Clash and Stiff Little Fingers. They made me think about things."

Of course Mark also had a love of the bubblegum element of punk: he carries one of Dee Dee Ramone's plectrums – snaffled at a gig in Bournemouth - around in his wallet.

In 1997 former Genghis Khan, Tokyo Blade, Shogun, Mr Ice and Pumphouse vocalist Alan Marsh became involved in the Yours Truly, Jack The Ripper show: "I had never done anything like that before. I'm glad Frogg made me do it. It was good fun – a different thing to do – it was enjoyable."

More recently Alan has been involved in the When The Lights Go Down DVD project, which seems to be quite closely related to the story of Tokyo Blade et al: "It's not based on it, but situations the band find themselves in are pretty much what I found myself in. Like most people's lives in bands – except for the lucky ones that get through - we picked ourselves up, dusted ourselves off and tried again… until it gets to the point where you're too bloody old to do it."

Tokyo Blade have recently reformed with a line up of Chris Gillen, Andy Boulton, John Wiggins, Andy Wrighton and Steve Pierce, and are recording a new album. To his former teachers' surprise, and despite having no qualifications or formal training on guitar, the Blade guitarist eventually had an opportunity to pass on his knowledge and skills at a high profile educational establishment.

Andy Boulton: "I was a musician by default really. I'm shit at everything. All I can do is play guitar, so I don't have much choice - I have to keep going at it. I ended up teaching guitar at Winchester College."

Meanwhile, the original Tokyo Blade recordings are still selling, especially in Europe – although the band members are not seeing a return.

Alan Marsh: "Go on Amazon and you can get anything you want. It's a bit annoying but without money you can't attack it and you probably wouldn't be able to prove one way or the other how much was missing or how many were sold."

Atilla has played keyboards with Cane (who later became Invisible Jesus), featuring Simon Berry of whom he says: "Simon is a flawed genius. At one stage we were really on it. Simon is a fantastic song crafter – there were some beautiful songs". Atilla has also played with Paul Di'Anno in Battlezone and covers band The Inbredz.

Atilla: "John Wiggins was involved with Paul in the original incarnation of Battlezone. They decided they didn't want to do straight ahead heavy metal and brought me into the studio to put in some samples, some grooves - some different sounds. Then they asked me

Andy Boulton

to come and do it live. About the same time the Almighty Inbredz came along, with Holton, just playing punk rock songs we liked and doing the odd gig."

More recently, Atilla has linked up with his former Mad Cow Disease colleague Jon Maple - the latter's first direct involvement in music for many years.

Jon Maple: "I've been looking with him at his project with Norwegian death metal and funeral doom – Legion Of Crows. We're currently working on a remake of Bullshit Acres."

Former Kinetic NRG vocalist and Un Deux Twang! drummer Alex Mundy recently left The Rhythm Blasters after twenty-five years, during which time he has also played with a number of side projects.

Alex Mundy: "The thing that a lot of Salisbury bands are good at is getting out and doing their own material. Considering Salisbury is a small town, a lot of bands play their own material. I don't think it necessarily means that a lot of the bands could have made it outside of Salisbury, or that they even wanted too, but the fact that you were able to shine in Salisbury has always been good."

"There has always been a lot of support for local bands. Thirty-two years on I would call myself a serious hobbyist musician and I love it. I have no regrets that I haven't taken it any further, but I want to be the best that I can, and I'm sure there's a lot of other musicians that feel the same way."

Alex has been working for Robert Fripp since 1997, at which time the former King Crimson man was still living in Broad Chalke.

Alex Mundy: "I had been plumbing on and off for years, and felt like I wanted to do something different, so I managed to get on to a sound engineering course at Salisbury College. As part of that we had to do our own work experience. Some people were getting placements in the Arts Centre or the Playhouse. I knew Robert Fripp lived in the area and was going to be doing some performances in Salisbury Cathedral. I found a number for his office in the phone book, which in fact should have been ex-directory. An American lady, Diane, answered the phone and after I explained I was looking for two weeks work experience, she said 'We're actually looking for someone full-time - do you want to come for a job interview?'"

"I met Robert at Broad Chalke. I remember being quite nervous. He asked me 'What do you do?' and I said 'I play drums' - he went 'Oh no!' I said 'I played a bit of guitar' - and he went 'Even worse!' I said 'I have done plumbing as well' and he said 'Oh - that could be useful'. By the time I got back home there was a message on my answer machine from Robert saying 'We would love to have you'. It's actually assisting David Singleton who is in partnership with Robert – mainly working on King Crimson and Robert's solo work, but they did release other artists' work including John Paul Jones and Bill Nelson."

After his later band Dennis folded, Alex's Kinetic NRG colleague Ian 'Skid' Browne moved away and managed pubs in London and Sussex – some of which are most politely described as 'dodgy'. Following his return he played with Cane and The Inbredz. He was also involved in the When The Lights Go Down DVD and still plays, with Pyeshoppe.

Skid: "The highlight in these last few years has been Endorse It In Dorset. We're all getting on a bit, we're all still playing really loud rock'n'roll music and we all end up camping in a field getting free tickets for a festival and getting completely trolleyed for the whole weekend, and having a laugh with a big gang of mates - which is what being in a band is all about."

Dave Taylor co-wrote Yours Truly, Jack The Ripper with Frogg Moody and has had plenty of fun in the Rhythm Blasters, with whom he still performs: "In the early days, with Alex and Colin [Holton], I have to say it was life threatening fun, because when they were together a side of them came out that was perhaps best put away."

"I have been in a Transit driving with no lights at night, in incredibly heavy rain, with both of them completely off their heads. At one point Colin just fell right out because he was trying to lean around and imitate the windscreen wipers - because there was no electrics. We had borrowed it from that one-armed bloke who used to dip wood in acid to get the paint off, but he didn't tell us it didn't have any electrics!"

"At some really, really high class party – the groom was called Tarquin - at Shrewton Stud we were the third part in the event, for the sort of hoi polloi in the evening. It was my fault - I was drunk. We were in this tent – better appointed than most people's houses - and at the end of every number someone would come up and say 'Can you play faster/slower/louder/softer'. It was really annoying."

"Tarquin came up and said 'Do you know anything from Grease?' Apparently, because I was drunk, I immediately retorted 'What do you mean? Fucking zither music?' knowing full well he meant the film. He said

ENDLESS BEAT
"I've got this great idea Clive!"

'No, no…the film…Grease'. My hand went back and Malc [Wilkinson] shot over and grabbed me and said 'Don't… we've not been paid!'"

In the early nineties former Don't Ask (amongst others) vocalist Johnny Fellows played in a fun band with Colin Gray, Barry Stevens, Graham Hughes and others but is no longer involved in music.

Johnny Fellows: "When Don't Ask split up, myself, Hughesy and Colin wanted to do some fun stuff. The first few gigs we did - for one we were called 'Fish From Outer Space' and another one was 'Nick Faldo's Haircut'…all these joke names. Myself and Colin are veering on the side of large hooters…and Colin's got a huge gut…we were jokingly saying we were going to be 'Guts'n'Noses' and our album was going to be 'Appetite For Lard', but it sort of stuck and people knew us as that. My daughter was born in '94 and it seemed like a natural conclusion."

Johnny has identified a contrast between the sources available to young musicians today and his own experiences in Amesbury back in the seventies.

Johnny Fellows: "I remember going down the Kings Arms - I was about seventeen. We had some songs we thought we might want to do so we went in there one Saturday lunchtime and, surreptitiously with a tape recorder, put stuff on the jukebox and tried to get close to the speaker to try and work out what keys they were in – we didn't want to have to go and buy the music book – and ended up horrendously drunk at half two and falling out. Compare that to just clicking on a download and getting it all!"

Others have contrasting views on the modern Salisbury scene.

Phil Manning: "It seems fairly vibrant but I have to say a lot of it is not to my taste. There was a period a number of years ago when every band in Salisbury wanted to be a thrash metal band - that can be a bit tedious if you've got three or four hours and its all pretty much of a muchness. I think it's changed a bit recently – people are getting into other things."

Chalky White: "It's always been interesting but unfortunately in recent times no one has really broken out of the city and 'made it'. However, every time I see a band in town now I'm impressed – the gear is a lot better and, although the sound is sometimes derivative, there has been some good bands around."

Given the seriousness of the brain haemorrhage he suffered whilst with Oglala Sioux, Kerry Waite's memory is extremely lucid and his subsequent achievements have been remarkable. Now living in Shepherds Bush, Kerry obtained a degree in music technology from Thames Valley University in the mid nineties and has worked live and in the studio with a range of artists including session musician Mike

Mickey Dyer and Andy 'Sprog' Ford

Sturgess and Cobalt of Zodiac Mindwarp. One of his greatest pleasures is teaching guitar, including in schools and prisons – a current pupil is the son of the late X-Ray Spex guitarist Jack Stafford (aka 'Jak Airport').

Kerry has recently been back in contact with his former Red Book and Dark Star colleagues Duncan Fulton and Andy 'Sprog' Ford, with a possible view to making a pure rock'n'roll album. He recalls how insular the old Salisbury scene could be.

Kerry Waite: "We knew every pub – 108 to my recollection: which ones to go in, who would be in there, what sort of people we would be talking to and why they didn't like us. We knew every single band: who was doing what, what they were going to do and where they had been playing. It was like a little cage and we were all rattling and trying to make more noise. We were introduced to ego: we believed we were the best, but I'm sure everybody feels exactly the same – that was the little baby egos that we all had."

Clive Roper has not played in a formal band since the end of Going Out With God: "I was about thirty-two then and had nothing – no wife, kids, picket fence – the mortgage rates soared but house prices plummeted and all of a sudden, for the first time in my life, I was in a position where I could buy a house - but I had to give things up."

"The last gig was supporting Hugh Cornwell [at the City Hall]. It went out on a bit of a high. Dave Marsh was intent on us going up and playing No More Heroes as the first song, which sounds very funny but we would have got murdered! We went down really well and Colin Holton wrote a review where he said 'Ropey Roper is keeping his end up with his much loved songs'."

Going Out With God had already crossed paths with a member of the headliner's band.

Clive Roper: "We had played in Box - Adam Heaton had taken over the Northey Arms, which was Hugh Cornwell's local. We did all the Stranglers' numbers and Hugh's keyboard player was there watching us. When we supported Hugh Cornwell the keyboard player said 'Oh my God…it's you boys…you're back!'"

"Basically my music came to an end…but not quite…I had one more card to play. Some bloke in town kept badgering me – 'I've got this great idea Clive'. He phoned and said 'I want to write a musical on Jack The Ripper'. Frogg came over and we started to do demos – taking Frogg's ideas and working them into songs."

As a songwriter Clive has great respect for the craft of two of his contemporaries in particular.

Clive Roper: "There were other bands that I really, really liked. There were two things which really stick in my mind. One was Newcombe and Roach's Pictures In The Rain. The other, which was much later, was Colour Me In With Your Pencils by

InSpired Events Presents

Hugh Cornwell

ex STRANGLERS

CITY HALL
Salisbury
ENTERTAINMENT CENTRE

Monday October 10th 8.00 p.m.

Supported by
"Going out with God"

Tickets £5.00

ENDLESS BEAT

"I can't believe he has come up with that – it's amazing!"

The Statues, which Sean Rice had written. I would be very happy if I could say I had written those two

public since 1987. When my father died he left me his guitars, which I actually play more now than keyboards.

some of that love of making music."

Former Toucantango vocalist Kurt Cooper didn't sing at all for fifteen years but is now trying to get a soul band together. He admits he was not always tolerant of other local acts' efforts.

Kurt Cooper: "I got asked to do a lot of judging in 'Battle of The Bands' competitions and a lot of local bands used my studio, so I saw a wide range of local music. Looking back I think I was probably too far up my own arse to appreciate anybody else."

"I always used to call the local band set 'musos' – they would form a band, split up, play for a year and then all change again. It just seemed to me they were going nowhere - they were

INNERVISION
Barry Stevens, Trevor Webb, Charlene Leverton, Steph Murray, Pete Leyland & Dave Walker

songs."

"I always thought I had punky credentials, but that was rubbish. I couldn't really do all that thrashy stuff. Everything I liked was really quite melodic – things like XTC – really clever pop songs. I could never do that…but I aspired to. My big thing wasn't so much the playing - I just really liked making noises. I also always had this terrible sensible streak that said 'Keep the job going'. There were times when enthusiasm turned into dreams of wealth, but you had to keep your feet on the ground."

Following the final split of Toucantango in late 1987, some members went on to form other bands.

Neil Leacy: "With swapping and changing line-ups Trevor [Webb], Pete Smith, Dave Walker and Nick Walker formed Who Is?, which eventually morphed into a very popular covers band called Pray - which became Innervision, a covers band that is still very much alive and kicking, with Trevor and Dave still playing together over thirty years after our first Stonehenge Inn Sunday afternoon sessions."

"I still have an enduring passion for music - playing, listening, seeing live - but have not played much in

Occasionally I write and record music for myself and maybe I will play in a band again, but for the moment I'm just happy to have seen my own children growing up, playing in bands, solo and in orchestras, and continuing

Jason Stuart, 'centre stage' with friends - The Plaza, Amesbury. Circa 1988

270

just feeding off each other to get something new…but there was nothing new. Hence I wanted to give Salisbury something different. I definitely had a look which nobody else had in Salisbury and I had a voice which I thought was better than anyone else. You have to have a certain amount of arrogance I think, and I had a lot of that at the time…but you're up there to be chopped down."

Steve Burton, Kurt's colleague in Shoot The Toux, is now a session player and producer.

Kurt Cooper: "Steve decided to move to London. He deserved to be somewhere else - he was drinking himself to death in Salisbury and I think going to London gave him the opportunity to show himself for what he really was – an excellent keyboard player."

What The Butler Saw and Shoot The Toux guitarist Simon Oxborrow has played on a number of sessions with Steve Burton. Another of his former band colleagues, Jason Stuart, went on to play keyboards with Hawkwind but sadly died in 2008.

Simon Oxborrow: "He was very lively on the keyboards - wonderful timing, a wonderful ear…sometimes you would be playing a song and would think 'I can't believe he has come up with that – it's amazing'."

Despite the band members having all dropped out of the music scene, Bubblegum Splash! - Salisbury's unlikeliest ever 'stars' - are now feted across the web for their 'perfectly punk' career.

Dave Todd: "You get people on the Internet saying the Bubblegum Splash! single summed up what that scene was all about - people who couldn't particularly play but had the enthusiasm, made one record and split up."

Bubblegum Splash! and original Jane From Occupied Europe drummer Alan Harrison lives with former Soundtracks columnist Sally Anne Lowe in Guildford. Although there were some negative aspects to her time as chronicler of the local scene – such as boarding a bus to be told by the driver 'My son hates you' and receiving death threats from a Bishop Wordsworth's schoolboy – Sally's memories are generally happy ones.

Sally Anne Lowe: "I have had some incredible experiences in music in Salisbury, made some life-long friends, and have some amazing memories. So much venom from people who didn't like what I wrote [but] it's how I met Alan and we're still together, so we have lots to thank the Journal for."

THE NUTHINS

Sally no doubt speaks for countless local musicians and fans when she recalls those she calls 'legends': "Ruth Jones was the woman I wanted to be when she was in The Kitchens - and many other bands. Colin Holton is just funny and talented and charismatic. Phil Manning - what can I say - same goes for Jolly Jon Maple. Roger Elliott must have been to more gigs than anyone. He didn't play in them but took the best pictures. I feel really lucky to know them and to have enjoyed their amazing creativity."

Dave Todd never played in another band after Jane From Occupied Europe folded, but also remembers the community spirit of the indie era: "We used to drink in the Star. Every Friday night there would be the bikers in one half of the bar and all us lot – Badgeman, Janies, Mayfields, Nuthins – all around the pool table at the other end."

"Jim [Harrison] lived around East Street with Kev [Russell] and Swannie. Then they moved to Woodstock Road and I moved there as well. Neale from The Badgeman unofficially lived there, so you had half of what we thought was the Salisbury music scene living in one house. We were playing a lot in London then, so you would come back to this sleepy street in Salisbury at three or four in the morning and get a load of gear out of the van. I think The Badgeman are the ones who should have gone further. When they signed up with Fire we were a bit envious -

ENDLESS BEAT

"It's a very hard job writing about local bands."

their records have stood the test of time."

The still incumbent Salisbury Journal photographer has taken countless pictures of local and visiting acts - and of course village fetes and Salisbury District League Cup Finals.

Roger Elliott: "Having a camera is very helpful because you have a purpose for being somewhere and nobody is going to look twice at you. One of the most amusing ones was when Eat Static played at the Arts Centre. I must have been the only sober person in the whole place. I spent most of the evening surrounded by young people with very large eyes - staring at me with curiosity. It's a bit difficult sometimes – you go into these things where the average age is about fifteen-sixteen and you do feel a bit odd."

Technology has of course changed the role of the photographer significantly.

Roger Elliott: "For twenty-two years I did nothing but take black and white photographs, develop films, make prints and mix up foul smelling chemicals. I don't do any of that anymore. My boss existed in this profession for forty-six years and nothing changed. Since I've been in charge it's turned on its head about half a dozen times. I'm a webmaster, I take digital photographs and use the computer all the time, and I don't have a darkroom anymore."

"Because everybody can take a good photograph now, the ones who are professional have to be that much better. I've always had this very strong belief that when I go and take somebody's photograph it's because they are doing something – it's not because of me. All I am doing is using my skill the best I can to capture whatever it is about in the best way I can. If I take a great 'Roger Elliott' photograph while I'm doing that, then that's a plus, but my job is to be in the shadows and just record what happens - but it's a great privilege to me to have documented all this stuff and I still get a buzz out of it."

During her time as the original Soundtracks columnist, Roger's wife Penny experienced some of the criticism hinted at by Sally Anne Lowe.

Roger Elliott: "I'm just the man who takes the pictures, but one of the reasons Pen stopped doing Soundtracks was she found you couldn't always say nice things about people you knew. She had a bit of a running battle with Jonathan Hyams – the director of the Arts Centre – carried out in public in the letters pages of the paper."

Penny Elliott: "In those days I did tend to speak my mind a bit. I can't really remember why I wrote what I did, but I put something about 'middle class posey people taking over the Arts Centre' and he wrote a nasty letter to the Journal. Of course I had to keep going to the Arts Centre because it was part of my job, and we used to wryly smile at each other for a while. Perhaps I didn't choose my words that carefully…but then you don't…it happens."

"I thought I was diplomatic. Looking back maybe I wasn't really but because I had to cover the older generation as well, which I had no interest in whatsoever, I tried to make every band look good - it wasn't my place to put a band down. If I did an interview with a band like, for instance, Tokyo Blade…I hate Heavy Metal but they were a good band and they were nice guys, so I didn't say anything nasty about their music. Maybe when I reviewed their performances I wasn't as kind as I could have been, but I always said 'That's my opinion' it wasn't their creative skills I was criticising but it was just not my scene."

Roger Elliott: "It's a very hard job writing about local bands. If you're going to see Oasis or whatever you can write about it 'til your heart's content – nobody's going to come back to you like if you write about a local band. I remember one band – it was all on college notepaper, obviously all the fans of this band had sat around in the common room during break time and written letters to Penny in protest."

"When we started Soundtracks it was a very Utopian vision. What we wanted to do was provide an organ of communication for all the musicians of Salisbury, regardless of whether they were a club band or played dub reggae or whatever. It was to be somewhere where any musician could get their gig publicised and read about other musicians."

"You couldn't do it these days because it just was not a financially viable operation. It only worked because we actually loved doing it and we had a sub in Carol Grant who basically gave us complete freedom to design the page every week."

Penny Elliott: "The Soundtracks era was a precious moment in time, which could never be again in an age of mobiles, e-mails etc. Part of the fun was scribbling interviews in pubs and turning up in weird places unexpectedly. I met some really good people, some of whom I have stayed friends with and to pick favourites, or judge who was particularly talented, is impossible."

Penny believes the vibrant eighties scene compares favourably with that of today.

Penny Elliott: "There was a lot more live music in pubs. I also think

Pictured here are members of the ten bands playing at the Arts Centre this Friday night for the Rocking For Peace gig. All the money raised will go to CND and, as it is on the eve of the big CND rally in London's Hyde Park, it will be a good warm-up for the big day. The fun starts at 7.30 pm and tickets are £2 in advance and £2.50 on the door. The event is being organised by members of What The Butler Saw.

ENDLESS BEAT

"... you had to decide how far you wanted to stick your head above the parapet."

there was a lot more music at the Arts Centre. It's diversified a bit since then – you wouldn't see a band every week at the Arts Centre now. The best gigs have to have been the benefits. I know that sounds self-righteous, but Salisbury turned out in force for Ethiopia and the miners, and also in a more personal way when they did a gig for Colin Harding's family. Colin was a local musician and artist and a big personality on the Salisbury scene."

We wholeheartedly agree with Mark Palmer's comments about Penny - without Soundtracks, researching Endless Beat would have been much more difficult.

Mark Palmer: "If she was here now I would buy her a drink. Without her what record would there be of music in Salisbury? There wouldn't be any. So I think we have to raise our glasses to Penny and say 'Well done!'"

After Penny's three and a half year stint, the Soundtracks column was taken on by Howard Gibbons, and then Sally Anne Lowe, Dan Clayton and Jon Maple, who was by far the longest incumbent, and probably the most respected.

Roger Elliott: "Jon Maple did it for ten years. He had very thick skin – he wouldn't mince his words with anybody, but it did become rather more focussed on the sort of thing that he would go and see. I mean you wouldn't catch him going to see a country and western band at Redlynch Social Club for instance. James Shepard used to dread his reviews of Larmer Tree Festival because he loathed anything vaguely hippyish - but that was Jon's persona and we love him dearly really, he did an awful lot for the Salisbury music scene."

Jon Maple: "I was originally taken on by the Blackmore Vale magazine. The Journal noticed this, because that was quite an outspoken column, and the editor approached me. I didn't really feel able to analyse musically what was going on as I had no theory behind me. I took the approach that I would just listen to what it sounded like and say 'Does that noise appeal to me and why?' With rock the performance is more than just music anyway – it's to do with lifestyle, politics, tribalism – so you're reviewing the whole bit."

"I got in to trouble a few times for speaking my mind, but I felt it wasn't my job to give people a warm, woolly blanket of comfort. I felt if they really meant what they were doing and progressed on to national releases and tours, then they would get reviewed by the music press, which was ultra-scathing. NME and Sounds didn't pull any punches, they didn't cut any slack at all - they were heavy. I thought that was my job – sort the men from the boys, the sheep from the goats and tell it like you think it is."

"Certainly there has always been an attitude in me which was piss-taking – even a band I liked – like pub banter you know? I knew a lot of these people as well, which didn't help. If somebody you knew quite well had just performed a load of shit, and you knew it, you had to decide how far you wanted to stick your head above the parapet - because you knew you were going to bump into this person within days and would then be called upon to defend yourself."

There was one occasion when Jon's writing incurred the wrath of supporters of The Statues' Sean Rice.

Jon Maple: "He had quite a loyal bunch of mates did Sean. I don't know that they were 'fans' - but they were mates and they were loyal to him. I remember writing words to the effect that 'this man cannot hold a song in a bucket', which was true – that night he was all over the place, slaloming around the melody line. I don't know whether that was just a bad night but there were people laughing at that performance."

"I remember thinking 'That's gonna cause a fuss' and sure enough… Somehow they got my number – I was ex-directory at the time – phoned and gave me an awful ear bashing, which I thought was a bit of an intrusion really, and a certain individual came up to me in the street and said 'You're proper cruel Maple'. He was a big bastard and I thought he was going to fell me with one blow, but that's all he had to say - but my attitude was that you didn't care about that if you were going to be effective and true to yourself…in both music and journalism."

"As a general rule newspapers love controversy - it stirs things up and keeps the newspaper itself in the news, and at a local level advertisers know it has been read because they are getting feedback from letters. One was encouraged in fact to be controversial but of course there were limits – you were writing in a family publication so not too much about coke habits or sexual deviancy – and no swearing [laughs]."

"In the end I got very tired of going to gigs and not enjoying them because I was looking at them in an objective way – like I was reading a book that I later had to write about in an exam. I wasn't enjoying that as an experience - I was involved in it as work."

Jon's last Soundtracks column was

8: **The Beat Goes On**

THE PROPHECY

published in May 1999. Vicky Woodhall had started the paper's monthly arts supplement Grapevine in the nineties, which was taken over by Roger Elliott although by then he had to use younger journalists as he no longer "understood youth music"… but does he have any favourites from when he did understand it?

Roger Elliott: "I loved The Prophecy - one of the most original bands I've ever heard. Jon Baggeley plays in bands with his kids now and he's involved in the Branksome China Company in Fordingbridge, and I met the lead singer behind the souvenir counter of the National Gallery some years ago!"

275

ENDLESS BEAT

"... there were too many bands trying to play in too few pubs!"

Penny Elliott: "It was Andy Brewer - he of the dress - who we bumped into working in The National Gallery! I liked their quirky songs and the fact they sang about their friends a lot! He is still making music somewhere as he sent a CD to the Journal a couple of years ago."

Roger's former Journal colleague also remembers the band.

Jon Maple: "The Prophecy were interesting. They were kinda prog, kinda psychedelic, kinda arty - completely uncompromising. They changed their name to Farley 708, which was somebody's landlord's phone number or something crazy. They were very much in that indie mould derived from that sort of northern miserablist, Mark E Smith, raincoats and second-hand clothes – a sort of anti-fashion thing…Woodbines and working men's clubs but doing this kind of art rock."

THE PHENOBARBITONES

The rather brilliant Prophecy - who begat Farley 708, who begat Farley Ridge - should have been featured in Endless Beat: we tried but the trail ran dry. Another 'unfeatured' band worth mentioning here are The Phenobarbitones, as Robert Howes of that band has gone on to record tracks for Hollywood movies such as Blade 2 and Matrix Revolutions under the name of Overseer.

Perhaps not best described as 'a band', we feel it is unlikely that The Grey Wolves would be overly disappointed at not having been featured in this book – they surely wouldn't consider themselves to be a part of any 'local scene'?

Formed in Amesbury in 1985 by Dave Padbury and Trevor Ward, they have been credited with pioneering the Death Industrial sub-genre. Their work has also been described as Dark Ambient and Power Electronics. They have also engaged in 'Cultural Terrorism', issuing manifestos and pamphlets as well as many tapes of their own music.

The Grey Wolves also created the Death Pact International label, under whose name anyone was free to record their own work. Each member also operates their own cassette label focusing on industrial music. They have gained notoriety for their use of fascist imagery and have been criticised for this aspect of their presentation. Whilst acknowledging the criticism, the group does not apologise for this, instead insisting it is an integral part of their critique of society.

Wiggy: "I would say their influences were the likes of Throbbing Gristle and Whitehouse, while some of their more well known peers would be Test Department, SPK and Einsturzende Neubauten - although The Grey Wolves made these look like pop groups! The term 'avant-garde' would be far too bourgeois for this lot - lots of white noise, found sounds and things being broken, with screams, shouts, recordings of Charlie Manson, the Jonestown Massacre etcetera and occasional bouts of self-mutilation on stage."

"They were scary and uncompromising - and would probably say they don't care to be included [in the book] or not. Lots of people thought they were fascists but they weren't. Very important in their field internationally and a shady presence in the history of Salisbury music - or 'anti-music'!"

Although she is now uncertain of who the band in question were, we suspect Penny Elliott might be thinking of The Grey Wolves when she recalls some rare moments of self-censorship: "I can't remember ever being censored…although I can't remember ever being that controversial. I was aware I was writing for the Salisbury Journal and not the NME – I wasn't Julie Burchill [laughs]. There were some anarchists who produced some sort of music, who lived in Amesbury. The music was a mass of obscenities. I never discouraged them or encouraged them but I did see them at the Arts Centre. They were very anarchistic and I knew they wouldn't get in [the paper], so I would mention they had a gig and leave it at that…but they were always contacting me with the anarchist 'A' on their literature."

The Morrigan have continued to play and record occasionally. Their most recent album, Hidden Agenda, was issued in 2002. The previous year had seen the release of Colin Masson's solo album Isle Of Eight and the follow up, The Mad Monk and The Mountain, is due soon.

After many years of non-involvement in music, one time 'anarchist poet' Chris Hartford made use of a non-refundable ticket to America for a blown out appointment, by photographing, filming and writing a soundtrack for his trip. He has repeated the process over subsequent years.

Chris Hartford: "It wasn't aimed at anyone – it's just languishing on my hard drive and only five or six people have ever seen it. I'm obsessed with production values now, which is very different to how I used to be. My influences are Lalo Schifrin and all that type of stuff – Bullitt soundtrack, Morricone, John Barry – I love the whole genre."

As well as playing in local bands, Nick Heron was involved in the local scene offstage: "The scene was pretty frustrating in some ways. There were way more bands about than I'd have expected for a town the size of Salisbury, the trouble is there was hardly anywhere to play. The pubs that had the sort of clientele that would want to listen to live music were generally too small to put bands on. I once did a gig in the infamous Star, where I think we had to set up in a space that meant no one could get to the loos for the entire time we played. In short there were too many bands trying to play in too few pubs so you'd have to slap off to places like the Saddle Rooms, which put on gigs

ENDLESS BEAT

"The Salisbury Journal once called us 'The Sly and Robbie of Salisbury'!"

pretty much every week."

"The best place to do a gig was of course Salisbury Arts Centre. Depending on how good you were - or more likely who you were supporting - you could play on the big stage to a fairly large audience, or to a smaller audience in the café/bar area. I thought it used to have a pretty nice atmosphere and reasonably good acoustics so the audience could get to listen to how good - or not - you were."

"I did various jobs in the Arts Centre over a three year period, but mostly working with bands, theatre groups etcetera - setting them up, doing their sound, lighting. Apart from the very small wage it was a great place to work."

"The Arts Centre tended to stage their bigger events on Fridays and Saturdays. As I was playing in various bands at the time and was aware of the lack of anywhere to play, I managed to convince the management we should put on local bands on Thursday nights. The deal was the band took the money on the door and the Arts Centre would make money on the bar. Everyone seemed happy! So I started up and was the 'promoter' of 'Another Thursday Night' for a while. This really wasn't too hard because pretty much every band wanted to play there."

"There were a lot of bands around - some were very good but most were fairly average. I suppose in some ways, the band I most admired - rather than liked - was Tokyo Blade. They were the only band I can remember that had a real mission to break into the big time, and they worked really hard at it. Any heavy metal band that would play country and western in working men's clubs - to earn the money to play the music they wanted to - deserve some praise. They also made me laugh because there was a bit of Spinal Tap about them."

"The trouble with most bands around at the time was they took themselves far too seriously and could suffer from being pretentious. For that reason I tended to like the bands that did what they did for the sheer enjoyment of it. You could kind of tell just by watching them…bands like Un Deux Twang! and The Rhythm Blasters come to mind. Another band I liked were Soupdragon. Caroline [Holt-Keen] had a great stage presence and Duncan [Howell] was a very solid guitarist. I also rated The Horizontal Bulgarians with their great encore number, Don't Call Me Chicken Head."

"I should mention Dave Marsh. All the bands I played with in Salisbury had Dave on drums at one time or the other. The Salisbury Journal once called us 'The Sly and Robbie of Salisbury' which, while very flattering, somewhat overestimated our musical ability! Dave managed to do all this despite having to have dialysis twice a week and a couple of failed kidney transplants. I was very sad to hear he died a few years ago."

Passenger Club co-founder Ant Roberts is now the Director of Colchester Arts Centre. He has fond memories of his time in Salisbury: "The thrill of live performance is that you experience it in the here and now. You are in a particular place at a particular time to witness a particular event. Some of the gigs burn brighter than others in the memory - time and subsequent reputations distort those memories: Napalm Death were so crisp, so new, so unfathomable then - they ain't now."

"In those two years I was learning my job in Salisbury, Colin [Holton] and I put on the likes of Milk, Cud, The Shrubs, Robert Lloyd and The New

SOUPDRAGON - left to right: Nigel Finn, Caroline Holt-Keen, Jim Blackwell and Duncan Howell

Caroline Holt-Keen

Four Seasons, John Wesley Harding, Tanita Tikaram and Napalm Death, alongside Rose Coloured Nightmares, The Phenobarbitones, Culture Shock, Chris Hartford and a string of local bands so glorious and transitory in their being."

"The Passenger Club remains one of the projects I have been most proud to be a part of. These projects are the product of a rare mix of people, places, artists and luck. The luck for me was that I became a passenger in the whirlpool of energy that surrounded me for those two brief years."

A former Mayfield, Swannie, now runs the £sD collectors shop in Wilton, in partnership with a former Nuthin, Bob Taylor.

Swannie: "We've been doing it now for ten years. I was always into vinyl but I never got heavily into it until Parma split up in 1998. Within two years of buying lots of records I had so many I decided to open a shop up – to get rid of all the ones I didn't want."

Not all of the items in the shop are for sale.

Swannie: "It's a treasure trove of local bands – Ten Feet Five pre-Troggs singles, Dave Dee, Dozy, Beaky, Mick and Tich signed promotional postcards, programmes, posters and flyers, demos and acetates – it's a museum of localness. We wouldn't part with it because we love it – it's almost like a pension scheme that we'll probably hand down to someone rather than cash it. It's a passion – we're not in it for the money. We were never in it for the money with The Mayfields or any of the bands, we just did it because we wanted to do it, and we have exactly the same outlook with the record shop."

ENDLESS BEAT

"When I look back the most fun time was in Salisbury."

Some of Swannie's own efforts would not be out of place in the 'museum' - a Mayfields demo cassette has sold for over £50 on Ebay - and he recently made a surprise return to the recording scene.

Swannie: "I thought my musical career was over and now it's not. I'm in conjunction with Urban Roots. It's a collective of people who all contribute to the songs and we've got a sixteen track album coming out of reggae/trip hop/soul/funk – with many different artists including Brinsley Forde – ex-Aswad. We've supported people like Dreadzone, Dub Pistols and we do a lot of VJ-ing for these bands. I'm just doing it because I love it – so it's not yet over…the story continues…."

Whilst living in Landford, Jon 'Mojo' Mills of The Nuthins started a garage/psych/power pop/mod/folk/soul/rock'n'roll fanzine named Gravedigger. Mojo later moved to London and set up a new publication along similar lines - Shindig! - now published by Volcano as a glossy, high street magazine covering a whole range of great artists not normally found in the other nationals. He recalls the Salisbury scene with fondness.

Mojo: "For a small town there were plenty of other bands we drank with at The Pheasant - our local, where we also often played and packed. Before we started venturing off to Portsmouth, then London and overseas, we played often with Jane From Occupied Europe and The Badgeman on the home turf. Although more contemporary and embracing indie music they also had similar touchstones to us, which resulted in that slightly-delic Salisbury vibe."

In geographical terms, The Nuthins probably had as widespread a fan base as any band that ever came from the Salisbury area. However, their only motivation had ever been looking and sounding right, and there are no regrets over what might have been.

Bob Taylor: "We're all still friends, there was never any problem, it just came to an end. I joined Marlboro County Fair and did the record shop with Swannie – which has been great because that keeps my music alive. Mojo went to London and did quite well with Shindig! He does quite a bit of radio and for Record Collector. Richie I think is a physicist and mathematician – that's taken him to universities all over the world. Carol now lives in Nottingham. Lee Tea is in Sweden. Andy is in London – I think he's a lawyer. We all did bits of music afterwards but never that serious."

Mojo: "Andy Cornick - from the final era of The Nuthins, Richie Walker and I played in a band called Little Bare Big Bear and issued one psychedelic single on Spanish label Butterfly in 2001. Lee Tea is heading a few garage bands including The Branded, who have had an album (along with The Exciters) issued on London label Dirty Water… a club which The Nuthins played at regularly - It all spins around in circles!"

The former members of Suicide King have also stayed in touch with one another.

Gary James: "New bands came out of it all and the three of us continued making music together on and off up until about 2005. Nick still lives in London, Ray has his own tattoo studio in Kent and I live in Suffolk with my wife and two children. We still all make music, are still in contact and still good friends."

Gary James (above & right), with the Holloway Sisters (top right)

After moving to London, Alexa Mackenzie and Mark Kenchington recorded demos with a 'shoe-gazing' sound, which briefly attracted the attention of 4AD Records.

Alexa Mackenzie: "I knew this place in Golders Green - like a squat but you paid £27 a week each. Ken went back to driving buses and I was serving coffee in this god-awful restaurant. Before we left Salisbury, to cushion the blow financially, we made hundreds of papier mache brooches. We only ever sold one – and our car broke down on the way back from the trade show – so it cost us about £200!"

THE GURUS

Mark 'Kenny' Kenchington and Alexa MacKenzie

"London was terrifying. Salisbury was a nice size with a really lively music scene - it was fun to be part of. Coming to London and trying to make it, and taking it so seriously, took all the fun out of it. When I look back the most fun time was in Salisbury and in Capetown looking for respect from your peers - the industry separates you out and it all becomes too contrived."

Alexa and Ken decided to go back to rock'n'roll and got a drummer in. They supported Oasis but didn't stay to watch them because, Alexa says, "we didn't know they were famous". The pair then formed a band named Fancy with Ash Watson on drums, signed to Big Life records and released a single.

Alexa appeared in The Face and the band incessantly fly-posted all around Camden, but there was a lack of record company support. Big Life was predominantly a dance label and was not sure how to promote an indie band and Alexa became disillusioned: "I think I can safely say we all found the being signed experience crushingly disappointing". Alexa next briefly joined a girl band but has since written music for television and corporate events with Ken, and worked in film and video.

Since Martin James' failed attempt to organise such an event in 1974, the possibility of a 'Salisbury Pop Festival' had continually raised its head and continually been rebuffed – perhaps the closest the suggestion came to reality was in the early nineties when The Prodigy and Black Grape were pencilled in for an event at the city's racecourse. Colin Holton was involved and believes that a "fear of the convoy" scuppered the licence on that occasion.

There is of course the Salisbury

ENDLESS BEAT

"Salisbury has always been conservative with a big C but also with a small c."

International Arts Festival, established in 1973. However, although Colin Holton set up the Salisbury Live 'fringe' in 2000, the 'pop' element has been all but non-existent.

Jon Maple: "The Festival started, as I recall, as classical music and high arts, elitist and centred round the Cathedral Close, with very what you might call 'highbrow' stuff going on - for the bourgeoisie and educated. It was simultaneously a social event, so there are people that go for other reasons than to watch something culturally interesting – they also go because it's a place where they can hobnob with their social set…as if it were Glyndebourne or Henley Regatta, or Ladies Day at Ascot. I had written some piece giving forth my ideas about how hopeless it was as an arts festival and decrying it…I remember somebody writing in to the Journal and describing me as 'an oik with a typewriter'."

"Then Helen Marriage came on the scene and wanted to revamp the whole thing - and quite right too. I was a bit slow to take her on board to be honest because I thought she was just another Oxford graduate art mogul sent down to ponce about…but Helen tried very hard. She was used to dealing with these Governmental agencies – rather gentle people that promote mime artistes - and was confronted suddenly by the sheer cynicism, criminality and shark-like behaviour of the music business, so she couldn't get decent quotes for this that and the other. It was a brave effort on her part. It took me a long time to accept her but she had an edge. She went on to do similar things in London with some success."

As well as problems with budgets, there was also resistance to Helen's proposals from the establishment.

Jon Maple: "I imagine it was memories of Stonehenge which were behind the institutionalised opposition, because they were at that stage a bunch of buffers who had a handle on the throttle of power in Salisbury. She tried her best but failed and I think if a woman like that - with that kind of drive and intellect – couldn't do it then it would be very hard for anyone else to."

Roger Elliott: "Salisbury is a conservative place. It doesn't like disruptions. It's quite feasible to have a festival without destroying a town you know – and there are some great locations around here where you could have a festival."

Mark Palmer: "There was an anti-Royal Wedding gig at the Arts Centre. As an act of revolution that's probably as close as it got in Salisbury. Salisbury has always been conservative with a big C but also with a small c. I have so much respect and admiration for anyone who has been involved in music in Salisbury throughout the ages, because I think it has always been in spite of the city. I think the burghers of Salisbury would be happy if there was no music scene…but equally we don't want the city or the State to actually help us too much, because that stifles creativity."

The Bass Connection project ended up having six rooms at Grosvenor House, with more than thirty bands coming in to use them.

FLINTLOCK COUNTRY BAND

8: **The Beat Goes On**

Keith Gale estimates that 70% of Grosvenor's progeny are still connected with music in some way - as musicians, tour managers and guitar salesmen they have been signed, toured across Europe and America and supported Kasabian at Wembley.

Skid: "When I was a teenager Grosvenor House was a dodgy youth club – you went up there and got bumped out the front by somebody from up the Heath sort of thing - but now they have got all the rehearsal and recording studios up there it's fantastic."

Bass Connection has an annual award showcase gig at the Arts Centre and Keith is also involved with The Unit – a Ruth Jones initiative aimed at promoting young people's activities. Despite these positive notes, Keith feels there are reasons why the local scene has in fact been in decline in recent years.

Keith Gale: "The Arts Centre closed for refurbishment - if you asked any of the bands before they would say 'This is a proper venue'. Yes your foot stuck to the beer on the floor but we felt as if we were in a proper venue - now it feels more like a theatre. It's a lovely place to play – dressing rooms and all that – but it lacks the atmosphere, and rock music is a lot to do with atmosphere. In those two years it was closed...in the past Bass Connection could generate the next generation of rock goers but that disappeared."

"The venues in Salisbury have become very expensive to hire. In the old days, if I put on a gig and only sold a hundred tickets I wouldn't make a loss. If I did it now I would be frightened of the loss I would make. We have got to have particular security and that doesn't help – in the old days we had our own people badged up, but

ESPRIT DE CORPS - left to right: John Ulicsny, Nigel Bailey, David 'Diddy, Savage and Jeff Bundy

DESMOND DEKKER - live in Salisbury

283

ENDLESS BEAT

"Anything you play I'm gonna play back at you twice as fast and twice as good!"

you're not allowed to use local people now."

A giant, in every sense of the word, of the Salisbury scene, has similar views to Keith.

Colin Holton: "The Arts Centre was a brilliant venue. People would come there even though it was off the beaten track. When it opened up again venues had cropped up in other major cities and that's where the big bands go now."

As well as lecturing in music at the Salisbury campus of Wiltshire College, Colin is responsible for Salisbury Live events held in the city each May and also still plays with The Strugglers and Pyeshoppe.

Colin Holton: "Everything I did revolved around music. I lived and breathed music. I've never had a big record collection – I used to tape stuff off John Peel or blag it – but I was just into all kinds of music…anything…"

One of Colin's projects involves a former member of Big Bird, who has evidently forgiven Colin for any part he may have had in the debacle of that band's only gig.

Neale Hancock: "I don't hate Colin – I'm in his band now…well, he's in mine anyway…I bumped into Holton outside a pie shop and that is genuinely why it's called 'Pyeshoppe'."

Colin's contribution to the Salisbury music scene over the last thirty-five years is immeasurable. Although his name is mentioned many times in the book, we have not come anywhere near covering all the things he has done, and continues to do, for the local scene. If anyone has deserved more 'success' it is Colin…but what would have been lost if that success had taken him away from this city?

Jon Maple: "He's a huge character, a natural humourist and a natural musician. He was born to be on stage and has done tremendous work for the music scene and the youth of Salisbury generally."

Pete Lucas and Reggie 'Dave' Maggs are still playing with The Troggs. After Amey-Gair-Mason folded Robin Gair continued to sing solo, with local bands and in duos with Eddie George and Roy Moore, who was tragically killed in a car accident. From the early nineties Robin has, with his children, been involved in running the En Masse singing group, singing schools and pop academies.

Robin Gair: "I realised that even though I dreamed of being a successful songwriter, I didn't have the talent. I can write a reasonable song, but in that market you've got to write great songs. I knew my singing was my strength and the Christmas song was the thing that kicked me off on the teaching side of things. I got involved with Downton School children to record that and I was mentoring them – teaching them the harmonies and the song itself. I realised I had a bit of a gift for passing this on, so it got me thinking."

en masse

"I decided I was going to start a singing school and got a grant from the Enterprise Agency - £40 a week – and it built from there. I realised in a very short space of time that all these people wanted an outlet for their singing and that's when I started to think about forming the group."

Aside from the personal satisfaction that encouraging hundreds of singers has given him, Robin's success stories include Stephanie Hatchman (daughter of John), who has worked with Limahl, and Peter Saul – who landed a leading role in Les Miserables.

Robin Gair: "It did bring more than a tear to my eye when I saw him. When you consider that he came to me at thirteen years old – it was something else. In my own career Amey-Gair-Mason was the thing – no shadow of a doubt, but in terms of kudos for my talents the Southern School of Popular Singing, En Masse and the two academies we have in Southampton and Salisbury are the things that I guess I will be remembered for more than anything."

Robin's Amey-Gair-Mason cohort Peter Mason formed a band with Paul Beavis and Gordon Haskell, but found things difficult because: "I was just doing my own thing. People weren't playing their own songs – they were just taking covers all the time of the American stuff, and I wasn't really into that. There came a time when it was just hard going – I was paying the band and not earning anything out of it myself."

Peter has since concentrated mainly on song writing with his material having been recorded by a range of artists including Rachel Sweet and Ellen Foley. His debut solo album, A Long Haul, was issued in 2008 on Salisbury Records. Among a number of Salisbury-connected credits on the album is Tich Amey, who played guitar and provided a photograph for the inner sleeve.

In the mid eighties Peter's former band member Gordon Haskell, who

THE PETER MASON BAND - left to right: Gordon Haskell, Paul Beavis, James Ferguson and Peter Mason (front)

had once been with King Crimson and would achieve a surprise number 2 hit with How Wonderful You Are in 2001, played a residency at the South Western Hotel in Tisbury.

The Peter Mason Band went through many personnel changes and at one stage included an unlikely bass player fresh from punk band The QTs.

Colin Holton: "There's me coming from being gobbed at and shouting and swearing to this – but they were good songs and I learnt about a new style of music, and that put me in good stead. They were people that would really stretch you to be better. It was like being with Salisbury royalty being with that band and we got to play in Europe. That's when I told work to stuff it up their arse and did music properly."

Yan Webber: "Peter Mason said 'I've got a band together - the trouble is the other guitarist is very competitive and hates other guitar players'. The other guitarist turned out to be Steve Cowan. When I first clapped eyes on Steve he looked at me as if to say 'Anything you play I'm gonna play back at you twice as fast and twice as good' - he had that attitude. However, he soon learned I was never going to be a threat to him [laughs] and from that moment we got on like a house on fire."

"We did a mini-tour of Holland, which was enormous fun. By that time Nigel Dixon had left and been replaced by Colin Holton and I have got to say I have never laughed in all my life so much as I did when we went around Holland. We were anarchic – to the chagrin of poor old Peter, who was trying to hold it all together. At the end of the tour he said 'Yan, I got you in this band because I thought being older than the rest you would be more sensible – you're the worst of the lot!"

"I learned from the band because Peter had the talent to surround himself with some really good musicians. When you have got people with the calibre of Paul Beavis – who is now with Andy Fairweather Low, Steve Cowan and Peter himself, you just can't help being raised, and when you have got bass players of the ability of people like Nigel Dixon and Colin it lifts you."

Yan was involved with a reformed Amey-Gair-Mason who, after a twenty-five year break, got back together again for a charity show at the City Hall, with Nigel Dixon on bass and Paul Beavis on drums.

Yan Webber: "They gobsmacked

ENDLESS BEAT

"It opened a big door of learning about music..."

Ken Lailey, Ruth Jones and David Taylor

me by asking me to play, because these were people that I had been stood at the back of the crowd of in the seventies, open mouthed in awe. I was so honoured. That to me was one of the best gigs of my life because my heroes were back together again and I was a part of it."

Yan also played with Tich in Itch - a name coined by Yan - an anagram of Tich, of course, but also because it was a 'scratch' band, with a line up that also included Nigel Dixon, Eddie George and Stuart Marshall.

More recently Yan has played with Payday and in a duo with Pat Lynch using backing tracks. His 'Music For Fun' nights have sought to revive the spirit of the seventies Musicians Union Band Box Balls, and he feels his current band, 22nd Street, recaptures the 'family feeling' he enjoyed in previous bands. On reflection he regrets some aspects of his younger playing days.

Yan Webber: "Music appeals to me on several levels socially, creatively and emotionally but it used to be a product of my ego. As Noddy [Dudman] once eloquently described it 'You were all show and no go'…and he was absolutely right. I was a posey little git who had a long guitar lead, didn't wear shoes and stood on tables just to get attention. I would die now if anybody had taken a video of that. I wasn't good enough to be influenced by anybody, I learned all the basic chords and to me – I'll hang my head and admit it – the guitar was just a means to pose."

James Ferguson also played with Peter Mason before doing some solo work, including playing clubs in Norway in an area where "the army doesn't let you go out because your lungs freeze!" James has since had a range of jobs including working as a film and TV extra, appearing in The House Of Elliott and Casualty.

Since the late eighties, former Obvious Action, View From A Bridge and Don't Feed The Animals drummer Steve Christey has played with some big names in the old and new waves of progressive rock.

Steve Christey: "I started to take lessons with a guy called Joe Rothman in London. I met up with a band called Jadis who were doing a lot of European gigs. They had just finished a support tour with Marillion - they weren't massive but they were doing okay. I was going from playing straight ahead rock music to very complex time signatures - influenced by Genesis and King Crimson - so it was a big culture shock. What you have got to do is put yourself in these predicaments. It was a fantastic learning curve – barking mad time signatures, ten minute songs - and I really had to pull my socks up."

"It opened a big door of learning about music and getting involved with other members of different bands. The sound guy of Jadis had a girlfriend who was friends with John Wetton, so I got a phone call asking if I would be interested in touring with the John Wetton Band. When you start dealing with King Crimson and UK tracks it's a scary time…but it went well."

"John was a good friend of Ian McDonald from Foreigner and Ian was drafted in to play saxophone and keyboards on a Japanese tour, and also John Beck from It Bites on piano, which was fantastic because I was a really big It Bites fan. That opened up a door with Ian McDonald – recording and touring."

After the implosion of Big Bird,

Ken Lailey and sax players: Tim Collinson, Andy Sheppard and Jav

Simon 'Wiggy' Wigglesworth went to Exeter University and then moved to Bristol, whilst fellow Badgeman Neale Hancock became a family man. For a brief period in 1998 the pair were reunited with Badgeman drummer Tim Kerley in The Original Howling Gods, a sort of Salisbury indie supergroup, which also featured Jim Harrison, Daz Blake and Matt Venn. Playing garage rock'n'roll and sea shanties with a West Country slant whilst wearing sharp suits, the band were memorably described by Jon Maple as 'six drunk men at a wedding'.

The Badgeman's work still has a great – if anything enhanced – reputation, particularly in the case of the second album Ritual Landscape.

Neale Hancock: "Wiggy has done most of the work on myspace and the feedback he has got from that is flattering. People are saying 'I've got this album and it's brilliant'. I loved making it – I would make it again… and we have been offered to… by Kramer. He's an American producer-cum-musician who has formed a band called Bongwater. He picked up on Ritual Landscape and wants to re-master it."

Wiggy: "It's nice to get offers like that but its not gonna happen because (a) we don't know where the masters are (b) finance and (c) why not do something else instead?"

Neale Hancock: "Wiggy brought me back down to earth with the logistics and finance of it, but I would be more than happy – who knows?"

Wiggy: "The reputation of the album, which flopped so badly when it came out, has just grown and grown. I always suspected Julian Cope had a copy. He's much better than us and I'm not saying he copied us, but you can sort of tell when people are exchanging ideas with you – even if you don't know them. I'm a big fan of Cope and one day I was looking on his Head Heritage website, and we were his unsung album of the month!"

In a lengthy appraisal Wiltshire resident Cope described Ritual Landscape as 'a work of brutal but gargantuan beauty, a quintessentially-English heathen folk racket of the most muscular post-punk variety'. Copey raved that he hadn't heard this blend played so convincingly since his Teardrop Explodes days, when he performed alongside Joy Division and Echo and The Bunnymen. He felt the Badgeman album had been 'criminally under-investigated' on its release but was positive that time would prove it to have been a work of 'enduring genius' with its 'effortlessly epic and life-affirming declarations'.

ENDLESS BEAT

"... people's teeth seem to stay the same... if they've got any left."

Wiggy: "It went bananas – our myspace was getting hundreds of hits every day with people writing and trying to get records. You could pick up copies of Ritual Landscape quite easily prior to that. You'll struggle now to find a copy but you can have it for nothing – we've got a website called badgemandiscography.com - you can go there and everything we have ever done you can download – help yourself. I don't care about the money, I don't care about the fame, but there are discerning people that I really respect – like Kramer and Julian Cope – who say 'This is a great album'."

Neale and Wiggy have fond memories of Salisbury's thriving indie scene.

Wiggy: "That six years or so from 1988 was phenomenal for Salisbury. To think we had The Badgeman, Jane From Occupied Europe, Mad Cow Disease, Nuthins, Mayfields – and a bit earlier Bubblegum Splash! How many places with such a small population could produce that many bands who were regarded nationally and internationally as really good bands? We were sending a lot of bands out to the world."

Neale Hancock: "Almost every week in the NME or somewhere there would be a little snippet on Salisbury bands – so and so has done a single, so and so has done this or that."

Wiggy: "One of the main reasons that period in Salisbury had bands transcending the local scene was Jon Maple – I genuinely believe that. We had someone treating local music seriously - a good writer with standards that he expected from people. Why should you say someone is good just because they are local?"

Andy Sheppard, who had started

Andy Sheppard

his jazz career with the Salisbury-based band Sphere, went on to achieve worldwide renown as a saxophonist: "All kinds of people that I listened to then, I am now friends with and work, record and tour with – it's really weird."

Andy's 'weirdest' experience in this regard came at an Island Records anniversary show at Pinewood Studios in London: "I had been playing with George Russell that night, at the London Jazz Festival, and I got sent a car because John Martyn wanted me to come and play in his band. He said 'Come and meet the band'. I went in the dressing room and there was Ringo, Eric Clapton, Andy Summers and Lee 'Scratch' Perry! We were all playing onstage together and you think 'Gee, this is like being in Madame Tussauds'."

Despite these brushes with the limelight Andy still has time to play the occasional hometown gig and has continued to play for the same reasons that he started out in the first place: "We [Sphere] had a reunion gig recently, which was really weird because suddenly I'm in a room with people I haven't seen for twenty-five years - but people's teeth seem to stay the same…if they've got any left."

"Every time I've been in a really tight corner - and I've been in quite a few – you get a gig. I've been a professional musician for thirty years. I've played with a complete cross-section - all from having a dream about playing a saxophone and saying 'I'm a musician'. I'm bringing up two kids, got a couple of ex-wives, all the usual story, but I've always lived off playing my music, my way, not being in a function band or playing in the West End or something."

"Thank God I've never been sucked into a straight music job, like playing Andrew Lloyd Webber, that would just…I would be dead. You have got to do your own thing and…make something happen. That's what we did in Salisbury – we made a band, we found some gigs, we discovered the language of jazz."

The former managers of Dave Dee and DBM&T, Ken Howard and Alan Blaikley, continued to write songs and music for a number of years, ranging from songs for Elvis Presley (I've Lost You, which achieved a gold disc in 1970, and Heart of Rome) to West End musicals (Mardi Gras and The Secret Diary of Adrian Mole) to successful TV scores, particularly The Flame Trees of Thika, By the Sword Divided and Miss Marple (the Joan Hickson version).

Alan Blaikley: "People we have written songs for include Lulu, Eartha Kitt, Matthews Southern Comfort, Frankie Howerd, Englebert Humperdinck, Rolf Harris, Sacha Distel - I guess we are old-fashioned 'tunesmiths' who have always enjoyed the challenge of writing the right material for the right person."

In late 1999 Dave Dee rejoined Dozy, Tich, Tony 'Beaky' Carpenter and John 'Mick' Hatchman for a full UK tour – their first 'home' gigs together for fourteen years. As well as running the Queen Anne period guest house (with resident ghost) Antrobus House in Cheshire, Dave was also by now serving as a magistrate, on the Macclesfield Bench.

The reconvened band's billing occasionally caused some internal disquiet, but this didn't lessen the impact of their performances.

John Hatchman: "We were already established as Dozy, Beaky, Mick and Tich but everybody assumed it was 'Dave Dee and his band'. They used to call it 'Dave Dee and Co' because they couldn't be bothered to spell out 'Dave Dee, Dozy, Beaky, Mick and Tich'. That was why – in some respects – we used to like working on our own… because we were a unit, we stuck together – but there was no malice between the band and Dave."

"I can honestly say I don't think half of them would walk across the road to see us, but a lot of people have seen us in circumstances where they didn't want to be there in the first place and at the end of the evening they're gob smacked – 'My word! I didn't think you were that good!' We get this all the time and I'm thinking 'Well, where have you been for the last thirty years?'"

A highlight for The Boys was taking to the hallowed stage of the London Palladium.

John Hatchman: "To actually walk on at the Palladium - when you consider who has trod those boards – that means a lot for musicians…more than say somebody giving me a hundred grand, because that goes down in folklore. When you sat as a small boy and watched Sunday Night at The Palladium - that was the epitome."

In 2001 DDDBMT were in the midst of preparing for another major tour when Dave was told he had cancer. The disease was in its early stages and it was decided to delay treatment until after the tour. Both the tour and, initially, the treatment were a success.

As well as their own shows, DDDBMT were regular stars of the Solid Silver Sixties tours of the UK. Alongside performing with The Boys, Dave joined another regular live project in 2004, the Reelin'n'Rockin' tour, featuring a band fronted by

ENDLESS BEAT

"... as an entertainer he was second to none."

combinations of sixties lead vocalists singing their old hits.

No doubt spurred by their live reputation, the early years of the 21st century saw a rise in the profile and recorded archive output of Dave Dee, Dozy, Beaky, Mick and Tich. All their original material has been issued on CD, as well as a great collection of BBC material, on which their choice of cover versions perhaps shows the direction they might have preferred to follow. There have also been a series of DVDs of old television footage.

The band has benefited from reappraisals, particularly of their more psych-pop offerings, in the music press and – almost unbelievably – in 2007 Quentin Tarantino used their recording of Hold Tight! for a pivotal scene in his movie Death Proof.

In March 2008 the city of Salisbury paid a lasting tribute to Dave Dee, Dozy, Beaky, Mick and Tich. Following a nomination by Frogg Moody, Salisbury Civic Society erected a blue plaque at the entrance to the City Hall in recognition of the band's achievements, in particular The Legend Of Xanadu reaching Number 1 in the charts: the fortieth anniversary of which was then approaching.

Perhaps surprisingly, the Civic Society had immediately accepted Frogg's proposal, stating it had proved to be one of the most popular the committee had ever considered. This was only the eleventh plaque awarded - and the first ever in recognition of people that were still alive. The band appeared genuinely touched by the affection shown to them at the unveiling ceremony - and the emotional standing ovation when the award was announced by Nigel Gibbons during their Solid Silver Sixties Show-stealing set at the venue that evening. What was not known then was that this would be the last DDDBMT show in Salisbury.

The climax of all this activity was an unexpected return to the charts with the Very Best Of compilation. Along with the hits, this collection included a selection of recordings of favoured in-concert covers. As well as finally allowing Dave to record Roy Orbison's It's Over, this also let the band give vent to some of its harder tendencies in a medley of Stairway To Heaven with Pinball Wizard, alongside a take on the Vanilla Fudge arrangement of You Keep Me Hanging On. In particular these tracks gave an opportunity for one of the most underrated and versatile of British guitarists to let fly: in the new millennium Tich is still using a black Les Paul Gibson Custom purchased in Manchester in 1967.

John Dymond still lives in Spain, while Mick Wilson is still in the Salisbury area but – at least in terms of music – prefers to keep a low profile. Paul Bennett, who had been the second 'Beaky' between 1989 and 1992, passed away in September 2002, on the day after his 56th birthday. He had continued performing up until his death, most notably in a duet named Grapevine, with the singer Melanie.

Although nobody would have guessed from watching his energetic shows, Dave Dee's cancer recurred over a number of years. He finally succumbed in January 2009, at the age of 67.

John Hatchman: "There's not a day goes by when I don't think of Dave. Our first gig without Dave was quite hard. It's hard to explain really…we knew we had to do the show and like all musos - whether you have backache, toothache or whatever – 'the show must go on'. It felt strange for me when it came to certain parts, like when Tich said 'Our next number is going to be a song we had a number 1 with…' It would all start coming back because Dave would have said that… and to not see Dave there with the whip…little things like that flash through your mind while you are actually on stage."

Dave Dee's death sparked a quite surprising, but nonetheless deserved, range of affectionate tributes in the rock and mainstream media. In his obituary of Dave for The Times, former manager Alan Blaikley said 'unlike some of his musical contemporaries he had no pretensions to high art, followed no guru and spouted no political or philosophical message…but as an entertainer he was second to none'.

Despite Dave's passing, the five boys who had first got together in the early sixties at the Wilton Road Palais and St Francis' Church Hall, and on the 819 to Amesbury, had by now long become immortal…and their voices will forever be heard, on the wind, across the sand…

Appendix 1
Local Bands

As far as we know this is the most comprehensive list of local pop and rock bands of the era covered by this book and their personnel that has ever been published. Some of this information is also included within the main text, but has been repeated here for ease of reference. The Salisbury scene was very incestuous; it was a long time ago, and we have found some information regarding personnel to be contradictory - dates should be treated as approximate. Any additions or corrections would be gratefully received.

Acrospire
Bishop Wordsworth's School sixth form prog/rock band circa 1977.
Dave Tee *(guitar and vocals)*; **Blaise White** *(guitar and vocals)*; **Dean Piacentini** *(bass)*; **Steve Smith** *(drums)*.

Afro Dizzy Acts - Mid-1980s. The Sarum Savannah Sound.
Included **Jonathan Hyams** *(guitar and vocals)*; **Charlie Davis** *(guitar)*; **Dave Taylor** *(guitar)*; **Malcolm Wilkinson** *(guitar)*; **Nick Heron** *(bass)*; **'Mike The Bike'** *(trumpet)*; **Julie Hyams** *(saxophone)*; **Tim Collinson** *(saxophone)*; **Andy Glashier** *(keyboards)*; **Nick Heron** *(bass)*; **Dave Marsh** *(drums)*.

After Four - Late 1980s.

Against The Wall - 1980s New Wave from Gomeldon.
Grahame 'Chalky' White *(vocals and guitar)*; **Nick Wells** *(vocals and bass) (replaced by* **Dicky Watts***)*; **Gary Holton** *(drums)*.

Aku Aku
Included **Mike 'Jackboot' Jones**.

Alienation - Late 1980s metal from Winterslow.

All In The Mind - Mid 1970s.
Included **Colin Maple** *(bass)*.
The last band to play at the Alex Disco.

The Amazing Exploding Trouser Band - 1980s.
Kurt Cooper *(vocals)*; **Jo Charrington** *(backing vocals)*; **Chris Binns** *(guitar)*; **Steve Burton** *(keyboards)*; **Pete Leyland** *(bass)*; **John Nicholas** *(drums)*.
Chris Binns: "We were 'The Commitments' a good few years before the film - tuxedos, bad behaviour and a lot of fun... although the headmistress of Godolphin might not agree!"

Ambulance Beat - 1980s.
Neil Dalziel *(vocals)*; **Chris Binns** *(guitar)*; **Pete Leyland** *(bass)*; **Steve Barker** *(drums) (replaced by* **John Nicholas** *and then* **Jon Stone***)*.

Amey-Gair-Mason - Mid 1970s.
Robin Gair *(vocals)*; **Ian 'Tich' Amey** *(guitar and vocals)*; **Peter Mason** *(vocals and guitar)*; **Nigel Dixon** *(bass)*; **Reg Maggs** *(drums)*.

The Aquatic Weasel Band - 1980s.
John Gent *(vocals) (replaced by* **Andy Morris***)*; **Walter Eddowes** *(guitar)*; **Ted Eddowes** *(bass)*; **Phil Urquhart** *(drums)*.

The Associates - 1970s.
Included **Yan Webber** *on guitar.*

Asterisk - 1970s.
Included **Yan Webber** *on guitar.*

Astral Plain - 1982/83.
Steve Thompson *(vocals and multi instrumentalist)*; **Neil Leacy** *(keyboards)*; **Mark Hogarth** *(bass)*; **Charlie Marsden** *(drums and vocals)*.
Astral Plain was a covers show band and went through many changes in personnel well into the 1990s. One later line up comprised **Steve Thompson** *with:* **Pat Lynch** *(guitar)*; **Yan Webber** *(guitar)*; **Wendy ?** *(keyboards)*; **Ron Jowell** *(saxophone)*; **Adrian Courtney** *(bass)*; **Stuart Marshall** *(drums)*.

The Avonaires - Early 1970s.
Ken Dodson *(saxophone and vocal)*; **Dave Adams** *(guitar and vocals)*; **Jim Hoppe** *(keyboards)*; **Chris Glover** *(bass)*; **Terry Francis** *(drums)*
A later version: **Ann Marie** *(vocals)*; **Paul Simmonds** *(guitar and vocals)*; **Tony Carrier** *(guitar)*; **Jack Simmonds** *(accordion)*; **Chris Glover** *(bass)*; **Terry Francis** *(drums)*.
Also included **Dave Bennett** *on drums at one stage.*

The Badgeman - Late 1980s/early 1990s psychedelic indie types.
Neale Hancock *(vocals and guitar)*; **John Packwood** *(guitar and vocals)*; **Simon 'Wiggy' Wigglesworth** *(bass guitar and vocals)*; **Tim Kerley** *(drums)*.
Evolved from Hunny Monsturs.

Banderlog - Early 1980s.
'Jaws' *(vocals)*; **Ian 'Skid' Browne** *(guitar)*; **Frogg Moody** *(keyboards)*; **Gary Clements** *(bass)*; **Alex Mundy** *(drums)*.

Band Of Gold - 1975-76. Disco and Funk.
John Hatchman *(vocals)*; **Pete Lucas** *(guitar)*; **Steve Clasby** *(keyboards)*; **Steve Collinson** *(bass)*; **John 'Beaky' Dymond** *(drums)*.

Bangkok - 1982-83.
Johnny Fellows *(vocals)*; **Colin Crook** *(guitar)*; **Chris Lucas** *(bass) (replaced by* **Simon Viney***)*; **Reg Maggs** *(drums). Later joined by* **Colin Gray** *(guitar)*.

Bedridden - Mid 1970s covers.
Neil Dalziel *(vocals)*; **Tom Pugh** *(guitar)*; **Chris Lucas** *(bass)*; **Lloyd Collinson** *(drums)*.

Bethany - Late 1960s-Early 1970s.
Bob Rynn *(vocals)*; **Pete Lucas** *(guitar)*; **Chris Lucas** *(bass)*;
Keith Small *(drums)*.
Later joined by **Dave Church** *(guitar). Became* **Jenny Lynn**.

Between The Eyes - 1978-81.
Johnny Fellows *(vocals)*; **Colin Crook** *(guitar)*;
Mike Lavender *(guitar)*; **Graham 'Chunky' Jenkins** *(bass)*;
Keith Evans *(drums)*.

Big Bird - 1990s. Demos and half a gig.
Neale Hancock *(vocals and guitar)*; **Ian 'Skid' Brown** *(guitar)*;
Darren 'Dazman' Blake *(guitar)*; **Mickey Dyer** *(guitar)*;
Simon 'Wiggy' Wigglesworth *(bass)*; **Tim Kerley** *(drums)*.

The Big Easy - Early 1990s.
Included **Caroline Holt-Keen** *on vocals.*

Big House - Early 1980s.
Duncan Fulton *(guitar and vocals)*, **Nick Marchant** *(guitar)*,
Tim Collinson *and* **Ruth Jones** *(saxophones)*; **Colin Holton** *(bass)*;
John Nicholas *(drums)*.

The Biscuits - See 'Cookie and The Biscuits'.

Blind Harvest - Early 1970s hard rock.

Blind Panic - Late 1980s.
Included **William Collins** *on vocals.*

The Blips - Early 1980s
Steve Ryall *(guitar and vocals)*; **Andy 'Sprog' Ford** *(guitar)*;
Ruth Jones *(bass)*; **Mike Buxton** *(drums)*.

The Blue - Late 1980s.
Bob Rushing *(vocals)*; **Sid Berry** *(guitar)*; **'Weazle'** *(bass)*;
Tim Clissold *(percussion)*.

Blue Haze - 1979.
Dave Wood *(bass guitar and vocals)*; **Dave Walker** *(guitar)*;
Neil Leacy *(keyboards)*; **Trevor Webb** *(drums)*.
Durrington rock covers rehearsals band. Evolved into **Snowblind**.

Blue Mondays - 1990s.
Included **Alex Mundy** *on drums.*

Bob James Band/Music - 1960s-1970s.
Ricky Hunt *(vocals)*; **Bob Dolman** *(trumpet and vibes)*;
Jim Driscoll *(baritone saxophone and trumpet)*;
John Mills *(saxophones)*; **Jim Hoppe** *(piano)*; **Alex Hayter** *(guitar)*
(replaced by **Steve Collinson***)*; **Chris Glover** *(bass) (replaced by*
Dave Farnham*)*; **Terry Francis** *(drums)*.
Also included **Dave Bennett** *on drums at one stage.*

The BOFs - See 'Grandma Moses'.

The Bolt-on Parsnips - Irreverent 1990s covers.
Included **Mervyn Baggs** *(vocals),* **Dave Lodder** *(guitar) and* **Michael 'Archie' Stone** *(drums).*

The Bonds - 1987.
Duncan Fulton *(guitar and vocals)*; **Nick Marchant** *(bass)*;
Andrew Lovelock *(drums)*.

The Bottlebank Band - Mid 1990s Folkies
Matt Carter *(banjo and mandolin)*; **Steve Lightfoot** *(melodeon)*;
Dave Rawlinson *(fiddle)*; **Ray Jones** *(keyboards)*;
Mike Reid *(guitar)*; **Jim Barrett** *(bouzouki)*.
Played numerous pubs and barn dances. One gig at the Arts Centre was played with Dave Marsh on drums: "The first man to ever play a drum solo at a barn dance" (Steve Lightfoot).

Britz - 1980s.
Lynden Williams *(vocals)*; **Bob Cooke** *(guitar)*; **Yan Webber** *(guitar)*; **Henk Leerink** *(bass)*; **Andy Golden** *(drums)*.
Later became **The Faith Healers** *for a while.*

BTF - Late 1980s Amesbury based crusty punk thrash.

Bubblegum Splash! - 1986-1987. Post C-86 Indie.
Nikki Barr *(vocals)*; **Jim Harrison** *(guitar)*; **Marty Cummins** *(tambourine, backing vocals)*; **Dave Todd** *(bass)*; **Alan Harrison** *(stand up drums) (no relation to Jim).*

Bullfrog - 1971.
Anton Hayman *(guitar and vocals)*; **Steve Collinson** *(bass)*;
Andy Golden *(drums)*.

Cadence - Late 1980s indie pop.
Lesley Hallett *(vocals)*; **Sean Rice** *(guitar)*; **Ian Rudolf** *(bass)*;
Dave Marsh *(drums)*.
According to Sean, their most memorable appearance was at the PALS dogs' home!

Camera In Paris - Late 1980s.
Clive Roper *(vocals and guitar)*; **Alan Grist** *(bass)*;
Dave Bullis *(drums)*.

Cane - 1990s.
Included **Simon Berry** *(vocals)*
and **Ian 'Atilla' Marshall** *(keyboards).*

Carfax and The Heretic - Late 1980s.
Evolved out of **Shadowlands**.

Cast Iron Shores - Late 1990s.

Casualty Victims - Early 1980s New Wave.
Included **Nick Kemp** *(guitar and vocals),* **Jez Kemp** *(bass and vocals) and* **Lloyd Collinson** *(keyboards).*

The Catalogue Men - 1983.
Neil Dalziel *(vocals and guitar)*; **Tim Madden** *(guitar and vocals,)*;
Nick Heron *(bass)*; **Dave Marsh** *(drums)*.

Censored - Late 1980s.

Chicken Pox - Late 1970s.
Included **Chic Duggan** *and* **Colin Holton**.

The Colin David Set - 1975-1993.
Colin Mitchener *(keyboards, saxophones and vocals)*;
Dave Adams *(guitar and vocals)*
(replaced by **Paul Longhurst** *but on keyboards)*;
Alan Young *(guitar and vocals)*
(replaced by **Andy Hill** *and then* **Chris Giddings***)*;
Colin Maple *(bass and vocals)*;
Dave Goddard *(drums and percussion)*.

Cookie and The Biscuits - Very early 1980s.
John Hatchman *(vocals);* **Lynden Williams** *(vocals);*
Bob Cooke *(guitar);* **Yan Webber** *(bass);* **Andy Golden** *(drums).*

Cooler - Mid 1970s.
Neil Dalziel *(vocals and guitar)* *(replaced by* **Neil Pedley***);*
Steve Le Hardy *(guitar);* **Colin Holton** *(bass);*
Lloyd Collinson *(drums).*

Cosa Nostra - Mid 1980s.

The Country Club Four - 1970s.
Included **Steve Terry** *and* **Terry Francis***.*

The Courgettes - Late 1980s.
Ruth Jones *(vocals and bass);* **Grahame 'Chalky' White** *(guitar);*
Lloyd Collinson *(drums)* *(replaced by* **Graham Hughes***).*
Initially briefly known as **Mission Impossible***.*

C Planes - 1990s.
Included **Alex Mundy***,* **Frogg Moody** *and* **Paul Abbott***.*

Craze - 1980s. Amesbury based.
Des Lynch *(vocals);* **Pat Lynch** *(guitar);* **John Junkin** *(?) (bass);*
Chas Sainsbury *(drums).*

Crazy Daisy - 1991.
Had a one-off track on the **God's Great Tape Head Cleaner** *compilation cassette.*
Dave Todd: *"Crazy Daisy was* **Lee Walker***, a lad from Swindon who moved down to Salisbury to work at the Arts Centre doing lighting. He nearly became* **Jane From Occupied Europe's** *guitarist a couple of weeks before we recruited* **Dave [Ware]***, but he and we felt it was going to be difficult to work around his work patterns".*

The Crimmos - Late 70s New Wave.
Nick Kemp *(lead guitar and vocals);*
Barry Stevens *(keyboards);*
Jez Kemp *(bass and backing vocals);*
Lloyd Collinson *(drums).*

Dance Factor - 1983.
Niki True *(aka* **Nick Walker***) (vocals);*
Steve Burton *(keyboards and programming).*

Dangerous When Wet - Late 1980s.

Dan-I & The Freedom Fighters - Incl. Richie Scott on guitar.

Dark Star - 1980s.
Caroline Holt-Keen *(vocals);* **Andy 'Sprog' Ford** *(guitar);*
Kerry Waite *(guitar);* **Duncan Fulton** *(bass);* **Jim Blackwell** *(drums).*

The Dave Charles Sound - 1970s.
Included **Dave Bennett** *on drums.*

David - Early 1970s.
Dave Dee *(vocals);* **Peter Mason** *(guitar and backing vocals);*
Ian England *(keyboards)* *(replaced by* **David Rose***);* **David Martin** *(bass)* *(replaced by* **Bob Taylor***);* **Phil Edwards** *(drums).*
Not really a 'Salisbury band' but included as they were **Dave Dee's** *backing band.*

Dave Dee, Dozy, Beaky, Mick & Tich
1974 Version:
David 'Dave Dee' Harman *(vocals);* **Trevor 'Dozy' Davies** *(bass);*
John 'Beaky' Dymond *(drums);* **Peter Mason** *(guitar);*
Ian 'Tich' Amey *(guitar).*

1980s/90s Version:
David 'Dave Dee' Harman *(vocals);* **Trevor 'Dozy' Davies** *(bass);*
John 'Beaky' Dymond *(drums);* **Pete Lucas** *(guitar) (replaced by* **John Hatchman** *(drums – Beaky moved onto guitar, but was then replaced by first* **Paul Bennett** *and then* **Tony Carpenter***);*
Ian 'Tich' Amey *(guitar).*

Dennis - Early 1990s.
Mickey Dyer *(bass and vocals);* **Ian 'Skid' Browne** *(guitar);*
Sarah McCauley *(violin);* **Andy Clements** *(drums).*

The Didicoi Quartet - 1990s.
Included **Colin Holton** *(bass) and* **Jim Blackwell** *(drums).*

The Dishevellers - 1992.
Mad Cows and lady friend in one off Levellers spoof incident.

Disturbance
Included **Jimmy Hutton** *on bass.*

Don't Ask - Mid-1980s.
Included **Johnny Fellows** *(vocals);* **Matt West** *(guitar);*
Micky Norris *(keyboards);* **Mike 'Spike' Pizing** *(keyboards);*
Simon 'Min' Viney *(bass);* **Graham Hughes** *(drums).*

Don't Feed The Animals - 1980s Indie.
Karen Baker *(vocals);* **Colin Holton** *(guitar and vocals);*
John Ulicsny *(guitar);* **Frogg Moody** *(keyboards);* **Nick Heron** *(bass)* *(replaced by* **Clive Roper** *and then* **Nick Shirfield***);*
Dave Marsh *(drums) (replaced by* **John Nicholas** *and then* **Alex Mundy***,* **Steve Christey** *and* **Jim Blackwell***). Also included* **Grahame 'Chalky' White** *at some stage…and maybe others!*

Down Amongst The Dead Men - Late 1980s.
David 'Diddy' Savage *(vocals);* **John Ulicsny** *(guitar);*
Peter 'Bam Bam' Stone *(bass);* **Michael 'Archie' Stone** *(drums).*

Dozy, Beaky, Mick & Tich (aka DBMT, DBM&T)
Early 1974 Version:
Trevor 'Dozy' Davies *(bass guitar & vocals);*
John 'Beaky' Dymond *(guitar & vocals);*
Michael 'Mick' Wilson *(drums);* **Ian 'Tich' Amey** *(guitar & vocals).*

1980s/90s Version:
Trevor 'Dozy' Davies *(bass guitar);* **John 'Beaky' Dymond** *(lead vocals and drums);* **Pete Lucas** *(guitar) (replaced by* **John Hatchman** *(drums – Beaky moved onto guitar, but was then replaced by first* **Paul Bennett** *and then* **Tony Carpenter***);*
Ian 'Tich' Amey *(guitar).*

Electric Sparrow - 1970s electric folk.
Brian Billen *(vocals);* **Brian Saunders** *(guitar);* **Chris Glover** *(bass).*

The Elite - Late 1970s.
Included **Dave Tee** *(guitar) and* **Mike 'Jackboot' Jones** *(drums).*

Elliott Ness and The G-Men - Christmas 1976.
Included **Jon Maple** *(vocals) and* **Tim Darlow** *(guitar).*
Seemingly Salisbury's first punk band – literally for one night only!

ENDLESS BEAT

The Emulsions
See Matt Vinyl & The Emulsions.

ESB Band - 1986-Now.
Tom Thatcher *(vocals and guitar)*; **Bobby Wallace** *(guitar and vocals)* *(replaced by* **Bob Shearn** *and then* **Pete Catlin***)*; **Rob Burton** *(keyboards)* *(replaced by* **Mark Skerritt***)*; **Colin Lee** *(bass and vocals)*; **Syd Guppie** *(drums)* *(replaced by* **Jon Nicholas** *and then* **Chris Williams**, **Keith Evan** *and* **Andy Golden***)*.
Honorary Member: **Noddy Dudman** *(roadie).*
Chris Binns *also appeared briefly on guitar.* **Sarah Shivells** *(vocals)*, **Dominic Thatcher** *(saxophones) and* **Keith Evans** *(occasionally, on drums) have all played with the latest incarnation.*

Escapade - Late 1980s.

Eskimo - 1973-74.
John Priestley *(guitar and vocals)*; **Steve Priestley** *(piano)*; **Steve Collinson** *(bass)*; **Reg Maggs** *(drums). Various lead guitarists including* **Nick Kemp** *and* **Pete Catlin**.

Esprit De Corps - 1980s Electropop.
David 'Diddy' Savage *(vocals)*; **Nigel Bailey** *(backing vocals, bass and keyboards)*; **Phillip Seago** *(keyboards)*; **John Ulicsny** *(guitar)*; **Jeff Bundy** *(drums).*

The Exit Band - Mid 1970s.
Tremayne Roden *(vocals)*; **Nick Kemp** *(lead guitar)*; **Jez Kemp** *(guitar)*; **Colin Holton** *(bass)*; **Steve Hutchinson** *(drums).*
An early rehearsal incarnation included **Colin Holton**, **Mickey Morris**, **Tremayne Roden** *and* **Tony Warr**.

Fairlane - Mid 1970s.
James Ferguson *(vocals, guitar and bass)*; **Tommy Pugh** *(vocals, guitar and bass)*; **Steve Hutchinson** *(drums).*
James would play guitar and Tommy the bass on a set of original material – then they would swap over during the drum solo for a set of covers. Later joined by **Chic Duggan** *and* **Colin Holton**.

Farley 708 (later 'Farley Ridge') - Late 1980s-Early 1990s.
Andy Brewer *(vocals)*; **Piers Moore** *(guitar)*; **Jon Baggeley** *(keyboards)*; **Frank Cross** *(bass)*; **Steve 'The Bear' Greenaway** *(drums).*
Once **The Prophecy**. **Mickey Dyer** *stood in on bass for a few gigs when Frank couldn't make it back to Salisbury.*

Fear Of Music
Chris Binns *(vocals and guitar)*; **Tom Heightman** *(bass)*; **Richard Jackson** *(drums).*
Augmented with London brass and backing vocals by **Rosie Highstead**.

Ferry - Mid 1970s duo.
Andy 'Brad' Bradbury *(vocals and guitar)*; **Andy Golden** *(bass, rhythm guitar and harmony vocals).*

Fester and The Vomits

Floyd Jones Groovy Train - Early 1990s
Johnny Bell *(vocals & guitar)*, **Simon 'Sox' Oxborrow** *(guitar)*, **Jason Stuart** *(keyboards)*, **'Tack'** *(bass) and a three piece brass section, as well as others (there were often eleven or twelve people on stage at any one time).*

The Fondell Brothers - Late 1980s jazz duo.
Kurt Cooper *(vocals)*; **Steve Burton** *(electric piano)*

Forbidden Fruit
Included **Neil Dalziel**, **Chris Binns** *and* **Steve Collinson**.

Force 5 - 1970s. - *Included* **Yan Webber** *on guitar.*

4AM
Included **Kurt Cooper** *(vocals)*, **Mickey Norris** *(keyboards)*, **Pete Leyland** *(bass)*, **Pete Smith** *(guitar) and* **John Stone** *(drums).*

The Freedom AKA - Dub-Roots.

The Freedom Fighters
See Dan-I and The Freedom Fighter.

Freeway - 1970s.
Included **Dave Bennett** *on drums.*

Friction - 1990s.
Included **Alex Mundy** *on drums.*

The Funeral Directors - Early 1980s.

Genghis Khan (1) - Metal. Formed in 1975.
Alan Marsh *(vocals)*; **Alwyn Lovell** *(lead guitar)*; **Eddie Johnson** *(guitar)*; **Rob Boston** *(bass)*; **Trevor Harris** *(drums).*
In 1976 **Ray Dismore** *joined the band on guitar for a brief period when Eddie went to University. Ray was replaced by* **Ian Frost** *in 1977. Trevor Harris also left the band in 1977 and was replaced by* **Tommy Mafflyn**. *In 1978 Alan Marsh, Eddie Johnson and Tommy Mafflin were replaced by* **Johnny Butcher** *(vocals)*; **Jimmy McTurk** *(guitar) and* **Billy Morrison** *(drums). Billy and Jimmy were replaced in 1979 by* **Dave Pounds** *and* **Dave Irwin** *respectively. This band split later that year.*

Genghis Khan (2) - 1983 NWOBHM.
Alan Marsh *(vocals)*; **Andy Boulton** *(lead guitar)*; **Ray Dismore** *(guitar)*; **Andy Robbins** *(bass)*; **Steve Pierce** *(drums).*
Chapter Five explains why there have been two Genghis Khans.

Gettysburg Address - Early 1980s.
Steve Rushton *(vocals)*; **Chris Walsh** *(guitar)*; **Frogg Moody** *(keyboards)*; **Gary Clements** *(bass)* *(replaced by* **Mickey Dyer** *and then* **Mark 'Ken' Kenchington***)*; **Andy Clements** *(drums)* *(replaced by* **Jon Nicholas***)*.

The Ghosts (1) - 1979-1980.
Johnny Butcher *(vocals)*; **Alwyn Lovell** *(guitar)*; **Rob Boston** *(bass)*; **Mick Corby** *(piano)* - *plus a session player on drums.*

The Ghosts (2) - Mid-1980s Landford Youth Club Garage Covers.
Included **Jon 'Mojo' Mills** *on guitar.*

Gland Band - 1971-73.
Tom Thatcher *(vocals and guitar)*; **Peter 'Evvy Pedro' Smith** *(vocals and bass)*; **Bob 'Megaton' Milner** *(drums).*
Became **Lizard**.

God's An Astronaut

Going Out With God - 1980s.
Clive Roper *(vocals and bass)*; **Richard 'Buzzard' Atkinson** *(guitar)*; **Martin Green** *(guitar)*; **Frogg Moody** *(keyboards)*; **Dave Marsh** *(drums).*

Government Property - 1983-1985.
Tom Thatcher *(vocals and guitar)*; Mike Durkee *(guitar and vocals)*; Colin Lee *(bass and vocals)*; Keith Evans *(drums and vocals)*.

Grandma Moses
1973-1983. Prog through funky blues to the new wave with various line ups:

1 *(1973-1975)*:
Andy 'Brad' Bradbury *(vocals and guitar)*; Nigel Goode (replaced by Bob Cooke) *(guitar and vocals)*; Chris Glover *(bass)*; Andy Golden *(drums and vocals)*.

2 *(1975-1978)*:
Andy 'Brad' Bradbury *(vocals and guitar)*; Paul McElhatton *(guitar and vocals)*; Tom Thatcher *(keyboards, guitar, mandolin and vocals)*; Chris Glover *(bass)*; Andy Golden *(drums and vocals)*.

3 *(1979-1981)*:
Andy 'Brad' Bradbury *(vocals and guitar)*; Tom Thatcher *(guitar and vocals)*; Marion Birch *(flute and vocals)*; George Hart *(bass)*; Andy Golden *(drums and vocals)*; Andy Cole *(occasional guest vocals)*.

4 *(1981-1983)*:
Andy 'Brad' Bradbury *(vocals and guitar)*; Tom Thatcher *(guitar and vocals)*; Tim Hedges *(keyboards and vocals)*; Henk Leerink *(bass)*; Andy Golden *(drums)*.

5 *(1983)*:
Andy 'Brad' Bradbury *(vocals and guitar)*; Tom Thatcher *(guitar and vocals)*; Colin Lee *(bass)*; Chris Williams *(drums)*.

Honorary Member: Noddy Dudman *(roadie from around 1980)*. The band also played in various permutations of this line-up and had several loud and exuberant reunions as **'The BOFS'**, with Brad, Tom, Andy and George Hart.

Grassworks - Late 1980s-Early 1990s.
Included Duncan Howell *on guitar*.

The Grey Wolves - Early 1980s to present.
Dave Padbury; Trevor Ward

'A Manifestation Of The Cultural Terrorism Network' in the form of uncompromising experimental industrial punk noise from Amesbury.

The Gurus - Late 1980s.
Alexa Mackenzie *(vocals and bass)*; Mark Kenchington *(guitar)*; Peter Wilks *(keyboards)* (replaced by Frogg Moody and then two guitarists).

Guts'n'Noses - 1990s.
Johnny Fellows *(vocals)*; Colin Gray *(guitar)*; Mark Robinson *(bass)* (replaced by Bob ? and then others); Barry Stevens *(keyboards)*; Graham Hughes *(drums)*.

The Haemorrhoids - Late 1990s.
Dan Foot *(vocals and guitar)*; Lee ? *(bass)*; John Birch *(drums)*.
Became Sweet Children.

Handcart - 1980s.

Charlie Harwood & The Pub Beats
- Mid-1970s ad-hoc pub band.
A revolving line up that at times included Ian 'Tich' Amey, John 'Beaky' Dymond, Trevor 'Dozy' Davies, Peter Mason *and* Pete Lucas.

The Heretic
See entry under Carfax and The Heretic.

Highway 5 - Late 1970s Bishop Wordsworth School cover band
Pete Gallagher *(vocals)*; Kurt Cooper *(guitar and vocals)*; Mark Sheldon *(lead guitar and vocals)*; Jon Murley *(bass and vocals)*; Jon Stone *(drums and vocals)*.

Later became Sheen *and then* Trax *when Jon Murley was replaced by* Pete Leyland *(bass and vocals) in 1978. Became* Xtrax.

The Hopback Blues Band - 1990 to now. Blues (of course!)
Trevor Kay *(guitar and vocals)*; Pete Catlin *(guitar)* (briefly before Pete Sherburn); Rick Wells *(bass)*; Duncan Brown *(saxophone)*; Charlie Marsden *(drums)*.

Horizontal Bulgarians - Early 1980s.
Phil Manning *(vocals)*; Matthew Finn *(guitar)*; Tim Darlow *(upside down five string guitar)*; Mickey Dyer *(bass)*; Miscellaneous Drummers.

Became Newcombe and Roach.

Horse Latitudes - 1981-84.
Included: Nick Kemp; Jez Kemp; Steve Collinson; Barry Stevens; Trevor Tanner; Tim Collinson; Caroline Holt-Keen *and* A Drum Machine.

Hot Water - 1990s covers.
Christine Taylor *(vocals)*; Linda Taylor *(vocals)*; Pete Sherburn *(guitar)*; Yan Webber *(guitar)*; Geoff Cooper *(keyboards)*; Nigel Dixon *(bass)*; Stuart Marshall *(drums)*.

Huggy Thunder and The Allstars - 1980
Steve Lightfoot *(vocals)*; Phil Edmonds *(guitar)*; Mickey 'Metal' *(guitar)*; Simon Viney *(bass)*; Graham Hughes (aka 'Huggy Thunder') *(drums)*.

Played two gigs: Alderbury Village Hall and Bishop Wordsworth's School hall

Hunca Munca - 1986.
Tom Thatcher *(vocals and guitar)*; Rob Vowles *(keyboards and vocals)*; Rick Wells *(bass and vocals)*; Paul Weldon *(drums)*.

The Hunny Monsters - Mid 1980s indie.
Neale Hancock *(vocals and guitar)*; John Packwood *(guitar and vocals)*; Simon 'Wiggy' Wigglesworth *(bass guitar and vocals)*; Tim Kerley *(drums)*.

Became Badgemen.

Identity Crisis - 1977-1980 New Wave.
Neil Dalziel *(vocals)*; Nick Marchant *(guitar)*; Steve Collinson *(bass)*; Lloyd Collinson *(drums)*. Later joined by Colin Gray *(guitar)*, Tim Collinson *and occasionally* Andy Sheppard *(saxophone)*!

The Inbredz - 1990s Punk Covers
Included Paul Di'Anno *(vocals)*, Colin Holton *(guitar)* *and* Ian 'Atilla' Marshall *(keyboards)*.

Innervision - From 1999
Teresa Taylor *(vocals)* Dave Walker *(guitar)*; Karl Knowles *(keyboards)* Pete Leyland *(bass)*; Trevor Webb *(drums)*.

ENDLESS BEAT

Inside Job - 1986.
Tom Thatcher *(vocals and guitar);*
Bobby Wallace *(guitar and vocals);* **Rob Vowles** *(keyboards and vocals);* **Rick Wells** *(bass and vocals);* **Syd Guppie** *(drums).*

Intensive Care
- Late 1970s/Early 1980s punks from the streets of Breamore and Fordingbridge.
Included **Neil Hotston**, **Steve Marlowe** and **Shaun Marlowe**.

The Jamesons - 1993-98.
Included: **Grahame 'Chalky' White**, **Gary Holton**, **Mark Blamey**, **Ruth Jones** and **Steve Collinson**.

Jane From Occupied Europe - Late 1980s-Early 1990s Indie.
Jim Harrison *(guitar and vocals);* **Colin 'Simod' O'Keefe** *(guitar);*
Dave Todd *(bass);* **Alan Harrison** *(drums) (replaced by*
Philip Eason*); **David Ware** joined later on guitar, organ and vocals.
Formed out of **Bubblegum Splash!**

Jeep   Late 1970s/early 1980s cover band.
Keith Daubney *(vocals);* **Yan Webber** *(guitar);*
Simon Reid *(bass)(replaced by* **Nigel Dixon** *and then* **Ian Miller***);*
Dave Smith *(drums) (replaced by* **Ray Sparrow***).*

Jenny Lynn - Early 1970s.
Bob Rynn *(vocals);* **Pete Lucas** *(guitar);* **Dave Church** *(guitar);*
John Ackroyd *(keyboards);* **Chris Lucas** *(bass);*
Keith Small *(drums).*
Formed out of **Bethany**.

Jerusalem - Early 1970s Metal.
Originally a three-piece: **Paul Dean** *(bass and vocals);*
Chris 'Kef' Skelcher *(guitar);* **Ray Sparrow** *(drums).*
Then augmented by **Bill Hinde** *(guitar).*
Chris was then replaced by **Bob Cooke** and the band were joined by **Phil Goddard**, who was later replaced by **Lynden Williams**.
Later reincarnated as a three-piece: **Pussy**.

Junk DNA - Late 1990s.

Kanz - Mid 1970s.

Killer - Late 1970s/Early 1980s Metal.
Alan Marsh *(vocals);* **Andy Boulton** *(guitar and vocals);*
Andy Robbins *(bass);* **Steve Pierce** *(drums).*
Became **Tokyo Blade**.

Kinetic NRG - Late 1970s New Wave.
Alex Mundy *(vocals);* **Ian 'Skid' Browne** *(guitar);*
Gary Clements *(bass);* **Andy Clements** *(drums).*

The Kitchens - Late 1970s New Wave.
Duncan Fulton *(bass and vocals);* **Fred Phillips** *(guitar);*
Andy Lovelock *(drums).*
Fred left to be replaced by **Paul Kelly** then **Colin Holton** came in on bass, leaving Duncan on vocals. After Colin left they reverted to a three piece with Duncan back on bass. Then Paul left, Duncan took over on lead guitar, **Gavin Lear** and **Ian Stramm** came in on rhythm guitar and bass respectively. Then Gavin left and was replaced by **Andy 'Sprog' Ford**. Ian left and it was back to a three piece, before **Ruth Jones** came in to complete the classic line-up of Fulton, Ford, Jones and Lovelock... but then Sprog left and they went back to being a three-piece. It's all quite straightforward really.

Language Of Thieves
Bob Rushing *(vocals);* **Walter Eddowes** *(guitar and vocals).*
Initially a duo before being joined by
Andy James *(keyboards),*
Todd ? *(bass) and*
Paul Batchelor *(drums).*

Laser
Sid Grace *(vocals and guitar);* **Kevin Smith** *(guitar);*
Mick Young *(replaced by* **Jimmy Hutton***) (bass);*
Keith Small *(drums).*

Last Orders - Early 1980s Punk.
Dave Boyes *(vocals and guitar);* **Colin Mundy** *(guitar);*
Mark Palmer *(bass);* **Ian Hamilton** *(drums).*
Morphed into **Obvious Action**.

Liquid Lloyd and The Lozenges

Lix n Trix
Widge Collins *(vocals);* **Walter Eddowes** *(guitar);*
Ted Eddowes *(bass);* **Phil Urquhart** *(drums).*
Formed out of the **Aquatic Weasel Band**.

Lizard - 1973-75.
Tom Thatcher *(vocals and guitar);* **Paul McElhatton** *(guitar);*
Peter 'Evvy Pedro' Smith *(vocals and bass);*
Bob 'Megaton' Milner *(drums).*
Formerly **Gland Band**. Split up when Pedro went to the USA to take up lectureship in Edmonton and Bob left to work on the Airbus. Tom and Paul then joined **Grandma Moses**.

Love In The Asylum - Late 1980s.

The Lozenges - See 'Liquid Lloyd and The Lozenges'.

Mad Cow Disease - 1990s grunge monsters.
Jon Maple *(vocals);* **Colin Holton** *(guitar and backing vocals);*
Grahame 'Chalky' White *(guitar) (replaced by* **Dan Bunce***);*
Ian 'Skid' Browne *(bass) (replaced by* **'Mad Mark' Andrews** *and then* **Ally Gamble***);* **Ian 'Atilla' Marshall** *(keyboards, samples and backing vocals);* **Rob Arney** *(drums) (replaced by* **Jim Blackwell***).*

Mad Dogs - 1970s.
Tom Shread; **Danny Shread**; **Nick Kemp**;
Steve Hutchinson *(drums and darts).*

Magical Pig

The Magnificent - 1990s Punkish rock.
Gary James *(vocals);* **Colin Mundy** *(guitar);*
Nick Shirfield *(guitar);* **Kev Barnes** *(bass);*
Ian Rudorf *(drums) (replaced by* **Ray Hunt**,
and **Jim Blackwell** *possibly also played at some stage).*
Formed out of **The Stand**.

Major Barbara - 1972.
Barbara Flippance *(vocals);* **Mike Flippance** *(guitar);*
Yan Webber *(guitar);* **?** *(bass);* **Roger Targett** *(drums).*

Marble Orchard - Late 1960s-Mid 1970s.

1970s Line up:
Martin James *(drums and vocals)*;
Mick Pinney *(guitar)*
(replaced by **Ethem Cetintas** *and then* **Dave Eppel***)*;
Pete ? *(keyboards)*
(replaced by **Mick Smith***)*;
Ernie Parsons *(bass)*
(replaced by **Keith Batten***)*.

Marlboro County Fair - 1990s to now.
Mark Featch *(guitar and vocals)*; **Steve Lewis** *(guitar and vocals)*;
Bob Taylor *(keyboards)*; **Nigel Finn** *(bass)*.

Didn't have a drummer for years until **Tim Kerley** *joined.*

Marseilles Frame - Early 1980s.
Mike Vickers *(vocals)*; **Mark Sheldon** *(guitar, keyboards and backing vocals)*; **Ady Courtney** *(bass)*;
Jon Nicholas *(drums and backing vocals)*.

Mason - 1972-73.
A nucleus of **Ian 'Tich' Amey**, **John 'Beaky' Dymond** *and* **Peter Mason** *on guitars and vocals, joined by*
Bob Taylor *(bass)*, **David Rose** *(keyboards)* *and* **Martin 'Cuddles' Smith** *(drums)*.

Ian England *(piano)*, **Chas O'Brien** *(drums and vocals)*,
Judie Tzuke *(harmony vocals)*, **John Weider** *(fiddle)*
and **Mox Gowland** *(harmonica) also joined the band in the studio.*

Peter Mason Band
Various line ups including: **Peter Mason** *(vocals and guitar)*;
Steve Cowan *(guitar)*; **Yan Webber** *(guitar)*; **Nigel Dixon** *(bass)*
(replaced by **Colin Holton***)*; **Paul Beavis** *(drums)*.

Matt Vinyl and The Emulsions

The Mayfields - Late 1980s/Early 1990s Indie.
Kevin Russell *(vocals and guitar)*;
Adrian 'Swannie' Martin *(tambourine and vocals and later bass)*;
Paul McDowell *(guitar)*; **Iain Lindsey** *(bass)*; **Mark Freeth** *(drums)*.

Bob Taylor *was an original member and according to Swannie 'literally about fifteen or twenty people' passed through the ranks over the years.*

The Men Of The Doomsbury Lifeboat - 1980s.
Lynden Williams *(vocals)*; **Bob Cooke** *(Guitar)*;
Colin Lee *(bass) (replaced by* **Henk Leerink***)*;
Andy Golden *(drums)*.

Had rehearsed and played one gig as **'Rocky Cockerel'** *without Lynden Williams. Later became* **Oxoxox***.*

The Menthol Jaggers - 1980-81.
Duncan Fulton *(guitar and vocals)*; **Nick Marchant** *(bass)*;
Andrew Lovelock *(drums)*.

Mercedez - 1983. 'Futuristic funk'.
Nick Walker (aka Niki True) *(vocals)*; **Dave Walker** *(guitar and synthesiser)*; **Neil Leacy** *(keyboards)*; **Mark Hogarth (aka Marco Hirst)** *(bass)*; **Trevor Webb** *(drums)*.

The Merry Macs
First formed in the 1940s, various line ups of the Macs - lead by
Pete Maple *from the drum stool - kept people dancing into the 1990s.*

The Midnite Ramblers - 1970s country rock.
Ted Collinson *(vocals)*; **Ray Gulliver** *(guitar)*;
Tony Griffiths *(bass)*; **Phil Bryant** *(drums)*.

Mission Impossible
See **The Courgettes***.*

Money For Guns - 1982-84.
Johnny Fellows *(vocals)*; **Colin Gray** *(guitar)*;
Mickey Norris *(keyboards)*; **Simon 'Minn' Viney** *(bass)*;
Jon Nicholas *(drums) (replaced by* **Jon Stone***)*.

The Morrigan - 1980s to now (sort of). Eccentric Electronic Folk Freakery.
At various times included: **Cathy Alexander**, **Melanie Byfield**,
Mervyn Baggs, **Tom Foad**, **Colin Masson**, **Cliff Eastabrook**,
Jon Hayward, **Dave Lodder**, **Matt Carter**
and **Michael 'Archie' Stone***.*

Mr Ice - 1990s Metal.
Alan Marsh *(vocals)*; **Andy Boulton** *(lead guitar) (replaced by*
Steve Kerr*)*; **Danny Gwilym** *(guitar)*; **Colin Riggs** *(bass)*;
Ian 'Atilla' Marshall *(keyboards)*; **Marc 'Jocker' Angel** *(drums)*.

Mrs Taylor's Mad - 1984-1986 Indie.
Dave Ware *(vocals and harmonica)*; **Andy Ware** *(guitar and vocals)*;
Tom Power *(saxophone)*; **Paul Read** *(bass)*; **Trevor George** *(drums)*.

Mystic Sister - 1990s. All female band from Tisbury.

The Nearlymen - 1990s.
Clive Roper *(vocals and guitar)*; **Frogg Moody** *(keyboards)*;
Mark Blamey *(bass)*; **Gary Holton** *(drums)*.

Never Bend Over - 1972-73.
Anton Hayman *(guitar and vocals)*; **Jerry Collinson** *(guitar)*;
Ernie Cartmell *(synthesiser)*; **Steve Collinson** *(bass)*;
Reg Maggs *(drums)*.

Newcombe and Roach - 1982-1986.
Phil Manning *(vocals)*; **Matthew Finn** *(guitar)*; **Tim Darlow** *(upside down five string guitar)*; **Mickey Dyer** *(bass)*; **Alex Mundy** *(drums)*.

Evolved from **Horizontal Bulgarians***. When Tim Darlow moved to Spain,* **Ian 'Skid' Browne** *took over his guitar duties.*

The New Sarum Sound - 1970s.
Included **Yan Webber** *on guitar.*

Next Of Kin - Late 1980s.
Alec Slatter *(vocals)*; **Nick Hinton** *(guitar)*; **Nigel Fawcett** *(bass)*;
Kieran Osmond *(keyboards)*; **Rob Fisher** *(drums)*.

Nicomachus Yagi - Formed at BWS in 1966, still going into 1970.
Gerald Hunt *(guitar)*; **Andrew 'Ted' Parton** *(bass)*;
Andrew Lovelock *(drums)*; *Someone else played vibes for a bit.*

Influenced by Hendrix and Family. Played one gig in 1970 in a hall on Bemerton Heath.

Nighthawk - 1982.
Nick Walker *(vocals)*; **Graeme Pinder** *(lead guitar)*;
Ray Goodge *(rhythm guitar)*; **Graham Rose** *(bass)*;
Trevor Webb *(drums)*; **Dave Walker** *('sound and vision')*.

Nightlife - Circa 1982-1989.
Steve Ainsworth *(vocals)* *(replaced by* **Pete Lawrence***);* **Pete Catlin** *(guitar);* **Yan Webber** *(guitar);* **Dennis Robbins** *(keyboards);* **Henk Leerink** *(bass);* **Andy Golden** *(drums)* *(replaced by* **Chris Williams** *and then* **Stuart Marshall***).*

Nosferatu - Early 1980s. Gothy Metal.
Mike Vickers *(vocals);* **Graeme Pinder** *(guitar);* **Ray Goodge** *(guitar)* *(replaced by* **Ray Dismore***);* **Graham Rose** *(bass);* **Nigel Emm** *(drums).*

The Nuthins - 1990s Garage Psych.
Mike Brunt *(vocals);* **Lee 'Lee Tea' Thornton** *(vocals and guitar);* **Jon 'Mojo' Mills** *(guitar and vocals);* **Carol Galpin** *(bass);* **Bob Taylor** *(keyboards and vocals);* **Richie Walker** *(drums and percussion).*
Mike quickly left. Lee was replaced by **Marcus** *and then when he quit they reverted to a four-piece with Mojo on lead vocals. Carol was later replaced by* **Andy Cornick**. **Ian Allen** *played harmonica on the Nuthins album.*

Obvious Action - 1980s Punks.
Dave Boyes *(vocals and guitar);* **Colin Mundy** *(guitar);* **Mark Palmer** *(bass);* **Steve Christey** *(drums).*
Developed out of **Last Orders**. *Dave later concentrated on vocals and Mark switched to guitar and* **Nick Shirfield** *came in on bass. Dave, Nick and Steve left and* **Kev Barnes** *came in on bass, with* **Russ Whatley** *on drums – Mark took over the vocals but then left and was replaced by* **Steve Marlowe**.

The Officers In The Gaming Room - Late 1970s.
Nick Kemp *(vocals and guitar);* **Bob Cooke** *(guitar);* **Neville White** *(bass);* **Steve Hutchinson** *(drums).*

The Off Switch - Early 1980s acoustic.
Included **Neil Dalziel**, **Duncan Howell** *and* **Russell ?**

Oglala Sioux - Late 1980s.
Kerry Waite *(guitar and vocals);* **Nigel Finn** *(bass);* **Jim Blackwell** *(drums).*

Open Defiance - New Wave type rock
Tim Hedges *(keyboards and vocals);* **Ray Dismore** *(guitar);* **Mick Hargraves** *(bass and vocals);* **Trevor Harris** *(drums).*

The Orchard - Early 1980s.
Lesley Hallett *(vocals);* **Duncan Howell** *(guitar and vocals);* **Nigel Finn** *(Bass);* **Jimmy Blackwell** *(drums).*

Original Howling Gods - 1998 Indie supergroup.
Neale Hancock *(vocals and guitar);* **Jim Harrison** *(guitar);* **Darren 'Dazman' Blake** *(guitar);* **Matt Venn** *(keyboards);* **Simon 'Wiggy' Wigglesworth** *(bass);* **Tim Kerley** *(drums).*

Oxoxox - *See* 'The Men Of The Doomsbury Lifeboat'.

Parma - 1990s.
Kevin Russell *(vocals and guitar);* **John Packwood** *(guitar and vocals);* **Adrian 'Swannie' Martin** *(bass and backing vocals);* **Tim Kerley** *(drums).*

Pauline Taste - 1970s.
Neville Anderson; **Nick Kemp**; **Bob Cooke**; **Andy Golden**

Peacewave - 1972-78.
Keith Daubney *(vocals);* **Yan Webber** *(guitar);* **Simon Reid** *(bass);* **Dave Smith** *(drums).*

The Perfect Squares - Mid 1980s.

Period - Late 1960s-Early 1970s. From Enford.
Mike Bird *(vocals and guitar);* **Anthony 'Biddles' Phillimore** *(bass);* **John Hatchman** *(drums).*

Peter Pod and The Peas

Phantom Pholk - Mid 1970s Amesbury Youth Club band.
Peter Chalk; **Anthony Leavy**; **Paul Cody**; **Peter Adams**; **Lynda Taylor**; **David Gough**; **Rolf Adams**; **Robert Garnett**; **Debbie Watts**.

The Phenobarbitones - Late 1980s.
Included **Dan Clayton** *and* **Robert Howes**.

Physical Jerx 1990 93.
Grahame 'Chalky' White; **Gary ?**; **Steve Collinson**.

Planc Crash - *Included* **Duncan Fulton**.

Plastic Penny - 1970s. Amesbury based incarnation of former hit makers.
Bob Rynn *(vocals);* **Harvey Cormack** *(guitar);* **Tony Murray** *(bass);* **Keith Small** *(drums).*

Pope Shenouda & The Coptic Orthodox - Circa 1983-84.
Included **Jon Maple** *(vocals);* **Phil Manning** *(backing vocals);* **Matthew Finn** *(guitar);* **Ian 'Skid' Browne** *(guitar);* **Mickey Dyer** *(bass).*

The Prams - 1980-1983. Heavy Rock in suits.
Rob Boston *(bass and vocals);* **Alwyn Lovell** *(lead guitar);* **Eddie Johnson** *(guitar);* **Nicky Boston** *(drums).*

Pray - mid 1990s to 2000 cover band
Kerry ? *(vocals)* *(replaced by* **Nick Walker** *and then* **Teresa Taylor***);* **Dave Walker** *(guitar);* **Richard Stickler** *(keyboards);* **Pete Smith** *(bass)* *(replaced by* **Dave Martin***);* **Trevor Webb** *(drums).*
Became **Innervision**.

The Premiers - 1970s.
Included: **David O'Reilly (aka David York)** *(vocals);* **Brian Saunders** *(guitar);* **Yan Webber** *(guitar);* **Steve Terry** *(organ)* *(replaced by* **Mike Reason***);* **Chris Glover** *(bass);* **Terry Francis** *(drums)* *(replaced by* **Adrian Annetts***).*
Later reformed as **Reform**.

The Processors - Early 1980s 'electronic space pop'.
Karen Baker *(vocals);* **Sarah Baker** *(vocals);* **James Ferguson** *(guitar and vocals);* **Frogg Moody** *(keyboards);* **Chris Walsh** *(bass).* *Lyrics by* **Peter Bown**.

The Prophecy - Mid 1980s.
Andy Brewer *(vocals);* **Piers Moore** *(guitar);* **Jon Baggeley** *(keyboards);* **Frank Cross** *(bass);* **Steve 'The Bear' Greenaway** *(drums).*
Became **Farley 708**.

The Pub Beats - *See* 'Charlie Harwood and The Pub Beats'.

Pumphouse - 1990s Metal.
Alan Marsh *(vocals);* **Jez Lee** *(lead guitar);* **Colin Riggs** *(bass);*
Marc 'Jocker' Angel *(drums). Augmented by* **Ian 'Atilla' Marshall**
on keyboards and samples.

The Purefinders - 1990-98.
Phil ?*;* **Ruth Jones***;* **Pete Maxfield***;* **Steve Collinson***;*
Grahame 'Chalky' White.

Pussy - Early 1970s Metal.
Paul Dean *(bass and vocals);* **Bob Cooke** *(guitar);* **Ray Sparrow** *(drums).*
A short lived later incarnation of **Jerusalem***, later reformed with*
Brian Goff *replacing Bob Cooke on guitar.*

The QTs - 1970s New Wave.
Mike Vickers *(vocals);* **Chris Walsh** *(guitar) (replaced by*
Andy 'Sprog' Ford*);* **Frogg Moody** *(keyboards);*
Colin Holton *(bass);* **Mike 'Jackboot' Jones** *(drums).*

Rat-a-Tat Tank - Early 1980s.
Kurt Cooper *(vocals);* **Nick Marchant** *(guitar);*
Colin Holton *(bass);* **Jon Nicholas** *(drums).*

Recorded Delivery - 1970s.
Included **Brian Billen** *(vocals);* **Mick Lecky** *(guitar);*
Don Reynolds *(organ);* **Adrian Lucas** *(bass);* **Geoff Lucas** *(drums)*
(replaced by **Cliff Fry***).*
And also... **Jimmy Trigwell** *(guitar) and* **Dave Bennett** *(drums).*

Red Book - Early-Mid 1980s.
Duncan Fulton *(vocals and bass);* **Andy 'Sprog' Ford** *(guitar);*
Kerry Waite *(guitar);* **Andy Gridge** *(drums) (replaced by*
Jim Blackwell*).*

Reform - 1970s.
David O'Reilly (aka David York) *(vocals);* **Brian Saunders** *(guitar);*
David Gay *(guitar);* **Chris Glover** *(bass);* **Adrian Allinson** *(drums).*
Also included **Dave Bennett** *on drums at one stage.*
Formerly **The Premiers***.* **Brian Billen** *filled in to honour a few*
outstanding dates following David O'Reilly's tragic death.

The Rhythm Blasters - Early 1980s to now. Blues.
Dave Taylor *(vocals and guitar);* **Malcolm Wilkinson** *(guitar);*
Colin Holton *(bass) (replaced by* **Andy Sylvester** *and then*
Henk Leerink, **Ruth Jones** *and* **Chris Foster***);* **Alex Mundy** *(drums).*
Occasionally joined by **Pete Catlin** *on guitar and* **Rick Wells** *on bass.*

Rocky Cockerel
See 'The Men Of The Doomsbury Lifeboat'.

Rook - 1990s.
Sean Rice *(Vocals and bass);* **Chris Walsh** *(guitar);*
Frogg Moody *(keyboards);* **Colin Watteston** *(drums).*

Room 237

Romantic Warriors
Mick Hargraves *(bass and vocals);* **Paul Andrews** *(guitar);*
Trevor Harris *(drums).*

Rose Coloured Nightmares - Late 1980s Goth-Glam-Punk.
Gary James *(vocals);* **Maugan Rimmer** *(guitar);*
Mark House *(bass);* **Richard Walker** *(drums).*

The Sackville Baggins - Late 1980s.
Rob Arney*;* **Scud***;* **Cath***;* **Jonny Blamey***;* **Jon 'Mojo' Mills.**

Saigon - Early 1990s metal.
Andy Boulton *(vocals and guitar);* **Neil Parsons** *(guitar and vocals);*
Dave South *(bass and vocals);* **Andrew Batchelor** *(drums, percussion*
and vocals).

The Salisbury Big Band - 1970s.
Ken Palmer *and* **Ray Barratt** *(trombones);* **Don Forder**,
Mervin Dukes, **Bob Dolman** *and* **Ted Haines** *(trumpets);*
Bob Newman *and* **Les Many** *(saxophones);* **Tony Lawrence** *(bass);*
Terry Francis *(drums).*
Augmented by members of the **2A Royal Artillery Mounted Band**
from Larkhill Garrison.

Sarajevo - Early 1990s Metal.
Pete Lacey *(vocals);* **Baz Strokosz** *(guitar);* **Mark Straker** *(guitar);*
Jakey Findlay *(bass);* **Ed Danielle** *(drums).*

The Scream Room - Mid 1990s Power Pop.
Sean Rice *(vocals and guitar);* **Simon Dickenson** *(lead guitar);*
Debbie Fulton *(guitar);* **Dave Wilds** *(keyboards);*
Mark Torokwa *(bass);* **Dave Marsh** *(drums).*
Previously **The Statues.**

Seeing Red - 1980s.
Included **Steve Rushton, Chris Walsh, Micky Dyer,**
Gary Holton *and* **David Barrington-Brown.**

Shadowlands - Late 1980s.
Became **Carfax** *and* **The Heretic.**

Sheen - Late 1970s BWS cover band.
Described by Tich Amey as a 'Highly Polished Band'! Became **Trax.**
See entry for **Highway 5.**

The Shining Hearts Band - Early 1970s.
Included **Steve Ryall, Fred Phillips, Duncan Fulton**
and **Mike Buxton.**

Shogun - Late 1980s Hair Metal.
Alan Marsh *(vocals);* **Danny Gwilym** *(lead guitar);* **David Gochaux**
(bass) (replaced by **Toby Martin**, *then* **Andy Wrighton** *and then*
Andy Robbins*);* **Bob Richards** *(drums) (replaced by* **Steve Pierce***).*
Later joined by **Ian 'Atilla' Marshall** *(keyboards).*

Shoot the Toux - Late 1980s Pop, soul and funk.
Kurt Cooper *(vocals);* **Simon 'Sox' Oxborrow** *(guitar);*
Steve Burton *(keyboards);* **Pete Smith** *(bass);* **Trevor Webb** *(drums).*

Shot In The Dark - early 1980s
Neil Dalziel *(vocals),* **Colin Crook** *(guitar);* **Pete Leyland** *(bass);*
Alex Mundy *(drums).*
Aka 'The Bartlett Brothers', rehearsed at the Kemp brothers'
Wilton home, which Neil was renting, and performed a handful
of local pub gigs. Alex left to join **The Rhythm Blasters***.*

The Shrine

The Singing Nuns of Alcatraz - 1978 punky power pop covers.
Included **Ian 'Skid' Browne** *(guitar) and* **Andy Clements** *(drums).*

ENDLESS BEAT

Single Factor - Late 1980s.

The Siren - Early 1980s.

Six Miles From Huesca - Late 1980s.
Sally Anne Lowe *(vocals and tambourine);* **Duncan Howell** *(guitar);* **Mark Palmer** *(bass);* **Alex Sharpe** *(drums).*

Slainte - 1992-93. Celtic folk.
Sean Rice *(vocals);* **Tim Madden** *(vocals and acoustic guitar);* **Doug Sheriff** *(accordion);* **Matt Carter** *(tenor banjo and mandolin).*

Smolensk

Snakespear

Snowblind - 1980-82.
Adrian Weeks *(vocals – but only very briefly)* (replaced by **Nick Walker**); **Dave Walker** *(guitar);* **Andy Shepherd** (?) *(guitar);* **Neil Leacy** *(bass and keyboards);* **Trevor Webb** *(drums).*
A rock covers band who evolved out of **Blue Haze**. *Only played 2 gigs.*

Sonofabitch - Mid 1970s Metal.
Tremayne Roden *(vocals);* **Roy Shergold** *(guitar),* **Jez Kemp** *(guitar),* **Maxwell Strange** *(bass),* **Trevor Frampton** *(drums);* **Peter Dennis**.

The Soupdragon - Early 1980s.
Caroline Holt-Keen *(vocals);* **Duncan Howell** *(guitar);* **Nigel Finn** *(bass);* **Jim Blackwell** *(drums).*

Sparrow - Circa 1969-1973.
Included **Brian Billen** *and* **Jon Walters**.

Sphere - 1970s Modern Jazz.
Andy Sheppard *(saxophones);* **Geoff Williams** *(piano);* **Pete Maxfield** *(bass); Various drummers.*

The Spoils - 1990s.
Christian Emmerson (vocals); Tim Waterman (guitar); Nigel Coulson (guitar); Adrian 'Swannie' Martin (bass); Tim Kerley (drums). Kevin Russell was a founder member on vocals and guitar.

The Stand - Late 1980s punks.
Colin Mundy *(guitar and vocals);* **Kev Barnes** *(bass);* **Terry Whatley** *(drums)* (replaced by **Rich Walker**).
Nick Shirfield *and* **Clive Roper** *later played guitar, "On a Peter Shilton/Ray Clemence rotation scheme- you have to be of a certain age!" (Colin Mundy).*
Morphed into **The Magnificent**.

Stan Holton's Immaculate Conception

The Statues - Mid 1990s Power Pop.
Sean Rice *(vocals and guitar);* **Simon Dickenson** *(lead guitar);* **Mark Torokwa** *(bass);* **Dave Marsh** *(drums).*
Added some members and changed their name to **Scream Room**.

Stormfly - Late 1990s.

The Strugglers - 1980s-1990s.
Colin Holton *(guitar and vocals);* **Frogg Moody** *(keyboards);* **Clive Roper** *(bass);* **Dave Marsh** *(drums).*
An occasional Stranglers/New Wave 'tribute band before tribute bands existed': A side project from **Don't Feed The Animals**.

Suicide King - Early 1990s. Fuzzy grunge guitar type stuff.
Gary James *(vocals and guitar);* **Nick Shirfield** *(bass);* **Ray Hunt** *(drums).*
Formerly **Swing Syndicate**.

Sweet Children - Late 1990s.
Dan Foot *(vocals and guitar);* **Pete Viney** *(bass);* **John Birch** *(drums).*
Became **Uncle Brian**.

Swing Syndicate - Early 1990s.
Gary James *(vocals and guitar);* **Nick Shirfield** *(bass);* **Ray Hunt** *(drums).*
Became **Suicide King**.

Table Talk - Late 1980s.

The Taylor-Gair Band - 1979-1981.
Robin Gair *(vocals);* **Linda Taylor** *(vocals);* **Christine Taylor** *(vocals),* **Yan Webber** *(guitar),* **Nigel Dixon** *(bass),* **Andy Golden** *(drums);* **John Hatchman** *(percussion and vocals).*

The Steve Terry Duo - 1970s.
Steve Terry; **Terry Francis**.

Theodore Watkins - Early 1970s.
Robin Gair *(vocals);* **Steve Clasby** *(organ and guitar);* **Jack Horner** *(bassoon and bass);* **Mike Stevenson** *(drums).*

Thick Dick & The Green'eds - 1979-88. DIY Indie Punk Rock.
Jeff Watkins *(vocals);* **Richard Grocott** *(guitar);* **Dave Notley** *(bass);* **Carl Hutson** *(drums);* **Andy Murphy** *(drums/keyboards). Also included* **Jim Clay** *and* **Andy Moores**.

Tokyo Blade - 1980s Metal Godlets.
Alan Marsh *(vocals)* (replaced by **Vic Wright** *and then* **Carl Sentance**); **Andy Boulton** *(guitar and vocals);* **Ray Dismore** *(guitar)* (replaced by **John Wiggins**); **Andy Robbins** *(bass)* (replaced by **Andy Wrighton**); **Steve Pierce** *(drums).*
Renamed 'Andy Boulton's Tokyo Blade' *with a new line-up:*
Peter Zito *(vocals);* **Andy Boulton** *(guitar and vocals);* **Chris Stover** *(bass);* **Alex Lee** *(drums and vocals).*
Then there was a 'German' *version:* **Michael Pozz** *(vocals);* **Andy Boulton** *(guitar and vocals);* **Michael Machwitz** *(keyboards);* **Dave Sale** *(bass);* **Astor** *(drums).*
And next a 1990s reformation: **Alan Marsh** *(vocals);* **Andy Boulton** *(guitar and vocals);* **John Wiggins** *(guitar);* **Colin Riggs** *(bass);* **Marc 'Jocker' Angel** *(drums).*

Toucantango - 1983-1987 'Pure Pop Funk'.
Kurt Cooper *(vocals)* (replaced by **Mike Vickers**); **Sarah Tolley** *(backing vocals)* (replaced by **Carol Chu**); **Dave Walker** *(guitar)* (replaced by **Pete Woo**, *then* **Andy Webley** *and* **Chris Binns**); **Neil Leacy** *(keyboards);* **Mark Hogarth** *(bass)* (replaced by **Pete Smith**); **Trevor Webb** *(drums);* **Dan Webb** *('sound and vision').*
Claimed to be the first local band with a Simmonds electronic drum kit. Were originally to be named 'Something Else' before Kurt's wife Jackie suggested 'Toucantango'.

Tracer - Late 1990s.

Tracker - Mid 1970s.
Ian 'Tich' Amey *(guitar and vocals);* **Pete Lucas** *(guitar and vocals);* **Trevor 'Dozy' Davies** *(bass and vocals) (replaced by* **Steve Collinson***);* **John Dymond** *(drums and vocals) (replaced by* **Reg Maggs***).*

Trax - Late 1970s BWS cover band. *Became* **Xtrax**.

The Trouser Devils - Late 1980s.
Phil Manning *(vocals & percussion);* **Jon Maple** *(vocals, harmonica & accordion);* **Matthew Finn** *(guitar);* **Ian 'Skid' Browne** *(guitar);* **Mickey Dyer** *(bass);* **'Red Ant'** *(drums).*

Uncle Brian - Late 1990s.
Dan Foot *(vocals and guitar);* **Pete Viney** *(bass);* **John Birch** *(drums)*
Formerly **Sweet Children**.

Un Deux Twang! - 1982-1984.
Candy Hill (aka Candy Box) *(vocals and keyboards);*
Phil Hill (aka Pheel Ill) *(vocals and guitar);* **Nikki Kozak** *(vocals);*
Malcolm Wilkinson *(guitar);* **Neil Nicholson** *(trumpet & saxophone);*
Colin Holton *(bass);* **Alex Mundy (aka Alex Rene)** *(drums).*

Unhealthy Fixation - Early 1990s.

Uno Rufo - Early 1980s.

Urban Kids - Early 1980s schoolboy punk.
Included **Dave Boyes**.

The Mike Vickers Band
Mike Vickers *(vocal);* **Richard Reeves** *(guitar);* **Terry Parkinson** *(bass) (replaced by* **Ady Courtney***);* **Ray Sparrow** *(drums).*

View From A Bridge - Mid 1980s.
Clive Roper *(vocals and guitar);* **Frogg Moody** *(keyboards);*
Richard 'Buzzard' Atkinson *(bass);* **Steve Christey** *(drums).*

Vulture Squadron - Late 1980s Metal.
Kevin Whale *(vocals);* **George Lennon** *(guitar);*
Peter 'Bam Bam' Stone *(bass);* **Michael 'Archie' Stone** *(drums).*

Wacchus Bacchus - Late 1980s.

What The Butler Saw - Late 1980s/Early 1990s
Johnny Bell *(vocals and guitar);* **Simon 'Sox' Oxborrow** *(guitar);*
Steve Burton *(keyboards);* **Andy Penny** *(bass);*
Steve Christey *(drums)*

White Diamond - Late 1970s Metal.
Steve Rushton *(vocals);* **Andy Boulton** *(guitar);*
Andy Robbins *(guitar);* **Martin Robbins** *(bass);*
Steve Pierce *(drums).*

Who Is? - 1990s Poppy Stuff.
Nick Walker *(vocals);* **Colin Crook** *(guitar) (replaced by* **Dave Walker***);* **Pete Smith** *(bass);* **Barry Stevens** *(keyboards);*
Trevor Webb *(drums).*
Colin suffered a stroke and was unfortunately unable to continue playing.

Wolfbane - 1980s Metal.
Chris Moon *(vocals);* **Jem Mills** *(guitar) (replaced by* **Walter Eddowes** – *who was also a later lead vocalist);*
Derrick Hocking *(guitar);* **Graham Andrews** *(bass) (replaced by* **George Lennon***);* **Phil Urquhart** *(drums).*

Woodsmoke - Mid 1970s Country Rock duo.
Trevor 'Dozy' Davies *(guitar and vocals);*
Phil Boardman *(guitar and vocals).*

Xtrax - Late 1970s - 1981 covers band.
Pete Gallagher *(vocals);* **Mark Sheldon** *(guitar);*
Kurt Cooper *(guitar);* **Pete Leyland** *(bass);* **Jon Stone** *(drums) (replaced by* **Jon Nicholas***).*
Also featured various keyboard players - **Ken ?**, **Rob Martin** *and* **Rick Northwood**. **Martin James** *came out of 'drumming retirement' for one gig at St. Paul's Club in 1980).*
Formerly **Highway 5**, **Sheen** *and* **Trax**.

Zebeck - Mid 1970s.
Chris Walsh *(guitar and vocals);* **Simon Kuczera** *(bass);*
Frogg Moody *(keyboards);* **Mike 'Jackboot' Jones** *(drums).*

Zero - 1980s.
Included **John Gent** *(vocals) and* **Walter Eddowes** *(guitar).*

Appendix 2
Discography

This discography concentrates on recordings from between 1970 and 1999, with the occasional demo and later releases for the sake of completeness or where they are of particular interest. Imports and compilation appearances are normally only noted for recordings not issued elsewhere. Recordings made by Salisbury artists after they 'left town' have not been included. Any additions or corrections would be gratefully received.

AFRO DIZZY ACTS

7" SINGLE

Open Your Eyes/Hide Your Love *(Shiki Ye Ye) (AFDA 001) (Picture Cover) (1984)*

THE BADGEMAN

7" SINGLES

Go Insane! *(Track on split flexidisc with The Mayfields) (Compact & Bijou C&B 001) (Picture Cover) (1988)*

Crystals/P.A.F *(Paperhouse PAPER 002) (Die Cut Company Sleeve) (1990)*

English Road Song/Auto Da Fe *(Paperhouse PAPER 019) (Picture Cover) (1992)*

12" EP

THE CURSE OF THE BADGEMAN *(Throwback; Magic Bullet; Drought; Crop Cycle) (Paperhouse PAP 009 T) (Picture Cover) (1991)*

ALBUMS

KINGS OF THE DESERT *(The Secret Diary of Jim Morrison's Bastard Son Aged 19¾; Crystals; Sean's Seen The Light; Extraordinary Girl; Cupid's Exploding Harpoon; False Yellow Eyes; King Of The Desert; Make Me Feel; Montezuma's Revenge; Goinsaneagain) (Paperhouse PAPLP 003) (Vinyl) (Paperhouse PAPCD 003) (CD with extra tracks: My Flash On You; P.A.F.) (1990)*

RITUAL LANDSCAPE *(Grey Area; Liturgy; Black Song; Seethe Shanty; Auto Da Fe; Tumuli; Swarm) (Paperhouse PAPLP 012) (Vinyl) (Paperhouse PAPCD 012) (CD with extra tracks: Drone; Magic Bullet; Crop Cycle; Drought; Andagain) (1992)*

COMPILATION APPEARANCE

HEAVEN AND HELL VOLUME 3 *(Velvet Underground tribute CD including 'Sister Ray') (Imaginary Records ILL CD 022) (1992)*

BIG BIRD

CASSETTE

Road; Rock'n'Roll; Sleepwalk; Worried Worried; Spooky; Three Chords To Heaven *(Home produced cassette with colour inlay) (1993)*

BUBBLEGUM SPLASH!

CASSETTE

BUBBLEGUM SPLASH! *(Plastic Smile; One Of Those Things; Room With A View) (1986)*

FLEXIDISC

If Only *(Track on split flexidisc with Darling Buds) (Bonk ON 001) (Given Away With 'So Naïve' Fanzine) (1987)*

7" EP AND SINGLE

SPLASHDOWN *(EP) (Plastic Smile; Fast Of Friends/Just Walked Away; One Of Those Things) (Subway Organisation SUBWAY 13) (Picture Cover) (1987)*

COMPILATION APPEARANCE

SURFIN' IN THE SUBWAY *(LP including 'Someone Said' and 'The 18.10 To Yeovil Junction') (Subway Organisation SUBORG 04) (1987) (both tracks were later also issued on the 'Take The Subway To Your Suburb' CD (Subway Organisation SUBORG 1CD) (1993)*

THE COLIN DAVID SET

ALBUM

LIMITED EDITION *(Stick By You; Baker Street; You're The One That I Want; Lovers Dawn; Look Through Any Window; You Were On My Mind; Rhythm Of The Rain; Me And You; The Difference It Makes; Theme From 'The Deer Hunter'; One Way Ticket; Without You) (Arny's Shack Records AS 044) (1981)*

CRAZY DAISY

COMPILATION APPEARANCE

GOD'S GREAT TAPE HEAD CLEANER *(Salisbury compilation cassette including 'Pens And Pencils') (7% GGTH 1) (1991)*

DAVE DEE, DOZY, BEAKY, MICK AND TICH

7" SINGLES

She's My Lady/Babeigh *(Antic K 11510) (1974)*

Do Wah Diddy/Waiting *(Global 104 986) (Picture Cover) (Germany 1983)*

La Leyanda De Xanadu (Live)/What'd I Say (Live) *(Discos Victoria VIC69) (Picture Cover) (Spain 1983)*

Staying With It/Sure Thing *(Atlantic A9757) (Picture Cover) (1983)*

Here We Go/Here We Go Again *(White Label Promo only) (1985) (Credited to 'The Boys')*

LP

DAVE DEE, DOZY, BEAKY, MICK AND TICH *(Hold Tight!; Save Me; Okay; Zabadak; The Legend Of Xanadu; Touch Me, Touch Me; The Wreck Of The Antoinette; Hideaway; Here's A Heart; Last Night In Soho; Bend It; It's So Hard To Love You) (all re-recorded versions) (Heartbreak Hotel HH 2) (1984)*

CDS

The 2006 CD reissue of the 1969 'Together' album *(Repertoire REPUK 1053)* includes the following as bonus tracks: She's My Lady; Babeigh; Do Wah Diddy; Waiting; Stayin' With It; Sure Thing.

COMPILATION APPEARANCE

HEROES AND VILLAINS *(LP including live versions of 'The Legend Of Xanadu' and 'What'd I Say' (the latter with Chris Farlowe and Cliff Bennett also on vocals) recorded at the 'Heroes and Villains' fundraising concert) (Dakota OTA 1001) (1982)*

DAVE DEE

7" SINGLES

My Woman's Man/Gotta Make You Part Of Me *(Fontana TF 1074) (1970)*

Annabella/Kelly *(Fontana 6007 021) (1970)*

Everything About Her/If I Believed In Tomorrow *(Philips 6006 061) (1970)*

Wedding Bells/Sweden *(Philips 6006 100) (1971)*

Hold On/Mary Morning, Mary Evening *(Philips 6006 154) (1971)*

Swingy/Don't You Ever Change Your Mind *(Philips 6006 180) (1971)*

The Ballad Of Bulldog Bobby/ The Ballad Of Bulldog Bobby *(Instrumental Version) (Panache Music PAN 2) (1982) (credited to 'Dave And The Bulldogs')*

CDs

UNFINISHED BUSINESS *(Captured; Where Did I Go Wrong; Promised Land; What's On Your Mind; Serious Action; Cry Surrender; Change Is Gonna Come; Falling; Not Made Of Stone; So Alive; It's Over) (Dave Dee Records DD CD001) (1995)*

'Boxed' a 100 track 4-CD Dave Dee, Dozy, Beaky, Mick and Tich compilation, issued in The Netherlands in 1999 *(BR Music 1009-2)* included the A and B sides of all Dave Dee's 1970s solo singles, alongside two previously unreleased tracks, Goodnight Ma and Stars.

The 2008 Dave Dee, Dozy, Beaky, Mick and Tich 'BBC Sessions' compilation CD *(BR Music BS 8026-2)* includes versions of 'Wedding Bells' and 'Sweden'.

KLAUS AND KLAUS AND DAVE DEE

7" SINGLE

ZABADAK *(Karakakora)/Tronkenbold (Teldec 247006-7) (Germany 1989)*

DAVE DEE AND MARMALADE

7" SINGLE

SCIROCCO/I DON'T BELIEVE IN LOVE ANYMORE *(Hansa 6127) (Germany 1989)*

DAVE DEE AND MARMALADE

12" SINGLE

SCIROCCO *(Long Version)/Scirocco (Single Version); I Don't Believe In Love Anymore (Hansa 126127) (Germany 1989)*

COMPILATION APPEARANCES

THOMMY'S CHRISTMAS PARTY *(CD including 'I Believe In Father Christmas' and 'Let's Hear It For Christmas') (Ariola 74321 21687 2) (Germany 1994)*

THE SIXTIES STORYBOOK *(CD including 'The Wall' by Dave Dee, Sandy Newman and Chip Hawkes) (Fairy Dust Records Dust 001) (1999)*

SIXTIES SING NINETIES *(CD including 'Don't Look Back In Anger') (Harry's Records) (1999)*

DAVID *(Featuring Dave Dee and Peter Mason)*

7" SINGLE

I'm Going Back/Selppin *(Fontana TF 1081) (1970)*

CD

The 2006 CD reissue of the Dave Dee, Dozy, Beaky, Mick and Tich 'Together' album *(Repertoire REPUK 1053)* included 'I'm Going Back' and 'Selppin' as bonus tracks.

DOZY, BEAKY MICK AND TICH *(aka DBM&T)*

7" SINGLES

Mr President/Frisco Annie *(Fontana 6007 022) (1970)*

Festival/Leader Of A Rock And Roll Band *(Philips 6006 066) (1970)*

I Want To Be There/For The Use Of Your Son *(Philips 6006 114) (1971)*

They Won't Sing My Song/Soukie *(Philips 6006 198) (1972)*

You've Got Me On The Run/Rock And Roll *(WEA 18099) (Germany/Netherlands 1979)*

In The Coven/I Can't Stop Wanting You *(Earlobe ELB S 103) (1981)*

Matthew And Son/Matthew And Son *(Instrumental Version) (Friend 190.036) (Holland 1986)*

ALBUM

FRESH EAR *(Mr President; Too Much; She Was A Raver; Mystery Rider; World; Rain; Soukie; Leader Of A Rock And Roll Band) (Philips 6308 029) (1971)*

CDs

The 2006 CD reissue of 'Fresh Ear' *(Repertoire REPUK 1054)* included all the original single and album tracks listed above, plus both sides of the 1969 single 'Tonight Today/Bad News' and a bonus track, Sarah.

The 2008 Dave Dee, Dozy, Beaky, Mick and Tich 'BBC Sessions' compilation *(BR Music BS 8026-2)* includes versions of the following: Tonight Today; Bad News; Talk To You; Mr President; Rain; Leader Of A Rock And Roll Band; Helplessly Hoping; Bluebird.

DENNIS

COMPILATION APPEARANCE

GOD'S GREAT TAPE HEAD CLEANER *(Salisbury compilation cassette including 'Emma (Mild Thing)') (7% GGTH 1) (1991)*

THE DISHEVELLERS

CD SINGLE

Crusty Girl *(Solstice Ritual Folksong); Crusty Girl (Gator Mix); Crusty Girl (Live Mix) (PC) (Catalina CATL 70012) (1992)*

DON'T FEED THE ANIMALS

7" SINGLE

Wealthy Man/Hostages *(Rod Records ROD S1) (Picture Cover) (1985)*

FARLEY 708

7" FLEXIDISC

Andy Wilson's Trousers/Andy Wilson's Coat *(Trip-Trip To A Dream Dragon Trip 1) (1987) (sold separately, but also distributed free with 'Candy And A Currant Bun' fanzine from Marlborough.)*

FARLEY RIDGE

COMPILATION APPEARANCE

GOD'S GREAT TAPE HEAD CLEANER *(Salisbury compilation cassette including 'Ballad Of The Six- Legged Millipede') (7% GGTH 1) (1991)*

ROBIN GAIR

7" SINGLE
Why Do We Have To Wait 'Til Christmas? / Don't Throw Our Love Away *(PVK Records PV32) (1979) (A-side credited to Robin Gair and Downton School Choir)*

GENGHIS KHAN (1)

7" SINGLE
Love You/Lady Lady/Mongol Nation/Gone For A Drive *(Wabbit Records WAB 61/63) (Double Single Picture Cover) (1983)*

GENGHIS KHAN (2)

7" SINGLE
DOUBLE DEALIN' *(If Heaven is Hell/Highway Passion/Midnight Rendezvous/Mean Streak) (Genghis Khan GK 1) (Double Single Picture Cover) (1983)*

After this single the band used the name 'Tokyo Blade'. They repackaged the singles they had left over into two new separate sleeves and stuck labels onto the discs. The repackaged discs were named 'If Heaven Is Hell' and '2nd Cut' respectively.

GETTYSBURG ADDRESS

COMPILATION APPEARANCE
YOUNG BLOOD *(Peninsula PENCV 1002) (LP including 'Dance Feat') (1984)*

GRANDMA MOSES

7" EP
GRANDMA MOSES *(Rolling Down The Country; Like A Thief In The Night/Cancelled Out; Rainbow Chaser) (Ongoing Situation OS 001) (Picture Cover) (1981)*

COMPILATION APPEARANCE
INFLUX ONE *(Zygo) (LP including 'One Dying Beetle' & 'Think') (1980)*

THE GREY WOLVES

7" SINGLES
A Wealth Of Misery/Lest We Forget *(Numbered limited edition, orange vinyl, poster cover with black card envelope sealed by sticker) (XN Recordings XNR 002) (Italy 1995)*

Zero Tolerance/Dominate Her *(Numbered limited edition, picture disc with t-shirt) (Membrum Debile Propaganda MDP 6000-08) (Germany 1996)*

CASSETTES
INTOLERABLE *(split cassette with Con-Dom) (includes Programmed To Kill, recorded live at Amesbury Sports Centre) (Control Domination) (1986)*

NO NEW JERUSALEM *(The Tell Tale Heart; Golgotha Requiem; Pagan Easter; Gillick; Pyrrhic Victory; The Passover) (V1) (1986)*

ATROCITY EXHIBITION *(The Skin Area; Rune Filled Eyes; Obscene Mannequin; Left Orbit + Temple; Unidentified Female; Orifice; Suite Mentalle; A Terminal Posture; Auto Erotic; The Him; An Existential Yes; Concentration City; The Weapon Range; The Image Maze; Beach Fatigue; Autogeddin; The Atrocity Exhibition) (Artaman 30) (1988)*

DEATH PACT 2 *(split cassette with Kapotte Muziek) (includes one untitled Grey Wolves track) (Death Pact Mailmusic DPMM 2) (Netherlands 1988)*

PRELUDE TO TERROR *(with special envelope and graphics scroll) (The Cultural Terrorist; Mindfuck; Meltdown; Brutal Love; Highrise; Submerge; Orgasm Aid; Body Control; Final Solution; Final Moments Of 3rd Reich; The Cross On Trial) (Banned Productions) (1988)*

RED TERROR BLACK TERROR *(Let The Night Roar; Terminal Extract; Co Existance No Existance; Rockwell Rising; Rise!; Black; Disektion; Stonehenge Attack; Air Amerikkka; Drums Of Dissent; Operation Wipeout; Chaos Warped Confusion) (Strength Through Awareness) (1988)*

SUFFERANCE *(Comprises two untitled tracks) (Not On) (1988)*

CHAOS OV CREATION *(Comprises two untitled tracks) (Cold Spring CS 004) (1989)*

BLOOD ON SAND *(Comprises twelve untitled tracks) (Strength Through Awareness) (1990)*

SPASM *(Lebensborn; Class War; Decadence Dance; Anima Christi II; Sufferance; Discharde No79; Shitlife; Pure Hatred; Religion; Into Oblivion; Caring Society; Crush; Rise O Christi Corps; Bloodpulp; Savage Sex; Powerpulse) (Minus Habens MHT 01) (Italy 1991)*

INCARCERATION *(Passage Of Demons; Eternal Suffering; Disektion; The Chaos Of Creation; Lebensborn; Restraint; Fist Of Steel; Disintegration) (Slaughter Productions SPT 13) (Italy 1995)*

ALBUMS
PUNISHMENT *(Operation Ranch Hand; Klandestine AmeriKKKa; Deprivation Chamber; Blind Faith; Impulse Over Order; Destination Death; Eurofascist (Overcome With Hate); Collapse; Split Womb) (Tesco Organisation TESCO 011) (Germany 1992)*

THE AGE OF DISSENT *(Art Of The State; Crawl; Empty Threat; Destructive State; Aura Of Violence; State Of The Art; The Age Of Dissent; Skin Hunger; Low Level Transmission; New World Dis/order; Bodycount) (Tesco Organisation TESCO 024) (Germany 1995)*

CD
HOLY COMMUNION *(split live CD with Con-Dom) (includes Ready Or Not...; ...Here We Come; New Luddities; Age Of Dissent / Star Of David) (Nuit Et Brouillard NB CD 01) (France 1998)*

The Grey Wolves also appeared on numerous compilations.

CHRIS HARTFORD

COMPILATION APPEARANCE
GOD'S GREAT TAPE HEAD CLEANER *(Salisbury compilation cassette including 'Fat') (7% GGTH 1) (1991)*

THE HORIZONTAL BULGARIANS

COMPILATION APPEARANCE
'Pictures In The Rain' was possibly released on a compilation tape from Yorkshire.

HORSE LATITUDES

7" SINGLE
Solo 015 Side A - European Nights (P) Solar Sound Ltd. Side B - Run, Run, Run (P) Solar Sound Ltd.

JANE FROM OCCUPIED EUROPE

CASSETTE
JANE FROM OCCUPIED EUROPE *(Just Like Holden Caulfield; Love Lies Killed; Blue Boar Row; She Comes Tomorrow) (1988)*

7" SINGLE

Ocean Run Dry/Annabel Lee; Kingdom By The Sea *(7% JANE 001) (Picture Cover) (1989)*

12" SINGLE

Little Valley Town; Parade/Walking Around; Horizons In Blue *(7% JANE 1202) (Picture Cover with free 'Roachomatic' postcard) (1990)*

ALBUM

COLOURSOUND *(Mourning Glass; Parade; Drift 13; Loss; Trash-A303; God's Sonic Telephone; Obsession; Synaesthesia) (7% JANE 003) (With free poster) (1991)*

COMPILATION APPEARANCES

MIT SONNENSCHIRMEN FINGEN WIR DEN BLÜTENZAUBER *(LP including 'Just Like Holden Caulfield' Frischluft Tonträger FRL 002) (Germany 1989)*

HEOL *(Cassette including 'Untitled') (Heol Records) (Germany c1991)*

JERUSALEM

SINGLE

Kamakazi Moth/Frustration *(Deram DM 358) (1972)*

ALBUM

JERUSALEM *(Frustration; Hooded Eagle; I See The Light; Murderers Lament; When The Wolf Sits; Midnight Steamer; Primitive Man; Beyond The Grave; She Came Like A Bat From Hell (Deram SDL 6) (1972)*

CD

The Jerusalem album was reissued in the USA in 2008 by Rockadrome *(Vintage ROCK014-V-2)* with the following additional tracks: Kamakazi Moth; Primitive Man (demo version); Beyond The Grave (demo version); Hooded Eagle (single version); I See The Light (mono version)

THE KITCHENS

7" SINGLE

The Death Of Rock'n'Roll/Lies; 'A' Bomb *(Red Square Records RS 001) (Picture Cover) (1979)*

MAD COW DISEASE

12" EP

SELECTIVE MORALITY *(Thrills And Disease (Remix)/ Brown (Morality Mix); Bullshit Acres) (Catalina CATL 60026) (Picture Cover) (1994)*

CD EPs

COSTERMONGERIN' *(Jesus Wants Me For a Vegetable; Body Bag; Slop; Master Of The Universe) (Catalina CATL 60012) (Picture Cover) (1992)*

SELECTIVE MORALITY *(Thrills And Disease (Remix); Brown (Morality Mix); Bullshit Acres) (Catalina CATL 60022) (Picture Cover) (1994)*

ALBUMS

GOAT LUNG (THE MEXICAN APPROACH) *(Brown; Sin Song; Meat; Iron; Symptoms; Jesus Wants Me For a Vegetable (Damascene Conversion Mix); Genital Torture; Decomposition; Sky Burial; Thrills And Disease) (CD has additional 'hidden' track: Jesus Wants Me For a Vegetable (Countrified Version)) (Catalina 10012) (1993)*

TANTRIC SEX DISCO *(My Death Squad; Craw; As Good A Place As Any; Goat Sucker; Exit; White Dove; The Annie Leibovitz Version; Keep Smiling; Elevator; Unicycle; Plague Song; The Epic Departure) (Catalina 118052) (1995)*

MASON

SINGLES

When Freedom Comes/It's All Gone Wrong *(Pye 7N 45231) (1973)*
Fading/It's Alright *(Dawn DNS 1040) (1973)*
Follow Me/Peacefully *(Antic K 11505) (1974)*

UNRELEASED ALBUM

STARTING AS WE MEAN TO GO ON *(Fading; Don't You Ever Change Your Mind; To 50 From 45; Love's Evening Song; Lordy; Rise With The Morning; J'Ann Here Is A Song; 48 Now To Each Day; It Was Me Who Left Her; My Country Home; You've Gotta Get Up) (Dawn DNLS 3050) (1973)*

CD

The Mason album was finally released on Cherry Tree *(CRTREE008)* in 2010, with the eleven tracks listed above plus three more: When Freedom Comes; It's All Gone Wrong; It's Alright.

PETER MASON

7" SINGLES

Rock 'n' Roll *(Look What You've Done To My Life)/Me And Clancy (CBS) (Germany) (1980)*
Bergen Blue Eyes/Easier Said Than Done *(Slager Records HS 138) (Picture Cover) (Norway 1989)*

CD SINGLE

Walking On A Tightrope; Lorraine *(Salisbury Sound Records) (1998)*

THE MAYFIELDS

7" SINGLES

All You Ever Say *(Track on split flexidisc with The Badgeman) (Compact & Bijou C&B 001) (Picture Cover) (1988)*
Deeper Than The Ocean/Feels Like Yesterday *(Bus Stop BUS 005) (Picture Cover) (1989)*
World Of Your Own/Call My Name *(Ambition AMB 001) (Picture Cover) (1989)*

CASSETTE

MAY THE FIRST *(Call My Name; Out To Sea; I Don't Dream) (Home produced cassette with colour inlay) (c1987)*

COMPILATION APPEARANCES

OUT OF THE BLUE *(Cassette including 'I Don't Dream' and 'Rain-Bird')*
ARE YOU READY? *(Cassette including 'I Don't Think So')*
SOMETHING BURNING IN PARADISE *(Cassette including 'Seasons Pass')*
POSITIVELY TEENAGE!! *(Cassette including 'Out to Sea' and 'World of Your Own')*
EVERLASTING HAPPINESS *(Cassette including 'Seasons Pass' and 'I Don't Dream')*
GOD'S GREAT TAPE HEAD CLEANER *(Salisbury compilation cassette including 'Private Universe') (7% GGTH 1) (1991)*

THE MEN OF THE DOOMSBURY LIFEBOAT

7" SINGLE

Goodnight Roxy

MERCEDEZ

CASSETTE
THE BREAK *(Too Much; Women Of My Dreams; Reactionary Situation)* (1983)

THE MIDNITE RAMBLERS

ALBUM
THE MIDNITE RAMBLERS *(Love Of The Common People; Streets Of Baltimore; Teach Your Children; Anne; Send Tomorrow To The Moon; Cotton Jenny; Sundown; Kentucky Woman; Ride Me Down Easy; Ruby; Shelley's Winter Love)*

THE MORRIGAN

CD EP
WAR IN PARADISE *(Throwing It All Away; War In Paradise; The Miner's Song; Spirit Of The Soup (Live)* (1993) (Picture Cover) (NSM 1000)

CASSETTES
SPIRIT OF THE SOUP *(Cold Haily Windy Night, Fingal's Cave/Spirit of the Soup; TurtleDove; Executioner's Song; Off The Rails; Agincourt; Cold Blows The Wind; Silent Seasons; Dribbles of Brandy-Johnny Get Brose; The Great Sun)* (1985) (Reissued on vinyl in Spain (circa 1996) and on CD in 1999 (English Garden ENG1023CD))
WRECKERS *(The Miller's Dance; Yarrow; The Wreckers; Banks Of Green Willow; Cold Haily Windy Night-Drowsy Maggie; The Agincourt Carol-La Rotta; Cold Blows The Wind; Wheels Turning; When The Rain Comes Down; Dark Girl Dressed In Blue; The Doubting Page)* (1996) (Reissued on CD in 1996) (English Garden ENG 1018CD)

ALBUM
THE MORRIGAN RIDES OUT *(The Morrigan Rides Out; Night Comes Closer; The Rakes of Kildare-Bedtime Stories; The Black Nag; Girls Will You Take Him-Four Times Over; The Well Below The Valley; Buskett's Folly; Corpus Christi; Tom O'Bedlam-Allemande* (NSM) (1990) (Reissued on CD in 1997 with extra track: Well Below The Valley) (English Garden ENG1024CD)

CDs
MASQUE *(Masque; Dever The Dancer; Blarney Pilgrim; Moonghost; Merrily Kissed The Quaker's Wife; The Traveller; Dribbles Of Brandy; The Lykewake Dirge; The Demon Lover; She Moved Through The Fair* (1998) (English Garden ENG 1021CD)

MR ICE

CD EP
HAVE AN ICE DAY *(Hot Breath; Poor Little Rich Kid; Women And Love; More Than A Pretty Face; Boyz Will Be Boyz; Young, Bad And No Good)* (1990)

CDs
MR ICE *(Billed as a 'new' Tokyo Blade release, this included all the tracks from the 'Have An Ice Day' EP)* (Zoom Club CD ZCRCD6) (1998)
THE NIGHT BEFORE *(This Tokyo Blade compilation again included all the tracks from the EP)* (Zoom Club ZCRCD7) (1998)

COMPILATION APPEARANCE
UNBROKEN METAL *(CD including 'Sting In The Tail (Demo)') (Unbroken Metal)* (1998)

MRS TAYLOR'S MAD

CASSETTE
BRAIN DRAIN *(with booklet) (tracks included: Fat Bastard On A Motorbike)* (1985)

THE NUTHINS

7" SINGLES AND EPs
Allergic Kiss/Colour Trip *(Merry Go Round MERRY 2) (Picture Cover)* (1992)
MODESTY BLAIZE *(EP) (Modesty Blaize; Ain't Gonna Miss Ya!/Paid The Price; Alternative Medicine) (Dionysus ID 074556) (Picture Cover)* (1994)
CEMETERY CHEMISTRY *(EP) (Cemetery Chemistry; Missing Link/Ages (I've Been Waiting); You're To Blame) (For Monsters FMR 005) (Picture Cover with free sticker) (Italy 1995)*
MISTAKE *(EP) (Mistake; There Must Be A Way/20/20; I Won't Deny It) (Detour DR 047) (Picture Cover - Red Vinyl)* (1996)
Thoughts And Visions/You've Got To Hide Your Love Away *(Twist 23/Lost Treasures 1) (Picture Cover)* (1999)

10" EP
THE HELLRAISERS VOL. 2 *(Split 10" EP with Maryland Cookies including: She's Gone; Girl Has Gone; Just A Man) (Rockin' Bones RON 026) (Picture Disc with Insert) (Sweden 2002)*

ALBUM
ONE STEP FORWARD *(Ain't Gonna Miss Ya; Next Of A Kin; Hey Joe; Cold As Ice; You Can't Have Me; Everyday; I Feel Fine; Why Do I Love Ya; One Step Forward; Boy Or A Girl; Shut And Close Case; Hang 9; I Scream Alone; Good Time Spot) (Twist TWIST BIG 11)* (1996)

COMPILATION APPEARANCES
MAHOI PRODUCTIONS *(7" EP including 'I Scream Alone') (Mahoi Productions MP 002) (Numbered Picture Cover) (France 1996)*
TRANSWORLD GARAGE SCENE VOL. 1: EUROPE *(LP including 'Sick And Tired') (Misty Lane MISTY 024) (Italy 1996)*
TRANSWORLD GARAGE SCENE VOL. 2: USA VS EUROPE *(LP including 'Put Down') (Misty Lane MISTY 033) (Italy 1996)*
TAKIN' A DETOUR *(Album including 'The Harder I Try') (Detour DRLP 006) (Pink Vinyl) (Detour DRCD 006) (CD)* (1996)

THE PRAMS

7" SINGLES
A's Okay/Don't Drop Any Bombs On Me *(Wabbit WWS 102S) (Picture Cover)* (1981)
How About Emee?/Cat That Walked Alone *(Wabbit WAB 7)* (1983)

ALBUM
WHAT'S THE TIME MR WOLF? *(A's Okay; Perpetual Suburbs; Hypocrite; Exploded; I'm Going Crazy; Don't Make A Fuss; Don't Drop Any Bombs On Me; Mongolia; The Sun The Sun; Mirror Mirror; Do The Pram; Twilight Hours) (Wabbit Wecords WWL 101A)* (1982)

THE PROPHECY

CASSETTE

THE PROPHECY *(Introducing Andy Wilson; Flunky Car Cloth; Butlins; Andy Wilson's Coat; Boppers Delight; Flares; Pieces Of Eight; Scenes Portraying Carvings/Andy Wilson's Job; Stoffs Wilp; Bob (Trotters Of The Pigs); Martin's Bed; Ortofon (Live); Andy Wilson's Citroen; Ballade Of The Six-Legged Millipede (Home produced cassette with black an white card inlay) (1986)*

PUSSY

SINGLE

Feline Woman/Ska Child *(Deram DM 368) (1972)*

THE QTs

7" EP

Savage In The City; Mummy Is A Wino/Yesterdays Tomorrow; Chance it *(Picture Cover) (SRTS/79/CUS 429) (1979)*

SAIGON

CD

SOUL SHAKER *(Dogs Of War; Little Queen; Bad Girl Fever; Soul Shaker; Mama Never Told Me; All I Want; In Too Deep; Ain't That A Shame; Never Had A Chance) (CD SAIG 1) (c1993)*

SARAJEVO

CD

TOMORROW IN THE HANDS OF YESTERDAY'S MAN *(Sarajevo; Tear Of Fury; Princess Of The Masquerade; Last Train Outta Town; Never Too Late For love; S.O.S.; Breakdown In Paradise (Elastic Cat CDEC2) (1993)*

SHOGUN

7" SINGLES

High In The Sky/When The Lights Go Down *(Picture Cover) (Attack ATA 913) (1986)*

Cloak And Dagger/Too Late For The Hunter *(Picture Cover) (Jet 7049) (1987)*

Voices From The Heart/ Cold Truth *(Picture Cover) (Jet 651472 7) (1987)*

12" SINGLES

Cloak And Dagger/Too Late For The Hunter; Tokyo Girl *(Picture Cover) (Red Vinyl) (Jet 12049) (1987)*

Voices From The Heart/ Cold Truth; Time Will Tell *(Picture Cover) (Jet 651472 6) (1987)*

ALBUMS

SHOGUN *(Too Much To Love; Time Will Tell; Too Late For The Hunter; TV Hero; Burning Down the Night; When The Lights Go Down; Tokyo Girl; Only The Lonely (Attack ATA 006) (1986) (reissued on CD in 1999 on Zoom Club Records with extra track: High In The Sky).*

31 DAYS *(Cloak And Dagger; Shock To The Heart; Voices From The Heart; You Are What You Are; Love Is A Game; Cold Truth; If Tomorrow Comes; Can't Live Without Your Love; First Time; Out Of Love Again) (Jet JET LP 248) (1987)*

SUICIDE KING

CASSETTE

GO GO JUICE *(Narcoboudoir; Hater; Bleed Everything; I've Chosen You Again; Doing Wrong; Like A Setting Sun; Numb; Another Plane; Season To Season; Alfie's Song) (Hourglass Music hg001cass) (1995)*

THICK DICK AND THE GREEN'EDS

CD

DUM DE DUM DE DUMB *(1999)*

TOKYO BLADE

7" SINGLES

If Heaven Is Hell/Highway Passion *(Picture Cover) (Blade Records) (1983)*

2ND CUT: Midnight Rendezvous/Mean Steak *(Picture Cover) (Blade Records) (1983)*

Powergame/Death On Main Street *(Picture Cover) (Powerstation OHM 2) (1983)*

12" SINGLES AND EPs

MIDNIGHT RENDEZVOUS EP *(Midnight Rendezvous; Mean Streak/ If Heaven Is Hell; Highway Passion) (Picture Cover) (Powerstation OHM 4T) (1984)*

Lightning Strikes/Fever; Attack Attack *(Picture Cover) (Powerstation OHM 7T) (1984)*

THE CAVE SESSIONS *(OFFICIAL BOOTLEG) EP (Shadows Of Insanity; School House Is Burnin'/Jezebel; Monkey's Blood (Picture Cover) (Powerstation LEG 1T) (1985)*

Undercover Honeymoon; Stealing The Thief/Playroom Of Poison Dreams; Bottom End *(Picture Cover) (TB BLADE 1) (1985)*

Movie Star/Tokyo City; Heartbreaker *(Picture Cover) (Areba ERA 1) (1987)*

ALBUMS

TOKYO BLADE *(Powergame; Break The Chains; If Heaven Is Hell; On Through The Night; Killer City; Liar; Tonight; Sunrise In Tokyo; Blue Ridge Mountains Of Virginia) (Powerstation LP AMP 1) (1983) (reissued on CD on Lemon CDLEM 165 in 2010 with bonus tracks: Death On Main Street; Madame Guillotine; Breakout; Love Struck; Midnight Rendezvous; Mean Streak; If Heaven Is Hell; Highway Passion; Shadows Of Insanity; School House Is Burning; Jezebel; Monkey's Blood)*

NIGHT OF THE BLADE *(Someone To Love; Night Of The Blade; Rock Me To The Limit; Warrior Of The Rising Sun; Unleash The Beast; Love Struck; Dead Of The Night; Lightning Strikes (Straight Through The Heart)) (Powerstation AMP 4) (1984) (reissued on CD on High Vaultage HV-1012 in 1997)*

WARRIOR OF THE RISING SUN *(Madame Guillotine; Fever; Night Of The Blade; Breakout; Unleash The Beast; Attack Attack; Lightning Strikes (Straight Through The Heart); Warrior Of The Rising Sun; Someone To Love; Mean Streak; If Heaven Is Hell; Break The Chains; Dead Of The Night; Powergame; Highway Passion; Midnight Rendezvous; Sunrise In Tokyo; Killer City; Liar; Death On Main Street) (Raw Power RAWLP 005) (1985)*

BLACKHEARTS AND JADED SPADES *(Dirty Faced Angels; Make It Through The Night; Always; Lovin'You Is An Easy Thing To Do; Undercover Honeymoon; You Are The Heart; Blackhearts And Jaded Spades; Tough Guys Tumble; Dancing In Blue Moonlight; Playroom Of Poison Dreams; Monkey's Blood) (TB TBR 1) (1985) (reissued on CD on Zoom Club ZCRCD 13 in the 1990s)*

AIN'T MISBEHAVIN' *(Heartbreaker; Too Much Too Soon; Watch Your Step; Movie Star; Hot For Love; Tokyo City; Love And Hate; Don't Walk Away; Ain't Misbehavin') (Scratch 805336) (1987) (reissued on CD on Jimco HMI 3002 in 1989)*

ENDLESS BEAT

NO REMORSE *(1000 Years (Intro); The Eye Of The Storm; Chains Of Love; Dark Night Over Paradise; Moonlight In Martini; 5 Inch Catwalk; Crystal Gold; Angel; Tears Are Not Enough; Shadows Of Insanity; Call Me Angel; Fever; Stop It Or Drop) (Apocalypse Records AP89 001 1) (1989) (also issued on CD (AP89 001 2)).*

A different version of this album was released in the same year and on the same label, with the same catalogue numbers, but with a different cover and less tracks ('1000 Years (Intro)', 'Dark Night Over Paradise' and 'Moonlight In Martini' having been omitted).

CDs

TOKYO BLADE *(Heartbreaker; Too Much Too Soon; Watch Your Step; Movie Star; Hot For Love; Tokyo City; Love And Hate; Don't Walk Away; Ain't Misbehavin'; 1000 Years (Intro); The Eye Of The Storm; Chains Of Love) (Laserlight 12 131).*

BURNING DOWN PARADISE *(Burning Down Paradise; Friend In Need; Flashpoint Serenade; Kickback; Wing And A Prayer; Hot Breath; Head Full Of Bad Wiring; Papering The Cracks; Get Out Of My Face; Only The Strong; Woman And Love; Dead End Kid) (SPV/Fresh Fruit SPV 085-12122) (Germany 1995)*

MR ICE *(Hot Breath; Poor Little Rich Kid; Women And Love; More Than A Pretty Face; Boyz Will Be Boyz; Young, Bad And No Good; No Resistance To Love; 1000 Nights; Passion And Emotion; One White Lie (Live Rehearsal); Young, Bad And No Good (Live Rehearsal)) (Zoom Club CD ZCRCD6) (1998)*

THE NIGHT BEFORE *(Night Of The Blade; Warrior Of The Rising Sun; Unleash The Beast; Love Struck; Attack Attack; Fever; Dead Of The Night; Breakout; Madame Guillotine; Someone To Love; Hot Breath; Poor Little Rich Kid; Women And Love; More Than A Pretty Face; Boyz Will Be Boyz; Young, Bad And No Good) (Zoom Club ZCRCD7) (1998)*

PUMPHOUSE *(Like You Not – Not; The Ultimate High; Gerald's Game; Pay The Man; Wrong Chair; It's Only Money; Character Assassination; S.O.S; All Work No Play; SNAFU; Having A Bad Day) (Zoom Club) (1998)*

BOOTLEG

ONE NIGHT IN LUDWISBURG VOL.1 *(Intro; Night Of The Blade; Someone To Love; Lightning Strikes; Guitar Solo; Fever; If Heaven Is Hell; Rock Me To The Limit; Love Struck; Dead Of The Night; Tough Guys Tumble (Recorded at Rockfabrik, Ludwisburg, West Germany, 17 March 1985)*

TOUCANTANGO

CASSETTES

MINUTES LATER... *(Crush My Hip; Spirits; I Know, You Know) (1984)*
TOUCANTANGO *(Get That Feeling; Crush My Hip; Change Of Heart; Confusion; Hand In Hand; Too Good To Be True; On Broadway / Turn It Up; Spirits; Is This Love; Taking Over My Feet; Can't Stop Dancing (I Know, You Know); I Know, You Know (Reprise)) (TCA 01) (1984)*

NIKI TRUE

7" SINGLE

Too Much/Woman Of My Dreams *(Sad Frog) (1983)*

UNHEALTHY FIXATION

COMPILATION APPEARANCE

GOD'S GREAT TAPE HEAD CLEANER *(Salisbury compilation cassette including 'King of The Hippies') (7% GGTH 1) (1991)*

VISITING ACTS

Material from **David Bowie's** set at Salisbury City Hall on 14 June 1973 was issued on the bootleg CD **'Quaaludes and Red Wine'**.

Material from **Hawkwind's** set at the Stonehenge Free Festival in 1976 was issued on the bootleg LP **'Live At The Watchfield And Stonehenge Festivals 1976'**.

Material from **Hawkwind's** set at the Stonehenge Free Festival in 1984 was issued on a 12" EP issued with the LP **'This Is Hawkwind, Do Not Panic'** *(Flicknife SHARP 022) (reissued on CD by Cleopatra in 2002)*

Material from **The Cardiacs'** set at Salisbury Arts Centre on 30 June 1990 was issued on the CD **'All That Glitter's Is A Mare's Nest'** *(Alphabet Business Concern ALPH CD 018).*

Appendix 3
Videography

This videography concentrates on film recorded between 1970 and 1999 and released on either VHS or DVD (where there has been a straight DVD reissue the original VHS details are not noted). Any additions or corrections would be gratefully received.

The DDDBM&T DVDs feature a vast number of clips (45 and 16 respectively) of the band appearing on various UK and European TV shows. There is a limited amount of duplication but they are both worth getting hold of. Although mainly covering the 1960s, each disc also contains some later DBM&T and Dave Dee solo material.

DAVE DEE, DOZY, BEAKY, MICK AND TICH
GREATEST HITS *(DVD) (BR Music BD 3010-9) (Holland 2003)*
Includes 'Staying With It' (from 'The Rod and Emu Show' 1984)

DAVE DEE
RENTADICK *(DVD) (Network DVD)*
Dave Dee recorded the theme song to this 1972 film with **The Kings Singers**.

DAVE DEE, DOZY, BEAKY, MICK AND TICH: GREATEST HITS *(DVD) (BR Music BD 3010-9) (Holland 2003)*
Includes 'My Woman's Man' (two versions, from 'Top Of The Pops' 1970 and 'Disco' 1971) and 'Wedding Bells' (from 'Disco' 1971)

DAVE DEE, DOZY, BEAKY, MICK AND TICH: THE LEGEND OF XANADU *(DVD) (Universal 982 948-8) (Holland 2005)*
Includes 'The Windmills Of Your Mind' (from 'Meet Judith Durham' 1970), 'My Woman's Man' (from 'Disco' 1971) and 'Wedding Bells' (from 'Disco' 1971)

DOZY, BEAKY, MICK AND TICH (aka DBM&T)
DAVE DEE, DOZY, BEAKY, MICK AND TICH: GREATEST HITS *(DVD) (BR Music BD 3010-9) (Holland 2003)*
Includes 'You've Got Me On The Run' (from 'Disco' 1980)

TOKYO BLADE
LIVE AT THE CAMDEN PALACE *(DVD) (Magada International) (2005)*

VISITING ACTS

THE CARDIACS
A Cardiacs concert filmed at Salisbury Arts Centre on 30 June 1990 was issued on VHS as 'All That Glitter's Is A Mare's Nest' (Alphabet Business Concern).

HAWKWIND
In 2004, the Hawks' set from the 1984 Stonehenge Free Festival was issued on DVD by Cherry Red as 'Hawkwind: The Solstice At Stonehenge 1984.

NAPALM DEATH
A Napalm Death concert was filmed at Salisbury Arts Centre on the same date as The Cardiacs - 30 June 1990 and issued later that year on videocassette as 'Live Corruption' (Fotodisk LFV 115). In 2001 the footage appeared on a compilation DVD 'Napalm Death: The DVD' (Earache). As well as looking for themselves in the brief glimpses of the moshpit, Salisbury punters might enjoy the inter-song interviews with the band, filmed in the grounds of the venue.

STONEHENGE FESTIVAL
In 1989, parts of the sets performed by Roy Harper, Hawkwind and The Enid at the 1984 festival were issued on VHS (Jettisoundz JE 134).

The 1984 festival was also subject of the 'Stonehenge 1984: A Midsummer Night Rock Show' DVD issued in 2009 (Voiceprint VPDD 50). This featured different footage of the same three acts plus part of the set performed by Here & Now and a short documentary, Where Have All The Crusties Gone?

Appendix 4
Concerts

This is an attempt at a list of all of the 'pop' or 'rock' shows at Salisbury's four main venues during the period covered by our book - the City Hall, the Alex Disco, the College of Technology and The Arts Centre, plus a few interesting gigs from smaller venues such as The Grange Hotel and The Fisherton Arms, as well as the acts that appeared at the Stonehenge and Larmer Tree Festivals.

We would not be confident enough to claim it is complete, but we believe it is close to being so and, as far as we know, this is the most comprehensive list of this information that has ever been published. We have only included the shows where we are confident of having established the correct date, so some of those mentioned within the main text of the book are not actually listed here. Any additions or corrections would be gratefully received.

1970

Saturday 10 January 1970
Alex Disco
Savoy Brown Blues Band

Saturday 17 January 1970
Alex Disco
Steamhammer

Saturday 24 January 1970
Alex Disco
Chicken Shack

Friday 30 January 1970
College of Technology
McArthur's Park; The Five Degrees

Saturday 31 January 1970
Alex Disco
Sir Percy Quintet

Saturday 7 February 1970
Alex Disco
Manfred Mann Chapter III

Saturday 14 February 1970
Alex Disco
Shy Limbs

Saturday 28 February 1970
Alex Disco
The Keef Hartley Band

Saturday 7 March 1970
Alex Disco
Egg

Saturday 14 March 1970
Alex Disco
Chicken Shack

Friday 20 March 1970
College of Technology
Uriah Heep

Saturday 21 March 1970
Alex Disco
Juicy Lucy

Saturday 21 March 1970
City Hall
Jelly Bread; Wedgwood Wing; The Night People

Saturday 28 March 1970
Alex Disco
Yes

Saturday 4 April 1970
Alex Disco
High Tide

Friday 10 April 1970
College of Technology
Aardvark

Saturday 11 April 1970
Alex Disco
Caravan

Saturday 18 April 1970
Alex Disco
Mandrake

Saturday 25 April 1970
Alex Disco
Procol Harum

Friday 1 May 1970
College of Technology
Mighty Baby

Saturday 2 May 1970
Alex Disco
Steamhammer

Saturday 9 May 1970
Alex Disco
The Greatest Show On Earth

Saturday 16 May 1970
Alex Disco
Black Sabbath

Friday 22 May 1970
Salisbury College of Technology
Uriah Heep

Saturday 23 May 1970
Alex Disco
James Litherland's Brotherhood

Saturday 30 May 1970
Alex Disco
Keef Hartley

Saturday 6 June 1970
Alex Disco
Edison Lighthouse

Saturday 13 June 1970
Alex Disco
Savoy Brown

Saturday 20 June 1970
Alex Disco
Caravan

Saturday 4 July 1970
Alex Disco
Flaming Youth

Friday 10 July 1970
College of Technology
Image

Saturday 11 July 1970
Alex Disco
Uriah Heep

Friday 17 July 1970
College of Technology
Gypsy; Bethany

Saturday 18 July 1970
Alex Disco
Heaven

Saturday 25 July 1970
Alex Disco
US Flattop and The Travelling Band

Saturday 1 August 1970
Alex Disco
Skid Row

Saturday 8 August 1970
Alex Disco
Merlin Q

Saturday 15 August 1970
Alex Disco
Shy Limbs

Saturday 22 August 1970
Alex Disco
Elias

Saturday 29 August 1970
Alex Disco
Root and Jenny Jackson

Saturday 12 September 1970
Alex Disco
The Greatest Show On Earth

Friday 18 September 1970
Alex Disco
Stackwaddy; Ian Davis; Marble Orchard; Wedgwood Wing 'plus many friends'

Saturday 19 September 1970
Alex Disco
Orange Air

Friday 25 September 1970
College of Technology
Raw Material; Slipped Disk; Mike Rogerson-Smith

Friday 25 September 1970
City Hall
Caravan; Trevor Billmuss;
Jackson Heights

Saturday 26 September 1970
Alex Disco
Elkie Brooks and Da Da

Friday 2 October 1970
Alex Disco
Country Club Four

Saturday 3 October 1970
Alex Disco
Megatun Flea

Saturday 10 October 1970
Alex Disco
Aardvark

Saturday 10 October 1970
City Hall
River Bottom Band; September Tree

Saturday 17 October 1970
Alex Disco
Warm Dust

Saturday 24 October 1970
City Hall
Folksouth 70 (Folksong, dance and music festival)

Saturday 31 October 1970
Alex Disco
Gentle Giant

Friday 6 November 1970
College of Technology
Jigsaw; Johnny Diamond

Saturday 7 November 1970
Alex Disco
Shy Limbs

Saturday 14 November 1970
Alex Disco
Dando Shaft

Saturday 21 November 1970
Alex Disco
Marjorine

Tuesday 24 November 1970
City Hall
Mick Abrahams' Band; Jeff Dexter's Sounds; Strife

Saturday 28 November 1970
Alex Disco
Merlin Q

Saturday 5 December 1970
Alex Disco
US Flattop and The Travelling Band

Saturday 12 December 1970
Alex Disco
Killing Floor

Monday 14 December 1970
Alex Disco
Jerusalem; Worth

Thursday 17 December 1970
College of Technology
Heaven; Generation

Friday 18 December 1970
City Hall
Dave Dee and David; Bethany; Five Degrees

Saturday 19 December 1970
Alex Disco
Windmill

Thursday 24 December 1970
Alex Disco
Everyday People

Saturday 26 December 1970
Alex Disco
Birth

1971

Saturday 9 January 1971
Alex Disco
Shy Limbs

Saturday 16 January 1971
Alex Disco
The Equators

Saturday 23 January 1971
Alex Disco
Genesis Creation

Friday 29 January 1971
College of Technology
Image

Saturday 30 January 1971
Alex Disco
Goliath

Friday 5 February 1971
College of Technology
Bliss with Bram Stoker; Brownhill Stamp Duty

Saturday 6 February 1971
Alex Disco
Kansas Hook

Thursday 11 February 1971
College of Technology
Stray

Saturday 13 February 1971
Alex Disco
Skid Row

Saturday 20 February 1971
Alex Disco
Warm Dust

Saturday 27 February 1971
Alex Disco
Cupid's Inspiration

Saturday 6 March 1971
Alex Disco
Everyday People

Friday 12 March 1971
College of Technology
Jerusalem; Winter In A White Dress

Saturday 13 March 1971
Alex Disco
Joyce Bond Review

Thursday 18 March 1971
College of Technology
Alan Bown; Aubrey Small; Mushroom

Saturday 20 March 1971
Alex Disco
Ashton, Gardner and Dyke

Saturday 27 March 1971
Alex Disco
Madrigal

Friday 2 April 1971
College of Technology
Satisfaction; Marble Orchard

Saturday 3 April 1971
Alex Disco
The Perishers

Saturday 10 April 1971
Alex Disco
Kansas Hook

Saturday 17 April 1971
Alex Disco
US Flat Top and The Equators

Saturday 24 April 1971
Alex Disco
Pebbles

Saturday 1 May 1971
Alex Disco
Orange Air

Saturday 8 May 1971
Alex Disco
Genesis Creation

Saturday 22 May 1971
Alex Disco
Madrigal

Saturday 29 May 1971
Alex Disco
Marjorine

Tuesday 1 June 1971
City Hall
The Pretty Things; The Pink Fairies

Saturday 5 June 1971
Alex Disco
Chancery Lane

Tuesday 8 June 1971
Alex Disco
Mick Abrahams Band

Wednesday 10 June 1971
Alex Disco
John Peel; Image

Saturday 12 June 1971
Alex Disco
Killing Floor

Saturday 19 June 1971
Alex Disco
Shy Limbs

Saturday 26 June 1971
Alex Disco
Thin Lizzy

Saturday 3 July 1971
Alex Disco
Felix

Friday 9 July 1971
Alex Disco
Time Dynasty

ENDLESS BEAT

Saturday 10 July 1971
Alex Disco
Hurricane Smith

Sunday 11 July 1971
Alex Disco
Uriah Heep

Thursday 15 July 1971
City Hall
Steamhammer; Smiling Hard; Spinning Wheels Disco

Saturday 24 July 1971
Alex Disco
Macaroni

Saturday 31 July 1971
Alex Disco
Warm Dust

Saturday 7 August 1971
Alex Disco
Bell and Arc

Saturday 14 August 1971
Alex Disco
Quiver

Saturday 21 August 1971
Alex Disco
Stackridge

Saturday 28 August 1971
Alex Disco
Pebbles

Saturday 4 September 1971
Alex Disco
Madrigal

Friday 10 September 1971
City Hall
The Premiers; Midnite Ramblers

Saturday 11 September 1971
Alex Disco
Lindisfarne

Saturday 18 September 1971
Alex Disco
Gift

Saturday 25 September 1971
Alex Disco
Cupid's Inspiration

30 September 1971
City Hall
Rory Gallagher; Period

Saturday 2 October 1971
Alex Disco
Paul Brett's Sage

Saturday 9 October 1971
Alex Disco
Quiver

Saturday 16 October 1971
Alex Disco
Joyce Bond Review

Monday 18 October 1971
Alex Disco
King G Boss; Laurel Aitken

Saturday 30 October 1971
Alex Disco
The Red River Band

Monday 1 November 1971
Alex Disco
King G Boss, Laurel Aitken

Saturday 6 November 1971
Alex Disco
Shy Limbs

Sunday 7 November 1971
City Hall
Van Der Graaf Generator; Genesis

Saturday 13 November 1971
Alex Disco
Felix

Saturday 20 November 1971
Alex Disco
US Flat Top and The Matumbi

Saturday 4 December 1971
Alex Disco
Finian's Rainbow

Saturday 11 December 1971
Alex Disco
Chancery Lane

Wednesday 15 December 1971
City Hall
Led Zeppelin

NB: Cancelled and rescheduled for 21 December 1971 due to Jimmy Page being ill, although the scheduled support acts Marble Orchard and Jerusalem still played.

Saturday 18 December 1971
Alex Disco
Slade

Tuesday 21 December 1971
City Hall
Led Zeppelin

NB: Rescheduled from 15 December 1971.

Friday 24 December 1971
Alex Disco
Yorubas Merchant

Monday 27 December 1971
Alex Disco
Geer

1972

Saturday 1 January 1972
Alex Disco
Stackridge

Wednesday 5 January 1972
Alex Disco
The Delroy Williams Show

Friday 14 January 1972
Alex Disco
Atomic Rooster; Nazareth

Saturday 22 January 1972
Alex Disco
Portrait

Friday 28 January 1972
Alex Disco
Ellis

Saturday 29 January 1972
Alex Disco
Lindisfarne

Tuesday 8 February 1972
City Hall
Status Quo; Paul Brett's Sage

Saturday 12 February 1972
Alex Disco
Patto

Wednesday 16 February 1972
City Hall
Free

Saturday 19 February 1972
Alex Disco
Genesis

Saturday 26 February 1972
Alex Disco
US Flattop

Saturday 4 March 1972
Alex Disco
The Sensations

Saturday 11 March 1972
Alex Disco
Pebbles

Saturday 18 March 1972
Alex Disco
Yorubas Merchant

Saturday 25 March 1972
Alex Disco
Gift

Saturday 1 April 1972
Alex Disco
Love Affair

Saturday 8 April 1972
Alex Disco
Noel and The Fireballs

Friday 14 April 1972
College of Technology
Silverhead

Friday 14 April 1972
City Hall
The Embers; The Five West Brothers

Saturday 15 April 1972
Alex Disco
Portrait

Wednesday 19 April 1972
City Hall
Wishbone Ash; Cast Iron

Saturday 22 April 1972
Alex Disco
Madrigal

Wednesday 26 April 1972
Alex Disco
The Equators

Friday 5 May 1972
City Hall
The Swinging Blue Jeans; The Country Club Four; The Rain

Saturday 6 May 1972
Alex Disco
The Matumbis

Saturday 13 May 1972
Alex Disco
Stackridge

Saturday 20 May 1972
Alex Disco
Skid Row

Tuesday 23 May 1972
City Hall
Uriah Heep; Mike Maran

Friday 26 May 1972
Cit Hall
Grant's Tomb; The Midnight Ramblers

Saturday 27 May 1972
Alex Disco
The Del-Hems

Friday 2 June 1972
Alex Disco
The Country Club Four

Saturday 3 June 1972
Alex Disco
Rock And Roll All Stars

Thursday 8 June 1972
City Hall
Jerusalem; Silverhead

Saturday 10 June 1972
Alex Disco
US Flattop and The Dynamics

Saturday 17 June 1972
Alex Disco
Capability Brown

Friday 23 June 1972
City Hall
Asquard; Marble Orchard

Saturday 24 June 1972
Alex Disco
Van Der Graaf Generator

Friday 30 June 1972
City Hall
The Premiers; The Country Club Four; Logie

Saturday 1 July 1972
Alex Disco
Hackensack

Saturday 8 July 1972
Alex Disco
East Of Eden

Friday 14 July 1972
City Hall
Savoy Brown; Roxy Music

Saturday 15 July 1972
Alex Disco
Vinegar Joe

Saturday 22 July 1972
Alex Disco
Genesis

Friday 28 July 1972
City Hall
The Bay City Rollers; Cliff Bennett; The Country Club Four

Saturday 29 July 1972
Alex Disco
Stray

Friday 4 August 1972
Alex Disco
Amazing Blondel; Hoedown; The Premiers

Saturday 5 August 1972
Alex Disco
Felix

Saturday 12 August 1972
Alex Disco
String Driven Thing

Saturday 12 August 1972
City Hall
Desmond Dekker; Mustard

Friday 18 August 1972
City Hall
East Of Eden

Saturday 19 August 1972
Alex Disco
Sunshine

Friday 25 August 1972
City Hall
Gary Glitter; Paul Brent and Mike Piggott

Saturday 26 August 1972
Alex Disco
FleshSaturday 2 September 1972
Alex Disco
Stackridge

Saturday 16 September 1972
Alex Disco
Aphrodite

Friday 22 September 1972
College of Technology
Quicksand; Music Machine

Saturday 23 September 1972
Alex Disco
The Red River Band

Monday 25 September 1972
City Hall
Arthur Brown's Kingdom Come; Hackensack

Saturday 30 September 1972
Alex Disco
Silverhead

Saturday 7 October 1972
Alex Disco
Demick Armstrong

Thursday 12 October 1972
City Hall
Lynx; Grandma Moses; Straw Dogs; John Brocklehurst

Saturday 14 October 1972
Alex Disco
Finian's Rainbow

Friday 20 October 1972
College of Technology
Blue; Foxey

Friday 27 October 1972
City Hall
Stackridge; Roy Young Band

Saturday 28 October 1972
Alex Disco
Madrigal

Saturday 4 November 1972
Alex Disco
Brian Auger's Oblivion Express

Saturday 11 November 1972
Alex Disco
Genesis

Saturday 18 November 1972
Alex Disco
West Coast Consortium

Saturday 25 November 1972
Alex Disco
Hobnail

Saturday 9 December 1972
Alex Disco
Snake Eye

Friday 15 December 1972
College of Technology
Quiver; Havana Boys Steel Band

Saturday 16 December 1972
Alex Disco
Flesh

Saturday 23 December 1972
Alex Disco
Raw Material

Friday 29 December 1972
City Hall
Love Affair; The Debonaires

Saturday 30 December 1972
Alex Disco
Rescue Co No 1

1973

Friday 12 January 1973
College of Technology
The Pink Fairies; Grandma Moses

Saturday 13 January 1973
Alex Disco
East Of Eden

Saturday 20 January 1973
Alex Disco
Blind Harvest

Friday 26 January 1973
City Hall
Blackfoot Sue

Saturday 10 February 1973
Alex Disco
Capability Brown

Saturday 10 February 1973
St Martins Church Hall
Slack Alice; Andy Sheppard

Thursday 15 February 1973
City Hall
Savoy Brown; Hemlock; Holy Mackle

Friday 16 February 1973
City Hall
The Swinging Blue Jeans

Saturday 17 February 1973
Alex Disco
Madrigal

Saturday 24 February 1973
Alex Disco
Emperor Rosco

Saturday 3 March 1973
Alex Disco
String Driven Thing

ENDLESS BEAT

Saturday 10 March 1973
Alex Disco
Pussy

Thursday 15 March 1973
City Hall
Jazz Festival: Terry Lightfoot;
Johnny Lawrence and His Band;
The Dixielanders

Saturday 17 March 1973
Alex Disco
US Flattop and The Dynamics

Saturday 24 March 1973
Alex Disco
Blind Harvest

Thursday 29 March 1973
City Hall
The Sweet

NB: Cancelled due to Brian
Connolly
being ill. Rescheduled for 26
April 1973.

Saturday 31 March 1973
Alex Disco
Budgie

Saturday 7 April 1973
Alex Disco
Jo'berg Hawk

Saturday 21 April 1973
Alex Disco
Whispering Wind

Thursday 26 April 1973
City Hall
The Sweet

NB: Rescheduled from 29 March
1973

Saturday 28 April 1973
Alex Disco
Brinsley Schwarz

Thursday 3 May 1973
City Hall
Blackfoot Sue; Quicksand; Rufus

Friday 4 May 1973
City Hall
Chicory Tip; The Fairground; The
Premiers

Saturday 5 May 1973
Alex Disco
Ramrod

Saturday 19 May 1973
Alex Disco
Greyhound

Saturday 26 May 1973
Alex Disco
Sam Apple Pie

Wednesday 30 May 1973
City Hall
Nazareth; Robin Trower

Friday 1 June 1973
City Hall
Grandma Moses; Anywayn

Wednesday 6 June 1973
City Hall
The Spinners

Saturday 9 June 1973
Alex Disco
Redhead

Thursday 14 June 1973
City Hall
David Bowie

Saturday 16 June 1973
Alex Disco
Blackfoot Sue

Saturday 23 June 1973
Alex Disco
Blind Harvest

Friday 29 June 1973
City Hall
Heinz and The Wild Boys; Bob Jams
and His Music; Frogmore

Saturday 30 June 1973
Alex Disco
Muggwump

Wednesday 4 July 1973
City Hall
JSD Band; John St Field

Saturday 7 July 1973
Alex Disco
Back Door

Saturday 14 July 1973
Alex Disco
Whispering Wind

Tuesday 17 July 1973
City Hall
Man; John St Field

Friday 20 July 1973
City Hall
Chris Barber and His Band;
Theodore Watkins

Saturday 21 July 1973
Alex Disco
Felix

Saturday 28 July 1973
Alex Disco
Pebbles

Friday 3 August 1973
Alex Disco
Randy Andy's Women; Jenny
Lynn; Slack Alice

Saturday 4 August 1973
Alex Disco
Necromandus

Friday 10 August 1973
City Hall
Now

Saturday 11 August 1973
Alex Disco
String Driven Thing

Friday 17 August 1973
Alex Disco
Wanky Doodle's Women; Jenny
Lynn

Saturday 18 August 1973
Alex Disco
Bees Make Honey

Friday 24 August 1973
City Hall
Edison Lighthouse; Twilight
Zone;
The Premiers

Saturday 25 August 1973
Alex Disco
Budgie

Saturday 1 September 1973
Alex Disco
Jack The Lad

Friday 7 September 1973
Alex Disco
The Midnite Ramblers; Theodore
Watkins

Saturday 8 September 1973
Alex Disco
Hookfoot

Friday 14 September 1973
City Hall
Christie; Fairground; Kestrel
Show Band

Saturday 15 September 1973
Alex Disco
Brinsley Schwarz

Friday 21 September 1973
City Hall
Acker Bilk; Adge Cutler and The
Wurzels

Saturday 22 September 1973
Alex Disco
Judas Priest

Saturday 29 September 1973
Alex Disco
Budgie

Saturday 6 October 1973
Alex Disco
Mason

Saturday 20 October 1973
Alex Disco
Madrigal

Saturday 27 October 1973
Alex Disco
Contraband

Friday 2 November 1973
Alex Disco
Country Club Four; Dinger Dell

Saturday 3 November 1973
Alex Disco
Whispering Wind

Friday 9 November 1973
Alex Disco
The Penny Arcade

Saturday 17 November 1973
Alex Disco
Smith

Saturday 24 November 1973
Alex Disco
Performance

Saturday 6 December 1973
Alex Disco
Kilburn and The High Roads

Tuesday 11 December 1973
City Hall
The Sensational Alex
Harvey Band

Friday 14 December 1973
College of Technology
Greenslade; Mason; Kanz

Saturday 15 December 1973
Alex Disco
Back Door

Monday 17 December 1973
Alex Disco
The Debonaires

Thursday 20 December 1973
City Hall
The Dave Gearing Showband;
Country Club Four; Dinger Dell

Saturday 22 December 1973
Alex Disco
Wild Angels

1974

Saturday 12 January 1974
Alex Disco
Paul Young's Paradox

Saturday 19 January 1974
Alex Disco
Dr Marigolds

Friday 25 January 1974
Alex Disco
Force 5; Dinger Dell

Saturday 26 January 1974
Alex Disco
Mandarin Kraze

Saturday 9 February 1974
Alex Disco
Jack The Lad

Saturday 16 February 1974
Alex Disco
DJ Nigh: Mick C International Roadshow

Thursday 21 February 1974
City Hall
Bandbox Ball: The Avonaires;
The Country Club Four; The
Dave Charles Sound;
Jenny Lyn; The Merry Macs;
Theodore Watkins

Saturday 23 February 1974
Alex Disco
Blind Harvest

Friday 1 March 1974
City Hall
The Premiers; The Midnite Ramblers

Saturday 2 March 1974
Alex Disco
Embers

Thursday 7 March 1974
Alex Disco
Gas Works; Ansazan

Friday 8 March 1974
College of Technology
John St Field; Andy Sheppard

Saturday 16 March 1974
Alex Disco
Chateau

Saturday 23 March 1974
Alex Disco
All In The Mind

NB: This was the last gig at The Alex.

Wednesday 27 March 1974
College of Technology
Merlin Lynx

Friday 5 April 1974
College of Techology
Global Village Trucking Co

Wednesday 10 April 1974
City Hall
The Swinging Blue Jeans; The
Dave Woodbury Four; Dinger Dell

Thursday 18 April 1974
City Hall
Theodore Watkins; City Hall

Wednesday 5 June 1974
Playhouse
Quadrophonic rock record
'concert' featuring Pink Floyd's
Dark Side Of The Moon

NB: Not a live show but an interesting experiment in presenting the new technology.

Thursday 20 June 1974
George Hotel, Amesbury
Sharks; Never Bend Over

June 1974
Stonehenge Free Festival
Zorch; Basil Brookes.

Friday 19 July 1974
City Hall
The Johnnie Walker Road Show;
Samura Khan; Crystal;The
Sounds of Mr Kazoon

Friday 26 July 1974
College of Technology
Andahma

Wednesday 31 July 1974
City Hall
The Debonaires; The Associates;
Peacewave

Wednesday 21 August 1974
City Hall
Tangerine Dream

Monday 9 September 1974
Playhouse
An evening of quadrophonic sound:
Mike Oldfield's Tubular Bells

NB: Another playing of an album as opposed to a live show.

Friday 27 September 1974
City Hall
Love Affair; The Country Club Four;
The Merry Macs

Friday 4 October 1974
College of Technology
Steve Tilston; Andy Sheppard;
Nigel Evans

Tuesday 5 November 1974
City Hall
Leo Sayer

Friday 6 December 1974
City Hall
Alex Welsh and His Band; Penny Arcade

Wednesday 11 December 1974
City Hall
Ray McVay and His Orchestra;
The Premiers

Monday 16 December 1974
City Hall
The Premiers; The Night Hawk;
The Phantom Pholk

1975

Wednesday 22 January 1975
City Hall
Barclay James Harvest;
Julian Brook

Thursday 20 March 1975
City Hall
Band Box Ball:
Asterisk; Associates;
Force Five; Peacewave;
Theodore Watkins;
John Poole Set;
Sounds Blue Show Band;
Southampton All Stars

Tuesday 8 April 1975
City Hall
Manfred Mann's Earthband;
Clancy

Monday 21 April 1975
Playhouse
Magna Carta

Wednesday 7 May 1975
City Hall
Love; Dog Soldier

Wednesday 14 May 1975
City Hall
Be Bop Deluxe; Grandma Moses

June 1975
Stonehenge Free Festival
Hawkwind; Here & Now;
Zorch;
Tracker;
Laughing Sam's Dice;
Wandering Spirit

1976

Monday 8 March 1976
City Hall
Man

June 1976
Stonehenge Free Festival
Hawkwind; Lightning;
Sphere;
Jupiter's Child;
Solar Ben;
The Shining Hearts Band;
Here & Now;
Fairlane

Saturday 2 October 1976
College Of Technology
Lamplight

ENDLESS BEAT

1977

Wednesday 16 March 1977
College Of Technology
(Rag Ball)
The Pink Fairies; Blue Angel

Monday 13 to Saturday
25 June 1977
Stonehenge Free Festival
Hawkwind; Richie Havens; Here & Now; Tim Blake; The Bombay Bus Company; Six; Warp 111; The Kitchens

Friday 1 July 1977
City Hall
The Pat Travers Band;
Doctors of Madness

1978

Friday 20 January 1978
College Of Technology
The Pirates

Sunday 5 March 1978
College Of Technology
The Boyfriends; Advertising

NB: This gig was possibly cancelled.

Wednesday 15 March 1978
College Of Technology
Advertising

Saturday 13 May 1978
City Hall
The Pirates; Sixteen

June 1978
Stonehenge Free Festival
Hawkwind; Alternative TV; Here & Now; Keith Christmas; Nik Turner and Sphinx; Warp III; Gross Catastrophe; The Mob; Seventh Angel; Bronz.

Friday 22 September 1978
College of Technology
Adam and The Ants

Tuesday 24 October 1978
City Hall
XTC; Push

Saturday 25 November 1978
College Of Technology
Alternative TV; Here & Now

NB: This gig was cancelled and replaced with the two below.

Saturday 25 November 1978
Sarum 76
Here & Now; Blank Space

NB: This gig and the one below replaced the cancelled one above.

Saturday 25 November 1978
College Of Technology
Gong

NB: This gig and the one above replaced the cancelled one above that.

Wednesday 20 December 1978
College of Technology
The Bishops

NB: This gig was cancelled.

Wednesday 20 December 1978
College Of Technology
The QTs

Thursday 21 December 1978
City Hall
Martin James 'Christmas Spectacular'.
Dozy, Beaky, Mick and Tich;
Taylor Gair Band;
Shelley Lane; Xtrax

1979

Thursday 22 March 1979
College Of Technology
Thieves Like Us

Wednesday 23 May 1979
College Of Technology
(Common Room)
The QTs; The Crimmos

June 1979
Stonehenge Free Festival
Gong; Here & Now;
The Funboy Five;
Keith Christmas; Nik Turner's Inner City Unit; Looney Q

Thursday 20 December 1979
City Hall
The Stilettos

1980

Friday 29 February 1980
College of Technology (Common Room)
Program; The Crimmos

Thursday 27 March 1980
College of Technology
(Common Room)
The Wait; The Kitchens

Friday 28 March 1980
College of Technology
Plain Characters

Friday 25 April 1980
College of Technology (Common Room)
Animals And Men; Moskow

NB: Cancelled.

Thursday 22 May 1980
City Hall
Blazers; The QTs

Monday 16 to Tuesday 24 June 1980
Stonehenge Free Festival
Hawkwind; Crass; Poison Girls; Nik Turner's Inner City Unit; The Mob; The Epileptics; Eggheads; Androids of Mu; Thursday's Children; Asphmatics; Suicide Victims; The Snipers; The Crimmos; White Bird On Red Rice; Thandoy and The You; The Torpedoes; The Vulgar Brothers; Animal Magic; Rocking Timbo; The Roustabouts; The Larry Millar Band; Entropy; The Spacemen 3; Psycho Hamster Meets The Killer Doughnuts From Mars; Ruts DC; The QTs

Wednesday July 1980
College of Technology
No Class

Friday 10 October 1980
College of Technology
Supercharge; Program

NB: Punishment Of Luxury were originally billed as headliners.

Friday 31 October 1980
City Hall
Restaurant For Dogs;
Martian Schoolgirls;
David Marx and The Mix

Friday 7 November 1980
College Of Technology
The Passions; The Crimmos

Monday 17 November 1980
City Hall
David Essex

Thursday 18 December 1980
College Of Technology
Bad Manners

1981

Friday 23 January 1981
College Of Technology
Here and Now; The Prams

Thursday 26 February 1981
City Hall
Diamond Head

Thursday 9 April 1981
College Of Technology
John Otway; The Europeans

Saturday 25 April 1981
Grange Hotel
TV Personalities; The Crimmos

Friday 19 June 1981
Stonehenge Free Festival
Hawkwind

Saturday 1 July 1981
College Of Technology
Weapon Of Peace; Ebony Rockers

Sunday 10 September 1981
City Hall
Hazel O'Connor; Bumble And The Beez

Sunday 17 September 1981
City Hall
Showaddywaddy

Tuesday 19 September 1981
Grange Hotel
Talisman

NB: In aid of 'Salisbury No Nukes'.

Thursday 1 October 1981
Grange Hotel
Crass; Dirt; Annie Anxiety

Friday 2 October 1981
College Of Technology
Hambi and The Dance; The New Brendas

Monday 9 November 1981
Grange Hotel
Jools Holland; Gettysburg Address

Friday 13 November 1981
College Of Technology
Wasted Youth; Gettysburg Address

Friday 4 December 1981
Grange Hotel
Peter and The Test Tube Babies;
The Crimmos

Thursday 17 December 1981
Arts Centre
Chase; The Zion Band

1982

Saturday 16 January 1982
Grange Hotel
Here & Now; Matt Vinyl
and The Emulsions

Friday 5 February 1982
Arts Centre
Seven States

Monday 8 February 1982
City Hall
Showaddywaddy

Friday 26 February 1982
College of Technology
The Prams; Inland Revue

Friday 5 March 1982
City Hall
Matt Vinyl and The Emulsions;
Four People I Have Known

Saturday 24 April 1982
Grange Hotel
Black Roots

Saturday 15 May 1982
Arts Centre
Abacush; Jam Today

June 1982
Stonehenge Free Festival
Hawkwind; Androids Of Mu

Friday 23 July 1982
Arts Centre
Pookiesnackenburger

Friday 30 July 1982
Arts Centre
Horizontal Bulgarians;
Banderlog; A Slap In The Belly

Friday 15 October 1982
College Of Technology
B-Movie; The Loved One

Friday 26 November 1982
College Of Technology
Animal Nightlife

Friday 17 December 1982
College Of Technology
Supercharge

1983

Friday 14 January 1983
College Of Technology
Jo Boxers; The Top Shop

Saturday 5 February 1983
Churchill Rooms
Doris and The Dots; Un Deux
Twang!

Friday 25 February 1983
College Of Technology
Chelsea; Last Orders

Friday 25 March 1983
College Of Technology
Blue Midnight; Impossible
Dreamers

Friday 15 April 1983
Arts Centre
Doris and The Dots; Un Deux
Twang!

Wednesday 15 to
Tuesday 28 June 1983
Stonehenge Free Festival
Hawkwind; The Impossible
Dreamers; Carol Grimes;
Here & Now; Poison Girls;
Urban Shakedown;
Orchestre Jazzira; The Enid;
Doctor and the Medics;
Roy Harper; Urban Warrior;
Ted Chippington; Flux of Pink
Indians; The Tibetan Ukrainian
Mountain Troupe; Benjamin
Zephaniah; Chumbawumba;
Passion Killers; Disturbance
From Fear.

Saturday 18 June 1983
Arts Centre
Horse Latitudes

Saturday 18 June 1983
High Post Hotel
Pinkertons Assorted Colours

Thursday 7 July 1983
Arts Centre
Midsummer Rock Frolic
Two Fingered Zen; Nine
Unknown Men; Paul Henry

Friday 15 July 1983
City Hall
Big Country

Friday 26 August 1983
Arts Centre
Micro Chip and The Word
Processors

Saturday 3 September 1983
Arts Centre
Mike Westbrook

Monday 12 September 1983
Arts Centre
The Soupdragon

Saturday 17 September 1983
Arts Centre
The Flying Picketts

Thursday 27 October 1983
Arts Centre
John Cooper-Clarke; Red Money

1984

Saturday 4 February 1984
Churchill Rooms
Doris and The Dots; Un Deux
Twang!

Thursday 16 February 1984
Arts Centre
Money For Guns

Friday 13 April 1984
College Of Technology
Twelfth Night

Friday 27 April 1984
High Post Hotel
Dozy, Beaky, Mick and Tich

Saturday 28 April 1984
High Post Hotel
Nashville Teens

Friday 11 May 1984
Arts Centre
Harvey and The Wallbangers

Thursday 14 to Thursday 28 June
1984
Stonehenge Free Festival
Hawkwind (two sets); Roy
Harper; The Enid; Nik Turner's
Inner City Unit; The Liberators;
The Wystic Mankers

Thursday 2 August 1984
Arts Centre
Toucantango

Friday 5 October 1984
College Of Technology
Roman Holliday; Toucantanago

Friday 23 November 1984
College Of Technology
New Model Army;
Obvious Action

1985

Thursday 7 March 1985
Arts Centre
Fear Of Darkness

Saturday 6 April 1985
Arts Centre
The Subhumans;
Don't Feed The Animals;
Obvious Action;
The Grey Wolves

Saturday 13 April 1985
Arts Centre
Rock for Ethiopia
Dark Star;
Seeing Red;
Afro Dizzy Acts;
Newcombe and Roach;
Chris Hartford;
Colin Harding

Friday 19 to Sunday 21 April
1985
Arts Centre
Folk Under Aries
Included: Country Remedy;
Innominata;
Lallan;
Wareham Down;
Jones and Co;
Portsmouth Shanty Crew;
Strong Country Band

Saturday 31 May 1985
Arts Centre
Hi-Life International

Sunday 22 June 1985
High Post Hotel
Dave Dee, Dozy, Beaky,
Mick and Tich

Saturday 5 July 1985
Arts Centre
999; Obvious Action

Sunday 28 July 1985
Arts Centre
Hugh Masekela

Thursday 1 August 1985
Arts Centre
The Siren; I Am 7

Sunday 4 August 1985
Arts Centre
Don't Feed The Animals

ENDLESS BEAT

Tuesday 27 and Wednesday 28 August 1985
Arts Centre
Music For Today:
Rock Band Contest (Heats)
Included: The Pat Masha Band;
Run Of The Millar;
Thick Dick and The Green 'Eads;
Bully For Garbo;
Nightshade;
Aces High;
Never Never;
The Protectors;
Obvious Action;
The Perfect Squares;
Wolfbane;
Random Gender.

Sunday 15 September 1985
Arts Centre
Music For Today:
Rock Band Contest (Final)
Included: Wolfbane;
Random Gender
(plus bands from Swindon Heats).

Saturday 21 September 1985
Arts Centre
The Troggs

Friday 27 September 1985
Arts Centre
Explorer; Dark Star; Wolfbane

Saturday 28 September 1985
Arts Centre
Rock For Ethiopia
The Splodges;
The Rhythm Blasters; \
Don't Feed The Animals;
Obvious Action;
The Boogie Brothers

Thursday 3 October 1985
Arts Centre
Dumpy's Rusty Nuts;
Don't Feed The Animals

Saturday 26 October 1985
Arts Centre
The Screaming Blue Messiahs;
Rave To The Grave

NB: The Men They Couldn't Hang were originally billed as headliners for this gig.

Wednesday 18 December 1985
Arts Centre

The Men They Couldn't Hang

1986

Thursday 21 August 1986
Arts Centre
Newcombe and Roach;
The Prophecy;
Bubblegum Splash!

Wednesday 27 to Saturday 30 August 1986
Arts Centre
Music For Today:
Rock Band Contest
Included: Bubblegum Splash!;
Cosa Nostra;
DB Five;
Snowdrops From
A Curate's Garden;
The Merry Marias;
Deo Vacente;
Against The Wall;
Frontiers;
The Perfect Squares;
Kizmet.

Thursday 11 December 1986
Arts Centre
Toucantango
(playing at a Spare Fishe Fashion Show)

1987

Saturday 14 March 1987
Arts Centre
Simon Nicol and Ric Saunders

Friday 10 April 1987
Fisherton Arms
Blyth Power

Thursday 16 April 1987
City Hall (Alamein Suite)
Bubblegum Splash!; The Hunny Monsturs; The Prophecy; Thick Dick and The Green'eds

Wednesday 26 to Saturday 29 August 1987
Arts Centre
Music For Today Contest
(Heats and Finals)
Included: The Hunny Monsturs;
No 4 Joystreet;
Ulterior Motive;
Blind Panic;
The Aquatic Weasel Band;
Mr 10 and His Amazing Men;
What The Butler Saw;
Refugee;
After Four;
Cutting Edge;
Table Talk

Wednesday 9 September 1987
Arts Centre
Patrick Street

Friday 11 September 1987
City Hall
Dr and The Medics

Saturday 12 September 1987
Arts Centre
Desmond Dekker

Friday 18 September 1987
Arts Centre
Gasper Lawal

Saturday 19 September 1987
Arts Centre
Qulmantu

Thursday 22 October 1987
Arts Centre
The Frantic Flintstones;
The Phenobarbitones

Thursday 19 November 1987
City Hall (Alamein Suite)
The Groove Farm;
The Mayfields;
The Phenobarbitones

Thursday 26 November 1987
Arts Centre
Mr 10 And His Amazing Men;
Farley 708

Friday 27 November 1987
Amesbury Sports Centre
Children In Need Dance
The Fourmost;
Brian Poole;
The Electrix;
Peter Podd And The Peas

Sunday 29 November 1987
Arts Centre
Leon Rosselson

11 December 1987
Arts Centre
Groovin' With The Mayor
(Mayor's Appeal Fundraiser)
Newcombe and Roach;
Don't Feed The Animals;
Mr 10 And His Amazing Men;
The Rhythm Blasters;
Pope Shenouda and The Coptic Orthodox

1988

Thursday 7 January 1988
Arts Centre
The Phenobarbitones;
Next Of Kin; True South

NB: First 'Passenger Club' gig.

Thursday 21 January 1988
Arts Centre
The Crop Dusters; The Stand

Thursday 28 January 1988
City Hall (Alamein Suite)
14 Iced Bears;
Pope Shenouda & The
Coptic Orthodox;
Wacchus Bacchus

NB: Bubblegum Splash! were originally due to appear

Thursday 4 February 1988
Arts Centre
The Cranes; Twelve 88 Cartel

Sunday 28 February 1988
Arts Centre
Chrome Molly; Nobody's Fools

Wednesday 2 March 1988
City Hall
Fairport Convention

Thursday 3 March 1988
Arts Centre
The Shrubs; The Hunny
Monsturs; Dogfish

Thursday 17 March 1988
Arts Centre
Flik Spatula; Chris Hartfield

Thursday 31 March 1988
Arts Centre
Spacemen 3; Jane From Occupied Europe

Thursday 21 April 1988
Arts Centre
The Morrigan; Chris 'Quack' Foster

Thursday 28 April 1988
City Hall (Alamein Suite)
The Rosehips; Mega City Four;
The Mayfields; Jane From
Occupied Europe

Friday 29 April 1988
Arts Centre
Gasper Lawal; The Africa
Ore Band

Appendices

Saturday 30 April 1988
Arts Centre
The Meteors

Thursday 5 May 1988
Arts Centre
Blyth Power; Crowforce; Grey Wolves

Thursday 19 May 1988
Arts Centre
Wolfbane; Mr 10

Friday 27 May 1988
Arts Centre
Dumpy's Rusty Nuts; Zero

Saturday 4 June 1988
Arts Centre
Dean Friedman; Tanita Tikaram

Friday 17 June 1988
Arts Centre
Blue Aeroplanes; The Courgettes

Saturday 25 June 1988
College of Technology (Common Room)
Razorcuts; The Mayfields; Jane From Occupied Europe

Thursday 30 June 1988
Arts Centre
The Cropdusters; Carfax and The Heretic

Friday 1 July 1988
Arts Centre
Bam-Bam and The Calling; Who's In The Kitchen

Thursday 7 July 1988
Arts Centre
Culture Shock; BTF; Sharon Tate's Children

Saturday 16 July 1988
Arts Centre
Jasmine Minks; The Mayfields; Rose Coloured Nightmares

Thursday 4 August 1988
Arts Centre
John Hammond

Tuesday 16 August 1988
Reuben Langford Wine Bar
Mike D'Abo

Thursday 18 August 1988
Arts Centre
Huw Lloyd Langton

Friday 19 August 1988
Arts Centre
Basil Gabbadon's Bass Dance Reggae Band

Wednesday 24 to Saturday 27 August 1988
Arts Centre
Music For Today Contest (Heats and Finals)
Included The Hunny Monsturs

Friday 16 September 1988
City Hall (Foyer)
Blow Up; Jane From Occupied Europe

NB: Next Of Kin were also billed but cancelled due to illness.

Wednesday 21 September 1988
Arts Centre
The Wishing Stones; The Claytown Troupe

Thursday 20 October 1988
Arts Centre
Cud; The Phenobarbitones; Raza Dolls

Friday 21 October 1988
Old Sarum Car Park
Cud

Saturday 5 November 1988
Arts Centre
Robert Lloyd and The New Four Seasons; Chris Hartford

Thursday 10 November 1988
City Hall (Foyer)
The Jazz Butcher; Farley 708; Next Of Kin

Friday 18 November 1988
City Hall
Children In Need Benefit
Included: The Mayfields, Rose Coloured Nightmares, Alienation, The Aquatic Weasel Band, The Hunny Monsturs and Censored

1989

26 January 1989
Arts Centre
The Wolfhounds; The Badgeman

Thursday 23 March 1989
Arts Centre
Close Lobsters; Jive Turkey; Jane From Occupied Europe

Thursday 13 April 1989
Arts Centre
UK Subs; BTF

Thursday 4 May 1989
Arts Centre
We Are Going To Eat You; Thee Hypnotics

Sunday 4 June 1989
City Hall
Hawkwind

Thursday 20 July 1989
Arts Centre
The Levellers

Thursday 24 August 1989
Arts Centre
The Fuzztones; The Stand

Wednesday 13 September 1989
City Hall
Toyah Willcox, Robert Fripp and Sunday All Over The World

Thursday 2 November 1989
Arts Centre
The Telescopes

Thursday 9 November 1989
Arts Centre
Senseless Things; Who's In The Kitchen?

Thursday 7 December 1989
Arts Centre
Mega City Four; Watch You Drown; The Stand

1990

Thursday 25 January 1990
Arts Centre
Carter The Unstoppable Sex Machine; Dennis

Thursday 1 February 1990
Arts Centre
The Parachute Men; The Gurus

Thursday 8 February 1990
Arts Centre
The Levellers

Thursday 15 February 1990
Arts Centre
Blyth Power; Read 'em and Weep

Thursday 22 February 1990
Arts Centre
The Da Vincis; Inner Daze

Wednesday 11 April 1990
Arts Centre
Ride

Thursday 12 April 1990
Arts Centre
Greenpeace Benefit: What The Butler Saw; Jane From Occupied Europe; Fear Of Music; Unhealthy Fixation

Thursday 3 May 1990
Arts Centre
The Milltown Brothers; Lakota

Saturday 12 May 1990
City Hall
Dr Feelgood; The Hamsters

Saturday 19 May 1990
Arts Centre
Jane Pow!; Don't Feed the Animals; The Gurus

Thursday 14 June 1990
Arts Centre
Carter The Unstoppable Sex Machine; Blab; Jane From Occupied Europe

Saturday 30 June 1990
Arts Centre
Napalm Death; The Cardiacs

Thursday 12 July 1990
Arts Centre
Five Thirty; Dennis

Saturday 14 July 1990
Larmer Tree Festival, Larmer Tree Gardens, Tollard Royal
Dick Heckstall-Smith Sextet; Geoff Williams/Jerry Underwood Band; The Barrelhouse Allstars with Johnny Mars; Tim Laycock; Bristol School of Samba; The Roots Quartet; Mayapi with Patricia Romero

Saturday 22 September 1990
Arts Centre
John Otway; The Magnificent

Thursday 1 November 1990
Arts Centre.
The Levellers; Manic Street Preachers

Friday 7 December 1990
Arts Centre
Bark Psychosis; Nikola VI; Cobalt Blue

319

ENDLESSBEAT

1991

Thursday 10 January 1991
Arts Centre
The Badgeman; The Mayfields

NB: Launch night of the bands' split flexidisc

Thursday 17 January 1991
Arts Centre
Silverfish; Milk

Thursday 24 January 1991
Arts Centre
B Boat

Thursday 21 February 1991
Arts Centre
Dumpy's Rusty Nuts

Thursday 11 April 1991
Arts Centre
The Darkside; Unhealthy Fixation

Friday 12 April 1991
Arts Centre
John Otway and With Atilla The Stockbroker in Cheryl - The Rock Opera

Thursday 25 April 1991
Arts Centre
The Chocolate Milk Festival
Jane From Occupied Europe; Unhealthy Fixation; The Nuthins; Farley Ridge

NB: Also the night of the Jane From Occupied Europe 'Coloursound' LP launch

Sunday 28 April 1991
Arts Centre
The 25th of May

Thursday 23 May 1991
Arts Centre
Mucky Pup; Lord; Kaotika

Thursday 20 June 1991
Arts Centre
The Macc Lads

Saturday 13 and Sunday 14 July 1991
Larmer Tree Festival, Larmer Tree Gardens, Tollard Royal
Bert Jansch/Pete Kirtley; The Balham Alligators; Show of Hands; 200 Fingers; Rhythm Method; Victor Brox and the Barrelhouse Blues Band; Mayapi; Alfies Crash Bang Wallop; Nicki Hann; James Lewis; Teresa Laramy; The Rev Joe Potts

Saturday 17 August 1991
Arts Centre
Captain Sensible

Friday 30 August 1991
Arts Centre
McCavity's Cat

Thursday 12 September 1991
Arts Centre
The Phantom Chords

Thursday 10 October 1991
Arts Centre
The Levellers

Sunday 3 November 1991
Arts Centre
Roy Harper

1992

Thursday 16 January 1992
Arts Centre
PJ Harvey

Friday 7 February 1992
Arts Centre
Gong

Thursday 20 February 1992
Arts Centre
The Wedding Present; Venus Beads

Thursday 5 March 1992
Arts Centre
Levitation; Pop Am Good

Friday 13 March 1992
College of Technology
Manic Street Preachers

Tuesday 24 March 1992
Arts Centre
Curve; Adorable

Thursday 26 March 1992
Arts Centre
The Catherine Wheel; The God Machine; Dennis

Thursday 16 April 1992
Arts Centre
Godflesh; Mad Cow Disease

Saturday 23 May 1992
Arts Centre
John Otway; Atilla The Stockbroker

Saturday 20 June 1992
Arts Centre
House Of Love; The Rockingbirds

Saturday 3 October 1992
Arts Centre
Mad Cow Disease; Gunner's Daughter; Unhealthy Fixation

1993

Sunday 7 February 1993
Arts Centre
Tribal Hearts

Friday 19 February 1993
Arts Centre
Mad Cow Disease; Swing Syndicate

Thursday 8 April 1993
City Hall
Toyah

Friday 28 May 1993
Arts Centre
Blaggers ITA; Fun-da-Mental; Blade

Thursday 24 June 1993
Arts Centre
Buzzcocks; Fabulous

Saturday 26 June 1993
Arts Centre
The Big Easy; Statues; Cow Town; The Hoax

Saturday 3 July 1993
Arts Centre
Blyth Power; Amazing Windmills

Saturday 17 and Sunday 18 July 1993
Larmer Tree Festival, Larmer Tree Gardens, Tollard Royal
Swamp Rat (with Pierre la Rue); Alianza!; Tony Wetherill and Jeff Mead; Show of Hands; Afterhours; 200 Fingers and Dick Heckstall-Smith; Big Man Clayton with the Barrelhouse Blues Band; Carmina; Mike Butcher; James Lewis and his Flamenco Dancers; Paul Downes; Jay Turner; So What!; The Grassworks; Spank the Plank and the Broken String Band; Teresa Laramy; The Joyriders; David John O'Leary and Sugarcane; Yellow Taxi; Dave Marchant; Annexe; HTG; Winton Wonder Band; Trio Hysteria

Friday 25 September 1993
Arts Centre
Mad Cow Disease; Pumphouse; Suicide King

Thursday 22 October 1993
Arts Centre
The Family Cat

1994

Wednesday 6 January 1994
Arts Centre
Orange Deluxe; The Nuthins

Saturday 9 and Sunday 10 July 1994
Larmer Tree Festival, Larmer Tree Gardens, Tollard Royal
Edward II; Toyah Willcox Band; Chris Wood and Andy Cutting; La Cucina; 200 Fingers; Flatville Aces; Chris Youlden and the Barrelhouse Blues Band; Europa String Choir; Roots Orchestral; Rhythm Method; Rhymers; Pinetop Boogie-Woogie Band; Yellow Taxi; Paul Hammond and Elwyn Jones; Tim Laycock; The Bewley Brothers; The Polygenes; Martin Ansell; Spank the Plank and the Broken String Band

Thursday 1 December 1994
Arts Centre
John Martyn

Saturday 3 December 1994
Arts Centre
The Waterboys

Saturday 10 December 1994
The Gallery Club
The Heads; The Tangerine Tea Company

1995

Friday 10 February 1995
Arts Centre
John Otway

Saturday 8 July 1995
Arts Centre
Sidi Bou Said; Suicide King; K.S. Kollectiv; Natural Orange

Friday 14 to Sunday 16 July 1995
Larmer Tree Festival, Larmer Tree Gardens, Tollard Royal
Bhundu Boys; Edward II; Show of Hands; Kangaroo Moon; Robin Williamson; Joe Le Taxi

and the Zydeco Specials; Lost T-Shirts of Atlantis; Ben Waters; Don Mescall; Gordon Haskell; Paul Downes; Pressgang; The Rattlers; Malcolm Brittain; Jim Couza; New Bushbury Mountain Daredevils; Rhythm Method; Rhythm Blasters; Don't Untie The Drummer; Yellow Taxi; Rhymers; Bottlebank Band; Pronghorn; Some People

Sunday 23 July 1995
Arts Centre
Roy Harper

1996

Thursday February 1996
Arts Centre
The Sweet

Tuesday 27 February 1996
Arts Centre
Chumbawamba

Friday 12 to Sunday 14 July 1996
Larmer Tree Festival, Larmer Tree Gardens, Tollard Royal
Oysterband; Shooglenifty; Baka Beyond; Banyumas Bamboo Gamelan; Coope, Boyes and Simpson; Kora Colours; Roots Progress Ceilidh; Old Rope String Band; Joyce Gang; Waulk Elektrik; The Wrigley Sisters; Kitchen Girls; Don Mescall; Outcast Band; Keith Donnelly; Wholesome Fish; Ashley Reed & J Owen Williams; Paul Downes; The Fold; Souls of Fire; Reg Meuross; Graham Russell; Keith Christmas; Yellow Taxi; Scary Red; Pronghorn; The Huckleberries; Lance Riley and the Pulse Party; Fin Gunn; Foo Foo and The Boys; Dreamcatcher; Some People; Absolute Darlings

Saturday 12 October 1996
Arts Centre
The Wedding Present; The Delgados

Friday 15 November 1996
Gallery Club
999; Life Stuff; Sweet Children

Thursday 12 December 1996
Gallery Club
Sidi Bou Said; Monorail; Sweet Children

Friday 20 December 1996
Arts Centre
The Hoax

Saturday 21 December 1996
Gallery Club
The Mad Professor

1997

Saturday 8 March 1997
Gallery Club
Kerbdog; {S.I.C}

Saturday 22 March 1997
Gallery Club
PA.I.N.; Concrete Fuzz

Sunday 20 April 1997
Arts Centre
Billy Bragg; The Mutton Birds

Thursday 24 April 1997
Gallery Club
A; Twist; Sweet Children

Saturday 17 May 1997
Arts Centre
Carter The Unstoppable Sex Machine; Groop Dog Drill.

Saturday 31 May 1997
Arts Centre
Hurricane #1; Super 8; Cane

Monday 2 June 1997
St Mary's Cathedral
Robert Fripp

Tuesday 3 June 1997
St Mary's Cathedral
Robert Fripp

Wednesday 4 June 1997
St Mary's Cathedral
Robert Fripp

Thursday 5 June 1997
St Mary's Cathedral
Robert Fripp

Friday 11 July 1997
Gallery Club
Smog U.K.; Sweet Children; Snub

Friday 11 to Sunday 13 July 1997
Larmer Tree Festival, Larmer Tree Gardens, Tollard Royal
Jazz Jamaica; Rory McLeod; Tartan Amoebas; Flook!; Rajasthani Folk Musicians; Big Jig and the Groove Dept; Vulcheva-Jenkins Incident; Anam; The Bushbury Mountain Daredevils; Waulk Elektrik; Pipin' Hot; Elephant Talk; The Boat Band; Eddie Martin; The Positively Testcard; Helen Watson; The Daily Planet; Keith Donnelly; Reg Meuross; Clarion; Roxy's Tool Box; Anna Ryder; Shine; Dahomey Dance; The Dolmen; The Hedgemonkeys; Shak Shak; Pronghorn; The Huckleberries; The Aqua Sisters

Saturday 12 July 1997
Gallery Club
Albaroot; U.K. Players

Friday 12 September 1997
Arts Centre
Ian Hunter

Saturday 13 September 1997
Arts Centre
Midget; Shining Silva Spaceship; Starsky

Saturday 27 September 1997
Arts Centre
All Folked Up!
Included: Blyth Power; Souls Of Fire; Chrstine Collister; Pressgang; Kevin Dempsey and Tom Leary

Friday 17 October 1997
Gallery Club
Tribute To Nothing; Room 237; Scruffhog

Friday 14 November 1997
Arts Centre
The Hoax; Mullitt

Saturday 6 December 1997
Arts Centre
Ebb

Sunday 14 December 1997
City Hall
Fish

1998

Tuesday 20 January 1998
Art Centre
Spritualized; Vex

Thursday 22 January 1998
City Hall
Richard Thompson

Saturday 24 January 1998
Arts Centre
The Catherine Wheel; Feline; Radiator

Sunday 25 January 1998
Old Ale House
Blyth Power; Wob

Wednesday 28 January 1998
Arts Centre
John Martyn

Sunday 15 February 1998
Arts Centre
Blyth Power

Friday 27 February 1998
Arts Centre
Groop Dogdrill; Junk DNA; Subtext

Friday 29 May 1998
The Tavern
999; Snub; Sweet Children; Inline Sk8ing Barbies; One Shot Nothing

Sunday 7 June 1998
City Hall
Jools Holland

Friday 12 June 1998
The Tavern
The Young Offenders; Subtext; Buster Move

Friday 10 to Sunday 12 July 1998
Larmer Tree Festival, Larmer Tree Gardens, Tollard Royal
Shooglenifty; Edward II; Black Umfolosi; Eliza Carthy Band; The Flatville Aces; Beware of the Dog; Sally Barker; Jackie Leven; Sarah Allen and Chris Thompson; Hank Dogs; Mukka; The Hoax; Carmina; Gilly Darbey; Keith Donnelly; Pete Lawrence; Space Otter; Kath Tait; Anna Ryder; Shine; Soca Fire; Pronghorn; Magic; Wob; Jig-Saw; Yellow Taxi; Foo Foo and The Boys; The Huckleberries; Pumproom; Dorset Youth Jazz Orchestra

Saturday 22 August 1998
Arts Centre
Goober Patrol; Worm; Sweet Children; Snub; One Shot Nothing

Wednesday 26 August 1998
City Hall
Supergrass

ENDLESS BEAT

Monday 28 September 1998
Arts Centre
Babybird; Tin Star

Thursday 19 November 1998
City Hall
The Stranglers

1999

Monday 8 February 1999
Arts Centre
Heather Nova

Friday 12 February 1999
Arts Centre
Radiator; Tribute To Nothing; Stormfly

Friday 26 February 1999
Arts Centre
The Creatures

Thursday 4 March 1999
City Hall
The Hollies

Friday 5 March 1999
Arts Centre
Gene

Thursday 18 March 1999
Arts Centre
Spunge; Euphoria; Uncle Brian

Thursday 1 April 1999
Arts Centre
Mad Cow Disease

Saturday 20 March 1999
Arts Centre
Whole Lotta Led

Friday 7 May 1999
Arts Centre
The Fall; Rico

Monday 31 May 1999
City Hall
Marc Almond

Wednesday 16 June 1999
Arts Centre.
Marianne Faithfull; Marlboro County Fair

Friday 25 June 1999
Arts Centre
Ash; Chicks

Thursday 8 to Sunday
11 July 1999
Larmer Tree Festival, Larmer Tree Gardens, Tollard Royal
Jools Holland and his Rhythm & Blues Orchestra; Martyn Bennett and Cuillin Music; Black Umfolosi; Lunasa; Tarika; Kavana, McNeil, Lynch and Lupari; Loyko; Peatbog Faeries; Daily Planet; Chris While and Julie Matthews; Kangaroo Moon; Europa String Choir; Keith Donnelly; Jackie Leven; Arnie Cottrell and Mo Thomas; FOS Brothers Acoustic; Rhythm Collision; Souls of Fire; Shine; Madra Rua; Soca Fire; Madigan; Global; Connie Lupino's Voodoo Kitchen Sound System; Wob; The Producers; Huckleberries; Pronghorn; Machine Breakers; Wise Children; Lou Taylor; Yellow Taxi; Harry Skinner and Dave Saunders; Woman Wants Tall Man

Friday 16 July 1999
Old Ale House
Hugh Cornwell; The Jamesons

Friday 17 September 1999
Arts Centre
Monkey Seven; Cane; Marlboro County Fair

Thursday 21 October 1999
Arts Centre
Ringworm; 16 Bronsons; Spankboy; TV Logic

Saturday 6 November 1999
Arts Centre
Earthtone 9

Monday 22 November 1999
City Hall
Morrissey; Sack

Thursday 25 November 1999
Old Ale House
Spunge; Stormfly

Thursday 16 December 1999
Old Ale House
Goldblade; Spankboy

Saturday 18 December 1999
Arts Centre
Buzzcocks

Special Thanks

Frogg would like to thank Petrina.

Richard would like to thank Anne and his Mum and Dad and family.

We would both like to thank Sarah Minshull and Kim Chittick.

Credits and Resources

Individuals

Without these people this book would have been merely a (small!) regurgitation of facts, figures and press cuttings. We offer them our sincere thanks.

Ian 'Tich' Amey; Michel Bands; Peter Beasley; Dave Bennett; David 'Benge' Bennett; Hannah Billen; Chris Binns; Alan Blaikley; Rob Boston; Andy Boulton; Mick Box; Ian 'Skid' Browne; Ethem Cetintas; Steve Christey; Steve Collinson; Bob Cooke; Peter Coombs; Kurt Cooper; Ron Cooper; Neil Dalziel; Paul Dean; Penny Elliott; Roger Elliott; Johnny Fellows; James Ferguson; Terry Francis; Duncan Fulton; Robin Gair; Keith Gale; Ian Gillan; Andy Golden; Neale Hancock; Pete Hancock; Perry 'M' Harris; Trevor Harris; Alan Harrison; Jim Harrison; Chris Hartford; John Hatchman; Nick Heron; Colin Holton; Gary Holton; Roger Hutchinson; Gary James; Mike 'Jackboot' Jones; Ruth Jones; Trevor Kay; Nick Kemp; Mark 'Ken' Kenchington; Simon Kuczera; John Lakeman; Neil Leacy; Steve Lightfoot; Alwyn 'Coke' Lovell; Sally Anne Lowe; Alexa Mackenzie; Phil Manning; Colin Maple; Jon Maple; Nick Marchant; Alan Marsh; Ian 'Atilla' Marshall; Adrian 'Swannie' Martin; Peter Mason; Jon 'Mojo' Mills; Colin Mitchener; Alex Mundy; Colin Mundy; Andy Nicklen; Dave Notley; Simon 'Sox' Oxborrow; Mark Palmer; Barbara Parker; Sandra Pollard; Andy Pringle; Barry Pritchard; Roger Raggett; Robert Read; Sean Rice; Mike Robins; Tremayne Roden; Clive Roper; Ant Roberts; Brian Saunders; Andy Sheppard; Keith Small; Bob Taylor; Dave Taylor; Tom Thatcher; Dave Todd; Tom Vague; Herman van Gaal; Mike Vickers; Kerry Waite; Andy Ware; Dave Ware; Yan Webber; Mike Wedgwood; Grahame 'Chalky' White; Simon 'Wiggy' Wigglesworth.

Photographs

All attempts have been made to contact copyright holders of photographs, where known. Apologies are offered to any copyright holders who we have not been able to contact. Where this is the case, please contact us and we will rectify matters in the event of any future editions of this book.

Resource Centres

The members of staff of the Salisbury Local Studies Library have been as helpful as always.

However, we would like to explicitly not thank Wiltshire Council for the failure to promptly replace or repair the library's microfiche viewer.

Newspapers and Magazines

Almost Grown; Candy And A Currant Bun; Channel 4; Convoy News; Due South; Fabulous 208; Family Entertainment; New Musical Express; Point Of View; Pramzine; The Rambler; Record Collector; Record Mirror; Salisbury Journal; The Second Coming; So Naïve; Submerge; Sussed; The Times; Vague; Wobbly Jelly; Zabadak *(available from Ron Cooper, Domaine des Palmiers, 124 Av Maurice Chevalier, Appt 103 Bat B3, 06150 Cannes La Bocca, France. E-mail: ron.cooper@neuf.fr)*; Zig Zag.

Salisbury Newspapers

We are particularly grateful to the Salisbury Newspaper Group for the use of photographs.

ENDLESS BEAT

Books

Kelly's Directories of Salisbury and Neighbourhood
(Kelly's Directories/IPC Business Press Limited - Various Editions)

The Politics of Pop Festivals
(Michael Clarke) (Junction 1982)

The Great British Mistake: Vague 1977-92
(Vague 1994)

Rock's Wild Things: The Troggs Files
(Alan Clayson and Jacqueline Ryan) (Helter Skelter 2000)

The Look: Adventures In Pop And Rock Fashion
(Paul Gorman) (Sanctuary 2001)

Up Yours!: A Guide To Punk, New Wave and Early Post Punk
(Vernon Joynson) (Borderline Productions 2001)

British Hit Singles and Albums - Edition 18
(Guinness 2005)

The Battle Of The Beanfield
(Edited by Andy Worthington) (Enabler 2005)

The Tapestry Of Delights Revisited: The Comprehensive Guide To British Music Of The Beat, R&B, Psychedelic And Progressive Eras 1963-1976
(Vernon Joynson) (Borderline Productions 2006)

Sleevenotes

Brian Protheroe: Pinball And Other Stories
(CD) (EMI 2006) (Richard Dodd, Brian Protheroe and Kieron Tyler)

Jerusalem
(CD) (Rockadrome 2008) (Uncredited)

Stonehenge 1984: A Midsummer Night Rock Show
(DVD) (Voiceprint 2009) (Leo Robinson)

Mason: Starting As We Mean To Go On
(CD) (Cherry Tree 2010) (David Wells and Peter Mason)

Tokyo Blade
(CD) (Lemon 2010) (Dave King)

Websites

We have looked at countless websites for research purposes, but these have been particularly useful:

www.dddbmt.com
(The official Dave Dee, Dozy, Beaky, Mick and Tich site)

www.davedeedozybeakymickandtich.nl
(A Dave Dee, Dozy, Beaky, Mick and Tich fan site with a remarkable array of picture sleeves)

www.petermasonmusic.co.uk
(The official Peter Mason site)

www.tokyoblade.com
(The official Tokyo Blade site)

www.angelfire.com/rock3/tokyoblade/home.htm
(A Tokyo Blade and related bands fan site)

www.themorrigan.co.uk
(The official Morrigan site)

www.vaguerants.org.uk
(Vague in cyberspace)

www.ukrockfestivals.com
(A great site with tons of stuff on the Stonehenge Free Festival)

Index

INDEX OF PERSONAL AND BAND NAMES IN MAIN TEXT
(NB: a small 'p' indicates a photograph)

101ers 87, 101
10cc 234
22nd Street 286
999 179

Abbott, Paul 261
AC/DC 47
Ackroyd, John 11
Acrylics 143
Adam and The Ants 65-66, 69, 106, 153, 178
Adamson, Stuart 155-156
Afro Dizzy Acts 148, 174-175
Against The Wall 179-182
Aku Aku 263
Alexander, Cathy 234, 237, 238, 239
All In The Mind 29, 64
Allen, Ken 102
Allenby, Jofie 49, 50
Ambrose Slade 3
Ambulance Beat 168-169, 168p, 263
Amen Corner 142
Amey, Ian 'Tich' 18, 21, 22-23, 43, 45, 46, 47, 48, 51, 52, 54, 55, 79, 85, 91, 92, 210, 211, 255, 284, 286, 289, 290
Amey-Gair-Mason 51-55, 53p, 90, 254, 284, 285
Andrews, Barry 88
Angel, Marc 'Jocker' 144, 145, 146
Angelwitch 121
Ansell, Dave 220, 222, 261
Arctic Monkeys 250
Arden, Don 142
Arney, Rob 227, 241
Arnold, Tony 47, 48, 54, 165, 173
Arthur's Mother 16
Ash 264
Asia 18
Aston, Jay 195
Astral Plain 195, 234
Aswad 280
Atilla (see Marshall, Ian)
Atkinson, Richard 'Buzzard' 183, 225, 226
Atom Heart Mother 233
Auger, Brian (and The Trinity) 15

Austin, Jane 66
Avengers, The 176
Avonaires, The 10
Aylett, Tim 68, 69

Babe Ruth 65
Babys, The 126, 127
Back Door 2
Bad Manners 153
Badgeman, The 207, 223, 224, 225, 247-252, 248p, 251p, 253, 271, 280, 287-288
Baggeley, Jon 275
Baggs, Mervyn 239
Baker, Karen 159, 160, 179, 182
Baker, Roger 159
Baker, Sarah 159, 160
Ban Jyang 233
Band Of Gold 48, 49, 49p, 51, 52, 91, 210, 211
Bangkok 111, 169-170
Barclay James Harvest 49
Barker, Steve 168
Barlick, Eddie 8
Barnes, Kev 178, 179, 225, 226
Barr, Nikki 206
Bassey, Shirley 23
Battlezone 146, 266
Be Bop Deluxe 39, 40
Beaky (see Dymond, John)
Beasley, Peter 110, 118-119, 152, 154-155
Beatles, The 19, 159
Beaton, Cecil 254
Beavis, Paul 254, 284, 285
Beck, John 286
Beer, Nick 146, 233
Bell, Eric 259
Bell, Johnny 193, 194, 194p, 195
Bemerton Boys, The 79, 81
Benn, Tony 16
Bennett, Dave 10-11
Bennett, David 'Benge' 9
Bennett, Paul 255, 290
Berry, Dave 62p
Berry, Simon 266
Best, George 211
Bethany 11, 11p, 47, 91
Between The Eyes 85, 169
Big Bird 252-253, 284, 287

Big Country 155
Big House 162
Big Num 265
Billen, Brian 50, 51
Billen, Hannah 50-51
Binns, Chris 168-169, 204, 254, 263-264
Birch, John 253
Black Grape 281
Black Sabbath 2, 14, 142
Blackburn, Tony 76
Blackmore, Ritchie 13, 15
Blackwell, Jim 162, 165, 169, 191, 193, 227
Blaikley, Alan 18, 19, 20, 21, 22, 43, 47, 289, 290
Blake, Darren 'Dazman' 252, 287
Blamey, Jonny 241
Bley, Carla 34
Blind Heart 144
Bloodvessel, Buster 115p, 153
Blow Up 214
Blue Haze 195
Blue Oyster Cult 140, 141
Blur 249
Boardman, Phil 91
Bob James Band/Music 10, 10p, 41, 42p
Bolan, Marc 23
Bolder, Trevor 24
Bolt-on Parsnips 239
Bombay Bus Company 103
Bond, Graham 95
Bond, Ronnie 87, 254
Boney M 88
Bongwater 287
Bonham, John 5, 6
Boshell, Bias 17
Boston, Beau 265
Boston, Luke 265
Boston, Nick 129, 176
Boston, Rob 119-120, 120-121, 122-123, 124-125, 126, 127, 128, 129, 130, 131-132, 146, 176, 264-266
Boston, Vic 265
Boulton, Andy 127, 129, 132, 133-134, 135-136, 137-138, 138-140, 140-141, 142, 144-145, 146-147, 148, 149, 266, 266p
Bowers, Billy 210
Bowie, Angie 24
Bowie, David 23-24, 69, 255
Bowley, Alf 90

325

Bowley, Mark 90
Bown, Peter 159, 160
Box, Mick 2
Boyes, Dave 176, 177, 178
Bradbury, Andrew 'Brad' 35, 37, 38, 40p, 89, 90, 160, 161p
Branded 280
Brewer, Andy 276
Brignel, Luke 153
Brilleaux, Lee 38
Britton, Chris 254
Britz 161-162, 257
Brown, Andy 225
Brown, Duncan 234
Brown, Joe 126
Browne, Ian 'Skid' 86, 108, 109, 113, 141, 152, 188, 225, 252, 267, 283
Brunt, Mike 240, 242
BTF 228, 241
Bubblegum Splash! 206-208, 207p, 208p, 209p, 214, 219, 220, 244, 249, 271, 288
Buckland, Judith 31
Bucks Fizz 195
Budgie 69
Bullfrog 41-42
Bullis, Dave 87, 193
Bullis, Dennis 87
Bullis, Ronnie (see Bond, Ronnie)
Bunce, Dan 227, 233
Burden, Colin 262
Burden, Steve 88, 219
Burnell, Bob 146
Burr, Pauline 202
Burton, Hannah 226
Burton, Steve 193, 194, 196, 204, 205, 271
Butcher, John 123, 124, 125, 126, 132
Butler, Martin 68
Butler, Simon 76
Buxton, Mike 86
Buzzcocks 62, 176
Byfield, Melanie 238

Cabaret Voltaire 168
Cadillac Babies 266
Cameras In Paris 193
Cane 266, 267
Caravan 2, 16-17, 17p, 38, 258
Cardiacs, The 215
Carpenter, Tony 255, 289
Carter The Unstoppable Sex Machine 215, 220, 222, 225

Carter, Hal 80, 81, 82
Carter, Matt 236
Cartmell, Ernie 42
Cast Iron Shores 254
Castle, Roy 10p
Catalogue Men, The 263p
Catlin, Pete 234
Cave, Nick 141
Cetintas, Ethem 4-5, 7-9, 30, 39-40, 148
Charlie Harwood and The Pub Beats 47
Chelsea 177
Chicken Pox 60, 75
Chicken Shack 2
Chillum 18
Chinatown 142
Christey, Steve 177-178, 183, 184, 193, 286
Chu, Carol 201, 201p
Church, Dave 11
Church, The 209
Clapton, Eric 289
Clark, Pete 17
Clarkson, Sharon 66, 68
Clasby, Steve 48
Clash, The 87
Clay, Jim 175
Clayden, Tony 178
Clayden, Vincent 155, 178
Clayton, Dan 274
Clements, Andy 86, 108, 156, 225
Clements, Gary 85, 86, 156
Cliff, John 162
Coasters, The (Salisbury band) 55, 176
Cobalt (of Zodiac Mindwarp) 269
Cockney Rebel 35
Cole, BJ 17
Cole, Richard 4
Coletta, John 13
Colin David Set, The 156
Collins, Joan 90
Collins, Phil 255
Collinson, Jerry 41, 42
Collinson, Jo 41
Collinson, Lloyd 56, 57, 59, 65, 83, 120, 219
Collinson, Luke 97p
Collinson, Steve 41-42, 43p, 47, 48-49, 75, 83-84, 84p, 96, 101, 186, 254-255, 261, 263
Collinson, Ted 41
Collinson, Tim 84p, 94p, 162, 171, 175, 234, 287p
Colquhoun, Fergus 30

Compton, Dave 146
Conroy Sect, The 57
Conway, Russ 218
Cooke, Bob 12-13, 14, 15, 35, 38p, 161, 257, 258, 259
Cooler 56, 57, 59, 60
Coombs, Peter 4, 5, 6, 7-8, 31, 42
Cooper, Alice 142
Cooper, Jackie 198
Cooper, Kurt 192, 194, 197, 198, 199, 201, 202-204, 204-205, 270-271
Cope, Julian 287, 288
Copeland, Miles 17
Coppin, Johnny 39
Corby, Mike 126
Cornick, Andy 247, 280
Cornwell, Hugh 269
Courgettes, The 88, 218p, 219, 235
Cowan, Nick 125
Cowan, Steve 285
Cowley, Liz 12
Cox, Christina 38
Cox, Paddy 41
Crass 101, 106, 108, 153-154
Crazy Gods Of Endless Noise 233
Crimmos, The 72, 84, 186, 264
Crompton-Batt, Alan 208
Crook, Colin 85, 111, 169, 170
Cross, Mark 69, 76
Cud 2 14, 278
Cult, The 141
Culture Shock 279
Cummins, Marty 206, 219
Curry, John 132, 174
Curved Air 16, 47

Dacre, Jack 12
Dakotas, The 234
Dallon, Mickey 13
Dalziel, Neil 56-57, 56p, 59, 62, 83, 84, 168, 169, 263
Damned, The 141
Dance Factor 196
Dark Star 163-165, 164p, 191, 260, 269
Darling Buds 207
Darlow, Tim 64, 184-185, 186, 188, 190
Darts 222
Daubney, Keith 9
Dave Charles Sound, The 10
Dave Dee, Dozy, Beaky, Mick and Tich 18-19, 21, 43, 45-47, 46p, 92, 211, 289-290
David 19, 44

Index

Davidson, Jim 200, 201
Davies, Trevor 'Dozy' 21, 23, 43, 47, 48, 91, 92, 211, 255, 289
Davis, Charlie 174, 175
DBM&T 18, 21-23, 43, 47, 92, 210, 210p, 211, 255, 289
Deakin, Graham 16, 17, 36p
Dean, Johnny 256
Dean, Paul 12, 13, 14, 15, 16, 257-258
Dean, Zoe 12, 13, 16, 38
Decameron 39
Dee, Dave 18-21, 19p, 28, 43, 44, 45, 46, 47, 52, 55, 65, 92, 209-210, 211, 255, 289, 290
Dee, Kiki 17
Deep Purple 12, 13, 14, 16, 38, 54
Dekker, Desmond 283p
Dell, Dinger 50
Denning, Chris 197
Dennis 186, 225, 267
Dennis, Peter 119
Denver, John 48
Di'Anno, Paul 146, 265-266
Diamond Head 118
Dickenson, Simon 237
Dio 136
Dishevellers, The 232
Dismore, Ray 120, 165
Distel, Sacha 89
Dixon, Jolyon 2 54
Dixon, Nigel 52, 90, 254, 285, 286
Dodson, Ken 10
Doghouse Boys, The 11
Dolenz, Mickey 17
Domino, Fats 255
Don't Ask 170-171, 170p, 268
Don't Feed The Animals 178, 180p, 181p, 182-184, 182p, 183p, 191, 226, 286
Doors, The 59
Dormannu 68
Downes, Geoff 258
Doyle, Beth 254
Dozy (see Davies, Trevor)
Dozy, Beaky, Mick and Tich (see DBM&T)
Dr Feelgood 38, 61-62, 92
Dreadzone 280
Dub Pistols 280
Dudman, Noddy 148-149, 286
Duffy, Billy 141
Duggan, Chic 59, 60, 253
Dumpy's Rusty Nuts 182
Dyer, Mickey 69, 81, 184, 185, 187, 188-190, 225, 252, 268p

Dymond, John 'Beaky' 21, 43, 44, 45, 46, 47, 48, 51, 52, 92, 210, 211, 255, 290
Eason, Phil 220
Eastabrook, Cliff 237, 238, 239
Eat Static 272
Eavis, Jean and Michael 96
E-Coli 232
Eddie and The Hotrods 61-62, 182
Edwards, Ken 30
Edwards, Phil 19
Eglington, Mick 16
Ekland, Britt 126
Electric Light Orchestra, The 142
Elite, The 263
Elliott Ness and The G-Men 64-65
Elliott, Penny 28, 148, 166-168, 174, 179, 200, 239, 273-274, 276, 277
Elliott, Roger 24, 28-29, 34, 111, 143, 166, 168, 173, 209, 239, 271, 272-273, 274, 275, 276, 282
Emm, Nigel 165
En Masse 284
Enfield, Harry 149
England, Ian 19, 44
Enid, The 112
Eno, Brian 88
Entwhistle, John 16
Epileptics, The 106-108
Episode Six 12
Eppel, Dave 40
Ertegun, Ahmet 40
ESB Band, The 149, 259
Eskimo 42, 47, 48, 57, 84
Esprit De Corps 283
Essex, David 255
Eugenius 252
Everard, Clews 116
Exciters, The 280
Exit Band, The 56, 58-59, 60, 119, 125
Ezrin, Bob 142

Fairlane 59, 60, 102-103, 159
Fairport Convention 14
Fairweather Low, Andy 285
Faith Healers, The 257
Fall, The 168
Family 14, 44
Fancy 281
Farley 708 244, 244p, 276
Farley Ridge 276
Fast Company 11
Features, The 209
Feldman, Marty 21

Fellows, Johnny 85, 101, 111, 169-170, 169p, 170-171, 268
Ferguson, James 59-60, 60p, 102-103, 159, 286
Ferry 37
Ferry, Bryan 17
Fieber, Fred 222
Finn, Matthew 184, 188, 190
Finn, Nigel 169, 191, 193, 217
Firefall 211
Fist 126
Flashback V, The 247
Flintlock Country Band 282p
Fluffy Vikings, The 132
Flux of Pink Indians 106
Foley, Ellen 284
Folk Blues Incorporated 55
Fondell Brothers, The 204
Foot, Dan 253
Forbidden Fruit 263
Ford, Andy 'Sprog' 71, 72, 73, 82, 162, 165, 268p, 269
Forde, Brinsley 280
Forecastle, Dave 132
Foreigner 286
Frampton, Trevor 119
Fraser, Andy 28
Freddie and The Dreamers 51
Free 6-7, 28, 90
Freeman, Alan 15, 230
Freeway 10
Fripp, Robert 76, 88, 254, 264, 267
Frogg (see Moody, Jeremy)
Frost, Ian 120-121, 122
Fry, Colin 133, 142
Fry, Liz 118
Fry, Rod 118, 127, 133, 141, 144, 179, 183
Fulton, Debbie 237
Fulton, Duncan 69-70, 71-72, 71p, 73, 84, 98, 103, 162, 163, 163p, 164, 165, 180, 260, 264, 269
Fuzztones, The 215, 215p, 225, 240, 242

Gair, Robin 51-52, 54, 55, 90, 208-209, 284
Gale, Keith 2, 5, 253-254, 283-284
Gale, Richard 253
Gale, Rose 253
Gallagher, Rory 6, 6p, 7, 48
Galpin, Carol 242, 247, 280
Gamble, Ally 229, 233
Gang Of Four, The 231
Genesis 2, 69

327

ENDLESS BEAT

Genghis Khan 118p, 119-127, 122p, 123p, 125p, 126p, 127-128, 129, 130, 132, 143, 146, 165, 166, 176, 264, 265, 266
Genghis Khan (Marsh-Boulton band) 127
Gentle Giant 18, 44
George, Christopher 262
George, Eddie 284, 286
George, Trevor 205
Gettysburg Address 155, 156-159, 157p, 158p
Ghosts, The (Landford band) 240
Ghosts, The (Mike Corby band) 126, 265
Gibbons, Howard 274
Gibbons, Nigel 290
Gibbs, Peter and Roger 49
Gill, Andy 231, 233
Gillan, Ian 12, 13, 14, 15, 15p, 16, 38, 54, 257-258
Gillan, Pauline 257
Gillen, Chris 266
Girlschool 147, 192
Gland Band, The 35
Glashier, Andi 174
Glaxo Babies 65
Global Village Trucking Co 41
Glover, Chris 35, 37, 89
Glover, Roger 13
Gochaux, David 142
Goddard, Dave 156
Goddard, Phil 12, 13
Goff, Brian 15, 257
Goff, Ivan 15
Gogan, Barbara 153
Going Out With God 226, 269
Golden, Andy 23, 24, 25p, 28, 35, 37, 38-39, 41, 42, 89, 90, 149, 160, 161, 259
Gong 112
Goode, Nigel 35
Goodge, Ray 165
Gorgeous George 132
Government Property 259
Gowland, Mox 44
Grandma Moses 35-39, 39p, 41, 89-90, 149, 160-161, 257, 259-260
Grant, Carol 273
Grant, Katy 201-202
Grant, Peter 4, 5
Grapevine 290
Gravity Hill 233
Gray, Colin 84, 170, 268
Gray, Oliver 76-78
Green, Alan 41
Green, Mick 259

Grey Wolves, The 276-277
Gridge, Robert 162
Grocott, Richard 175
Groove Farm 214
Groundhogs, The 40, 69
Gulliver, Paul 261
Gurus, The 217-218, 281p
Guts'n'Noses 268
Gwilym, Danny 142, 144

Haas, Rainer 92, 211
Haemoerrhoids, The 253
Hahn, Ollie 146
Halcyon 40
Hamilton, Ian 177
Hamilton, Michael 30, 105
Hamilton, Nick 169
Hamilton, Sam 15
Hamlin, Laurie 16
Hancock, Neale 247, 248, 249, 250, 251, 252, 253, 271, 284, 287, 288
Hancock, Terry 247
Hannett, Martin 169
Happy Mondays 182
Harding, Colin 274
Harding, John Wesley 279
Hardwick, Jules 263
Hardy, Roger 31
Harman, David (see Dee, Dave)
Harper, Roy 111, 112
Harpo (and The Banana Band) 32
Harris, Perry 'M' 61, 63, 66, 68, 69, 73, 111, 153
Harris, Rolf 289
Harris, Trevor 119, 120, 122p
Harrison, Alan 206, 214-215, 219, 220, 271
Harrison, George 19
Harrison, Jim 206, 207, 208, 219-220, 221p, 222, 223, 244, 271, 287
Hart, George 16, 18, 37p, 89
Hart, Tim 18
Hartford, Chris 152, 152p, 239-240, 277, 279
Hartley, Keef 42
Harvey, Alex 69
Haskell, Gordon 284, 285
Hastings, Pye 38
Hatchman, John 7, 48, 52, 90, 91, 210-211, 255, 284, 289, 290
Hatchman, Stephanie 284
Hatherley, Charlotte 264
Havens, Richie 95, 103-104

Hawkwind 104, 112, 271
Hayes, Jeremy 144
Hayman, Anton 41, 42, 43p, 101
Hayman, Sam 42
Hayward, Jon 238
Hayward, Justin 168
Hayward, Richard 168
Heap 16, 18, 89
Heaton, Adam 226, 269
Heavy Metal Kids, The 47
Heckstall-Smith, Dick 216
Heffernan, Terry 30
Hellspawn 143
Henry, Stuart 32, 132
Here and Now 103, 110, 112
Heron, Nick, 63, 175, 182, 183, 277-278
Higgins, Alex 'Hurricane' 211
High Voltage 13
Hill, Candy 171, 173, 174
Hill, Phil 171, 173, 174, 234
Hinde, Bill 12, 13, 14, 258
Hogarth, Mark 196, 198, 201p, 202
Holder, Noddy 3
Holland, Jools (and The Millionaires) 155
Hollies, The 46, 47
Holloway Sisters, The 233, 280p
Holman, Pamela 14
Holt-Keen, Caroline 163-164, 163p, 165, 233, 278, 279p
Holton, Colin 56, 57, 58-59, 60, 65, 70, 71, 73p, 75, 75p, 76, 78, 81, 82, 85, 86, 124, 125, 144, 162, 171, 173, 180, 182, 183, 184, 213, 214, 215, 227, 228, 229, 230, 232-233, 234, 235, 239, 252, 253, 254, 256, 261, 267, 269, 271, 278, 281, 282, 284, 285
Holton, Gary 179, 180
Homosexuals, The 42
Hopback Blues Band, The 233-234
Hope, Wally (Philip Russell) 96, 98-101
Hopgood, Steve 142
Horizontal Bulgarians, The 184-186, 186p, 278
Horse Latitudes 264p
House Of Love, The 216
Howard, Ken 18, 19, 21, 22, 43, 47, 289
Howell, David 50
Howell, Duncan 64, 219, 278
Howerd, Frankie 289
Howes, Robert 276
Howles, Rosemary 262
Hugg, Mike 21
Hughes, Graham 170, 171, 219, 268
Hull, Rod 211

Humperdinck, Englebert 289
Hunny Monsturs, The 247, 248, 249
Hunt, James 211
Hunt, Marsha 15
Hunt, Ray 226, 227, 233, 280
Hutchings, Ashley 18
Hutchinson, Steve 58, 59
Hutson, Carl 175
Hyams, Jonathan 174, 175, 273
Hyams, Julie 174

I Am 7 202
Identity Crisis 69, 83-84, 83p, 169, 170, 263, 264
Inbredz, The 266-267
Inner City Unit 106
Innervision 270, 270p
Innes, Neil 31, 131
Inside Job 149
Invisible Jesus 266
Iron Maiden 121, 265
Irwin, Dave 125, 126
Irwin, Sandra 29, 30
It Bites 286
Itch 286

Jackboot (see Jones, Mike)
Jadis 286
Jagged Edge 134
James, Bob 19, 46
James, Gary 226, 227, 233, 280, 280p
James, Martin 5, 7, 8-9, 40, 41, 148, 154, 154p, 281
James, Sid
James, Steve 131-132
Jamesons, The 260p
Jane From Occupied Europe 219-223, 244, 271, 280, 288
Jav 194p, 287p
Jazz Butcher, The 214
Jelly Bread 2
Jenny Lynn 11
Jensen, David 'Kid' 15
Jerusalem 4, 12-15, 12p, 14p, 35, 38, 41, 258
Jesus Jones 222
John Paul II (Pope) 265
John, Elton 17, 18
Johnny Johnson and The Bandwagon 21
Johnson, Chris 66
Johnson, Derek 106
Johnson, Eddie 119, 120, 129, 131, 264-265

Johnson, Jilly 209
Johnson, Martin 231
Johnson, Wilko 38
Johnstone, Davey 17
Jonathan the Jester 226, 237
Jones, Chris 192, 193
Jones, Gethyn 202
Jones, John Paul 267
Jones, Mike 'Jackboot' 57, 58, 63-64, 73, 74, 86, 263
Jones, Ruth 71, 71p, 72, 88-89, 157, 162, 217p, 218-219, 235-236, 260-261, 271, 283, 286p
Jones, Sandra 166
Joy Division 176
Juicy Lucy 14
Junk DNA 254
Just Us 16

Kamen, Nick 18
Kasabian 283
Kay, Trevor 233-234
Keane, Feargal 259
Kelleher, Dan 87
Kelly, Paul 70, 71
Kemp, Jeremy 'Jez' 56, 58, 59, 84, 85p, 119, 111p, 186, 264
Kemp, Nick 42, 56, 57, 58, 59, 72, 84-85, 84p, 85p, 111, 111p, 186, 264
Kenchington, Mark 'Kenny' 157-159, 217, 218, 280-281
Kenny 65
Kerley, Tim 247, 248, 251, 252, 287
Kerr, Steve 145, 146
Key, Robert 223
Kid Charlemagne 202
Killer 127
Kinetic NRG 85-87, 86p, 156, 188, 267
King Crimson 267, 285, 286
King's Singers, The 21
Kings Of Lounge, The 264
Kinky Machine 226
Kirkconel, David 49-50
Kirke, Simon 90
Kitchens, The 68p, 69, 69p, 70-73, 70p, 75, 82, 85, 87, 88, 162, 166, 218, 260, 271
Kitt, Eartha 289
Korner, Alexis 44
Kozak, Nikki 171, 173, 174, 174p
Kramer 287, 288
Kramer, Billy J 234
Kuczera, Simon 29, 56, 57-58, 66, 73, 75-76, 80, 87-88, 89

Lailey, Ken 234, 286p, 287p
Lakeman, John 29-30
Lamb, Pete 222, 225, 246
Las, The 225
Last Orders 176-177, 176p, 178, 266
Lavender, Micky 85
Lawrence, Wendy 234
Le Hardy, Steve 59
Leacy, Neil 195-197, 195p, 197-198, 200-202, 204, 205, 270
League of Gentlemen, The 88
Lear, Gavin 71
Led Zeppelin 4-6, 7, 12, 23, 40, 69
Lee, Jez 146
Leerink, Henk 161
Legion Of Crows 267
Lemmy 147-148, 148p
Lennon, John 19
Levellers, The 116, 216, 232
Leyland, Peter 168
Liberators, The 112
Limahl 284
Lindisfarne 2
Ling, Chris 90
Liquid Lem 104
Little Bare Big Bear 280
Lizard 35
Lloyd, Robert (and The New Four Seasons) 278
Lockyer, Frank 102, 105
Lodder, Dave 239
Loder, John 108
London Cowboys, The 209
Lord, Jon 13
Lords Of The New Church 192
Lovell, Alwyn 'Coke' 119-120, 121p, 122, 123, 124, 126, 127-128, 129, 130, 132, 146., 265
Lovelock, Andrew 69, 70, 72, 162, 260
Loveridge, Simon 68
Lowe, Sally Anne 143, 208-209, 219, 220, 225, 271, 273, 274
Lowry, Dave 119
Lucas, Pete 11, 47, 48, 79, 91, 92, 210, 227, 254, 284
Lucas. Chris 11, 85, 169
Lulu 289
Lumley, Grace 101
Luther, Paul 254
Lynch, Pat 286
Lynott, Phil 4, 156, 156p

Macc Lads, The 226
MacDonald, Amy 254
Mackenzie, Alexa 216-218, 217p, 280-281
Mackerel, Bill 'Tiny' 2, 50, 154
Mad Cow Disease 188, 227-233, 228p, 229p, 230p, 267, 288
Mad Mark 227, 229
Madden, Tim 236
Maddock, Superintendent 108
Mafflyn, Tommy 121, 122
Maggs, Reg 'Dave' 42, 43p, 47-48, 52, 83, 101, 169, 254, 284
Magic Power 210-211
Magnificent, The 226-227, 226p
Major Barbara 9
Mama's Boys 134
Man 28, 44-45
Manfred Mann (Chapter III) 2
Manfred Mann 21
Manic Street Preachers 216, 216p
Manning, Phil 112, 184-186, 186-188, 190, 256, 268, 271
Mant, Les 10
Maple, Colin 29, 64, 156
Maple, Jon 64-65, 108-109, 113, 116, 188, 190-191, 215, 217, 218, 222, 227, 229, 230-231, 232, 233, 267, 271, 274, 276, 282, 284, 287, 288
Maple, Pete 29, 64
Marble Orchard 4-5, 5p, 7-9, 8p, 39-40, 148
Marchant, Nick 83, 84, 162, 174, 264
Marlboro County Fair 280
Marlowe, Steve 179
Marmalade 255
Marriage, Helen 282
Marriott, Steve 126
Marsden, Charlie 195, 234
Marseilles Frame 165, 165p
Marsh, Alan 119, 120, 121, 122, 123, 127, 128, 129, 132, 133, 134-135, 136, 137p, 138, 139p, 140, 141-142, 144, 145, 146, 261, 262, 266
Marsh, Dave 174, 182, 183, 226, 237, 252, 253, 269, 278
Marshall, Ian 'Atilla' 143-144, 145, 146, 147, 228, 229, 230, 231, 232, 261, 266-267
Marshall, Stuart 286
Martian Dance 154
Martian Schoolgirls, The 73, 87-89, 218, 219
Martin, Adrian 'Swannie' 223-225, 271, 279-280

Martin, David 19
Martin, George 159
Martyn, John 289
Mary My Hope 233
Mason 44-45, 44p, 45p, 47
Mason, Peter 19-20, 21, 43-44, 44-45, 46, 47, 51, 52, 54, 55, 90, 92, 210, 255, 255p, 284-285, 285p (Band), 286
Masson, Colin 234, 237, 238, 239, 277
Matlock, Glen 209
Matthews Southern Comfort 289
Maxfield, Pete 34
Mayall, John 12
Mayfields, The 207, 222, 222p, 226, 244, 249, 271, 279, 280, 288
McCauley, Bootsy 188
McCauley, Sarah 222, 225
McColl, Kirsty 218
McDonald, Ian 286
McElhatton, Paul 35, 89
McLaren, Malcolm 62
McManus, Mick 81
McMordie, Ali 266
McTurk, Jimmy 123, 124, 125
Meatloaf 144
Meddy Evils, The 44
Mega City Four, The 214
Melanie 290
Men of the Doomsbury Lifeboat, The 259
Menswear 256
Mental, The 178
Menthol Jaggers, The 162
Mercedez 196-197, 196p
Merry Macs, The 10, 29, 64
Metallica 136
Midnite Ramblers, The 41, 41p
Milk 278
Miller, Adrian 126, 127
Mills, Jon 'Mojo' 240-242, 244-246, 245p, 247, 280
Minnear, Kerry 18
Mission Impossible 219
Misty In Roots 111
Mitchener, Colin 156
Mob, The 106
Mojo (see Mills, Jon)
Mojos, The 44
Money For Guns 170
Monty Python's Flying Circus 17, 31, 230
Moody Blues, The 168
Moody, Carl 86
Moody, Jack 57

Moody, Jeremy 'Frogg' 57, 58, 73-74, 75p, 78-79, 80-81, 82, 82p, 85, 147-148, 148p, 155, 156-157, 159-160, 173, 182-183, 184, 218, 226, 261-263, 266, 267, 290
Moonrakers, The (Denver band) 59
Moonrakers, The (Salisbury band) 247
Moore, Roy 284
Moores, Andy 175
Moreton, Tony 9, 11, 197
Morrigan, The 234, 237-239, 237p, 277
Morris, Steve 255
Morrison, Billy 123, 124, 125
Morrison, Paddy 101
Morrissey 256
Morrow, Rob 89p
Moss, Edward and Jerry 5, 6
Most, Mickie 4
Mother Gong 110
Motorhead 148
Move, The 142
Mr Ice 144-145, 146, 266
Mrs Taylor's Mad 205-206, 206p
Mundy, Alex 85, 171, 173-174, 183, 184, 186, 187, 234, 235, 267
Mundy, Colin 176-177, 177p, 178-179, 226-227
Murphy, Andy 175
Murray, Tony 91
Muscampf, Mike 68
Musy, Jean 47

Nagasaki, Kendo 32
Nail, Jimmy 18
Napalm Death 215-216, 278, 279
Nash, Richard 61, 215
Nelson, Bill 267
Never Bend Over 42, 48, 96, 96p, 97p
New Animals, The 44
New Model Army 178
New Overlanders, The 16
Newcombe and Roach 186-190, 187p, 188p, 189p, 190p, 207, 225, 269
Newman and Baddiel 240
Newman, Colin 64
Newman, Denny 259
Newman, Sandy 255
News, The 131
Nicholas, Jon 86, 127, 157, 162, 182, 201
Nicholson, Neil 171
Nicholson, Paul 254
Nicklen, Andy 3, 5, 79, 92, 208
Nighthawk 195, 196

Index

Nixon, Kevin 133
Norcott, Jim 121
Nosferatu 165-166, 166p, 167p, 195
Notley, Dave 175
Nugent, Chris 66
Nuthins, The 223, 224, 226, 240-247, 240p, 241p, 243p, 246p, 247p, 250, 271, 271p, 279, 280, 288
Nutz 32, 132

O'Brien, Chas 44
O'Hare, Brendan 250
O'Keefe, Colin 219, 220
O'Reilly, Dave (aka Dave York) 50, 51p
Oasis 256, 281
Obvious Action 177-179, 178p, 202, 225, 226, 266, 286
Oddie, Bill 65
Offord, Eddie 23
Oglala Sioux 191-193, 191p, 192p, 268
Oldfield, Mike 27
OMD 263
Original Howling Gods 287
Osbourne, Ozzy 136, 142
Overlanders, The 16
Overseer 276
Owen, Bronwen 30
Owen, Mark 254
Oxborrow, Simon 'Sox' 193-195, 194p, 205, 261, 271
OXOXOX 259

Packwood, John 247, 248, 249, 251-252
Padbury, Dave 276
Page, Jimmy 4, 5
Palin, Michael 230
Palladino, Pino 155
Palmer, Dave 176
Palmer, Ken 10
Palmer, Mark 176, 177-178, 179, 219, 266, 274, 282
Paramore, Graham 262
Paramore, Sue 261
Parma 225, 279
Parr, Mike 50
Parsons, Ernie 40
Partridge, Andy 85
Partridge, Joe 17
Passions, The 153
Pathfinders, The (see Vernon, Ricky)
Patrician, Richard 132
Paxman, Mike 18, 18p
Payday 286

Peacewave 9-10, 9p, 33, 90
Peel, John 76, 161, 222, 228, 229, 249
Peel, Philip 262
Pembroke, Lord 104-105
Pendragon, John 112, 114
Penny, Andy 193, 194
Penny, John 9
Percy, Chris 120
Period 7, 7p, 48
Perry, Lee 'Scratch' 168, 289
Persian Risk 140
Peter Pod and The Peas 168
Phenobarbitones, The 276, 276p, 279
Phillips, Fred 69, 70
Pierce, Steve 127, 134, 137, 138, 142, 147, 266
Pinder, Chas 254
Pinder, Graeme 165
Pine, Wilf 142, 144
Pink Floyd 27, 142
Pinney, Mick 7
Pippins, The 41
Pirates, The 69, 259
Pizing, Mike 'Spike' 170
Plant, Robert 5, 6
Plastic Penny 11
Poffley, Simon 153
Pogues, The 18
Poison Girls, The 106, 108
Police, The 165
Pooh Sticks 225
Pook, John 69
Poole, Tony 12
Pooley, Ruth 183
Pope Shenouda and the Coptic Orthodox 190-191
Popees, The 16
Pounds, Dave 125, 126, 132
Powell, Peter 259
Power, Tom 205
Prams, The 128, 128p, 129-132, 129p, 176, 264, 265, 265p
Pray 270
Premiers, The 50, 50p
Presley, Elvis 289
Presley, Reg 227, 255
Press Gang 238
Preston, Shelley 195
Priestley, John 42, 43p, 48, 83
Pringle, Andy 31-32, 260
Prior, Maddy 18
Pritchard, Barry 101, 102, 106, 108, 110, 112-113, 115-116

Processors, The 159-160, 159p, 160p
Procol Harum 2
Prodigy, The 281
Prophecy, The 275-276, 275p
Protheroe, Brian 55-56, 57
Psychedelic Furs, The 208
Pugh, Tommy 59, 103
Pumphouse 146, 266
Purge, The 4, 15, 38, 257, 258
Pyeshoppe 267, 284

QTs, The 69, 72, 73-82, 73p, 77p, 78p, 79p, 81p, 83, 85, 86, 87, 156, 165, 173, 188, 261, 263, 285

Radcliffe, Mark 247
Raggett, Roger 3-4, 5, 24, 52, 55, 90
Ramone, Dee Dee 141, 266
Ramone, Joey 141
Ramones, The 141
Rawle, Sid 96, 105, 113
Rawlings, Cass 29, 30
Razorcuts 223
Read, Paul 205
Recorded Delivery 10, 50-51, 51p
Red Book 162-163, 269
Red Hot Chilli Peppers 231
Red River Group, The 41
Reform 10, 50
Reid, Simon 9
REM 254
Reynolds, Don 50, 51
Rhythm Blasters, The 234-236, 235p, 267-268, 278
Rice, Sean 5, 116, 236, 237, 261, 270, 274
Richard, Cliff 159, 255
Richards, Bob 142
Ride 225
Riggs, Colin 144, 146
Rigor Mortis 16
Rimbaud, Penny 101, 108
Roache, William 111
Robbins, Andy 127, 132, 134
Robbins, Martin 127
Roberts, Ant 213-214, 215-216, 227, 239, 240, 249, 278-279
Robertson, Brian 71
Robins, Mike 2, 30, 49-50, 154
Roche Sisters, The 88
Rocky Cockerel 259
Roden, Tremayne 58, 59, 119, 125
Roman Holliday 200

331

Ronson, Mick 24
Roper, Clive 87, 183-184, 188-190, 193, 225, 226, 233, 261, 269-270
Rose Coloured Nightmares 226, 241, 279
Rose, David 44
Rose, Graham 165
Rosehips, The 214
Rossiter, Ian 134, 137, 141
Rothman, Joe 286
Rudorf, Ian 226
Rushent, Martin 44, 47
Rushton, Steve 127, 156, 157, 159
Russell, George 289
Russell, Kevin 222, 223, 224, 225, 227, 271
Russell, Philip (see Wally Hope)
Ryall, Steve 69
Ryan, Barry 255
Rynn, Bob 11

Sackville Baggins, The 241
Saigon 146
Sandford, Chris 50, 80
Saul, Peter 284
Saunders, Brian 50, 51p
Sayer, Leo 29
Scallywag 48
Scarlet 254
Scott, Stan 54
Screens, The 65
Second Hand 18
Sentance, Carl 140
Sex Pistols 62, 68, 76, 131, 209
Shaar Murray, Charles 60, 92
Shady Lady 225
Sharks 28
Sharpe, Alex 219
Sheehan, Finbar 236
Sheldon, Mark 165
Shepard, James 216, 274
Shepherd, Andy 195
Shepherd, Brian 133
Sheppard, Andy 2-3, 10, 28, 33-35, 33p, 84, 234, 287p, 288p, 289
Sherburne, Pete 234
Shergold, Roy 119
Sheridan, Pat 63
Sheriff, Doug 236
Sherrin, Ned 21
Shining Hearts Band 69, 70, 86, 103
Shirfield, Nick 178, 183, 225, 226, 227, 233, 280

Shogun 141p, 142-144, 147p, 182, 266
Shoot The Toux 205, 205p, 271
Shrubs, The 278
Sidi Bou Said 233
Sights, The 257
Simons, Tim 6
Singing Nuns of Alcatraz, The 86
Singleton, David 267
Siren, The 239
Six Miles From Huesca 219
Skelcher, Chris 'Kef' 12, 13
Skid (see Browne, Ian)
Skids, The 155
Skin 134
Slade 2, 3
Slainte 236
Slik 51
Small, Keith 11-12
Smith, Dave 9
Smith, Delia 199
Smith, Don 115
Smith, John 2
Smith, Martin 'Cuddles' 44
Smith, Mike (band manager) 188, 191, 192
Smith, Mike (Marble Orchard) 16, 40
Smith, Pete 201, 202, 205, 270
Smith, Phill 256
Smith, Ray 161
Snafu 59
Snakespear 240
Snipers, The 106
Snowblind 195, 204
Somerville, Dave 68, 69
Somerville, Julia 262
Sonofabitch 119
Soupdragon, The 278, 278p
Spacemen 3 249
Spandau Ballet 175
Sparrow, Ray 12, 14, 15, 16, 257, 258
Spedding, Chris 28, 28p
Sphere 33p, 34-35, 34p, 289
Sphynx 110
Spicy Chutney 264
Spinal Tap 95
Spirit of St Louis 143
Spoils, The 225
Sprog (see Ford, Andy)
Stafford, Cliff 127, 145, 148, 240
Stafford, Jack 269
Stainer, John 2
Stand, The 215, 225, 226, 242
Stanford, Phil 186

Stapley, Baz 120
Starbecker, Ronnie 41
Starr, Ringo 17, 289
Statues, The 236p, 237, 270, 274
Status Quo 13, 18, 49, 180
Steamhammer 2
Steeleye Span 18
Stent, Spike 263
Stevens, Barry 268
Stevens, Cat 255
Stewart, Johnnie 21
Stewart, Rod 17
Stiff Little Fingers 266
Sting 165, 254
Stocken, Anthony 31, 72
Stocker, Frank 68
Stone Roses, The 214, 215
Stone, Archie 238, 239
Stone, Jon 86, 170
Stormfly 254
Stramm, Ian 71
Strand, David 4
Strange, Maxwell 119
Stranglers, The 65, 75, 269
Strugglers, The 183, 284
Strummer, Joe 87, 101
Struthers, Jon C 214
Stuart, Jason 270, 271
Sturgess, Mike 268
Styler, Trudie 254
Suicide King 233, 280
Sullivan, Big Jim 20
Summers, Andy 289
Supertramp 81
Sutherland, Steve 28
Sutton, Ian 31
Swannie (see Martin, Adrian)
Sweet 23
Sweet Children 253, 254
Sweet, Rachel 284
Swing Syndicate 227, 233

Tangerine Dream 28-29, 29p, 69
Tarantino, Quentin 290
Tatler, Steve 142
Taylor, Bob (Mason) 44
Taylor, Bob (The Nuthins) 224, 240, 242-244, 246, 247, 279, 280
Taylor, Christine and Linda 90
Taylor, Dave 148, 174-175, 234, 235, 261, 262, 267-268, 286p
Taylor, Stuart 143
Taylor-Gair Band 90-91, 91p, 149

Index

Tea and Symphony 11
Tea, Lee (see Thompson, Lee)
Tears for Fears 201
Teenage Fanclub 249-250, 252
Ten Years After 95
Terraplane 144
Thatcher, Dominic 259
Thatcher, Margaret 113
Thatcher, Tom 6p, 16, 35-37, 37-38, 36p, 37p, 39, 89-90, 148-149, 160-161, 161p, 259, 260
Theodore Watkins 51-52
Thick Dick and The Green'eds 175-176, 180
Thin Lizzy 2, 3-4, 71, 156
Thomas, Steve (see Vague, Tom)
Thompson, Lee 'Lee Tea' 240, 242, 247, 280
Thompson, Steve 195
Thorne, Joe 6
Thoughts, The 91
Thrower, Debbie 260
Thynne, Alexander (Lord Bath) 89
Thynne, Christopher 90
Tibetan Ukranian Mountain Troupe 112
Tich (see Amey, Ian)
Tikaram, Tanita 279
Ting Tings 263
Tiny (see Mackerel, Bill)
Tobias, Oliver 90
Todd, Dave 206-207, 214, 219, 220, 223, 271
Todd, Wendy 223
Tokyo Blade 127, 128, 132-141, 133p, 135p, 136p, 137p, 138p, 142, 143, 144, 145, 146-147, 148, 188, 266, 273, 278
Tolly, Sarah 197-198, 201
Toomer, Elwyn 127, 198, 202
Torme, Bernie 119
Torokwa, Mark 237
Toucantango 127, 195, 197-204, 198p, 199p, 200p, 201p, 203p, 204p, 205, 261, 270
Townsend, Roger 31
Toyah 153, 254
Tracer 254, 254p
Tracker 23, 47-48, 48p, 49, 51, 91, 92
Travis, John 141
Troggs, The 91-92, 210, 227, 254-255, 284
Trubridge, Horace 222
True, Niki (see Walker, Nick)
Turner, Nik 106
Tzuke, Judie 18, 44, 52

UFO 120
UK 286
Un Deux Twang! 171-172, 171p, 172p, 234, 235, 267, 278
Uncle Brian 253
Underwood, Austin 30
Urban Roots 280
Uriah Heep 2, 12, 18, 57, 145

Vague, Tom (Steve Thomas) 62, 65-66, 68-69, 106, 153-154
Van Der Graaf Generator 11
Vance, Tommy 132
Vapors, The 81
Vaselines, The 249
Venn, Matt 287
Vernon, Ricky (and The Pathfinders) 52
Vickers, Mike 74-75, 74p, 75p, 76-78, 81, 82, 82p, 165, 204, 261
View From A Bridge 183-184, 184p, 193, 225, 286
Viney, Simon 'Min' 169, 170
Violent Daffodils, The 89
Volcano, Jimi 264
Vulture Squadron 238

Waite, John 126
Waite, Kerry 162-163, 163-164, 165, 191-193, 268-269
Wakeman, Rick 65
Waldron, Tony 124
Walker, Dave 195, 196, 198, 201, 202p, 270
Walker, Nick (aka Niki True) 195, 196, 270
Walker, Richie 225, 241, 242, 280
Walking Seeds, The 249
Wallace, Bob 259
Walsh, Chris 57, 73, 74, 75p, 78, 80, 82, 119, 124, 156, 157, 159, 160, 261
Walton, Andy 65
Ward, Trevor 276
Wardman, Pete 20
Ware, Andy 205-206, 220-223, 225
Ware, Dave 205, 219, 220, 223, 225
Washington, Geno 2
Watkins, Jeff 175
Watson, Ash 281
Watts, Richard 'Dicky' 180
Webb, Barry 28
Webb, Trevor 195, 196, 198, 204, 205, 270
Webber, Paul 147

Webber, Pete 21
Webber, Yan 9-10, 33, 55, 90-91, 161-162, 162p, 285-286
Webley, Andy 204
Wedding Present, The 225
Wedgwood Band, The 259
Wedgwood Wing 35, 38, 74
Wedgwood, Mike 16-18, 35, 36p, 38, 39, 47, 258-259, 258p
Wedgwood, Reverend Keith 16
Weekes, Gareth 166
Weeks, Adrian 195
Weider, John 44
Weller, Paul 65
Wells, Nick 180
Wells, Rick 234
Wench 229
West, Matt 170, 171
Westwood, Vivienne 62
Wetton, John 286
What The Butler Saw 193, 205, 271
Whatley, Miss (Grosvenor House) 253
Whatley, Russ 178, 179
Whatley, Terry 225
White Diamond 127
White Trash 15
White, Grahame 'Chalky' 180-182, 219, 235, 268
Whitehorn, Brian 57
Who Is? 270
Who, The 7
Whyton, Wally 91
Wiggins, John 146, 266
Wigglesworth, Simon 'Wiggy' 188, 247, 248-249, 249-250, 250-251, 251-252, 252-253, 277, 287, 288
Wild Horses 71
Wilde, Marty 20, 40
Wilds, Dave 237
Wilkinson, Malcolm 171, 173, 175, 234, 235, 240, 268
Wilks, Peter 217, 218
Williams Geoff 33, 34, 34p
Williams, Chris 161
Williams, Jack 16
Williams, Lynden 12, 13, 14, 161, 162, 258, 259
Williams, Patrick 131
Williams, Tony 259
Williamson, Harry 110
Wilson, Mick 43, 92, 290
Winwood, Muff 219
Wire 64
Wishbone Ash 2

333

Wizzard 15
Wogan, Terry 55
Woo, Pete 202
Wood, Roy 15
Woodhall, Vicky 275
Woodmansey, Woody 24
Woods, Dave 195
Woods, Gay 18
Woods, Terry 18
Woodsmoke 91

Wright, Vic 136, 138, 140
Wrighton, Andy 134, 142, 266
Writz 263
Wynne, Gilbert 146
Wyper, Olaf 38

X-Ray Spex 269
XTC 69, 88
Xtrax 197, 197p

Yes 2, 23
York, Dave (see O'Reilly, Dave)
Young, Alan 156

Zebeck 56, 57-58, 60, 73, 74
Zevenbergen, Iggy 66, 68, 69

About the Authors

Jeremy 'Frogg' Moody was born in Salisbury where he still resides. In 2004 he formed The Salisbury Timezone Group to research and record social life and historical events from the city's past through books, theatre, music, lectures and exhibitions. www.timezonepublishing.com

Frogg is a Committee member of The Whitechapel Society, which promotes the study of the Whitechapel Murders of 1888 and of Victorian and Edwardian life and culture in the East End of London. Since the publication of Hold Tight! (Timezone 2007) he has co-authored If I Did It, I Don't Remember (Hob Nob Press 2008), edited Written and Red (Timezone 2009) and been involved – as editor - in the launch of a new Salisbury music magazine, Beat Route. In June 2010 Frogg was presented with the British Association for Local History Award for his contribution to the study of local history.

Frogg is also a talented musician and composer and a well-known face on the local music scene himself, having played with several local bands. He is also the musical composer of the internationally acclaimed stage musicals Yours Truly, Jack The Ripper and Daughter of Destiny - The True Titanic Love Story.

Richard Nash has spent most of his life in Downton. During the eighties and early nineties he produced The Rambler, which might loosely be described as a 'lifestyle' fanzine, and which remains something of a cult in the area. He has contributed articles, reviews and football match reports to Shindig!, Record Collector, Beat Route, the Salisbury Journal and various fanzines, and also operates www.southwilts.com/site/bluemoonraker, a website concerned with the history of the Salisbury music scene.

Since the publication of Hold Tight! Richard has co-authored the Downton Heritage Trail booklet (Downton Heritage Trail 2009) and launched a website about the buildings of Downton (www.southwilts.com/site/downtonbuildings).